ALSO BY CALDER WALTON

*Empire of Secrets: British Intelligence, the Cold War,
and the Twilight of Empire*

SPIES

THE EPIC INTELLIGENCE WAR
BETWEEN EAST AND WEST

★

CALDER WALTON

SIMON & SCHUSTER

NEW YORK   LONDON   TORONTO   SYDNEY   NEW DELHI

Simon & Schuster
1230 Avenue of the Americas
New York, NY 10020

First Simon & Schuster hardcover edition June 2023

SIMON & SCHUSTER and colophon are registered trademarks of
Simon & Schuster, Inc.

For information about special discounts for bulk purchases,
please contact Simon & Schuster Special Sales at 1-866-506-1949 or
business@simonandschuster.com.

The Simon & Schuster Speakers Bureau can bring authors to your live event.
For more information or to book an event, contact the Simon & Schuster Speakers
Bureau at 1-866-248-3049 or visit our website at www.simonspeakers.com.

Illustrations by Noma Bar
Maps designed by David Lindroth
Interior design by Alexis Minieri

Manufactured in the United States of America

1   3   5   7   9   10   8   6   4   2

Library of Congress Cataloging-in-Publication Data

Names: Walton, Calder, author.
Title: Spies : the epic intelligence war between East and West / Calder Walton.
Description: First Simon & Schuster hardcover edition. | New York : Simon
and Schuster, 2023. | Includes bibliographical references and index.
Identifiers: LCCN 2023010240 (print) | LCCN 2023010241 (ebook) | ISBN
9781668000694 (hardcover) | ISBN 9781668000700 (paperback) | ISBN
9781668000717 (ebook)
Subjects: LCSH: Espionage--History--20th century. |
Espionage--History--21st century. | Intelligence service--Soviet
Union--History. | Intelligence service--Russia (Federation)--History. |
Intelligence service--United States--History. | Intelligence
service--China--History. | East and West. | Cold War. | World
politics--1989- | BISAC: HISTORY / United States / 20th Century |
HISTORY / Military / Strategy
Classification: LCC JF1525.I6 W388 2023 (print) | LCC JF1525.I6 (ebook) |
DDC 327.124709/04--dc23/eng/20230321
LC record available at https://lccn.loc.gov/2023010240
LC ebook record available at https://lccn.loc.gov/2023010241

ISBN 978-1-6680-0069-4
ISBN 978-1-6680-0071-7 (ebook)

For Hayden

After such knowledge, what forgiveness? Think now
History has many cunning passages, contrived corridors
And issues, deceives with whispering ambitions,
Guides us by vanities.

—T. S. Eliot, "Gerontion"

CONTENTS

PART SIX
THE CLASH OF A NEW GLOBAL ORDER

CHAPTER ONE

THE HUNDRED-YEAR INTELLIGENCE WAR

The past is never dead. It's not even past.
–William Faulkner, *Requiem for a Nun*

THE SECRET REPORT ABOUT UKRAINE REACHED BRITISH INTEL-
ligence on a cold day in February. It came from an officer who had met a reliable agent, a Ukrainian nationalist exiled in neighboring Poland. According
to the agent, the Russians admitted they could only hold on to Ukraine by
force and that Ukrainians were "generally hostile to them and their ideas." As
a result, he continued, the Russians were unable to draw economic advantages
from Ukraine, which should be providing Russia with food. Instead, Russia
was obtaining nothing beyond what it seized by force in a narrow zone near
principal railways. The report continued: "My informant naturally looks
forward to the reconstruction of an independent Ukrainian state and was
anxious to know how such a state would be received abroad, and if it could
expect to receive any financial or other support. I pointed out to him that no
power would intervene against Russia now, and that the Russians en masse
would never permit the Ukraine to separate itself entirely from Russia."

1

This report was written not in February 2022 but February 1922, exactly one hundred years before. When it comes to Western intelligence, Ukraine, and Russia, what's old is new again.

What neither the British intelligence officer nor the Ukrainian agent knew was that the Soviet intelligence service, the Cheka—an abbreviation for Vladimir Lenin's Extraordinary Commission for Combating Counter-Revolution and Sabotage—was creating false Ukrainian nationalist groups to lure exiles back to be arrested, tortured, and shot. Soviet intelligence would continue to use bogus Ukrainian groups for years to target Western intelligence services, feeding them disinformation and arresting their operatives. Western intelligence services counterattacked, supporting exiled Ukrainians and sending some back. Ukrainian nationalists working for Western intelligence services would thereafter find their names high up on Moscow's assassination lists.[1]

Spies: The Epic Intelligence War Between East and West is the history of the intelligence conflict waged between Russia and Western countries, more or less continuously, for the last century. This war has been driven by Russia's political, economic, and military weakness and insecurity rather than by its strength. Although Russia professes to be a "great power," its leaders have always been keenly aware of its shortcomings compared to its Western rivals. By embracing espionage, sabotage, subversion, and information warfare, the Kremlin has attempted, before, during, and after the Cold War, to equalize the imbalance of resources between East and West.

This is also the story of how Britain and America mounted their own shadow war against Russia. It is a story of the best and the worst of mankind: bravery and honor, treachery and betrayal. Our narrative, and the characters we meet along the way, deserve the epithet "epic." The story shifts across continents and decades, from the freezing streets of Petrograd (St. Petersburg) in 1917 to the bloody beaches of Normandy in World War II; from coups in faraway lands to present-day Russian and Chinese use of synthetic warfare, internet bots unleashed during the coronavirus "infodemic" pandemic. It is about the intersection of structural forces and human action and their impact on global affairs; about the rise and fall of superpowers, Russia's past, present, and future, and the ascendance of China.

This book was written against the backdrop of Russia's invasion of Ukraine in February 2022. Russia ignited a war in Europe—terrifying words, which I, like most people, thought were consigned to the dustbin of history. And yet here we are, amid a kind of historical throwback, learning daily about Russia's war through a twenty-four-hour news cycle. The scenes reach the West on television and social media—Ukraine is the first TikTok war, with videos coming live from its front lines. They teleport us to what seem like horrors from the last century: bombings, destruction, burning tanks and vehicles, pillage, plunder, deportations, bodies in streets, and mass graves. As a historian, it is impossible to see pictures of the war emerging from Kyiv, Kharkiv, and Odesa and not think how these same places suffered a similar fate under the Soviets in the 1930s, the Nazis ten years later, and then under the Soviets again for decades after 1945.

We see agony in the faces of fleeing mothers and children as they kiss goodbye those who are bravely staying behind in Ukraine to fight. We read and hear about soldiers raping women, hundreds of thousands of civilians forcibly deported, Orwellian state propaganda describing Russia's "special military operation," and atrocities against Ukrainian civilians, perhaps even genocide. Russian forces are known to operate mobile crematoria for disposing of their own fallen soldiers and potentially to eradicate evidence of their war crimes. Vladimir Putin's political thugs have descended into Stalinism, as a matter not of rhetoric but of precedent. Putin's invasion of Ukraine is a strategic disaster for Russia, arising from an intelligence failure, similar to Stalin's mishandling of intelligence before the Nazi invasion of the Soviet Union in 1941. The spectacle of Putin publicly rebuking and humiliating the director of Russia's foreign intelligence service (SVR), Sergey Naryshkin, at the bizarre televised (and prerecorded) National Security Council meeting on the eve of the invasion of Ukraine in February 2022 was a window into the crippling sycophancy that Russia's leader demands, as did those in the Kremlin before him. In Putin's palace, there is no room for telling truth to power, just as there was none during Stalin's reign.[2]

Russia's war in Ukraine became personal for me when I heard about the fates of two of my researchers for this project. One fled over the Ukrainian border to the West. The other stayed in Kyiv and took up arms; as I write this, he is alive and fighting—a man who just weeks before had had no military experience. Two of my other researchers were in Moscow: one escaped with his family to Armenia as Putin's rule slid from autocracy to dictatorship; the other stayed on, attempting to resist from the inside in whatever way possible. Meanwhile, as this goes to print, Putin is threatening the use of a tactical nuclear weapon over Ukraine. Escalating to de-escalate is a long-standing Russian military strategy. Western powers, led by the United States, are undertaking nuclear brinkmanship with Putin not dis-similar to that used in the Cuban Missile Crisis at the height of the Cold War. According to CIA director William Burns, Ukraine is a war that Putin cannot afford to lose. The more that Ukrainians win on the battlefield, the more likely Putin is to use a tactical nuclear weapon. We may know whether this horror becomes reality by the time you read this. Perhaps by then Putin will no longer be in power in Russia. One can only hope.

The Bolshevik Revolution in Russia in 1917, Western intervention in it, and the ensuing Russian Civil War laid the foundations for a century of clandestine plots between Russia, Britain, and the United States. For most of the period, the services of those Western powers were on the back foot, reacting to Russia's secret war against them. You have probably seen flashes of this war in news headlines in recent years—espionage, disinformation, spy swaps, election meddling, assassinations—but these frequently lack context. This book provides that context. It is about the underhanded activities that all governments conduct, in the same way that robbers rob banks and soldiers carry guns. The difference is how those weapons are used—their ends.

In Western democracies like Britain and the United States, intelligence agencies have broadly operated within a rules-based system of checks and balances, with a free press investigating their activities, even when agencies themselves were secret and non-avowed, as they were in Britain for most of the twentieth century. In liberal democracies, intelligence agencies exist to protect their citizens; in authoritarian states they operate to prop up and support the regime in power. Of course, there have been epic failures and abuses of intelligence in Western democracies; harebrained operations in faraway lands that did little to contribute to either side's grand strategies, and probably detracted from them. The difference between Western countries and Russia, past and present, is that in the former, for the most part we eventually reckon with those mistakes and abuses. Intelligence services in Russia have operated without checks and balances, the rule of law, political oversight, accountability, or an independent free press investigating their activities. As a Russian defector put it to me, the only limitation for the Russian security service (FSB) is operational effectiveness—not legal, ethical, or moral considerations.[3]

Although this book describes a conflict between "East and West," it is really a story about two superpowers, the Soviet Union and the United States, and another global power, Britain, which remained preeminent in the intelligence world even as its military dominance diminished. The reason why I have chosen these countries to study is, first, because of availability of records, and second because they were leading intelligence powers during the Cold War. Soviet intelligence had a commanding role over its allies in Eastern Europe. "We didn't dream of doing anything significant without instructions from Moscow," one defector from the Czech intelligence service (StB), Ladislav Bittman, told me. When it came to foreign intelligence, Soviet spy chiefs viewed Britain's MI6, and then the CIA, as their primary opponents. That alone is a good enough reason to study KGB-MI6-CIA shadow operations. Equally significant, in the West, British and U.S. agencies themselves had uniquely close intelligence relations. They were the first two, and drivers, of the "Five Eyes" alliance—the three other later eyes being Australia, Canada, and New Zealand. Five Eyes was the most important Western intelligence effort during the Cold War and lasts to the present day. This is not to say that other agencies in the West and East, and different actors, were not important, but any study must have its limits. Some important players, like French intelligence, only have walk-on roles in the space available here.[4]

I use the phrase "the West" throughout. The West I am referring to is not a geographical area but a collection of ideas and alliances, and a form of government centered on liberal democracy, which includes freedoms of speech, political association, and the rule of law. This exists in contrast to the world's first major one-party state, the Soviet Union, and Russia today, where there is no independent judiciary, or free press, and where intelligence agencies operate to serve the regime and subdue its people. I use "the East" as shorthand for the Soviet Union's form of rule, careful, of course, not to conflate it with "East" in the orientalist sense—generalizing about the languages and cultures of Asia. Intelligence in the Soviet system, as in all authoritarian states, had built-in dysfunctions; intelligence chiefs only provided, often on pain of death, information that their leaders were willing to hear. The fact that Moscow's intelligence services operated largely without checks, and Western societies were open, meant that there was a fundamental asymmetry of arms between the two sides of intelligence during the Cold War. The CIA had to spend millions of dollars to steal Soviet secrets on subjects like its missiles. Soviet spies could pick up a copy of *Aviation Week & Space Technology*.[5]

My aim here, then, is to figure out what the hell is going on with Russia and its intelligence services. I speak of an "intelligence war": the Bolsheviks considered themselves at "war" with Western democracies long before the Cold War started. Their war was both ideological and practical, with intelligence services acting as foot soldiers. Lenin, leader of the Bolsheviks and first head of the Soviet Union, proclaimed himself to be applying history scientifically. He used the nineteenth-century writings of Karl Marx to create a regime that would defeat Western capitalist "bourgeois" powers and replace them with a universalist socialist utopia. It was a struggle for the future world order. The major targets of Soviet intelligence, the vanguard of the Soviet communist revolution, were Britain, the world's greatest imperial (and thus capitalist) power, and then the United States. The latter entered World War I, and global affairs, the same year the Bolsheviks seized power in Russia. America's democracy and huge economic resources placed it on an ideological and geopolitical collision course with the Soviet regime thereafter, no matter how hard Washington tried to stay out of world politics. Britain and the United States have also continued to be major Kremlin targets in the twenty-first century. From 1917 onward, these three powers, the Soviet Union in the East, and Britain and the United States in the West, have thus waged an intelligence war based on two competing ideological systems, vying for global supremacy.

Four themes run like dark threads throughout our story below. The first three are the action parts of intelligence agencies: espionage (stealing secrets), subversion, and sabotage. The latter two of these constitute covert action, as it is known in the West, or—in Russia—active measures. Added to these "kinetic" activities of intelligence services in East and West is a fourth theme, and part of the secret world, the role of analysis: understanding an opponent's aims and capabilities. All four of these ventures are as old as history, but they were taken to new levels by superpowers during the Cold War. Today the action elements are also carried out in the cyber domain, which provides a new medium for what is much older tradecraft. As we shall see, these three components—espionage, subversion, and sabotage—continue to be in play even when relations ostensibly improved between East and West.

Along the way in our story, we come to understand what motivated people to spy for another country—in other words, human drama. After all, one side's traitor is the other's hero. This account, however, ultimately involves more than Russia and the West. Its conclusions relate to China. The story of the twentieth century's Cold War offers an urgent warning about the intelligence conflict that the Western world, particularly the United States, is already confronting with respect to China, the world's new superpower. As far as intelligence and national security are concerned, the United States is already in a Cold War with China. Once again, as in the previous conflict, intelligence services are on the front line of the struggle for the future world order, this time between democracy and authoritarianism, as President Joe Biden has correctly framed it. Since the eve of the war in Ukraine, China and Russia have been in an alliance with "no limits." It constitutes an axis expressly geared against Western liberal democracy. China appears to be on the verge of providing Russia with lethal aid for Ukraine. If that happens, any doubts about a new East-West Cold War will surely dissipate. The last century's Cold War certainly is not a perfect analogy for the overall unfolding clash between the United States and China, which is even more complex than the former Cold War. China's economic weight, and the implications of its integration into world markets, makes the country a more challenging—and arguably dangerous—adversary than the Soviet Union ever was. China and its spies are like the Soviet Union on steroids. In 2021, the FBI was opening a China-related investigation every twelve hours.[6]

This is necessarily a long book. I know only too well that each of us, every day, is bombarded by a twenty-four-hour news cycle, which in my experience too often degenerates into doomscrolling in an endless Twitterverse in the middle of the night. If you are, like me, overwhelmed by sensory overload, then it will help to have a preview of the principal conclusions of *Spies* up front. I view these not as *arguments*, which to my mind (as a former barrister) can suggest something contrived, but instead as my *assessment* of the situation, based on seven years of research on four continents and reading tens of thousands of pages of previously secret records in British, American, Russian, and some former Soviet bloc intelligence archives. What follows is my interpretation of events and their meaning.

Here, then, are the book's three principal conclusions:

First, the Cold War started before we tend to imagine. It is conventionally considered to have begun after 1945, amid seismic shifts in the grand strategies between East and West. In fact, it began earlier. Western governments were stuck in a Cold War long before 1945—they just did not realize it. Revelations about Soviet espionage and subversion in the West that came to light after 1945—which became defining episodes of the Cold War—really exposed what had long been taking place. Successive postwar Soviet spy scandals were like alarms triggered after a bank robbery—though in this case, the robbers had hacked into police communications and bribed key members of the police force. The British and Americans were woefully unprepared after 1945, effectively coming to the ensuing gunfight with the Soviet Union armed with a toy bow and arrow. Moscow's spies had been targeting them for years, stealing as many of their secrets as possible as part of their effort to prepare for what Marxist-Leninists perceived as an "inevitable" conflict with Western imperial powers. By 1945, Soviet spies had stolen plans for the greatest wartime secret of the Western Allies, the atomic bomb, and in so doing permanently changed postwar international security. Stalin's spies in the West allowed him foreknowledge of most major Western strategic initiatives. The Cold War, as we usually consider it, thus emerged from a previous wartime and prewar assault by Soviet intelligence.

The intelligence conflict between East and West was asymmetric, with built-in advantages for the former against the latter. It was also persistent, continuing even when East-West relations apparently improved and were reset: during World War II, during what came to be popularly termed détente, and after the Soviet Union's collapse. In fact, at these moments of thawed relations, Soviet and Russian intelligence services scaled up their assault on Western countries, pushing at an open door while Western defenses were down or strategic attention was focused elsewhere. The war against Nazi Germany, during which the Soviet Union became allies with Britain and the United States, made little difference to Stalin's intelligence onslaught against them. In fact, it allowed his spy chiefs to strengthen their attack. After the war, Britain and the United States were on the defensive, racing to catch up in a struggle they had not known they were in. They were left trying to understand the scale of the secrets the Soviets had stolen, and assess Stalin's mindset, objectives, and capabilities. Only slowly after 1945 did the challenge facing the West from the Soviet Union become clear.

Second, contrary to assumptions in the West at the time, the Cold War did not end neatly in 1991 with the Soviet Union's collapse. That was a mirage. Russia was humiliated on the world stage following the Soviet empire's demise, and so its intelligence services became, if anything, more aggressive. Nothing breeds cold aggression like disgrace. Russia's post-Soviet intelligence services changed their names, but little else. The same former KGB officers, tradecraft, and even agents embedded in the West continued to operate, now under Russia's new FSB and SVR. In hindsight, it was a tragedy for the West, for Russians themselves, and for the countries sharing borders with Russia—its "near abroad"—that its intelligence services were not fully dismantled in 1991. Their disproportionate influence in post-Soviet Russia was the surest guarantee that the country would not—could not—develop along liberal democratic lines. Instead, it continued as a police state. The FSB and SVR grew into a state within a state, especially when a former low-level unsuccessful KGB officer, Vladimir Putin, became head of the FSB in 1998 and then Russian leader the next year. Once in the Kremlin, Putin surrounded himself with "men of force," *siloviki*—those with backgrounds in military and intelligence services. Since entering the Kremlin, now more than two decades ago, Putin has unleashed tradecraft straight from the KGB's old playbook: espionage, deep-cover illegals, assassinations, disinformation, and other so-called active measures. Russia's intelligence services, once called its "new nobility," publicly praise their Soviet past, providing carefully sanitized—and largely imaginary—versions of its dark history.[7]

If we look closer, however, we find that although there are continuities between Russia past and present, its intelligence services today are also significantly different. Since Putin came to power, they have been vehicles for massive state-run organized crime. (Putin came to prominence in St. Petersburg, the epicenter of the Russian mafia.) The FSB has helped Putin, and a small number of oligarchs, accumulate vast wealth. Anodyne terms describing Russia's renewed place in the world—"great power competition," "resurgence of great powers"—much discussed in Washington these days, especially among excitable political scientists, are too polite by half; they do not do justice to the ugly reality of Putin's gangster regime. The FSB helps Putin run Russia as a mafia state.

Putin's genius was to convince Western powers after 9/11, during the war on terror, that he was not pursuing two agendas at the same time. He assisted with Western counterterrorism, but all the while was pushing a grand strategy to make Russia great again and correct the "injustices" inflicted on it by the Soviet collapse. He held out one hand in friendship, while stealing with the other. In doing so, Putin was following in the tradition of his predecessor in the Kremlin, Joseph Stalin. The Western Allies naively thought that Stalin was their ally, when he was really as devious as their Nazi enemies. Flash forward six decades. During the war on terror, as the digital revolution was underway, the resources of the U.S. intelligence community and its allies were overwhelmingly focused on counterterrorism and the wars in Iraq and Afghanistan, not on threats from rising powers like Russia. In the Kremlin, Putin was surely laughing to himself.

This takes us headlong into a debate that has ignited politicians, pundits, and scholars since Russia's invasion of Ukraine in February 2022: Who is to blame for Russia's increasingly militant foreign policy in the twenty-first century, the expansion of the North Atlantic Treaty Organization or Russia itself? The answer, though frustrating for those who want explanations to be monocausal, is both. NATO's enlargement eastward after 1991 triggered Russia's long-standing fears about encirclement and Western subversion of its domestic affairs. These fears long predated NATO expansion, but the successive admission of countries into NATO (Poland, Hungary, and the Czech Republic in 1999, the Baltic states next, with others in Eastern and Central Europe thereafter) made them worse. New light is shed by British records opened in 2021. Tony Blair's foreign secretary, Robin Cook, and his defense secretary, George Robertson, wrote to the prime minister in 1997, on the eve of the first three former Warsaw Pact countries joining NATO: "If [enlargement] decisions look to Russia like the beginning of a landslide which will stop only at her borders, then she will react adversely." There is little point arguing whether NATO expansion actually posed a threat to Russia. It is like arguing logic with a drunk. Those in the Kremlin believed, and still think, that it did. That is what is important.[8]

At the same time, Russia's militarist aggression was homegrown, the result of dysfunctions in its society and a style of government veering between dictatorship, autocracy, and oligarchy. This book's gloomy conclusion is that the West has a long-term Russia problem, not just a Putin problem. He personifies the Russian government's malfunctions. But many others in the Kremlin, even more hard-line than him, share his hatred of the West. If Putin were to disappear, it is unlikely that Russia's relations with the West would be normalized any time soon.

A cursory look at the power of the intelligence services in Russia in the 1990s, their creeping criminality and corruption, and then their use as personal tools for Putin's rule and enrichment, shows it is a fantasy to suppose that Russia would have been a peaceful partner in the international world order without NATO expansion. Under Putin, Russia and its "special services" have been the hooligans of international relations. His grand design has been to correct what he sees as the "catastrophe" of the Soviet Union's collapse, to reclaim its sphere of influence over countries like Ukraine, and to take on its nemesis, the United States—known within the Kremlin as the "Main Adversary" (*glavny protivnik*). Far from being an unprecedented attack, as many claimed, Russian election meddling in the U.S. presidential election of 2016 followed in a long tradition of Soviet efforts to interfere in American politics. Russia used new means—social media—but relied on older tactics and strategies. Russia's "sweeping and systematic" intelligence attack, to use special counsel Robert Mueller's phrase, was part of Putin's strategy to wage a war on democracies, undermining how they, and Western institutions like NATO, function, while turning Russia into the great power that Putin's messianic ethnonationalism believes is destiny. We are seeing Putin's revanchist project play out in blood in Ukraine. President Barack Obama once criticized Mitt Romney for being stuck in the past when it came to Russia. The Cold War appeared over. In this case, however, Obama was too quick to dismiss the notion of being stranded in history. The man in the Kremlin today really does want to return to the 1980s—and overturn their results.

My **third** conclusion answers the question: "So what?" The book ends by showing that the history of Russia's epic, hundred-year intelligence war against the West provides a stark warning about China. Once again, with China, Western countries, particularly the U.S., face a persistent, asymmetric intelligence threat from a superpower seeking global dominance. Chinese intelligence services are deploying tradecraft (in terms of espionage and covert actions) similar to the Soviet Union's—but taking it to new levels. The history of the world's first superpower conflict thus informs what Western countries can expect in the twenty-first century. "Every day we are fighting an onslaught from China, which we hope does not turn into hot war," one senior Australian signals intelligence official told me. The U.S. and its Western allies are again now racing to catch up and to understand the intentions and capabilities of a closed-regime police state.

In the first two decades of the twenty-first century, China's intelligence services undertook an unprecedented onslaught on Western countries, hacking into and stealing their commercial and government secrets. Some of these activities are certainly the kind that all states undertake, but when it comes to the secret world, Chinese intelligence is different in nature, scope, and scale than anything deployed by the West: the U.S. government does not undertake industrial espionage for the benefit of American companies. In China, by contrast, intelligence and commerce are integrated. In 2012, Keith Alexander, the head of the National Security Agency (NSA), publicly warned that Chinese hacking constituted the greatest transfer of wealth in history. The resources that China has thrown at espionage make the Soviet efforts during the Cold War look low energy.[9]

Understanding U.S. tradecraft against the Soviet Union helps us to see what is needed against Chinese intelligence. Equally important is appreciating mistakes made in the twentieth century's Cold War. Transparency about the nature of the threat facing the West is key—Chinese spies are real, as were Soviet spies. But that does not mean that all Chinese Americans are spies, any more than liberal or left-leaning Americans were Soviet agents. Also key is not withholding relevant information from U.S. citizens when there are few valid security reasons for doing so. If the U.S. government had been transparent about its knowledge of Soviet espionage early in the Cold War, much of the tragedy of McCarthyism could have been avoided. The United States must not repeat this mistake with China.

A word of caution, however. The past, alas, only takes us so far. History never repeats itself, though it does rhyme, as Mark Twain is believed to have said. The past is a mess. It would be dangerous to think that previous intelligence and national security policies can be simply grafted onto the present challenge from China, incorporating the best hits from the twentieth century. Instead, what is required is forward thinking and imagination: open-source intelligence collection, machine learning, artificial intelligence (AI), and supercomputing. These are the future of Western intelligence and national security when it comes to the challenge of China. Harnessing imagination is the true lesson from the history of Western intelligence in the Cold War.

◆

The following pages cover a broad tapestry, which I have arranged both chronologically and thematically. A comprehensive book about the hundred-year intelligence war between Russia and the West would stretch to multiple volumes. Instead, I have emphasized particular cases, and incidents, which I believe, based on my research, are important to understanding this story. Inevitably, I have had to make hard editorial decisions about what to include, with entire countries falling by the wayside. But rather than leaving material on the cutting-room floor, I have created a website where you can discover more: www.spieshistory.com.

A few words of warning about what the ensuing pages are *not*: their

theme is the Cold War, but this is not a history of that conflict. That story
has been expertly told elsewhere. It is also not comprehensive. Some subjects, like the KGB's sponsorship of Middle Eastern terrorism, and Eastern
bloc–supported assassins, like Carlos the Jackal, lie outside its scope. Some
questions necessarily remain unanswered: Was South African leader Nelson
Mandela an MI6 agent? One renegade former MI6 officer has claimed as
much. MI6 does not (yet) release records from its own archives. It thus
largely remains an historical enigma. The published writings of Michael
Burleigh, Max Hastings, and Jonathan Haslam have been especially helpful
for me.[10]

I have arranged this story in six parts. The first, "The Clash Between
Dictators and Democracies," sets the stage, stretching from the Bolshevik
Revolution to the end of World War II. These years revolutionized intelligence work, laying foundations that have lasted to the present day. Behind
the war against the Axis powers, Britain and the United States were the
targets of another sustained secret war—waged by Stalin.

Part two, "The Clash of Civilizations," reveals how intelligence services became the vanguard of two competing strategies for a new global
order. Soviet spies in the West, like the Cambridge Spies in Britain and
the similar Ivy League spies in the United States, had buried themselves
as moles deep inside Western governments. Thanks to them, Stalin was
far better informed about Western secrets in the early years of the Cold
War than the West ever was about Stalin's. London and Washington were
effectively and inadvertently practicing open diplomacy toward Moscow as
the Cold War set in, with Stalin privy to some of their most closely held
secrets. Meanwhile, the United States had to create peacetime intelligence
capabilities from scratch, following the dissolution of its wartime agency,
the OSS (Office of Strategic Services). The early Cold War also saw two
apparently incompatible developments that would plague liberal beliefs
and opinion in Washington for decades: Soviet espionage in the United
States was real and posed a threat to national security; and the claims made
by Senator Joseph McCarthy, in what was called the Red Scare of the

1950s, were inaccurate, overblown, and hugely damaging, leaving countless innocent victims. Due to a lack of reliable information, most American policymakers and citizens ended up failing what F. Scott Fitzgerald called the test of a first-rate mind: the ability to hold two contradictory ideas in one's head and still function. In reality, Soviet spies were real *and* Joe McCarthy was wrong.

In part three, "The Clash of Arms," we follow a succession of failures on the part of the U.S. and British intelligence communities to recruit spies behind the Iron Curtain and "roll back" the Soviet bloc in Eastern Europe through covert actions. Consequently, they turned to state-of-the-art scientific and technological intelligence to understand the intentions and capabilities of those in the Kremlin. The standoff between the world's two superpowers reached its apex—the most dangerous moment in history—during the 1962 Cuban Missile Crisis. The brinkmanship between President John F. Kennedy and Soviet premier Nikita Khrushchev over the Soviet Union's placement of nuclear missiles in Cuba nearly resulted in a nuclear war. The fact that the Cuban Missile Crisis was resolved successfully, without war breaking out, occurred despite, not because of, Soviet intelligence. The same was true of some of the Kennedy White House's intelligence initiatives during the crisis. President Kennedy's decisions during the crisis were shaped by briefings he received from a combination of human and technical intelligence, but he was also more cavalier than posterity tends to remember.

Part four, "The Clash of Empires," shows how the world's two superpowers used their respective intelligence services as proxies in the Third World. They launched coups, bribed governments, and churned out disinformation in foreign countries with the hope of aligning them in their respective camps. U.S. and British covert actions, and the Soviet equivalent, active measures, did more to embitter relations between the two sides than anything else in the Cold War, to say nothing of the damage inflicted on targeted countries themselves. Our story here is about superpowers in the Third World, which does not negate the importance of local actors there, who of course had agency of their own and used secret services ɩ pursue their own agendas.[11]

In part five, "The Clash of Reigning Superpowers," we delve into what became the final showdown between the CIA, MI6, and the KGB. We see that, contrary to appearances at the time, the Cold War did not end with the unwinding and collapse of the Soviet Union between 1989 and 1991. In fact, Russia's intelligence services expanded and modernized old Soviet tradecraft. While Western governments aspired to bring democracy to Russia, its intelligence services ruthlessly pursued their national interests—even more vigorously than before, with Russia now humiliated on the world stage, having lost its empire and in economic ruin. If we must assign blame, there is enough to go around. Western politicians, particularly in Washington, convinced themselves that Russia was reformed. Under Putin, who rose like a meteor to become head of Russia's domestic security service and later the president, the government reverted to its long-standing tradition of autocracy, ultimately leading to dictatorship. Unlike in the twentieth century, however, when the Kremlin at least had the Politburo to offset a Soviet leader, in this century Putin has ruled alone by personal despotism. He fused Russian intelligence and security services with the Russian mafia and organized crime. In this noxious mix of Russian intelligence, and mafia types whose surnames end with vowels, we meet in part six the 2016 U.S. Republican presidential nominee, Donald J. Trump.

◆

Intelligence has traditionally been termed the "missing dimension" of statecraft and diplomacy in the twentieth century. That is no longer entirely the case. It is a vibrant area of research. Despite those advances, however, and insatiable popular interest in spies and spying, intelligence continues to be missing from history books in several ways. Notable scholars who comment frequently about intelligence matters in op-eds, and on Twitter, inexplicably omit those same subjects from their scholarship—or treat them as unserious footnotes. In the past, they could claim a lack of archival records, but that is no longer the case. There are now *too many* declassified records to work with, many available at the click of a mouse.[12]

Consider the role of signals intelligence (SIGINT), for example. No history of World War II could now be written without incorporating the work of Allied code breakers, particularly at Britain's Bletchley Park, which decrypted Axis communications. When it comes to the history of the Cold War, however, otherwise excellent studies either overlook the role of code breakers entirely or make passing reference to them; this is true even of those written after the revelations of former NSA contractor Edward Snowden, which made the agency a household name. In reality, code-breaking agencies on both sides of the Cold War—Britain's GCHQ, America's NSA, and the Soviet Union's KGB—were the largest components of their intelligence communities. At the height of the Cold War, Soviet SIGINT employed about three hundred thousand personnel. NSA, the largest part of U.S. intelligence, was also massive (though smaller than the KGB): it employed about one hundred thousand U.S. officials. SIGINT shaped, and in some cases warped, the foreign affairs of each side of the Cold War.[13]

Take another example: histories of the Global South invariably mention the activities of the CIA in instigating coups and assassinations. But they habitually fail to mention the Soviet equivalent. The overall problem is revealed by a quick look at databases like the standard search engine for academic publications, JSTOR, or the Society for Historians of American Foreign Relations. They reveal fleetingly few results about Cold War signals intelligence, for example, in their millions of online records. The Stanford political scientist Amy Zegart, one of the few scholars to take the subject of intelligence seriously, has noted that between 2001 and 2016 the three most highly regarded academic journals in political science published just five articles, out of a total of 2,780, in which intelligence was a topic. University departments in the United States, driven by their research agendas, also treat intelligence as a marginal issue. At a U.S. university, as Zegart has noted, you are more likely to learn about U2 the rock band than U-2 the 1950s high-altitude spy plane. This has a knock-on effect on the field of public policy. The U.S. Congress has more members who are experts in powdered milk than intelligence.[14]

There are several reasons why intelligence does not occupy the position that, in any reasonable view, it should in major U.S. research institutions. The first relates to publicly available records. Western intelligence agencies were traditionally poor at disclosing their secrets. The CIA, for instance, has countless operations like the one recounted in the 2012 film *Argo*, but it has been poor at releasing records containing similar stories from its archives. Another part of the explanation why intelligence is a sideshow at U.S. universities relates to lingering suspicions about U.S. intelligence agencies, stretching back to the 1960s and 1970s, when they were found to be spying on American citizens and dissident groups. The winds of suspicion on U.S. campuses about clandestine agencies blew harder with the recent exposure of intelligence abuses: catastrophic errors about Iraq's weapons of mass destruction, CIA "rendition" of terrorists, and torture of detainees, during the war on terror. Piled onto this came Edward Snowden's unauthorized disclosures in 2013 about NSA and GCHQ "mass surveillance"—more accurately, bulk data collection. (The war in Ukraine in 2022 may be changing post-Snowden lingering suspicions. U.S. intelligence successfully stole Putin's secrets about the invasion, and then, by disclosing them, undermined his ability to concoct excuses, or "false flags.") Then there is the nature of the subject itself, which makes observers unsure how to separate fact from fiction. Intelligence attracts nut jobs, hacks, and conspiracists like moths to a flame. Finally, there is the James Bond effect. Intelligence is one of the few, if only, fields where a fantasy literature has taken hold before a serious one. Now, however, it is possible to study the history of intelligence in a meaningful way. Hitherto secret archives give us the goods—in some cases, literally receipts from covert operations. As I seek to do in this book, it is now possible to use original documents to analyze significant subjects about intelligence—for instance, its impact on the Allied war effort and the riddle of ABLE ARCHER, in 1983, when the world may have stumbled to the brink of nuclear war. My research, which became a quest, hopefully offers a corrective to the overwhelming lack of public policy understanding about the history of intelligence.

Our subject here, in essence, is about the interaction of human affairs and structural forces in history—whether men and women make history or history makes them. In recent years, academic historians have increasingly focused on structural, socioeconomic causes to explain major historical turning points, relegating the "great men" school of history to an antiquarian past. That is a mistake. No one would suggest that we are not creatures of the times in which we live, subject to forces beyond our control—though not in the Jedi sense. At the same time, no serious person (outside of, perhaps, university history departments) would argue that the personalities of leaders are not important. If Stalin had not become leader of the Soviet Union after Lenin, or Khrushchev after Malenkov and Stalin, the Soviet Union would have been a different place. Who would argue that Russia today would be different if Putin had not entered the Kremlin? The same is true of Winston Churchill for Britain's war, or Margaret Thatcher, Ronald Reagan, or Mikhail Gorbachev in helping end the Cold War. Leaders matter.

Let's also get one other major point out of the way up front: most of the time, intelligence was not decisive in international relations. Occasionally, however, in the right circumstances, it was. This occurs when an agency collects timely, relevant, and accurate intelligence and delivers it to a decision maker who is willing to listen. As this book shows, this happened during the Cuban Missile Crisis in October 1962, the most dangerous moment of the Cold War, and also two decades later, when the British and U.S. governments received intelligence from an MI6 spy in the KGB, Oleg Gordievsky, who revealed the extent to which Soviet leaders were genuinely afraid of the United States. In these two cases, human intelligence revealed its true potential significance. Espionage involves the collision of human agency and structural forces. In rare instances, it has global consequences. To borrow Otto von Bismarck's famous phrase, all great powers are traveling on the "stream of Time," which they can neither control nor direct, but which they can navigate with skill and experience. Espionage is an acute example of the interaction between the flow of history and experience—human actors can help steer the stream of Time, when it is acted upon.[15]

I can hear a skeptical reader muttering, "You would say this, wouldn't you, about your own subject?" A scholar of any topic, be it the history of balloons or ballet, will inevitably conclude that his or her subject is important. The archives of intelligence agencies are particularly problematic in this respect, not least because they contain seductive subjects; the files on which this book is based have an allure. They are stamped SECRET, with instructions for how they are to be handled and, in some cases, destroyed. We find code names, assassins lurking within them, transcribed telephone and bugged conversations otherwise lost to history. Files declassified for this book from the Czech state intelligence (StB) archives even contain bugged audio recordings of its surveillance targets, whose disembodied voices take us to meetings long ago, whose attendees thought were private. A social history, using them, is waiting to be written. We also find refreshingly non-politically correct judgments in British records, written at a time when the country's intelligence services were not officially acknowledged (avowed). British intelligence desk officers in the first half of the twentieth century never thought their reports would see the light of day. There is no political veneer in their records, because there was no need for it in a nonexistent secret agency. Sometimes, scrawled in the margins, we find curse words about the subject of a file written in ancient Greek or Latin. Reading the thumbed, yellowing intelligence dossiers, it is tempting to think one has found Britain's crown jewels of state secrets. The reality is frequently more pedestrian, alas. Much material in them is from openly available sources, like newspaper reports. But every once in a while, there is indeed something startling. Who would have thought that British intelligence would bug diplomatic negotiations for colonies gaining independence from Britain during the Cold War, as we see in part four? It is essential to read dossiers critically, but it is also fair to say there is surely something significant in records that governments from both sides of the Cold War, and beyond, have done their best to keep secret. Some of the files used for this book were only declassified in 2022.

I have done my best to place the role of intelligence agencies within the broader context of the governments of which they are a part. They are the tools of policymakers, whether in the Kremlin or the Oval Office or Downing Street, and it is only by seeing how they were used and abused that we can assess the impact of intelligence on international relations. The wartime OSS officer Arthur Schlesinger Jr., later a close adviser to President Kennedy, wrote: "Intelligence is only as effective as its dissemination . . . Even the best-designed dissemination system cannot persuade busy people to read political analysis unless it affects the decisions they are about to make." In this book, I have tried to focus on the moment when intelligence made a difference—or should have. Decision makers have reams of information coming at them. Sometimes intelligence delivered a margin, sometimes it did not. It's important to understand why. Some of the stories below are bound to be familiar to specialists, though new light can be shed by placing them on a broader hundred-year canvas. This book is concerned with the Cold War as an East-West superpower conflict, as opposed to a global one, which recent research has highlighted. A fresh view of the twentieth century's East-West superpower conflict is not only possible using newly available archival records, but urgently needed given the revival of an East-West superpower clash today.

At the end of the Cold War, prominent historians debated the extent to which its history would need to be rewritten with the opening of secret archives. They speculated that there were unlikely to be revelations like the ULTRA secret, which forced the history of World War II to be revised in key respects. They were correct. There was not an intelligence breakthrough by one side that gave it a revolutionary competitive advantage over the other—nothing similar to breaking the German Enigma code in World War II, though that was the perpetual quest of both sides. Instead, the true intelligence successes of Western powers during the Cold War are measured by omissions, like Sherlock Holmes's dogs that did not bark. The greatest contribution that British and U.S. intelligence made to the Cold War was to help prevent the outbreak of a hot war, World War III. By contrast, Soviet intelligence services broadly failed to provide leaders in the Kremlin with accurate intelligence. They also effectively kept Soviet society imprisoned. In doing so, they prolonged the Cold War.[16]

It may, at this point, be helpful for you to know something about me, your historical guide. My own introduction to this unusual field of research, the secret world, started two decades ago, when I was a graduate student at Cambridge University. My doctoral supervisor, Christopher Andrew, the world's preeminent historian of intelligence and national security, offered me a remarkable (and then confidential) opportunity: to work on MI5's official hundred-year history, which he was commissioned to write, using intelligence archives at its London headquarters. It was an irresistible offer, the opportunity of a lifetime.

Walking through the circular doors at Thames House on my first day changed my understanding of international relations. My part-time work on that project, for seven years, took me through the looking glass into the secret world: giving me privileged access to archives of the world's longest continuously running security intelligence service. I learned who spies were and how intelligence services worked. Having peered into this world, my overwhelming conclusion was that for the most part, events commonly ascribed to the work of the hidden hand of British intelligence were really the result of accident, mistakes, and failures. Although there were genuine conspiracies by Britain's intelligence services (some of which are discussed below), for the most part I found screwups, not conspiracies.

Put another away, those who tend to see the work of a conspiracy tend to overestimate the competency of those in Whitehall. "If only they knew how bad we are," not a few people inside Britain's secret services said to me in interviews over the years. The succession of British intelligence failures presented in these chapters, I believe, disabuses any suspicions that in working on MI5's authorized history I got too close to my subject. I describe events as I see them.

Years later, at Harvard, the idea for this project really took hold. As I watched British and American spy scandals unfold in the wake of Edward Snowden's disclosures in 2013, I wanted to understand how and why those two governments developed such close intelligence relations. For good and bad, Britain's and America's intelligence agencies have been the preeminent Western intelligence agencies and have shaped global affairs, past and present. But it was the seismic geopolitical shocks of 2016, from Brexit to Trump's election, which drove me to refocus and reconceive the parameters of this book. Various media outlets approached me to write about Russia's "unprecedented" meddling, its active measures campaign against the United States in 2016. I replied that I could not because they were not unprecedented. The more I looked, the more I realized that my original idea, about British and U.S. intelligence, was only one half of what needed to be told. What I *really* needed to do was understand not just them, but also Russian intelligence—both sides of the story.

My research thus became an odyssey to uncover secret service archives from both sides of the conflict, East and West: in Britain, the United States, and the Soviet Union. It expanded to include some archives in former Soviet bloc countries. I have woven together archival records, as well as the Russian-language memoirs of former Soviet intelligence officers. One source has been immensely helpful: the archive compiled and smuggled to the West, with MI6's help, by a former senior archivist in the KGB, Vasili Mitrokhin, parts of which are now publicly available in Cambridge, England. Indeed, the declassified parts of the Mitrokhin Archive, comprising typescript notes on secret KGB records, make Cambridge one of the two places in the world holding such material, the other being the KGB's archives in Moscow, which are not open—to say the least.[17]

Before beginning our story, we need to understand the names of the intelligence agencies that appear below. The intelligence world thrives on acronyms, with three-letter agencies producing a confusing alphabet soup. I have tried my best to minimize their use, but some are inescapable. HUMINT refers to human intelligence—that is, espionage: information from a human source, an agent, or a spy.* SIGINT refers to the interception of communications sent over cables, radio waves, and so on. IMINT is imagery intelligence, reconnaissance from spy planes and satellites. Then we have a multitude of three-letter agencies, abbreviations that governments love to use: KGB, MI6, MI5, CIA, FBI, NSA, all of which are characters in our narrative. In Britain, foreign intelligence was—and is—collected by MI6. It is known formally as the Secret Intelligence Service, SIS; within British government records, informally as "the friends," and its reports as *CX* (C standing for chief). It has traditionally been a straight human intelligence (espionage) service. Britain's SIGINT service is GCHQ (the oddball, with four letters: Government Communications Headquarters), successor to Britain's famous wartime Bletchley Park. Britain's Security Service, MI5, is responsible for security intelligence—counterespionage, sabotage, subversion, and terrorism. MI5 ("P.O. Box 500") is broadly analogous to the FBI in the United States, though its responsibilities are wider; its officers embark on preemptive investigations in ways that would be difficult, if not impossible, under the U.S. Constitution. The FBI was, and is, primarily a law enforcement

---

* The term *agent*, or *spy*, used in this book, covers a spectrum of engagement and knowledge: from someone knowingly working as a recruit of a foreign service, to someone being unknowingly cultivated. It is perfectly possible for a target to be recruited and not know for whom she or he is really working (so-called "false flag" recruitments). The fact that someone is given a code name by a foreign intelligence service, for potential recruitment, does not mean she or he knows this—and should not be taken to imply any illegal activity on his or her part.

agency. The CIA, which was not founded until later in our story, in 1947, is a foreign intelligence collection agency, like Britain's MI6, though with a much broader scope, and vastly more resources. The largest intelligence agency in the United States responsible for SIGINT, the NSA, is fused, as we shall see, with Britain's GCHQ.[18]

In the Soviet Union, Soviet intelligence consisted of two branches: the KGB and military intelligence, known as the Razvedupr, later the Fourth Department and then the GRU. The KGB went through a succession of different names—the Cheka, OGPU, NKVD—but, as we shall discover, its responsibilities remained broadly consistent. It was the self-styled "sword and shield" of the Communist Party of the Soviet Union (CPSU), charged with slaying its enemies and defending the motherland at home and abroad. The KGB's overwhelming focus was domestic, policing (read: suppressing) the Soviet population. Its foreign intelligence collection department, the First Chief Directorate (FCD), a body that runs like a thread throughout this book, was an offshoot of the KGB's domestic secret police functions. At its height, the KGB is thought to have employed 480,000 people, the largest secret police force to that point in history. If we include agents, that number likely exceeded a million. It was responsible for everything from running Soviet concentration camps, the Gulag, to deploying elite deep-cover "illegals" in Western countries. During the Cold War, the First Chief Directorate employed around twenty thousand people, broadly similar in size to the CIA at the time. Britain's MI6 and MI5 were smaller, at some points pathetically so. On both sides of the Cold War, SIGINT agencies squared off against each other, taking the majority of resources. In Russia today, the KGB's successors are the FSB and the SVR, which see themselves as its heirs. Russian military intelligence, now called the GU, not GRU, is today known for conducting incompetent and reckless assassination attempts on European soil, like when its operatives used a weapons-grade chemical agent, Novichok, to try to assassinate a former MI6 spy, Sergei Skripal, in Salisbury, England, in March 2018.[19]

What, then, is this book about, on an operational level? Consider these two incidents, one from the 1970s, and one from our more recent past:

On an otherwise unremarkable day in April 1971, a Russian man walked into Hampstead's police station in north London. He announced that he was a member of the Soviet trade delegation and wished to speak to someone in authority: "I have important information," he added. He was soon speaking to a Special Branch officer, who, upon hearing the man's story, called in MI5. The Russian, a man named Oleg Lyalin, revealed that his position in the Soviet trade delegation in Britain was a cover; he knew nothing about importing knitwear, as his official job suggested. In fact, he was a senior Soviet intelligence officer, working in the KGB's unit specializing in sabotage and covert attacks, Department V. Facing turmoil in his personal life, conducting two separate extramarital affairs, and terrified of being recalled to Moscow, where he faced an unknown fate, he offered information in exchange for his defection. Over the coming four months, in debriefings at MI5 safe houses in London, Lyalin revealed that the KGB was making contingency plans for sabotaging Britain's critical infrastructure, upon instructions from Moscow. "The poison gas canisters will be released by agents in tunnels under London," he said. "Our aim is to terrorize the British government and population, bringing them to their knees." His network of agents, some of whom were later prosecuted, communicated with the KGB in Moscow in Morse code, using Sony radio sets.

In September 1971, Lyalin was arrested for drunk driving in London. He decided this was the moment to defect. His intelligence caused consternation when senior Downing Street officials were briefed. On the other side of the Atlantic, Henry Kissinger, the U.S. national security adviser, informed the president of the United States, Richard Nixon, about Lyalin and the KGB's sabotage plans. At that exact moment, the president was trying to initiate better relations with Moscow: détente. In response to Lyalin's defection, the British government sanctioned the mass expulsion of 105 Soviet intelligence officers posing as diplomats in London—the largest such expulsion in history. Top secret Soviet records reveal that doing so degraded Soviet intelligence operations in Britain, marking a major turning point in Cold War counterespionage. Afterward Britain was, for the first time, a hard target for Soviet spy chiefs.[20]

In 2020, the centenary of the foundation of Soviet foreign intelligence, Russia's intelligence services conducted a massive nine-month-long supply chain hack on an American software company, SolarWinds, which provided software services to 250 U.S. federal agencies and most of America's largest companies. It has not been publicly disclosed whether Russia's cyber intrusion moved beyond reconnaissance to the sabotage of sensitive systems: inserting malware and back doors into networks, including those of government agencies, corporations, the U.S. electric grid, and laboratories developing and transporting new generations of nuclear weapons. In the cyber world, distinctions between reconnaissance and sabotage are slight: it is the difference between observing and changing data, altering computer code. The failure of U.S. intelligence to detect Russia's SolarWinds hack ranks among the worst in American history. The U.S. government apparently did not, however, sit on its hands in the aftermath. Informed commentators have pointed to power cuts that Moscow experienced soon after the SolarWinds attack as evidence of a U.S. counterattack.[21]

These two incidents, separated by fifty years, at first seem worlds apart: the first involved sabotage in the physical world, the second collection and perhaps sabotage in today's digital world, where operatives can move seamlessly across domains. In the past, the KGB undertook physical reconnaissance of targets in Western countries, hiding weapons and arms caches in unassuming urban and countryside locations in the United States, Britain, and other Western countries, for activation when instructed by Moscow.

In today's cyber age—using bytes rather than bullets—it is easier, quicker, and cheaper than ever for states and individuals to conduct espionage and sabotage. In our new digital world, spies can reconnoiter critical infrastructure and orchestrate sabotage operations from the safety of their own jurisdictions, vaulting over national boundaries and firewalls. While the environment for these clandestine activities has changed, the underlying strategies behind them have not: to spy on, disrupt, and degrade enemy states. *Spies* tells that story.

PART ONE

THE CLASH
BETWEEN DICTATORS
AND DEMOCRACIES

CHAPTER TWO

CHILL IN THE EAST

. . . a permanent state of "cold war" . . . a "peace that is no peace."
–George Orwell, *You and the Atomic Bomb*

IN OCTOBER 1945, IN THE WAKE OF THE TWO ATOMIC BOMBS dropped by the U.S. on Hiroshima and Nagasaki, bringing World War II to an end, the British author George Orwell wrote an essay about the fundamental geopolitical change that atomic weapons created. The changes underway, as Orwell pointed out, had begun over a dozen years before. Atomic bombs were new, devastating tools for a longer-term ideological conflict between East and West. As usual, Orwell was correct. As this first part of *Spies* reveals, Western powers were effectively engaged in a Cold War with the Soviet Union long before they knew it.

Vladimir Lenin's grand strategy for the Soviet regime was anchored in his application of the writings of Karl Marx. Inevitable historical forces, both Marx and Lenin believed, would lead to a revolution of the proletariat, capitalism's exploited working class, sweeping away bourgeois capitalist powers and replacing them with a unified "socialist" society. ("Socialism" in the Soviet Union had little to do with socialism as understood in Western European liberal democracies—as little as conservatism relates to fascism.

It was an anodyne term for communist dictatorship, which Marx described, and Lenin created. But because of the Kremlin's hijacking of the term, there began a long and tiresome conflation, especially in the United States, of "socialism" and "communism.") At the time of the Bolshevik Revolution and then the bloody Russian Civil War, history seemed to be on the side of Lenin's revolutionaries. The age of the great European powers appeared over. World War I led to the collapse of four European empires. Royal families who were not bayoneted escaped into exile. The crumbling of the great empires in Central and Eastern Europe raised Bolshevik hopes to fever pitch to create a new world order. Russia was to be the tinderbox for a global conflagration.

WAR AND SOVIET TERROR

Russia's intelligence services today trace their origins to immediately after the Bolshevik Revolution. Six weeks after seizing power in November 1917 (October in the traditional Russian calendar), Lenin established the Cheka, the predecessor to the KGB. The Cheka functioned as the vanguard of the Bolshevik Party, slaying its enemies and defending its people, domestic and foreign. Although the Cheka would be renamed with different acronyms before KGB—OGPU, NKVD—its functions remained the same. Intended to be temporary ("extraordinary"), in fact it became a permanent, central fixture of the Bolshevik regime for the next seven decades. Cheka officers served as frontline soldiers for Lenin, Stalin, and their successors in the Kremlin. Their overwhelming priority was domestic, protecting the regime against counterrevolutionary "enemies of the people." Some were real. The Bolsheviks faced armed Western intervention to depose them. Many other enemies were phantoms. Lenin and the Cheka also feared, from their reading of Marx, an inevitable conspiracy by Western capitalist powers against them. The Cheka soon established a foreign intelligence branch to conduct espionage, subversion, and sabotage abroad.[1]

Today, Russia's intelligence services present carefully sanitized versions of their history, lionizing the early successes of Soviet foreign intelligence, and airbrushing away its murders, mass repressions and imprisonments, and gross violations of human rights. It serves the purposes of today's Kremlin, under Vladimir Putin, to present the Cheka as a professional intelligence service whose officers, Chekisty, had "warm hearts, a cool head, and clean hands," as they claimed. In reality, the hearts of Cheka officers were murderously cold, their heads warped hot by Lenin and Stalin's conspiratorial worldviews, and their hands bloodied.[2]

The Cheka's first head was Felix Dzerzhinsky. Born to a wealthy Polish family, he became a fanatically hard-line Bolshevik, one of Lenin's closest advisers. A bespectacled, bookish-looking man in a party of many such types, Dzerzhinsky was the selfless Knight of the Revolution, in later retelling, who slew counterrevolutionary enemies. The Cheka did indeed conduct astonishing coups against the regime's opponents at home and abroad, but this was only a small part of its work. Starting with Dzerzhinsky, the Cheka grew into the largest secret police in the twentieth century. Dzerzhinsky's successors, men like Genrikh Yagoda, Nikolai Yezhov, and Lavrenti Beria, served as Joseph Stalin's loyal hangmen, carrying out the Great Terror, the greatest repression in modern peacetime European history. Omitting the story of mass repression from the Cheka's history, as Putin's regime tries to do, is akin to describing Adolf Hitler as a failed Austrian painter.[3]

Contrary to later Soviet depictions, the Bolsheviks did not come to power in a popular uprising. They seized power in a coup. Before Lenin returned to the country in 1917, he did not believe that Russia, where two-thirds of the population was made up of poorly educated peasants, was ready for a workers' revolution. Germany, with its industrialized society, was a more obvious birthing ground. Lenin hailed from Russian nobility; with his characteristic goatee, he was an urbane polyglot, more at home in the cafés and libraries of Munich, London, and Geneva than on Moscow's streets. The fact that the Bolsheviks seized power, and then, against all odds, held on to it—largely due to the Cheka's reign of terror—can blind us to how events seemed to contemporaries at the time. News of the Bolsheviks' seizure of power made little immediate impression in the Western press. The *Times* of London, for example, asserted confidently the week after the coup that the Bolsheviks would not be in power long.

Less than four months later, in March 1918, the Bolsheviks signed a peace treaty with imperial Germany, at Brest-Litovsk, that pulled Russia out of World War I. It was humiliating but necessary, in Lenin's view, and controversial in Russia, splitting the ruling coalition between Bolsheviks and the leftist Socialist Revolutionary Party. The latter then targeted its former allies for assassination.

To gain peace, one-quarter of Russia's empire passed to imperial Germany. In the aftermath, the Bolsheviks became "communists" and relocated their base of operations from Petrograd (changed from the former name of St. Petersburg because "burg" sounded too German) to Moscow. This meant, for the newly styled communists, turning their back on Russia's Europeanized and culturally rich city, the Venice of the North. The Cheka requisitioned a former Russian insurance building, the Lubyanka, as its headquarters in Moscow. The Lubyanka's basement became infamous as the site of gruesome Cheka torture, akin to a chamber of horrors.

Bolshevik rule was born in a crucible of internal and foreign intrigue. The Red Army fought a civil war against a coalition of "White" anti-communist forces, white being a color traditionally associated with the Romanov tsars. They scythed down pro-monarchists ("former people"), as well as members of the bourgeoisie ("class enemies"), saboteurs ("fifth columnists"), "wreckers" (a loose term, effectively meaning all who opposed the Bolsheviks), and spies, some sponsored by Western powers—but not as many as Lenin believed. The ensuing Russian Civil War resulted in the deaths of approximately 3.3 million people. The war, and foreign subversion in it, would shape the thinking of successive Soviet leaders and their secret police. By 1922, the Red Army was victorious. The Russian Soviet Republic became the centerpiece of the Union of Soviet Socialist Republics (USSR), eventually a federation of sixteen republics carved out of the former tsarist empire, stretching from the Arctic north to subtropical southern areas in the Caucasus. The Bolsheviks would eventually rule over and terrorize six hundred million people.

The Bolsheviks faced armed Western hostilities. The Western Entente powers overtly intervened in Russia to try to strangle Lenin's regime at birth. In March 1918, an advance party of British marines landed at Archangel, on the White Sea, some seven hundred miles northeast of Petrograd. The invasion, which included American warships, was enthusiastically and publicly backed by Britain's wartime first lord of the admiralty, Winston Churchill. The landing party was part of an Allied wartime strategy to destroy the Bolshevik regime, restore the wartime eastern front, and thus relieve pressure on the Allies on the western front. Scholars have described U.S. intervention in the Russian Civil War as a secret war against Bolshevism and even the "first Cold War." There is much to this. As well as facing *overt* military intervention, the Cheka also uncovered *covert* Western plots to unseat the Bolsheviks, some initiated by Britain's foreign intelligence service, MI6 (then known as MI1c). These plots by the British, Americans, and other Western powers confirmed Lenin's worst fears. Evidence of Western secret conspiracies left a burning impression in the hallways of the Kremlin that lasted throughout the Soviet era. Its echoes still reverberate there today.[4]

According to later Cheka valorizations, one British operation, known as the envoys plot, was part of a clandestine conspiracy by Western powers to depose the Bolsheviks. The truth was different. MI6's archives reveal that it had little intelligence from inside Russia in the first chaotic months of Bolshevik rule. Even if it wanted to, it would have been unable to orchestrate a plot to depose Lenin. MI6 in Russia relied on adventurers, con men, and informants, some of whom were left-leaning journalists like Arthur Ransome (known as "S76"), later the author of *Swallows and Amazons*. His mistress was Trotsky's secretary. Most of his "intelligence" was devoted to getting her out of Russia. There was, then, a vast gulf between the intentions and capabilities of Western services when it came to spying on and subverting the Bolsheviks. Soviet leaders from Lenin onward never grasped that. In August 1918, the Cheka stormed the British embassy in Petrograd in retaliation. Robert Bruce Lockhart, a hard-drinking Scottish thirty-three-year-old diplomat associated with the plot, was imprisoned at the Lubyanka for a time. A British MI6 agent, Sidney Reilly (code-named "ST1"), a womanizer and philanderer, the so-called "ace of spies," escaped in disguise. Rumors have rumbled ever since that Reilly, who seems originally to have come from Ukraine, was really a Soviet Cheka agent. It is impossible to know; the documentary evidence is incomplete. But that story seems too clever by half.[5]

For eighteen months, Britain and Soviet Russia were effectively at war, as Britain intervened militarily, supporting White Russian forces. In Lenin's mind, with justification, Soviet Russia was a "fortress besieged by world capital," which conjured up memories of Napoleon's invasion in 1812 and European intervention in the Crimea in the 1850s. The Bolsheviks could justifiably call themselves the defenders of Russia against foreigners. In reality, however, there was no unified Western conspiracy against the Bolsheviks. If there had been, the regime surely would have lost the civil war. Those Western troops that did intervene militarily in support of White Russian forces were too few to affect the war's outcome, but numerous enough to convince the Bolsheviks that they were defending the regime against Western imperialism.[6]

At the end of August 1918, while Lenin was recovering from the third assassination attempt that year, he authorized what became known as the Red Terror: "it is necessary secretly—and urgently—to prepare the terror," he instructed. In September he issued a decree that sanctioned "mass shooting" to be "inflicted without hesitation." As he faced threats on his life, Lenin's bent toward institutional terror became unrestrained. The size and role of the Cheka, the chief instrument of the terror, grew dramatically. In March 1918, there were 120 Chekists; by 1919 the number had swollen to more than 100,000, making it one of the largest parts of the early Soviet state. The Cheka devised ingenious methods of torturing victims during the Red Terror. Each local Cheka *rezidentura* (station) had its own specialty. In Kharkiv, where the *rezident* was an alcoholic drug addict, they used the "glove trick"—burning victims' hands in boiling water until the blistered skin could be peeled off, leaving the torturers with "human gloves." In Voronezh, south of Moscow, they rolled naked victims in barrels with protruding nails. In Kyiv, they resorted to medieval torture, attaching a cage full of rats to a victim's torso, which they heated up, so that, panicked, the rats ate their way through the victim to escape the flames. In Odesa, they chained victims to planks and pushed them slowly into a giant cauldron of boiling water. A favorite Cheka winter torture was to pour cold water on naked victims in subzero weather until they became living ice sculptures. Many of the horrors later attributed to Stalinism were really initiated under Lenin. In the autumn of 1918, Lenin established a concentration camp in the Solovetsky Islands, in the White Sea. Lenin also used the Cheka to terrorize the Russian Orthodox Church. That is again sanitized from Putin's version of the past today, which makes much of the connections between "Chekists" and religion—Russia's "spiritual security." Putin is framing Russia's war in Ukraine as a "holy war."[7]

Before seizing power, the Bolshevik Party had been largely an illegal, conspiratorial, underground organization. Once in power, the party did not change its stripes. It continued to rely on informants, blackmail, and deception. Bolshevik leaders continued to use their prerevolutionary aliases; Vladimir Ilyich Ulyanov used his pseudonym, Lenin, while the Bolshevik Georgian seminary dropout and former bank robber, Joseph Dzhugashvili, continued to be known as Stalin (he also liked being called Koba, after a folk hero from his native Georgia). Some of the intelligence methodologies used by Lenin and other Soviet leaders was adopted from techniques previously employed against them by the tsarist secret police, the Okhrana. They knew firsthand its use of agents provocateurs—undercover officers used to entrap targets. Some have suggested that Stalin himself had previously been an Okhrana informant, although that is impossible to substantiate given incomplete records from the time. Stalin's own Okhrana dossier was conspicuously gutted once the Bolsheviks gained power. By 1921, the Soviet bureaucracy was ten times as large as under the tsars.[8]

As the Bolsheviks fought for their survival during the Russian Civil War, the Cheka began to send undercover officers and agents behind enemy lines. By June 1919, the number of these so-called illegals was large enough to justify their own department within the Cheka. In December 1920, on the third anniversary of its founding, the Cheka created a new foreign intelligence department, called the INO, to direct all operations beyond Soviet borders. The INO, led by Artur Artuzov, grew from 70 men in 1922 to 122 seven years later, of whom 62 served abroad.[9]

Illegal officers were essential to the Cheka INO's initial work. During its early years, the Soviet Union was an international pariah. It had few diplomatic relations with foreign countries, which meant it was unable to send intelligence officers overseas under diplomatic ("legal") cover. The United States refused to open diplomatic relations with the Soviet Union until 1933. It did, however, open trade relations with the Soviets earlier. As the Soviet government established commercial relations with Western powers, it used trade offices to open illegal intelligence stations in foreign capitals, by default operating without diplomatic protection. They were headed by a *rezident* (head of station). In the early years, such residencies (*rezidentury*) served both the Cheka and Soviet Red Army military intelligence (later known as the GRU), though later they would separate.[10]

In March 1919, the Soviet government established the Communist International (Comintern) to export revolution overseas. Its president, Grigori Zinoviev, boasted that "within a year all Europe will be communist." The Comintern imposed rigid military-like discipline on overseas communist parties, which were obliged to respond to Moscow's instructions. Despite their later protests to the contrary, local communist parties, and the Comintern itself, facilitated Soviet espionage. The Comintern provided technical support, safe houses, courier networks, and orchestrated the illicit transfer of funds for Soviet agents overseas, as well as paying secret subsidies to communist parties in the West.[11]

The basic structure of Soviet foreign intelligence, with *rezidentury* overseas reporting to headquarters in Moscow—called "the Center," known to readers of John le Carré as Moscow Center—was thus established in the early years of the Soviet Union. It would remain in place throughout the seven decades of its existence. Even after the Cheka could create legal *rezidentury*, with the opening of diplomatic relations, it continued to operate illegals. They were cut off from a Soviet embassy, out in the cold, who worked without the benefit of diplomatic protection. This meant that if they were caught, they could be arrested, as opposed to expelled, which diplomatic cover afforded. Illegals were, and still are, viewed as Russia's foreign intelligence elite; they use complicated codes, hollow coins, hidden deposits ("dead drops"), and suchlike. The INO would later be transformed into the KGB's foreign intelligence branch, known as the First Chief Directorate.[12]

The Cheka's use of agents provocateurs was part of a longer-term Russian military doctrine of *maskirovka*: using military camouflage and disguise. It was closely aligned with the use of disinformation (or *deza*, disseminating false or misleading information whose authorship is concealed). The INO ran a disinformation unit from at least 1921, whose stock in trade was faking memoranda purportedly from the Soviet ruling body, the Politburo, and Red Army orders of battle, and then planting them among their enemies, drawing them out into the open, at which point they could be eliminated. During the Russian Civil War, Cheka officers used these tactics to impose Soviet rule. One arena where they did so was Ukraine, a huge country at the crossroads between Europe and Russia, and the latter's historical heartland. With its rolling wheatfields, Ukraine was, and is, the breadbasket of Europe, something that the Bolsheviks quickly grasped. After 1918, however, much of the countryside in Ukraine was in open revolt against the Bolsheviks. Its subsequent bloody "pacification" by the Cheka and Red Army—masterminded by Leon Trotsky, one of the original seven Bolshevik Politburo members and the head of the Red Army—was integral to the creation of the Soviet Union in 1922.[13]

One particularly imaginative and successful Soviet deception operation was known as TREST (or "Trust" in English), which took place from 1921 to 1927. The Cheka—OGPU, as it was renamed in 1923—established a bogus Russian tsarist underground, the Monarchist Association of Central Russia. Soviet officers posed as its members and traveled abroad to ensnare anti-Bolshevik supporters. The main victim of the TREST deception was MI6's former operative in Russia, Sidney Reilly. TREST was a well-executed operation against a second-rate opponent, the British. In September 1925, the Monarchist Association (that is, the OGPU) lured Reilly back to Russia, where he was immediately arrested. Under brutal OGPU interrogation, Reilly promised to reveal all he knew about British intelligence and Russian émigrés in the West. Six days later, he was taken for a walk in the woods near Moscow and, without warning, shot from behind. The OGPU later put Reilly's body on display in the Lubyanka, where, to this day, it is rumored to lie under a courtyard.[14]

BRITAIN'S SECRET SERVICE

There are good reasons why Britain's intelligence services have not featured significantly in our story so far. In Soviet Russia, the Bolsheviks continued to be at "war" even after the armistice brought World War I to an end in 1918. Wartime policies like mass surveillance and deportation, which all major powers had undertaken to varying degrees, became permanent features in the new Soviet state, used to suppress and terrorize the population. By contrast, the resources of Britain's intelligence services were slashed after the war. The famed reputation of Britain's secret service owed more to fiction than fact. In Europe and North America, myths abounded about the prowess of Britain's service stretching back to the Elizabethan period, a narrative encouraged by writers like William Le Queux and Rudyard Kipling. Intelligence may have been "the great game that never sleeps day or night," as Kipling claimed, but in reality, after 1918, Britain's intelligence services were largely asleep.[15]

Britain's security and foreign intelligence services, MI5 and MI6, respectively, had been established on the eve of World War I, in 1909. MI5's founding director general, Vernon Kell (known as "K"), a former general in the British army, continued at its helm until World War II. This made him the longest-serving head of any British government department. By the signing of the armistice in 1918, MI5's staff had grown to 844. A year later, amid demobilization of the largest army in British history, MI5 had a staff of just 151. Just over five years later, in 1925, it had a total staff of just 35. For the two decades after 1920, MI5's counterespionage department had an average of just five officers. Its annual budget shrank from about £100,000 in 1919 to £35,000 a year later. MI5 eked out a threadbare existence at its headquarters on Cromwell Road, opposite the Natural History Museum in London. According to a secret in-house history, MI5's pay was so meager that it could only rely on officers with private incomes.[16]

Britain's foreign intelligence service—MI6, or SIS—fared little better. It suffered a similar slashing of resources. MI6 had broad responsibilities, to collect foreign intelligence for the British government from human sources. Its actual capabilities, however, were negligible. In the 1920s, it had 33 stations overseas, mostly one-man operations. Its officers worked under diplomatic cover, as British passport control officers, in embassies and consulates. Britain's government at the time approached intelligence in the same way the Victorians did sex: it was not a subject fit for discussion in polite society. The government did not publicly avow the existence of MI5 or MI6 for the next seven decades. This had benefits for both services, allowing them to create an aura of mystique. The British public had a seemingly insatiable appetite for espionage—something shared with Russians—devouring the writings of former British intelligence officers like W. Somerset Maugham, in his story collection *Ashenden*.

In real life, some of the eccentric personalities in MI6's service could have come straight from a novel. Its first chief, Mansfield Cumming, cultivated an enthralling image around the service. Cumming had lost a leg during the war in a road traffic accident, hacking it off with a penknife. MI6's postwar chief, Hugh "Quex" Sinclair, was a *bon viveur*, frequently seen in London's clubs. He drove a Lancia sports car and wore a bowler. MI6 chiefs were known by the letter *C*—whether that also stood for Cumming remains unclear—a tradition lasting to this day. They signed their correspondence with the letter *C* in green ink. MI6's headquarters were located, from 1926, and for the next three decades, in the Broadway Buildings, near St. James's Park Underground, in the heart of London. *C*'s office, on the fourth floor, had a green light above the door to let visitors know when they could enter. The service's budget, £200,000 a year in the late 1920s, was more than MI5's, probably because its operations involved payments to recruit foreign agents. Like MI5, it received its budget from a "secret vote" in Parliament. Overall, however, MI6's budget was minuscule compared to other parts of Britain's defense industry. On the eve of World War II, its budget was less than the annual maintenance cost of one of His Majesty's destroyers berthed in home waters.[17]

While Britain's intelligence services were under-resourced and understaffed, they did better than agencies on the other side of the Atlantic. After World War I, the U.S. government did not even have a dedicated foreign intelligence agency. In 1929, the secretary of state, Henry Stimson, famously closed the U.S. government's code-breaking department, the Black Chamber, on the grounds that "gentlemen do not read each other's mail." Washington thus entered the 1930s without the benefit of a dedicated, single SIGINT agency.[18]

SOVIET ESPIONAGE FRONT GROUPS

It was precisely because the Soviet state was so weak that it resorted to aggressive foreign intelligence. Some activities were like those that all states conduct—to know the secrets of opponents and shape foreign affairs in advantageous ways. But Lenin's spy chiefs did much more. They integrated intelligence with other components of the Soviet state, and commerce, in ways without parallel among contemporary Western powers. Soviet intelligence stole as many Western secrets as possible, especially in the military and industrial sectors, to prepare for what Marx predicted would be the inevitable conflict between communism and capitalism. The Soviet regime's efforts to steal Western secrets, and subvert Western governments by clandestine means, grew in reverse proportion to the actual impact that communist parties had in countries like Britain. In October 1931, eleven years after its establishment, the Communist Party of Great Britain (CPGB) was a spent force, receiving approximately just seventy thousand votes in the general election that year and failing to gain a single seat in Parliament. What the Soviet Union could not do openly through communist parties, it did secretly.

In 1920, the young Bolshevik regime, fighting for its existence, sent a trade delegation to London. It was a masterstroke by Lenin, resulting in the first de facto recognition of the regime by a Western power. Among the delegation were undercover intelligence officers. (Operatives would accompany such delegations time and again over the coming decades.) Nicolas Klishko, secretary and official translator on this trip, appears to have been the first Soviet *rezident* in Britain. Spying and buying were essential for the Soviet state from the start.[19]

Britain's government, led by Liberal prime minister David Lloyd George, knew from intercepted communications—SIGINT—about the trade delegation's hidden agenda. For a decade after the Bolsheviks seized power, Soviet government communications were insecure, vulnerable to the skillful work of British code breakers. One, former tsarist code breaker Ernst Fetterlein, known as "Fetty," had escaped to Britain after the Bolshevik Revolution and been recruited by Britain's new peacetime code-breaking department, the Government Code and Cypher School (GC&CS), established in 1919 under MI6's jurisdiction. ("School" was meant to suggest something harmlessly academic.) Fetterlein, a large, bearish, taciturn man, attacked Soviet codes with the same relentless dedication he had previously unleashed on British communications, when he worked for the tsarist code-breaking black chamber (*cabinet noir*). Between 1920 and 1923, GC&CS provided senior policymakers in London with 13,000 intercepts, roughly 290 per month. Britain's foreign secretary, Lord Curzon, recognized the importance of GC&CS's work. They were, he wrote, "without doubt the most valuable source of our secret information respecting their [the Soviet government's] policy and actions. They provide the most accurate and, withal, intrinsically the cheapest, means of obtaining secret political information that exists."

Lloyd George took personal charge of the negotiations with the Soviet trade delegation, and in so doing received a constant flow of decrypts, which he annotated with pencil markings in the margins. Among the decrypts was a blunt warning from Lenin to Soviet trade negotiators about the prime minister himself: "that swine Lloyd George has no scruples or shame in the way he deceives. Don't believe a word he says and gull him three times as much."[20]

British decrypts revealed that the Soviet government was illicitly subsidizing the British Communist Party, established in 1920, and using Comintern agents as couriers to launder money in Britain. At the same time, they showed the slender prospects of success that the Bolsheviks had for inciting revolution in Britain. This gave Lloyd George the confidence, despite Soviet rhetoric about sponsoring subversion in the West, to make a trade agreement with the Soviet government in March 1921. A permanent Soviet trade office opened in London soon thereafter, becoming a defining feature of Anglo-Soviet relations in the coming decades. It was a den of spies, conducting espionage, subversion, and sabotage.

Unfortunately for British code breakers, the authentic Soviet reports they decrypted also included deliberately planted forgeries. In October 1924, a document about Soviet subversion in Britain contributed to the downfall of Britain's first Labour prime minister, Ramsay MacDonald. The so-called Zinoviev letter, named after the Comintern leader, purported to be instructions to the CPGB to put pressure on their sympathizers in the Labour Party to engage in seditious activities. The provenance of the letter is still debated. It may have been genuine but was more likely a forgery, possibly the work of anti-Bolshevik White Russians, possibly a British forgery (as the Kremlin to this day maintains). It may even have been an elaborate Soviet forgery designed to whip up an anti-Soviet backlash in Britain, allowing the Kremlin to present itself as an innocent victim. Whatever its origin, the Zinoviev letter did not contain anything that could not be found in genuine Comintern messages, decrypted by GC&CS, showing Soviet subversion in Britain. It was published by the *Daily Mail*, four days before Britain's general election in October 1924, helping to bring down MacDonald's government, but probably not decisive in doing so.[21]

The Soviet government also used its state-run news agencies as cover for espionage. These included the Russian Telegraph Agency (ROSTA), which had a presence in London beginning in 1920 and still exists, under the name TASS. Soviet intelligence services likewise used front groups to conduct espionage—dummy outfits that ostensibly had nothing to do with the Soviet government and thus provided cover for conducting illicit activities. Soviet commercial groups that opened in Britain seemed to MI5 to have dual uses. One such was Russian Oil Products (ROP), established in 1924. It seemed to allow the Kremlin to weaponize its oil supplies. All of ROP's shareholders were Russian, and one-third were members of the British Communist Party. While it had legitimate business interests (selling Russian oil), it seemed to be a Soviet intelligence front. Its network had sites dangerously close to British fuel depots—later designated "critical national infrastructure"—which MI5 concluded could be used for sabotage by driving oil tankers into them. ROP was placed on a list of businesses subject to police regulation in the event of a "national emergency," meaning the outbreak of war. Such measures were later known in Britain as protective security.[22]

Another Soviet front group was the innocent-sounding Federated Press of America, or FPA, which opened in 1923 with offices in London's oil-lamp–lit Outer Temple, near the Strand. MI5's surveillance of the FPA revealed its connections with another outfit, the All-Russian Co-operative Society (ARCOS), based at 49 Moorgate, in London. Its ostensible purpose was to promote trade between Britain and Russia. In fact, it was a Soviet espionage front. In March 1927, a disaffected former ARCOS employee informed MI6 that ARCOS had a copy of a classified British document. MI5 and MI6 spent the next six weeks checking the informant's reliability. Then, with approval from both the director of public prosecutions and the prime minister, Stanley Baldwin, MI5 authorized the Special Branch to raid 49 Moorgate. It was an aggressive move, violating diplomatic privileges attached to ARCOS.

The raid was bungled. No incriminating British classified documents were found. But it caused a sensation in the House of Commons, where a group of anti-Soviet Conservative backbenchers, and some ministers, including Winston Churchill, pushed the government to take a tough stance against the Soviets. Baldwin complied. He severed diplomatic relations with the Soviet Union.[23]

With nothing to show from the ARCOS raid, however, Baldwin panicked and resorted to drawing on top secret intercepts to prove his case. In an unprecedented move, at the end of May 1927, he rose to his feet in the House of Commons and read from four SIGINT intercepts—or as the cabinet nicely put it, "secret documents of the class which is not usual to quote" that had "come into the possession of His Majesty's Government." Baldwin quoted excerpts from one intercept from the Soviet chargé d'affaires to Moscow.[24]

In the aftermath, the Soviet spy ring centered on FPA was rolled up, though the British authorities decided not to prosecute because of the challenge of revealing intelligence. Much worse followed. Disclosing top secret intelligence publicly in the House of Commons proved disastrous for Britain's intelligence efforts against the Soviet Union.

The Soviet government thereafter adopted a new method for encrypting its communications, using virtually unbreakable onetime pads—a system that uses a randomly generated private key, known solely to the sender and receiver of a message. As the name suggests, it is used only once, making it effectively impossible to crack. As a result, from 1927 until the end of World War II, British code breakers at GC&CS were hardly able to read any high-grade Soviet communications, although they had some success with

Comintern communications. SIGINT, the best source of intelligence on the Soviet Union, dried up, leaving Britain with few windows into Stalin's aims or capabilities. MI6 managed to obtain some insights into Stalin's rule when Boris Bazhanov, his aide and the party secretary, defected in 1928. He was the first high-ranking Soviet party official to defect to the West after the revolution. Bazhanov provided MI6 with 140 pages of information. As would happen on countless later occasions, however, he was found to be exaggerating his importance.

In Moscow, MI6 was nonexistent. Britain reopened diplomatic relations with the Soviet Union in 1929, but that did not include an MI6 presence there. In 1936, Britain's wonderfully named ambassador in Moscow, Aretas Akers-Douglas, better known as Viscount Chilston, refused to allow MI6 to open a station inside the embassy there on the grounds that it was "liable to cause embarrassment." Subsequent British ambassadors in Moscow felt the same. So, too, would later U.S. ambassadors about their own intelligence service, the CIA. When the U.S. government opened relations with the Soviet Union, in 1933, its new embassy was easy prey for Soviet intelligence. It had virtually no security and initially used no ciphers. George Kennan, one of the embassy's founding staff, recalled that telegrams were transmitted through the regular telegraph office and lay on tables for locally employed Soviet staff to see.[25]

Two days after the British government cut off diplomatic relations in 1927, the Soviet Politburo decreed that using illegals would be a normal practice beyond its borders, in Western Europe and farther afield. In the United States, the Soviets also used front groups, and illegals, living under false identities ("legends"). A major Soviet intelligence racket there was Moscow's first trade mission to the U.S., the American Trading Corporation (or AMTORG). It was similar to, and connected with, ARCOS in Britain.

Incorporated in New York, AMTORG was established in 1924, with help from the Russian-descended American businessman Armand Hammer, known as "Lenin's capitalist" due to his relationship with the first Soviet leader and his willingness to launder money for the Soviet government.

From 1924 to 1933, AMTORG had disproportionate influence as a principal channel between the U.S. and Soviet governments, as they did not have diplomatic relations. As the sole purchaser for the Soviet government in the U.S., the organization was designed to facilitate trade between the two countries. From its offices at 165 Broadway in Manhattan, not far from Wall Street, Soviet intelligence officers had perfect cover for seeking Americans interested in doing business in Russia—and then stealing their scientific and technical secrets. A common Soviet tactic was to dangle a lucrative deal in Russia's vast untapped market, acquire a target company's commercial secrets, then scuttle the deal.[26]

AMTORG would become a major center of Soviet espionage in North America throughout the Cold War. Its roster of executives and employees included both GRU and KGB officers.[27]

STEALING CODES

Code-breaking sometimes occurs through the work of brilliant minds, as we see in the movies. But it also is accomplished in more pedestrian ways: foreign code books can be stolen, or clerks recruited. This continues today. Contemporary intelligence services refer to "human-derived SIGINT": when a spy discloses secrets that make code-breaking possible.[28]

The Cheka was far ahead of Western intelligence services in recognizing the importance of recruiting well-placed agents with access to code books. In May 1921, at the height of the Red Terror, Lenin established an independent SIGINT body run jointly by the Cheka and the Soviet Red Army (military) intelligence. It was housed not in the Lubyanka but in the foreign affairs building on Kuznetsky bridge, a brief drive from the Kremlin. The "special department," or SPEKO as it was known, was then the largest and best-resourced SIGINT agency in the world. It was led by an officer named Gleb Boky, a veteran of the St. Petersburg revolutionary underground. Boky, a trained hydrologist in his fifties, carried the scars, both physical and mental, of being repeatedly imprisoned and tortured by the tsarist secret police, the Okhrana, for his revolutionary activities. Tall, with piercing blue eyes and the emaciated look of a tuberculosis patient, he walked with a pronounced stoop. He kept his door closed throughout the workday, using a peephole to survey those knocking for admittance before letting them in. Female staff viewed him with disgust as Boky prided himself on his sexual athleticism and arranged weekend sex "retreats" at his dacha. Under his command, SPEKO successfully decrypted diplomatic traffic from Britain, Austria, Germany, Italy, and almost certainly the U.S. government. No Western SIGINT agency during the 1920s and 1930s collected as much political and diplomatic intelligence.[29]

Lenin and Stalin viewed Britain as the world's most powerful country after World War I. Britain's "capitalist" empire, spanning the globe, inevitably made it the primary ideological target for them. In 1924, just two years after the Soviet Union was established, the Cheka's foreign intelligence branch, the INO, achieved its first penetration of Britain's foreign service, recruiting Francesco Constantini (assigned the code name DUNCAN), an Italian messenger working in the British Embassy in Rome. For more than a decade, Constantini provided diplomatic documents and cipher materials to his Soviet handlers, who paid him handsomely. The material he stole was invaluable for the SPEKO in decrypting British communications. Soviet intelligence headquarters ranked Constantini as its most important foreign agent. That year, he provided, on average, 150 pages of classified material a week.[30]

Five years later, in 1929, the OGPU recruited a cipher clerk who worked in the British Foreign Office communications department. Ernest Holloway Oldham was a walk-in, as the intelligence world calls those who volunteer their services. He approached the OGPU *rezident* in Paris, while he was in the city with a British trade delegation, and offered to sell Foreign Office ciphers in exchange for money—a lot of it. To the fury of his superiors in Moscow, the *rezident* failed to follow up on Oldham's offer. The Center, as Soviet intelligence headquarters in the Lubyanka would always be known, dispatched one of its most flamboyant deep-cover illegals, Dmitri

Bystroletov (code-named HANS, then ANDREI), to track Oldham down. According to a carefully sanitized hagiography of Soviet foreign intelligence published in 2021, to mark the Cheka's centenary, Bystroletov was one of the most successful of the so-called Soviet Great Illegals, more on whom below. He was indeed successful. But Bystroletov was also grimly efficient.

Born in 1901, Bystroletov was the illegitimate son of a Cossack mother and, as Bystroletov convinced himself, the novelist Alexei Tolstoy (distantly related to Leo Tolstoy). Bystroletov's name in Russian roughly means "fast flying." He certainly was. Extroverted and strikingly handsome, he was a master of disguise. During his career, he successfully impersonated a Hungarian count, a British nobleman, an American gangster, and a Dutch artist. His method of obtaining foreign state secrets was to seduce female staffers in embassies and foreign ministries who had access to them. The "Romeo spy" also employed what intelligence professionals call "false-flags," the technique of recruiting targets while posing as a businessman and other cover occupations.[31]

Bystroletov tracked Oldham down in a Paris bar and, pretending to be an impoverished Hungarian aristocrat who had fallen into the clutches of Soviet intelligence, won his trust. The spy portrayed himself to Oldham as a sympathetic friend. Oldham agreed to provide his new chum with Foreign Office ciphers, which Bystroletov offered dutifully to pass on to Soviet intelligence, helping both of them out of a bind, as his story went. For his services, Oldham was given a down payment of $6,000 (approximately $103,000 today), a second payment of $5,000, and then $1,000 a month. Bystroletov was accompanied to some of his meetings with Oldham by the OGPU illegal *rezident* in Berlin, Boris Bazarov (code-named KIN), who posed as an Italian communist. The two Soviet spies would meet their new recruit at the Oldhams' London home, in Kensington's Pembroke Gardens, and in France and Germany, where they played good cop, bad cop. Bystroletov won over Oldham's wife, Lucy, putting their relationship on what an OGPU report described as "an intimate footing." The Oldhams' marriage was soon over. Ernest hit the bottle.[32]

In September 1932, Oldham, unable to withstand the pressures of his double life, announced his resignation from the Foreign Office, although he continued to go into work after giving notice. His MI5 dossier reveals that in July 1933, he was under intense suspicion because of his erratic behavior. On one occasion, he was found in the cipher room by the nighttime cleaning staff at eleven o'clock, having gained entry using a key copied from an impression on a bar of soap.

If Oldham believed that resigning from the Foreign Office would convince his aristocratic Hungarian friend, and Soviet intelligence, to leave him alone, he was fatally wrong. Over the next year, Bystroletov relentlessly pressured Oldham to give him details about his former colleagues, in the hope of recruiting one. The Center's harassment of Oldham drove him to despair. By July 1933, MI5 had placed him under surveillance, intercepting his telephone calls and mail. The "handsome" man meeting with Lucy Oldham, noted in her husband's MI5 file, was likely Bystroletov. At this point, both Oldham and the Center were convinced that British intelligence was on to the two men (MI5 did correctly suspect that Oldham was up to something) and that British operatives would try to eliminate Oldham (which MI5 and MI6 were not in the business of doing).

The Center supplied Bystroletov with a rifle, which he believed he needed to protect himself from (nonexistent) British assassins. In one MI5 report in September 1933, written by an undercover officer watching Oldham as he drank at a pub, the officer noted: "In my opinion, OLDHAM is rapidly heading for a breakdown." Four days after the report, and almost a year to the day after Oldham resigned from the Foreign Office, he committed suicide, sticking his head in the gas oven of his flat in Pembroke Gardens. The thirty-nine-year-old was rushed to the hospital but pronounced dead on arrival. The Center concluded that he had been murdered by British intelligence. It refused to acknowledge the tragic truth: that the pressure imposed on him by the Center contributed to his suicide. Soviet intelligence had extracted as much information as possible from him, then discarded him, careless about the impact on his state of mind. This was the ugly human reality of Soviet espionage. MI5 only later, in 1940, discovered the true nature of Oldham's spying from a Soviet defector.[33]

During Stalin's Great Terror, the homicidal maelstrom unleashed in 1936, Bystroletov was recalled to Moscow, tortured with a large ball bearing swung on a steel cable, tried on false charges of being a foreign spy, and sent to the Gulag. His wife slit her own throat with a kitchen knife. His elderly mother poisoned herself. Bystroletov somehow survived his sentence, but was left crippled. He deposited his memoirs, describing his ordeal, in a library in St. Petersburg, where they were held in secret special storage.

STALIN'S REGIME

By the end of the 1920s, it was clear that the workers' revolution was not forthcoming in West European countries like Germany. In 1929, Stalin thus began to build socialism at home, transforming the preindustrial country the Soviets had seized into an industrial society. It was to be the world's first worker state—a radical experiment in social engineering. Stalin instigated crash industrialization. The OGPU (renamed the NKVD in 1934) was the vehicle to bring that about. The Soviet Union would catch up with capitalism not in fifty years, but ten. Stalin's first Five-Year Plan forced nine million farmers to move into industrial cities and zones. "Shock brigades" militarized production, while the OGPU forced the collectivization of peasant farmers and purged the *kulaks,* or "richer" peasants, loading them onto cattle cars and deporting them to the frozen ends of the red empire. In the Soviet Union, a richer peasant might simply be someone who had an extra cow or who dared to put a tin roof on his hovel. Stalin's enforced farm "modernization" through centralized collectives led to crop failures across the country, then famine. When his policies sparked a revolt in Ukraine, he ordered the NKVD to confiscate all available food. Ukrainians were reduced to eating bark, berries, and rats. In the Holodomor ("death by hunger") that followed, around four million people are thought to have starved to death.[34]

Stalin's rule was one of history's most brutal dictatorships. But this did not stop communist fellow travelers and sympathizers in the West, squinting hazily from afar, from supporting his regime. The British socialist Beatrice Webb found little to criticize because, as she wrote, Stalin had "cut out the dead wood" in Soviet society and was building a new civilization. These sympathizers were enraptured by the myth of the Soviet state. The historian Philip Toynbee, who became a communist at Oxford, said that the hellish existence in the Western world drove him to invent an earthly paradise somewhere else. In their hearts, some must have known it was an illusion. Among the faithful who made pilgrimages to the Soviet Union were those who willfully looked away from the evidence of terror in front of their eyes. Other Westerners who traveled to the socialist utopia, where Soviet propaganda proclaimed that "life has become more joyful," found themselves arrested, sent to work colonies, or executed.[35]

Stalin's regime orchestrated a disinformation campaign (code-named TARANTULA) that depicted Soviet industrialization as a staggering success. Some intelligence services in the West fell prey to it, and to other Soviet disinformation about the strength of its industry, leading to inflated Western assessments about Soviet capabilities in the 1930s. Lack of reliable intelligence, confused by Soviet disinformation, would become a recurring theme in Western intelligence assessments of Soviet military capabilities throughout the Cold War.

SOVIET GREAT ILLEGALS

The Wall Street crash of 1929 set off the worst ever global depression. Western democracies appeared broken, unable to feed their citizens. In the three years after the crash, worldwide gross domestic product fell by about 15 percent. The Soviet Union seemed to offer a panacea to the failures of Western capitalism. In Britain and the United States, some would take their disillusion one step further. They became Soviet agents.

"Turning" them was the careful work of a talented group of cosmopolitan Soviet intelligence officers, later known in the Kremlin as the Great Illegals. Bystroletov, who recruited Oldham for cash, was one such. Another was a Hungarian, Theodore Maly (code-named MANN), who went by the alias Paul Hardt. As an MI5 report later noted, he was like something from a novel: a six-foot-four ex-monk, former cavalry officer, and lady killer. With two gold teeth shining under a large mustache, Maly recruited and ran agents posing as an executive from a fictitious Dutch bank. But arguably the most important of the great Illegals was Arnold Deutsch, who recruited agents in Britain not for financial reward but through ideological conviction: those who believed communism offered a better system of government and even civilization.[36]

Deutsch went by the alias Stefan Lange and the code name STEFAN (later OTTO). He was the chief recruiter of the five "Cambridge Spies," the most successful—and damaging—group of foreign agents ever recruited by the Soviet Union. Its members, H. A. R. "Kim" Philby, Guy Burgess, Donald Maclean, Anthony Blunt, and John Cairncross, rank among the greatest spies in history. It was Deutsch, a Slovakian-Austrian Jew, who had the idea of recruiting young, idealistic university graduates and then sending them off to penetrate the halls of power, like viruses entering the body politic. It was a more sophisticated and patient approach to agent recruitment than anything contemporary by the West. In his three years in Britain, from 1934 to 1937, Deutsch recruited seventeen agents in this fashion.[37]

There are now movies, television shows, and entire shelves in libraries devoted to the Cambridge Spies. Fresh light is cast on them, however, by the recent opening of British records, some only in 2022. They show how close British intelligence came to identifying the Cambridge espionage network and that Soviet intelligence let them down. Deutsch was an outstanding multilingual academic. He held a doctorate in chemistry, which he obtained with distinction from the University of Vienna in 1928, aged just twenty-four. He had also studied psychology, which gave him valuable insight into human behavior. A committed communist revolutionary, he was recruited by the INO after finishing his studies. Russian intelligence today remembers Deutsch as a towering figure, but in truth, his espionage tradecraft at the time was often primitive. As his now unsealed British intelligence dossier makes clear, Deutsch arrived in Britain in April 1934 under his own name, with the assistance of his millionaire cousin in Britain, Oscar Deutsch, who founded Odeon Cinemas. The Soviet spymaster moved to Hampstead, home to many progressive artists and authors, where Deutsch lived in a block of modernist apartments, the Lawn Road Flats. It was a poor choice for a home. Known communists and other Soviet agents also lived in the same building (as would Agatha Christie, then finishing *Murder on the Orient Express*). Had Deutsch not been recalled to Moscow in 1937, amid Stalin's Great Terror, MI5's ongoing surveillance of the Lawn Road Flats, as a home of known communists, likely would have placed him on its radar. As the dossier on him makes clear, however, it was only after he left Britain that MI5 discovered Deutsch's true identity.[38]

At London University, Deutsch enrolled in a psychology course, an easy pursuit given his previous academic expertise. It was the perfect cover. Soviet intelligence archives reveal that Deutsch and Maly recruited at least three agents from Oxford. One was code-named SCOTT, now identified as a sallow postgraduate student, Arthur Wynn, who acted as a talent spotter for Soviet intelligence. Another was Bernard Floud (later an MP) and a third was a redheaded academic, Jenifer Williams (later Hart). According to her MI5 dossier, opened in 2022, Williams's Soviet controller was Wynn, along with a "central European man," whom she later identified as Deutsch. After a few clandestine meetings, however, she had second thoughts about working as a Soviet recruit and broke off contact. Williams aced the civil service entrance exams in October 1936, with the highest score by a female candidate to that point. In March 1939 she became private secretary to the permanent undersecretary at the Home Office. In 1940, she was asked by MI5's acting director, Jasper Harker, who was unaware of her communist background, to recommend names for MI5 recruits. If Williams had still been a NKVD agent at that time, it would have been a phenomenal achievement for Soviet intelligence. It was a lucky escape for British security.[39]

As it transpired, it was not Oxford, nor London University, but Cambridge that was to become the source of Deutsch's greatest achievement for Moscow. During a walk in Regent's Park on a balmy day in June 1934, he successfully recruited a high-flying recent Cambridge graduate: Kim Philby. They sat on the grass together, speaking in German, seated at angles to keep an eye out for MI5 "watchers." They need not have bothered. Nobody was watching.[40]

Philby, a dapper young man with a predilection for booze and womanizing, was a committed communist by the time he graduated from Trinity College, Cambridge, the previous year, 1933. He and the others in what became the Cambridge network were inspired by the promise of communism; they believed it offered a brighter alternative to capitalism. Later, they believed it to be the best bulwark against fascism. On Philby's last day at Cambridge, he asked his tutor, Maurice Dobb, a fellow there in economics and a well-known communist, what he could do to serve the communist cause. Dobb suggested he could work for a relief organization in Austria, which was a Soviet front group. Philby did so. While there, he fell in love with and married Litzi Friedmann, an Austrian communist. It was through Friedmann that Philby was introduced to Deutsch, leading to their fateful conversation in Regent's Park. The meeting would change Philby's life forever. It also set in motion a process that wrecked British national security for decades. Soviet intelligence assigned Philby the code name SONNY: SYNOK in Russian, or SÖNCHEN in German.[41]

Philby acted as a talent spotter for Deutsch, providing him with the names of people he knew from Cambridge, including Guy Burgess and Donald Maclean. Deutsch built the network from there. They in turn led to the recruitment of a Trinity academic, Anthony Blunt (unimaginatively code-named TONY), and John Cairncross, an academically brilliant Scot. Unlike the others, all of whom hailed from privileged backgrounds, Cairncross's origins were more humble. The son of a Scottish ironmonger, he got to Cambridge on an academic scholarship.

Maclean was the gifted son of a former Liberal cabinet minister. He graduated with a First Class degree in modern languages in 1934, intending to teach in the Soviet Union. Over the summer, he changed his mind, probably with Deutsch's encouragement, and instead decided to sit for the entrance exam for the Foreign Office. Deutsch initially assigned him the code name ORPHAN (SIROTA in Russian, WAISE in German), a reference to the death of his father two years earlier. When Maclean passed the entrance exam with flying colors, he became the first member of the network to penetrate Britain's foreign policy establishment. It was an epic success for Soviet intelligence, albeit one assisted by an equally epic failure of British security. The Cambridge Spies were effectively pushing at an open door. At the time, background checks (vetting) for British government departments with access to state secrets were primitive. Before World War II, the Foreign Office did not employ a single security officer, let alone a security department. Vetting did not involve proactive investigations into an applicant's background but instead relied on information contained in MI5 records, derived from its surveillance of groups considered to pose security threats, like the British Communist Party. Deutsch had the good idea to instruct his Cambridge recruits to break off contact with the CPGB, which he correctly assumed was under close MI5 surveillance. Thus there were few traces in MI5's files against their names.[42]

To a man, the members of the Cambridge network were originally inspired by the intellectual ideas of Marxist communism—not anti-fascism, though that is what their communism became in the later 1930s. But they were armchair communists. Their Marxism-Leninism was academic, the stuff of debates at the Cambridge University Socialist Society, discussions at the elite intellectual group the Apostles, while lounging in their college rooms, sitting by the banks of the River Cam, or padding around Trinity's Great Court. Deutsch offered them something seductive: the opportunity to make a practical difference, secret work for the Comintern underground, to help advance its cause. It is unlikely they considered themselves as pawns of Soviet intelligence or understood the work of the OGPU, NKVD, or KGB. Instead, Deutsch promised them the reward of important secret work. Two of the Cambridge Five were gay (Burgess and Blunt), and one bisexual (Maclean), at a time when homosexuality was illegal in Britain. They thus already led secretive lives. All of the Cambridge Five were, in their own ways, rebelling against the strict class structure of prewar Britain. Deutsch accepted them, affirmed their sexual and social liberation, and helped them on their way.[43]

On the eve of World War II, thanks to its Cambridge recruits, Soviet intelligence perversely had more graduates of British universities than Britain's own intelligence services, MI5 and MI6, whose few officers had military backgrounds, not university educations. Soviet intelligence used similar tactics on the other side of the Atlantic. In the prewar years, however, the U.S. was not the priority for Soviet spy chiefs that it would later become. The economic might of the United States at the time of the Bolshevik Revolution—as the only creditor on the planet—and its sense of messianic destiny about democracy, first espoused by President Woodrow Wilson, placed it on a collision course with the Soviet Union under the Bolsheviks. The two world powers, in the East and West, had universalist, but utterly divergent, ideologies about the future of the world. That divergence was only revealed during World War II.[44]

CHAPTER THREE

NEMESIS

An Intelligence Service ought to act as a kind of agency
operating in the interests of the various formations which are–in
effect–its customers. . . . It should be the business of Intelligence
to anticipate their needs, and to provide the required facts
even before they are demanded. It should circulate to each all
relevant information as soon as it is available.

–Marc Bloch, *Strange Defeat*

WORLD WAR II IS THE FULCRUM OF OUR STORY, THE EPIC
intelligence war between East and West. During the conflict, each of the
three powers, the Soviet Union, Britain, and the United States, galvanized
intelligence and national security institutions, and tradecraft, which would
shape their subsequent postwar relations. It is impossible to understand
intelligence during the Cold War without appreciating their wartime experiences. In the West, Britain and the United States were schooled in espionage
during the war. They achieved unprecedented wartime intelligence successes.
The war turned them from amateurs into players. It also created alliances
between them lasting to the present day. For the Soviet Union, wartime
espionage against its wartime Western *allies* would shape its subsequent

relationship with them. The war started, however, with a series of intelligence disasters for each of the powers in the East and West.

When wars begin is subjective, rarely fitting neatly into schoolbook timelines. As the historians Rana Mitter and Richard Overy have shown, from the perspective of China—the West's forgotten wartime ally—World War II began in December 1937, when the Japanese attacked and destroyed Nanjing, the capital of the Chinese nationalist government. Japanese forces massacred somewhere between 100,000 and 300,000 people, raping women and murdering the city's inhabitants in all manner of ammunition-saving ways—beheading, crucifying, having dogs tear them apart, and unleashing poisoned gas. For Europe, the war began with the Nazi and Soviet invasions of Poland in 1939. Britain stood alone for two long years. The year 1941 was the war's geopolitical turning point, when, with Hitler's attack on the Soviet Union, the Japanese attack at Pearl Harbor, and Hitler's declaration of war on the U.S., it became a global conflagration. The currents flowing toward world war arose from colossal intelligence failures on the part of each of the players in our story, Britain, the Soviet Union, and the United States. The experiences of each country, all three of which were ill-prepared for surprise attacks, would shape their governments in the postwar years—and far beyond.[1]

Despite their famed reputations, Britain's intelligence services were spying blind at the outbreak of war in Europe in September 1939. MI5 and MI6 did not even know the name of Germany's foreign intelligence service, the Abwehr, let alone run any significant operations against it. As MI5's top secret in-house history put it: "In 1939 we had no adequate knowledge of the German organizations which it was the function of the Security Service [MI5] to guard against. . . . We in fact had no definite knowledge whether there was any organized connection between the German secret service and Nazi sympathizers in this country, whether of British or alien descent."[2]

At the beginning of hostilities in Europe, British code breakers at the

Government Code and Cypher School were unable to read German traffic, which used highly complex Enigma machines for enciphering. In fact, the situation was even worse: German naval intelligence (B-Dienst) had cracked one of the Royal Navy's codes. Starved of resources, MI6 did not succeed in recruiting an agent with access to Hitler's thinking. It also made egregious tradecraft errors. Two months after the war's start, two MI6 officers stationed in the Netherlands traveled to meet "anti-Nazi" agents at Venlo, a town on the German border. In fact, the contacts were German provocations. The MI6 officers, traveling in an ostentatious Lincoln-Zephyr, were met by an armed German security service (SD) snatch squad, dragged across the border, and arrested. For reasons unknown, one of the MI6 officers brought a list of his agents to the meeting. The Gestapo quickly arrested and liquidated them. The MI6 officers were imprisoned, but survived.[3]

British intelligence failed to warn decision makers on Downing Street about events as the world slid into war: the Nazi-Soviet pact in August 1939, which saw the two dictatorships divide and conquer countries in Eastern Europe; Nazi and Soviet parallel combat operations in Poland; the Nazi invasion of Norway; and Stalin's disastrous winter war in Finland, which nearly sparked a war between Britain and the Soviet Union. Britain's spy chiefs also failed to predict Hitler's Blitzkrieg in Europe in the spring and summer of 1940, overrunning Scandinavia, the Netherlands, Belgium, and France. Britain stood alone, facing what appeared an imminent Nazi invasion. Spy fever swept the country. Under strain put on them by the public, flooding them with reports about sightings of enemy "spies," Britain's intelligence services ground to a halt and collapsed. Britain also seemed on the brink of war with the Soviet Union.[4]

Meanwhile, in the Far East, MI6 was an equally sleepy organization. It had some successes against the Comintern before the war, but MI6 officers spent more time placing bets at Hong Kong's Happy Valley racecourse, or sipping sundowners on the teak verandas at Raffles Hotel in Singapore, than doing humdrum but essential intelligence work like cross-referencing names in file registries. To be fair to MI6, its superiors in London had not tasked it with collecting intelligence on Japan. The Joint Intelligence Committee (JIC) did not turn its attention to Japanese intentions until May 1940. Its assessment then lamely noted that MI6 was "not functioning in Japan." Britain's intelligence failures were disastrous during Japan's sweltering drive forward by land in late 1941 and early 1942. In Singapore, Britain's outpost in the Far East, the administration was so ill-prepared for the Japanese attack, two months after Pearl Harbor, that its guns were infamously pointing the wrong way, expecting an invasion from the sea. A hundred thousand British soldiers surrendered in Singapore, the worst military defeat and capitulation in British history, as Churchill thundered. Japan's war of conquest splintered Britain's empire in Asia, never to recover.[5]

——

Approximately six thousand miles away, in the Kremlin, Stalin was responsible for one of the worst intelligence catastrophes in history: the Soviet Union's failure to prepare for Hitler's invasion, BARBAROSSA, on June 22, 1941. Chief responsibility for the Soviet disaster lay with Stalin himself. The swarthy, curly-haired dictator was his own obsessive intelligence analyst, believing he knew better than his spy chiefs. As he paced in his office, the "little corner," in the Kremlin, puffing on his pipe in the stifling summer heat of 1941, Stalin refused to believe that Hitler would break their two-year-old nonaggression pact—at least not yet.[6]

Stalin ignored a stream of intelligence landing on his desk. German deception and provocations made assessing them difficult. Even so, the statistics about intelligence that Stalin dismissed speak for themselves. In the three months before the Nazi attack, NKVD stations in Ukraine sent at least fifty reports to the Center about the accumulation of Nazi forces on the border and Nazi scouts crossing it. According to reports obtained from Ukrainian archives for this book, some warnings passed the desk of the party's boss in Ukraine, future Soviet leader Nikita Khrushchev. Born on the Russian-Ukraine border, Khrushchev had grown up in Donetsk.

Stalin also dismissed intelligence from a celebrated Soviet military-intelligence illegal in Japan, Richard Sorge (code-named RAMZAI, or RAMSAY). Operating undercover as a German journalist in Tokyo, Sorge befriended the German military attaché at the embassy there, who disclosed to him military secrets including the planning of BARBAROSSA. When Stalin received Sorge's warnings, however, he not only dismissed them but denounced them. He claimed that they were German disinformation from a lying "shit who has set himself up with some small factories and brothels in Japan." Sorge's accurate intelligence was placed in a folder of "dubious and misleading reports."[7]

On June 16, the NKVD delivered a warning about the Nazi invasion from one of its principal agents in Germany, an officer in the Luftwaffe. The following is Stalin's response to it, written in green rather than Stalin's usual red or blue pencil:

You can tell your "source" in German airforce headquarters to go fuck himself. He's not a "source," he's a disinformer. J. Stalin.[8]

The day before BARBAROSSA, Lavrenti Beria, the head of the NKVD, ordered that agents who sent reports contradicting Stalin's unshakable faith that Germany would not attack should be "ground into labor camp dust." Stalin also dismissed intelligence given to him by Britain's leader, Winston Churchill. Although Churchill did not disclose its nature, his intelligence came from Bletchley Park decrypts, code-named ULTRA. It was fortunate that Churchill did not disclose its source. Stalin's willingness to appease Hitler in their nonaggression pact doubtless meant he would have betrayed Churchill's secret to the Nazis if he knew it.

Churchill sent a deliberately "short and cryptic" warning to Stalin, disguising his source, ULTRA, on April 3, 1941. Churchill also then passed warnings to Stalin about BARBAROSSA through Britain's ambassador in Moscow, Stafford Cripps, and to the Soviet ambassador in London, Ivan Maisky. Other messengers were Britain's foreign secretary, Anthony Eden, and Churchill's trusted Foreign Office adviser, Alexander Cadogan. When Eden presented

Maisky with intelligence on June 13—nine days before the Nazi attack—the Soviet ambassador said that he "did not believe in the possibility of a German attack against Russia." Stalin squandered all these warnings. He only believed information stolen, not freely given. He was convinced that his old nemesis, Churchill, who had tried to unseat the Bolsheviks after 1917, was trying to drag him into a war against Hitler. There was, Stalin's court sycophants told him, a conspiracy of spies trying to undo him, all organized by the "center of centers." Stalin's mind was a macabre labyrinth.[9]

Stalin, whose name means "man of steel," ruled the country and his Kremlin court with an iron fist. Given the terror he instigated, it is remarkable that he received the flood of intelligence about BARBAROSSA, which foreign agents bravely sent. Before the war, the Soviet leader had annihilated precisely those he would need most when war came: in suicidal self-destruction, he ordered half of the Red Army's officer corps, approximately thirty-five thousand men, shot or imprisoned. Ninety percent of its generals were "purged," an aseptic term meaning killed or sent to their deaths in camps. They were thrown into the back of NKVD vans, Black Marias, and driven to NKVD headquarters, never to be seen again. Similar fates befell most of the NKVD's talented foreign intelligence officers, the Great Illegals. One of them, Ignace Reiss, was machine-gunned by an NKVD hit squad in Switzerland. The recruiter of the Cambridge Spies, Arnold Deutsch, was recalled to Moscow but somehow survived his imprisonment in Siberia. Another NKVD officer, Alexander Orlov (SCHWED, or "Swede"), escaped only by blackmailing his boss, Nikolai Yezhov, saying that he would reveal what he knew about Stalin's spies in the West, including their code names, if his family were harmed.[10]

Precise figures of those purged or liquidated during the Great Terror are still debated by historians. It started with show trials, where depositions and confessions were splattered with blood, but then metastasized into "national operations" against counterrevolutionary anti-Soviet elements. In one order, number 00447, in July 1937, the NKVD shot 72,950 people. Another order, signed by Stalin, sealed the fate of 6,600 people—more than all political opponents executed during the century before the Bolshevik coup. In total, during the Great Terror about 650,000 Soviet citizens are thought to have been shot, with millions sent to the Gulag. About a million died from starvation, exhaustion, or exposure in camps scattered around the edges of the Soviet empire, in freezing Siberia or the boiling deserts of Kazakhstan. Stalin's willing executioners were his successive NKVD heads, first Genrikh Yagoda, who was replaced and purged by Nikolai Yezhov. The Great Terror was known as the "Reign of Yezhov" (Yezhovshchina). The purpose of the Great Terror—for most mass murders have a rationale—is still unclear. It seems to have been Stalin's demented way of instilling loyalty to him.

"Better to do too much than not enough," Yezhov told his NKVD officers. Yezhov, a tiny man known as the "poison dwarf," was himself purged in a show trial. He was shot (along with his wife, sister, and brother-in-law) by the NKVD in a basement with a sloping floor that Yezhov himself had designed for ease of mopping up after executions. Yezhov's replacement was Beria, a pince-nez-wearing killer and sexual predator.[11]

In these horrific conditions, Stalin effectively institutionalized intelligence failure. NKVD officers feared death when providing any intelligence that contradicted his thinking. Under Stalin, the NKVD's foreign intelligence branch, the INO, did not even have an analytical department. In 1938, the INO was in such a state of decimation and disarray that, for 127 consecutive days, it did not forward a single intelligence report to Stalin.[12]

Stalin refused to believe that Hitler would break their August 1939 nonaggression pact. After "pouring buckets of shit over each other's heads" for years, as Stalin put it, the two dictators secretly agreed to divide Eastern Europe between themselves, in spheres of influence. We do not know what intelligence was shared in secret SS-NKVD meetings thereafter, which Putin's Kremlin would prefer erased from history. Britain's MI5 discovered some instances of intelligence collaboration between Moscow and Berlin.* The two despots duly invaded Poland in September 1939. Behind the

---

* For information about an American spy who was a Soviet and Nazi agent, Tyler Kent, see this book's website: www.spieshistory.com.

advancing Wehrmacht, SS formations undertook "pacification" operations, shooting Polish civilians, including Jews. This started a process of Nazi mass murder in occupied Europe that would lead to the Holocaust. Meanwhile, Stalin's Red Army moved westward into Poland, allegedly to protect ethnic Russians, later conquering the Baltic states. The Soviets would eventually deport about 1.25 million Polish citizens to the Soviet interior. The NKVD also carried out mass executions in occupied Poland. They shot an estimated 22,000 Poles in trenches in a forest at Katyn, near Smolensk, in April 1940. Others were executed in a basement by an NKVD major wearing an apron and elbow-length gloves, to avoid splattering blood on his tunic. Stalin claimed the victims had gone missing in Manchuria.[13]

◆

The U.S. had even worse intelligence than either Britain or the Soviet Union. Before the war, Washington lacked both a dedicated foreign human intelligence (espionage) service and a SIGINT agency. Army and naval SIGINT agencies were so antagonistic that they were barely on speaking terms. Instead, Washington lumbered under a maze of competing intelligence branches and bureaucracies. Its fragmented intelligence architecture directly contributed to America's day of infamy: Japan's surprise attack on Pearl Harbor, the greatest disaster in U.S. naval history.

After the start of the war in Europe, before Pearl Harbor, President Franklin Delano Roosevelt tried—unsuccessfully—to galvanize the branches of U.S. intelligence. For guidance, the president turned to the British, who he believed were the world experts in spying. The British did not disabuse the American president of this idea. In July 1940, Roosevelt dispatched William "Wild Bill" Donovan, a friend from Columbia Law School, to Britain. Donovan's mission was to assess Britain's handling of the war and to learn what might be in store for America. A World War I hero and a Wall Street lawyer, he was a trusted adviser of Roosevelt's in spite of his political affiliation: Donovan was a Republican.

MI6 rolled out the red carpet for Donovan. He met its chief, Sir Stewart Menzies, at MI6 headquarters, at the Broadway Buildings, and Britain's other intelligence chiefs. Donovan witnessed Britain's gritty determination to fight on. Their efforts were not doomed, as the U.S. ambassador in London, Joseph Kennedy, believed. The father of the future U.S. president stood firmly on the wrong side of history, trying to do his best to keep America out of the war. Partly thanks to Donovan's favorable ensuing report, Roosevelt looked beyond Kennedy and agreed to transfer fifty mothballed U.S. destroyers to help defend Britain's sea-lanes. In return, Britain agreed to lease naval and air bases in the Caribbean and western Atlantic to the U.S. This was the forerunner to the Lend-Lease Act of March 1941, which made the United States into "the Arsenal of Democracy" eight months before it entered the war.[14]

Much of MI6's influence in America was due to its dapper man in New York, William Stephenson. Stephenson later cultivated the image that he was one of the founding fathers of U.S. intelligence. His influence in Washington about secret affairs was indeed supreme. He was the first non-American to obtain the Medal for Merit. "Little Bill" Stephenson, as he was known, was a wealthy Canadian industrialist with longstanding connections to MI6. He had swanky offices on two floors of Rockefeller Center, on Fifth Avenue, operating under the deliberately bland title British Security Coordination, or BSC. From his Manhattan perch, Stephenson charmed Roosevelt's men, especially Donovan, over martinis.

With Britain fighting alone, Churchill instructed Stephenson to use all manner of dirty tricks to help bring America into the war on Britain's side. This involved planting favorable stories in U.S. newspapers about Britain's war effort, suborning a radio station to broadcast British-friendly programs, stealing polling data to shape propaganda, and smearing "isolationist" U.S. politicians and groups like "America First."* British officials in Washington

---

* For more about British dirty tricks in the United States before Pearl Harbor, see this book's website: www.spieshistory.com.

had a secret fund for countering Nazi activities on U.S. soil. Furthermore, as in World War I, Britain's code breakers were intercepting and reading U.S. traffic. Before Pearl Harbor, America was more of a target than an ally for British intelligence.[15]

In July 1941, the month after the Nazi attack on the Soviet Union and six months before Pearl Harbor, Roosevelt's effort to bring cohesion to U.S. intelligence branches led to the creation of a new position: the coordinator of information (COI). Thanks in no small part to Stephenson's suggestion, Roosevelt appointed Donovan to the post. Although the title COI would suggest coordinating all intelligence, Donovan's responsibilities did not extend to U.S. SIGINT. That omission from the role would have direct, disastrous consequences. The U.S. Army's SIGINT unit, the Signals Intelligence Service, was locked in bitter disputes with the corresponding U.S. naval cryptanalytic section, OP-20-G. Perennially arguing over resources, they could not agree on which messenger would deliver decrypts to Roosevelt. As the NSA's in-house previously classified history notes, the two branches were so entrenched that in August 1940 they could only agree on an absurd procedure: the army would deliver decrypts to the president on even dates in the calendar, and the navy on odd dates.[16]

American code breakers delivered strategic warning to Roosevelt that war with Japan was coming. Decrypts revealed Japan's aim to dominate Asia, driven by a belief in racial superiority—not dissimilar to Nazism—but they failed to show where or when a Japanese attack would come. We can now see why. In September 1940, U.S. Army code breakers managed to break Japanese diplomatic codes, code-named RED, later PURPLE. Due to their ability to work apparent miracles, the code breakers were given the nickname "magicians." The name MAGIC thereafter stuck for Axis decrypts.

Crucially, however, the Japanese government never provided its own overseas diplomatic missions forewarning of the Pearl Harbor attack—leaving nothing in diplomatic communications for U.S. code breakers to intercept. Japan's imperial conference on November 5, 1941, when Tokyo made its decision to project a force halfway across the Pacific to Hawaii, passed by U.S. Army code breakers. On December 3, four days before Pearl Harbor, Churchill was given an ominous decrypt by Bletchley Park. It was from Japan's foreign ministry to its ambassador in London, instructing him to destroy his cipher machine. Something was coming that would require the ambassador to cut off contact. But where? Other intelligence about Pearl Harbor was held by a British double agent code-named TRICYCLE. Such clues, however, are only painfully obvious with the benefit of hindsight.*

Japanese naval communications, which American code breakers named JN-25, did carry messages about the Japanese fleet steaming toward Pearl Harbor. However, U.S. naval SIGINT (OP-20-G) failed to crack that code (JN-25) and the Japanese variant introduced in December 1940 (named JN-25B). In her celebrated study of Pearl Harbor, the scholar Roberta Wohlstetter argued that the attack was the result of a U.S. failure of analysis—a failure to distinguish signals from noise. That is only partly true. In fact, Pearl Harbor resulted from a failure to collect intelligence—Japanese naval codes. According to the NSA's own study, America's failure to break JN-25 was due solely to a shortage of resources. For three years before Pearl Harbor itself, OP-20-G on average had only two officers (and never more than five) assigned to all Japanese codes and ciphers. If more resources had been thrown at JN-25, it is likely that U.S. cryptanalysts would have cracked it before Pearl Harbor, as they were able to do after, working with the same tools—pencil and paper. Even if there had been sufficient resources, however, it is doubtful whether the relevant decrypts would have found their way through Washington's labyrinth of competing bureaucracies to decision makers. Pearl Harbor was, then, a failure of U.S. intelligence collection *and* analysis. On December 7, 1941, the Japanese attacked Pearl Harbor, sinking eighteen American ships, destroying two hundred aircraft, and killing approximately 2,400 Americans. To this day, oil still seeps into the ocean waters from the USS *Arizona*.[17]

---

* For the story of TRICYCLE, see this book's website: www.spieshistory.com.

ENIGMA

Britain's code breakers—GC&CS—were based at Bletchley Park, a manor house fifty miles north of London. MI6's chief, the debonair Hugh Sinclair, had purchased the fifty-five-acre site in Bedfordshire for use by MI6 and GC&CS, which came under the former's jurisdiction, at the outbreak of war. Sinclair was GC&CS's nonoperational director; its operational head, Alastair Denniston, was a veteran Scottish code breaker (and Olympic hockey player). Sinclair had chosen Bletchley because it was roughly equidistant from Cambridge and Oxford, having correctly predicted that recruits would be drawn from both when war broke out.

Sinclair died of cancer in November 1939, literally writing reports on his deathbed. His successor, Menzies, an Old Etonian officer in the Grenadier Guards, was a brave veteran of World War I, having earned the U.S. Legion of Merit, though even his supporters would admit he was more of a jolly good chap than smart. He came from landed gentry, had a private income, and enjoyed long liquid lunches in London's clubland (his entry in *Who's Who* reads: "*Clubs*: White's, St. James's"). Menzies was the beneficiary of Sinclair's and Denniston's work. He was the messenger for Bletchley Park ULTRA decrypts. He brought them to Churchill daily, locked in a red buff case with the instructions "Only to be opened by the Prime Minister in person." Menzies and Churchill had the only keys (Churchill kept his on his personal key ring). Today, we can see the volumes of decrypts that Churchill read. He initialed them with his characteristic red "WSC" signature. Over the course of the war, Menzies is thought to have met Churchill a thousand times. When Churchill traveled to meet Roosevelt off the coast of Newfoundland in August 1941, where they drew up the Atlantic Charter of Allied war aims, MI6 flew ULTRA decrypts by plane to him, carried in a lead-weighted case to sink into the sea if anything happened to the plane.[18]

Bletchley—known as Station X—was built on the pioneering work of Polish code breakers. The Poles and British achieved their initial breakthroughs on German communications through human ingenuity. The scale of the challenge was head-spinning. Enciphering communications on Enigma machines, which used three mechanical rotors, produced so many millions of variations that they were effectively unbreakable. But Bletchley achieved the impossible. The breakthroughs came with the mechanization of code-breaking, using electromechanical devices, or "bombes," to attack Enigma key combinations. Each bombe, about six feet tall, contained thirty-six banks of high-speed, electrically driven key-finding machines. In May 1940, as Britain faced the Battle of Britain, Bletchley cracked the German Luftwaffe Enigma cipher, which it then read effectively without interruption for the rest of the war. The following spring, it mastered the German navy Enigma, and, in September 1941, the Wehrmacht. Bletchley's nine intercept stations in Britain (with 260 wireless sets) and seven stations overseas (with 75 sets) brought a daily avalanche of raw messages for the bombes to attack.[19]

Luckily for the Allied war effort, Britain had obtained a new leader at precisely the same moment when Bletchley's intelligence came on line. Winston Churchill was more interested in secret service than any inhabitant of Downing Street, before or since. He had been obsessed with spies since his youth, had helped establish MI5 and MI6 in 1909, and oversaw SIGINT as First Lord of the Admiralty when war broke out in 1914. Now sixty-five years old, Churchill was the man for the moment. Most of us have an instantaneous picture of Churchill in our mind's eye, the man who led Britain's finest hour: his chubby face, incessant cigars, soaring rhetoric, bow ties, bulging midriff, velvet "siren suits" made by Turnbull & Asser, famous *V* for victory sign. His work ethic was gargantuan, causing him two heart attacks and pneumonia. He drank heavily, as his receipt chits in his personal papers show.

Churchill was the first prime minister to visit GC&CS. On a warm day in September 1941, he met Alan Turing, a Cambridge mathematician working there, and saw Bletchley's famous code-breaking huts. Standing on a pile of bricks outside one of them, he gave an impromptu speech to assembled code breakers: "You all look very innocent; one would not think you are involved in anything secret." He told them that he called them "the geese who laid the golden egg and never cackled." Although Bletchley's staff, whose average age was twenty-three, grew to number approximately ten thousand during the war, its members did not cackle—for a long time. ULTRA was the best-kept secret in British history. Only twelve of Churchill's thirty-five ministers knew about it. Bletchley's role in the Allied war effort would remain a secret for three decades after the war ended. A month after Churchill's visit to Bletchley, a relatively junior code breaker, Stuart Milner-Barry, was dispatched to Downing Street with an urgent plea for more resources. Churchill personally intervened with a now celebrated "ACTION THIS DAY" memo: "Make sure they have all they want on extreme priority and report to me that this has been done."[20]

As the historian Paul Kennedy has shown, American industrial might was the primary engineer of Allied victory. Intelligence was part of that might. Bletchley Park industrialized intelligence for the first-ever time; it was another wartime factory, one that mechanized the acquisition of foreign secrets and clanked them out. Building bombes became a straight industrial effort. OP-20-G threw resources at doing so, announcing in September 1942 that it would build them by the hundreds (at the time, the British had just thirty-two). When the Germans introduced a new cipher for their teleprinter communications, Tunny, Bletchley's mathematicians, linguists, and engineers responded by building, in 1943, the world's first electromechanical computer, Colossus, a breakthrough in the history of cryptology. It attacked German teleprinter (*Geheimschreiber*) radio traffic, which in the war's last two years produced more intelligence than Enigma, even though its recipients knew it all as ULTRA. Bletchley's decrypts grew from about 50 to 250 per day in the winter of 1940–41 to around 3,000 to 4,000 per day in mid-1943. Some German communications from the eastern front made their way to Churchill—after interception, decoding, and translation—before they reached their intended recipients, Hitler's high command.[21]

Churchill also energized British intelligence in other ways. He demanded an overhaul of its analytical machinery. He insisted the services provide him with collective assessments ("appreciations"), as opposed to individual ones. A week after becoming prime minister, he instructed his chief of staff, Hastings "Pug" Ismay, to make the JIC into the centerpiece of British intelligence, instructing it to provide him, as well as the war cabinet and chiefs of staff, with assessments "at any time of day or night." Under pressure from Churchill, Britain's secret services for the first time became an "intelligence community."[22]

British intelligence contributed to the Allied war effort in three operational theaters. The first was in the six-year-long Battle of the North Atlantic, where ULTRA gave the Royal Navy an edge fighting the Germans. The U-boat peril in the dark waters of the North Atlantic was, as Churchill later admitted, the one matter that really frightened him during the war. German U-boats attacked Allied transportation ships, bringing desperately needed matériel across the Atlantic—Britain's lifeline with the New World. Apart from a nine-month period when the Germans introduced a new code variant (SHARK), Bletchley Park and American code breakers used ULTRA and radio direction finding techniques to pinpoint U-boats and safeguard Allied transport ships. Doing so allowed convoys to be rerouted to avoid U-boats and thereby kept open the Atlantic supply chain.[23]

The second theater where intelligence contributed to Allied victory was in the moonlike desolation of North Africa. From June 1941, Bletchley was reading Enigma traffic that highlighted both Germany's poor fuel supplies in North Africa and the logistical problems of Germany's commander there, Erwin Rommel, "the desert fox." His counterpart, Britain's Bernard "Monty" Montgomery, used ULTRA as he defended Egypt from Rommel's breakout attack at the Battle of Alam el Halfa. In August 1942, Rommel sent his order of battle to Hitler in an Enigma message. Within forty-eight hours, after being deciphered at Bletchley, it was in Monty's hands, delivered by MI6 Special Liaison Units (SLUs) on the ground. ULTRA also played a role in Monty's better-known victory during the Second Battle of El Alamein, in October and November 1942. Monty did not mention ULTRA in his memoirs, which he wrote with a pencil after the war. It was still secret. His insufferable ego, however, prevented him from giving ULTRA's cover story, BONIFACE, or ULTRA itself, any credit for his wartime successes even after its secret was exposed.

The third operational theater where intelligence assisted the Allied war effort lay with the invasion of Europe on D-Day, on which more below.

Britain's official historian of wartime intelligence, F. H. "Harry" Hinsley, of Cambridge University, once claimed that ULTRA shortened World War II, perhaps by two years. As much as we should admire Hinsley as the doyen of intelligence history, he was not an impartial observer on this point, as he was a Bletchley wartime recruit himself. More recently, scholarship has cautioned against Hinsley's claim. Bletchley's band of brothers and sisters performed miracles, but neither ULTRA nor any other single intelligence source was decisive in winning the war for the Allies. Furthermore, until about 1943, the intelligence war between the Allies and the Axis powers was more evenly matched than mythologies about Bletchley tend to describe. As GCHQ's official history now shows, ULTRA was more like something that tipped the advantage to the Allies, offering a tiebreaker in otherwise locked conflicts. German intelligence was initially able to read the U.S. diplomatic code, for example, which provided Rommel with advantages against Montgomery. The Germans only lost their "Good Source," as they described their American decrypts, when the Americans plugged the leak, having been informed by Bletchley, which identified it from reading German ULTRA.[24]

Churchill's boundless enthusiasm for spying had a dangerous flip side: it led him to act impulsively and unpredictably. He meddled in, and outright interfered with, military operations based on his reading of intelligence. Britain's great man was, after all, a renegade—he changed political parties twice—and was never afraid to attack conventions or leap to conclusions. As the flow of ULTRA from Bletchley turned into a torrent, Churchill wanted to see everything, and only by going head-to-head with him did Menzies convince him otherwise. On occasion Churchill also wanted to use intelligence publicly, or pass information to Stalin, leaving MI6's chief having to talk him out of it.

As the war progressed, Alan Brooke, chief of the Imperial General Staff and a stubborn military bureaucrat from Ulster, increasingly expended energy on containing Churchill's ill-judged enthusiasms. Churchill was a prima donna. From July 1941, the chiefs of staff were given updates from Bletchley three or four times a day, to help insulate them from Churchill's "proddings." At the end of the war, Cadogan, letting off steam in his diary, wondered how they ever managed to run the war "with the PM spending *hours* of his and other people's time simply driveling, welcoming every red herring so as to have the pleasure of more irrelevant, redundant talk."[25]

ENTER THE AMERICANS

Six months after Pearl Harbor, Roosevelt finally whipped long-overdue reforms of U.S. intelligence into action. In June 1942, the president created the Office of Strategic Services (OSS) and appointed Wild Bill Donovan as its director. For the first time, America had a dedicated foreign intelligence collection (espionage) and sabotage service. Given the influence of MI6's Bill Stephenson, the OSS was unsurprisingly drawn up along British lines, though it was modeled more on Britain's wartime sabotage agency, the Special Operations Executive (SOE), than MI6, which focused on espionage.

It is easy to criticize the OSS, but Donovan was attempting to do something that no other wartime power had to: create an intelligence service from a standing start. The OSS would eventually employ about thirteen thousand Americans, plus foreigners. It enjoyed almost unlimited funding for agents, weapons, planes, cars—and endless parties, earning it the sobriquet "Oh So Social." By the end of the war, it had a budget of $57 million, of which $37 million could be spent without provision. A joke in neutral Portugal was that, when one saw happy people on the streets, it was payday for OSS informants.

The service attracted adventurers, the children of American dynasties, and movie stars. Behind the seemingly continuous cocktail parties, however, the OSS did have some significant intelligence achievements. The head of station in Switzerland, Allen Dulles—who went by the alias "Mr. Burns," official OSS code name "11"—recruited a valuable source in the German foreign office, Fritz Kolbe. Code-named GEORGE WOOD, he provided Dulles with about sixteen hundred pages of German secrets, including information about V-1 and V-2 weapons and a German agent, CICERO, operating at Britain's embassy in Turkey.

The OSS also established a research and analysis division that was second to none in the world. It would eventually house nine hundred analysts, drawn from university campuses across the United States, including the economist Walt Rostow, the historians Crane Brinton and William Langer, and the Sinologist John King Fairbank. Many OSS officers held left-wing views, especially academics in the service's research division. Donovan tolerated them, once quipping that he would put Stalin on his payroll if it ensured the defeat of Hitler. He was more right than he knew.[26]

Unlike in Britain, where MI6's chief was given responsibility for SIGINT and human intelligence, Roosevelt did not give Donovan access to U.S. SIGINT, which remained the purview of the military; but he did finally unify the fighting factions of U.S. Army and Navy signals intelligence. Army SIGINT (SIS), which grew to a staff of seven thousand during the war, was given jurisdiction over the interception of all foreign military and diplomatic communications, while the navy's OP-20-G focused on foreign naval traffic. In the endless Washington merry-go-round about the importance of being the messenger, the navy's representative was still allowed to deliver decrypts to the president.

Six months after Pearl Harbor, SIGINT helped turn the tide of the war in the Pacific. The ability to decipher Japanese communications first proved valuable for U.S. commanders in the Pacific at the Battle of the Coral Sea in May 1942, revealing Japanese strategic and tactical intentions. The battle effectively ended Japan's advance toward Australia. But MAGIC's major contribution occurred at the Battle of Midway the following month. The commander of the U.S. Pacific Fleet, Chester Nimitz, used SIGINT to gain sufficient confidence to launch a surprise attack on the Japanese fleet, which itself thought it had the advantage of surprise. The U.S. naval forces destroyed four of the six Japanese aircraft carriers that had carried out the attack on Pearl Harbor. The battle forced Isoroku Yamamoto, commander in chief of the Japanese Combined Fleet, onto the defensive and began America's sweltering island-hopping advance across the Pacific. In April 1943, Nimitz authorized U.S. fighters to shoot down Admiral Yamamoto, whose flight details were detected from MAGIC decrypts, even though his midair assassination could have compromised their ongoing use.[27]

SIGINT was where the British and American governments developed the closest wartime intelligence relations, closer than any previous two nations. Before Pearl Harbor, Roosevelt's navy secretary, Frank Knox, and secretary of war, Henry Stimson, both favorably disposed to American intervention in the war, supported sharing intelligence with the British. At a meeting in August 1940 in London, amid the Battle of Britain, the head of the American Observer Mission, George V. Strong (later Eisenhower's head of army intelligence, G-2), suggested a free exchange of intelligence with the British. Soon thereafter, a delegation led by a British scientist, Henry Tizard, traveled to the United States to discuss sharing technical secrets between the two countries, including SIGINT. It became the beginning of what some called the "wizard war," in which science and technology, including radar, aeronautics, and code-breaking, were harnessed for the Allied war effort. Tizard's mission won Stimson's support and that of the U.S. Army SIGINT service, SIS.[28]

Building on the Tizard mission's success, in February 1941 a four-man American delegation traveled to Bletchley Park. To show their sincerity in sharing secrets, the Americans revealed to their British hosts the U.S. Army achievements (through SIS) against the Japanese diplomatic code PURPLE. They even brought with them a replica PURPLE machine that the Americans had reverse-engineered. The British in turn disclosed secrets of Bletchley's bombes; but they initially refrained from sharing something even more closely guarded, decryption of the Luftwaffe Enigma. The senior military code breaker at Bletchley Park, John Tiltman, was aghast: to make collaboration sincere, he argued to Menzies and Denniston, the British had to show similar good faith. He succeeded in convincing them. Nearly a year before Pearl

Harbor, Churchill authorized Bletchley to disclose the ULTRA secret to the American delegation, who were required to sign oaths of secrecy and only orally brief their superiors in Washington. It turned out to be the beginning of the Anglo-American SIGINT relationship that lasts to the present day.[29]

After Pearl Harbor, Roosevelt agreed to a free exchange of SIGINT with British intelligence. It started informally between services, cautiously, but then in 1943 became wholehearted. When Dwight Eisenhower visited Britain in 1942, Churchill personally briefed him on ULTRA. In May 1943, the two governments formalized their SIGINT exchange in a top secret agreement known as BRUSA (later known as UKUSA). London and Washington deemed the agreement so sensitive that it took them seven decades to declassify its text. BRUSA was signed in Washington by Bletchley's new director, Edward Travis, and George Strong, then the head of U.S. military intelligence. From 1943, British and American cryptanalysis of naval Enigma was carried out according to a single program coordinated by Bletchley Park. U-boat tracking rooms in London, Washington, and (from May 1943 onward) Ottawa communicated via direct lines. The SIGINT relations between the three Western Allied governments became so close that, according to Britain's official history of wartime intelligence, for the remainder of the war "they operated virtually as a single organization."

By the end of the war, two hundred American officers were stationed at Bletchley. They were more than liaison officers; they were cryptanalysts and translators. They included William Bundy, later the U.S. national security adviser, who worked at Bletchley's Hut 6 at the center of the attack on German army Enigma. GC&CS likewise stationed officers in Virginia at Arlington Hall, a former junior college for women, now turned U.S. Army SIGINT center. Like Bletchley, it came to look like a factory assembly line, which led some to call it the "salt mines," though most preferred "the mother ship" because of its worldwide network of SIGINT stations. Antagonism between U.S. Army SIGINT at Arlington Hall and U.S. Navy SIGINT, never far from the surface, meant Bletchley also had to station liaison officers with the latter. U.S. Army and Navy counterparts were frequently more willing to collaborate with the British, valued outsiders with no skin in Washington's game, than between themselves.

COVERT ACTION

The war also taught the Allies the darker arts of intelligence, what they politely termed "political warfare." This referred to a sliding scale of under-handed activities, from propaganda, bribery, and burglary, to various degrees of paramilitary actions, all the way to assassinations. While the Soviets had already mastered such arts, the British and Americans had hitherto used them only piecemeal. The war institutionalized them, now with entire bureaucracies in London and Washington dedicated to carrying them out. It had lasting repercussions in the East-West intelligence war after 1945.

In Britain, the agency tasked with carrying out political warfare was SOE, established in July 1940 with Churchill's enthusiastic backing. He famously tasked it to "set Europe ablaze." It was initially led by Hugh Dalton, a Labour MP and former lecturer at the London School of Economics. From its headquarters at 64 Baker Street, London, the "Baker Street irregulars" expanded during the war to cover six acres of office space from the Baker Street tube station to Portman Square. It attempted to ignite popular uprisings against Nazi occupation throughout Europe. Many of SOE's exploits have become legends. The individual bravery of agents para-chuted into the dark skies over occupied Europe cannot be overstated. In one operation conducted in 1943, British-trained Norwegian agents sailed down into occupied Norway and destroyed a heavy-water plant at Vermork, which the Allies feared the Nazis were using to build an atomic weapon. After the Germans rebuilt it, SOE agents sabotaged a ferry, using explosive mines, carrying railway tanker wagons laden with 15,000 liters of the heavy water destined for Germany. Before and after D-Day, as Patton's Third Army blasted toward Berlin, SOE and OSS networks attacked German lines of communication. OSS Jedburgh teams (named after the town in Scotland where they trained) dropped behind enemy lines, sabotaged German lines of communication, and sent back intelligence to advancing Allied forces.[30]

SOE files reveal that it bribed politicians across the Middle East. Churchill signed off on bribing officials in neutral countries like Spain and Portugal. Meanwhile, in Britain's information war against the Axis powers, its propaganda unit, the Political Warfare Executive (PWE), orchestrated "black propaganda," in which London's hands were hidden. PWE created bogus newspapers, such as *Das Neue Deutschland*, and "freedom" radio stations, including one called Nationalist Fascist Radio, to distribute fake news in occupied Europe and the Far East. According to PWE's once secret in-house history, its black-radio stations "purported to be of enemy origin with the object of discrediting him [the enemy] and producing action of different kinds." PWE, run by Robert Bruce Lockhart, the British diplomat who had tried to unseat the early Bolshevik regime, did not speak of "disinformation" but "deception," "rumors," "whispers," and "sibs" (from the Latin for "hiss," *sibilare*).[31]

Was SOE worth it? The answer is unquestionably "yes." Certainly the "ministry of ungentlemanly warfare," as SOE was called, failed to set Europe ablaze, but that was an impossibly high standard. Its value was seen in sabotaging Nazi atomic bomb plans, destroying Axis supply routes before D-Day, and supporting resistance groups in occupied Europe and the Far East. Yet despite the bravery of individual agents, an unsentimental analysis must conclude that SOE was not decisive in the Allied war effort. The same could be said of OSS efforts. Not for nothing, Douglas MacArthur, leader of U.S. forces in the Pacific, banned the OSS from his theater. Once the Soviet Union and the United States joined the struggle, the war was destined to be won through military and industrial might.

The distinction between the myth and reality of special operations can be seen in the Balkans. Allied strategy was to use them as a distraction from its operations in the Mediterranean, to keep Hitler tied up there, and to prevent him from transferring forces to the eastern front, thereby relieving pressure on Stalin. SOE and OSS relations grew increasingly fraught, however, with jurisdictional battles revealing deeper differences between them about the future of the Balkans. As research by the historians Max Hastings and, more recently, Halik Kochanski has shown, SOE and the American OSS were also pulled into what was effectively a civil war between the Croats and Serbs, the latter led by a conservative royalist leader, Draža Mihailović, who after the war was convicted of war crimes and executed by firing squad. For two years, SOE backed Mihailović, and his Yugoslav Chetniks, despite their collaborating with Italian fascists against communists under Josip Broz, known as Tito. In 1943, SOE switched allegiances to Tito, backed by OSS. Whatever SOE and OSS thought they were doing on the ground, many locals hated each other even more than the Axis powers. It was a story that would be replicated across Eastern Europe.[32]

Like in the Balkans, OSS and SOE found themselves supporting opposing wartime sides in Asia. The actors they supported, in Indochina and India, reflected divergent views of the British and U.S. governments about the postwar world, especially over the future of the British and European colonial empires. In August 1941, Churchill and Roosevelt had enunciated their vision for a postwar world, the Atlantic Charter, reached in a meeting onboard the USS *Augusta*, off the Newfoundland coast, as we have seen. Churchill, however, rejected the idea that self-determination, as described in the charter, applied to Britain's empire. Indeed, as the war progressed, he viewed the British services, SOE and MI6, as actors who could help reimpose British colonial rule—opening valuable markets for the City of London. By contrast, Roosevelt and OSS supported anti-colonial forces, while similarly eyeing markets for Wall Street. When it came to anti-colonial groups, SOE and OSS were little more than allies of a kind.[33]

What about assassinations? In June 1942, SOE-trained agents killed one of the architects of the Holocaust, Reinhard Heydrich, in Prague. The operation, ANTHROPOID, however, revealed the inherent dangers of supporting partisan warfare, to say nothing of assassination plots: mass reprisal killings. Hitler exacted terrible revenge on those believed responsible for murdering his deputy, Heydrich, razing an entire city in Czechoslovakia, Lidice, which the Gestapo thought was harboring the perpetrators. (German troops shot the town's entire male population, while the women were sent to Ravensbrück, a female concentration camp in northern Germany. Some of the town's children were sent to gas chambers. Wehrmacht engineers then blew up the town's buildings; tombstones in the cemetery were taken away for building materials; and the village pond was filled with rubble.) Two years later, the head of SOE's German section, R. H. Thornley, opposed plans to assassinate Hitler (Operation FOXLEY) because he believed it was in the Allied interest for Hitler to remain in power, rather than someone else with a potentially clearer military head.[34]

Eight decades after the war, the Kremlin produced documents suggesting that Soviet intelligence successfully thwarted an attempt by Nazi intelligence to assassinate the Allied "Big Three" leaders, Churchill, Roosevelt, and Stalin, when they met at Tehran in November 1943. Contrary to the Kremlin's claims, however, Operation LONG JUMP was not as real as Stalin claimed when he revealed it to his two Western Allies. Its alleged leader, a Waffen SS officer named Otto Skorzeny, later said there was no meaningful plot. Instead, LONG JUMP was a classic ploy by Stalin, giving him the excuse, on security grounds, for insisting that Roosevelt stay in the well-fortified Soviet embassy compound in Tehran rather than in the less-protected U.S. legation. Inevitably, the Soviet building was thoroughly bugged.[35]

SOE's official historian, M. R. D. Foot, once told me that its greatest success was to "give resistance movements in occupied countries the moral courage to fight." This was something they did not forget in the postwar years. In this respect, as Max Hastings has correctly noted, the true achievement of SOE was felt after the war, not during it: "Never could enemies of democracy claim that Britain and the United States had abandoned the occupied nations to their fate."[36]

WAR OF ANNIHILATION

While Stalin had dismissed Richard Sorge's reports about BARBAROSSA, he did believe the reports from his key agent in the Far East indicating that

Japan would not attack the Soviet Union—that it would stick to its neutrality pact signed with Moscow in April 1941. This was further confirmed by Soviet SIGINT. In the autumn of 1941, reassured by this intelligence, Stalin moved forces from the Far East to fight Germany on the eastern front, to take on the Nazi army in what became the bloodiest war in history.

World War II was overwhelmingly fought and won on the eastern front. The numbers of combatants and civilians slaughtered there are desensitizing. In total, the Soviets lost somewhere on the order of 28 million people. Four out of every five Germans killed lost their lives on the eastern front. By comparison, the British suffered about 450,000 total wartime casualties, the Americans approximately 418,500. Reflecting on the rivers of Soviet blood spilled, Stalin decreed that in communist lexicology, the word "revolution" should be synonymous with "nation." The duty of all communists was to defend the Soviet nation. It is not for nothing that Russians still speak of a Great Patriotic War.

Intelligence played a role on the eastern front but was not decisive. The war there effectively came down to combat—and Stalin's willingness to send limitless numbers of Soviet soldiers and citizens to their deaths. BARBAROSSA unleashed Germany's war of racial annihilation on the Soviet Union. Hitler's strategy was to conquer an empire in the East for living space (*Lebensraum*), then repopulate with biologically "superior" *Volk*. The Soviet Union's Slavs would become slaves. It was an existential war to destroy the Soviet Union, as well as Jews, which in Hitler's nightmare were synonymous. Hitler's attack achieved both tactical and strategic surprise. In the boiling summer months, German forces advanced into Soviet territory at breakneck speed. It was a three-pronged attack: to the north, toward Leningrad; in the center, toward Moscow; and in the South, toward Ukraine, with its promising wheat fields; and onward to oil reserves in the Caucasus.

Just as Stalin failed to grasp BARBAROSSA, so Hitler failed to predict Soviet resistance. As in the Kremlin, sycophancy in Hitler's court meant German intelligence provided him with "loyal" information. The magnitude of Soviet resistance, with Stalin dragooning citizens, was revealed during the siege of Leningrad. German forces besieged and starved the city, whose inhabitants were forced to eat glue, wallpaper paste, leather belts, and even each other to survive. But they refused to surrender. Despite Germany's rapid early advances, in the autumn its army ground to a standstill in mud and early snow. In December, forward Wehrmacht teams could see the Kremlin through field glasses. But they would never enter the city. Temperatures plummeted at night to −40 degrees. The German army was left to fight the war on the eastern front in its summer denim kit, so certain was the German high command that the war would finish before winter. The snow ran red with blood. Body parts flew through the air, as NKVD officers machine-gunned suspected collaborators, "partisans."[37]

Soviet intelligence ran some successful espionage networks in Western Europe, which assisted Stalin's war effort. One such spy ring, established before the war, was the so-called RED ORCHESTRA (ROTE KAPELLE in German), a network comprising 117 agents in Germany, France, Belgium, and Switzerland. The conductor of the "orchestra," known as Le Grand Chef, was a Polish Jew named Leopold Trepper. In late 1942, the Abwehr managed to track down the radio operators, "musicians," in the network using radio direction finding. The Nazis executed eleven members of the network in December 1942. Gallows were ordered before the trials had even begun. The GRU also ran a spy ring of illegals in Switzerland, known as the RED THREE (ROTE DREI), after its three main radio transmitters, which were out of reach of German intelligence and continued to work until 1943, when the Swiss shut the group down. One of the GRU officers in that network was Ursula Kuczynski, code-named SONYA; she reappears in our story below as the handler of a Soviet spy, Klaus Fuchs, who stole secrets of the Anglo-American atom bomb. Contrary to later claims by Soviet historians, the ROTE KAPELLE and the ROTE DREI were not decisive in the Soviet war effort. They did not, for example, warn Soviet headquarters of the German sweep in the south in the summer of 1942 toward Stalingrad on the Volga River. The NKVD's SIGINT section, housed in the old Select Hotel on Dzerzhinsky Street in Moscow, never achieved anything comparable to ULTRA.[38]

Stalin's intelligence services also orchestrated some successful strategic deception operations on the eastern front. They were modeled on the Cheka's earlier deception, the TRUST. In an operation code-named MONASTYR ("Monastery" in English), Soviet intelligence fabricated a fake pro-German underground supposedly in the heart of Stalin's high command, the Stavka. A central figure in this deception was a Soviet Red Army officer, Alexander Demyanov (code-named HEINE), who volunteered for the Abwehr and provided apparently genuine intelligence on the Soviet order of battle. His intelligence became important in September 1942, when the German Sixth Army, under General Friedrich Paulus, entered Stalingrad. In November, in what Stalin called "the decisive moment of the war," the Soviets began a counteroffensive.

The NKVD–Red Army deception operation was designed to prevent Germans from moving reinforcements from its central army group, west of Moscow, to support Paulus's encircled Sixth Army group at Stalingrad. Surviving reports in German archives from Alexander Demyanov's bogus agent network, whose purpose was to deceive the Germans, show that it successfully dissuaded the German high command from moving more forces to Stalingrad. The head of German intelligence on the eastern front, Reinhard Gehlen, was convinced for the rest of his life that Demyanov's deception about the Soviet order of battle and strategy was genuine. The retaking of Stalingrad opened the Soviet Army's push westward into Romania, Bulgaria, Hungary, and toward Berlin. Stalin's famed general Georgy Zhukov led a merciless advance.[39]

In August 1941, Stalin had issued Order 270, which instructed the Red Army to "fight to the last," and proclaimed Soviet officers who fell into German hands would not be considered prisoners of war, but "malicious deserters," and treated as such, while families of rank-and-file Soviet soldiers who fell into German hands would forfeit rations, effectively condemning them to starvation. Subsequently, in Order 227, in July 1942, Stalin ordered the Red Army to take "not a step back." He authorized the deployment of blocking detachments to prevent Soviet soldiers from retreating. Red Army conscripts thus faced German guns in front of them and NKVD guns behind them. In defending Stalingrad, General Vasily Chuikov shot an estimated 13,500 of his own men as a morale-stiffening exercise, as the historian Michael Burleigh has noted. By the end of the war, about 300,000 Red Army soldiers had been killed by their own army for attempted flight or desertion. One NKVD tactic was to parachute agents into forward operation zones, dressed in German uniforms, and then liquidate local partisans who helped them.[40]

From the eastern front, crackling German radio waves carried messages revealing the horrors of the Holocaust. Bletchley Park decrypted some of them. Its operators were effectively eavesdropping on hell. Some decrypts unambiguously revealed Nazi atrocities in occupied Eastern Europe and the deportation of Jews, including children, from far-flung corners of Europe—what the Nazis euphemistically called the "Final Solution to the Jewish Question." We can read those horrendous decrypts today, leaving us to imagine the fates of the souls described. Approximately six hundred ULTRA and U.S. MAGIC decrypts exist in British and American archives relating to the Holocaust, in which six million Jews—more than one-third of contemporary Jews in the world—were murdered. Two months after the Nazi invasion, Churchill decided to use ULTRA intelligence about it publicly. Against the advice of Bletchley Park's directors, he made a chilling radio broadcast. In his instantly recognizable voice, Churchill warned that German police troops were carrying out mass executions on Russian soil. It was, Churchill said, a crime without a name. After his broadcast, as Bletchley feared, the head of the Nazi Order Police forbade his troops from communicating "secret Reich matters" over the radio, namely anything relating to killing Jews, which thenceforth was described in bland terms. Churchill's use of intelligence raised a moral question still haunting us today: whether to disclose crimes against humanity discovered from secret intelligence, when doing so may jeopardize its further use.[41]

Bletchley Park was only able to decrypt somewhere between a quarter and a half of all the messages intercepted; consequently, its code breakers could not grasp the full picture of what the Germans were perpetrating.

The decrypts also replicated the deliberately vague and bland language in the original messages, describing "actions" against Bolsheviks, plunderers, partisans, and bandits as "liquidations" and "special measures." Nazi mass murder was based on secrecy and deception, though its horrors were more widely known in Germany and occupied territories than many claimed after the war. Details about mass killings at Auschwitz II (Birkenau) did not reach London or Washington until the summer of 1944, two years after they began. While decrypts contained descriptions of massacres, they did not reveal the deliberate policy of genocide.[42]

The NKVD never industrialized killing, though they did establish shooting galleries to streamline it. Stalin's knowledge of the Holocaust is a secret still hidden in Russian NKVD archives, with little prospect of ever being released. The deportation and liquidation of entire ethnic groups, however, would not have been alien to Stalin, the "breaker of nations." Beria, whom Stalin called "my Himmler," carried out ethnic cleansings. He demolished autonomous regions within the Soviet Union, dispatching entire populations like the Karachays in clinking rail cars to hellish ends of the Soviet empire. In February 1944, he authorized the deportation of approximately 460,000 Chechens and Ingush. The NKVD burned villagers alive in homes, stables, and mosques. Chechnya and Ingushetia were wiped off the map. Three months later, in May 1944, the NKVD carried out a massive deportation of Crimean Tatars, sent on trucks into oblivion. By the time Stalin met with Churchill and Roosevelt at Yalta on the Crimean Peninsula in February 1945, there was probably not a single Tatar remaining in Crimea.[43]

The eastern front's barbarity had been revealed back in August 1941, when the German Sixth Army advanced on Kyiv. Stalin refused to order its evacuation. Once the German army was inside the city, with much of Kyiv ablaze from fierce bombardment, NKVD saboteurs remotely detonated mines in the city center's buildings. In retaliation, the SS and German military—supposedly fighting "Judeo-Bolshevism"—took 33,771 Jews to the Babi Yar ravine near the city. They shot their victims over two days, using 100,000 rounds of ammunition. German army engineers then blew up the sides of the ravine, burying the bodies. By April 1942, there were only about twenty Jews left in Kyiv.[44]

STRATEGIC DECEPTION: TOWARD VICTORY

The most important British intelligence body during World War II was one that you have probably never heard of: the London Controlling Section (LCS), which orchestrated strategic deceptions against the Axis powers. The LCS was established in September 1941 by an officer named Oliver Stanley, a barrister and conservative politician. It was later run by an Eton- and Oxford-educated British army officer, John Bevan. Although he is not a household name, like Alan Turing, Bevan was a key wartime British intelligence officer. Under his control, the LCS prepared "deception plans on a worldwide basis with the object of causing the enemy to waste his military resources," according to its charter.[45]

The idea of using disinformation to degrade Germany's war effort took root in the arid soils of North Africa and grew outward from there. British intelligence deceived the German high command before the Allied invasion of Sicily in 1943 into thinking that the attack from North Africa to southern Europe was not coming to Sicily (as was blindingly obvious to anyone with a map) at the foot of Italy, but Sardinia to its northwest and Greece in the eastern Mediterranean. Conceived by British naval intelligence, the operation, known as MINCEMEAT, involved dropping a dead body from a London morgue (the "man who never was") into the sea off the coast of neutral Spain, with a forged map of plans for an Allied invasion of Sardinia, when the true target was Sicily. Spanish officials found the body and passed it to the Germans. ULTRA showed that the German high command believed the map was genuine. It convinced Hitler to divert forces to Sardinia. As a result, the Allies invaded Sicily (HUSKY) with fewer casualties than expected.

Operation ZEPPELIN created a fictitious British army in the Egyptian desert, which induced Hitler to maintain twenty-two divisions in Yugoslavia and Greece to repel a supposed Allied landing that never materialized. Other Allied campaigns in the eastern Mediterranean, likewise buttressed by deception, bogged down Axis forces that Hitler needed on the eastern front.

Into these strategic deception operations entered MI5's astounding counterespionage feat, its so-called double-cross system. It was the most successful deception of the war—and probably in the history of warfare. Thanks to ULTRA, London's intelligence chiefs identified every wartime Axis agent sent to Britain, approximately one hundred and fifteen in total. MI5's counterespionage outfit, B Division, captured and turned thirty of them into double agents, using them to send disinformation back to the Axis powers in Europe, the Middle East, and Asia. As MI5's wartime director general put it at the end of the war: "The full story can perhaps never be told but if it could be, it could perhaps gain acceptance as truth on the grounds that it seems stranger than fiction." We can now tell the story—and it is stranger than fiction.[46]

MI5 was assisted by the fact that, unlike Soviet agents, German wartime spies dispatched against the Allies were generally not ideologically committed. Once captured, they broke relatively easily under interrogation. MI5's orchestra of double agents was conducted by a talented officer, T. A. "Tar" Robertson, a handsome Scot, who delighted his MI5 colleagues when he came to work wearing Scottish trews or a kilt. Robertson reported to an MI5 body, the Twenty Committee, so-called because the two letters for double-cross, "XX," were the Roman numerals for twenty. This code name was thought up by its witty chairman, a willowy, cricket-playing Oxford don, John Masterman. Bletchley Park was integral to the double-cross system's operation. Without ULTRA, it would have been impossible for MI5, and above it the LCS, to know whether the German high command was being deceived. By delivering carefully selected information, and tracing it through ULTRA as it spread to Berlin, Britain's spy chiefs were able to plant stories they wanted inside the files of German intelligence, as Robertson put it. German intelligence became a delivery system for British disinformation. ULTRA also confirmed that no unaccounted German agents operated in Britain during the war. As Masterman later recalled: "we actively ran and controlled the German espionage system in this country."[47]

When MI5 first briefed Churchill on the double-cross system, he was inevitably fascinated: "In wartime, truth is so precious that she should always be surrounded by a bodyguard of lies." Successful deception relies on an audience already believing something to be true, not in conjuring ideas out of nothing. As the poet Samuel Coleridge said, no stage play can be successful without a "willing suspension of disbelief" among the audience. Disinformation, or deception, works in a similar way: helping a target along the way. This happened with the Allied deception campaign surrounding D-Day, FORTITUDE, in which MI5's double agents took a lead. American and British code breakers provided D-Day's planners with a window into Hitler's strategic thinking: they were reading diplomatic messages (PURPLE) from Japan's ambassador in Berlin, Baron Hiroshi Ōshima, one of Hitler's close allies. In his dispatches back to Tokyo, Ōshima reported Hitler's belief that the major Allied assault force in Europe in 1944—which everyone knew was on the way—would come not to Normandy but to the Calais area. Enter MI5's double agents to support that belief.

MI5's star wartime double agent was a Spaniard, Juan Pujol Garcia. In a nod to his star-like quality, the British code-named him GARBO. Although GARBO's story is now relatively well known, it still makes one's hands sweat when told. GARBO delivered false information before and after D-Day. With the help of his MI5 handler, a Spanish-speaking London art dealer, Tomás Harris, GARBO radioed false information to his German handlers about the Allied invasion, which the German high command believed. Less well known is the case of Nathalie "Lily" Sergueiew (code-named TREASURE). She was a Russian-born anti-Bolshevik who lived in France, where she worked as a journalist. After France fell in 1940, she was recruited by German intelligence, and, in November 1943, was dispatched to Spain. But there, in Madrid, she secretly gave herself up to the British. Her British handler thereafter was MI5's Mary Sherer. They became the only British female agent and case officer duo during the war.

TREASURE's case reveals the pedestrian human drama at the heart of wartime counterespionage, which posterity tends to forget. It centered on her dog, Frisson, which she had been forced to leave behind in Gibraltar when leaving for Britain. TREASURE was a valuable agent, but her MI5 files also describe her as "temperamental." The loss of her dog gnawed away at her. She told her boyfriend that she was a British double agent, and threatened to quit unless MI5 arranged for her dog to be brought from Gibraltar. Matters came to a head in the month before D-Day, May 1944, when Sergueiew learned that her dog had died. She told MI5 that she had a secret signal that would indicate to her German commanding officer that she was under British control, and she threatened to use it in revenge for her dog's death. After a tumultuous meeting with Robertson, she eventually backed down and gave him the secret code. She continued to work for MI5 through D-Day, sending radio messages describing Allied troop concentrations in southeast England, preparing for an invasion of the Calais area (when really they were in the southwest, destined for Normandy). Her antics, however, made her replaceable for the British; a week after D-Day, MI5 let her go, although it continued to transmit messages, supposedly sent from her, for several months.[48]

GARBO and TREASURE's disinformation confirmed what Hitler and the German high command already believed. Their deception reached a climax with the Allied invasion of Europe (OVERLORD) on June 6, 1944. By that time, the Supreme Commander for the Allied Expeditionary Force, Dwight D. Eisenhower, was drinking twenty cups of coffee a day and chain-smoking Camels. The Allied deception operation (BODYGUARD) surrounding the invasion of northwest Europe, on D-Day, involved one of the largest phantom forces in military history. The First U.S. Army Group (FUSAG), nominally under General George Patton's command, never existed: it was a collection of balsa-wood tanks and dummy aircraft in fields in southern England designed to deceive Luftwaffe overhead reconnaissance. It did as planned.

At this point, GARBO entered history. Before and after D-Day, he radioed transmissions from his "agents" in Britain that helped convince Berlin that the Allied invasion was coming not to Normandy but to the Calais region—specifically, to the Pas de Calais, 175 miles north of the Normandy peninsula. Britain's intelligence chiefs watched with pride and relief as ULTRA revealed that the German high command had swallowed the bait, diverting Panzer tanks to Calais to wait for the bogus Allied invasion force that would never arrive. GARBO was awarded the German Iron Cross, his German handlers told him, to his and MI5's delight.

Three months before D-Day, Bletchley was able to read the communications between Berlin and the commander of German forces in France, Gerd von Rundstedt. His communications, and other ULTRA decrypts, revealed that Hitler exaggerated Allied forces in Britain by almost 200 percent. As it turned out, Hitler kept his Panzers in Calais longer than even British deception planners predicted—through July. Meanwhile, Ōshima's intercepted dispatches to Tokyo dutifully reported Hitler's order of battle and the Führer's continued belief that the major Allied assault would come to the Calais area. Churchill read the decrypts avidly as they came in.[49]

D-Day would have succeeded without Anglo-American deception—but at a higher cost in Allied lives. Eisenhower's crusade into Europe, as he called it, depended on 160,000 brave Allied troops who landed on Normandy's beaches. Some 4,400 were cut down by German fire on that first day of the invasion alone—terrible numbers, but small by the standards of the eastern front. Intelligence, according to Eisenhower himself, "saved thousands of British and American lives, and, in no small way, contributed to the speed with which the enemy was routed and eventually forced to surrender." The U.S. commander secretly wrote to Bletchley Park at the war's end, thanking its staff for their "magnificent services," which had been of "priceless value" to him. Ike's message to Bletchley, more than anything else, reveals the value of intelligence to the Allied war effort.

One of Eisenhower's aides concluded about ULTRA: "Very few Armies ever went into battle better informed of their enemy." In short, intelligence did all that could be hoped for with D-Day, providing the Allies with an advantage. The rest came down to the strategies of commanding officers and the fearless combat of troops. Two weeks after OVERLORD, the Soviets on the eastern front launched BAGRATION, the largest Allied offensive of the Great Patriotic War.[50]

CHAPTER FOUR

STALIN'S WARTIME ASSAULT

Tangle within tangle, plot and counter-plot, ruse and treachery,
cross and double-cross, true agent, false agent, double agent, gold
and steel, the bomb, the dagger and the firing party, were interwoven
in many a texture so intricate as to be incredible and yet true.
–Winston Churchill

FOR STALIN, THE WAR AGAINST NAZI GERMANY WAS A CUR-
rent fight for his country's survival; the future, as he saw it, was the "inevitable" conflict with the world's imperialist, capitalist powers in the West.
Stalin deftly used his intelligence services to propel his long-term grand
strategy against them, even as they remained focused on defeating Nazi
Germany. He wanted to discover whether they were secretly negotiating a
separate peace deal with the Axis powers, a conspiracy he was convinced of
but could not prove. He also tasked his intelligence services with stealing
scientific and technological secrets from his Western Allies on an industrial
scale, to be used after the Third Reich's defeat. In fact, Stalin assigned a
greater priority to espionage against his Western Allies than he did Nazi
Germany. His greatest wartime intelligence successes were not conducted
against the German high command but at Britain and the United States.

Stalin's moles were breathtakingly successful, able to burrow their way into the Allies' most sensitive military programs. Their espionage meant that during and after the war, London and Washington were effectively conducting open diplomacy with Moscow.[1]

Hundreds of Americans and British subjects spied for the Soviet Union during the war. Most did not penetrate sensitive positions in the British or American governments. But some, like the Cambridge Five, did.

The identity of some wartime Soviet agents remains a mystery to this day. We do not know, for example, who the agent code-named NOBILITY was. We know that he or she was at the center of a GRU espionage ring in Britain, the X-Group, but that is all. One of X-Group's known agents was Ivor Montagu, hailing from a wealthy banking family. Educated at Cambridge, an intellectual and a committed socialist as well as a member of the left-wing Fabian Society, Montagu was one of the foremost promoters of Britain's film industry. He visited the Russian filmmaker Sergei Eisenstein in Hollywood and was a successful film producer in his own right, collaborating with the director Alfred Hitchcock on movies like *The 39 Steps*, *Secret Agent*, and *Sabotage*. In this case, life imitated art. Montagu was a secret agent himself.

Montagu's openly communist views and membership in the Communist Party of Great Britain had placed him squarely on MI5's radar by the time of the war's outbreak. The service amassed a thick file on him, containing intercepted letters and bugged telephone conversations. What British intelligence did not know was that Montagu was in fact working as a Soviet agent, right under its nose. As Britain's spy chiefs would later discover, Montagu was recruited by Simon Kremer, the GRU *resident* in London, and given the code name INTELLIGENTSIA. His spying never reached the level of Stalin's other Cambridge-educated Englishmen. His espionage appears to have petered out by 1943, although some of the secrets he betrayed are still locked in GRU archives in Russia. Montagu had connections with people at the heart of wartime British intelligence. His brother, Ewen, was the Royal Navy representative on MI5's wartime double-cross committee, where he played a prominent role in MINCEMEAT, the Allied deception that persuaded German forces to shift reinforcements to Sardinia and Greece. Did Ewen let slip MINCEMEAT's secrets to his brother, the Soviet agent? Did that information get forwarded to Moscow? We do not know.[2]

THE CAMBRIDGE FIVE

In their recruitment of agents in Britain, Stalin's spy chiefs cast their net wide in the hope of reeling in a major catch. They needed just one, but hoped for more. In Britain, they caught five, as we saw in chapter two. During the war, the Cambridge Five penetrated every major section of Britain's secret state: MI5, MI6, SOE, Bletchley Park, the Foreign Office, and the wartime atomic bomb project. Members of the Cambridge Five were hemorrhaging British secrets to Moscow before June 1941. Luckily, Stalin did not disclose them to Hitler, whom he was desperate to appease. In 1942 alone, material supplied by one of the Cambridge Five, Donald Maclean, from inside the Foreign Office, filled forty-five volumes in the NKVD's Moscow archives. KGB records reveal that between 1941 and 1945, Anthony Blunt provided his handlers in London with 1,771 documents from within MI5. In the first six months of 1945, Guy Burgess (code-named HICKS) provided 389 British documents classified top secret.[3]

According to documents recently released by Russian intelligence, one of Burgess's principal sources of information was Dennis Proctor, private secretary to Anthony Eden, inside Churchill's wartime cabinet. Proctor disclosed sensitive information to his friend Burgess—and thus to Moscow—about Churchill and Roosevelt's wartime plans to open a second front in Europe. Meanwhile, the "fifth man," John Cairncross (LIZT, or "List" in English), was responsible for two betrayals: first, from inside the Foreign Office, he exposed atomic secrets, and then, after moving to Bletchley Park, he disclosed ULTRA to Stalin. The most important ULTRA decrypts he provided were German preparations for the Battle of Kursk in July 1943, when the Red Army defeated Hitler's last offensive on the eastern front. (The documentary record is unclear about the intelligence that Churchill delivered to Stalin, in disguised form, about Kursk.) Stolen ULTRA secrets allowed Stalin to launch massive preemptive strikes against German airfields. Meanwhile, in 1944, Arnold Deutsch's original Cambridge recruit, Kim Philby, became the head of MI6's new wartime department for investigating Soviet espionage. A Soviet spy was thus at the helm of Britain's espionage effort against the Soviet Union. From his position at the epicenter of Western intelligence efforts against the looming Soviet threat, Philby was able to sabotage British and American counterespionage investigations from the inside. The wreckage he caused would last for decades.[4]

Russia's foreign intelligence service today, the SVR, calls the Cambridge Spies the "Magnificent Five": heroes of the Soviet regime. Indeed, they were, from Russia's perspective. From the British perspective, their achievements represent astonishing failures of security. In earlier chapters we saw the primitive nature of British vetting. But Britain's failure to counter Soviet intelligence went deeper. When the Soviet Union was pulled into the war in June 1941, forming the Grand Alliance, the Foreign Office placed a moratorium on all intelligence collection on its new ally in the East. The Foreign Office strategy was based on a gentlemanly but naive belief that allies do not spy on allies. Stalin, of course, showed no such restraint. MI6 did not have a station in Moscow, nor a single agent worth the name in the Soviet Union during the war—or for years after. The KGB's continued ability to run the Cambridge Spies for years is evidence enough of that; a well-placed British agent in Moscow would have revealed them.

After London's embargo on collecting Soviet intelligence, Bletchley Park likewise was not allowed to monitor or attack Soviet communications. This caused consternation among Britain's spy chiefs, who warned that the Russian tiger had not changed its stripes. Guy Liddell, MI5's senior chain-smoking counterespionage desk officer, confided to his diary in the middle of the war that he felt certain that Russian espionage continued: "and sooner or later we shall be expected to know all about it," he wrote.[5]

Liddell was more accurate than he knew. His diary reveals that Anthony Blunt frequently swung by his office for friendly chats. MI5 tried to find a way around the Foreign Office ban by increasing surveillance on the British Communist Party. After the Soviet Union entered the war, MI5 installed bugs in the CPGB's headquarters in Covent Garden. That strategy was not futile. Soviet intelligence did foolishly maintain connections with the party. "The Soviet authorities have from time to time," noted a wartime MI5 report based on bugged conversations, "obtained information from most of the leading members of the Communist Party who have shown various degrees of willingness to do this work." MI5's strategy paid off modestly. In June 1943, it rounded up a Soviet spy ring led by a CPGB senior member, Douglas (Dave) Springhall, who acquired classified material from the Air Ministry, SOE, and a secretary in MI6. Springhall was prosecuted in 1943, receiving seven years. The dossier of one of his agents, Mary Sheehan, in the Air Ministry, opened in 2022, suggests that British authorities kept her trial secret to protect political fallout with Britain's wartime ally in the East.[6]

Monitoring the CPGB was, however, never going to be sufficient to identify clever Soviet agents. The Cambridge Five purposefully kept their distance from it. Worse, they sabotaged the fledging efforts by British intelligence to detect wartime Soviet espionage. As a result of Blunt's espionage inside MI5, Moscow knew about its intensified surveillance on British communists. We do not know if Moscow Center warned the CPGB. Evidence in bugged transcripts from inside the party suggests not. Thus began a game of chess, move and countermove, between East and West that would become a hallmark of the Cold War.

Like MI5, Bletchley Park tried to work around Britain's ban on collecting Soviet traffic by collecting intercepted *German* communications about the Soviet Union. Once again, Stalin's spies sabotaged those efforts. At Bletchley, John Cairncross betrayed its efforts to the Kremlin. Meanwhile, in May 1943, MI6 began considering its postwar strategy, and established a new department on Soviet communism, Section IX. It, too, was fatally compromised when, in 1944, Philby became its head. All in all, it is difficult to imagine a picture of greater desolation than Britain's wartime intelligence services when it came to the Soviet Union.[7]

PARANOID TENDENCIES

Britain's government was spared the full damage of wartime Soviet espionage by Stalin's own crippling paranoia. Despite the breathtaking capabilities of intelligence collection, which saw his agents' work only limited to the amount of material they could steal, their espionage against Britain was squandered by Stalin's insistence on being his own chief intelligence analyst. His conspiratorial mind was shaped by his memory, not entirely unreasonable, of Churchill's crusade to unseat the Bolshevik regime just twenty years earlier. This meant that sometimes Stalin disregarded even the best intelligence from his agents in the British government. In the middle of the war, when the Cambridge Five were stealing the most secrets, Stalin and Beria decided that their spies were part of an elaborate British deception operation against them. The Center's paranoia ran so deep that in 1943 it even dispatched an NKVD surveillance team to London to monitor their own agents—the Five. The team clumsily tailed them in the hope of catching them in the act of treachery for the British.[8]

The more Stalin learned about the workings of MI5's double-cross system and other deceptions, the more he distrusted his agents' reports stating that British intelligence was not targeting the Soviet Union. Despite a 1942 Anglo-Soviet agreement on war collaboration, Stalin was convinced that Churchill was deceiving him: secretly trying to strike a deal with Nazi leaders, leaving the Third Reich and the Soviet Union to fight to the death.[9]

Stalin was obsessed by the bizarre flight to Britain in May 1941 by Hitler's deputy Rudolf Hess. He believed the flight was part of a plot between Hess and British intelligence to hatch a separate peace between Britain and the Third Reich. In fact, as Hess's thick British intelligence dossier reveals, MI5 and MI6 were taken by surprise when the Nazi leader crash-landed in Scotland after flying solo across the North Sea while high on a cocktail of drugs. His mission was the work of an unsound mind, the British reasoned. When he was arrested, he was dressed in leather and clutching twenty-eight different medicines. Contrary to what Stalin believed, there was no secret peace treaty being brokered between the British and Hess. The Kremlin to this day insists that the British government is hiding documents about such a plot.[10]

Fuel was added to this fire years later, after the Soviet Union's collapse, with the declassification of a British military assessment called UNTHINK-ABLE, carried out at the end of the war. In May 1945, with Germany close to defeat, Churchill asked his chiefs of staff to consider whether Western powers could continue with military action, now against the Soviet Union, to compel Stalin to make concessions about territories he wanted to incorporate into the Soviet orbit. According to the authorized history of Russian intelligence, published in 2014, UNTHINKABLE proves Churchill's true intentions about the Soviet Union, and thus, by implication, proves that Stalin's fears of the British leader were correct. That is nonsense.

It is unclear whether Stalin knew of UNTHINKABLE. Guy Burgess, then working in the Foreign Office, may have disclosed some of its details to his Soviet handlers. If it did indeed reach Stalin, UNTHINKABLE would have fed his inner demons. In fact, however, UNTHINKABLE proves the opposite of what Russia's official intelligence historians today claim: the danger of acquiring pieces of intelligence, without their proper, broader context. UNTHINKABLE was a contingency plan against potential Soviet aggression in Europe. Churchill detested the Soviet Union but was not going to initiate hostilities against the Soviets and risk starting World War III. Such nuances, however, would have been lost on Stalin. The most important part of UNTHINKABLE was its conclusion: a war against the Soviet Union would probably fail. For Britain, UNTHINKABLE was true to its name—unthinkable.[11]

WITH AN ALLY LIKE THIS

Stalin's intelligence services unleashed a similar assault on the United States. After America's entry into the war, the NKVD and the GRU exploited the

Roosevelt administration's focus on its wartime enemies in Europe and the Far East to collect as much intelligence as possible. As in Britain, Soviet intelligence penetrated and compromised the U.S. government: Soviet spies breached every major branch of the administration, including the Oval Office. At key strategic moments of the war, Stalin was better informed about American wartime secrets than antagonistic branches within the U.S. government themselves.

Before the war, when Arnold Deutsch was recruiting spies from Cambridge, Soviet intelligence was recruiting a group of like-minded Ivy Leaguers to enter into the hallways of power in Washington: Laurence ("Larry") Duggan, Alger Hiss, Harry Dexter White, Duncan Chaplin Lee, and more. One Soviet agent, Julian Wadleigh, who entered the State Department in 1936, later wrote: "When the communist international represented the only force effectively resisting Nazi Germany, I had offered my services to the Soviet underground in Washington as one small contribution to help stem the fascist tide."[12]

In early 1942, after America signed the Lend-Lease Act and entered the war, Moscow became second only to Britain as a recipient for U.S. wartime aid. The Soviet government received $11 billion in total, delivered in hellish journeys, bobbing over hostile seas, which took the lives of about five thousand Allied sailors. As part of these loan arrangements, U.S. authorities allowed the Soviet government to increase the size of its diplomatic staff, and open logistical offices in the United States to administer the incoming aid. The Soviet government opened organizations like Machinoimport, based in New York, and the Soviet Government Purchasing Commission, which established offices in several American cities. AMTORG, which was originally set up in New York, as we have encountered, expanded its offices to the West Coast.

It was all too easy for Soviet spy chiefs to exploit American goodwill and naivete. Soviet Lend-Lease offices in America did administer aid, but they also housed undercover intelligence officers. Ironically, because the new Soviet offices were subsidized by American Lend-Lease aid, the U.S. government was effectively funding espionage on itself. The Soviet government opened a new consulate on the West Coast, giving Soviet intelligence a total of three legal *rezidentury* in the United States: in New York, Washington, and San Francisco. The Soviet offices established during World War II, as well as a web of illegal officers, agents, and couriers, would last into the twenty-first century.[13]

The NKVD wartime illegal *resident* in the United States, working without diplomatic cover, was Iskhak Akhmerov. An ethnic Tatar, Akhmerov cut a dapper figure, with a thick head of hair and well-tailored suits. He had served in the U.S. since 1935, when he arrived, posing as a student, on a doctored American passport. He went under various aliases, including Michael Green. Based in New York and later Baltimore, Akhmerov set up cover employment in the fur and clothes business. His wife, Helen Lowry, was the niece of Earl Browder (HELMSMAN), leader of the Communist Party of the United States of America (CPUSA), illustrating the connections between the party and Soviet intelligence.

Akhmerov's espionage was prodigious; he met agents over meals at diners, in train stations, and at the Longchamps restaurant chain. In just one year, his illegal *rezidentura* increased the number of microfilm rolls acquired nearly fourfold, from 59 in 1942 to 211 in 1943. He received the microfilms, containing documentation stolen by agents across the United States, via Elizabeth Bentley (MIRNA, then UMNITSA, "clever girl" or "good girl" in Russian), a Vassar graduate and NKVD courier. Akhmerov used Bentley and other couriers as "cutouts," or intermediaries, between himself and agents. Every fortnight, she would deliver microfilms from agents to him, which she hid in her knitting bag.[14]

None of Stalin's wartime American spies defected to the Soviet Union. Some of his most important agents, like Harry Dexter White in the Treasury, or Larry Duggan in the State Department, died before they could be prosecuted. This led to endless subsequent speculation about their guilt. Soviet intelligence archives—both officially opened, and those smuggled to the West—as well as contemporary U.S. and British SIGINT intercepts now establish their actions and guilt beyond doubt.

Like the Cambridge Spies, most Soviet agents working in the heart of America's wartime administration were ideologically committed communists. They saw themselves as secret warriors against international fascism. Before the war, the Spanish Civil War had radicalized some fellow travelers to become Soviet agents. The NKVD used the civil war between communists and fascists there to talent-spot Western recruits. British and U.S. authorities only later discovered the civil war's significance for Soviet intelligence. (Unbeknown to ideologically motivated recruits, Stalin used Spain as a hunting ground to eliminate ideological deviants, "enemies of the people," like Trotskyists, who disappeared into a crematorium operated by the NKVD *rezident* there.)

Some Soviet agents were also driven by money, like the New York Democratic congressman Samuel Dickstein. He demanded, and received, the princely sum of $12,000 (about $240,000 today) between 1937 and 1940 for betraying secrets in his possession. The NKVD, in a fit of inspiration, aptly code-named him CROOK. His work for the Soviets was only later uncovered. He died in 1954, as a sitting New York State Supreme Court justice.[15]

Unbeknown to the president, Roosevelt's administrative assistant, Lauchlin Currie, was a Soviet agent (code-named PAGE). Currie's Oval Office position earns him the distinction of being the highest-ranking Soviet agent ever inside the U.S. executive branch. Born in Canada, Currie earned a doctorate in economics from Harvard, which propelled him into Roosevelt's New Deal administration. During the war, he became the president's economic adviser, which afterward led to prestigious postings at the World Bank. Among the secrets that Currie is known to have delivered to his NKVD handlers was that, in 1945, the "Americans were on the verge of breaking the Soviet code." Moscow was aghast at Currie's intelligence, but on further investigation, its fears dissipated. Currie's warning to the Center was derived from an episode in late 1944 when the Americans obtained a fire-damaged Soviet code book. At the end of hostilities between Finland and the Soviet Union in 1944, Finnish intelligence officers escaped to neighboring Sweden, knowing that Soviets would be returning to the Baltic in overwhelming force. There, in Sweden, they set up what amounted to a garage sale of intelligence products related to Finland's wartime enemy, the Soviet Union. In an operation known as STELLA POLARIS because of its northern origins, the Finnish sold their wares to the highest bidder. In stepped Uncle Sam. The OSS purchased a Soviet code book for $63,000— approximately $1.2 million today.

Currie learned about the purchase of the code book, but jumped to the wrong conclusion. In fact, the Americans were not on the verge of cracking Soviet codes. Far from it. When Roosevelt's business-savvy secretary of state, Edward Stettinius Jr., and OSS director Donovan discovered OSS trying to spy on their wartime Soviet ally, they ordered the code book returned. Donovan's decision showed him at his naive best. A Soviet diplomat at the embassy in Washington, Andrei Gromyko, later the Soviet foreign minister, happily received the book. The Soviet head of foreign intelligence in Moscow, Pavel Fitin (VICTOR), doubtless perplexed, sent Donovan his thanks.[16]

The GRU, rather than the NKVD, had run the major prewar Soviet espionage networks in America. The man who built the GRU, known as the "Fourth Department," was Jan Berzin. With a chiseled, lined face and piercing blue eyes, Berzin had been a principal organizer of the early Soviet Red Terror. Berzin's officers and agents in the U.S. centered on émigré communities in New York City, particularly Latvians. The GRU ran money-laundering schemes and collaborated with the CPUSA in the same way that Soviet intelligence did with the British Communist Party. The defection of a GRU courier, Whittaker Chambers, however, gave the NKVD an excuse to take over most of the GRU's American networks. This only intensified the bitter rivalry between the two branches of Soviet intelligence, as each vied for Stalin's approval.

The GRU still continued to run some important agents in the U.S., like Larry Duggan (code-named 19). Duggan, a Harvard-educated official in the U.S. State Department, had a crisis of faith following the 1939 Nazi-Soviet pact. Despite his misgivings, Duggan was pressured by his Soviet handler, Akhmerov, to resume work once the U.S. entered the war with the Soviet

Union in 1941. Duggan rose to become chief of the State Department's Latin America division. From there, he provided his Soviet case officers with secrets about Washington's wartime and post-war strategy for South America—and how Moscow could sabotage it.[17]

Harry Dexter White (KASSIR, "cashier") was an equally important Soviet source of political intelligence inside the U.S. government. To the delight of Akhmerov, White's career was meteoric. His spectacular academic credentials—educated at Columbia and Stanford, with a doctorate in economics from Harvard—paved his way to the U.S. Treasury, where he rose to become its assistant secretary. He became a key adviser to Treasury Secretary Henry Morgenthau Jr. White represented the U.S. government at the Bretton Woods Conference in 1944. Today Bretton Woods is remembered for the founding of the West's postwar economic strategy. White played a significant role in it, helping to create two Bretton Woods institutions: the International Monetary Fund and the World Bank. Thanks to White, Stalin had a ringside seat to it all. The Soviet leader chose to remain outside the collaborative global economy that Bretton Woods produced, instead pulling down, to use Churchill's famous phrase, an Iron Curtain across Europe.[18]

Duggan and White nearly delivered Stalin an epic wartime intelligence coup. Roosevelt's vice president during his third term in office, from 1941 to 1945, was Henry Wallace. Wallace later said that if Roosevelt had died during his third term, which was not unlikely due to his ill health, and Wallace had become president, he would have appointed Duggan his secretary of state and White as his secretary of the Treasury. In that case, Soviet agents would have held two of the most senior positions in the U.S. government. As it transpired, Roosevelt lived into an unprecedented fourth term in office and replaced Wallace with Harry Truman for the 1944 election.

Soviet intelligence also penetrated the OSS. Donovan's confidential assistant, Duncan Lee, was, as we have seen, a Soviet agent (KOCH). A well-spoken former Rhodes scholar at Oxford, where he may have been recruited, Lee was the highest-placed Soviet agent ever to operate inside U.S. intelligence. Donovan's relaxed attitude toward Soviet intelligence was revealed when OSS opened a liaison station in Moscow in 1944. Wild Bill traveled there in the dead of winter, December 1943. He met the head of NKVD foreign intelligence, Pavel Fitin, and visited the NKVD's headquarters.

At a subsequent reception, whose guests included America's ambassador in Moscow, Averell Harriman, the Americans and Soviets toasted the opening of the OSS Moscow station. Britain's SOE mission head in Moscow had caustic comments about Donovan's trip. According to a secret SOE cable back to London, Donovan's meetings "resulted largely in a disclosure to the N.K.V.D. of the O.S.S. organization, accompanied by any undue modesty about their powers, and in return he received from the N.K.V.D. practically nothing." Donovan went even further, however. He wanted to allow the NKVD to open an official liaison office in Washington. When the FBI director, J. Edgar Hoover, heard about Donovan's proposal, he shot it down. Hoover suspected OSS was compromised by Soviet intelligence. He was right.[19]

Soviet intelligence also penetrated Britain's outfit in the United States, the BSC. One of its officers, Cedric Belfrage, a Cambridge graduate and Hollywood film critic, was a Soviet agent. This produced ironic results. Due to Stalin's festering conspiracies about the Cambridge Spies, who seemed too good to be true, in the middle of the war Soviet intelligence actually ranked Belfrage (CHARLIE) as more important than them. Although Belfrage betrayed some Allied secrets, in reality his espionage was not in the same class as the Cambridge Five.[20]

Due to his spies in the West, when Stalin met Churchill and Roosevelt at successive wartime conferences of the Big Three, he was better informed about them than they ever were of him. Stalin's intelligence about the Western leaders, with whom he was negotiating, probably surpassed that of any leader in history.

The Big Three meetings—at Tehran in November 1943, Yalta in February 1945, and Potsdam in July 1945—settled the fate of postwar Europe. Using the superior intelligence available to him, Stalin achieved his main strategic objective during these summits: recognition of a large Soviet "sphere of influence." At Tehran in 1943, the first time that Stalin and the U.S. president met, Roosevelt was determined to reach an agreement with the Soviet big boss. Stalin made the president travel six thousand miles to meet him, by sea and air, while he flew south (accompanied by three fighter squadrons). He insisted on housing Roosevelt, as we saw in the previous chapter, in the Soviet compound, embellishing a story of an assassination plot. In fact, the "discovery" of the plot gave Stalin an excuse to separate Roosevelt from the rambunctious Churchill, who stayed in the British compound, and bug Roosevelt's conversations. Stalin received transcripts of Roosevelt's private conversations each morning at eight o'clock. Revealingly, the Soviets code-named the Tehran conference EUREKA.

Stalin extracted a major concession from the Western Allies at Tehran: they agreed to give the postwar Soviet Union its 1941 frontiers back. This allowed Stalin to recover his territorial gains obtained when he and Hitler dismembered and occupied Poland and the Baltic states. In addition to bugging Western delegates, Stalin may have received intelligence from Roosevelt's close wartime adviser, Harry Hopkins, one of the many U.S. officials who indulged Uncle Joe. No compelling evidence has emerged that Hopkins was a Soviet agent, but he was certainly an asset. He is known to have provided Soviet officials in America with information about FBI wartime surveillance. Charles "Chip" Bohlen, later the U.S. ambassador to the Soviet Union, who acted as the American interpreter at Tehran, described Hopkins's influence on the president at the Tehran summit as "paramount." It is not impossible that Hopkins deliberately or inadvertently provided Stalin with information that helped Stalin's negotiations in Tehran. Those secrets, if they exist, remain hidden in Moscow archives.[21]

It was at the Big Three's meeting at Yalta, however, when Stalin's espionage truly paid off. Using the excuse that poor health prevented him from traveling, the generalissimo pressured Churchill and Roosevelt—who was genuinely sick and would die two months later—to make the arduous journey to the Crimea in February 1945. Hosting the conference on Soviet territory allowed Stalin to control its physical aspects. The British and American delegations at Yalta were housed in the ornate Vorontsov and Livadia Palaces, a former residence of Tsar Nicholas II. The hosts laid out banquets of caviar and Crimean wine, all in grand Italian Renaissance settings. The NKVD of course extensively bugged both palaces. These operations were overseen by Beria's son, Sergo, who later recounted that he used directional microphones to pick up, from fifty to one hundred meters away, the conversations of American and British delegations strolling on the grounds of the palaces. Sergo Beria provided Stalin with transcripts of the bugged conversations, which meant they knew at least some of what the U.S. and British delegates were saying and thinking. It also meant the delegates' wildest whims could be accommodated. Churchill's daughter Sarah, who accompanied him to Yalta, mentioned in the Vorontsov Palace that lemon juice went well with caviar. Overnight, a lemon tree laden with fruit appeared in the orangery. Stalin's British and American guests would have been alert to such surveillance, but human nature being what it is, there were endless possibilities for careless remarks. Churchill's spy chiefs, anticipating the worst, told him that he could not receive his ULTRA messages at Yalta. But he did get lemons with his caviar.[22]

The U.S. delegation at Yalta contained someone well known to Soviet intelligence: Alger Hiss, an agent code-named JURIST, then ALES. Hiss, forty years old at Yalta, had movie-star looks and charm. He was tall, often sported a bow tie, and carried the air of seriousness of a young academic. A graduate of Johns Hopkins and Harvard Law School, he was a highflier within the U.S. State Department, which he had joined in 1936, the same year he was recruited by the GRU. During the war, Hiss became a special adviser on Far East affairs to then secretary of state Cordell Hull. In late 1944, doubtless to the delight of his Soviet handlers, Hiss was pulled in to prepare the American side for the Yalta summit. He then joined the hundred-person delegation itself. A photo from the conference shows Stalin looking across a crowded round table at Roosevelt, to whose left sits Hiss.

Perched quietly in the hazy light behind Roosevelt at the conference, Hiss
made his own set of notes on conversations that took place. Along with
Chip Bohlen's notes, they became the official U.S. record. The GRU later
expressed its gratitude for the intelligence that Hiss provided at Yalta.[23]

Unsurprisingly, given the NKVD's extensive bugging and its mole inside
the U.S. delegation at Yalta, Stalin again achieved his key strategic objectives there. Churchill and a visibly ailing Roosevelt tried to extract from
Stalin the concessions previously agreed to in Tehran about Poland's fate.
Bedecked in a mustard yellow suit, Stalin outmaneuvered his Western Allies.
Knowing that the president and prime minister attached great significance
to Poland having "democratic" future elections, Stalin appeared to concede
to this graciously, while extracting their consent to accept the reality of a
Soviet-dominated postwar Poland. He knew that a "democratic" Poland
could easily be bent to his will if he installed a puppet regime—exactly what
happened. Poland's democratic future, and much of Eastern Europe's, died
on the Crimean vine at Yalta.[24]

G-MEN

The FBI expanded dramatically during the war, from 2,280 people in 1941
to about 15,000 in 1945, including 5,000 special agents (as FBI *officers* were
and still are known). These were America's G-men, as the tabloids dubbed
them. The Roosevelt administration had evidence of Soviet spies in its midst
from the earliest point of the war. On the first day of the war in Europe,
September 1, Whittaker Chambers confessed what he knew about Soviet
espionage to Adolf Berle, the assistant secretary of state and an adviser to
Roosevelt. Berle drew up a memorandum that listed Alger Hiss, Harry
Dexter White, and Lauchlin Currie (misspelled in Berle's memo) as Soviet
agents. Roosevelt's advisers, however, took no action. The case was a low
priority. The FBI did not interview Chambers until 1942. After the Soviet
Union and America became wartime allies in 1941, political winds were

blowing hard against such counterespionage investigations. Gaik Ovakim-
ian, an undercover Soviet intelligence officer in America, operating out of
AMTORG in New York, was detected by the FBI in 1941, but to avoid
a diplomatic fallout, the State Department intervened to prevent charges
being brought against him. The Soviet army, after all, was killing more
Nazis than the United States or Britain combined. The British and U.S.
governments were willing to dine with the Devil to defeat Nazism.[25]

Like Britain, the U.S. government failed to conduct any meaningful
wartime foreign intelligence collection on the Soviet Union. Donovan's
relaxed attitude to his Eastern ally was a gift to Moscow's spies. On American soil, the FBI monitored American communists and Soviet officials
in the hope of detecting Soviet espionage, but this was a sideshow to the
Bureau's overwhelming focus on the Axis powers. As in Britain, monitoring
American communists was never going to be sufficient to catch Soviet spies
who purposefully distanced themselves from the party. But it was not futile.
Soviet spy chiefs in America did stupidly rely on the CPUSA to assist with
espionage, thereby exposing them to FBI surveillance. The wartime NKVD
rezident in the U.S., Vassili Zarubin, drew on the CPUSA for recruits.
Despite the party's subsequent protests to the contrary, it provided a support
network for Soviet espionage, subversion, and sabotage on American soil.[26]

Through the connections between the CPUSA and Soviet agents, FBI
special agents obtained their first indication about the greatest ever failure
of American security: Soviet espionage at the heart of the U.S. atomic bomb
project. In March 1943, FBI surveillance on an American communist would
change history. The bureau was tapping the phone of Steve Nelson—born
Stephen Mesarosh in Croatia—a communist on the West Coast, as well as
bugging his home in Oakland. Amid the trawl of his daily conversations,
one recording stood out. It revealed Nelson talking with a scientist from
Berkeley's radiation laboratory who told him that thousands of people were
working on a nationwide uranium enrichment project, with facilities at Los
Alamos, New Mexico, and Oak Ridge, Tennessee.

The FBI tailed Nelson as he met with a Soviet official, who turned out to be Zarubin (MAKSIM). Zarubin was visiting the Soviet consulate in San Francisco. At that point, FBI director Hoover suspected Zarubin's true identity as a Soviet intelligence officer, though he could not yet confirm it. Hoover himself had not yet been indoctrinated into the MANHATTAN Project. His bugs in Nelson's home opened up a Pandora's box of American secrets. When he was briefed in broad terms on the atomic bomb project a few weeks later, it seemed to confirm Hoover's worst fears: the existence of a conspiracy operating against the United States, with underground links between Soviet intelligence and American communists. It would shape Hoover's view of Soviet communism long after the war.[27]

Hoover soon opened two major investigations into Soviet espionage: CINRAD (Communist Infiltration of the Radiation Laboratory) and COMRAP (Comintern Apparatus). He devoted significant resources to both. Beginning in May 1943, about fifty FBI special agents were assigned to these investigations in New York, an equal number in Washington, and about 125 to field offices across the country. They tailed Soviet officials, tapped telephone lines, ran informants, and staked out AMTORG's offices in New York. One team, nicknamed the Bucket Squad, set up a permanent observation post in the Pierre, a luxurious New York hotel, to monitor the Soviet consulate on East Sixty-First Street. They used a 35mm newsreel camera to film Soviet diplomats coming and going. What they were monitoring was the FACTORY, as Moscow had code-named the New York *rezidentura*, which occupied the top three floors of the Soviet consulate. It was appropriate given the volume of intelligence it produced. In 1944, the Factory was churning out so much material that its officers were running out of microfilm.

The truth of wartime Soviet intelligence in the West was that it relied on the dedication of its local communist agents, not the sophistication or professionalism of Soviet officers, as the Kremlin today likes to portray. Many Soviet wartime officers in the West were duds and dotards.

While Soviet intelligence undertook a broad effort to steal as many American science and technology (S&T) secrets as possible, the most important was their theft of atomic research (ENORMOZ, "enormous"). Stalin had received intelligence on Britain's TUBE ALLOYS atomic project in September 1941, but at the time he and his military leadership were focusing on defending Moscow from the German advance. Six months later, however, in March 1942, Beria sent him a detailed report on Britain's atomic weapons plans.

In June of that year, Roosevelt and Churchill discussed pooling their resources to build an atomic bomb. It would take a year for their governments to formally agree on integrating their nuclear projects: TUBE ALLOYS was ultimately subsumed into the MANHATTAN Project. The NKVD learned about Churchill and Roosevelt's discussions the same month they took place. By the end of 1942, following consultations with Soviet scientists, Stalin made the monumental decision to build an atomic bomb of his own. Doing so amid the Battle of Stalingrad, as the Soviet regime fought for its survival, revealed that the Soviet leader was already considering his strategy for the postwar world. Stalin assumed that Churchill and Roosevelt would never give him the atomic bomb. He therefore set about stealing it.[28]

ENORMOZ

Soviet intelligence conducted a broad assault on U.S. and British wartime S&T, including radar, sonar, aeronautics, and jet propulsion. Atomic research was, however, the true prize. According to documents recently declassified by Russia's foreign intelligence service, the SVR, the NKVD began targeting British atomic research at least since 1938. While these records need to be treated cautiously, parts of them can be corroborated from Western sources. Britain was a birthplace of atomic scientific research—and thus a significant target. There were two principal centers of atomic research there. At the Cavendish Laboratory in Cambridge, Ernest Rutherford, the Nobel Prize–winning physicist who split the atom, and his colleague James Chadwick led pioneering teams researching nuclear fission. Meanwhile, at

Birmingham University, two émigré nuclear physicists, Otto Frisch and Rudolf Peierls, made a groundbreaking calculation in March 1940 that a "super-bomb" could be built. Alarmed by Hitler's description of a German "secret weapon," Churchill created a committee, known as MAUD, to determine the feasibility of creating a nuclear fission weapon.[29]

The Soviets had an agent in the Cavendish Lab: Austrian nuclear physicist Engelbert Broda. Code-named ERIC, Broda had emigrated to Britain in 1938. Against MI5's advice, Broda was employed on the British atom bomb project. Soviet intelligence also appears to have run a source inside Birmingham University's research team. The key intelligence to reach Moscow about Britain's atomic bomb project, however, came not from scientists, but from John Cairncross, who had unique access to British atomic secrets. Cairncross had initially been at the Foreign Office, but during the war he became private secretary to the long-serving—and equally long-winded—cabinet secretary, Maurice Hankey.[30]

Through Cairncross, Soviet intelligence struck gold. Churchill appointed Hankey to be head of a scientific advisory committee, responsible for overseeing new technologies for the war effort. Hankey's group liaised closely with the MAUD committee. Because of Cairncross, Soviet intelligence discovered Britain's greatest wartime secret within days of Churchill's decision in September 1941 to build an atomic weapon. Cairncross was handled by the NKVD London *rezident*, Anatoli Gorsky (VADIM), who by the end of 1941 was complaining that Cairncross was producing so many classified British documents—reports from the war cabinet, assessments from MI6, the Foreign Office, and the military—that he could not transmit them in cipher.[31]

In June 1942, Roosevelt decided to build a U.S. atomic weapon and to collaborate with the British to do so. Within a month of the opening of a top secret laboratory at Los Alamos, New Mexico, in March 1943, the NKVD knew of its existence. The Center then initiated an all-out attack to steal as much information about it as possible. This was overseen by the NKVD's head of S&T intelligence, Leonid Kvasnikov (ANTON), who in January

1943 relocated from the Center to New York. From there, he reported to Stalin's atomic bomb project director, Igor Kurchatov.[32]

Los Alamos contained an awesome assembly of brainpower, including twelve scientists who would become Nobel laureates. It also soon included Soviet spies. Even now, over seven decades later, secrets about Soviet espionage at Los Alamos are still being uncovered. The small band of seventeen British-based scientists selected to join the MANHATTAN Project included a GRU agent: Klaus Fuchs (REST, later CHARLES). A brilliant physicist, Fuchs was a refugee to Britain from Nazi Germany, where he had been sentenced to death for his opposition to Hitler. He became a naturalized British subject and studied under two leading physicists of the day, Nevill Mott at Bristol University and another German émigré, Max Born, at Edinburgh. Rudolf Peierls, at Birmingham, coauthor of the watershed 1940 report about creating an atomic chain reaction, invited Fuchs to be part of TUBE ALLOYS. His invitation was a godsend for the Kremlin.

Fuchs first had to be vetted by MI5. The service had two adverse contemporary pieces of information on file about him: a letter from the Gestapo about Fuchs's communist activities and a British report stating that, while interned by the British government as an "enemy alien" at the start of the war, he associated with a known German communist. Both pieces of information were circumstantial. Nazi police tended to label all political opponents "communists," as MI5 knew, and Fuchs's association with a German communist while in internment was not surprising given their shared heritage and hatred of Nazism. MI5 knew that Fuchs was anti-Nazi, but not that he was pro-Soviet. In his favor, Fuchs had outstanding academic references to support his application, and his technical capabilities were crucial for TUBE ALLOYS. Excluding scientists with communist affiliations would have been catastrophic for it. MI5 made a judgment call, allowing Fuchs to work on Britain's atomic project. It proved to be disastrous.[33]

In reality, Fuchs was a committed communist who believed that Stalin would save Europe from Nazism. At university he had been an avowed member of the German Communist Party. Unlike others, his communist faith remained intact even after the 1939 Nazi-Soviet pact. In late 1941, Fuchs asked the leader of the German Communist Party underground operating in Britain, Jürgen Kuczynski, for help so he could pass secret information from TUBE ALLOYS to Soviet authorities. Kuczynski taught at the London School of Economics and lived in Hampstead. He introduced Fuchs to the GRU's London *rezident*, Simon Kremer, who recruited him. (Kremer had also recruited the agent we met earlier, INTELLIGENTSIA.) Fuchs's GRU handler thereafter became Jürgen Kuczynski's sister Ursula Kuczynski (SONYA), whom we encountered earlier as a member of the GRU's wartime Red Three network in Switzerland. Fuchs almost certainly never realized the family connection between Ursula and Jürgen. Ursula's marriage to a British man, also a GRU agent, gave her a British passport. She set up shop in the small village of Banbury, in the rolling Oxfordshire countryside, where she claimed to be a Jewish refugee from Nazi Germany. In fact, she was one of the GRU's most successful officers. She became the only woman ever to be made an honorary colonel of the Red Army.[34]

Fuchs had to go through British vetting again in 1943 to gain clearance to join the MANHATTAN Project. Again, MI5, relying on a system of negative vetting, and with no positive evidence against him on file, cleared Fuchs. When he transferred across the Atlantic to work on the MANHATTAN Project, Fuchs was secretly passed from the GRU to the NKVD, though it made no difference to him for which branch of Soviet intelligence he was spying. Fuchs initially worked on part of the MANHATTAN Project at Columbia University, where he made calculations on gaseous diffusion, essential for making a nuclear bomb.

Fuchs had his first meeting with his NKVD controller, Harry Gold (code-named GOOSE, later ARNO), in February of 1944 in New York, over dinner at a steakhouse, Manny Wolf's, not far from Grand Central Terminal. Fuchs was instructed to identify himself by carrying a tennis ball in his hand, and to look for a man carrying another and wearing a pair of gloves. Gold was an industrial chemist born in Switzerland to Russian parents; in the U.S., he reported directly to the NKVD S&T chief, Kvas-nikov, at the New York *rezidentura*.

Gold was known to Fuchs as Raymond. He would continue to be Fuchs's controller after the scientist was transferred to Los Alamos. There he worked in its Theoretical Division under the physicist Edward Teller. In New Mexico, Fuchs was at least outwardly living the American dream: he dated women, saw movies, drank margaritas, went horseback riding, and got a tan. But he also made secret trips to nearby Santa Fe, where he met Gold and handed over top secret MANHATTAN Project reports. The NKVD's clearinghouse for classified material coming out of Los Alamos was a drugstore in Santa Fe.[35]

Another central figure in Soviet wartime S&T intelligence in America was Semyon Semyonov, who arrived in Cambridge, Massachusetts, in 1938 as a twenty-six-year-old Soviet exchange student studying at the Massachu-setts Institute of Technology. His studies were a cover. In fact, Semyonov was an NKVD illegal officer (code-named TWEN, "Twain"), born in Odesa. Semyonov had graduated from the Moscow Textile Institute with a specialty in power systems engineering. Short and stocky, with a "duck nose, and large eyes," as one of his Soviet colleagues described him, Semyonov remained in America after graduating in June 1940. He worked for AMTORG and Machinoimport. Semyonov convinced the NKVD *resident* in the U.S., Zarubin, to make him Harry Gold's contact and go-between.[36]

By the end of 1944, the head of NKVD S&T, Kvasnikov, was reporting to the Center from New York about a web of Soviet agents being spun at Los Alamos. In addition to Fuchs, there was David Greenglass (BUMBLE-BEE, CALIBER, later ZINGER), a machinist at Los Alamos, who had been recruited by his wife, Ruth (WASP). David Greenglass's sister was Ethel Rosenberg, whose husband, Julius (ANTENNA, later LIBERAL), was then a twenty-seven-year-old from New York with a degree in elec-trical engineering. Yet another Soviet agent at Los Alamos was the preco-ciously brilliant nineteen-year-old Harvard physicist Theodore "Ted" Hall. Inspired by the myth of the Soviet Union as the world's first worker state, Hall was convinced that an American monopoly on nuclear power would threaten postwar peace. For him, passing secrets of the MANHATTAN Project to Moscow was thus a way to "help the world, as well as the Soviet Union." Soviet intelligence gave him the unimaginative code name MLAD ("young"). In March 1945, Hall delivered to his Soviet contact in Santa Fe the design of the atomic bomb, which he copied onto a newspaper, using milk as ink. The failure of the FBI and the U.S. military, which ran Los Alamos, to detect Rosenberg's and Hall's communist affiliations proved to be a disaster equal to MI5's failure with Fuchs.[37]

Each of Stalin's spies at Los Alamos was ignorant of the existence of the others. For some reason, however, Harry Gold acted as courier for both Fuchs and Greenglass. It was lamentable spycraft. A basic rule in intelligence is to compartmentalize; the same person should not be the contact for two networks, because exposing that person would jeopardize both. This was in fact exactly what later happened. But for the time being, the Soviet agents at Los Alamos produced a tsunami of intelligence for the Kremlin. The rolls of microfilm sent by Akhmerov's illegal *rezidentura* to the Center in Moscow jumped from 211 in 1943 to 1,896 in 1945. Some of the Los Alamos intelligence was delivered by a new courier employed by the New York *rezidentura*, Leontina "Lona" Cohen (code-named LESLIE), who was recruited by her husband, Morris. Thereafter they became a husband-and-wife deep-cover Soviet illegal team. She traveled to meet Hall and receive documentation from him in Santa Fe. The Kremlin would later give the Cohens high decorations for their espionage. Meanwhile, Julius Rosenberg's handler was another Soviet intelligence officer, Alexander Feklisov.[38]

Even now, secrets about Soviet espionage in the MANHATTAN Project are still being disclosed. One figure to emerge recently from Los Alamos's shadows is a GRU officer, George Koval (code-named DELMAR). Koval grew up in Iowa and obtained a degree in electrical engineering from the University of Iowa. Before the war his family moved to a Jewish autonomous region, near the Soviet border with Manchuria. He then obtained a degree from the Mendeleev Institute of Chemical Technology in Moscow. Given his American upbringing, he was an obvious recruit for Soviet intelligence, which did so and sent him back to the U.S. In February 1943, he joined the U.S. Army, and, in 1944, with his background in engineering, he was enlisted into the MANHATTAN Project, first at Oak Ridge and then at another laboratory, in Dayton, Ohio, where plutonium initiators were being manufactured. Koval thus became the only Soviet intelligence *officer*, as opposed to a Soviet *agent*, to penetrate the atomic bomb project. He would remain in the U.S. after the war, later emigrating to the Soviet Union, leaving the FBI chasing his ghost.[39]*

The final stages of the war saw some of the most significant Western secrets arrive at the Kremlin. In February 1945, right after the Big Three met at Yalta, Soviet intelligence submitted a detailed report on atomic intelligence to Stalin's spy chief, Beria, based on reports from inside Los Alamos. Five months before the Western Allies tested the first atomic bomb in southern New Mexico, the Center thus acquired intelligence about its construction. Fuchs and Hall then independently provided Moscow with the actual plans of the first atomic bomb, which was successfully tested in July 1945. The Center was able to cross-check the plans against each other. Six decades later, Vladimir Putin would posthumously name the GRU's officer in Los Alamos, Koval, a "Hero of Russia." According to Russia's defense ministry, when the Soviet Union detonated its first atomic weapon in 1949, it was prepared according to the "recipe" provided by Koval. The Soviet bomb was an exact replica of the one tested by the United States in New Mexico.

———◆———

Toward the end of the war, there were two moments that, with the benefit of hindsight, reveal the remarkable intelligence that Stalin received about his Western Allies. The first was at the international conference held in San Francisco, between April and June of 1945, which created the United

---

* For another Soviet atom spy who has not received the attention he deserves, Arthur Adams, see this book's website: www.spieshistory.com.

Nations. The UN's founding charter, signed by fifty allied nations, expressed the importance of ending war and safeguarding human rights. The *New York Times* hailed it as a watershed moment in civilization.

But the San Francisco conference was also an intelligence coup for Stalin. Sitting onstage next to the UN secretary-general, Gladwyn Jebb, who presided over the conference of 850 delegates, was a smartly dressed man with swept-back hair. He wore a double-breasted suit and polished oxfords, and to his other side was Secretary of State Edward Stettinius. The stage backdrop was an assemblage of the world's flags. Photos show the man shaking hands with President Truman. He was none other than Alger Hiss. Worse still for Western security, the U.S. delegation included another Soviet agent, Harry Dexter White. Stalin thus had two spies in pride of place at the UN's founding.

Back in Washington, Britain's embassy dutifully reported to London British and U.S. strategies for the new UN body. A senior official at the embassy there, at the forefront of Anglo-American policymaking, was yet another Soviet agent: Donald Maclean. He provided 191 secret documents, of which 141 were sent to Stalin. Through their espionage, there was little that Stalin did not know about British and U.S. postwar policies for the UN.[40]

Another moment with acidic irony, and profound geopolitical implications, occurred during the final wartime meeting of the Allies, in July 1945, at the Cecilienhof Palace in Potsdam, on Berlin's ruined outskirts. Stalin traveled there in his usual armored luxury train, with NKVD guards stationed every hundred yards of the journey. At the summit, Harry Truman, who had recently become president following Roosevelt's death in April, received news of the first atomic test explosion in the New Mexico desert. It produced a mushroom cloud reaching almost forty thousand feet in the air and was so powerful that a blind woman was reportedly able to see light. At the conference, Truman took a bullish approach to Stalin, revealing that the U.S. now had "a new weapon of unusual destructive force." Stalin seemed unimpressed, as Britain's new prime minister,

Clement Attlee, noted at the time. We now know why. Stalin already knew about the atomic bomb. Twelve days before it was assembled at Los Alamos, the NKVD secured descriptions of the bomb from its Washington and New York *rezidentury*. In fact, Stalin had known about it *years* before Truman, who was only told about the MANHATTAN Project when he became president, three months before. Stalin also knew about ULTRA before Truman, who was only indoctrinated into that wartime secret when he sat behind the Resolute Desk in the Oval Office. The Cold War was already underway; unfortunately for the Western Allies, they did not yet realize it.[41]

PART TWO

THE CLASH OF CIVILIZATIONS

CHAPTER FIVE

FROM WORLD WAR
TO COLD WAR

There's an east wind coming all the same, such a wind as never
blew on England yet. It will be cold and bitter, Watson, and a
good many of us may wither before its blast.
—Arthur Conan Doyle, *His Last Bow*

IN SHARP CONTRAST TO THE KREMLIN'S WARTIME INTELLI-
gence assault on the West, in 1945 Britain and the United States had no
significant intelligence whatsoever about Stalin's plans. Britain's MI6 did
not begin policy discussions to open a station in Moscow until 1948, while
President Truman was so naive about America's need for foreign intelligence
that, immediately after the war, in September 1945, he closed the OSS,
bowing to criticism that it was an American "Gestapo." Britain's new Labour
government under Prime Minister Clement Attlee nearly disbanded MI5
on similar grounds amid war demobilization, but instead allowed it to limp
on with staff and resources slashed. By 1947, MI5 had fewer than a hundred
officers and MI6 had approximately the same. Five years later the KGB would
be the largest intelligence service in the world, with approximately 200,000

officials in the Soviet Union. The GRU was the world's second-largest. There was, then, an inequality of secret arms as the Cold War set in.[1]

◆

At the end of the war, in the rubble of the Third Reich, British and U.S. intelligence agencies focused on hunting down Nazis and bringing them to justice. The U.S. Army apprehended one of the principal Nazi mass murderers, Ernst Kaltenbrunner, an architect of the Final Solution, in a remote cabin in the Austrian mountains, disguised as a hunter. Holding false papers, he was preparing to flee. The scar-faced, six-foot-four SS general, former chief of the Reich Security Main Office (RSHA), was extensively interrogated by U.S. military intelligence (G-2) and later British intelligence. Kaltenbrunner's British intelligence files, which have since been opened, contain chilling documents: Nazi party papers and mug shots taken in captivity, revealing the remorseless eyes of a killer.

Having obtained as much intelligence as they could from Kaltenbrunner, his American and British interrogators handed him over to prosecutors at Nuremberg, where he was tried, found guilty of war crimes, and, on October 16, 1946, executed. Hitler's deputy Heinrich Himmler, SS Reichsführer, was caught in disguise, using forged papers, by a British border patrol as he tried to escape Germany. Using a cyanide capsule hidden in a false tooth, he managed to kill himself in prison before he could be interrogated or tried. To end speculation about Hitler's death, MI6 dispatched Oxford historian and wartime recruit Hugh Trevor-Roper to Berlin to investigate. His report about Hitler's final days later became a bestselling book.[2]

Many of the captured Nazis offered up secrets about the Soviet Union. Here we encounter a disturbing chapter in the postwar years: the recruitment by Western intelligence services of former Nazis. One such case involved the former Gestapo intelligence officer Horst Kopkow, who was responsible for the death and torture of countless wartime resistance members and Allied saboteurs in occupied Europe. Arrested by British soldiers in the Baltics in May 1945, he told his captors that he had valuable information: he had been responsible for arresting two major Soviet spy rings, ROTE KAPELLE and ROTE DREI. MI5 and MI6 interrogated him over the next year; he avoided the gallows at Nuremberg in return for information. After MI5 and MI6 had squeezed everything they could from him, they announced his "death" to the world. But Kopkow lived and died twice. MI6 gave him a new identity and exfiltrated him to West Germany, where he lived under an alias. He never faced trial for his crimes.[3]

"THE MAN WHO STARTED THE COLD WAR"

A month after the United States dropped atomic bombs on Hiroshima and Nagasaki, ending World War II, the Allies at last discovered that Stalin had acquired secrets of America's atomic bomb. This devastating news broke on September 5, 1945, when a twenty-six-year-old GRU cipher clerk stationed in Ottawa, Igor Gouzenko, defected. He brought with him more than one hundred sweat-soaked secret GRU communications between Soviet *rezidentury* in North America and Moscow. They showed that during the war, Soviet intelligence had established sophisticated espionage networks in North America, with the U.S. and Canadian Communist Parties working hand in glove with the Kremlin to facilitate them.

Gouzenko's documents revealed that Soviet intelligence had an agent working in Ottawa as confidential secretary to Britain's high commissioner, Malcolm MacDonald; that a Canadian MP was a Soviet spy; and, most alarmingly for Western governments, that a Soviet agent and scientist in the MANHATTAN Project, code-named ALEC, had secretly provided Moscow with "documentary materials of the atomic bomb: the technological process, drawings, calculations." Gouzenko's disclosures exploded postwar international relations and security.[4]

Gouzenko has been called "the man who started the Cold War." Really, he did not start anything, but he did reveal to Western governments that,

whether they wanted to admit it or not, they were already locked in a geopolitical struggle with the Soviet Union. The question was now what the
Western Allies would do about it. As MI5's Guy Liddell bluntly noted after
Gouzenko's defection: "Do the British, Canadian and U.S. Governments
want to have a show-down with Russia or not?" Now-opened British foreign
office records reveal that Gouzenko's espionage led to deliberations at the
highest levels of those Western governments. The cipher clerk's disclosures
led to a scramble as Attlee in London, Truman in Washington, and Canada's
prime minister in Ottawa, William Lyon Mackenzie King, tried to limit
the damage done and find a way forward, somehow salvaging the wreckage
from the disintegrating wartime Grand Alliance. Gouzenko's intelligence
prompted momentous decisions, as Western leaders shifted attention from
the rubble of the Axis powers to the surging Soviet Union. The issue for
them then, as for later governments, was whether to go public about an ugly
intelligence scandal and risk diplomatic fallout, or deal with it privately,
using it in negotiations with the perpetrator. Unfortunately, the situation
was far worse than anyone in the West then knew.[5]

Papers held by Gouzenko's family reveal that his motivation for defecting
from the GRU with his wife, who was also a GRU officer, was not, as some
accounts suggest, a rushed response to having been recalled to Moscow after
he left some confidential paperwork unattended in the Soviet embassy. As
his unpublished diary shows, he and his wife carefully thought through
their defection, which they did for ideological reasons. Gouzenko knew
from the GRU cables he saw, and transmitted, that by the end of the war
Stalin already had atomic secrets in his hands, which the Americans and
British had been concealing from the Kremlin on the grounds that the
world would be more dangerous if a murderous dictator like Stalin had a
nuclear weapon. For Gouzenko, it was imperative that Western governments
know that Stalin already had their atomic secrets. The memoir also reveals
that, while living in Canada, he and his wife realized that the true "workers' paradise" was North America, not the Soviet Union, as he had been
indoctrinated to believe from a young age. After his defection, Gouzenko

spent two long days hiding from Soviet KGB (NKVD) henchmen as they ransacked his apartment, because Canadian officials initially disbelieved his story. When the Canadian police finally recognized Gouzenko's significance, he was kept under guard day and night by three officers, and continuously shuttled around.

For Clement Attlee, Gouzenko's disclosures came at a fraught moment. The prime minister needed Truman's support. While Britain had won the war, it had bankrupted itself in the process. When MI6 chief Stewart Menzies first briefed Attlee on Gouzenko, on September 8, the prime minister was focused on negotiating a loan from the U.S. government. Attlee initially thought Gouzenko could be useful in the negotiations for that loan, revealing the nature of a shared threat from the Soviet Union. Britain's tough-talking, no-nonsense foreign secretary, Ernest Bevin, pushed hard to take a tough public response against the Soviet Union, including prosecutions of Soviet agents in the network. Attlee, ever the pragmatist, was more restrained, knowing that ultimately the decision on how to proceed, as well as Britain's financial future and the atomic bomb project, was in U.S. hands.[6]

President Truman, however, was "fogged as to what had apparently so soon and so darkly clouded the atmosphere of Potsdam," where just two months earlier he had apparently amicably met Stalin. Mackenzie King was similarly dumbfounded, yet more clear-eyed, writing in his diary that he could barely believe that the Soviet embassy, "just a few doors away," was the "center of intrigue." While Canadians had been doing "all we can to foment Canadian-Russian friendship, there has been one branch of the Russian service that has been spying" on Canada, the prime minister wrote. "The amazing thing is how many contacts have been successfully made with people in key positions in government and industrial circles."

Reading the flurry of correspondence between London and Washington, we are left with an inescapable conclusion: that Truman buried his head in the sand when it came to what Gouzenko revealed. The Grand Alliance was dead, and the Soviet Union had never been the ally he thought. Truman, a Midwesterner plunged into the presidency with no experience in international relations, was not sure what to make of foreign intelligence. His shuttering of the OSS occurred just two weeks after Gouzenko defected. Stalin assumed that the U.S. president would never give him the secrets to an atomic bomb. Truman, the only man in history to decide whether to use a nuclear bomb to kill people, in fact wanted to place the horrendous new weapon under UN control. He wanted to reach an agreement with the Soviets about atomic energy and would not allow a Canadian defector to get in his way.

When Prime Minister Attlee traveled to Washington two months later to finalize loan agreements, Truman still refused to make a decision about Gouzenko. "It makes me despair," lamented Bevin to the Foreign Office's avuncular permanent undersecretary, Alexander Cadogan, that Truman and his secretary of state, James Byrnes, a largely ineffective statesman from South Carolina, were optimistic about upcoming Council of Foreign Ministers' meetings between Britain, America, and the Soviet Union. At their initial opening in September 1945 in London, the Soviet foreign minister, Vyacheslav Molotov, blurted out to Byrnes, "We have the bomb." Byrnes did not believe him. At the Potsdam Conference, Truman had remarked that Stalin was a "fine man who wanted to do the right thing." For Truman's White House, "mutual coexistence" between East and West seemed feasible in the postwar years, overlooking the ugly reality that, in the Marxist-Leninist dialectic, "peaceful coexistence" meant the continuation of class warfare.[7]

Gouzenko's intelligence revealed the secrets that ALEC, the GRU agent, had betrayed, but not his identity. ALEC had worked at a Canadian branch of the MANHATTAN Project, a heavy-water plant at the Chalk River in Ontario. He or she had even supplied small samples of uranium to Soviet intelligence, which it transmitted to Moscow: an enriched specimen of uranium 233 in a glass tube and a deposit of uranium 235 wrapped in platinum foil. From descriptions in Gouzenko's documents, ALEC was soon identified as the British physicist Alan Nunn May. He was a Cambridge-educated physicist who had been a contemporary of Donald Maclean's at Trinity Hall.

Nunn May had already returned to Britain, where he held a research post at King's College London. Gouzenko's stolen cables revealed that the scientist was scheduled to meet his Soviet controller in London the following month, October, by the British Museum. Like something from an espionage novel, ALEC was to carry a copy of the *Times* under his left arm, and his Soviet intelligence controller was to carry the *Picture Post* under his. They were to identify themselves by asking for the shortest way to the Strand, ending their exchange with the words "Best regards from Mikhail." This gave MI5 a prized opportunity: to catch Nunn May in the act of espionage. It would need this evidence to prosecute him—an English court would dismiss Gouzenko's stolen documentation as unreliable hearsay evidence. MI5 placed Nunn May under close surveillance, including tapping his calls and opening his mail. Its undercover officers lay in wait for the British Museum rendezvous. But neither the scientist nor his Soviet case officer appeared. Britain's spy chiefs were left wondering what happened.[8]

Britain's initial inquiries into Nunn May were handled by MI5's liaison officer in Ottawa, Cyril Mills, a wartime recruit and counterespionage officer (and the son of British circus owner Bertram Mills). MI6's representative in Washington, Peter Dwyer, traveled to Ottawa to assist with Gouzenko's debriefing. The major player in Britain's handling of the Gouzenko case, though, was William Stephenson at BSC in New York. Stephenson was brilliant at promoting Britain and MI6's interests in the United States, and equally his own. The stream of cables between Ottawa, Washington, and London about Gouzenko were all routed through Stephenson's secure cipher at BSC headquarters and sent personally to Stewart Menzies ("CSS") in London. Unfortunately for British and Western counterintelligence, one of the select few officers who received Stephenson's cable traffic within MI6 was none other than the Soviet spy, Kim Philby. As head of MI6's Section IX, Philby was legitimately in the thick of Britain's investigation into a major Soviet intelligence defector. MI5 and Foreign Office records now lay bare that Philby used his MI6 position to try to sabotage Britain's investigation into Gouzenko from the inside. He also warned Soviet agents in the network that they were in danger.[9]

Philby's cover had nearly been blown by a Soviet defector in Istanbul, Konstantin Volkov, in 1945. He offered documents to the British embassy there, which, he claimed, revealed that Soviet intelligence had two high-level agents in the Foreign Office (doubtless a reference to Maclean and Burgess), and seven inside "the British intelligence system," including one "fulfilling the function of head of a section of British counter-espionage" (undoubtedly Philby). Philby, who saw the cable about the defector at MI6's headquarters in London, realized that Volkov's intelligence was a reference to himself. He sent an urgent warning to Moscow. Philby skillfully persuaded his MI6 bosses to allow him to oversee the case personally and travel to Istanbul. In fact, his warning to Moscow had already done the trick: an NKVD hit squad kidnapped Volkov and his wife and spirited them away, heavily sedated on stretchers, on a plane back to Moscow, where Volkov was brutally interrogated and executed. Philby drafted a misleading report for MI6, and the Foreign Office, about Volkov. Reading it today, it drips with sarcasm. Philby stated that it appeared Volkov had been a genuine defector, but "unfortunately" it was "exceedingly difficult to guess which parts of his statement were true and which parts exaggerated or false." As Philby later wrote after he defected to Moscow, the Volkov case "proved to be a very narrow squeak indeed."[10]

Philby similarly tried to sabotage the Gouzenko case. Unlike Volkov, who was NKVD, Gouzenko was a GRU officer. Philby thus did not have inside information, from his NKVD handlers, about what secrets Gouzenko had. He had to act quick. He soon had a plan. Philby tried to take over the entire British investigation into Gouzenko's defection. (Gouzenko was code-named CORBY by the British, apparently because that was the favorite whisky of British officers in New York on the case.) Philby's efforts to drive the British side of the case earned an angry response from MI5, whose desk officer, Roger Hollis, pointed out to Philby that because the Soviet official had defected in Canada, a British Dominion (Commonwealth) country, it was MI5, not MI6, which had responsibility for the case. MI5 had responsibility for security intelligence in Britain's empire and the Commonwealth, while MI6's jurisdiction was intelligence collection in foreign countries.

Failing to insert himself into the British investigation, Philby set about stalling communications from MI6 that would have been useful for MI5. He also provided misleading reports to Foreign Secretary Bevin and Britain's chiefs of staff. Philby's reports minimized the role of the Canadian Communist Party in the case, information that may have led the authorities to sanction enhanced investigations into Britain's Communist Party. Philby suggested that the documents Gouzenko had stolen did not reveal much that Western powers would not imagine the Soviet Union to be doing anyway. It was hardly surprising that Moscow was spying, he pointed out. All that was left to do, Philby misleadingly suggested, was to tie up leads.[11]

Philby also diverted the one MI6 officer who, more than anyone, he feared: Kathleen Jane Sissmore (later, through marriage, Archer). An Oxford graduate who joined MI5 in the prewar years, and trained as a barrister, Archer had a ferocious intellect, which quickly led her to outshine her MI5 superiors. In early 1940, when the Soviet Union and Nazi Germany were effectively allies, Archer interrogated a GRU defector, Walter Krivitsky, in London. As MI5's authorized history notes, her interview of Krivitsky was a model of its kind—the first professional debriefing of a Soviet intelligence officer on either side of the Atlantic. Her intellect, however, ended her career at MI5 when she denounced the incompetence of a boss. She was sacked and transferred to MI6, where she landed with Philby in Section IX. He admired her. She was, Philby later recalled, "perhaps the ablest professional intelligence officer ever employed by MI5." Archer was "a woman after my own heart, tough minded and rough-tongued," though Philby added: "Jane would have made a very bad enemy." Her interview of Krivitsky produced a scrap of intelligence about a Soviet agent who was an English journalist sent to Spain during the Spanish Civil War. Philby alone immediately recognized that as a reference to himself.[12]

When it became clear that a British officer needed to travel to Ottawa to debrief Gouzenko, Philby made sure that it was not Archer. She was indispensable in London, Philby claimed, preferring to keep her close. He diverted her formidable energies into analyzing a mass of nonincriminating intercepted radio communications from Eastern Europe. Meanwhile, Hollis, Philby's opposite number in MI5 (and later its director general), traveled to Ottawa to interview Gouzenko. The FBI's liaison officer in Ottawa joined the interrogations. Hoover put seventy-five special agents on the case. As a cipher clerk, Gouzenko also provided technical information about Soviet codes to British code breakers. Bletchley Park's liaison officer in Washington, Eric Jones (later GCHQ director), interrogated him, as did American SIGINT official Frank Rowlett. According to the NSA's now-declassified in-house history, Gouzenko offered otherwise unknowable information about Soviet codes and accelerated American code-breaking effforts.[13]

It was almost certainly Philby who sent a warning to Alan Nunn May not to appear at his rendezvous outside the British Museum. Years later, Nunn May admitted that he had been warned by Soviet intelligence—but refused to say by whom. Despite Philby's efforts, the London Special Branch and MI5 interviewed Nunn May and managed to secure a confession from him. This was the work of MI5's trilby-wearing principal interrogator, Jim Skardon, and a Special Branch officer, Leonard Burt. Without his confession, Nunn May could not have been prosecuted.

At the trial, the judge threw the book at the scientist: he received a ten-year sentence, handed down on the same day Churchill delivered his Iron Curtain speech. Nunn May never revealed who had recruited him to Soviet intelligence. MI5 believed it was someone at the Cavendish Laboratory in Cambridge, the chief culprit believed to be Engelbert Broda. Soviet archives, however, reveal Nunn May's Soviet recruiter was in fact a "man without a shadow," Yan Chernak (JACK), a GRU illegal operating in Britain who managed to obtain 142 pages on Britain's bomb effort from Nunn May—and on whom MI5 does not appear to have had any record.

Papers held by Nunn May's family reveal that he first started passing atomic secrets to the undetected Soviet official (now identifiable as Chernak) in meetings in London in 1941. After his release from jail, Nunn May remained unrepentant, refusing to describe his espionage as treachery. He felt he had "made a contribution to the safety of mankind" by preventing America's monopoly on atomic weapons. He returned to research—kept far away from classified information—and later moved back to Cambridge, where he shuffled around Trinity Hall until his final days.[14]

As the Gouzenko and Nunn May cases unfolded, the Soviets not only had Philby in a key role at MI6 but also Donald Maclean, stationed at Britain's embassy in Washington. Maclean had been entrusted by Britain's ambassador, Lord Halifax, with access to British and American secret post-war atomic planning documents. With Stalin's access to Anglo-American nuclear secrets, it is little wonder that successive meetings of foreign ministers broke down. In London and then Moscow, the British and the Americans suggested that atomic energy should be controlled by international agreement under the new United Nations organization. Stalin and his foreign minister, Molotov, knew Britain's and America's negotiation positions and refused to be derailed from their determination to acquire their own nuclear weapons. At a subsequent London conference, thanks to Stalin's spies, some Foreign Office documents appear to have reached Soviet ambassador Ivan Maisky before they reached their intended British recipients.[15]

Truman's hand was finally forced in January 1946, when information about the Gouzenko case was leaked, apparently by the State Department. One of America's best-known columnists, Drew Pearson, alluded to the Soviet defector on NBC. The following month, the Canadian government belatedly established a Royal Commission to investigate. But after five months of delay following Gouzenko's defection, as Canadian, British, and American leaders dragged their feet over what to do, the Soviet spy network had already been dissolved. The GRU *rezident* in Ottawa, Nicolai Zabotin, was recalled to Moscow, where he succumbed to a fate frequently suffered by those who failed Stalin—he died of a "heart attack" shortly after arrival. Meanwhile, the Royal Canadian Mounted Police resettled Gouzenko and his wife under new identities. He lived in constant fear of Soviet intelligence taking reprisals ("active measures") against him. In Moscow, the KGB interrogated Gouzenko's mother so harshly in the basement of the Lubyanka that she died. When Gouzenko later spoke publicly about the terror of Stalin's regime, he did so wearing a paper bag over his head to protect his identity. The KGB never succeeded in eliminating Gouzenko, as it had Volkov in Istanbul.[16]

RED SPY QUEEN

Two months after Gouzenko's defection, another important Soviet agent fell into the arms of Western intelligence when she walked into an FBI field office: Elizabeth Bentley, whom we met earlier and whose Soviet code name, UMNITSA—"good girl"—became a painful choice for the Center. Bentley had been a courier for an important Soviet intelligence officer in America during the war, the NKVD's illegal *rezident* based in New York, Jacob Golos (code-named ZVUK, meaning "sound," a play on his surname in Russian, "voice"). Golos, a Ukrainian-born immigrant, had been one of the founders of the U.S. Communist Party and thereafter became a link between it and Soviet intelligence. That connection revealed how poor Soviet tradecraft could be. In fact, it exposed Soviet spies to the FBI, which kept the Communist Party under tight surveillance. Worse for the NKVD, in 1938 Golos and Bentley became lovers, their romance blossoming during a New York snowstorm. Golos, whom Bentley knew as "Timmy," dressed like the businessman that in many ways he was: he set up and ran a lucrative travel business for the CPUSA, World Tourists, which was the ideal cover for his espionage. He used it to orchestrate surreptitious travel for Soviet agents, providing them with funds, tickets, visas, and passports. Golos's cover at World Tourists, which had offices in New York and Dupont Circle in Washington, DC, was similar to that of the deep-cover Russian spy protagonists in the popular FX TV series *The Americans*.[17]

The emotional and physical toll on Golos, working eighteen hours a day as a Soviet intelligence officer while running a travel agency and assisting the CPUSA, proved fatal. He died from a heart attack on Thanksgiving in

1943. Bentley, distraught, blamed Moscow for working him to death, and soon had a falling-out with her new NKVD handler, Anatoli Gorsky, who, having moved on from his London post, was now *rezident* in Washington. Gorsky, code-named VADIM, had run the Cambridge Five. A grimly efficient, humorless, hard-line Stalinist, Gorsky had somehow survived Stalin's prewar homicidal purge of NKVD and GRU ranks. His career advanced on the basis of a lethal form of the Peter Principle: climbing over piles of corpses, he owed his rapid promotion to the liquidation of his colleagues. Known to Bentley as "Al," Gorsky soon alienated her, criticizing her "Americanness" when they had scheduled meetings at New York diners. Gorsky's incompetence pushed Bentley toward the FBI. She became disillusioned with underground work, and in fact for the entire Soviet enterprise to which she had devoted her life. In August 1945, Bentley approached the FBI's field office in New Haven, Connecticut, about defecting, which she did in November.[18]

After the FBI checked Bentley's bona fides—her heavy drinking made believing her a challenge—she became the bureau's clever girl. J. Edgar Hoover soon assigned 227 agents to her investigation. It was the biggest counterespionage case in FBI history, with special agents chasing down leads in field offices across the country. In interviews with the FBI over the coming weeks, months, and eventually years, Bentley claimed that nearly 150 Americans spied for the Soviet Union, including 37 within the U.S. federal government. She identified 80 in total. In May 1946, Hoover sent a hair-raising report to Truman stating that Soviet agents in the U.S. government included "an assistant to the Secretary of State" (doubtless a reference to Alger Hiss), as well as Harry Dexter White, Duncan Lee in the OSS, and Roosevelt's former aide Lauchlin Currie. Bentley's information confirmed the prewar testimony of GRU messenger Whittaker Chambers.[19]

The FBI team handling Bentley convinced her to make contact with Gorsky again so they could try to catch him in the act of espionage—much like MI5 was attempting to do with Alan Nunn May. After renewing contact with him, Bentley met Gorsky at a Bickford's cafe in Midtown

Manhattan in November 1945. They agreed to meet again in January, but that proved to be their last encounter: Gorsky disappeared. The reason for his vanishing is revealed in now-opened British intelligence files. Hoover told MI6's representative in New York, Stephenson, about Bentley's defection. Stephenson then duly notified MI6's head of Soviet affairs: Kim Philby. Yet again, we can see Philby's hidden hand at work. Thanks to a warning from Philby, Gorsky broke off contact with Bentley, just as Soviet intelligence did with Nunn May in Britain. By the time of Gorsky's scheduled meeting with Bentley, he was back in Moscow. The FBI was left chasing ghosts.[20]

For several years, Stalin feared that the FBI would uncover sufficient evidence for prosecutors to bring a major spy case to trial based on Bentley's evidence. But that never happened. Although Bentley produced voluminous leads for the FBI, not one resulted in a prosecution. With Philby's warning, the Center recalled two other officers in the United States, a legal and an illegal *rezident*, and warned its agents against contacting *rezidents* still there. The bureau failed to catch any agents in the act of passing classified information. The information it did acquire on Soviet agents, from wiretaps, which Truman authorized Hoover to undertake in general terms ("electronic surveillance"), was unusable in court. In July 1948, three years after her defection, Bentley agreed to go public with her evidence, appearing before Congress at the House Un-American Activities Committee (HUAC), where she gained instant celebrity as the "Red Spy Queen."

The HUAC, established before the war, would become the postwar public theater for investigating the communist ties of Americans. Bentley was skillfully questioned by a young Republican congressman from California, Richard Nixon. Hoover allowed Nixon to read FBI files and he thus knew the answers to his questions in advance. Among the people Bentley publicly accused of being Soviet agents were Lauchlin Currie and Harry Dexter White, who, to Hoover's consternation, had become head of the International Monetary Fund. White resigned from the IMF and died of a heart attack immediately after testifying. Bentley's testimony polarized

Americans. She became the target of liberal media smear campaigns in which she was widely, but mistakenly, ridiculed.[21]

The following month, Whittaker Chambers, the former GRU operative who was now a senior editor at *Time* magazine, testified before HUAC, where he publicly accused Hiss of being a Soviet agent. Bentley and Chambers seem to have calculated that, although they lived in fear of Soviet retribution, they were safer hiding in the open than in the shadows. The KGB did indeed consider ordering Bentley's assassination, but concluded that it would be reckless, even for Stalin, to sanction a hit on U.S. soil given her public profile. Although the U.S. government did not publicly disclose it at the time, Bentley's and Chambers's evidence about Soviet espionage was confirmed by highly sensitive U.S. SIGINT coming on line, decrypts later known as VENONA, as we shall see in the next chapter.

THE CREATION OF U.S. NATIONAL SECURITY

President Truman faced huge geopolitical events in the postwar years, but never really knew what he wanted from U.S. intelligence. Nonetheless, he was instrumental in establishing the institutions and architecture of postwar American intelligence and national security. What he did has shaped them up to the present day. Ironically, it was precisely because Truman was inexperienced in world affairs that he demanded things of U.S. agencies that others, more versed in world affairs, probably would have considered unnecessary. Asking simple questions can force fundamental policymaking.

The centerpiece of Truman's policy was his creation by presidential order in January 1946 of the office of the Director of Central Intelligence (DCI). *Time* magazine called it the end of America's "historical innocence" in intelligence. The DCI's function was to direct a small analytical branch, the Central Intelligence Group (CIG), whose job was to collate and analyze intelligence collected by other U.S. government branches and then disseminate assessments to the president. As Truman's White House advisers grasped, coordinating intelligence within the warren of competing Washington intelligence bureaucracies was essential to avoid repeating Pearl Harbor. The first DCI—the acronym applies to both the office and the officeholder—was the head of naval intelligence, Rear Admiral Sidney Souers, a wealthy Democratic Party honcho from the Midwest. Souers made little secret of the fact that he did not want the job. At a White House reception to celebrate the DCI's creation, the president presented his guests with black cloaks, hats, and wooden daggers, announcing that his friend Souers was to become "the director of centralized snooping."[22]

Though purely humorous, the incident revealed deeper issues about Truman's attitude toward U.S. intelligence. Truman informed Souers that what he wanted from his new DCI was, above all, a short digest of intelligence each day summarizing the pile of overseas cables, often two feet high, that his desk groaned under each morning. Although Truman's request for a digest led to further tiresome wrangling about which department's information would be included, only solved by Truman again intervening, it was a milestone: Truman instigated the so-called intelligence daily summary, the forerunner of today's President's Daily Brief. For many presidents since the 1960s, the PDB has been one of the first documents read each morning.[23]

The CIG was, however, hamstrung from the outset. It was subordinate to entrenched foreign policy bureaucracies like State, War, and Navy, which provided the CIG's budget, staff, and raw data. The group's lack of independence meant that it was difficult, if not impossible, to overcome the infighting between the departments and deliver assessments that were critical of them. Speaking truth to power could mean biting the hands that fed it. The CIG's lack of autonomy was graphically illustrated right after its creation, in March 1946, when it tried to produce its first coordinated intelligence evaluation. Prompted by growing concern over Stalin's actions, Truman directed the army, navy, and U.S. Army Air Forces to assist the CIG and "produce the highest possible quality of intelligence on the USSR in the shortest amount of time." The report, bogged down in bureaucratic battles, took two years to complete. Souers barely lasted one hundred days as DCI.

The CIG's inherent flaw, its lack of autonomy—beholden to all, master of none—was addressed head-on by the man who replaced Souers: Hoyt Vandenberg. The nephew of Arthur Vandenberg, the influential Republican senator from Michigan, Hoyt was as energetic as he was handsome. He was later described by Marilyn Monroe as one of the three men in the world with whom she would like to be shipwrecked. Vandenberg was determined to bring the CIG greater independence by giving it the ability to produce its own intelligence. When he took over, the CIG was like a sewing club, he complained. It was staffed with prevaricating one-handed lawyers.[24]

Vandenberg hired new analysts to produce independent research "not being performed by other departments." To give it further independence, he expanded the CIG from its initial mandate of *collation* into *collection*— namely, to spy. He gave it "muscle," in his own words. He founded the Office of Special Operations (OSO) within the CIG, composed of about one thousand former wartime OSS officers. When Truman signed away the OSS's existence, a residual workforce of analysts quietly transferred to the War Department, where they lived on as the Strategic Studies Unit (SSU). Of the approximately 10,000 OSS officers at the end of the war, just 1,970 remained employed in the SSU and other corners of the government by year's end. The CIG's new operational function, the OSO, drawn from the OSS's ashes, gave the Director of Central Intelligence some—though not sufficient—independence about the intelligence provided to the Oval Office. Thus was also born another characteristic of U.S. intelligence ever since: an alphabet soup of three-letter government bodies.[25]

Truman's dawning realization that world affairs were ugly, and required spies, arose from sweeping changes to the geopolitical landscape in the years 1946 and 1947. The Soviet Union seemed to many in Washington to be following Nazi Germany's expansionist path. Soviet troops had protracted their occupation in Iran, and Stalin supported communists in Greece, where a civil war erupted, as also happened in the Philippines. Meanwhile, NKVD shock troops subjugated the new governments of Poland, Hungary, and Romania. In March 1947, Truman appeared before a joint session of Congress and asked

for $400 million to help save Greece and Turkey from becoming commu-
nist bridgeheads in Europe, after a bankrupt British government informed
Washington it could no longer support them. The president's speech became
known as the Truman Doctrine: "I believe that it must be the policy of the
United States to support free peoples who are resisting attempted subjuga-
tion by armed minorities or by outside pressures." For the next forty years,
"containment" would be America's grand strategic doctrine with respect to
the Soviet Union. Truman demanded and won approval from Congress for
the great undertaking of the reconstruction of Europe, later known as the
Marshall Plan: $13.7 billion in aid over five years to help Europe. The Marshall
Plan also provided lucrative opportunities to U.S. contractors.[26]

Truman overhauled U.S. intelligence with a momentous piece of legislation in July 1947: the National Security Act. "For the first time in the
history of the nation," Truman later wrote, "an over-all military establishment was created." In six paragraphs, the act created, for the first time, a
dedicated, autonomous, peacetime foreign intelligence agency for the U.S.
government: the Central Intelligence Agency (CIA). It was designed to
solve the problems that had previously beset the CIG. Under the terms of
its new charter, the CIA's head was also the president's Director of Central
Intelligence—twin roles, head of the CIA and head of U.S. intelligence,
that DCIs would hold for the rest of the twentieth century.

Just over two years after becoming president, Truman had finally recognized that the U.S. government needed a professional spy agency, like Britain
and the other major Western democracies already had, to say nothing of the
Soviet Union in the East. The United States had thus taken a major leap,
joining the other world powers. The National Security Act also created the
National Security Council (NSC), a cabinet advisory committee wherein
different branches of government, the armed forces, and the State Department
were given equal weight, with the hope that they could not play each other off.

The Director of Central Intelligence advised the NSC but reported
directly to the president himself. The National Security Act replaced the
War Department with a new Department of Defense, bringing together

the army, the navy, and the newly established U.S. Air Force—which Vandenberg, Truman's DCI, would lead the following year. The model that Truman's advisers turned to was the British cabinet, whose objective, they noted, was consensus-building, streamlining, and minimizing work: "It is a mark of successful Secretariat work [in Britain] if the committee does not have to meet at all," a report to Truman noted. That lesson never crossed the Atlantic to Washington.[27]

The same year, Truman also issued a sweeping executive order, which established an "employee loyalty program" for more than two million U.S. federal workers. It was an unprecedented peacetime attempt to give the U.S. government maximum protection against disloyalty in its ranks. But it was also good politics for Truman. There is no evidence that he introduced the loyalty program on the basis of an investigation into its merits, which suggests something else lay behind it. The loyalty program allowed Truman to fend off criticism from Republicans that he was soft on communism: his program would purge communists from government.

Following the exposure of Soviet atomic espionage, the White House pushed Britain to adopt a similar loyalty program, involving proactive investigations into the backgrounds of employees engaged in sensitive work. Britain resisted doing so until its intelligence community was decimated by the exposure of the Cambridge spy ring in 1951. Truman's administration also indicted the leaders of the U.S. Communist Party, under sedition legislation, on the (correct) grounds that they had facilitated Soviet espionage.

One of Truman's final acts before leaving office was to sign, in October 1952, a secret executive order creating the National Security Agency, which would become the Western world's largest intelligence agency. Headquartered at Fort Meade, Maryland ("the Fort"), it would become home to the world's biggest and most complex computer systems during the Cold War. We shall return to the NSA's establishment, and its impact on U.S. national security, in our story below.

Truman would later deny that he intended for the CIA to be a "cloak and dagger" agency. In fact, in a series of directives, he gave the agency responsibility for conducting covert political and paramilitary activities. He was the first U.S. president to establish a peacetime U.S. covert action agency. Facing a communist takeover in Czechoslovakia and rising tensions in Berlin, which soon led to its blockade by Soviet forces, Truman's newly minted team of "national security" advisers realized that the time for *implying* authorization of U.S. covert action was over: it needed *express* presidential sanction.[28]

The thorny question was whose responsibility covert activities should be, particularly "psychological warfare," which Truman recognized would play a significant role against Soviet communism. The president initially thought they should fall to the State Department. But the secretary of state, George Marshall, was vehemently opposed: any direct links between covert activities and the State Department would be disastrous for U.S. foreign policy and his plan for postwar recovery in Europe. At the same time, Marshall recognized their importance. Indeed, a central part of the U.S. grand strategy against the Soviet Union would be creating a "Marshall Plan of the Mind," a war of wills, to win over populations in Europe falling under Moscow's shadow.

Ultimately, in directive NSC 4-A, such covert activities became the responsibility of the CIA, their logical home. In May 1948, George Kennan, now head of the State Department policy planning staff, proposed an expansion of U.S. covert action, calling for the "inauguration of organized political warfare" and the creation of a new clandestine service to conduct covert operations against the Soviet Union worldwide. For Kennan, the Marshall Plan, the Truman Doctrine, and CIA covert operations were all complementary and interlocking parts of America's strategy against Stalin's growing empire. A month later, "taking cognizance of the vicious covert activities of the USSR, its satellite countries and Communist groups to discredit and defeat the aims and activities of the United States and other Western powers," Truman signed a directive, NSC 10/2, which ordered the creation within the CIA of a department to plan and engage in "propaganda; economic warfare . . . sabotage," anti-sabotage, "demolition and evacuation measures; subversion against hostile states . . . and support of indigenous anti-Communist elements in threatened countries of the free world." America's spies had come of age.[29]

The president's directive placed one explicit restriction on CIA covert actions: that its operations were "so planned and executed that . . . the U.S. government can plausibly disclaim any responsibility for them." With a flick of Truman's pen, the principle of plausible deniability thus entered U.S. foreign policy. Contrary to the maxim prominently displayed on Truman's desk, "The BUCK STOPS here," as far as covert action was concerned, the buck would not reach the Oval Office.

In August 1948, Truman approved NSC 20/1, authorizing guerrilla operations behind the Iron Curtain using Soviet émigrés recruited in the West. Within the CIA, covert action was housed in the innocuously named Office of Policy Coordination (OPC). Revealing the importance that the State Department attached to covert action for U.S. foreign policy, although the OPC was formally within the CIA, it reported to the secretary of state. The first head of the semidetached OPC was Frank Wisner, a corporate lawyer and former OSS station chief in Romania. From his nondescript headquarters—a cluster of temporary wartime Nissen huts flanking the Washington Monument and Capitol Reflecting Pool—Wisner built the OPC into an empire. He had an almost maniacal level of energy. One of the officers he recruited, William Colby (later DCI in the Reagan administration), recalled that "Wisner landed like a dynamo, read all the intelligence and set out to form a clandestine force worldwide."

Unlike Britain's corresponding foreign intelligence service, MI6, which only had a small paramilitary function, the CIA in the 1950s focused primarily on covert action. It received more than half of the agency's budget and an explosion of personnel. Between 1949 and 1952, Wisner's covert action outfit grew from 302 staffers to 2,812, with an additional 3,142 overseas contract personnel. Its budget shot from $4.7 million to $82 million. Its foreign stations grew from seven to forty-seven. It became the shadow arm of U.S. foreign policy. In 1954, Eisenhower further clarified U.S. covert action by issuing National Security Directive 5412. It gave the CIA sole responsibility for conducting covert action, to be overseen by the "5412 Special Group" of the National Security Council. Eisenhower's directive was one of the most secret documents in the U.S. government.[30]

Those present at the creation of the U.S. national security establishment—to borrow Secretary of State Dean Acheson's phrase—were a relatively small Georgetown cocktail set of "wise men": U.S. statesmen like Charles Bohlen (U.S. ambassador in Moscow), David Bruce (former OSS head in London and later U.S. ambassador there), James Forrestal (first secretary of defense), and Robert Lovett (undersecretary of state and later secretary of defense). Wisner's colleague Richard Helms (later DCI under presidents Johnson and Nixon), who specialized in the CIA's clandestine collection (espionage), said that Wisner burned with "a zeal and intensity which imposed, unquestionably, an abnormal strain" on him. These were indeed wise men. But they were also mental prisoners to the "lessons" of Munich, which required "strength" against new Hitlers popping up around the globe.

None of the Georgetown set suffered the strains of a colossal workload thrust upon him like Forrestal. In March 1949, he resigned as America's first secretary of defense and suffered a mental breakdown on his last day of work, complaining that he had not slept in weeks. He was admitted for psychiatric treatment to Bethesda Naval Hospital, where he calmed himself by studying ancient Greek. One night, he was writing out the chorus from Sophocles's *Ajax*. He got to the word "nightingale." He then went to the window and threw himself to his death from the sixteenth floor. NIGHT-INGALE was the code name of an operation involving Ukrainian exiles, including former Nazi collaborators, whom the CIA parachuted behind the Iron Curtain to fight Stalin.[31]

ASYMMETRY OF ARMS: EAST-WEST SPIES

As relations between East and West broke down after 1945, there was a vast gulf between each side's intelligence capabilities. Britain and the United

States were essentially bringing toys to a gunfight. At the end of the war, and for years after, neither country had any significant agents behind the Iron Curtain. In 1948, the CIA had a grand total of twelve analysts who spoke Russian. Britain was also handicapped. In 1945, its senior official at the Foreign Office, Alexander Cadogan, ruled that MI6 should only attempt to penetrate the Soviet Union from outside, not establish an espionage capability on the inside, for fear of repercussions if exposed. Under Stalin, even relatively simple matters like posting a letter to an agent in the Soviet Union were elaborate exercises.[32]

Britain's intelligence services, and senior Whitehall policymakers, mused about using Soviet agents who had been caught to recreate the wartime double-cross system, in this case against the Russians. This was fantasy. The linchpin in British wartime deception, the London Controlling Section, continued to operate into the postwar years (under a new official name, the Hollis Committee). Hopes for recreating past triumphs against the Soviets, however, were soon dashed when it became clear that Soviet spies, unlike their wartime German predecessors, were ideologically committed and thus more difficult to turn. The British also lacked the equivalent of ULTRA, which made MI5's wartime successes possible. Not only was there to be no new double-cross system, but for years after the end of the war, the British had no significant intelligence on Stalin's Soviet Union at all.[33]

In London, the Joint Intelligence Committee was conspicuously silent on the Soviet Union during the geopolitical realignment from World War to Cold War. The JIC did not directly address the Soviet Union between December 1944 and March 1946, precisely when we would imagine it would have been essential to do so. When it did belatedly provide senior Whitehall policymakers with an assessment about Soviet strategy, it bluntly concluded that it was speculating, because it lacked meaningful intelligence on Stalin's aims and military power.

Worse still, the March 1946 JIC report was almost certainly drafted with the assistance of MI6's "expert" in Soviet affairs, Kim Philby, who would have passed it on to the Kremlin. In the wake of Gouzenko's defection, Britain's foreign secretary queried whether taking action against Soviet agents in the West would lead to reciprocal actions against British agent networks in the Soviet Union. MI6's pathetic answer was revealing. There was no need to worry, it told Ernest Bevin: MI6 did not have any such networks.

Britain and the United States were thus again spying blind in 1945, this time about the Soviet regime. As Richard Helms, an OSS officer and later the head of the CIA, put it: "In the beginning, we knew nothing." At the end of the war, MI5's official in-house historian, John "Jack" Curry, concluded that MI5 was roughly in the same position regarding the Soviet Union as it had been with the Axis powers in 1939. Given its lack of intelligence then, this was a dire, but as it turned out accurate, admission. As late as 1951, an official inquiry into Britain's intelligence services by the cabinet secretary, Norman Brook, concluded that MI6's efforts against the Soviet Union were inadequate and disappointing.[34]

In contrast to Britain's and America's intelligence famine, Stalin's agents kept him abreast of major geopolitical milestones in the West. He used his spies to formulate a grand strategy toward the Western powers. Stalin was confident in the inevitable long-term victory of communism over liberal democracies. But he did not want war with them—yet. Stalin himself was a wreck at the war's end, exhausted, now aged sixty-five, his teeth yellowing, his pockmarked face graying, and his once full mustache now scrawny. He did not have a master plan for Europe. He hoped that the Grand Alliance would last for several years after 1945, giving him time to rebuild the Soviet economy and industry. Cities like Kyiv were uninhabitable ruins. There were millions of starving orphans in eastern Europe coming under his control.

Stalin used the intelligence that came to him from his Western spies to wage a war of nerves with his former wartime Allies, pushing and squeezing to get what he could. His Marxism and Leninism told him that inherent greed would soon send the Western capitalist powers to war among themselves. He would watch as they committed fratricide. He demanded territorial concessions from Turkey and sought geopolitical gains around the Mediterranean rim. In Greece, he supported guerrillas in its ongoing civil war—which British code breakers, it seems, detected. Stalin delayed the withdrawal of Soviet troops from wartime-occupied Iran and Manchuria. In February 1946, he delivered a blistering speech, blaming capitalism for the war. He declared that it would inevitably precipitate a third world war.[35]

Soviet espionage produced a kaleidoscope of ironies in postwar international relations. Following Gouzenko's exposure of Soviet atomic espionage, the U.S. Congress passed the McMahon Act (1946), which closed atomic intelligence sharing with foreign powers, including Britain. The raised American drawbridge was only lowered due to the fancy footwork of British diplomats and spy chiefs. The United States, with its vast accumulation of wartime wealth, was, by the early 1950s, the unmistakable senior partner in transatlantic intelligence relations, even as the CIA learned on the job. In this atmosphere, with London nervous about sharing potentially damaging intelligence with Washington, Stalin was sometimes better informed about Anglo-American intelligence relations than the two Western governments themselves.[36]

Despite the intelligence he received, Stalin was capable of massive strategic miscalculations. This happened in Berlin, where the Allied armies met in 1945, and which remained divided between occupying powers. In 1946, Stalin proclaimed: "All of Germany must be ours, that is, Soviet, communist." The Soviets expropriated property wholesale in East Germany, while Red Army soldiers between 1945 and 1947 raped as many as two million German women. In the Western sector of Berlin, to combat inflation, the occupying powers introduced a new currency, the Deutschmark. Stalin and his foreign minister, Molotov, responded by blockading the city. They miscalculated Western resolve. America's newly formed CIA correctly told Truman that Stalin was trying to extract concessions, not start World War III. Western governments instigated an unprecedented airlift of supplies to the besieged city, flying in twenty-four-hour shifts.[37]

West Germany was established twelve days after the end of the blockade, in May 1949. Stalin had responded to Truman's announcement of the Marshall Plan with the formation of a new Communist Information Bureau, Cominform, in September 1947. It was a continuation of the prewar Comintern, but as we have seen, Stalin's wartime dissolution of the Comintern had made little practical difference, as he continued to use communist parties and networks for Soviet clandestine foreign policy. What was most important for the United States was the creation of NATO in 1949. Eschewing the warnings of the Founding Fathers about "foreign entanglements," Truman joined the military alliance with Western Europe. It was a turning point. The United States agreed to the peacetime defense of Europe. It was the moment when the Cold War moved from ideological to military conflict between two armed blocs, East and West. The Soviet government responded by creating the Warsaw Pact.

Historians have devoted enough ink to the origins of the Cold War to fill entire libraries: how and why the conflict arose, which side was responsible for it, and whether it was inevitable. When seen from the perspective of intelligence, the history looks significantly different. The Soviet Union's wartime intelligence assault on Britain and the United States, only gradually revealed after 1945, was so profound that it is difficult to see how Britain and the U.S. could *not* have responded with grand strategies of their own. Stalin's espionage against them constituted an attack on their sovereignty, undermining their ability to function effectively, which no country could tolerate. The fact is, the Soviet Union conducted wartime espionage, and stole Western military and industrial secrets, in ways that lacked any equivalence by the West. FBI reports indicating the scale of Soviet espionage, combined with evidence from Gouzenko, Bentley, and Chambers, as well as information from U.S. code breakers, eventually made it impossible for Truman to ignore. The president also exaggerated the threat of war from Stalin for domestic purposes. Anti-communism, being seen as strong against Stalin, was a useful political platform for him. The only way that Truman could have known Stalin's intentions was from secret intelligence—which he was wholly missing. Stalin's aims were unknowable mysteries.[38]

SUBVERSION: ELECTION MEDDLING

The intelligence conflict between the Soviet Union and the West did not just involve collection, but also subversion. The U.S. government termed it "covert action," the British "special political action," and the Kremlin "active measures," as we have seen. Both sides considered their efforts defensive, countering the covert intrusions of the other, both real and imagined, in what became a clandestine arms race.[39]

After the war's devastation, Stalin's initial strategic objective was to rebuild the Soviet economy and bring security to the heartland. He did so by subverting governments in Russia's "near abroad": forging the Soviet bloc in Eastern and Central Europe. The East German communist leader Walter Ulbricht announced to his inner circle after returning to Berlin from exile in Moscow in April 1945: "It's got to look democratic, but we must have everything under our control." Because a democratic facade had to be preserved in all the states of the new Soviet bloc, the open use of force to exclude non-communist parties from power had, so far as possible, to be avoided. Nonetheless, the Soviet military takeover of Czechoslovakia in early 1948, when tanks rolled into Prague, showed that Moscow was prepared to use open force when necessary to subjugate nonconforming governments. The last remaining non-communist in the Czech government, Jan Masaryk, its popular foreign minister, fell from a window to his death in a Prague courtyard, dressed in his pajamas—conveniently for Stalin.[40]

Moscow's establishment of communist-controlled security services was essential to the Eastern bloc's creation. They were made in the KGB's image and overseen by Soviet "advisers." While not all Eastern bloc regimes had the same vision of communism as Moscow, when it came to creating their security services, the Kremlin imposed its will. As one officer from the Czechoslovakian intelligence service, the StB, stated: "We did not do anything important without approval of the KGB." The StB requisitioned a former convent in Prague, near the Granite Bridge over the Charles River, as its headquarters; the convent's Sisters were sent to detention camps; its basement was converted to interrogation and torture cells; the attached church became a shooting range. One-party Stalinist regimes ruled by intimidation behind the scenes of Eastern Europe's so-called people's democracies—the epithet "democratic" being a telltale sign, to this day, that a government is *not* democratic. Stalin's wartime military counterintelligence body, SMERSH, purged East European governments of all visible opposition, deporting dissenters to fates unknown. Stalin's spy chiefs rigged elections in the "democracies" to create huge, and fraudulent, communist majorities.[41]

The first major postwar subversion battlefield between East and West intelligence was not, though, in Eastern Europe but in Italy, where in April 1948 both sides attempted to meddle in that country's free and democratic elections. Clandestine efforts there foreshadowed central characteristics of the Cold War elsewhere around the globe, as both sides tried to subvert the "alignment" of foreign governments. While Stalin was imposing Soviet rule in Eastern Europe, he also threatened the security of Western Europe from within. In the first postwar Western European elections, communists made inroads everywhere. Responding to requests for assistance from the American embassy in Rome, in November 1947 Truman issued instructions in the first document issued by his new National Security Council. NSC 1/1 proclaimed: "The Italian Government, ideologically inclined toward Western democracy, is weak and is being subjected to continuous attack by a strong Communist party." The directive authorized a U.S. program to "actively combat Communist propaganda in Italy by an effective U.S. information program and by all other practicable means, including the use of unvouchered funds." America's spy chiefs were getting to work.[42]

America's "forward defense" against communism in Italy was both overt and covert. The Truman administration approved shipments of wheat and other commodities to the destitute European nation, distributed from Italian ports with trucks emblazoned with the Stars and Stripes. Truman's spies also ran clandestine, non-avowed activities there.

Just three months after its establishment, the CIA set to work to ensure the defeat of communists in Italy. The agency's newly created clandestine psychological warfare unit—the Special Procedures Group (SPG), part of the OSO—used bribery, forgery, and disinformation to help the U.S. embassy "get out the vote" for non-communist candidates. Lifting tradecraft derived from the OSS days, and from British intelligence, it disseminated posters, pamphlets, and stories in newspapers, encouraged speeches backing non-communist candidates, and forged documents purporting to have come from the Italian Communist Party. The wiry CIA chief of station in Rome, James Angleton, Yale poet and OSS veteran, did as NSC 1/1 authorized and funneled unvouched funds to support moderates: he used $10 million from captured Nazi gold to bankroll anti-communist politicians in Italy. This involved handing Italian politicians cases full of cash. Some of it made its way to the Italian prime minister, Alcide De Gasperi, helping the campaign of his moderate Christian Democratic Party.[43]

While the CIA provided cash, MI6 also lent support—a recurring theme in Anglo-American postwar joint covert actions. Britain's propaganda unit, the Information Research Department, distributed pamphlets smearing Italian communists. The combination of overt and covert actions was a major lesson, which subsequent White House administrations, and the U.S. intelligence community itself, often failed to appreciate: to be effective, a covert action had to complement, not replace, broader U.S. policy.[44]

As Soviet intelligence archives show, the Kremlin was also active trying to subvert the general election in Italy, providing secret subsidies to the Italian Communist Party and individual candidates there. Despite their best efforts, Italy's moderate Christian Democrats won the election by a comfortable margin. Truman regarded this as a victory for the CIA and sent his personal congratulations to his new Director of Central Intelligence, Admiral Roscoe "Hilly" Hillenkoetter. It remains unclear whether U.S. and British covert actions really were significant, let alone decisive. One way to determine a covert action's impact is through non-avowed polling, which

CIA and British intelligence do not appear to have undertaken in Italy—but they subsequently would in other regions and countries. De Gasperi's political fortunes soon declined, indicating a short-term impact, whatever it was. Despite a lack of solid evidence, the CIA's experience meddling in Italy's democracy enshrined a misguided belief in Washington that it could achieve otherwise impossible things for American statecraft.[45]

Enthusiasm for covert action grew in Washington as the weapon of choice in what Secretary of State Dean Rusk once called the back-alley struggles of the Cold War. Meanwhile, the U.S. government institutionalized CIA covert funding to non-communist groups elsewhere in Europe. Although we do not usually learn this in school, the Marshall Fund for the reconstruction of Europe had a secret annex for the CIA. It devoted about 5 percent of its $13.8 billion fund ($685 million) to the agency for its clandestine activities in Europe. This was the centerpiece of America's "organized political warfare" against communism, requiring measures short of war, as Cold War strategist George Kennan put it.[46]

Stalin's "special services," the KGB and the GRU, had disproportionate advantages when it came to subverting Western democracies with their freedoms of press, speech, and political association. It was impossible for U.S. and British intelligence to unleash similar, corresponding political warfare on the closed police states of the Soviet bloc. They had no free press to manipulate. This was not lost on Stalin. As he faced U.S.-financed reconstruction in Europe, and a collision with Western powers over the city of Berlin in the summer of 1948, he shifted strategy from Russia's sphere of influence to undermining the United States itself. He attempted to interfere in the U.S. presidential election that year to unseat Truman.

Russian archival records obtained for this book show that Stalin colluded with his favored U.S. candidate in 1948, Henry Wallace, Roosevelt's Soviet-friendly former wartime vice president.[47]

The nature of Wallace's relationship with the Kremlin has long been a subject of speculation. Soviet intelligence is known to have unimaginatively code-named the vice president CAPTAIN'S DEPUTY during the war. But no evidence has ever emerged that Wallace was recruited as a Soviet agent. He was, however, we can now discern, a Soviet tool. He sincerely believed that "peaceful coexistence" between the Soviet Union and the United States not only could be achieved, but was essential for world peace. All the while, he looked away from (and naively followed Soviet propaganda denying) the existence of Stalin's mass forced labor and terror programs. According to Truman's counsel Clark Clifford: "It was never clear to me how aware he [Wallace] was of the uses to which the Communist Party was putting him, but whether he knew it or not, he was following the communist line, serving communist ends, and betraying those Americans who supported him as a serious alternative to the two main candidates." Wallace's naivete about Soviet communism turned him into an asset for Stalin, if not a recruited Soviet agent.[48]

Wallace decided to run in the 1948 U.S. election as the Progressive Party nominee. In April and May that year, he secretly liaised with Stalin about public policies that would be advantageous for the Soviet Union, coordinating his public statements with the dictator. Wallace secretly met with the youthful Soviet ambassador to the UN in New York, Andrei Gromyko, who dispatched the candidate's messages to the Soviet foreign minister, Molotov, and to Stalin himself. In his memoirs, Gromyko admitted to meeting Wallace, but downplayed the meeting's significance, suggesting that after talking with him he considered that Wallace had lost contact with the pulse of American life. Archival documents in Moscow reveal that in fact Stalin took Wallace's position and candidacy seriously, approving his public positions, and answering questions that the former vice president put to him, which Stalin annotated in his distinctive pencil. Their alignment produced a published open letter from Wallace to Stalin, vetted by the Soviet leader in advance, to which Stalin then publicly replied, all as agreed between the two men.[49]

Wallace's presidential election bid in November 1948 dismally failed; he ended up getting barely 2 percent of the vote, while Truman, to his and the nation's surprise, won a second term. He defeated New York governor Thomas E. Dewey in one of the greatest upsets in U.S. presidential history.

Ironically, the staff of Wallace's failed 1948 campaign included none other than the Soviet atom spy Ted Hall. Following his unsuccessful White House run, Wallace had a crisis of faith in his pro-Stalinism. This may have been caused by his realization that Stalin had used and discarded him after the election. Stalin had gotten what he wanted from Wallace. In 1952, Wallace published an article, "Where I Was Wrong," describing "Russian Communism" as "utterly evil." The Kremlin and its intelligence services nevertheless learned an important strategic lesson for later in the Cold War: that it could use the freedoms inherent within American electoral campaigns to influence candidates favorable to the Soviet Union.[50]

CHAPTER SIX

PUZZLE PALACES

"Do you mean we're overhearing Portsmouth ships trying to talk to
each other—that we're eavesdropping across half South England?"

"Just that. Their transmitters are all right, but their receivers
are out of order, so they only get a dot here and a dash there.
Nothing clear."

–Rudyard Kipling, "Wireless"

MANY HISTORIES OF THE COLD WAR, EVEN THOSE RECENTLY
published, remain silent when it comes to SIGINT agencies and their
impact on foreign affairs. GCHQ and the NSA received the largest share of
funding of any of their governments' intelligence agencies during the Cold
War. A 1955 review by Britain's chief of the Imperial General Staff, Gerald
Templer, concluded that GCHQ produced about 90 percent of Britain's
intelligence, which underscores both the importance of SIGINT and the
herculean difficulty of acquiring human intelligence against a closed society
like the Soviet Union.[1]

British and U.S. code breakers, the "wizards" in their "puzzle palaces,"
tried to emulate their wartime successes with ULTRA and produce a second

breakthrough—cracking high-level Soviet codes. There is no evidence in the public domain that they managed to do so after 1948, a date whose importance is revealed later. Without the benefit of cryptanalysis against Soviet codes, the British and Americans instead focused their efforts on other SIGINT areas that were not reliant on it: one was traffic analysis, another was plaintext interception. These two areas were arguably GCHQ and NSA's major contribution to fighting the Cold War. Traffic analysis is a process of analyzing communications without gleaning their underlying contents, while plaintext is, as its name suggests, the analysis of unencrypted communications—in this case, Soviet civilian and military radio traffic. As one NSA study has put it, plaintext was a candle in the dark during the Cold War. Both of these methods allowed the British and Americans to build up a daily map of Soviet forces and capabilities, from which they could identify deviations in Soviet behavior and infer intentions. Soviet SIGINT efforts are meanwhile secrets under lock and key in Moscow, but we know that both sides threw resources at building computers capable of unlocking the other's encrypted communications.

SIGINT: ANGLO-AMERICAN SPECIAL RELATIONSHIP

The same month President Truman closed down the OSS, September 1945, he also secretly authorized SIGINT authorities to continue collaborating with the British. Six months later, the two governments came to an unprecedented peacetime agreement that would serve as a cornerstone of Western security for the rest of the Cold War and beyond. The seven-page agreement, signed by British and American delegations in Washington on March 5, 1946—the same day, as we saw, when Churchill delivered his Iron Curtain speech in Missouri and Nunn May was sentenced to imprisonment in London—provided for the free and complete exchange of all SIGINT collection, product, knowledge, and techniques. Illustrating its continuation of wartime collaboration, the agreement had the same name as its wartime predecessor: the British-U.S. Communication Intelligence Agreement, or BRUSA. While the Anglo-American "special relationship" has frequently been described in romanticized, chest-puffing terms, especially in London, when it comes to SIGINT there was, and is, something genuinely special. SIGINT is the most special part of the Anglo-American "special relationship."[2]

When Truman became president, on April 12, 1945, he was briefed about ULTRA, which gave him (and Churchill) a ringside seat to the final days of the Axis powers. It is difficult to determine Truman's attitude toward SIGINT; like other American and British statesmen at the time, he did not discuss it in his memoirs. However, it is likely that the insights he gained from ULTRA caused him to support continued postwar SIGINT collaboration with GC&CS (later known as GCHQ). The dirty secret of U.S. intelligence is that, just as the British shaped it during the war, they also guided postwar American SIGINT. BRUSA, soon to be called UKUSA, was not a single agreement but a series, modified and expanded a decade after its signing to incorporate other Western Anglophone countries in the Commonwealth: Canada, Australia, and New Zealand—constituting the Five Eyes SIGINT alliance that still exists today. At the time UKUSA was signed, "Britain" represented both the empire and its Dominions. British negotiators realized that the empire gave GCHQ a disproportionate influence in Washington. As successive White House administrations grasped, Britain's imperial outposts across the world, though diminishing in number in the postwar years, were vital bases for SIGINT collection on the Soviet Union.[3]

Seventy-five years after UKUSA's establishment, the Five Eyes partners finally publicly acknowledged their global SIGINT alliance and the significance it has played in international Western security. This represents a sharp reversal in policy, as UKUSA had been one of the British and U.S. governments' most closely held secrets. In some instances, the secrecy surrounding the agreement led British and American statesmen to conduct historical deception. When publishing the diaries of defense secretary James

Forrestal, for example, U.S. officials and his publishers excised sensitive passages from the text about SIGINT collaboration with the British. The blanket of secrecy around UKUSA allowed myths and conspiracy theories to emerge. One is that the agreement permits British and U.S. governments to sidestep their respective laws, using the other to intercept communications that would be illegal under their own laws. In fact, UKUSA's text expressly concerns foreign communications, which, by definition in the agreement, excludes British and American communications. London and Washington thus cannot use the agreement to get around legal prohibitions about, for example, collecting communications of each other's citizens. We can now safely slay this old conspiracy canard.

Anglo-American postwar SIGINT collaboration was not initially the well-oiled machine it would become. By the end of the war, GC&CS (Bletchley) had a staff of 8,902. A year later, amid postwar demobilization, its staff was slashed to 1,010. Bletchley had produced the most valuable intelligence during the war, but the Axis was now defeated and Bletchley's importance died. Many of Bletchey's talented wartime recruits went back to their previous professions. MI5 and MI6's staff numbers were similarly axed. In April 1946, GC&CS moved from Bletchley, its wartime headquarters, to Eastcote on the outskirts of London and thereafter, in the 1950s, to Cheltenham. At that point, GC&CS was officially renamed the Government Communications Headquarters, or GCHQ. Thereafter, "going to the West Country" became a euphemism, with a nod and wink among Whitehall insiders, for GCHQ.

Truman's order for rapid demobilization also saw massive SIGINT staff reductions. In 1945, the U.S. Army SIGINT agency (the SSA) and the navy's communications intelligence organization, OP-20-G, consisted of 37,000 military and civilian personnel and had 37 listening posts overseas. The SSA could read 350 diplomatic code and cipher systems belonging to 60 countries. Within four months of the end of hostilities, army and navy communications intelligence organizations lost 80 percent of their personnel.[4]

In the immediate postwar years, U.S. SIGINT witnessed a revival of the conflicts between army and naval cryptanalysts that had plagued SIGINT before the war and had contributed to Pearl Harbor. There was something close to open warfare between U.S. SIGINT agencies. With the dramatic decline of wartime naval SIGINT, OP-20-G's resources were downgraded. It tried to reclaim some of its prewar work on diplomatic traffic. The army's redesignated SIGINT agency, the Army Security Agency (ASA), based at Arlington Hall in Virginia, however, refused to surrender its monopoly of diplomatic decryption, simply, ASA claimed, to give residual U.S. Navy cryptanalysts "something to do." Further confusion was caused with the creation of an independent U.S. Air Force in October 1947. Its dapper chief of staff and the former DCI, Hoyt Vandenberg, insisted that it should have its own SIGINT capability.

In August 1948, a committee chaired by Rear Admiral Earl E. Stone, director of naval communications, was ordered to resolve the confusion between the three service SIGINT agencies. The attempt was a failure. After further wrangling, a new Armed Forces Security Agency (AFSA), headed by Stone, was set up in May 1949 to try to coordinate SIGINT operations by the three armed forces. AFSA made the existing confusion even worse. A top secret report in 1952 noted that, in place of two wartime SIGINT organizations, the army and navy, the U.S. government now had four—each of the armed services, plus AFSA. Worse, the Director of Central Intelligence was, contrary to his title, not the director of intelligence when it came to SIGINT. In fact, Truman's DCIs were deliberately excluded from the most important American code-breaking breakthroughs.[5]

Within the confusing mess of competing SIGINT agencies in Washington, British GCHQ liaison officers became steady and respected hands. The SIGINT rivalry in Washington placed GCHQ in the position of being an honest broker. U.S. SIGINT officials frequently found it easier to liaise with their British counterparts than among themselves. America's dangerously confusing state of postwar SIGINT would directly contribute to the failure to predict the outbreak of the Korean War in June 1950.

CIPHER WAR

According to the NSA's in-house history, U.S. SIGINT agencies started the postwar years in dire straits, disorganized and with "little experience, less money, and no expertise" when it came to Soviet codes. American army and navy chiefs all saw the need for collaboration on SIGINT but could not agree on how to achieve that. By pooling resources with the British through UKUSA, otherwise rival American cryptanalytic branches found ways to collaborate. In 1946, the year UKUSA was signed, the two countries were collaborating to attack 109 different foreign "units." Twenty were tackled by the British and thirty by the Americans, with the remaining shared. Their transatlantic work was code-named BOURBON. That same year, the British and Americans were decrypting twenty thousand messages from Soviet traffic per month. The goal was to create a second ULTRA that would even the odds of the escalating conflict with the Soviet Union.[6]

There were three sources for BOURBON. First were stolen Soviet communications. In 1944, the FBI burgled the New York offices of the American Trading Corporation to steal its messages with Soviet authorities. Though publicly available documentation does not reveal exactly how American and British code breakers used the stolen documents, they are known to have been valuable for BOURBON. Equally useful was the acquisition of Soviet code books, like that acquired in the STELLA POLARIS operation, which we encountered earlier. OSS director Donovan may have demanded that it be returned to the Soviets, but American cryptanalysts secretly broke his orders and kept a copy. In the coming years, this code book would become a valuable source for those working on Soviet traffic. Third, the defection of Igor Gouzenko in Canada in September 1945 provided British and American SIGINT with insights into Soviet cryptology.

BOURBON paid significant dividends for London and Washington. It was largely due to SIGINT that British and U.S. intelligence accurately warned their leaders during the Berlin crisis in the summer of 1948, when Soviet forces blockaded the city, that Stalin would not risk war.[7]

In October 1948, however, the Soviet government abruptly changed its codes, switching its communications to secure enciphered traffic, and diverting radio messages to landlines. Within the NSA, this was "Black Friday," or "the day the lights went off." The loss of Soviet codes actually took place incrementally over six months, but its effect was the same as if it had happened all at once. With virtually no human intelligence behind the Iron Curtain, the British and U.S. governments were now in the dark regarding Soviet intentions. It would take British and American code breakers two decades to recover from Black Friday.

American and British SIGINT only later discovered why the Soviets had changed their codes. It was the result of a Soviet spy working inside the U.S. Army SIGINT agency, the AFSA: William "Bill" Weisband. Today his name remains largely unknown, even to devoted students of intelligence history, due to the blanket of secrecy that U.S. authorities imposed on his espionage. Weisband, however, was one of the most damaging agents ever to breach American SIGINT.

Weisband, stocky and balding, looked like the shifty customer he was. He had been recruited as a Soviet agent before the war (code-named ZVENO, "link" in English) and joined the wartime U.S. Army SIGINT agency. The son of Russian-Ukrainian immigrants to the United States and himself a Russian speaker, Weisband was employed by AFSA as a linguist. He was known to colleagues to have Soviet sympathies and even placed on an FBI list of suspected communists. It is perplexing then, to say the least, that he obtained and maintained a security clearance. Coworkers at AFSA remember Weisband, forty years old in 1948, as a stroller, always walking its hallways and starting up conversations. He managed to get himself on circulation lists of reports that he had little legitimate reason to receive. One of those whom he befriended was Meredith Gardner, a brilliant code breaker in his early thirties from Texas. Gardner was an ascetic, whose only known indulgence was his impeccable tweed coats and Oxford shirts. He later recalled that Weisband took particular interest in his efforts to decrypt Soviet messages, peering over his bony shoulder with a pipe as he worked on them in 1946. It was because of Weisband's espionage that the Soviet Union knew to change its codes. His treachery reveals the damage that a single well-placed spy can inflict on intelligence collection.[8]

While Weisband's espionage fatally sabotaged BOURBON, American code breakers soon produced a windfall of their own—VENONA. This was the code name eventually given to almost three thousand intercepted Soviet intelligence and other classified telegrams dating from 1940 to 1948. Since 1927, the Soviet government had used onetime "pads," which, again, involve using a "dictionary" of unique random number sequences held only by sender and receiver. According to NSA insiders, these constitute a "perfect" form of encryption. Soviet authorities transmitted the number sequences via commercial telegram companies to and from the United States, confident that they were securely encrypted.

Although onetime pads offer perfect encryption, there are no perfect users. Soviet cipher clerks broke the cardinal rule and accidentally reused parts of the onetime pads, making them vulnerable to attack by Western cryptanalysis. Decrypting the messages was a monumental undertaking, a shot in the dark, with little prospect of success. It involved trawling mountains of material. If each pad were used once, the search would be fruitless, but if they were reused, there would be patterns. The brains behind VENONA in 1945 was Gardner. The Texan had mastered twelve languages, including Sanskrit. His talents had made him an obvious recruit for wartime U.S. SIGINT, where he worked on German ciphers. He continued to use his formidable skills after 1945, now on Soviet traffic.[9]

VENONA was probably the greatest single source of intelligence about Soviet espionage available to Western governments during the Cold War. It revealed that more than two hundred Americans had worked as Soviet agents during, and sometimes after, World War II, and that the leaders of the American Communist Party had colluded with Soviet intelligence. It was VENONA that revealed that every section of Roosevelt's wartime administration had been penetrated by Soviet intelligence—and identified Harry Dexter White and Alger Hiss as spies. It confirmed that the OSS had been thoroughly compromised. VENONA led to the discovery of Klaus Fuchs and Ted Hall. It also gave the British and the Americans their first clues to the identities of the most successful group of foreign agents ever recruited by the Soviet Union, the Cambridge Five. VENONA has been subsequently corroborated by archives opened in, and smuggled out of, Russia. All this despite the fact that only about 1 percent of VENONA communications intercepted before Soviet traffic went dark in 1948 were actually decrypted. To this day, VENONA decrypts contain code names of Soviet agents who have never been publicly identified. There are still secrets about 1940s Soviet espionage in the West.

The wartime ULTRA secret had been more closely guarded than any previous source of intelligence in U.S. or British history, known only to six ministers in Churchill's cabinet and probably even fewer members of Roosevelt's administration. VENONA was even more tightly held. It was so secret that its very existence was apparently even withheld from President Truman. This was an absurd situation. Until the end of Truman's administration, neither the National Security Council nor Roscoe Hillenkoetter, DCI from mid-1947 through most of 1950, was briefed on VENONA. The extraordinary restrictions placed on its material went beyond operational necessity about a cryptologic secret. They arose from bitter, and at times absurd, internecine rivalries in Washington.

While the FBI knew about VENONA, General Omar Bradley, chairman of the Joint Chiefs of Staff from 1949 to 1953, refused to share anything about it with Hillenkoetter. Bradley appears to have resented the fact that the CIA was not placed under the authority of the Joint Chiefs, as the OSS had been. Bradley and J. Edgar Hoover were also—not unreasonably—suspicious of CIA security, given Soviet agent penetration of the OSS, which they feared and then learned about from VENONA. The DCI was frequently one of Truman's first visitors of the day. That rivalry drove the chairman of the Joint Chiefs, on his own authority, to withhold the secret about VENONA from the CIA. Bradley also took it upon himself to keep the secret from the U.S. president and commander in chief—unless and until he deemed it necessary to inform Truman about the contents of a specific VENONA decrypt. Only by keeping VENONA from the president could Bradley be sure that it was kept from Hillenkoetter. It was a mess.[10]

It was not until 1952 that the DCI was finally briefed on VENONA. There is no evidence that Truman was ever informed about the decrypts, though his successor, President Eisenhower, a wartime admirer of SIGINT, as we have seen, was briefed. Had Truman known about VENONA, and that it confirmed testimonies of defectors like Elizabeth Bentley, it is unlikely his administration would have considered acts they did, like smearing her, or given credence to disinformation spread by the Communist Party in America about Alger Hiss's innocence. When Truman was asked at a news conference in August 1948 about Soviet spy scandals, he said he thought they were a red herring to divert public attention. In fact, Soviet spies were real, as VENONA would have revealed to him.[11]

On the other hand, American SIGINT agencies readily shared VENONA with their British counterparts at GCHQ. According to the NSA's history, by 1948 there was "complete and profitable US-UK cooperation on the VENONA project." GCHQ duly shared VENONA with Britain's other intelligence services, MI5 and MI6; it appears that Prime Minister Attlee and some of his senior ministers were also briefed on it. As such, before November 1952, a perverse situation arose: the British government was better informed about Soviet espionage in the United States than were the U.S. president and his DCI. Because of Weisband's espionage, Stalin knew about VENONA six years before the president or the CIA.

Despite VENONA's revelations, of the 206 Americans identified in the decrypts, only 15 were prosecuted. Forty Soviet agents managed to flee. The striking failure to prosecute was due to something that would torment agencies on both sides of the Atlantic over the coming decades: the decrypts could not be adduced as evidence in court, both for public policy reasons (potentially exposing the secret that Western governments had broken Soviet codes) and as a matter of legal evidence (decrypts were hearsay evidence, which, to have probative value, would require their Soviet authors, and the code breakers, to testify in court—both obviously fantasies).

Thus it was necessary to build cases against agents with sufficient evidence to meet standards of prosecution without using VENONA. Practically speaking, this invariably meant obtaining a confession. Bill Weisband's case was revealing in this regard. He was suspended from AFSA, but the FBI, guarding VENONA tightly, was unable to proceed against him in court, and he was never charged with espionage. He was convicted of contempt of court for failing to appear for a federal grand jury hearing about the Communist Party and sentenced to a year in prison. But Weisband thereafter remained at liberty, working as an insurance salesman until his death.

U.S. authorities encountered similar difficulties prosecuting an agent code-named SIMA. Judith Coplon was a petite twenty-seven-year-old Barnard graduate and communist. She was arrested in 1949 while meeting a Soviet intelligence officer on a Manhattan street corner. She was carrying a fake document on atomic research, which the FBI had planted at her work at the U.S. Department of Justice. When she was brought to trial, FBI special agent Robert Lamphere, to overcome the inability of adducing VENONA in court, testified that his suspicion had fallen on her from a reliable "confidential informant."

Coplon's defense attorney failed to undermine the prosecution's nebulous claim, and she was convicted. On appeal, however, her conviction was overturned due to irregularities in the Department of Justice's case—FBI special agents had listened to her conversations with her attorney. Coplon, erudite and well spoken, became a cause célèbre for the New Left that later emerged in the 1960s—viewed as an innocent victim of American show trials. As VENONA made clear, and as Lamphere knew, she was indeed a Soviet agent.[12]

THE TORMENT OF SECRECY

There were legitimate operational security reasons why VENONA was such a closely guarded secret. That secrecy, however, became a tragedy for public policy in the United States. Belief in the guilt or innocence of those accused of being Soviet spies became highly politicized: one of the most polarizing subjects in postwar American politics. In no case was this more true than that of Julius and Ethel Rosenberg, who were arrested in 1950, confessed to spying, and executed in the electric chair in June 1953 at Sing Sing. President Eisenhower refused to grant them clemency. If VENONA had been made public, Americans would have known that Julius Rosenberg was the organizer, with some assistance from Ethel, his wife, as we have seen, of a successful Soviet spy ring in New York that produced a wide range of scientific and technical intelligence—crucially, atomic secrets from Los Alamos. If the evidence had been made public, it is unlikely that Ethel would have been executed: the decrypts show that she played a minor role, facilitating her husband's espionage but little more. She did not even receive a Soviet code name. Meanwhile, the people who really fit the description of "central figures" for the theft of atomic secrets from Los Alamos, as the Department of Justice labeled the Rosenbergs, were Fuchs and Hall. Fuchs confessed; Hall never did so. Reading the FBI files on the Rosenbergs today, we are left with an inescapable impression that the DOJ pursued them with a vengeance because it lacked a prosecutable case against Hall.

Of course, while VENONA was still a secret there was no feasible way to adduce it in court. That was a nonstarter. The tragedy was, however, that the U.S. authorities continued to guard VENONA even when its secret was blown. The prolonged refusal by British and U.S. governments to declassify the VENONA decrypts left a generation and more of Americans with a distorted understanding of the early Cold War. For many, it became an article of faith that Julius and Ethel Rosenberg, like Alger Hiss, were innocent victims. The truthful testimony of Elizabeth Bentley and Whittaker Chambers, who had worked as GRU agents before and during

World War II, was widely ridiculed by American liberal commentators at the time. In fact, VENONA corroborated both.[13]

The U.S. and British governments continued to shroud VENONA in secrecy long after there were legitimate reasons for doing so. Stalin knew the VENONA secret through Weisband's espionage. U.S. intelligence would have suspected this when suspicion fell on Weisband in 1950. Whatever doubts there were, U.S. authorities would have had to assume that VENONA was blown by 1960. That year, the dramatic defection of two American NSA officials, William Martin and Bernon Mitchell, quashed any hope that VENONA was still unknown in the Kremlin. The two defectors gave a public press conference in Moscow in which they disclosed the nature and scale of U.S. SIGINT efforts. Any lingering doubts were obliterated three years later, in 1963, when Kim Philby defected to Moscow. As MI6 liaison officer in Washington in 1949, Philby had access to VENONA. But U.S. and British authorities continued to guard the secret, thus effectively deceiving the American public for another three decades. As special agent Lamphere, who led some of the major U.S. counterespionage investigations in the early Cold War, put it to the NSA director in 1950, "Who are you keeping the secret from? It's not from the KGB, it's from the American public."[14]

The secrecy surrounding VENONA allowed self-serving political demagogues to emerge. The most dangerous was the Republican senator from Wisconsin, Joseph McCarthy, who began leading an anti-communist witch hunt in 1950. He claimed in public that he had the names of 205 State Department communists who were "shaping" American foreign policy. McCarthy's claims were both dangerous and false, smearing reputations and wrecking the lives and careers of innocent people.

The two leading historians of VENONA and American communism, Harvey Klehr and John Haynes, have shown that the overwhelming majority of those named by McCarthy were not Soviet agents: of the 159 people McCarthy named, only 9 were Soviet agents identifiable in VENONA. The reality of Soviet espionage and Senator McCarthy is something that commentators have found difficult to grasp, that two opposing and apparently irreconcilable ideas were in fact correct: Soviet espionage was real, and presented a serious threat to American national security; *and* McCarthy's claims about it were false. President Truman was undoubtedly right when he stated in 1951 that the greatest asset the Kremlin had in the U.S. was McCarthy. As Lamphere put it: "McCarthy's star chamber proceedings, his lies and overstatements hurt our counterintelligence efforts."

To many Americans, the idea of an "enemy within" seemed plausible and helped to explain why the U.S. government, despite its immense power, seemed unable to prevent the onward march of communism and the emergence of the Soviet Union as a nuclear power. By January 1954, opinion polls found 50 percent of Americans with a favorable opinion of McCarthy, and only 29 percent opposed to him. Even Democrats, like the young congressman from Massachusetts, John F. Kennedy, found it opportune to adopt McCarthy's red-baiting slogans. He never denounced McCarthy. In fact, his brother, Robert Kennedy, briefly worked for McCarthy. Both sides of the political divide raced to outdo the other over anti-communism.[15]

HOT WAR IN KOREA

The Cold War's first hot conflict occurred in Korea. It sounded the alarm to the world about the dangers of two nuclear-armed superpowers squaring off against each other in a proxy conflict. The Korean War arose from intelligence failures and miscalculations.

When the war erupted, in June 1950, the U.S. government had no meaningful intelligence about the objectives and capacity of North Korean leader Kim Il Sung—grandfather of the country's current ruler, Kim Jong Un. Largely because of infighting, U.S. SIGINT agencies failed to provide advance warning of North Korea's invasion of the South. According to the NSA's previously secret history, when North Korean forces crossed the border, AFSA had "no person or group of persons working on the North Korea problem." It had no Korean linguists, dictionaries, traffic-analytic aids, or Korean typewriters. Incredibly, there were no documented high-priority U.S. national intelligence requirements in Korea until after the invasion began. The only requirement concerned tracking *Soviet* interest in the peninsula. Newly declassified records reveal that Korea was conspicuously absent from the intelligence assessments (the predecessor of the President's Daily Brief) given to Truman in the first six months of 1950. When those assessments finally did address Korea, on June 26, they did so through the prism of Soviet, not Chinese, involvement in Korea. According to Secretary of State Dean Rusk's later memoirs:

> After the attack occurred, some of our intelligence people, already
> bitten by Pearl Harbor, thumbed back through thousands of tidbits
> of information and found maybe six or seven items that seemed
> to point towards the invasion. They wanted to be able to say, "we
> warned you." That was just damn nonsense.[16]

Britain's intelligence services were caught similarly flat-footed. MI6 lacked human sources in North Korea (and the Soviet Union), while GCHQ's listening stations in Hong Kong and Japan were pointed not at Korea but the Soviet Union, and the violent communist insurgency that British forces were fighting to the southwest, in the colony of Malaya.[17]

After the start of hostilities, U.S. SIGINT and IMINT reconnaissance flights (using color-imagery intelligence for the first time) scrambled into action and provided valuable tactical, order-of-battle, and strategic intelligence about North Korean forces. The U.S. commander in Korea, General Douglas MacArthur, hero of America's Pacific campaigns during World War II, used SIGINT for his successful invasion in September 1950 of Incheon, near Seoul—one of the largest ever amphibious landings after D-Day. U.S. Army SIGINT (ASA) direction-finding antennae farms provided locations for combat against North Koreans. In the first month of the war, AFSA read one-third of all North Korean messages. By December, it was reading more than 90 percent.

MacArthur, habitually wearing a leather jacket, was stubborn. He used SIGINT when it suited him but dismissed it when he disagreed. As he drove his troops deep into North Korea through rice paddy fields and forest mountains, he insisted that China would not intervene: he ignored Chinese public statements about entering the war, as well as secret intelligence, from SIGINT, revealing the country's massing of troops on the border. Mac-Arthur delivered the same message to Truman when he met the president on Wake Island in October 1950. In November, Mao Zedong sent three hundred thousand troops over the Yalu River into the conflict against UN forces. The following month, Truman declared a national emergency. He later relieved MacArthur of his command. Combat in Korea became static trench warfare, roughly along the 38th parallel.

The war arose because of strategic miscalculations between East and West. Stalin allowed Kim Il Sung to attack the South because he misjudged U.S. grand strategy in Asia. Following America's failure to intervene to prevent Mao's communist victory in China in 1949, Stalin believed that the prevailing mood in Washington was to not interfere in Korea. He reached that conclu- sion by misinterpreting a stolen U.S. national security document—almost certainly supplied by Soviet agent Donald Maclean, head of the American desk in the Foreign Office—which excluded the Asian mainland from the U.S. defense perimeter. Stalin also knew from his spies in the West that Lon- don and Washington believed Moscow would not consider war before 1955. That was the earliest, they judged, that the devastated Soviet economy would recover from World War II. Having thus misinterpreted U.S. policy in Asia, and believing that he had until 1955 to maneuver freely, Stalin sanctioned a surprise attack by Kim on the South. Contrary to Stalin's assumption, however, Truman responded decisively to defend South Korea.[18]

On the U.S. side, it did not occur to intelligence agencies in Washing- ton that the outbreak of hostilities on the peninsula would come not from the Soviet Union, but from Kim Il Sung, through his request to Stalin. Washington fell into two classic analytical traps: mirror imaging and con- firmation bias. U.S. analysts understood the Soviets and North Koreans as reflecting what Washington would do, seeing what they wanted, not the reality. Both Britain and America thought that the Soviet Union did not want a conflict with the West because it was distracted by concerns in Europe (the lingering crisis over Berlin) and the Middle East (Soviet influence in Iran). Given the closed nature of Stalin's regime, the only way that U.S. or British intelligence could have known Stalin's true strategic calculations about Korea would have been from secret intelligence, which they woefully lacked. Second, the Truman administration mistakenly viewed communism in monolithic terms: that the Soviet Union ruled the entire communist world. The White House viewed China as a junior partner to the Soviet Union long after evidence indicated the contrary. It did not occur to the Truman administration that it would be Beijing, rather than Moscow, which would unleash its troops into the conflict. Washington's belief that communism was monolithic, and its refusal to recognize the power of nationalism alongside communism, would contribute to its subsequent grand strategy, the "domino theory" of communism in Asia, which would eventually justify the escalation of U.S. forces in Vietnam.[19]

SIGINT was essential in Korea due to America's failure of human intelligence there. While the CIA conducted some successful agent and paramilitary operations in the North, overall Korea was a CIA failure. In 1951, the agency proudly reported a growing number of agents operating in North Korea, overseen by Frank Wisner's CIA covert action outfit, the OPC. Matters, however, were not what they seemed. When John L. Hart, the agency's thirty-two-year-old new chief of station, arrived in Seoul in 1951, he was dismayed by what he found. Among the almost two hundred American personnel in the agency's station, there was not a single fluent Korean speaker. He soon discovered that most of the CIA's much-vaunted assets in the North were bogus—agents in fact controlled by North Korean forces. After instigating a program of polygraphing the "agents," he learned that much of their intelligence was simply North Korean disinformation. Although the agency was loath to admit it given its rivalries with other branches of military intelligence, the CIA acknowledged that it was unable to collect intelligence on North Korea. As Hart recalled, "SIGINT was almost the only intelligence worth having in Korea."[20]

Truman's new Director of Central Intelligence, Walter Bedell Smith, the fourth DCI in four years, took office in October 1950 and demanded results from the CIA in ways his predecessors had not. A slim, ashen-faced man who suffered no fools, Smith said what he meant and had a legendary temper. "Beetle," as he was known, had been Eisenhower's wartime chief of staff, and had represented the Allied Supreme Commander in Europe at the surrender of German forces. As U.S. ambassador in Moscow, Smith was a perfectionist and a workaholic, who pushed himself and others to the brink of physical collapse. He put both the DCI office, and the agency, on Washington's map, transforming it from an upstart organization with no real consequence to preeminent status within the U.S. intelligence community.

Within a week of taking office, Smith recognized that the organizational status of Wisner's semidetached covert action outfit, the OPC, was problematic and not getting results. Smith took personal control of it. But even that did not satisfy rumbling frictions between the OPC and the Office of Special Operations (OSO), whose function was clandestine collection—recruiting and running spies. In 1952, Smith created a new body in the CIA, the Directorate of Plans, which finally brought together OPC covert action and OSO agent recruitment. The new directorate's first head—called the Deputy Director of Plans (DDP)—was Allen Dulles, former OSS officer and Wall Street lawyer. Richard Helms was made head of the DDP's operations. Both Dulles and Helms would go on to become DCIs themselves. To complement the DDP, Smith consolidated the CIA's analytic functions into the Directorate of Intelligence (DI). Meanwhile, following a string of failures to provide policymakers with warnings of major global events, Smith created a new Office of National Estimates (ONE). Its task was to produce major intelligence assessments ("forecasts") based on collaborations of all sections of the U.S. intelligence community. By the end of November, ONE had a staff of fifty, led by William Langer, of Harvard, who had previously served as OSS head of research and analysis.

Smith's overhaul gave the CIA its shape for the next seven decades. Its principal strategic target was, and would remain, the Soviet Union. Smith, however, was not blinkered about the capabilities of human espionage in the Cold War. He fully recognized the difficulty of the task to be performed by the Directorate of Plans, recruiting agents with access to the secrets of decision makers in police states behind the Iron Curtain. He therefore embarked on a seismic shift within the agency to find technical solutions for collecting intelligence on the West's strategic enemy in the East. The West's intelligence struggle with the Soviet Union would thereafter be a "wizard" war, one of intelligence using science and technology, much as in World War II.[21]

As Eisenhower's wartime chief of staff, Smith had seen the benefits of SIGINT. His experience with ULTRA made him a firm believer, as DCI, in its value. Korea reinforced this. When he discovered U.S. SIGINT's lack of coordination, and his lack of jurisdiction over it as DCI, Smith wrote to Truman emphasizing the unique value of SIGINT. He declared himself "gravely concerned as to the security effectiveness with which the communications intelligence activities of the government are being conducted." In December 1950, Truman ordered an investigation into the status of U.S. SIGINT, headed by another New York lawyer, George Brownell. The Brownell Committee reported in June 1952, unusually quick by Washington standards.

Brownell's investigation provided a scathing indictment of U.S. SIGINT. "The Committee is convinced that the present organization of COMINT [communications intelligence] activities seriously impedes the efficiency of the operation, and prevents us from attracting and retaining as much top-quality scientific management manpower as this country ought to be investing in so important a field." It recommended giving AFSA effective authority over military-service SIGINT agencies that it hitherto lacked and allowing the DCI to oversee the coordinating of SIGINT with other intelligence activities.

That October, Truman signed a top secret eight-page presidential memorandum that put into effect the main recommendations of the Brownell Committee, with one significant addition: in keeping with AFSA's enhanced national authority, it was renamed the National Security Agency. The date of the NSA's founding was deliberately chosen as Election Day, November 4, 1952, when newswires were overrun with Eisenhower's presidential win. As he had been during the war, Eisenhower in the White House would be a strong supporter of SIGINT. The budget and personnel of the NSA—which would come to be known in Washington as "No Such Agency"—soon outstripped those of the CIA.

SOVIET SIGINT

Stalin observed Truman's colossal reforms in Washington and tried to centralize and unify his intelligence services. He created a new body, KI, to run both the MGB (or KGB) and military intelligence, GRU. He also attempted to bring cohesion to Soviet SIGINT, creating a new overall body, GUSS, in October 1949, two months after the first Soviet atomic bomb test. But GUSS would soon fizzle. Unlike in Britain and the United States, which had GCHQ and the NSA, the Soviet Union never had a permanent, single, dedicated SIGINT agency. Its code-breaking efforts during the Cold War were splintered between the KGB and the GRU.[22]

Stalin continued to prioritize human intelligence—espionage—over SIGINT. But VENONA broke the ascendency of Soviet espionage. It led to the collapse of networks in the United States and Britain, as the Center scrambled to exfiltrate key agents like Morris and Lona Cohen (code-named VOLUNTEERS), still at liberty, from the United States. In March 1951, a directive from the renamed KI instructed that every operative "must get it firmly into his head that the struggle against the Main Adversary [the United States] is no short-term undertaking but will constitute a fundamental substance of our work as a whole for a long time." Stalin's principal effort to advance Soviet cryptology was, inevitably, by stealing. In October 1951, the Soviet deputy minister of state security, Yevgeny Pitovranov, responsible for GUSS, directed all *rezidentury* to target for recruitment officials with access to British or American code books.[23]

Stalin knew perfectly well, however, that he could not cheat and steal his way to victory over Western cryptographers. From his spies in the West, the Soviet leader discovered Bletchley Park's wartime breakthroughs and realized that a key to the Soviet Union's struggle with the Main Adversary lay with electronic computing, building on Bletchley's work. The Cold War would thus become an East-West intelligence race to build the most powerful computers, capable of attacking each other's ciphers at speed. As the historian Jonathan Haslam has shown, Stalin established the Institute of Precision Mechanics and Computation Technology to build a Soviet computer for that purpose. The Kremlin had world-class mathematicians at its disposal for the calculations needed for such computers. Ultimately, however, such brains fell victim to the system of which they were a part. Under Stalinism, the characteristics of successful code breakers—imagination, creativity, and independent thought— were viewed as subversive. They were evidence of ideological nonconformity. Mathematicians and scientists who dared to think differently were reported by informants among their colleagues and came under blistering attacks from the regime. This suffocating and terrifying environment held back Soviet efforts to build powerful computers to attack encrypted Western communications.

Upon Stalin's death, on March 5, 1953, from a massive stroke, his experiment with unifying Soviet SIGINT also died. GUSS was liquidated and carved off between the MVD (KGB) and the SIGINT departments of the Soviet armed forces. Stalin had come to terms with what appeared to be an overall failure of Soviet foreign intelligence—both espionage and SIGINT. His networks were in disarray and his computers were second-rate. Stalin's death also brought the Korean War to an end, with an armistice signed in June 1953.

Stalin's death was protracted; in the four days prior, members of the Kremlin court, jockeying for power, had ample time to plan an overhaul of the broken state of Soviet foreign intelligence. On March 6, Beria, state security chief, consolidated the MGB and the MVD into a single organization under his command. His reign, however, was short-lived. In June 1953 Beria was arrested by order of Nikita Khrushchev, an ascendant player in the Kremlin. Beria, who himself had killed so many on falsified charges, was executed that December on false charges of being a British spy. He was shot, after falling to his knees and begging for his life. He thereafter became a nonperson, in grim Soviet lexicology. Subscribers to the *Great Soviet Encyclopedia* were advised to use a small razor blade to remove the entry for Beria and replace it with one on the Bering Sea. In March 1954, the consolidated MVD was renamed KGB. Its First Chief Directorate was responsible for foreign intelligence, and its Eighth Directorate for SIGINT. The GRU ran its own SIGINT department (also its Eighth Directorate). What they lacked in terms of cohesion, Soviet SIGINT made up for with manpower. By the later Cold War, it is thought that Soviet SIGINT dwarfed the size of U.S. and British SIGINT.[24]

BRITAIN'S SIGINT EMPIRE

When it comes to SIGINT, geography matters. In the postwar years, Britain's imperial holdings were vital for Western SIGINT collection. Britain's real estate across the globe offered valuable strategic locations for intercepting the shortwave, high-frequency, long-distance radio communications of the Soviet Union and communist China. Britain maintained a constellation of SIGINT installations in military sites, embassies, and consulates stretching from the dusts of Malta to Heliopolis, in Egypt; Sarafand, in Palestine; Habbaniya (near Baghdad), in Iraq; Abbottabad, in Pakistan (where years later Osama bin Laden would be found and killed); Delhi, in India; Kilindini, in Kenya; a site known as "HMS Anderson," near Colombo, in Ceylon (now Sri Lanka); and tropical Singapore and Stonecutters Island in Hong Kong. Aerial farms popped up in all these sites, pointed toward the Soviet Union. At a moment when Britain's military power was declining in the postwar years, SIGINT sites gave London inflated influence in Washington, as Whitehall's mandarins quickly realized. Britain's postwar grand design was to make itself indispensable to the United States in any way possible. Intelligence generally, and SIGINT in particular, was a golden ticket for London.[25]

Britain's empire and the Commonwealth were, from the outset, central to UKUSA. New light emerges on the origins of Five Eyes from now-declassified UKUSA records. The original engine room was the Anglo-American SIGINT relationship. It grew, however, into more than just an Anglo-American club—into an unprecedented *Western* intelligence alliance. The Dominions—Canada, Australia, and New Zealand—were incorporated as the Cold War set in because they had shared values about code-breaking and security in democracies. There were also practical reasons for their membership: they allowed for collaborating on round-the-clock, follow-the-sun collections. There was nothing comparable in the Soviet bloc and Warsaw Pact countries.[26]

Intelligence both shaped Britain's withdrawal from empire in the postwar years and also, in some instances, perpetuated its empire, amid a succession of counterinsurgency wars. Historians have long noted how the U.S. government picked up, adopted, and paid for remnants of Britain's empire amid the Cold War. As early as 1948, the CIA warned Truman that he would have to be prepared to do so. Its assessment was prescient. SIGINT was a striking example of how Britain was acting as Greece to America's Rome, to borrow Harold Macmillan's phrase. In Cyprus, the NSA funded British SIGINT collection sites. In the Indian Ocean, Britain's territory of Diego Garcia was so important for the United States that its inhabitants, the Chagos Islanders, were forcibly and illegally relocated. It was a shameful chapter, as a court case brought by the Chagosians against the British government as recently as 2021 shows. The U.S. national security adviser, Henry Kissinger, valued the importance of Diego Garcia to SIGINT so much that he permitted a British SIGINT official in Washington to attend a National Security Council meeting—something he would not have permitted for the citizen of any other country, as he emphasized.[27]

Britain's most important SIGINT outpost in Asia was Hong Kong. Following Mao's seizure of power in China in 1949, the U.S. government did not have an embassy in mainland China. This naturally made the neighboring British colony of Hong Kong vital. According to the CIA's head of Far Eastern affairs in the Office of National Estimates, Russell Jack Smith, "Hong Kong became an American watchtower on China."* The CIA was so bereft of intelligence on China that it resorted to buying fish and chips in Hong Kong, to read the newspapers from the mainland they were wrapped in. The Korean War escalated the colony's strategic importance for American SIGINT collection in Asia. U.S. SIGINT threw huge resources into British intelligence installations there. In London, a recurring nervous theme of Joint Intelligence Committee assessments became Hong Kong's vulnerability to attack by China's People's Liberation Army (PLA). What would happen if China invaded Hong Kong? British SIGINT installations were given detailed evacuation and "burn" instructions. When Britain eventually lowered its flag in Hong Kong at the end of the century, in 1997, British SIGINT facilities were transferred to Australia; the NSA also continues to run a vast facility with the Australian Signals Directorate, the ASD, near Alice Springs, known as Pine Gap.[28]

---

* National Intelligence Estimates were drafted by the staff of the Office of National Estimates; the Board of National Estimates revised and published them.

CHAPTER SEVEN

CLIMATE OF TREASON

"Were you a spy then?"

"Not quite." . . .

"Really I was still a thief. No great patriot. No great hero. They
had just made my skills official."

—Michael Ondaatje, *The English Patient*

FOUR YEARS AFTER AMERICA'S ATOMIC WEAPONS ENDED
World War II, the Soviet Union successfully tested its own nuclear bomb,
in August 1949. It caught British and U.S. intelligence by surprise, blew
apart the postwar international order, and permanently changed relations
between East and West.

It was just five months later, in January 1950, when Klaus Fuchs confessed to British intelligence that he had passed atomic secrets from the
MANHATTAN Project to Soviet intelligence. The next day, on the other
side of the Atlantic, Alger Hiss was sentenced to five years' imprisonment
for perjury before a grand jury—for lying about the nature and length of
his acquaintance with the GRU agent Whittaker Chambers. Barely a week
later, Fuchs was charged and imprisoned in London, leading to headlines
across the world that Soviet spies had delivered the atom bomb to Stalin.

The following week, Senator Joseph McCarthy aired his claims of communists crawling through the corridors of power. It was a climate of treason.[1]

In May 1951, Guy Burgess and Donald Maclean defected to the Soviet Union, revealing that Soviet spies had burrowed deep inside the most sensitive parts of Britain's government. Their defection initiated what would become the longest, and most complex, counterespionage investigation in British history, which would take thirty years to complete: the hunt for the five Cambridge Spies.

Within the Kremlin today, Soviet agents from early in the Cold War, like Fuchs and the five Cambridge Spies, occupy pride of place in the annals of foreign intelligence. The SVR showered them in hagiographical terms on its centenary in 2021. The reality is different. Contrary to the impression given by the SVR, these agents conducted their hugely damaging espionage for Moscow at times despite, rather than because of, the KGB and Stalin. The damage they inflicted on British and American national security was the result of their motivation and skill as spies, not the professionalism and methods of the KGB, which at times badly let them down. Furthermore, contrary to what the SVR portrays today, British intelligence came close to catching all of them.[2]

"THE MAN WHO STOLE THE ATOM BOMB"

Five days before the Soviet atomic test in Kazakhstan in August 1949, Roscoe Hillenkoetter, the DCI, told Truman that the earliest probable date for Moscow to detonate an atomic weapon was the mid-1950s. British intelligence made similarly mistaken predictions. The truth is, as we have seen, London and Washington lacked any meaningful intelligence on Stalin's secrets. The best intelligence they obtained on the secret Soviet atomic project came from radioactive particles wafting at high altitude in the Pacific, detected by U.S. sensor-equipped aircraft, which alerted Washington and the rest of the world that Stalin had detonated an atomic device. His acquisition of an A-bomb would embolden Stalin's strategic risk-taking. Without nukes, it is unlikely that he would have backed Northern forces in the Korean War in 1950.[3]

As we saw earlier, Klaus Fuchs provided the Soviets with information that accelerated their development of an atomic bomb. When news of his espionage broke, FBI director J. Edgar Hoover claimed that Fuchs "gave Stalin the atom bomb," and labeled it "the crime of the century." The reality was less straightforward. The Soviet atomic bomb was built by a huge *Soviet* industrial and engineering effort. Fuchs's espionage, and that of Stalin's other atom spies, helped Soviet scientists build a bomb more quickly and cheaply than otherwise, avoiding the trial and errors that Western scientists had experienced on the MANHATTAN Project. To this day, this remains the essence of scientific and technical intelligence collection: stealing military and industrial secrets saves money and expedites research and development.

Over his seven-year career as a Soviet agent, Fuchs transmitted to Moscow complex formulas for refining ordinary uranium into bomb-grade, as well as the technical plans for production facilities, and engineering principles for the "implosion" technique. This allowed Soviet scientists to build an atomic bomb using plutonium, a substance easier to manufacture than bomb-grade uranium. Fuchs's intelligence allowed Stalin's nuclear scientists to bypass building a uranium-based bomb, like the one dropped on Hiroshima, which required extensive mining and engineering to extract the uranium 235 isotope, and helped them move straight to developing a plutonium bomb, like the one dropped on Nagasaki. Alarmingly for the West, plutonium bombs required less time to build and were more easily replicable. The Soviet bomb was built through forced labor, with entire secret towns devoted to the dangerous work. The number of dragooned workers who died from radiation exposure remains unknown.[4]

Fuchs's espionage was discovered in the summer of 1949, when British and U.S. code breakers decrypted a VENONA message describing an atomic scientist code-named CHARLES. He was quickly identified as Fuchs, at that time working at Britain's own atomic research establishment at Harwell, in Oxfordshire. Fuchs had previously been on MI5's radar and went through its wartime vetting, as we saw in chapter four.[5]

When Fuchs was being vetted again after the war, Whitehall authorities were eager to ensure his participation in British nuclear research. In the wake of the McMahon Act, which prohibited the U.S. from sharing nuclear research with foreign countries, the British government needed Fuchs as much as the Soviets did. A cryptic note in Fuchs's MI5 dossier from October 1946, as he was being vetted, noted: "It would undoubtedly be said that, if FUCHS proves to be a dangerous customer, that his technical ability is such that [British] Atomic Energy would suffer very considerably if he were removed from his current employment." It was thus important for Britain that Fuchs was not denied access to Britain's nuclear research. He would play an important role, following Britain's decision, in 1947, to develop a nuclear weapon of its own. "We've got to have the bloody Union Jack on top of it," as the foreign secretary, Ernest Bevin, memorably put it—a secret so closely guarded within the British government that only a few members of Clement Attlee's cabinet knew.[6]

News that Stalin had tested an atomic weapon in 1949, combined with evidence the following month from VENONA that Fuchs had betrayed atomic secrets to the Kremlin, lit a fire under Attlee and Britain's military leaders. A now-declassified British military damage assessment put the situation in stark terms: the Americans were calling off trilateral talks on atomic cooperation, established to repair relations after the McMahon Act. Meanwhile, the report noted, the Russians, "starting from scratch," without the benefit of collaborating with America during the war, had beaten Britain to detonating a nuclear weapon. Fuchs's espionage now gutted Britain's primary strategy, "full integration and interchange of information with the Americans on atomic research." It also blew apart Britain's efforts to acquire a "stockpile of bombs in this country" before the Soviet Union. Britain, bankrupt and destitute, enduring bread rationing for the first time since the war, had failed to become a nuclear power.[7]

MI5 placed Fuchs under round-the-clock surveillance: it tapped his telephones, intercepted his mail, and had surveillance teams follow him wherever he went. Its investigations over the next four months amassed a wealth of information detailing his private life, contained in fifteen thick volumes of files, including details about an affair he was having and that he was a bad driver. Its surveillance, however, produced no evidence of espionage. There was, we now know, good reason for this: by 1949, the scientist had cut off contact with Soviet intelligence. There was nothing for MI5 to detect. By that year, he had achieved his primary espionage goal: the Soviet Union had obtained its own atomic weapon, which Fuchs believed was essential for advancing world peace and the communist revolution.[8]

MI5's breakthrough in the case came through the work of its lead interrogator, Jim Skardon. Over the course of four interviews with Fuchs in his office at Harwell, Skardon, a former Special Branch officer, gradually befriended him, gained his confidence, and then ultimately tricked him into confessing. Skardon let the scientist believe that if he confessed, he would be able to find a position at a British university. After stonewalling Skardon during the first three interviews, at the fourth, Fuchs abruptly broke down, evidently unable to continue lying. He gave Skardon a full confession, admitting that he had given the Russians "all the information in his possession about the British and American research in connection with the atomic bomb." He also revealed that during a trip to visit his sister in the United States in 1947, he had obtained information on a "hydrogen super bomb," which he handed to his Soviet handler in London, the NKVD *rezident* Alexander Feklisov, previously handler of Julius Rosenberg, a Soviet agent in Los Alamos, whom we met above. After confessing, Fuchs realized that Skardon had lied; no university position in Britain awaited him. In a trial lasting just ninety minutes at the Old Bailey, Fuchs was found guilty and sentenced to the maximum fourteen years' imprisonment. Like Alan Nunn May before, Fuchs failed to realize that, without his self-incriminating confession, British authorities would never have been able to prosecute him. Released from prison early, and stripped of his naturalized British citizenship, Fuchs resettled in East Germany, where he continued with nuclear research. He lived until the eve of East Germany's collapse.[9]

During a subsequent interrogation in prison, Skardon pushed Fuchs to explain how, as a matter of conscience, he was able to betray his friends, his colleagues, and the country that had taken him in as a refugee from the Nazis. Fuchs's answers gave investigators a chilling psychological profile of a professional spy. He said that he used his Marxist discipline to establish "two separate compartments" in his mind. The first was for his friendships and work colleagues and those he loved. The second, which he concealed from everyone around him, transcended all personal loyalties and was reserved for his secret work for Russia. It was, he told Skardon, a form of "controlled schizophrenia." It was one of the most alarming counterespionage insights that a Western intelligence service could encounter, an ideologically committed agent with a split personality, able to lock away his innermost feelings. There is little that any security intelligence agency could do to detect someone with such a devious, damaged psychology, capable of hiding his or her inner thoughts.[10]

When the Fuchs case broke, Kim Philby had risen to become MI6's liaison officer in Washington. That position gave him, and thus the Kremlin, access to VENONA. The American cryptologist, Meredith Gardner, later recalled the keen interest that Philby took in his work decrypting VENONA messages. Thanks to his access to VENONA, Philby was able to warn the Center that MI5 had identified Fuchs. The Center may have gotten a warning to Fuchs that he was under suspicion, which could have been the reason he broke off contact in 1949. If so, he would not have been able to admit this during his MI5 interrogation without revealing the existence of a Soviet agent inside British intelligence. It is impossible to know for sure if this transpired, because available records do not cast light on it. It is equally possible that Fuchs's mental instability caused him to disregard a KGB warning about his safety. It remains a mystery why the KGB failed to exfiltrate him.[11]

After Fuchs's confession, MI5 discovered that it had come within a whisker of detecting him three years earlier. In 1947, on the basis of information from a Soviet intelligence defector, MI5 had dispatched Skardon to interview Ursula Kuczynski—SONYA, whom we met above. The service correctly suspected that she was involved with Soviet wartime espionage. Interviewing Kuczynski at her home in Oxfordshire, on the edge of the Cotswolds, Skardon got nothing useful from her at the time. If MI5 had probed more deeply, it would have discovered that she was Fuchs's handler, the "woman from Banbury" to whom he had passed secrets, as Fuchs said in his confession. Skardon's interrogation of SONYA could have unmasked them both. Nor was this Fuchs's only close call. In an address book belonging to one of the agents identified by the Soviet defector Igor Gouzenko, there was an entry for a Kristel Heinemann. Had MI5 and the FBI cross-checked and found her maiden name, they would have discovered that she was in fact Fuchs's sister, married to a well-known communist in Cambridge, Massachusetts. Such seemingly unrelated strands in a web of espionage, however, only appear blindingly clear with hindsight.[12]

The Fuchs case strained Anglo-American intelligence relations to a breaking point. To FBI director Hoover's consternation, MI5 did not initially allow his special agents to interview Fuchs in London, claiming legal constraints. But a reading of the FBI-MI5 correspondence today leaves us with the inescapable impression that MI5 did not want the FBI looking through its dirty laundry. It was only when Hoover effectively threatened to shut down intelligence sharing with MI5 to a "mere formality" that the British service relented. The British government placated Hoover by granting him an honorary knighthood (KBE), at an investiture ceremony at Britain's embassy in Washington in the autumn of 1950.[13]

President Truman was also exasperated with the British government for other reasons. In January 1950, Attlee's government recognized the People's

Republic of China, while Truman's administration continued to support nationalist forces in Taiwan. But the president did not let such strategic differences with London, or Fuchs's espionage, escalate too far. When it came to Soviet espionage, Truman's White House had its own problems. Trilateral talks about atomic cooperation between the Americans, British, and Canadians, which Fuchs's case had derailed, were soon resumed.[14]

BUSTING THE ROSENBERG SPY RING

Fuchs's arrest was a disaster for the KGB (then known as the MGB). His prison interviews led the FBI to dismantle a major New York–based Soviet spy ring led by Julius Rosenberg. In prison, Fuchs identified his American KGB courier, Harry Gold (code-named ARNO). Gold confessed on May 22, 1950, and began cooperating with the FBI. (He was in fact already known to the bureau, as his name had been given to them by the Soviet defector Elizabeth Bentley.) The bureau chased down Gold's leads across the country, filling 108 now-declassified files. Its investigations soon led the FBI, in early June, to David Greenglass. He had been a U.S. Army technical sergeant; while at Los Alamos, David made implosion lenses for the plutonium bomb. Fearing that Fuchs's confession placed key Soviet agents in Greenglass's network in jeopardy, the Center instructed David and his wife, Ruth, also a Soviet agent, to flee to Mexico. The FBI, however, arrested the couple on the day of their planned escape. They immediately started cooperating. David was sentenced to fifteen years in prison, while Ruth avoided prosecution as part of their plea agreement. Greenglass's evidence led the FBI to his sister, Ethel Rosenberg, and her husband, Julius. The latter was arrested on July 17, 1950, his wife a month later. Using Greenglass's evidence, the Rosenbergs were tried in court, convicted, sentenced to death in 1951, and executed in June 1953—the only Soviet spies to be executed in America during the Cold War.[15]

For Soviet intelligence, Fuchs's confession acted like a series of time bombs, waiting to go off at any moment. Ultimately, the KGB's decision to use known communist sympathizers (like Rosenberg and Gold) as Soviet agents, and have Gold operate as a courier for both Greenglass and Fuchs, was their undoing. It was poor tradecraft. Once exposed, Gold brought down both networks. The FBI placed the other main agent in the atomic spy network, Ted Hall, under round-the-clock surveillance for almost a year. When interviewed, Hall deflected the FBI's questions and refused to confess. He concluded, correctly, that without a confession, the FBI would be unable to prosecute. The bureau had no choice but to let him go, although he was obviously barred from working on sensitive atomic research. Four decades later, after the Soviet Union's collapse, his name was revealed in published VENONA decrypts. Hall, unrepentant, admitted his espionage for the Soviet Union, crowing that he had carried it out to undo America's monopoly on nuclear weapons, which he saw as threatening global security.[16]

THE CAMBRIDGE SPIES

Washington got its first indication of the Cambridge Five—Donald Maclean, Guy Burgess, Kim Philby, Anthony Blunt, and John Cairncross—from VENONA in the spring of 1951. This derived from an old wartime decrypt mentioning an agent, code-named HOMER, who was working in the Foreign Office and whose wife was pregnant. After narrowing down potential culprits, HOMER was identified as Maclean. At that point, Maclean was the head of the American desk in the Foreign Office, a position that placed him at the apex of Anglo-American strategic planning regarding the Soviet Union and gave him access to atomic secrets. Britain's foreign secretary, Herbert Morrison, agreed to place Maclean under MI5 surveillance in the hope of catching him meeting his Soviet handler.[17]

MI5's plainclothes surveillance team followed Maclean as he went about his daily life. They tapped his phone at his Surrey home, opened his mail, and installed listening devices. On several occasions, Maclean met with Burgess, who had recently returned from serving in Britain's embassy in Washington. Burgess was already a worry to MI5 due to a spate of drunken escapades that had posed "security concerns" for the British. At the time, however, there was nothing suspicious about two Foreign Office colleagues getting together. Furthermore, there was nothing about Burgess's character that suggested he was a spy: his boorish, drunken lifestyle did not fit the profile of existing Soviet agents. MI5 attached little significance when its "watchers" tailed Maclean and observed him meeting Burgess in a pub on Friday, May 25, 1951. An MI5 officer followed the two men into the pub and tried to hear what they were saying. His report filed the next day makes for painful reading in retrospect. MI5 noted that Burgess "appears to have something on his mind and is, in fact, obviously deeply worried." The report went on: "He will order a large gin (his favourite tipple) and will then pace the bar for a few seconds, pour the neat spirit down his throat and walk out, or order another and repeat the performance. In the open he frequently shows indecision, with apparently his mind in turmoil." The report concluded: "With CURZON [Maclean] there is an air almost of conspiracy between the two." The MI5 undercover officer standing in the pub next to Burgess and Maclean that day had no idea how right he was. Later that same day, the two Soviet spies would defect to the Soviet Union. MI5 was standing next to two of the most damaging spies in British history on the day they disappeared.[18]

Their KGB handler at the London *rezidentura*, Yuri Modin, orchestrated an escape as the net tightened. Burgess and Maclean traveled on a tourist ferry (which did not require passports) from England's south coast to France and from there, via a circuitous route and equipped with KGB-provided false passports, they made it to Moscow. By the time MI5's watchers resumed work on that Monday morning, the two British diplomats were in fact already behind the Iron Curtain. Maclean's possessions, including his Foreign Office work diary, which MI5 trawled through, revealed nothing about his plans for disappearance. As far as their families, friends, and MI5 were concerned, the two men had vanished.

As British and U.S. intelligence would later discover, it was Kim Philby

(STANLEY) who warned Maclean that he been exposed. When Maclean was identified as HOMER from VENONA, which Philby had access to, Philby sent an urgent warning to him to flee. He did so through Burgess, who had been living as a lodger with Philby while working at the Washington embassy. Burgess's drinking and obnoxious behavior had alienated colleagues and American officials—and attracted the attention of the local Virginia police. He was being recalled to London in disgrace, which provided the opportunity to send a warning with him to Maclean in London. Philby and Burgess worked out their plan without involving the KGB *rezidentura* or the Center. Burgess dutifully passed a warning to Maclean, but failed to honor his other promise to Philby: to not defect with Maclean. Philby realized that if Burgess escaped with Maclean, suspicion would soon fall on Philby, given his close association with Burgess.[19]

The strain of living a double life as a Soviet agent had taken its toll on Maclean, who had suffered a mental breakdown and required psychiatric treatment. Far from easing the workload on him, as Maclean begged his Soviet handlers, the Center continued to pressure him to extract as much information as possible from inside the Foreign Office. When Burgess arrived in London, he, too, appeared to his KGB handler to be teetering on the edge of a nervous breakdown. Facing two apparently burned-out agents, the Center decided to extract them both. But it left Stalin's prize agent, Philby, dangerously exposed.

Philby sits in the pantheon of heroes of Russian foreign intelligence— one of the greatest spies in history. His portrait hangs in the historic Memory Room in the SVR headquarters. In 2018, Moscow's mayor dedicated a new square to Philby, near SVR headquarters. But these and other Russian descriptions of the Cambridge Spies are little more than historical theater, based on a carefully packaged and sanitized version of the past. In truth, the KGB badly let Philby down, and he, in turn, betrayed his fellow Soviet agents, Burgess and Maclean. This secret, now uncovered in opened British records, is one that Putin's Kremlin does not wish publicized. Philby lied to everyone to save himself.[20]

When Burgess defected with Maclean, Philby panicked. He sent an urgent request for a rendezvous with the KGB *rezident* in New York, Valeri Makayev (HARRY). But Makayev failed to appear. Philby was left to improvise on his own. As Philby had anticipated, Burgess's disappearance with Maclean immediately cast suspicion on himself. He set about doing his best to deflect the attention of Britain's spy chiefs.[21]

Philby initially told MI6 chief Stewart Menzies that it was inconceivable that Burgess was involved in espionage. However, a month after the disappearance of the two men, Philby changed his tune. He sent MI6 and MI5 a summary he claimed to have pieced together suggesting that the possibility Burgess was a Soviet agent could not be ruled out. While Burgess was living with him in Washington, Philby explained, he "had available the essential requirements of an espionage agent," such as a camera and a sunlamp (the latter could be used for exposing secret writing). Burgess was in the habit of working from home after office hours, frequently traveled to New York, and even left behind a book on the Marxism of Stalin, Philby claimed.

Each could have had an entirely innocent explanation, but taken together, Philby helpfully pointed out to British intelligence, they seemed to suggest a more sinister interpretation. He went further still. At a moment when British and U.S. intelligence were scrambling to locate the two missing British diplomats, Philby suggested that there may have been a "very early connection" between Burgess and Maclean since their time at Cambridge; it was "even conceivable that one recruited the other," Philby noted, and "if either had succeeded in getting wind of the investigation, it would be natural for them to concert a joint getaway." Distraught at Burgess's having disobeyed his instructions and thereby directed suspicion at him, Philby threw both Burgess and Maclean under the bus. Philby's letter was a masterful collection of lies and innuendo designed to save his own skin. He deliberately misspelled Maclean's name to insinuate how little he knew him.[22]

In fact, as Philby knew well, *he* had been responsible for Burgess and

Maclean's recruitment as Soviet agents, acting as a talent spotter for the KGB. *He* had been the one who, "getting wind of the investigation," had helped Maclean get away. Furthermore, Burgess's regular trips to New York were because Philby used Burgess as a courier with his KGB controller in New York, Makayev.

Despite Philby's best efforts, as he had predicted, his association with Burgess made his job in MI6 untenable. DCI Walter Bedell Smith informed MI6 that Philby was no longer welcome as its representative in Washington. He was recalled to London and, in December 1951, interrogated by MI5 about his connection with Burgess. His interrogator was Helenus "Buster" Milmo, a wartime MI5 officer, lawyer, and later a High Court judge. Milmo had earned his nickname from his combative cross-examination style.

In his interviews with Milmo, Philby drew on a long-standing speech stammer to disarm his inquisitor. Well versed in all of MI5 and MI6's interrogation techniques, Philby knew that without a confession, Britain's director of public prosecutions would lack the necessary evidence to bring a case against him in court. Philby also had loyal and powerful supporters within MI6, not least its new chief, John "Sinbad" Sinclair, who convinced himself that Philby was the innocent victim of unfortunate circumstances.

Philby was officially retired from MI6 with a golden handshake of £5,000 over lunch with the chief at the Savoy. He found work as a journalist, spending much of his time inebriated. Milmo nonetheless emerged from his interviews with Philby convinced that he was a Soviet agent. Speculation and disagreement continued to swirl between Britain's intelligence services and their American counterparts about whether Philby was indeed the "third man." Their suspicion increased as they looked back at the disclosures of Konstantin Volkov, the NKVD near-defector in Istanbul in 1945, and those of the earlier GRU defector in 1939, Walter Krivitsky, about a Soviet agent inside British intelligence. Such assessments remained in the realm of counterespionage, though, not evidence for a legal prosecution.

In November 1955, the British press reported that an MP in the

House of Commons had asked the government whether Philby was the third man. Britain's foreign minister at the time, Harold Macmillan, was forced to do the only thing that available evidence permitted: to clear Philby publicly. Philby held a triumphant press conference, serving beer and sandwiches to the media crammed into his mother's London apartment. He flatly denied that he was a Soviet agent. Lying through his teeth, he said: "The last time I spoke to a Communist, knowing he was one, was in 1934."[23]

With Burgess and Maclean's disappearances and assumed defections, MI5 was on the heels of Anthony Blunt and John Cairncross (the fourth and fifth men). As British intelligence discovered years later, Blunt broke into Burgess's apartment when the latter disappeared and ransacked it—they used to be roommates—to destroy incriminating evidence linking him to the other members of the Cambridge spy ring. Blunt, however, overlooked notes from a prewar Whitehall meeting. After MI5 questioned those present at the meeting, the author of the notes was identified as John Cairncross. He was placed under close MI5 surveillance. Watchers observed him acting erratically. In reality, as British intelligence later discovered, he was doing so because he was desperately trying to meet his KGB controller. MI5's Skardon interviewed Cairncross, but like Philby, the Soviet agent refused to confess, claiming that his suspicious behavior was the result of an affair he was having with an unnamed Frenchwoman.[24]

It did not take long for suspicion to fall on Blunt. Britain's intelligence services received a tip from a friend of Burgess's, Goronwy Rees, a fellow of All Souls College, Oxford. He claimed that Burgess had tried to recruit him and Blunt as Soviet agents before the war. The Soviets indeed thought they had recruited Rees, giving him the code name GROSS. As evidence piled up, some of Blunt's colleagues and friends in MI5 were shocked by the idea that this slight, erudite art historian, fellow of Trinity College, Cambridge, the King and later Queen's art curator, could be a Soviet spy. With hindsight, MI5 records reveal Blunt's duplicity and the damage he caused.

In the wake of Burgess and Maclean's disappearances, Guy Liddell, then MI5's deputy director general, turned to none other than Blunt himself for advice about them. Blunt must have known them from Cambridge, Liddell asked. Blunt was a paradigm of helpfulness to Liddell. Eventually Liddell realized that Blunt's Cambridge association with Burgess, Maclean, and Philby must make him a suspect too. As Soviet intelligence archives reveal, Blunt had used his MI5 position to help the KGB plan Burgess and Maclean's exfiltration from Britain. Blunt informed the KGB about MI5's surveillance, including the fact—extraordinary from today's perspective—that its watchers did not work after Saturday morning on the weekends. That allowed the KGB to plan their escape accordingly. MI5's watchers were being watched by the KGB.

After the exfiltration of Burgess and Maclean, Blunt kept the Center informed of Britain's investigation into the two missing diplomats as it unfolded. The Center instructed Blunt's handler, Yuri Modin, to encourage him to escape to Moscow as well. In a meeting at the Courtauld Institute of Art in London, where Blunt was the director, Modin tried to persuade him to flee. Blunt's response left him speechless: he was unwilling to exchange the comfortable, prestigious surroundings of the Courtauld Institute for the brutal gray reality of Stalin's Russia: "I know perfectly well how your people live," Blunt told Modin, "and I can assure you that it will be very hard, almost unbearable, for me to do likewise."

Blunt was ideologically committed to the myth of the Soviet Union but not to its reality. In April 1952, when MI5 interrogated Blunt, he refused to confess. Skardon sensed that he was holding something back but believed his secret had to do with his homosexuality, which was illegal in Britain at the time. As with its investigations into Philby and Cairncross, MI5 failed to gain prosecutable evidence against Blunt—not due to an establishment cover-up, as is often alleged, but because of an inability to assemble sufficient admissible evidence to bring a case against him.[25]

PURGE PROCEDURES

Burgess and Maclean's defections, and the suspicions harbored about Philby, fell like a wrecking ball on intelligence agencies on both sides of the Atlantic. In Britain, it led Whitehall, under increasing pressure from Washington, to redraw its entire security architecture for those employed on sensitive work. Following Fuchs's exposure in the autumn of 1950, Attlee's Labour government established a "purge procedure," officially known by its cabinet title, GEN 183, to prevent "subversives" (read: communists) with divided loyalties from engaging in work that allowed access to British state secrets. Up to that point, background checks for those working in sensitive posts were limited, as we have seen, to negative vetting. This amounted to checking a person's name against MI5 records. It was an inadequate security system that relied on MI5 having accurate, up-to-date, and identifiable information about a candidate's political associations. The exposure of Maclean, Burgess, and later Philby, all men with the "right" background, education, and class, revealed its fundamental flaw. They slipped by unnoticed.[26]

Britain's intelligence services, lacking manpower for the task, resisted positive vetting—proactive investigations. MI5 feared positive vetting would overwhelm it. Pressure from Washington to reform security vetting in Britain had increased after Fuchs, but then became acute after Burgess and Maclean's disappearances. In a meeting on atomic intelligence held in London between British, American, and Canadian governments two months after the two Soviet agents disappeared, the American delegation made clear that the U.S. government would not share secrets with any foreign government, even its former wartime allies, unless they used suitable background checks.

Positive vetting reformed Britain's civil service. It contributed to the decline of the old-boy network wherein school and university connections opened the doors of power in Whitehall. It meant, for the first time, that all those working in sensitive areas with access to state secrets had to undergo the same checks, irrespective of their education and social class.

Initially, MI5 was convinced that "just a few thousand officials" would require positive vetting. But by 1955, eleven thousand people working in nuclear weapons research had been positively vetted (with three thousand more on a waiting list); in other positions of government seven thousand people had been positively vetted (with six thousand more waiting).[27]

In the United States, Joe McCarthy's Red Scare led to widespread "purges" of the U.S. civil service: between 1947 and 1956, twenty-seven thousand federal employees were sacked and twelve thousand more resigned. All were publicly named. In Britain, the total for the same period was just 124. Not one of those sacked British civil servants was named. In most cases, those found to pose a security threat were moved to different, less sensitive positions. Positive vetting did not, however, offer perfect security; Soviet spies would still manage to penetrate Britain's most sensitive areas later in the Cold War.[28]

RING OF FIVE

In December 1961, a thirty-five-year-old KGB major, Anatoli Golitsyn, defected to the CIA. Stationed in Helsinki, Golitsyn simply walked into the U.S. embassy and asked for asylum in return for intelligence. Debriefed steadily through 1962 by the CIA, he claimed to know about an almost endless army of spies. He identified some genuine Soviet agents, though much of his information turned out to be "imprecise." Like many defectors determined to ensure their status, he was continually remembering new facts. He did, though, provide the first confirmation that Philby was indeed a Soviet agent.

Golitsyn told British intelligence that the Center called the Cambridge Spies the "Ring of Five," because all five had been at the university together. In fact, while they were all Cambridge graduates, they had not studied there at the same time. Even though Golitsyn (code-named KAGO by the British) admitted that he had not actually seen KGB files on the Cambridge

Spies, and despite his recognized tendency to exaggerate, key British and U.S. intelligence officers took his claims literally. The result was that the next two decades were spent chasing phantoms, nonexistent Soviet agents who matched Golitsyn's descriptions.[29]

The major breakthrough in the case against Philby came in July 1962, when a former wartime MI5 officer, Victor Rothschild, had a chance meeting at a cocktail party with a friend, Flora Solomon, at the Weizmann Institute in Israel. Outraged by anti-Israeli articles being published by Philby, who was living in Beirut working as a journalist covering the Middle East, Solomon—a Russian-born executive at Marks & Spencer—told Rothschild that Philby had attempted to recruit her as a Soviet agent before the war. As Solomon's MI5 dossier—declassified in 2022—reveals, she had appeared on MI5's radar a decade earlier, back in 1952, during its original investigation into Philby (whom MI5 code-named PEACH).

One of the MI5 officers who reviewed Solomon's case was Stella Rimington, later MI5's first female director general. In a sixty-seven-paragraph analysis, she concluded that there was something "very fishy" about Solomon. When MI5 interviewed her in 1962, Solomon stated that if she had been previously asked about Philby, she would have revealed his attempted recruitment of her. It was thus a missed opportunity for MI5. Nevertheless, now armed with this information, Philby's friend Nicholas Elliott, MI6's former head of station in Beirut, interviewed Philby in January 1963. According to Philby's KGB-sponsored memoirs, he refused to confess.

That was another lie, as newly opened British records reveal. In fact, according to notes taken by Elliott—only made public in 2019—Philby made a partial confession. As he sat in his apartment in Beirut, with traffic noise from an open window all but drowning out Elliott's tape recording, Philby admitted to working as a Soviet agent from 1936 to 1946. He claimed to have seen the error of his ways that year and to have broken off contact with Soviet intelligence. He admitted that he had indeed sent a warning to Maclean in 1951, but falsely stated that this was a one-off, done purely out of personal friendship. When news of Philby's confession reached MI5 and the FBI, they felt vindicated. However, they had once again been deceived. Less than a week after his confession, Philby vanished, only to resurface six months later in Moscow. At that point, the British and U.S. governments realized that Philby had in fact been a Soviet agent for nearly thirty years, until 1963. There is tantalizing, but inconclusive, evidence that Philby's friend Elliott may have allowed him to escape.[30]

Philby's defection caused British intelligence to look once again at Blunt and Cairncross. In early 1964, Arthur Martin, a senior MI5 officer investigating Golitsyn's Ring of Five, traveled to the United States, where, with permission from the FBI and the CIA, he interviewed Cairncross, who had a teaching position at Case Western Reserve University in Ohio. Martin persuaded Cairncross to confess that he had spied for the Soviet Union until 1951. Unsurprisingly, Cairncross refused MI5's offer to return to Britain and to be interviewed under caution.

The decisive breakthrough in the case against Blunt, meanwhile, came from the prominent American publisher, novelist, and patron of the arts Michael Straight (Soviet code name NOMAD, then NIGEL). Straight admitted to the Harvard historian Arthur M. Schlesinger Jr., as part of a routine background check for employment in the U.S. government, that Blunt had recruited him as a Soviet agent while he was an undergraduate at Trinity College, Cambridge. An MI5 officer, again probably Martin, traveled to the United States to interview Straight.

Once back in Britain, in April 1964 Martin interviewed Blunt at the Courtauld Institute and informed him about the information from Straight. According to Martin, Blunt was silent for several minutes. His right cheek was twitching. He poured himself a drink, and stood by the tall window in his office, looking out at Portman Square. He went back to his desk and sat down. After confirming his assurance from prosecution, Blunt confessed to being a Soviet spy.

Fifteen years later, in 1979, a book on the Cambridge Spies all but named

Blunt as the fourth man. That year the British government unmasked him in the House of Commons. Blunt was stripped of his knighthood, resigned from the British Academy, and was removed as an honorary fellow of Trinity College. Reading his memoir today—embargoed for twenty-five years after his death—it is apparent that he continued to deceive himself to the end of his life. He did not say for whom he was really spying. Not once did he mention the KGB in his memoir, instead deluding himself by stating he worked for the Comintern. Blunt did, however, admit that working for the Soviets was the greatest mistake of his life.[31]

By 1964, British intelligence had thus secured confessions, in varying degrees, from the third, fourth, and fifth men in the Cambridge spy ring. Unfortunately, however, they took at face value Golitsyn's claim that the Ring of Five had all been at Cambridge at the same time. It was not until the 1980s, when MI6 recruited a high-level agent of its own inside the KGB, Oleg Gordievsky, that British intelligence realized they had, in fact, already identified all five members of the ring three decades earlier.[32]

Burgess, Maclean, and Philby found the reality of life in the Soviet Union to be bitterly disappointing. Burgess cut a sad figure in Moscow, as depicted in Alan Bennett's play *An Englishman Abroad*: he missed England, continued to wear his Old Etonian tie, ordered clothes from his favorite tailor on London's Jermyn Street, enjoyed food baskets sent from Fortnum & Mason. He hung around the theater, ballet, and lobbies of Moscow hotels, hoping to encounter Westerners. Burgess drank himself to death in 1963. It was Maclean, who had never been close to his fellow spy, who was left to give the oration at his funeral service in Moscow. In accordance with Burgess's last wishes, his remains were returned to England, where he was given a small funeral service in Hampshire, with just five people present. It was a fitting tribute to a man who loved England but betrayed it, who became so unwelcome in the country of his birth that his remains had to be interred in secret.[33]

Philby's train of betrayals continued in Moscow, where he had an affair with Maclean's wife, Eleanor, destroying their marriage. He married her, then divorced her. Philby never forgave Burgess for defecting with Maclean, thereby casting suspicion on him, and refused to meet him in person in Moscow. Life there was not what he or his KGB handlers outwardly pretended. The KGB never really embraced Philby like the star he (and they) craved to be. Contrary to impressions Philby gave in his memoirs, Philby was never a KGB *officer*, only an *agent*. He was never made a Hero of the Soviet Union. Although Philby was loath to admit it, the KGB did not trust him enough even to allow him into the Center for fourteen years after his defection. (KGB foreign intelligence headquarters moved from Moscow's Lubyanka Square to the city's outskirts at Yasenevo in 1972.) KGB officers tasked with chaperoning Philby in Moscow recalled that the Soviet government treated him badly, giving him only a small pension and a dingy apartment, where he spent his time mostly in a drunken stupor. The KGB, and later SVR, papered over this and glamorized Philby's life. Philby died in 1988 on the eve of the Soviet Union's collapse.

WILDERNESS OF MIRRORS

In the wake of the revelations about the Cambridge Spies, intelligence agencies on both sides of the Atlantic tore themselves apart in mole hunts. The KGB masterfully exploited their confusion by feeding them disinformation about other Soviet moles. When these hunts produced little or no evidence, zealots took this as evidence of an even more elaborate hidden Soviet conspiracy at work. As the saying goes, the only difference between counterintelligence and paranoia is an index card.[34]

The Ring of Five raised the specter of other long-term Soviet agent penetrations in Western agencies. That suspicion ended careers of innocent and talented officers. Guy Liddell's association with members of the Cambridge network cut short his career at MI5. He retired in 1953 in the wake of Burgess and Maclean's defections, guilty only of having made bad friends. Similar career cannibalism befell a skillful MI6 officer, David Footman, whose friendship with Philby forced him to retire. He moved to Oxford, where he established the Russian and East European Centre at St. Anthony's College.

Philby and Burgess's friendships also cast suspicion on others in British intelligence, including Tomás Harris, whom we met earlier as the double agent GARBO's talented wartime case officer. Unfortunately for him, Harris owed his recruitment into MI5 in 1941 to Blunt. Harris was killed in a car crash in Majorca in January 1964, where he lived. It has been speculated, but cannot be proved, that he was himself a Soviet agent, and that the KGB assassinated him before MI5 got to him. No evidence has emerged in Harris's British dossier, opened in 2022, to support this claim. In fact, it appears that Harris was a *target* of Soviet intelligence, with Philby instructed to cultivate him to help Philby's own career in British intelligence.[35]

Philby's defection drove fear of Soviet penetration within Britain's intelligence services to fever pitch. His disappearance came on the heels of the exposure of another MI6 officer, George Blake, as a Soviet agent in 1961. MI5 and MI6 opened a small working group, code-named FLUENCY, led by Peter Wright, to investigate their own ranks. Wright's name, with his distinctive handwriting, features prominently in previously secret British records into the Cambridge Spies. The investigations drew MI5 into a tangled web, which led it ultimately to investigate its own deputy director general, Graham Mitchell, and director general, Roger Hollis. MI5's unprecedented investigation into its own head—Hollis led MI5 from 1956 to 1965—caused insidious internal damage, the kind of which the Kremlin could only dream.[36]

The investigation into Mitchell and Hollis was so sensitive that only three British ministers were told about it. President Kennedy and his brother Robert, the U.S. attorney general, were briefed on the British investigation—by the DCI, it seems. None of the FLUENCY investigations, which lingered on into the 1970s, produced evidence that Hollis or Mitchell was guilty. After retiring from MI5, Peter Wright published a sensational memoir, *Spycatcher*, which he wrote with the help of Paul Greengrass (who later directed some of the *Bourne* films). To the millions who read his book, Wright aired his conspiracy theory, fueled by Soviet defector Golitsyn, that Hollis was a Soviet agent. It is a theory that refuses to die. An investigation in 1974 by the respected British cabinet secretary Burke Trend concluded that there was no compelling evidence of Hollis's or Mitchell's guilt. No material has emerged from Russian archives.

Indeed, within the KGB, the Hollis conspiracy was viewed as so bizarre that some of its foreign intelligence (FCD) officers thought it derived from "some mysterious, internal British intrigue." However, there remains a possibility, impossible to disprove, that Hollis was a Soviet agent run not by the KGB but instead by the GRU. (The same could apply to Mitchell.) Disproving this theory would, by definition, require proving a negative, as Margaret Thatcher noted in a public defense of Hollis before Parliament. No evidence has emerged from GRU defectors, or GRU records opened in Russia. In fact, as Ben Macintyre has noted, the strongest evidence against the theory that the head of MI5 was a Soviet spy for nearly a decade, which rumbles on to this day, is that it would constitute an irresistible propaganda victory for the former KGB officer currently occupying the Kremlin, Vladimir Putin.[37]

Golitsyn's information led to similarly destructive mole hunts in the United States. After Philby's defection, his wiry friend and drinking partner James Angleton, the head of the CIA's counterintelligence staff, was drawn into a wilderness of mirrors—to use T. S. Eliot's phrase—from which the CIA officer never emerged. Angleton, an eccentric Anglophile who wore black suits and bred orchids, tore the CIA inside out for twelve years searching for a Soviet agent inside its ranks code-named SASHA. This was Angleton's "Monster Plot": that the CIA was penetrated. With life imitating art, Angleton's SASHA was a real-life counterpart to John le Carré's Karla, George Smiley's enigmatic Soviet nemesis. Golitsyn provided Angleton with the tip about SASHA, but like his information about the Ring of Five, it was confused. In fact, as the CIA later discovered, SASHA was, rather than a code name, a nickname: that of a Soviet agent and former CIA contractor in Germany, Alexander "Sasha" Orlov (whose true Soviet code name was RICHARD). When eventually identified, he was working as an art gallery owner in Virginia, far away from U.S. state secrets.[38]

Golitsyn's information led Angleton's CIA counterintelligence staff essentially to grind to a halt in the 1960s, as he turned away genuine Soviet defectors, believing they were provocations. When Golitsyn defected, he said that the KGB would send another false defector. Then that appeared to happen. In January 1964, a thirty-six-year-old KGB officer, Yuri Nosenko, defected to the CIA in Switzerland. Angleton believed that he was Golitsyn's Soviet plant. The CIA embarked on one of its most shameful episodes: to try to determine Nosenko's bona fides, it subjected him to cruel treatment—arguably constituting torture. He was detained without trial and kept in isolation for approximately three years. This is revealed in the CIA's formerly top secret report about its illegal activities: the "Family Jewels," written in Watergate's aftermath. Nosenko was eventually released, paid off, and given American citizenship and a new identity. Years later, he received an official apology from the CIA.[39]

Both Angleton and Peter Wright believed Golitsyn's most sensational claims: that Labour prime minister Harold Wilson was a KGB agent and that Henry Kissinger, U.S. national security adviser and later secretary of state, was under KGB influence. Like other conspiracy theories, Golitsyn's claims about Britain's prime minister and the U.S. secretary of state grew from a kernel, which then grew to grotesque proportions. Only now, through secrets smuggled from Soviet intelligence archives, can Golitsyn's claims be conclusively established as false. The KGB did have an agent development file on Wilson, to whom it assigned the code name OLDING, dating from his time on Britain's Board of Trade in the 1940s. Its cultivation of Wilson, however, never succeeded.

Meanwhile, as far as Kissinger was concerned, a KGB officer working undercover as a Soviet journalist, Boris Sedov, had contacted him while he was at Harvard. During the 1968 U.S. election campaign, Kissinger used Sedov to pass back-channel messages to Moscow—apparently tacitly acknowledging that Sedov's work involved more than journalism. Kissinger was never under KGB influence. After Nixon's inauguration, the FBI kept Sedov's activities under observation and briefed Kissinger on them. According to a senior KGB officer based in the United States, Oleg Kalugin, the KGB never thought of trying to recruit Kissinger as an agent, instead viewing him as a source of political information. Kissinger doubtless thought the same about Soviet intelligence.[40]

PART THREE

THE CLASH OF ARMS

CHAPTER EIGHT

BATTLEGROUNDS

Martins stood there, twenty yards away, staring at the silent
motionless figure in the dark side street who stared back at him.
A police spy, perhaps, or an agent of those other men, those
men who had corrupted Harry first and then killed him–even
possibly the third man?
–Graham Greene, *The Third Man*

THE EARLY BATTLEGROUNDS OF THE EAST-WEST INTELLI-
gence war, which formed a central axis of the Cold War, lay along what
Winston Churchill called the Iron Curtain. In his famous speech at Westminster College in Fulton, Missouri, in March 1946, Churchill said: "From
Stettin in the Baltic to Trieste in the Adriatic, an iron curtain has descended
across the continent." The previous month, Stalin had declared that war
between the East and West was inevitable. Churchill's words were intended
to underscore the threat that the Soviet Union and communism posed
to the postwar world. The many cities and sites of this shadowy Cold
War in Eastern Europe along the Iron Curtain would be vividly depicted
by novelists like as John le Carré and Graham Greene. As former MI6

officers, le Carré and Greene knew about the world of which they wrote. As is frequently the case with intelligence, however, reality is often stranger than fiction.

———◆———

A valuable recruit for Western intelligence services was Reinhard Gehlen, whom we previosly met as Hitler's former intelligence chief on the eastern front. Gehlen, an austere and taciturn figure, believed that the Third Reich's war with the Soviet Union was part of a larger, and unavoidable, clash between West and East. In captivity in 1945, he told the Allies that Western democracies needed all available help in their struggle with their Soviet nemesis. Sometime while in Allied hands, in 1945–46, he volunteered his services to U.S. military intelligence. He subsequently created a semiofficial "Gehlen Organization" for U.S. military intelligence, housed in a former Nazi headquarters building in Munich. The organization provided the U.S. military with voluminous intelligence about the Soviet Union. Some within the newly created CIA, founded in 1947, were horrified at the idea of using former Nazis to gain information and gather espionage, but ultimately those misgivings were frozen in the face of the Cold War's plummeting temperature. The Gehlen Org became a centerpiece of West Germany's first federal foreign intelligence service, the BND, which the CIA and MI6 helped to shape.

What the British and the Americans did not know was that Soviet intelligence had compromised the Gehlen Organization from the outset. British intelligence records kept secret for seven decades reveal that one of the MI6 officers working on the Gehlen case was none other than Kim Philby. It is a story worthy of a John le Carré novel: a Soviet mole deep inside a Western intelligence service overseeing a case involving a former Nazi taking on Soviet espionage. Philby helped his KGB handlers target the Gehlen Organization, and their efforts soon paid off handsomely. In 1951, Gehlen recruited a former SS officer, Heinz Felfe, as head of counterintelligence in the BND. But Felfe was in fact a Soviet agent (code-named

KURT). Like Philby in MI6, he inflicted devastating damage on West German intelligence.

According to Soviet intelligence archives, Felfe's activities, along with those of Philby and another Soviet agent in MI6, George Blake, allowed the KGB to "eliminate the adversary's network" of agents in East Germany between 1953 and 1955. In July 1954, Otto John, the head of West Germany's intelligence service, the BfV, dramatically defected to East Berlin. John had been involved in the bomb plot to kill Hitler in July 1944, had been a wartime MI6 agent, and then, with the agency's help, had risen up the ranks of postwar West German intelligence. He was also, MI6 discovered when he defected, a Soviet agent. Due to Soviet and East German penetration of West German intelligence, the Stasi arrested and killed countless Western agents (in an operation code-named LIGHTNING). After the arrest of their agents, MI6 withdrew its officer stationed in Berlin, Ruari Chisholm, in June 1955.[1]

SOVIET DEFECTORS

Back in 1946, a wartime Soviet defector, Victor Kravchenko, had published a scathing attack on Stalin and his crimes, *I Chose Freedom*. Secretly, British and U.S. intelligence chiefs tried to lure other Kravchenkos to defect. It was easier said than done, given Stalin's reign of terror and the fear of reprisals instilled in potential defectors. In Berlin's occupied sectors, British, American, and Soviet officials ran prisoner-of-war interrogation and exchange facilities to process millions of displaced and desperate people after the war. These people offered golden opportunities for both sides to recruit agents and insert them among refugees returning home.

Britain's first postwar defector was a Soviet expert in aerodynamics, Grigori Tokaev. Disillusioned with Stalinism by the time he arrived in June 1945 to work at the Soviet administration (Control Commission) in Berlin, he had previously joined a secret opposition group in the Soviet Union. Fearing this would be discovered, in October 1947 Tokaev deserted his position and crossed from the Soviet to the British sector in Berlin. There he soon found himself in front of MI6's head of station in Germany, Reginald Gallienne, who resettled him to Britain, where MI6 and MI5 debriefed him. Under the code name EXCISE, Tokaev provided British intelligence with a window, albeit narrow, into Soviet science and technology. Stalin was rearming for a future war against the West, Tokaev claimed, although he was not yet ready to initiate it.[2]

Tokaev's intelligence made its way to Britain's senior policymakers, including foreign secretary Ernest Bevin. With British permission, Tokaev went public with his denouncements of Stalin. When, in 1948, the Joint Intelligence Committee realized that Soviet defectors offered a unique opportunity to gain intelligence, it instigated a policy, DRAGON RETURN, to centralize control of Soviet defectors. Tokaev, however, was a flash in the pan. In 1951, the JIC noted that what it got from high-grade defectors was "the most valuable source of intelligence," but it said too that Britain's handling of defectors was "inadequate." Many of MI6's defections of Soviets across the Iron Curtain ended in shambles. One such example was that of Jason Davidovich Tasoev, who worked for the Soviet repatriation authority in Bremen. On the eve of the Berlin crisis of 1948, Tasoev volunteered to defect. An MI6 officer flew him to Britain, where he was debriefed in a safe house in London's Carlton Gardens. A month after arriving, however, Tasoev had a crisis of faith and wanted to *redefect* to Soviet authorities. When his story leaked to the press, Soviet officials claimed that the British had kidnapped Tasoev.[3]

Following the Tasoev debacle, MI5's head of counterespionage, Dick White (later its director general), ripped through records to find statistics about Soviet defectors to Britain. His ensuing report in 1948, which the British government kept under lock and key for six decades, revealed that just twenty Soviet officials had defected to Britain since 1926. They did so out of hatred of Stalin's regime, and out of "fear, love, or a desire for the western way of life." Repression and reprisals against family members were reasons why more did not defect. But another reason why so few Soviet officials took a leap of faith with the British was because, as Tasoev suggested in his debriefings, they widely believed that the British let down defectors. This was the poisoned legacy of Konstantin Volkov's botched defection in Istanbul four years earlier.

The CIA fared little better. In June 1951 it instigated a program, RED-CAP, to monitor Soviet officials posted overseas and encourage them to defect. In 1953, it managed to secure the defection of a KGB officer stationed in Vienna, Peter Deriabin, who escaped on a clinking freight train through Soviet-occupied territory near that city. He became a CIA asset, later authoring books about the KGB. But apart from a few apostles like Deriabin, REDCAP produced limited results. The same was true of the CIA's paramilitary infiltration operations in Eastern Europe.[4]

COVERT ACTIONS

Under President Truman, the U.S. government finally came of age with intelligence. America's overt grand strategy regarding the Soviet Union was containment, which, to observers at the time and since, suggested something defensive. But from the outset, containment had a clandestine offensive component. The father of containment, George Kennan, was clear-eyed about the need for the U.S. to pursue "political warfare" against the Soviet Union: to roll back communism. In his view, that meant carrying out all acts short of war, including psychological and paramilitary operations. The precedent he drew on was the OSS. In his later life, at Princeton, Kennan would disown the political-warfare child he created, calling it his greatest mistake. But at the time, he was unambiguous. It was at Kennan's urging that the U.S. government created the Office of Policy Coordination (OPC) in 1948 to carry out political warfare. Although the OPC was semi-detached from the CIA, taking orders from the State Department and Joint Chiefs of Staff, it was in spirit a CIA beast. It would formally come into the CIA in 1952. It thereafter ballooned into a clandestine paramilitary wing of the

U.S. government, as we have already noted. The CIA's strategy, code-named REDSOX, was to infiltrate émigré groups in Western countries and recruit agents to return to the Soviet Union to conduct paramilitary operations. The effort was modeled on wartime OSS Jedburgh paramilitary teams parachuted into enemy territory.[5]

In London, Britain's senior policymakers and civil servants were sharpening their own covert action knives. Labour foreign secretary Ernest Bevin was initially skeptical about letting MI6 and the CIA's dogs of war loose because of the reaction it might engender from Stalin. But Bevin's resistance toward covert action softened as he struggled with successive diplomatic failures with the Soviet Union at meetings of foreign ministers. He agreed to a policy of covert action in Eastern Europe. Its stated objective was to weaken Soviet rule by aggravating disaffected peoples inside Soviet territories, so that if hostilities broke out with the West—World War III—Moscow would be bogged down, requiring significant occupation forces to control them. In 1948, at the request of the Foreign Office's Orme Sargent, MI6 set out types of political warfare it could unleash on the Soviet Union. In a report kept classified for seven decades, MI6 chief Menzies offered a menu of dirty tricks, ranging from propaganda, bribery, and blackmail of Soviet officials in Western countries (planting evidence to smear them and encourage their recall to Moscow) to more sinister acts like arson, sabotage, kidnapping, and "liquidations"— apparently a euphemism for assassinations. We know that for five years, starting in 1950, Operation FLITTER used bogus radio transmissions to cast suspicion on Soviet officials with the aim of having them purged.[6]

Albania offered an early test case for subverting, and even "liberating," other countries behind the Iron Curtain. Momentum seemed on Britain's and America's side. In 1948, the leader of neighboring Yugoslavia, Tito, dramatically split from Stalin, developing his own style of communism outside the Soviet bloc.

Truman knew that Tito slaughtered his opponents, but the U.S. president valued the strongman's Soviet apostasy more than he deplored his

violence. Between 1950 and 1953, the Truman administration would pro-
vide approximately $336 million in aid to Yugoslavia. Old SOE hands like
David Smiley and Julian Amery suggested the time was right to overthrow
the communist leader of next-door Albania, Enver Hoxha, and install a
Western-friendly leader drawn from its old monarchy. They suggested tools
straight from SOE's wartime playbook, including blackmail and bribery of
Albanian officials. But bribes meant money, something in short supply in
Britain. Enter the Americans. Little wonder MI6 called its Albania operation
VALUABLE. The CIA's more didactic code name was FIEND. The CIA
carried out a series of covert actions against Albania, from propaganda to
paramilitary "rollback" activities.

In 1949, the British dispatched six teams, known as "Pixies," by boat
from Malta. Their mission was to link up with CIA teams, join partisan
groups in Albania, and subvert Hoxha's regime. The MI6-CIA attempt
to liberate Albania was, however, a dramatic failure. Soviet security forces
seemed to be lying in wait, as if they knew the U.S. and British teams were
coming—which they did. Unfortunately for MI6 and the CIA, Britain's
liaison officer in Washington at the time was Kim Philby. Yet again, we see
his hidden hand at work. When he arrived in Washington in September
1949, Philby's friend James Angleton briefed him on REDSOX generally,
and worse still, divulged the drop locations for teams being sent into Albania. Their imminent arrival exposed, the teams were easy prey for the KGB.
Regarding similar CIA teams dropped into Ukraine, Philby later—in his
KGB-sponsored memoirs—took credit for their betrayal, in a macabre
locution: "I do not know what happened to the parties concerned. But I
can make an informed guess."[7]

The CIA and MI6 failures cannot all be credited to Philby's masterful
espionage, as the KGB liked to claim. Stalin first heard of VALUABLE from
the NKVD London *rezident* in June 1949, before Philby arrived in Washington. This information probably came from loose-lipped émigré groups
used by the CIA for its rollback operations in several European capitals.
This was, then, poor CIA and MI6 operational security. Albania was not

so much a Soviet espionage success as a Western failure. MI6 and the CIA could not even agree about who should rule the country, once liberated. After the outbreak of the Korean War in June 1950, the Foreign Office became increasingly worried about the value of VALUABLE.[8]

U.S. and British covert actions in Eastern Europe generally were tactical and strategic failures. Their aim was "to get in there and do something that would put a frown on Uncle Joe's face," as one meeting of senior U.S. decision makers put it in 1952. They failed because neither government could agree on what a successful outcome would be: there was a seesaw between hawks, pushing for maximalist rollback, and others who favored a lesser defense against further Soviet expansion.[9]

Eisenhower's secretary of state, John Foster Dulles, no friend of Kennan, later said that containment, if that was to mean holding ground, was a non-moral activity, as it left millions to the plight of Soviet domination. As CIA and MI6 émigré teams parachuted into the night skies over Ukraine and other countries in Eastern Europe, it was thus not entirely clear what their measure of success was. The obliteration of British and American teams behind the Iron Curtain led to a major strategic revision, by Britain's government, of covert actions. After Albania, its strategy against the Soviet Union shifted from victory through liberation to disruption—"pinpricks" chipping away at Soviet rule by exploiting weakness, spreading discord, and creating nuisance behind the Iron Curtain, "throwing grit into the machine of Communist regimes," as one report noted. Moderation, not buccaneering rollback, would be Britain's covert action strategy behind the Iron Curtain thereafter.[10]

Moderation and patience were virtues largely absent in Washington when it came to the Soviet Union. In April 1950, President Truman signed a sixty-six-page National Security Council policy paper, NSC 68, which presented the Cold War as a Manichaean struggle between Western light and Eastern darkness. It restated Truman's strategic doctrine of containment. Egregiously, however, it went further than available intelligence in trying to gauge Stalin's intentions.

The only way that the National Security Council could have known

Stalin's objectives and capabilities for certain, given the closed nature of the Soviet police state, was from secret intelligence—which the NSC lacked. Instead of admitting this to their readers, the authors of NSC 68 at the State Department, led by Paul Nitze, a slick investment banker who had succeeded Kennan on the Policy Planning Staff, nevertheless claimed—with little evidence—that the Soviet Union had a master plan "for the complete subversion or forcible destruction of the machinery of government and structure of society in the countries of the non-Soviet world and their replacement by an apparatus and structure subservient to and controlled from the Kremlin." This was a dangerous overstatement. NSC 68 failed to distinguish between Stalin's ideological faith in the long-term triumph of communism and an actual plan for world domination, which it falsely suggested he had.[11]

In Washington, a struggle between good guys and bad guys, with the fate of the world hanging in the balance, was easy to sell—to voters, the military, and the business industry. As the historian Ernest May noted, NSC 68 "provided the blueprint for the militarization of the Cold War from 1950 to the collapse of the Soviet Union at the beginning of the 1990s." Nowhere in NSC 68 did its authors consider strategic empathy—namely, to take seriously Soviet fears, whether well founded or not, about the threat they perceived from the West. They failed to consider that U.S. "countermeasures" were capable of looking like aggression to the Kremlin. With ghastly irony, Stalin's spies in the United States and Britain—particularly those like Donald Maclean—almost certainly betrayed the contents of NSC 68 to the Kremlin, thus stoking the paranoia there that it described.[12]

The U.S. intelligence community failed to provide Truman's national security team with forewarning of a mass protest of about 370,000 East Germans in June 1953. Three months after Stalin's death, East Germans took to the streets to protest "Sovietization" measures enacted by Walter Ulbricht, who had been handpicked by Moscow. They protested work quotas imposed to build "socialism" in East Germany amid declining living standards. The East German regime, backed by the Soviet Union, crushed and killed many of the protesters. Four thousand miles away, Eisenhower, who had taken office less than five months earlier, politely, but forcefully, made his disappointment clear to the CIA about this missed opportunity to subvert a Soviet satellite state.[13]

As the former Supreme Allied Commander in Europe, Eisenhower managed his National Security Council like a military affair. He personally chaired 90 percent of its meetings during his two terms. Ike demanded that the CIA's Directorate of Plans should be arming underground organizations capable of launching sustained warfare in East Germany and other Soviet satellite countries. That summer, in his Project Solarium, so called because the meetings took place in the White House sunroom, the president gathered his most trusted national security advisers to strategize about the Soviet Union. On comfortable sofas, surrounded by plants growing in the sun, the men assembled included former DCI Walter Bedell Smith, George Kennan, Secretary of State John Foster Dulles, and the air force pilot who had led America's fire-bombing of Tokyo in 1942, James R. "Jimmy" Doolittle. In 1954, at Eisenhower's request, Doolittle delivered a report on CIA covert action. In it, he doubled down on NSC 68's dangerously mistaken hyperbole about the Soviet threat:

> It is now clear that we are facing an implacable enemy whose avowed objective is world domination by whatever means and whatever cost. There are no rules in such a game. Hitherto acceptable norms of human conduct do not apply. If the United States is to survive, long-standing American concepts of "fair play" must be reconsidered. We must develop effective espionage and counterespionage services and must learn to subvert, sabotage and destroy our enemies by more clever, more sophisticated and more effective methods than those used against us. It may become necessary that the American people be made acquainted with, understand and support this fundamentally repugnant philosophy.

Doolittle did not take the opportunity to question what constitutes success in covert action against the Soviet Union. Instead, he recommended that America conduct more covert action—and do it better. Washington needed "an aggressive covert psychological, political and paramilitary organization more effective, and more unique and, if necessary, more ruthless than that employed by the enemy."[14]

It was tough talk, but produced little tangible results. Eisenhower responded to the protests in East Germany by authorizing a covert action to assist resistance groups in satellite countries, falling short of full-scale rebellion. The language was suitably vague ("covertly stimulate acts and attitudes of resistance") to make success in the eye of the beholder. Its vague language reflected a deeper issue: the U.S. government did not have a coherent strategy for what covert action behind the Iron Curtain should be, what "success" would be.

Two years later, in October 1956, the CIA again failed to forewarn of or exploit another uprising, this time in Hungary. With few assets in the country, the agency failed to instigate a covert action to assist protesters—despite this being exactly the moment it had been waiting for. Instead, it resorted to using the U.S. propaganda organization, Radio Free Europe, to broadcast some messages of support. Those broadcasts, though fewer in number than history tends to remember, nevertheless led Hungarians to believe American help was coming. Instead the CIA stood by as Soviet troops, assisted by the KGB, crushed partisans in Budapest. About 2,500 were killed, 20,000 wounded, and countless others sent to Siberian camps. As far as Eisenhower was concerned, it was another moment of shameful inaction by the agency. The president courteously but acidly pointed out to his DCI, Allen Dulles, that if there were ever a need for covert, deniable, psychological warfare against the Soviets, it was in Hungary in November 1956. Frank Wisner sank into a deep depression after Hungary that would lead to his suicide a decade later. Meanwhile, to deflect from the bloodbath in Hungary, Khrushchev warned Britain and France that he would attack them with "rocket weapons" if they did not remove their forces from Egypt, where they were trying to overthrow its leader, Gamal Nasser. When they did withdraw, the Soviet leader wrongly believed that his bellicosity had worked. It would contribute to Khrushchev's later risk-taking.[15]

The successive failures of covert action in Europe forced Eisenhower to question whether he should really be poking the Soviet bear through its cage. After deliberating with his Solarium advisers, Eisenhower's New Look grand strategy (NSC 162/2) shelved the idea of detaching Soviet satellites. Instead, nuclear weapons would be the primary U.S. deterrence against Soviet expansionism. Overwhelming nukes, not spooks, would be Ike's strategy. Under Eisenhower, the U.S. developed B-52 bombers to deliver nuclear weapons, as well as intercontinental ballistic missiles (ICBMs) and submarine-launched ballistic missiles (SLBMs) to do so. U.S. nuclear weapons ballooned under Eisenhower, from 370 in 1950 to more than 40,000 at decade's end. Eisenhower's New Look strategy focused on nuclear weapons as a way of avoiding an American "garrison state" and the military-industrial complex about which he would later warn Americans. Meanwhile, for the Soviet ambassador in Budapest, Yuri Andropov, Hungary in 1956 showed the importance of acting decisively—and violently—against ideological subversion. It was a lesson he carried with him as he became KGB chairman and, eventually, leader of the Soviet Union.

SCALP-HUNTING

Covert action may have been the focus in the 1950s, but the CIA and MI6 continued trying to recruit spies behind the Iron Curtain. Security procedures inside the Moscow Center were head-spinning, minimizing the chance of documents being surreptitiously taken. Each document in a file was hand-sewn in by a senior officer on the case, sealed with wax, and locked in a safe each night. The CIA's Moscow station opened with a litany of failures, the result of both poorly trained officers and inept embassy security. CIA officers and other embassy officials were easily compromised by KGB honeypot operations. But the lack of success was not just due to CIA incompetence. Pervasive security in the Soviet Union made Moscow a suffocating environment to conduct espionage. The Soviet Union was effectively run like a prison, with about 200 million people in 1955 behind heavily guarded bars and over a million KGB officers and agents acting as jailers.[16]

European capitals were easier hunting grounds for CIA and MI6 agent recruiters, or scalp-hunters, as the British, adopting a phrase from le Carré, would later term those in the trade. Soviet embassies there offered a window into the otherwise-closed Soviet regime. Vienna, bombed and burned-out during the war, was a rich espionage hunting ground. It was there, on the cobbled banks of the Danube, that the CIA achieved its first major recruiting success against Soviet intelligence: a thirty-year-old GRU officer, Pyotr Popov. The first Soviet spy of lasting value to U.S. intelligence, Popov was recruited as part of the CIA's REDCAP operations, designed to encourage Soviet officials to defect, while remaining in place for as long as possible before doing so.

Code-named ATTIC by the CIA, Popov was a significant catch. His recruitment was the work of the CIA's chief scalp-hunter, George Kisevalter. Born in Russia, Kisevalter had been stranded in the United States as a child when the Bolsheviks seized power in 1917. His father was in the U.S. buying arms for the tsarist regime; his grandfather had been a tsarist deputy finance minister. Now a U.S. citizen, Kisevalter graduated from Dartmouth, and, during the war, joined U.S. military intelligence. After 1945, he worked with Gehlen and his organization in Germany, and in 1951, almost inevitably, he joined the CIA. He ran a special department, SR 9, to handle Soviet moles from CIA stations in Vienna and Berlin. It was only a matter of time before Popov, stationed in both cities for the GRU, came onto Kisevalter's radar.[17]

Like Berlin, Vienna was a city divided by the former wartime Allies. While the Soviet zone was rigorously segregated from the others, Vienna's old historic center was a carefully delimited International Sector, where Soviets and Westerners were allowed to mix. Spies stalked the streets. Using the alias Gary Grossman, Kisevalter recruited Popov in 1953, paying him $4,000 per month. But Popov was not only interested in the money—he was disgusted by the Soviet government's repression of its peasants, which included Popov's own family. He also wanted to advance his own stalled career. Married, with children, Popov was having an affair with a German communist. Like all good case officers, Kisevalter offered more than a professional relationship with Popov; he became his friend and confidant. Popov told him secrets about himself that he hid even from his family.

Over the course of five years, first in Vienna and then while stationed in East Berlin, Popov gave the CIA secrets from deep inside the GRU, about Soviet tanks, tactical missiles, and military doctrine. At the time, before the building of the Berlin Wall, if you had the correct papers, it was still relatively easy to travel between West and East Berlin by car, subway, or walking down the Kurfürstendamm. Kisevalter and Popov took full advantage.

When Popov was transferred to East Berlin, in 1955, he was assigned to work on GRU illegals—deep-cover agents—being sent to Western countries to spy. This was a jackpot for the CIA. In total, Popov betrayed the identities of 650 of his fellow Soviet intelligence officers. According to the CIA, Popov's intelligence saved the U.S. government billions of dollars in military research and development by ascertaining the Soviet Union's military capabilities.

But Popov was not a perfect spy. He drank like a fish, forgot things, and continued his love affair, even after promising his GRU superiors that he would end it. He was demoted and transferred back to Kalinin (now called Tver), his hometown, about one hundred miles northwest of Moscow. What or who brought him to the attention of KGB security, the Second Chief Directorate, remains unclear. It was probably George Blake, a high-level penetration agent inside MI6, whom we shall meet in more detail below. Blake provided the Center with a tip-off; the KGB was soon on Popov's case.

Poor FBI tradecraft may also have helped the KGB identify Popov. In 1959, using information he had supplied, the FBI placed two Soviet deep-cover illegals arriving in the United States under observation, but its surveillance was clumsy. The GRU and the KGB suspected that they had a mole in their midst who had alerted the Americans. In October of that year, Popov was arrested by the KGB and unimaginatively code-named JUDAS. The KGB tried unsuccessfully to use him to pass disinformation to the CIA, in Operation BOOMERANG. In January 1960, Popov was tried, and in June was executed by firing squad in the Lubyanka. For the CIA, his execution was the harshest reminder of the life-and-death stakes of East-West espionage.[18]

ANATOMY OF ASSASSINATIONS

Soviet intelligence services engaged in political murder in ways lacking comparison in Western intelligence services. In 1953, Stalin ordered the assassination of Tito. Pavel Sudoplatov, the former NKVD head of special tasks, was instructed to "sort out" the renegade leader of Yugoslavia once and for all. The man chosen for the job was Iosif "Grig" Grigulevich (code-named ARTUR, MAKS, and FELIPE). Grigulevich had helped to assassinate Stalin's nemesis Trotsky in 1940 and was now sent to dispatch Tito, posing as a foreign dignitary.* Grig's plan to kill Tito involved spraying him with pneumonic plague. He got as far as writing a farewell letter to his wife before the plot was called off at the last minute, following the death of Stalin.[19]

After Stalin's demise, Soviet leaders were more restrained with political assassination. But both the KGB and GRU kept professional assassins on the payroll. In September of 1953, the Soviet minister responsible for the KGB emphasized the importance of "recognizing the value of engaging in acts of terrorism," or active measures. The Center continued to operate a laboratory (the Kamera) specializing in poisons, which had been in existence at least since Genrikh Yagoda was head of the NKVD, from 1934 to 1936.[20]

Ukrainian nationalists were high on the Kremlin's hit lists. The new leader to emerge in the Kremlin, Nikita Khrushchev, former party secretary in Ukraine, had sanctioned poisonings there. (Between 1944 and 1953, the Soviets arrested six hundred thousand people in western Ukraine. About a third were executed, and those remaining were left to rot in jail or the

* For more about Grigulevich, see this book's website: www.spieshistory.com.

Gulag.) As Soviet leader, Khrushchev needed little persuading to continue "wet work." One of his bêtes noires was the hard-right wartime Ukrainian nationalist leader Stepan Bandera, whose anti-Semitism and hatred of the Soviet Union had driven him to collaborate with the Nazis during the war, before being imprisoned by them. Now in exile in West Germany, leading a faction called the Organization of Ukrainian Nationalists (OUN), his fire-breathing anti-Sovietism had driven him into the CIA's arms.[21]

The KGB ordered Bandera's liquidation. The weapon of choice was a specially made gun. About four inches long, it fired a poison gas, released from a crushed cyanide pill, which caused instantaneous cardiac arrest. The assassin? This would be a twenty-five-year-old Ukrainian, Bohdan Stashinsky (code-named OLEG). Traveling to West Germany on false papers, he was to track down and eliminate Bandera and another Ukrainian nationalist, Lev Rebet. As now-opened operational files in Ukrainian archives reveal, Stashinsky tested his weapon on a dog, which he tied to a tree in the woods near the KGB's station in East Berlin, Karlshorst. The dog went into convulsions and died. Stashinsky's superiors at the Center had chosen the elaborate murder weapon because they believed an autopsy was likely to rule the cause of death as a heart attack.

Now in West Germany, Stashinsky shadowed his two intended victims, getting to know their daily movements. In 1957, the moment came for Rebet. Lying in wait in the darkened hallway of Rebet's Munich apartment block, Stashinsky shot Rebet in the face with the poison vapor, killing him instantly. Next came Bandera. The assassin stalked him. Two years later, in October 1959, Stashinsky used a modified version of the weapon to slay Bandera. After again hiding in his target's apartment hallway, he approached Bandera, holding the weapon in a rolled-up newspaper, and shot him in the face. As he knew he would be, the killer was also exposed to the poison vapors, so he crushed antidote capsules that the KGB had supplied and inhaled their fumes. The murders were a success. At the time, West German authorities did not treat either Rebet's death or Bandera's as suspicious. As the Center had hoped, their demises were ascribed to heart attacks.[22]

In December 1959, after his successful hit jobs, Stashinsky was recalled to Moscow. KGB chairman Alexander Shelepin presented him with a high Soviet decoration, the Order of the Red Banner, for "carrying out an extremely important government assignment." Shelepin informed Stashinsky that he would next be sent to take a language course to perfect his English, and then posted on a three- to five-year assignment in the West to carry out further "special actions." Fate, however, intervened in a way that Soviet spy chiefs in the Center had not predicted: Stashinksy fell in love. He began to have second thoughts about his remit, and, at the urging of his East German girlfriend, whom he married in 1960, he agreed to flee with her to West Berlin, which they did in August 1961, the day before Soviet forces sealed the Berlin Wall.

Stashinsky gave himself up to West German authorities and confessed to the murders of Rebet and Bandera. At a trial fourteen months later, Stashinsky, then thirty, was found guilty and sentenced to eight years' imprisonment. The judge ruled, however, that the true culprit was the Soviet government, which had institutionalized political murder. Following his release, he and his wife disappeared, possibly to South Africa. Stashinsky reportedly underwent plastic surgery.[23]

Even before Stashinsky, KGB contract killers had become public embarrassments for the Kremlin. Back in September 1954, again on Khrushchev's instructions, the KGB dispatched an assassin to kill another leader of a Ukrainian nationalist group, the NTS, living under CIA auspices in West Germany. The killer was a blond, blue-eyed former actor, Nikolai Khokhlov, who was overseen and trained by Aleksandr Panyushkin, head of KGB foreign intelligence (the FCD) and former Soviet ambassador to the U.S. Khokhlov was also trained by a judo champion and a five-time national pistol tournament winner. Khokhlov's weapon was an electrically charged gun that fired cyanide-laced darts. The gun, and a silencer, were hidden in a cigarette packet.[24]

But Khokhlov also had a crisis of faith. When he appeared at his intended victim's apartment doorstep in Frankfurt in February 1954, he announced: "I've come to you from Moscow. The Central Committee of the Communist

Party of the Soviet Union has ordered your assassination"—and then explained that he had decided not to carry out the murder. Instead, Khokhlov defected to an initially skeptical CIA in April that year, was debriefed by MI6 in London, with Churchill's approval, and held a sensational press conference in which he revealed the assassination plot and displayed his lethal cigarette box to the world's media. Hiding in the open was his best defense against Soviet reprisals, Khokhlov believed. He published his memoirs, further humiliating the Kremlin. Soviet intelligence sought revenge. Two years later, the KGB tried to kill its former assassin using radioactive thallium (chosen because Moscow believed it would degrade after death). It made Khokhlov's hair fall out but was not lethal. Later, Putin's Kremlin would again use similar elaborate methods, including radioactive poison, to eliminate its enemies.[25]

Following these derailments, we might imagine Moscow would have curtailed similar hit jobs. But reason was largely lacking in Khrushchev's Kremlin. Nor did the KGB's new chairman, a yes-man named Vladimir Semichastny, offer restraint. In November 1961, Semichastny approved plans for additional KGB "direct actions," on the grounds that from 1954 to 1961, of the 329 instances of Soviet "treachery," only 29 traitors had been lured back to Russia to pay the price for their treachery. Semichastny thus authorized his own justice. Meanwhile, Bandera's ghost lived on in the Kremlin. Six decades after his assassination, in 2022, Putin, seeking to justify his war in Ukraine, called its leader, Volodymyr Zelensky, a Banderite "neo-Nazi" and "collaborator" with U.S. intelligence. Following in the KGB's tradition, Russian intelligence has attempted to assassinate Zelensky.[26]

ILLEGALS

We first met the American-born husband-and-wife Soviet undercover team Lona and Morris Cohen in chapter four as they transported stolen U.S. atomic secrets from Los Alamos. They continued their undercover work after the war, providing technical support for another major KGB illegal in New

York, William Fisher, who went by various aliases, including Rudolf Abel, made famous by the 2015 Steven Spielberg film *Bridge of Spies*. In 1952, following the trial of Julius and Ethel Rosenberg, the Center spirited the Cohens out of America on forged papers, via Canada, to the Soviet Union, where they received further training from the Soviet illegals section, Directorate S. Two years later, they appeared in Britain under new aliases: Helen and Peter Kroger. They purported to be a New Zealand couple, living quiet suburban lives in a residential street in Ruislip, in northwest London. They owned an antiquarian bookshop on London's Strand. Neighbors described the occupants of 45 Cranley Drive as friendly. The couple hosted parties. Under the cover of bland suburbia, in fact they ran a sophisticated deep-cover Soviet spy ring, as they had in the United States.

The Cohens' operation in Britain, known as the Portland Spy Ring, was the first Soviet illegal espionage network discovered in postwar Britain. MI5's fifty-four volumes of files on the network, declassified since 2017, are the first records from the archives of British intelligence to reveal how such an illegal network was detected.[27]

The tip-off to British intelligence came from a well-placed agent that the CIA was running in Polish intelligence, Michał Goleniewski, SNIPER, who later defected to the United States. Within the CIA, Goleniewski is known as its first "write-in" agent: there was no in-person contact with him, no meetings. Everything was done through the mail. Goleniewski chose to do it this way because he knew how many Soviet agents there were in Western services, so he wanted to keep his identity anonymous. Accepting him as an agent was a risk for the CIA, but it paid off. (It may have been for the best that he did not meet his CIA case officers. Goleniewski was a slightly mad figure, looking like someone straight from central casting: he had a large, oiled mustache, which he twirled. He also convinced himself that he was the last surviving son of Nicholas II and heir to the Russian imperial throne.) In April 1960, Goleniewski reported that Polish intelligence had recruited an agent in the British naval attaché's office in Warsaw. When that agent returned to Britain, he was handed from the Poles to the KGB.[28]

Thanks to the CIA's information, MI5 was soon on the case. The prime suspect was quickly identified as Harry Houghton, a clerical officer at Britain's Underwater Detection Establishment (UDE) in Portland, Dorset, on England's south coast. Houghton had previously served in Warsaw, until being sent home due to alcohol abuse. Embarrassingly for MI5, it discovered that Houghton had previously been on its radar. In 1956, MI5 had been asked to investigate whether Houghton was a security risk at the UDE. They were sent a report from Houghton's wife warning that he was revealing classified information. MI5's vetting section, however, had concluded, without serious investigation, that Mrs. Houghton had made her claim out of spite because of the breakup of their marriage. It was a striking failure. When they later questioned the former Mrs. Houghton, who had since remarried, she revealed that Harry used to bring classified papers home with him from work at the UDE and take them to London on the weekends, sometimes returning with bundles of cash. Mrs. Houghton had been too afraid to report his actions to the police because her husband was violent.[29]

Surveillance on Harry Houghton (whom MI5 code-named REVERBER-ATE) soon showed that he was having an affair with a recordkeeper at UDE, Ethel "Bunty" Gee, who had more access to classified documents than he did, including sensitive U.S. information on underwater technology. A spinster, with curly hair, glasses, woolly A-line skirts, Gee was unremarkable, a paradigm of Englishness at the time, far away from East-West espionage. But for that precise reason, the Soviets recruited her. It was a well-practiced espionage technique. Rather than focusing on recruiting senior officials, who were hard to land, better to enlist the help of lower-level secretarial staff with wide access to records. At the time, such staff were invariably women. Houghton and Gee's MI5 files show that in July 1960, the service's plainclothes officers followed the couple on a weekend trip to London. They were observed meeting a man, "A" in the initial surveillance reports, who was believed to be "an illegal agent working for either the Russian or Polish intelligence service." The man drove off after the meeting in a car registered in the name of Gordon Lonsdale.

MI5 and MI6 soon set to work finding out what they could about Lonsdale (code-named LAST ACT by MI5), placing an eavesdropping bug in his apartment in central London. It revealed him to be something of a playboy in 1960s London, driving fast cars (a large American-imported Studebaker) and dating faster women. With dark hair and a broad smile, Lonsdale was a ladies' man. He was a successful businessman. He managed several companies, one known as the White House, which imported American jukeboxes and bubble gum machines. One of his machines was known as the "Trump."[30]

But Lonsdale's life was a smokescreen. His real name was Konon Molody. He was a KGB illegal. The son of Soviet scientists, Molody seems to have been groomed from childhood to be a potential Soviet intelligence officer. In 1932, at the age of ten, he was sent to live with an aunt in California, where he became fluent in English and picked up an American accent. After returning to Moscow and serving in the NKVD during the war, he was sent to Canada, where he trained as an undercover agent. There he obtained the passport of what is known as a "dead double," someone who has died but whose identity can fraudulently continue to be used. In this case, the victim was Gordon Lonsdale. Born in Canada, he had emigrated with his family to the Soviet Union, where he passed away.

Assuming Lonsdale's identity and papers, Molody traveled to London, where he established the first postwar illegal *rezidentura*, using KGB funds to set up his companies. He later claimed that the businesses were so successful that he became the KGB's first multimillionaire undercover agent. With his American accent, he posed as a U.S. naval officer to recruit Gee and Houghton.[31]

MI5's undercover team kept Houghton and Lonsdale under close surveillance through the summer of 1960, as Cold War tensions spiked after a U.S. U-2 spy plane was shot down over Soviet territory. Houghton and Lonsdale's indiscretions sometimes simplified matters: one surveillance report notes that, after Houghton met Lonsdale near London's Old Vic Theatre in August 1960, they went into a cheap café, where MI5's watchers were able to overhear some of their conversation. Lonsdale spoke in a low voice, but Houghton was loud-mouthed. Their conversation included reference to "future meetings on the first Saturday of each month." On another occasion, Lonsdale was seen handing Houghton and Gee tickets to—what else?—the Bolshoi Ballet, which was visiting London.[32]

After a meeting between Houghton and Lonsdale in November, MI5 tailed Lonsdale to a house, which turned out to be Peter and Helen Kroger's home in Ruislip. The service set up an observation post in the house across the street and watched the Krogers (code-named the KILLJOYS) go about their lives. The case developed more urgency in January 1961 when the CIA's agent in Polish intelligence, Goleniewski, defected in Berlin. Britain's spy chiefs feared that if the KGB discovered that he knew about Houghton's espionage, they would recall their British agents. Britain's eavesdroppers, GCHQ, intercepted some of Lonsdale's incoming radio traffic.[33]

London's Special Branch police arrested Houghton, Gee, and Lonsdale, on Waterloo Road, on London's Southbank, after observing Gee (TRELLIS) hand over what turned out to be classified documents relating to British submarine technology. MI5 also decided to move on the Krogers, who were arrested in their home. It was found to be packed with espionage gear: seven passports, secret writing material, facilities to make and read messages hidden in microdots, and a cigarette lighter with a secret compartment containing cipher pads for encrypting radio transmissions. It was a house of secrets. The Krogers had been serving as Lonsdale's radio operators and technical support team. As they were being arrested, Mrs. Kroger asked if she could stoke the fire. A vigilant police officer stopped her, searched her handbag, and found letters from Lonsdale that contained microdot film, which she was attempting to destroy. Five days later, after tearing the house apart, MI5 discovered the Krogers' high-speed radio-transmission set, which they used to communicate with Moscow, hidden in a cavity under a floor.[34]

After their arrest, the Krogers' fingerprints were sent to the FBI, who established their real identities as Morris and Lona Cohen. There was also a breakthrough in establishing that Gordon Lonsdale was not the person he presented himself to be. This arose from something unique in the annals of intelligence history: a foreskin. "Lonsdale" was not circumcised, while the true Lonsdale was, according to the Royal Canadian Mounted Police and the FBI. So who was the person sitting in front of MI5? He revealed his true identity as Molody. At their trial in London in March 1961, all five of the Portland Spies were convicted. The presiding judge sentenced "Lonsdale" to twenty-five years' imprisonment, showing him no leniency because he was a "professional spy." The Krogers got twenty years each, and Houghton and Gee each fifteen. The Royal Navy later determined that the intelligence Lonsdale passed to Moscow from Portland had helped the Soviet Union manufacture a new, quieter generation of submarines, including advanced sonar technology from Britain's then only nuclear submarine, HMS *Dreadnought*.[35]

MI5's weighty files on the Portland Spy Ring reveal something that was kept secret for six decades: while in jail, Lonsdale suggested he was willing to work for the British as an agent. He offered this to the principal MI5 officer on his case, Charles Elwell, who visited and befriended him in jail. Lonsdale told Elwell he was making the offer "with eyes wide open." "He had burnt his boats" with the Soviet Union, noted Elwell. He was, Lonsdale growled, worried "about the fate that awaited him when he returned to Russia." Ultimately Lonsdale's offer to spy for the British got nowhere. This was because he refused to betray names of agents in his network, which was essential for British intelligence for a deal. Showing his sincerity, however, as now-opened MI5 files reveal, in August 1961 Lonsdale accompanied Elwell to visit the Krogers in jail, at Birmingham. He urged them to give information to MI5 for a reduced sentence. They refused to do so.[36]

The Krogers were released in 1969 in an East-West spy swap. They returned, flying first class, drinking champagne, to a heroes' welcome in the Soviet Union. Photos show Peter Kroger, wearing a dark suit, with white hair, triumphantly waving, while Helen Kroger, her hair in a bouffant, smoked and smiled. The Kremlin hosted dinners in their honor, and they received a high Soviet military decoration, the Order of the Red Banner. As with Philby, Soviet postage stamps were issued with their images and true names. After his death three decades later, Morris Cohen was given the posthumous title Hero of the Russian Federation by President Boris Yeltsin.

Meanwhile, Lonsdale had been released in 1964 in another spy swap, at the Staaken checkpoint in Berlin. His fears about his fate came true. He died in 1970, apparently from a heart attack after picking wild mushrooms in the Russian countryside. He did not have a history of heart problems. It is possible that the KGB killed him, having learned, from the Krogers, about his offer to defect to the British. If so, that has been edited out of the Kremlin's sanitized version of history. The KGB's successor, the SVR, continues to honor Lonsdale in the Soviet foreign intelligence hall of fame, glossing over the fact that his detection was a British and U.S. counterespionage success.[37]

In 1968, the KGB began deploying illegals against targets within Soviet bloc countries themselves, in what it code-named PROGRESS operations. When liberalizing pro-democracy reformists rose up against Soviet rule in Czechoslovakia that year in what came to be called the Prague Spring, KGB chairman Yuri Andropov used his men to brutally crush the uprising. Remembering his lessons from Hungary twelve years earlier, Andropov sent an army of illegals disguised as Western tourists, journalists, and businesspeople, equipped with money and false papers, to Czechoslovakia. Their mission was to inform on Czech protesters, who were then arrested or deported to the Soviet Union. The illegals used false-flag operations to justify Moscow's armed intervention. These included the "discovery" of an American arms dump and a forgery purporting to show a U.S. plot to subvert the Czech regime.

In Moscow, Prime Minister Alexei Kosygin publicly decried Western subversion in Prague. The KGB withheld accurate intelligence, obtained by its Washington *rezidentura*, which showed that U.S. intelligence was in fact not behind the Prague Spring. The CIA kept President Lyndon Johnson informed about the protesters in Prague, but with the Vietnam War grinding on, he was trying to avoid confrontation with the Soviet Union. He decided not to intervene. Over the coming decades, the KGB would deploy more illegals against dissidents within the Soviet bloc than it ever did overseas. With deadlock in Europe, between two armed camps, Western powers looked for new ways to collect intelligence on their enemy in the East.[38]

CHAPTER NINE

RISE OF THE MACHINES

The King hath note of all that they intend,
By interception which they dream not of.
–Shakespeare, *Henry V*, Act 2, Scene 2

EISENHOWER'S GREATEST FEAR FOR THE SECURITY OF THE
United States was a surprise attack like Pearl Harbor, but now with atomic
bombs. He was shocked when U.S. intelligence failed to warn his administration about the Soviet Union's detonation of a hydrogen bomb in November 1955, nine months after America's own first test of a thermonuclear
weapon. The Soviet Union appeared to have capabilities to deliver such
a weapon to the United States, having unveiled its new long-range heavy
bomber, the Bison, at Moscow's May Day parade back in 1954. "The number
[of new heavy bombers]," wrote CIA head Allen Dulles, "far exceeded what
was thought to be available." One Soviet bomber was thought capable of
carrying a thermo-bomb with an explosive force 250 times greater than the
Hiroshima bomb—several times greater than all Allied munitions dropped
on wartime Germany. A Soviet nuclear attack would be catastrophic, leaving
millions dead. In reality, as U.S. analysts later realized, the 1954 parade
had been a hoax: the same squadron of Bison bombers flew in circles,

reappearing every few minutes over Red Square, making it seem like it was a much larger force.[1]

Two months later, Eisenhower called in MIT president James R. Killian to study ways to prevent a nuclear Pearl Harbor. Killian's February 1955 report marked a turning point for U.S. intelligence: technology would now be favored over old-fashioned human espionage. "We obtain little significant information from classic covert operations inside Russia," the report said: "But we can use the ultimate in science and technology to improve our intelligence take."[2]

Eisenhower took Killian's advice and began to throw money, people, and other resources into a new "wizard war." For years, U.S. and British intelligence had dreamed about recreating the SIGINT triumphs of the previous war. The Brownell Committee, whose recommendations led to the creation of the National Security Agency in the fall of 1952, as we have observed, dismissed the idea. Moscow's use of onetime pads made its communications effectively unreadable. Another study, in 1957, led by William Baker, the vice president of research at Bell Labs, noted it would take "centuries" for a computer to succeed in a bulk attack on onetime pads with a prearranged key code, given the impossibly large number of potential permutations. Even if such a computer could be built, Baker's secret report explained, it would require more energy than scientists believed to exist in the universe. In these mind-spinning circumstances, the only realistic prospect of reading Soviet traffic was through cryptanalysis: an analysis of the language and encrypted text, educated guesswork about what those messages might say, assisted, where possible, by human intelligence. "One code clerk may be worth the value of a number of intercept positions run for a number of years."[3]

Stalin was similarly haunted by the fear of a surprise attack—an atomic BARBAROSSA. He attached greater weight to old-fashioned espionage than to science and technology, but in time, the Soviet spies in the West convinced him of the threat of supercomputers. If the Americans and the British were able to pull off a computing miracle, Soviet communications could be read. As East and West vied for dominance, each side hoped to render the other's encrypted communications useless.

SPY TUNNELS

If technology could not immediately deliver the results that intelligence agencies needed, it was always possible to steal the answer. MI6's head of station in Vienna, Peter Lunn, had an inspired plan for doing so. Lunn was an Old Etonian, a former champion alpine skier, and a wartime MI6 recruit. He devised a way to tap into Soviet telephone landlines. From the cover of a shop in Vienna selling tweed fabric, Lunn proposed that MI6 dig a tunnel to access underground Soviet telephone lines in the Austrian capital. Since the Soviets had changed their communications from radio to landline in 1948, tapping into the phone system was one of the few avenues the British (and the Americans) had left to gather intelligence. Lunn's Vienna operation, code-named SILVER, was a success. It inspired his superiors in London to attempt something far more ambitious: to tunnel from West Berlin into the Soviet sector of the city to tap its communications.

Berlin was the Cold War's front line. It was a city frozen in time: 1945, when it had been divided between the Allied powers. It was a center of espionage. It was also a hub for Soviet bloc communications carried over telephone lines. Tunneling to reach them, MI6's technicians realized, would require resources that only the Americans could provide. The CIA was already thinking similarly, and Lunn's operation showed it could be done. For MI6, carrying out a skilled operation like this with their American "cousins" would also help repair its damaged relations with the CIA after the defections of Burgess and Maclean, and Washington's suspicions about Kim Philby (later proved correct).

In December 1953, MI6 chief, John Sinclair, and the tweedy, pipe-smoking Allen Dulles, then newly installed as DCI, agreed to a joint operation, unimaginatively code-named JOINTLY. Churchill personally approved their plan, risky though it was, and so likely did Eisenhower. Surprisingly, given the technical nature of the operation, it was conducted by MI6 and the CIA rather than by GCHQ and the NSA. In fact, the CIA did not inform the NSA until the fall of 1955, doubtless in response to the NSA's having declined to bring the CIA into VENONA for so long. The CIA only informed the NSA when it needed its translation resources. The NSA was pissed.

The Berlin tunneling operation, which MI6 code-named GOLD, a step up from SILVER, was an awesome feat of engineering. Reinhard Gehlen, Hitler's former intelligence chief on the eastern front, provided the locations of underground telephone junctions running to Soviet military headquarters in Karlshorst (in Berlin's Soviet sector). From a disguised warehouse basement in Rudow (in the U.S. sector), British and American teams dug a six-foot-wide, 1,476-foot steel-lined tunnel east to Altglienicke (in the Soviet sector), running under one of the most heavily guarded borders on the planet. The CIA's man on the ground was William Harvey, a hard-drinking, pistol-toting former FBI agent who had little in common with the "nice Yale boys," as he called CIA officers. Short, fat, bald, and puce-faced, Harvey was a coarse but effective dynamo. In just eight months, the British and the Americans hauled away some 3,100 tons of dirt by wooden railway track, working quietly in shifts round the clock. At one point, they hit an undocumented cesspool, making the tunnel a literal shit show. On one cold morning, as a previously secret CIA history of the operation reveals, those in the tunnel could hear an East Berlin security guard stomping his feet above them. Sounds of steel-hoofed horses overhead reverberated through the iron tunnel walls.[4]

Finally, they reached their target under Soviet military headquarters. Excavating a vertical shaft, they hit their mark, a cable mere inches in diameter. Lunn, as MI6's man in charge, helped to lay taps at the top of the shaft into the three Soviet landline cables. Assisted by American and British military engineers, the CIA and MI6 had successfully built a secret tunnel that was the length of about five American football fields. The operation cost $6.7 million (approximately $74 million today), roughly the same cost as the entire Lockheed U-2 spy plane project, with most of the cost borne by the Americans.[5]

Operation GOLD came on line in the summer of 1955. For eleven months, it provided British and U.S. intelligence with a massive haul of Soviet communications. According to the CIA's report, the operation yielded about 50,000 reels of magnetic tape, weighing 25 tons, containing 368,000 fully transcribed conversations in Russian and German. Magnetic tapes were flown from Berlin each week to Washington, where a team of Russian- and German-speaking personnel, housed in a hut built for the purpose on the Washington Mall, transcribed the communications. At its peak, there were 350 people involved on the American side. In London, an MI6 team swelling to 317 people transcribed voice recordings in a safe house in Carlton Gardens, in central London.[6]

In April 1956, disaster struck. A Soviet foot patrol discovered the tunnel, and MI6 and the CIA had to shut it down. It took their teams two and a half years to clear the backlog of amassed material, which resulted in 1,750 reports (code-named REGAL). The trove of intelligence from the Berlin tunnel gave the British and Americans insights they had lacked since Soviet codes went dark in 1948; these included the Soviet order of battle, insights about Moscow's intentions and capabilities, and the architecture of Soviet intelligence and counterintelligence. Some significant intelligence to come from the phone taps, however, was gleaned from what was not said: they revealed no indication that the Soviet Union was preparing to start World War III. Coexistence, rather than conquest, appeared to be the keynote of Soviet foreign policy in the post-Stalin world. MI6 and the CIA toasted their success.

Or so it seemed. In fact, while the British were the operation's inspiration, they were also its undoing. As it transpired, GOLD had been betrayed to Soviet intelligence almost from the outset because of a Soviet spy deep inside MI6, George Blake. Blake was the last major agent we know of who spied for the Soviet Union because of ideology, as opposed to soldiers of fortune, those who did it for cash, or to seek revenge. When Blake joined MI6, the service did not yet have enhanced positive vetting. If it had, it is likely he would never have made it to an MI6 interview. Blake always considered himself an outsider. He later insisted that he was not a traitor, because he never even considered himself to be British. "To betray, you first have to belong," he said. "I never belonged."[7]

George Blake was born in the Netherlands in 1922; his mother was Dutch, his father a naturalized British subject, originally from Turkey. During the war, he joined the Dutch resistance. Disguised as a monk, he escaped the Netherlands and got to Britain, where he changed his birth name, Behar, to Blake. He enlisted in the Royal Navy and in 1944 was recruited into MI6. After the war, he completed Russian-language training, and, in 1948, was posted to Britain's embassy in South Korea. A year later, shortly after the outbreak of the Korean War, he was captured by North Korean forces. He spent three years in captivity, where he was interviewed by a KGB officer. Blake revealed that he was an MI6 officer and volunteered to work as a Soviet agent (thereafter under the code name DIOMID). He later claimed that witnessing American carpet bombing in Korea had convinced him to spy for the Soviets. Following his release from North Korean captivity in 1953, he went back to Britain and was permitted to return to work for MI6, first in London, then overseas. MI6 vetted Blake again— inadequately. A slight man, by then in his mid-thirties, bearded, tanned, with what others described as a sensitive face, he spoke with a plummy British accent, emphasizing his r's, but with a Dutch tinge that he kept to the end of his days. His English wife knew nothing of his communist "double life."[8]

By a stroke of good luck for Moscow, Blake landed right in the middle of Operation GOLD. He was present, and responsible for taking notes, at initial MI6-CIA planning meetings at Carlton Gardens. A junior CIA officer, Cleveland Cram, later recalled that after one meeting, he asked Blake, the corresponding junior MI6 officer, if he wanted to get lunch. Blake politely declined, saying he was too busy with the meeting's notes. Indeed, he was. In January 1954, Blake had a meeting with his KGB controller on the top of a London double-decker bus, during which he handed over the MI6 minutes he had thus far taken. His other meetings with his KGB handler took place about once a month in parks and train stations. Blake was careful not to seek classified papers outside his MI6 duties.[9]

Having learned about GOLD, the KGB orchestrated for the Berlin tunnel to be "discovered" by a Soviet foot patrol in April 1956. It thus happened that MI6 and the CIA's tunnel operation lasted less than a year. The Soviet commandant in charge at Karlshorst called a press conference, unveiling the spy tunnel, and displayed some of the machinery stamped "Made in England." The Soviets expressed righteous indignation about the West's "perfidy" and "treachery." The East Germans opened a snack bar at the tunnel's entrance. It became a tourist attraction. In the West, news that British and American spies had tunneled under the feet of the Soviet military was met with adulation. The *Washington Post* ran a headline "Hope It's True." The KGB would later get back at MI6's Peter Lunn by placing a bug in his office at a British embassy.[10]

To this day, the Kremlin claims that its intelligence services used the tunnel to disseminate disinformation to the British and the Americans. Western commentators at the time, and since, have widely assumed the same. Russia's foreign ministry repeated this claim when George Blake died, at the ripe age of ninety-eight, in Russia in 2020. It would have been a clever ploy for Soviet intelligence to use the tunnel for disinformation, but there is no evidence that it did so. In fact, it appears that the KGB let the tunnel operation run to protect Blake, its prize agent in Britain. In doing so, it seems to have disregarded the attendant threat to its rival service, the GRU, and to the Soviet army. The KGB's own communications were secure, running on a separate network that the British and Americans were not tapping. To protect its agent, the KGB let the British and the Americans vacuum up the GRU's communications. Meanwhile, Blake continued his espionage work inside MI6. He used a KGB-supplied Minox camera, about the size of a matchbox, to photograph roughly two hundred documents a month, betraying British, American, and West German intelligence operations and agents. His haul allowed the KGB to eliminate CIA and MI6 networks in East Germany. Although Blake would later deny having blood on his hands, MI6 calculated that Soviet authorities executed at least forty agents based on tips by him.[11]

It is frequently said that it is spies who catch other spies, not brilliant technical wizardry. This was the case with George Blake. Michał Goleniewski, the Polish intelligence officer working for the CIA who exposed the Portland Spy Ring, also tipped them off about Blake. Goleniewski's intelligence included a warning, in 1961, that Soviet intelligence had a mole in MI6. Early that year, Goleniewski defected to the CIA and provided further leads about the traitor. The CIA passed his intelligence on to MI6. With the assistance of GCHQ, which analyzed Soviet intercept traffic, MI5 identified Blake as the most likely culprit.

In April 1961, MI6's leading expert on Soviet affairs, Harold Shergold, interviewed Blake over three days in Carlton Gardens. Shergold repeatedly put it to Blake that he was a Soviet agent. On the third day, the interrogator finally had a breakthrough. When Shergold suggested that Blake had been tortured while imprisoned in Korea, and had been blackmailed to work for the KGB, he blurted out angrily: "No, nobody tortured me! No, nobody blackmailed me! I myself approached the Soviets and offered my service to them of my own accord." Armed with this at least partial confession, MI6 tried a new tactic. They took Blake to Shergold's countryside cottage, in a village in Hampshire, in the hope that a relaxed weekend atmosphere would get him to talk more.

Shergold and Blake were joined at the cottage—kept under close Special Branch observation—by MI6's head of counterintelligence, John Quine. Quine revealed details about Blake in a later, never-aired TV interview. Over the course of the weekend, the three men talked, while Shergold's wife cooked. They drank, went for walks, and slowly started to discuss the purpose of their weekend retreat: they all knew that Blake was a Soviet spy. Although most historians who have studied this case have not noticed it, Shergold and Quine appear to have been willing to offer Blake immunity from prosecution in return for a full, secret confession. With no law enforcement powers, MI5 presumably would have had to get the director of public prosecutions to agree before making such an offer. Three years later, MI5 would make the same offer to the Cambridge spy Anthony Blunt, having failed to secure sufficient evidence against him for a trial.[12]

As it transpired, they never had to negotiate such a deal with Blake. He voluntarily confessed. With a full confession, Blake was put on trial in May 1961 at the Old Bailey and found guilty. The lord chief justice gave him what was then the longest sentence ever imposed by an English court, forty-two years' imprisonment. It never seems to have occurred to Blake that had he not confessed, the prosecution would not have had a strong enough case to bring him to trial. He was proud of his work for the Russians.

Blake's trial caused an international media sensation. The government's official secrecy about its intelligence services at the time placed the prime minister, Harold Macmillan, in an absurd position. After Blake's trial, Macmillan wrote in his diary that the British public did not know "and cannot be told he belonged to MI6, an organization which does not theoretically exist. So I had a rather rough passage through the House of Commons." Initially Britain's intelligence services feared that Blake's case would wreck their special relations with Washington. The U.S. intelligence community, however, had problems of its own, which overshadowed Blake's case. His trial came a month after the CIA's inept attempt to invade Cuba at the Bay of Pigs and shortly after the humiliating defection of two disaffected NSA cryptographers, William Martin and Bernon Mitchell. They had both been polygraphed. They escaped through Mexico and Cuba; once in Moscow, they gave a public press conference revealing that the NSA was reading the communications of friends and enemies alike. When MI5's liaison officer in Washington briefed J. Edgar Hoover on the Blake case, the usually irascible FBI director took it surprisingly well. He said that even Christ had a traitor in his small band of twelve disciples.[13]

Blake only remained incarcerated at London's Wormwood Scrubs prison for little more than five years. In October 1966, he escaped through a broken bar on a landing window and climbed down from the prison wall, using a knitting-needle rope ladder supplied by someone on the outside. He crossed to the Continent hidden in a camper van and then went on to

Moscow. The secrets that he had were six years old, thus not jeopardizing any agents' lives, MI5 and MI6 were relieved to tell Harold Wilson, then prime minister. At the time of Blake's defection, John le Carré wrote:

> There is enormous propaganda value for the Russians in his escape. It highlights the inefficiency of Britain's prisons in that, after the full weight of British justice had been massed to sentence him for 42 years, he could only be kept inside for five. But, more importantly, it further discredits the Western secret service agencies in Western eyes. It must give the Russians great pleasure.

In Moscow, the Kremlin rolled out the red carpet for Blake. Unlike Philby, Blake was not only appointed a KGB officer but made a colonel and awarded the Order of Lenin. Having abandoned a wife and three children in England, he remarried and started a new family in Russia. Years later, on Blake's eighty-fifth birthday, Putin would grant him Russia's Order of Friendship. As with other Western intelligence defectors, however, Blake's life in the Soviet Union was a carefully choreographed Kremlin display. Below the surface, it was as gray and disappointing as Moscow's bleak architecture.[14]

A decade after defecting, Blake would have a spectacular falling-out with Philby in Moscow. During a drunken weekend at Philby's dacha, a KGB gift to him, Philby's son took photos of the two spies, which then leaked to the British press. They were printed with the headline "Traitors Philby and Blake, Both Now with Russian Wives, Meet Near Moscow to Talk Over the Legacy of Betrayal." The photo shows the two men with glum expressions, "pathetically anxious to dispel any impression that they were treated as third class citizens," as the article stated. Blake, so outraged that he refused to speak to Philby again, became obsessed with conspiracy theories to explain why he had been punished so much more severely by British justice than Philby or Blunt: "It was probably because I was of foreign origin, and I could more easily be made an example of. . . . They were members of the Establishment, and I was not." In fact, Blake only had himself to blame for his sentence. If he had not made a voluntary and unconditional confession, he could not have been convicted, and MI6 probably would have struck the same bargain with him that MI5 offered to Blunt.[15]

LISTENING DEVICES IN THE WALLS, INK STANDS, AND TELEPHONES

From the moment when the United States opened diplomatic relations with the Soviet Union back in 1933, its Moscow embassy became a sustained target for Soviet electronic surveillance. It would continue to be so throughout the Cold War—and beyond. Eavesdropping provided Soviet leaders with insights into Western foreign policies. It also gave Soviet SIGINT officials opportunities to attack Western communications traffic. The celebrated historian of code-breaking, David Kahn, has probably correctly suggested that the greatest breakthroughs for Soviet code breakers came not from painstaking cryptanalysis, but from bugs and spies betraying their Western countries.[16]

Toward the end of World War II, a U.S. Navy technician conducted the first sweep of the U.S. embassy in Moscow. He discovered 120 microphones hidden throughout the premises, planted in walls, chair legs, and chimneys. Between 1943 and 1946, the British discovered 28 microphones in their Moscow embassy. A later study concluded that Soviet security officials had likely taken advantage of the evacuation of foreign diplomatic staff during the Nazi advance to plant them. The most notorious incident of Soviet bugging was revealed in 1952, when George Kennan had the embassy and his ambassadorial residence, Spaso House, searched. As Kennan dictated the text of an old diplomatic dispatch, technicians in another room heard his voice being transmitted. Homing in, they found a small wireless bug embedded inside a wooden replica of the Great Seal of the United States, hanging in Kennan's office.

The seal had been a gift, presented by Soviet schoolchildren, to Averell

Harriman at the end of the war. The pencil-shaped bug inside it stunned Western technicians: it was a resonating device, powered by microwaves that Soviet officials aimed at it from nearby buildings. As such, it was capable of operating indefinitely, since it did not need its own power supply. The bug had relayed U.S. officials' words to Soviet eavesdroppers for seven years. The next two American ambassadors to the Soviet Union, Charles Bohlen and Llewellyn Thompson, thereafter wrote out their telegrams in longhand rather than dictating them. When they had something sensitive to discuss with colleagues, they passed notes.

The discovery of "The Thing," as it was called, did not bring Soviet eavesdropping to an end. A decade later, two Soviet defectors, Golitsyn and Nosenko, revealed that there were additional bugs inside the U.S. embassy. Sweepers found fifty-two microphones hidden in bamboo tubes built into the embassy walls, placed behind radiators to shield them from metal detectors. They had been installed, it transpired, when the U.S. government built a new embassy on Tchaikovsky Street. During its construction, U.S. security personnel had stood guard during the day at the site to prevent local workmen from installing bugs, but inexplicably did not remain on duty at night, leaving the embassy wide open. Soviet archives contain intercepted American embassy telegrams. An October 1964 U.S. damage report into bugging concluded that, although it was not possible to trace specific changes of Soviet policy to the bugging of U.S. embassies, it was safe to assume that it enabled the Soviets to read "most, if not all, of our telegraphic messages between Washington and Moscow and between Washington and posts in Eastern Europe."

The CIA and NSA developed countermeasures by creating lead-lined, soundproof "bubbles," raised from the ground like large camping trailers, in American embassies. These bubbles were usually constructed deep in concrete basements and are now known as Sensitive Compartmented Information Facilities, or SCIFs. But SCIFs did not stop the barrage of electronic spying by the Soviets, who found workarounds. As listening-device technology advanced with ever-smaller microphones, so did the sophistication of

Soviet eavesdropping. Three decades after The Thing was found in the U.S. embassy, the NSA discovered that the Soviets had installed sophisticated miniature electronic bugs in sixteen IBM Selectric typewriters used in U.S. embassies in Moscow and Leningrad, concealed inside innocuous-looking bars running the length of each machine.

The project was known as GUNMAN. Over a period of eight years, Soviet intelligence had been copying every communication typed on the machines, and transmitting them by VHF radio bursts to KGB listening posts nearby. They were powered by batteries and from the typewriter's own power. Other miniature listening devices, following in the tradition of "The Thing," were discovered to be powered by electromagnetic waves which the Soviets bombarded the U.S. embassy with—levels so great in Moscow that it once prompted Secretary of State Kissinger, to complain to the Soviet ambassador in Washington, Anatoly Dobrynin. Kissinger claimed that the U.S. ambassador, Walter Stoessel, had developed leukemia because of prolonged electromagnetic radiation exposure. On instructions from Moscow, Dobrynin assured Kissinger that the field around the embassy did not exceed Soviet health standards—on its own terms, not a reassuring statement. A later U.S. investigation came to similar conclusions as Dobrynin, though CIA insiders claim the investigation was a "white wash" as to the danger of Soviet electronic radiation fired at the embassy. Sickness among U.S. embassy officials in Cold War Moscow has eerie echoes of "Havana Syndrome" arising among U.S. personnel since 2017.[17]

British and U.S. intelligence agencies were not, however, innocent victims when it came to electronic surveillance. They bugged Soviet bloc embassies in their own Western territories and overseas, especially in the Third World. When he met with Khrushchev in 1959, Harold Macmillan remarked: "In every Embassy in the world there were listening devices in the walls, or the ink stands, or the telephones." It was an exaggeration, but not far-fetched.[18]

In *Spycatcher*, the renegade MI5 officer, Peter Wright, wrote that in the 1950s British intelligence bugged the Soviet consulate in London by breaking into a neighboring building and inserting a microphone probe into the wall. He also once gained entry into the Egyptian embassy in London disguised as a telephone technician and planted a listening device so sensitive that it could detect keystrokes used by the embassy's cipher clerk. GCHQ and the NSA discovered that cipher machines produced compromising acoustic and electromagnetic emanations, which could be detected from such well-placed receivers, producing a haul known as TEMPEST. Wright's bug in the Egyptian embassy allowed GCHQ to track Cairo's communications with the Soviet Union, as well as Egyptian traffic, which proved useful during Britain's Suez crisis in 1956. The FBI conducted similar burglaries and buggings.[19]

EAST-WEST RACE FOR COMPUTING DOMINANCE

The NSA received an influx of resources and staff during Eisenhower's administration. By 1956, its headquarters at Fort Meade, measuring 1.4 million square feet, had approximately 9,000 employees. Fifteen years later, it had 110,000 employees. In a project code-named LIGHTNING, in 1957, Eisenhower authorized the NSA to develop the leading computer-research program in the world. With a budget of $25 million over five years, it brought in the best brains available from the private sector and universities. It was the age of the military-industrial complex. LIGHTNING's goal was to expand computer capability by a thousand percent, which it successfully did.[20]

Under the guidance of the NSA's first director, Ralph Canine, and its long-serving deputy, Louis Tordella, Fort Meade became a major center of scientific and technical research. Through Project LIGHTNING, the NSA and its defense contractors developed computers that no longer relied on vacuum tubes for their calculations but instead used magnetic tape and tape drives. In the 1950s the NSA built a computer called SOLO, which for the first time used solid-state transistors. Another computer, HARVEST, which used a high-speed tape-drive system, was the first fully automated storage and retrieval system, and a precursor to modern storage systems. The NSA also used mainframes—huge computers that took up an entire room—dedicated to specific tasks. Within a decade, the NSA would have more than one hundred such computers.[21]

The resources that Eisenhower plowed into U.S. SIGINT changed not just East-West relations but the balance of power among the Western powers themselves. At the end of World War II, London was the undisputed leader when it came to SIGINT. A decade later, U.S. intelligence had overtaken Britain. The Americans outspent the British fifteen to one and devoted seven times the manpower to SIGINT. That imbalance was not lost on White-hall. By 1954, GCHQ had a special-purpose digital computer, OEDIPUS, joining the effort to crack Soviet codes. But Cheltenham, where GCHQ was based, from 1954, frequently depended on American hardware.

GCHQ's deputy director, Leonard "Joe" Hooper, recognized how important it was for the British to continue being valuable to Washington. Hooper was a Bletchley veteran and therefore knew firsthand the importance of Anglo-American joint efforts in intelligence. But although the British needed the Americans for their huge computing resources, the Americans were becoming "less dependent on us," Hooper noted. Later, as GCHQ director, Hooper would shape the organization's strategy toward making itself useful to the NSA.

To offer advantages to the Americans, GCHQ needed financial investment—unwelcome news for Britain's Treasury. Prime Minister Mac-millan was cutting costs wherever possible. In 1957, he ordered what he called "something of a Profit and Loss Account" of Britain's overseas empire to see what could be cut. "Supermac," as Macmillan was known after a cartoon of him as Superman stuck, forced Whitehall to cut its department budgets by 10 percent. The idea that the Treasury should spend *more* on its spies and intelligence services was anathema; the British government's total spending on SIGINT by 1962 was already as much as the whole of the Foreign Office, with all its embassies and diplomats overseas. As the historian Richard Aldrich has noted, GCHQ was being paid more than its master.[22]

It was during this impecunious time that the Treasury instigated an independent review of Britain's SIGINT capabilities. It was conducted by the Oxford philosopher Stuart Hampshire. On first impression, a philosopher might seem an improbable choice to review the future of Britain's technical code-breaking service. But Hampshire had a razor-sharp mind and had served in MI6 during the war, decrypting German radio communications.

Hampshire's probe of British SIGINT lasted ten months in 1963, including a six-week visit to NSA headquarters at Fort Meade. If the Treasury was hoping for the highbrow Oxford don to produce an audit whose obvious point would be to slash GCHQ's budget, they were disappointed. Hampshire concluded that SIGINT was so important for transatlantic relations that its funding could not be cut, but instead should be increased. SIGINT was one area where the government could exert disproportionate impact on U.S. strategy during the Cold War. According to Hampshire, SIGINT was a "hard" subject, a source of intelligence, not dependent on the soft, subjective uncertainties of human nature inherent in espionage. Reflecting on his wartime experiences, Hampshire argued, SIGINT provided the best opportunity for Britain to be the engine room of intelligence collection on the Soviet Union.

Hampshire found a valuable ally in Britain's newly appointed avuncular cabinet secretary, Burke Trend, who likewise saw the value of secret service work. With their backing, GCHQ scored a major victory. After 1962, the budgets of most British foreign departments went down by 10 percent. Hampshire's report caused Britain's SIGINT budget to go up by the same amount.[23]

The Soviet Union, under both Stalin and Khrushchev, was just as active in the search for another ULTRA. In July 1948, Stalin created the Institute of Precision Mechanics and Computer Technology in Moscow to build a powerful Soviet computer. Its first computer went operational by December 1951. Collaborating with the Advanced School of Cryptography, Soviet SIGINT efforts were led by a talented GRU officer, Nikolai Andreev. By the early 1960s, the KGB claimed to be reading two hundred thousand cables a year sent by fifty-one different governments. Despite the size of the Soviet

SIGINT enterprise, it was fragmented and disorganized. It was controlled by endlessly changing rival bureaucracies. The GRU's Eighth Directorate was responsible for decrypting military communications, while the KGB's own Eighth Chief Directorate attacked diplomatic and other civilian traffic. Later, the KGB's Eighth Directorate confusingly changed its name to the Sixteenth Directorate. Its perplexing iteration of titles revealed deeper issues about the confused state of Soviet SIGINT.

The Soviet Union boasted some of the world's best theoretical mathematicians and physicists, pioneers in the fundamental principles of computer science. But when it came to applying their theories in the research labs, as we have noted, they acted with trepidation due to the nature of the regime. By contrast, application of theory was where the U.S. excelled. As a result, the Soviet M-20 computer paled in comparison to the IBM Naval Ordnance Research Calculator (NORC)—the world's first supercomputer, using vacuum tubes and electronic tape. NSA and GCHQ both used NORCs. The heads of Soviet intelligence under Khrushchev knew this full well. In the early 1960s, they embraced a fateful decision to address it: to harness the best possible computing power, knowing they could not compete with Western providers, they made their equipment compatible with IBM hardware. This provided Washington with additional leverage in the East-West technology arms race. A decade later, for example, the U.S. government placed an embargo on the sale of American industrial hardware, including IBM computers, to the Soviet Union. Preventing an adversary from acquiring essential technology was just as important as innovation when it came to a race for computing. There are whispers that the Soviet Union's use of IBM technology allowed for U.S. supply chain sabotage operations.[24]

ENGINEERING A GLOBAL CRYPTO HACK

As Richard Aldrich has noted, until 2020 scholars of intelligence and international relations had been unable to piece together the history of signals

intelligence from Bletchley Park's time to the disclosures leaked by Edward
Snowden about British and U.S. bulk data collection. For anyone familiar
with Bletchley Park, Arlington Hall (headquarters of the wartime U.S.
Army SIS), and their postwar successors, the principle of bulk collection
revealed by Snowden—quickly and erroneously called "mass surveillance"
by pundits—was unsurprising. But how Washington and London developed those capabilities was anyone's guess. Scholars examined NSA and
GCHQ code-breaking efforts during the Cold War using a patchwork of
archival sources, which they skillfully wove together, but which were necessarily incomplete. GCHQ insiders confidently told me that its history
could never be officially written, because doing so would require disclosing
some major postwar secrets. When pressed about what such a tantalizing
comment meant specifically, they clammed up or became amnesiacs about
their Cold War work.

Spies at Cheltenham did commission and publish their history in
2019. But its otherwise intricately researched history, by a leading expert
in SIGINT, John Ferris, does not discuss a major revelation uncovered by
investigative journalists just one year later, in 2020: during the Cold War,
U.S. intelligence engineered a hack of global communications that lasted for
decades. It systematically rigged, and exploited, encryption machines made
by the world's leading manufacturer, a Swiss company, Crypto AG. The
exploitation of Crypto by U.S. intelligence constituted the longest-running
and most successful SIGINT operation in history. In the early 1950s, Crypto
entered into a secret agreement with the CIA and West Germany's intelligence service. Later the Swiss company became a wholly owned subsidiary of
Langley. Crypto's 250 employees at its headquarters near the lakeside town
of Zug did not know they were in fact working for the CIA. Its customers
trusted they were getting the best equipment that money could buy and
the guarantee of Swiss neutrality. They were all deceived.[25]

According to a leaked detailed in-house CIA history of the operation,
Crypto's hardware, which was sold to at least 120 different governments
during the Cold War, effectively operated as collection platforms for U.S.

and West German intelligence. The CIA initially called the operation THE-SAURUS. It was apt. Thanks to the use of Crypto machines, U.S. and West German intelligence analysts were able to read the communications of governments like books. This was the missing puzzle piece linking the history of code-breaking from the era of mechanical gears at Bletchley to the age of silicon chips and software in the decades that Snowden revealed. Journalists and historians had periodically stumbled upon clues pertaining to Crypto but were unable to complete the picture. As described in the top secret CIA history of the operation written for internal use: "It was the intelligence coup of the century. Foreign governments were paying good money to the U.S. and West Germany for the privilege of having their most secret communications read by at least two (and possibly as many as five or six) foreign countries." Even accounting for what we might assume to be inevitable exaggerations of an in-house history, it is hard to disagree with this conclusion.

How did this come about? In 1957, America's leading code breaker, William Friedman, who ran the research division of U.S. Army SIS, visited a close friend in Europe, Boris Hagelin, a Swedish manufacturer of encryption machines and the founder, in 1952, of Crypto AG. The two men were kindred spirits. Both were Russian-born and thus had a naturally gloomy outlook about mankind. They shared a fascination for encryption and decryption. They had known each other since the 1930s, but it was during World War II that the two men, one a code maker, the other a code breaker, began collaborating. As the Nazis surrounded Sweden in 1940, Hagelin, who was living there, escaped to America. He brought with him one of his encryption machines, a portable hand-powered device that looked like a fortified music box. He won a valuable contract with U.S. Army SIGINT to provide encryption machines for troops on the move. It made him wealthy. At the end of the war, Hagelin returned to Sweden, but he was forever grateful to the country that had welcomed him and made him rich. He remained in touch with Friedman.

In 1951 the two men met in Washington over dinner at Friedman's favorite haunt, the exclusive Cosmos Club. Friedman brought both a message and a proposal. His message: the U.S. stood on the brink of a precipice. Sophisticated commercial encryption machines offered by technology giants like Siemens were coming on the market and risked defeating U.S. code breakers. So Friedman made a proposal to his Swedish friend: to prevent Washington from "going dark," Hagelin could sell lower-grade encryption machines to third-party governments, which he would tell Friedman about, while selling superior machines to the U.S. and its trusted allies. Hagelin agreed; the two shook hands, having arrived at their ungentlemanly agreement. It evolved and was memorialized over the coming years, but its substance remained the same as that initially reached over dinner in Washington. Hagelin sold lesser-quality machines to all the world's governments except for a trusted inner circle, which included the Western Five Eyes nations.

Hagelin's motivations for entering the deal were manifold. He had moved Crypto to Switzerland for tax purposes and to escape what he considered a draconian Swedish law obliging collaboration with the Swedish authorities for purposes of national security. To his mind, Friedman's request on behalf of America, a country he was indebted and loyal to, was different. The Americans were the good guys, and Friedman was his friend. Hagelin was also a savvy businessman. He must have realized that having the U.S. government as a guaranteed business customer was an almost incalculably lucrative opportunity. The gentleman's agreement came with a $700,000 advance (about $8.6 million today).

Friedman and Hagelin refined their original agreement during subsequent meetings. They continued to fear that unbreakable ciphers would appear on the private market. The plot of Ian Fleming's *From Russia with Love*, published in 1957, was not far-fetched: it featured a Russian super-enciphered machine, the Spektor. In 1960, the CIA entered into a full-blown licensing agreement with Crypto (which it code-named MINERVA). The CIA paid Crypto $855,000. The other silent partner in the licensing agreement was the CIA's West German protégé, the BND. In 1970, they bought the company outright. Thus the world's leading encryption manufacturer became a front for Western intelligence collection during the Cold War, an operation now code-named RUBICON by the CIA.

The deal not only provided America's spies with a back door into Crypto hardware—it gave them a front door. The U.S. intelligence community was effectively blind-copied on every communication using Crypto machines. The NSA was initially lukewarm toward rigging Crypto's equipment. Fort Meade saw its primary objective as harnessing computing power to break into encrypted communications. It was skeptical that a deal with a foreign commercial entity could produce significant results. The CIA saw it differently. It eagerly took ownership of the operation and propelled it forward. RUBICON reveals a largely unappreciated reality of intelligence during the Cold War (and onward): signals intelligence and human espionage were not separated neatly between agencies like the NSA and the CIA. Langley's technical department, D Division, undertook SIGINT capabilities of its own. Another reason why the CIA took the lead in RUBICON was because it necessarily involved an element of human tradecraft. That was stock-in-trade for the CIA Directorate of Operations. The handful of Crypto executives who knew about its ownership by Langley worked with a CIA case officer. Agency officers posed as Crypto employees in boardrooms and government offices across the world. Rigging Crypto was both a human and an electronic espionage operation.

That said, the CIA's theft of global communications had limitations. America's and Britain's primary intelligence targets during the Cold War in the East, the Soviet Union and China, were never Crypto customers. The Kremlin discovered the West's secret manipulation of Crypto from its two spies inside the NSA, cryptologists Martin and Mitchell, who, as we have observed, defected in 1960, and others who followed in their footsteps. While Crypto did not, therefore, unlock Soviet and Chinese communications, it did so for Third World nations that formed the "non-aligned" movement during the Cold War. Reading their communications allowed intelligence analysts in Washington and London to see the extent to which countries in South America, Africa, and Southeast Asia (what today is called the Global South) were aligned with the Soviet Union. And in the Cold War's endless espionage game, the Kremlin would have known that the West was reading the communications of nonaligned countries. And so on.

At certain crisis points during the Cold War, RUBICON paid off handsomely, with direct results for leaders in the White House and Downing Street. In 1978, the NSA was monitoring the communications of Egypt's U.S.-friendly leader, Anwar Sadat, when he met President Jimmy Carter at Camp David to secure a peace accord with Israel. It did so, it seems, thanks to RUBICON. The haul from Crypto machines also produced some real-time intelligence about the fall of the shah of Iran in 1979—though evidently not enough to provide U.S. intelligence with forewarning—and the Falklands War three years later. In the later stages of the Cold War, RUBICON was responsible for producing 40 percent of all communications that the NSA decrypted.[26]

There is a more sinister question raised by publicly available documentation about the operation: Did the U.S. intelligence community know about human rights abuses, even atrocities, committed by regimes using Crypto, which it did not disclose to protect RUBICON? We have already encountered this moral maze—whether to publicly disclose crimes or protect a valuable intelligence operation—with Churchill and the wartime ULTRA decrypts in the face of Nazi killings in occupied Europe. If the CIA knew, from RUBICON, that Americans were in danger, then it would be legally required to warn those citizens. CIA insiders have suggested to me that during the Cold War, they deliberately leaked stories to investigative reporters about human rights abuses based on disguised Crypto intelligence. A full accounting of this story, however, can only be written once the relevant documents become available. Doing so will open a significant public policy debate about what the leaders of Western democracies prioritize: safeguarding state secrets during a geopolitical struggle or potentially jeopardizing them to save lives at risk.

SPIES IN THE SKY

President Eisenhower valued aerial reconnaissance, but he complained to his national security team about the lack of imagery intelligence (IMINT) on the Soviet Union compared to what military leaders in Europe and the Pacific theater had during World War II. One of the members of the committee led by James Killian, who we met earlier, was Edwin Land, the scientist who invented the Polaroid camera. On November 5, 1954, Land sent Allen Dulles a memorandum urging that the CIA become a "pioneer in scientific techniques for collecting intelligence" and that it seize the "opportunity for aerial photography." Three weeks later, the day before Thanksgiving, Dulles, Killian, and Land met with Eisenhower at the Oval Office to propose developing a high-altitude spy plane. No minutes were kept of the meeting. Although Eisenhower usually liked to sleep on important decisions, according to Killian's later account, the president authorized the U-2 spy plane program on the spot, stating: "Well, boys, I believe the country needs this information, and I'm going to approve it. But I'll tell you one thing. Some day one of these machines is going to be caught, and we're going to have a storm."[27]

Just half an hour after Eisenhower authorized the U-2 program, the CIA officer who was named to manage it, Richard Bissell, was summoned to the Oval Office. Eisenhower emphasized the paramount importance of secrecy. Bissell—pale, male, and from Yale—was the embodiment of the agency at that time, part of what was known as the Georgetown set, the well-connected, well-educated, well-to-do Cold War chess masters who helped shape American strategy. One can almost hear Allen Dulles, who shuffled around his office wearing slippers because of gout, and Bissell calling each other "old sport" in the CIA's halls.

A gawky economist, who taught intermittently at MIT, Bissell did not know much about aerial technology. But he was masterful at running big projects. He had previously been an administrator of the Marshall Plan, where he funded OPC (CIA) covert operations in Europe. Bissell was in a league of his own when it came to galvanizing Washington bureaucracy. He energetically moved the project from the drawing board to the runway in record time. Under a top secret contract signed with Lockheed Martin, the high-altitude plane was built in a California hangar called the Skunk Works, because no unauthorized personnel were allowed near it. The aircraft was built of lightweight aluminum, powered by two fuel-efficient engines mounted on its fuselage. Its glider-like wings allowed it to soar into the stratosphere at 70,000 feet. High-resolution cameras made by an electronics firm, Hycon Manufacturing, were mounted on board. Just seven months after the contract was signed with Lockheed, the U-2 flew its first test flight, in August 1955. Bissell brought the project in $3 million *under* budget. Its veil of secrecy was so tight that only about five hundred people—a small number for the construction of an entire new spy plane—knew about it.[28]

Test flights over U.S. airspace revealed that the U-2 plane shot past radar undetected. Edwin Land showed Eisenhower photographs from one such flight, which he displayed on large briefing boards. A photograph of San Diego, taken from seventy thousand feet, revealed automobiles on the streets; the president could see the lines separating spaces in the parking lots. With the U-2, Bissell later said, the U.S. intelligence community had the ability, within twenty-four hours, to cover any part of the earth within reach from American airfields and to do so in seventy-two hours for any place requiring refueling. America could surveil the globe.

For Eisenhower, spying was a last resort. If something could be done openly, and by mutual agreement, it should. Buoyed by the success of U-2 test flights, Eisenhower made a dramatic proposal, called Open Skies, during a four-way East-West summit in Geneva in July of 1955: that the United States and Soviet Union agree to allow each other right of aerial reconnaissance and make available a blueprint of their military establishments. Over cocktails after the conference session, Khrushchev told Eisenhower that his proposal was "nothing more than a bald espionage plot against the Soviet Union." Open Skies was grounded. But later in the Cold War, mutual overhead reconnaissance conducted by Soviet and U.S. space satellites would become essential for verifying East-West arms control agreements—the very principle that Eisenhower had suggested.

Secret overhead reconnaissance was now, in Eisenhower's view, the only way ahead to collect intelligence on the heavily guarded Soviet Union, given Khrushchev's refusal of Open Skies. U-2s would give the U.S. intelligence community and leaders a view into the darkness behind the Iron Curtain. Eisenhower personally reviewed and approved every U-2 mission, as papers at his presidential library reveal. Authorizing flights over Soviet territory provoked excruciating "soul searching," he wrote. If the secret missions were discovered, the political fallout with the Soviet Union would be immense. If a U-2 flight were detected, Eisenhower would have to disavow it, which would jeopardize his reputation for honesty throughout the free world. Khrushchev was looking for excuses to be belligerent.

To help reduce Eisenhower's angst about authorizing U-2 missions, Bissell proposed that they become a shared project with the British; its prime minister should also be allowed to authorize U-2 flights over the Soviet Union, suggested Bissell. Reflecting on the uniquely close relations between the two countries, and remembering successful wartime Anglo-American photo reconnaissance, in August 1958 Eisenhower agreed to Bissell's proposal. U-2 flights were so politically charged, however, that Harold Macmillan refused to allow them to take off from airfields in the British mainland. Instead, as a previously classified history of the U-2 project shows, they flew from overseas British bases. In late 1959, Macmillan authorized his first U-2 mission over the Soviet Union, flown by British RAF pilots, from the Middle East. Over the next two years, British pilots conducted twenty-seven such Soviet overflight missions.[29]

In addition to the geopolitical risks, Eisenhower was clear-eyed about the risks that the mission's volunteer pilots were taking. If they were shot down, and survived, they would have to choose between being captured or taking a poison pin, embedded in a coin, which they carried. "It was our expectation from the very beginning that someone would eventually get shot down," Bissell later said. Secretly he calculated that there was no chance of a pilot surviving if a U-2 were hit.

The first U.S. flight over the Soviet Union was in July 1956. It covered targets in the Leningrad area and long-range bomber bases in the western Soviet Union. The CIA's senior photographic-intelligence analyst, Arthur "Art" Lundahl, brought the photographs from the flight to Eisenhower, who pored over them with a magnifying glass. When the president asked whether the Soviets had tried to intercept the mission, Lundahl displayed photographs of MiG fighters trying desperately to reach the U-2, but falling back as their engines cut out at high altitude.[30]

The second U-2 mission, just twenty-four hours after the first, photographed Moscow and targets in southern Ukraine, outflying surface-to-air missiles. Between July 1956 and August 1960, U-2s flew fifty-one missions over the Soviet bloc, half of which were over Russia itself, according to CIA documents at the Eisenhower library. U-2 aircraft were also equipped with NSA equipment to detect electronic emissions, or ELINT: Soviet radar, microwaves, and ground communications. Doing so brought an end to the risky U.S. and British ELINT "ferret" mission flights that the two countries had previously flown, briefly skirting Soviet airspace to trigger Soviet radar for ELINT collection and analysis. About ninety personnel died in ELINT flights around the Soviet Union during the Cold War.[31]

The intelligence produced by U-2 spy planes shaped America's strategy toward the Soviet Union. They gradually exposed a myth in Washington that the Soviet Union possessed an intercontinental bomber force superior to that of the United States, the "bomber gap." In 1955, U.S. Air Force intelligence assessments claimed that by the end of the decade the Soviet long-range air force would be more powerful than U.S. Strategic Air Command. In 1956, Senator Stuart Symington, the first secretary of the air force and a Democrat from Missouri with presidential ambitions, convened three months of hearings on U.S. airpower. The architect of U.S. wartime strategic bombing in the Pacific, Curtis LeMay, testified that by 1958, the Soviets would be "stronger" than the U.S. government, and, once stronger, "may feel it could attack." U.S. Air Force intelligence estimated that the Soviet Union would be producing twenty-five of its Bear bombers per month by late 1956; and that, by 1959 or 1960, it would possess a fleet of six hundred to eight hundred of its four-engine Bison strategic bombers. U-2 IMINT caused these alarmist calculations to be scaled down. By 1959, the Soviets in fact possessed a combined total of fewer than two hundred Bison and Bear bombers.[32]

The U-2 catastrophe that Eisenhower feared occurred in May 1960, as he neared the end of his second term. With a four-power summit scheduled for June in Paris, he had been reluctant to authorize any U-2 flights, believing that it would be disastrous "if one of these aircraft were lost when we are engaged in apparently sincere deliberations." Nevertheless, he was persuaded to authorize one more mission, GRAND SLAM, by May 1. CIA pilot Francis Gary "Frank" Powers was to take off from a U.S. base in Peshawar, Pakistan, pass over Soviet nuclear plants in the Urals, fly over Stalingrad (now Volgograd), and land in Norway. It did not go as planned, as the film *Bridge of Spies* vividly portrays. As Khrushchev was reviewing troops at the May Day parade in Moscow, the commander of Soviet defense forces whispered in his ear that a U-2 had been downed by a Soviet surface-to-air missile.

Eisenhower received the news soon after. He and the CIA assumed that the pilot had been killed, and put out a cover story that the flight was a research plane. Five days later, May 5, Khrushchev gave a marathon address to the governing council of the Soviet Union, the Supreme Soviet, in which he announced, to thunderous applause, that an American "aggressor plane" had been shot down deep inside Soviet territory. Eisenhower modified slightly the cover story he had given, claiming that the pilot had lost consciousness and flown into Soviet territory. In fact, he fell into a trap that had been laid by the Soviet leader. On May 7, Khrushchev announced to even greater applause at the Supreme Soviet that Powers was alive, being held in captivity, and would stand trial.

Powers had survived because the Soviet surface-to-air missile did not hit the fragile U-2 plane fuselage, but exploded behind it, using a proximity fuse (based on technology that one of the wartime Soviet atom spies, Julius Rosenberg, had stolen from the MANHATTAN Project). Powers was thrown clear of the plane before he could activate the self-destruct mechanism, and parachuted safely to the ground. He did not use his suicide pin—though U-2 pilots were not required to do so. Eisenhower received the news that Powers was alive and being held in Soviet custody while he was at his Gettysburg house for the weekend.

Over the coming days, he agonized about whether to go public with the U-2 program and risk aggravating Khrushchev before the Paris Summit. He found himself placed in precisely the position he had wanted to avoid: either making an implausible denial or coming clean. In Moscow, Khrushchev feigned righteous indignation about U.S. aerial espionage, despite presiding over the KGB, the largest intelligence and secret police force in history. The KGB accompanied the news with active measures to discredit the U.S. government. It forged, and leaked, documents alleging that the U.S. government was using the U-2 to spy on allies. It also set out to discredit the DCI, Allen Dulles.[33]

Behind closed doors, Art Lundahl gave classified briefings on the U-2 missions to U.S. senators. He received a standing ovation. Allen Dulles was so taken aback that his pipe fell out of his mouth and his jacket started smoldering. Eisenhower, however, refused to go public with the U-2. On the eve of traveling to Paris, he held a press conference in which he defended intelligence work in general terms. It was "a distasteful but vital necessity":

No one wants another Pearl Harbor. This means that we must have knowledge of military forces and preparations around the world, especially those capable of massive surprise attacks.

Secrecy in the Soviet Union makes this essential. In most of the world no large-scale attack could be prepared in secret, but in the Soviet Union there is a fetish of secrecy and concealment. This is a major cause of international tension and uneasiness today. . . .

The Paris Summit was effectively over before it began. Khrushchev demanded an apology for the U-2 flights and a guarantee that they would cease. Eisenhower offered to return to his earlier Open Skies proposal. Back in the United States, the president finally went on national television to explain the events of the past two weeks. He had an opportunity to score a major public relations victory, by displaying U-2 photographs of Soviet targets that the CIA had prepared for him to use. But at the last minute, as the historian Christopher Andrew has noted, the president decided to show only pictures from inside U.S. airspace. He could have revealed to viewers the importance of imagery intelligence. Given the reception of the U-2 in the U.S. Senate, it seems likely that the American public would have rallied behind the idea that the Soviet missiles and bomber force should be monitored closely. In fact, the president could have turned the whole situation on its head and shown the success of U.S. intelligence in monitoring the Soviet nuclear strike force. His instincts as a military man, however, got the better of him. Eisenhower instead kept U.S. IMINT on the Soviet Union secret.[34]

Following the Powers debacle, Eisenhower did not authorize any more U-2 flights. He did, however, push forward another CIA project (code-named OXCART) to build an even higher-altitude spy plane, called the A-12. But Eisenhower also had another secret weapon to collect intelligence on the Soviet Union. Under James Killian's guidance, the U.S. government launched its first photo-reconnaissance space satellite (CORONA, whose cover name was *Discoverer*), a month after the downing of Powers's plane. For the first time in history, a Western intelligence agency could monitor another country's military bases and activities from space, which was, White House lawyers suggested, by definition beyond the jurisdiction of any nation on earth. Besides, the Soviets had established the principle of space overflight with Sputnik. The East-West intelligence war had gone orbital.[35]

U-2 IMINT allowed Eisenhower to resist pressure from the U.S. military-industrial complex to escalate military production in a race to catch up with the (nonexistent) bomber gap. But this was happening in secret. In public, U.S. weakness was widely debated. Democrats accused Eisenhower of it. Another myth took hold: that the U.S. trailed the Soviets in a "missile gap." The chief proponent of that claim was John F. Kennedy, who proclaimed—inaccurately—in his 1960 presidential election campaign that there was a "missile gap" favoring the Soviet Union. Considering the Soviet success of Sputnik, and the Luna 2 rocket to the moon in September 1959, this was plausible. But it was wrong, and was stoked by Soviet propaganda and disinformation. In reality, it was the other way around. (The U.S. also held a ten-to-one edge in nuclear warheads over Moscow.) Eisenhower knew from U-2 intelligence that Kennedy's claim was false, but he did not—could not—publicly correct him.[36]

To rein in Kennedy's unfounded claims, which were buoyed by Soviet propaganda about its arsenal, Eisenhower authorized Allen Dulles to brief "little boy blue," as Ike called Kennedy. Dulles did so in July 1960 at the Kennedy family compound in Hyannis Port, Massachusetts, and the Texas ranch of Kennedy's vice presidential running mate, Lyndon Johnson. According to Dulles's reports of the meetings, Kennedy was interested in the U-2 program and asked about "how we ourselves stood in the missile race." Dulles told Kennedy that the Defense Department was the competent body to answer that. The next month, as we can see in a paper trail at both presidents' libraries, Eisenhower authorized another briefing for Kennedy, now by the Department of Defense. According to the director of the Joint Chiefs, Earle Wheeler, who briefed Kennedy, when the candidate heard about the number of U.S. and Soviet operational missiles, he asked if there were any doubting Thomases within U.S. intelligence. Wheeler replied that it was the job of U.S. intelligence to be doubting Thomases.[37]

Even after Kennedy's classified briefings, he continued to refer to the missile gap in his campaign. This suggests a calculating, duplicitous side to the handsome young candidate who, driven by ambition, was willing to rely on dubious claims to further his political advantage. He won the presidency in 1960 in the closest election in American history to that point. His opponent, Vice President Richard M. Nixon, knew the reality of the nonexistent missile gap from intelligence briefings he received as Eisenhower's second-in-command, but could not correct Kennedy in public without revealing U-2 intelligence. It helped to poison Nixon's view of the CIA, which, he believed, had failed to take steps to counter Kennedy's false accusations. Once in power, Kennedy was briefed again on the "missile gap," a myth that he had helped perpetrate. In February 1961, his secretary of defense, Robert McNamara, told reporters in a briefing he thought was off record that there was no missile gap. When the story broke, McNamara offered to resign; Kennedy asked him to remain, but to allow the missile gap controversy to die away.[38]

CHAPTER TEN

THE MISSILES OF OCTOBER

Evaluation of enemy strength is not an absolute, but a matter
of piecing together scraps of reconnaissance and intelligence to
form a picture, if possible a picture to fit preconceived theories
or to suit the demands of a particular strategy. What a staff
makes out of the available evidence depends upon the degree
of optimism or pessimism prevailing among them, on what
they want to believe or fear to believe, and sometimes upon the
sensitivity or intuition of an individual.
–Barbara W. Tuchman, *The Guns of August*

ON AN APRIL MORNING IN MOSCOW IN 1962, WITH SNOW
still on the ground, a young British woman took her two young children for
a crisp walk along Tsvetnoy Boulevard. Pushing her youngest in a stroller, she
sat down on a park bench for a rest. Shortly thereafter, a burly Russian man
with a military bearing approached, stopped, and exchanged a few pleas-
antries with her, admiring her children. At the end of their conversation, in
a seemingly kind gesture, he placed a box of sweets in the child's stroller.[1]

The man was Oleg Penkovsky, who worked inside the GRU. Penkovsky
was one of the West's prize agents during the Cold War. And the mother he

met on that Moscow park bench? She was Janet Chisholm, the wife of MI6's head of station in Moscow, Ruari Chisholm. Under suffocating KGB surveillance in Moscow, Janet acted the part of an innocent-looking civilian. In fact, she was a cutout between Penkovsky and MI6. Inside the box of chocolates Penkovsky left in the stroller were seven rolls of developed Minox microfilm and two sheets of paper revealing secrets of the Soviet military arsenal. The exchange between Penkovsky and Chisholm that day was one of a dozen or so orchestrated by MI6. The intelligence that Penkovsky spirited to the West from deep inside Soviet military intelligence would have immense value six months later during the Cuban Missile Crisis, when the Soviet Union and the United States stood on the brink of nuclear Armageddon.[2]

THE HUMAN FACTOR

Penkovsky, deputy head of the GRU's foreign section, was a hugely productive spy. Working with a maniacal effort that at times alarmed his British and American case officers, he produced a total of ten thousand pages of classified GRU reports about Soviet missiles and military strategy. It took twenty CIA officers and ten MI6 officers to translate and analyze the voluminous material he stole. According to one account of his espionage, written with access to CIA records, Penkovsky saved the world during the Cuban Missile Crisis. That grandiose claim is misleading. But his espionage without question contributed to President Kennedy's decision-making and statecraft during the crisis. Penkovsky's intelligence about Soviet missiles made it possible for U.S. analysts to interpret photographs taken from U-2 spy planes over Cuba in October 1962, assess the nature of the Soviet missiles there, and determine how close they were to becoming operational. They provided the president with time to maneuver diplomatically with the Kremlin. The Cuban Missile Crisis reveals how human espionage and technical intelligence can be combined and used by a statesman to defuse a standoff between two nuclear superpowers.

Penkovsky was an only child, born in 1919 in a small town in the south-ern Caucasus Mountains, frequently described as the separation between Europe and Asia. His father, a mining engineer, had been a lieutenant in the White Army during the Russian Civil War. He disappeared during the fighting. To protect her son, Penkovsky's mother claimed that her husband died of typhus rather than in battle against Lenin's Red Army. A highly decorated artillery officer wounded in World War II, Penkovsky joined the GRU after the war. He was a close friend of Sergei Varentsov, who would become the Soviet Union's chief marshal of artillery.

After a stint at the Frunze Military Academy, the Soviet equivalent of West Point and the GRU's intelligence school, Penkovsky's career seemed assured. But then, in the late 1950s, rumors emerged that his father had been a White Russian military officer, and that Penkovsky had, unwittingly, lied on his intelligence school admission forms. Varentsov intervened to help. He got Penkovsky promoted to colonel, and appointed deputy chief of the GRU's foreign section, in charge of collecting scientific intelligence from the West.[3]

Penkovsky craved recognition. He was also disgusted by the Soviet system—a perfect combination for Western intelligence agencies. He was convinced that Khrushchev was leading the Soviet Union, and the world, down a dangerous path. (The Soviet Union conducted thirty-one atomic tests in a single three-month period in 1961.) Through GRU military secrets that Penkovsky had access to, he knew that Khrushchev's boasts about Soviet missile superiority over the United States were nonsense. It was imperative, Penkovsky felt, for the West to know that Khrushchev was bluffing about his claims that the Soviet government was churning out missiles like sausages. But his motivations for spying for the West were also more pedestrian: a ladies' man and natty dresser, he needed money for his social life. Working for the West gave him cash and also offered Penkovsky the opportunity to receive the praise he yearned for, which he knew he would never get from the Red Army.[4]

British and American intelligence agencies risked much when they accepted Penkovsky. In the previous two years before the Cuban Missile Crisis in October 1962, they had faced other defectors, traitors within their ranks, and provocations. This made it difficult to distinguish genuine agents from plants, fact from fiction, intelligence from disinformation. Spy fever gripped both sides of the Atlantic. Much to his chagrin as a gentleman born in the Victorian era, Harold Macmillan had to deal with scandals involving two subjects he detested—spies and sex. In January 1961, the CIA and MI5 dismantled the Portland Spy Ring. Four months later, and just two weeks before Penkovsky met his British and American handlers at a London safe house, George Blake confessed to having been a Soviet spy for the best part of a decade. To CIA officers, it was another instance of a spy being allowed to flourish within British intelligence. Soon after, it emerged that the KGB had blackmailed a gay cipher clerk at Britain's embassy in Moscow. U.S. agencies were facing similar humiliations. The abortive Bay of Pigs invasion of Cuba—more on which in the next chapter—occurred in April 1961, just a week before the CIA and MI6 secretly first met Penkovsky. The CIA and MI6 both desperately needed a win. Recruiting Penkovsky was a roll of the dice. Luckily for MI6 and the CIA, they cashed in.

Penkovsky had first tried to contact the CIA in Moscow by approaching American tourists and handing them an envelope to pass to the U.S. embassy. That failed. The agency did not even have a station in the U.S. embassy at that time. The U.S. ambassador there, Llewellyn Thompson, refused to allow one, not wanting his embassy to be used as a den for espionage. After pressuring Thompson, Langley was finally allowed to send one officer, COMPASS, to Moscow to assess Penkovsky. COMPASS, however, was woefully inexperienced. His cover was working as a janitor at the U.S. embassy. He achieved little more there than his cleaning duties. Penkovsky saw little fruit from his espionage offer to the Americans.[5]

Penkovsky then tried his luck with the British. His official GRU position involved a cover job at the State Committee for the Coordination of Scientific Research (GKKNIR), overseeing scientific and technical exchanges with Western countries. For the GRU, it was an ideal position from which to recruit Western agents to steal scientific secrets. Penkovsky inverted the process. He used the GKKNIR as a platform for his own espionage. During a GKKNIR meeting in Moscow, Penkovsky finally hit his mark. He asked a debonair British businessman, Greville Wynne, who was visiting Moscow to promote trade, to pass a letter to the British authorities and another to the U.S. government. Penkovsky addressed the letters to Queen Elizabeth and President Kennedy, offering to be their soldier behind Soviet lines. Wynne did as he was requested; he soon found himself at the center of a nail-biting Cold War espionage case, acting as a courier between MI6 and a major Russian spy. Given the oppressive security in Moscow, MI6 and CIA case officers did not want to risk trying to meet Penkovsky in person. There was another way, however. Penkovsky's message, delivered through Wynne, revealed that he would be traveling to Britain as part of a Soviet (GKKNIR) delegation in April 1961. MI6 and the CIA sent a message, through Wynne, back to Penkovsky. They agreed to meet him when he was in London. Their secret meetings duly took place at the Mount Royal Hotel, near Marble Arch.[6]

Knowing the risks they were taking, MI6 and the CIA's first task was to establish Penkovsky's bona fides. A team of four Anglo-American officers carefully cross-checked his statements about his known life story and activities. On the CIA side was Joe Bulik, of Slovenian descent and a fluent Russian speaker, who harbored suspicions of MI6 following U.S. concerns about Kim Philby; he was joined by George Kisevalter, the bearish CIA officer who had recruited Pyotr Popov. The British team was composed of Michael Stokes and Harold Shergold, who we met earlier as Blake's interrogator. A reserved, determined, and disciplined man, Shergy, as he was known within the service, had been a teacher at a well-respected English secondary school, Cheltenham Grammar School, before World War II. He had joined British military intelligence during the war, and afterward MI6, where he worked in occupied Germany. Following Russian language training, he became MI6's principal expert on the Soviet Union.[7]

It soon became clear to his MI6 and CIA handlers that Penkovsky was providing secrets that Western governments lacked about the Soviet Union, the kind prized by any intelligence service: insights into an adversary's aims and capabilities. Penkovsky was ideally placed to obtain such secrets. Varentsov trusted his protégé unreservedly and spoke unguardedly in front of him about Khrushchev. Penkovsky was also apparently close with GRU director Ivan Serov, later also KGB chairman. Penkovsky had even served as host and tour guide for Serov's wife and daughter during a three-week trip to London as part of a Soviet delegation. MI6 and the CIA had a winner on their hands. The CIA assigned Penkovsky the code name HERO.[8]

Penkovsky's espionage came on line as relations between East and West deteriorated. The cause was over the future of Berlin, a divided city inside a divided country. Khrushchev viewed Berlin, the only part of Germany where people could cross freely from East to West, as a thorn in the heart of communist East Germany, where 250,000 Red Army soldiers were stationed. The Soviet leader wanted a "peace treaty" with the West over East Germany, which for him meant the U.S. government recognizing East Germany diplomatically (which hitherto Washington had not). Khrushchev's threat was that, if the U.S. did not agree to a peace treaty, he would leave the fate of Berlin, which lay deep inside East Germany, to be settled "democratically" by the East German government. In 1956, Khrushchev had transferred control of East Berlin to the East German government—though Moscow still guided its satellite state. Following the Bay of Pigs, Khrushchev saw a moment to exploit the young and inexperienced new president to extract concessions over Berlin. The scene was set for a showdown at a summit held between the two leaders, which took place in Vienna in June 1961, just six weeks after the Bay of Pigs.[9]

Before leaving for Vienna, Khrushchev told the Politburo that the German question was "the key issue." He would have to be tough, he told them, because Kennedy was "a son of a bitch." At the summit, held in the U.S. ambassador's residence in Vienna, Khrushchev made true on his promise. He dominated Kennedy, belligerently thumping the table, bullying the American "boy in short pants," as he described him. Kennedy, at just forty-three, the youngest ever president, failed to achieve any of his goals in Vienna—a nuclear test ban accord or a working relationship with Khrushchev. Worse, he was humiliated. As he told the *New York Times* reporter James Reston, the Soviet leader "just beat the hell out of me." Khrushchev demanded the abolition of Berlin's three-power status, and a German peace treaty by the year's end. The Soviet leader had once graphically told Secretary of State Dean Rusk that Berlin was the testicles of the West, which he could squeeze at will. Khrushchev continued to squeeze hard after returning to Moscow.

The following month, July 1961, Penkovsky made a three-week trip to Britain on behalf of the GKKNIR. While there, he secretly met his MI6 and CIA handlers in Carlton Gardens, in St. James's, London; in Birmingham; and in Leeds, in northern England. Penkovsky revealed Khrushchev's strategy, which went to the heart of East-West relations: contrary to Khrushchev's bullish bravado, he was not ready for "war" with the United States, revealed Penkovsky. The Soviet leader was trying to intimidate the West into negotiating with, and officially recognizing, East Germany—to give the Soviet Union the recognition it craved on the world stage. Penkovsky provided a note that he wanted delivered to the president: "The firmness of Khrushchev must be met with firmness. . . . He is not prepared for a big war, and is waging a war of nerves." As now-opened notes from his CIA-MI6 meetings show, Penkovsky revealed to the British and Americans how to launch a knockout blow on the Soviet Union. He identified targets for decapitating Soviet military and security forces, which would leave Khrushchev unprepared for retaliation.[10]

Penkovsky confirmed what President Eisenhower and U-2 spy surveillance had suggested—that the supposed "missile gap" between the U.S. and the Soviet Union was an illusion. In fact, the Soviet Union had fewer than twenty-five operational Intercontinental Ballistic Missiles (ICBMs) in six silos capable of attacking targets in the United States, and they took hours to fuel—effectively reducing the number of Soviet missiles available to be launched at any given time to six. The missiles also suffered from fundamental problems with electronics and guidance systems for delivering payloads to a given target. Despite the Soviet Union's recent scientific and technological achievements—the launching of the world's first satellite, Sputnik, in 1957 and Yuri Gagarin's successful orbit of the earth in April 1961, barely a week before Penkovsky's initial meeting with MI6 and the CIA—the Soviet Union was thoroughly outgunned by the United States with its nuclear arsenal. Khrushchev knew he was bluffing. The U.S. could launch 1,000 missiles carrying 1,685 nuclear warheads, compared with the Soviet Union's 253.

These revelations constituted political dynamite in Washington. But the spy also included a warning: although the Soviet premier lacked an arsenal like that of the United States, if he thought world opinion was with him, he would be prepared to strike the Main Adversary anyway. Pushed by his CIA and MI6 handlers about what he meant by the word "strike," Penkovsky admitted that he did not know; he was reporting verbatim what his patron, Varentsov, had confidentially told him.

In July 1961, outgoing DCI Allen Dulles briefed Kennedy on Penkovsky. Existing records do not reveal exactly what was said; intelligence briefings are some of the most closely guarded secrets in government. It seems, however, that the president was captivated by Penkovsky's story and by the fact that the CIA had an asset so high up in the GRU. Kennedy asked to be updated on further reports. It is not difficult to see what would have grabbed his attention. Penkovsky's story involved betrayal and bravery at the intersection of world affairs. Kennedy's interest was probably also piqued by the involvement of British intelligence, which, for the president, like many others at the time, carried a mystique. The CIA's head, Allen Dulles, recalled that President Kennedy admired Ian Fleming and his creation James Bond, claiming that *From Russia with Love* was one of his favorite books. (The world premiere of Sean Connery as James Bond in *Dr. No* took place in London eleven days before U.S. intelligence detected Soviet missiles in Cuba).[11]

The CIA produced two series of highly classified reports, amounting to approximately eight thousand pages of transcriptions in total: IRON-BARK, based on documents stolen by Penkovsky from inside the GRU, and

CHICKADEE, which covered his oral briefings to MI6 and the CIA. By mid-July, U.S. satellite photography confirmed Penkovsky's initial report, that Khrushchev had fewer than twenty launch sites for ICBMs, and even fewer operational missiles.

Kennedy incorporated Penkovsky's advice on how to deal with Khrushchev in a tough address he made to the American public in July 1961, in which he threw down his own gauntlet. In his mesmerizing clipped cadences, the president described West Berlin as "the great testing place of Western courage and will," a "focal point" for the West's "solemn commitments," which would be protected by all means. He called on Americans to know what to do in the event of a nuclear attack, called up reserves, and announced a major increase in the U.S. defense budget. At a subsequent meeting with Penkovsky, the MI6-CIA team showed him a copy of Kennedy's speech. Penkovsky beamed. His information had influenced U.S. policy at the highest level. The spy was so elated that he asked to be photographed in both British and American military uniforms supplied by MI6 and the CIA. The photographs, now public, show him smiling with pride.[12]

Faced with Kennedy's tough resolve over Berlin in July 1961, Khrushchev backed down. In a six-and-a-half-hour speech before the Twenty-Second Congress of the Communist Party, he proclaimed that the Soviet Union was stronger than ever. In secret, though, the Soviet premier liaised with the hard-line East German leader, Walter Ulbricht, to find a solution to contain the exodus of East Germans fleeing to the West. In 1960, around 190,000 East Germans had crossed to West Berlin in search of greater freedom and better incomes. In March 1961, Khrushchev authorized a contingency plan for Ulbricht: to construct a barrier to seal off East from West Berlin. Then, in August, Khrushchev authorized the erection of the Berlin Wall, Operation ROSE, first with barbed-wire barricades; then, when Western security forces did not stop that from happening, officials on the Soviet side started building a brick wall. The operation was overseen by Erich Honecker, later himself East German leader. The wall was thirteen feet high, ninety-six miles long, and protected by guard towers, police dogs, mines, and troops with orders to shoot anyone trying to escape. The Berlin Wall was the visible manifestation of the Iron Curtain.

In Berlin, the crowds that witnessed the wall's construction included a young MI6 officer named David Cornwell, then stationed at Britain's embassy in Bonn, the capital of West Germany. Cornwell would be later known to millions of readers by his pen name, John le Carré. Two decades later, he would use Penkovsky as inspiration for his novel *The Russia House,* modeling the Russian spy Dante on Penkovsky and Bartholomew "Barley" Scott Blair, played by Sean Connery in the 1990 film adaptation, on the courier Wynne. (More recently, Wynne has been portrayed by Benedict Cumberbatch in the 2020 film *The Courier.*)

On the other side of the Berlin Wall, those who saw it go up included a young Russian student at the Institute of Foreign Relations, who was in the city on a six-month internship. This was Oleg Gordievsky, who would later become MI6's key agent inside the KGB. Two young men, who would become giants in Cold War intelligence, stared at events from either side of the Berlin Wall. It was a formative moment for both—spies who later came in from the cold. Two months after the Berlin Wall went up, in October 1961, the Soviet Union tested a 50-megaton "super H-bomb," the Tsar Bomba (emperor bomb), producing a flash that could be seen some six hundred miles away, greater than anything tested before or since. It was about 1,500 times the combined yields of the bombs dropped on Hiroshima and Nagasaki.[13]

In the spring and fall of 1961, Penkovsky's relationship with his MI6 and CIA handlers was intense. That is not uncommon in an officer-agent relationship. When secrets are shared, trust becomes essential. Penkovsky's MI6 and CIA handlers acted as his friends, confessors, facilitators, and psychologists. They paid him about $1,000 per month, which was put into an escrow account. The team conversed with him in Russian, playing to his egotism and need for praise, telling him that his work as their "soldier" was tipping the balance of world power.

During his secret meetings in Britain in July, Penkovsky asked to meet the minister of defense, a request that even MI6 could not pull off. He did, however, meet MI6 chief Sir Dick White. The service worked to keep him happy, providing him with small luxuries unavailable behind the Iron Curtain: medication, perfume, nail polish, and lipstick for his wife, and fountain pens for his colleagues. He went on a three-hour shopping trip with Wynne to Harrods, while his MI6 handler, Michael Stokes, who was roughly the same build as Penkovsky, was dispatched to Jermyn Street to buy a tailored suit for the spy.

On one occasion, his MI6 team provided Penkovsky with a bottle of cognac for Varentsov's sixtieth birthday, with a label forged by MI6 purporting to be from his birth year; Penkovsky reported that Varentsov had enjoyed the cognac immensely, to their amusement. On another occasion in London, after a long session of debriefing, MI6's Shergy, who controlled the service's purse strings, gave Penkovsky £50 in cash (almost $1,500 today) for a proper night out on the town. They even acted as pimp for the spy, one time arranging a prostitute for him. In total the CIA spent £30,000 running Penkovsky (approximately $1 million today). At their meetings with him in Paris in September, MI6 conjured up safe-house apartments in the 16th arrondissement that even impressed the two-man CIA team. MI6 also secured the services of a former racing driver to whisk them through the Parisian streets. Penkovsky left his CIA and MI6 handlers in Paris in October 1961. It would be the last time they ever saw him.[14]

Over the next ten months, the Soviet spy communicated with his intelligence handlers through MI6's courier, Wynne, leaving material and messages at dead drops in Moscow. They also used "brush-pass" meetings with MI6 officers stationed there, under lampposts and bridges—first with Janet Chisholm, and then Pamela Cowell, the wife of MI6's next head of station in Moscow.

The CIA belatedly established an operational presence in Moscow when U.S. ambassador Llewellyn Thompson relented and allowed the CIA to operate out of the embassy. Langley assigned one of its senior officers, Hugh Montgomery, formerly with the OSS and one of the CIA's "founding fathers," to handle Penkovsky. Montgomery, who held an undergraduate degree and doctorate from Harvard, ran Penkovsky under his cover as agricultural attaché at the embassy. In-person meetings were all but impossible given KGB surveillance of embassy staff. (One trick the CIA later developed to lose tails in Moscow was to send a two-person team out in a car, with one officer jumping out, in disguise, as it went around a corner. A plastic dummy lookalike, repurposed from a sex toy, would pop up in his or her place, like a jack-in-the-box, making it appear to the KGB following behind that the missing officer was still inside.)

Official diplomatic receptions for British, American, and Soviet dignitaries in Moscow offered some of the only opportunities for MI6 and the CIA to communicate with Penkovsky. He attended such evening parties in his official Soviet (GKKNIR) capacity. They were nerve-racking affairs. At cocktail parties at the British embassy, Penkovsky handed over Minox film and instructions, which Pamela Cowell would hide and retrieve in an MI6-devised tin of bathroom disinfectant that had a false bottom. They also swapped messages hidden in cigarette packets.

On one occasion, at a large Fourth of July party hosted by the U.S. ambassador, as Benny Goodman and his band performed for hundreds of guests, Montgomery's efforts to recover a Minox camera roll of film, containing photos of top secret documents, descended into farce. Penkovsky had taped the film, about the size of an acorn, in a waterproof bag and placed it inside a toilet cistern. The parcel had come unstuck and fallen into the cistern, which, in Russian plumbing tradition, was elevated on the wall. Scrambling to pull himself up, Montgomery's foot slipped into the toilet, leaving him with a soaked shoe and trouser leg; he then tried to climb onto the sink, which proceeded to come away from the wall. He eventually managed to recover the film. Montgomery, disheveled, with a soaking foot, emerged from the toilet, as he overheard another guest complaining that someone had "trashed" the bathroom. Within the CIA, Montgomery became known as the "Cistern Kid."[15]

On the eve of the Cuban Missile Crisis, MI6 and the CIA lost contact with their prize Russian spy. Penkovsky delivered what was to be his last microfilm of classified documents at a diplomatic reception in Moscow at the end of August 1962. He never appeared at a planned rendezvous the next month. Soviet archives show that the KGB, "the neighbors," placed him under surveillance, in an operation called OPEN SESAME. They also broke into his apartment, where they found his Minox camera, which he used to photograph documents.

We do not know precisely how, or when, KGB security first suspected that Penkovsky was a Western spy. They likely had a tip-off from George Blake, who we know identified Ruari Chisholm as an MI6 officer. As a result, the Second Chief Directorate began monitoring the Chisholms and probably identified Penkovsky during one of their brush-pass meetings. If so, MI6's use of the Chisholms to handle Penkovsky, when Blake had compromised their identities, was a terrible mistake, something the CIA had feared. At some point before his arrest, it is possible that the KGB used Penkovsky to pass disinformation to MI6 and the CIA. It is fanciful to suppose, however, as some KGB and GRU officers have claimed, that Penkovsky's espionage throughout was worthless. This is no more than face-saving on their part. The GRU secrets that he stole were too damaging and complex to be a Soviet deception. MI6 and the CIA assessed his authenticity through careful checks and cross-checks.[16]

Penkovsky was arrested on October 22, 1962, at the height of the Cuban Missile Crisis. MI6's courier, Wynne, was caught in Budapest the following month. He later claimed that he was traveling to Moscow on a rescue mission with a van equipped with a secret compartment, but that was an embellishment: nobody in MI6 or the CIA knew about such an escape plan. MI6's head of station in Moscow, Gervase Cowell, was declared persona non grata after Penkovsky's arrest, as was the CIA's Hugh Montgomery. In the spring of 1963, Wynne and Penkovsky were both subjected to show trials in Moscow, leading to Penkovsky's conviction and execution. He was probably shot in the Stalinist tradition, with a bullet to the back of his neck in the basement of the Lubyanka. Rumors—probably untrue—later surfaced that he was tied up with chicken wire, and cremated alive, in front of GRU officers as a warning to the fate awaiting others if they betrayed the motherland.[17]

Penkovsky's intelligence provided President Kennedy vital information during his nuclear standoff with Khrushchev over Cuba. According to the CIA's deputy director of plans, Richard Helms—across whose desk every bit of operational intelligence from Penkovsky passed—without the data he supplied, the precise capabilities of the Soviet missiles placed in Cuba (R-12s, or SS-4s under NATO designation) "could not have been made known to the President," nor would he have known "how much time he might have to negotiate before taking military action to destroy the missiles." Penkovsky's intelligence gave the president "extra days," according to Helms, between October 16 and 17, when the CIA estimated the missiles would become operational. "Never before in history have two powers come together on a collision course like that," recalled Robert Amory, CIA deputy director, "and one power known exactly what the other had." CIA hands like Helms and Amory of course had an interest in emphasizing Penkovsky's role during the crisis, but even allowing for this, we can see that his espionage did produce tangible results.[18]

One of the documents smuggled by Penkovsky from the GRU was an operating manual for Soviet SS-4 missiles. Without that manual, and other information on Soviet missile procedures and site construction, U.S. imagery analysts at the CIA's National Photographic Interpretation Center (NPIC) would not have been able to understand how close to being operational the Soviet missiles on Cuba were. NPIC principal analyst Dino Brugioni considered Penkovsky's espionage operation to be "one of the most productive" in history.

As we can now see, all of the major U.S. assessments about the Soviet missile threat in Cuba supplied to the president's advisers, in what came to be called the Executive Committee of the National Security Council (ExComm), drew on Penkovsky's intelligence. To this day, his intelligence in those assessments is easy to overlook; they are stamped "IRONBARK" at the top, the code name given to Penkovsky's photographed documents. On at least one occasion, CIA director John McCone referred to Penkovsky's oral briefings by their code name, CHICKADEE, in a meeting with White House decision makers. Kennedy's advisers evidently knew what IRONBARK and CHICKADEE meant. Two easy-to-miss code names, in fact representing the product of intricate, high-stakes espionage.[19]

THE CUBAN MISSILE CRISIS

In 1959, Khrushchev claimed that communism would bury capitalism. But he knew he was outgunned by the United States. His strategic aim in dispatching nuclear missiles to an island ninety miles off America's coast was to redress that imbalance. He decided to sidestep his lack of ICBMs by placing midrange missiles in Cuba, which since 1959 had been led by a newly minted communist, Fidel Castro. From Cuba, such missiles could strike major American cities and the main U.S. Strategic Air Command bases. Khrushchev's strategy was to underscore the M in MAD, or mutually assured destruction. (The physicist Robert Oppenheimer, often called the father of the atom bomb, famously described MAD as two scorpions in a glass jar.) Khrushchev used missiles in Cuba to counter equivalent U.S. missiles deployed in Britain, Italy, and Turkey—NATO's southern flank, which threatened the Soviet heartland. It was time, as he later thundered, to give the Americans "a taste of their own medicine."[20]

Khrushchev's decision to turn Cuba into a nuclear encampment, he subsequently claimed, came to him in a flash of inspiration on vacation at the Black Sea. The move offered the Soviet Union several strategic advantages: threatening the main adversary's heartland (throwing a hedgehog down Uncle Sam's pants, as Khrushchev liked to say); supporting a communist ally in America's backyard; and displaying Soviet strength on the world stage, especially in the face of China's bid to show that it was the true leader of Marxism-Leninism against American imperialism. Contrary to the Soviet regime's claims that its missiles in Cuba were "solely for the purposes of defense," Khrushchev informed his Politburo colleagues that they were an offensive policy. After the U.S. midterm elections in November 1962, the Soviet premier planned to broach once again the issue of Berlin becoming a "free city," turning to the UN, if necessary, for assistance.

U.S. and British intelligence failed to detect the Soviet transfer of 40 medium-range missiles, about 43,000 troops and airmen, and logistical matériel to Cuba in June 1962. Khrushchev later added 80 nuclear-tipped cruise missiles, 6 atomic bombs, and short-range tactical missiles that could be used against an American invasion force. The failure of U.S. intelligence and that of its closest ally, Britain, ranks as one of the worst in the twentieth century. As the NSA's in-house history put it, the Cuban Missile Crisis "marked the most significant failure of SIGINT to warn national leaders since World War II."[21]

The U.S. intelligence community had considered the potential of the Soviet Union introducing offensive missiles to Cuba on four separate occasions in the first nine months of 1962. On each occasion, they had judged it doubtful. The latest assessment came on the eve of the crisis, when a U.S. Special National Intelligence Estimate, from the Office of National Estimates (ONE) we met earlier, dated September 19, 1962, considered the possibility that the Soviets would introduce medium- and intermediate-range ballistic missiles to Cuba. It assessed the threat as unlikely, on the mistaken grounds that doing so "would be incompatible with Soviet practice to date," and would "indicate a far greater willingness to increase the level of risk in U.S.-Soviet relations than the USSR has displayed thus far, and consequently would have important policy implications with respect to other areas and other problems in East-West relations." It was a classic case of continuity bias and mirror imaging—relying on an adversary's previous actions to predict its future behavior. The authors failed to appreciate that what they understood to be Khrushchev's motivation for restraint was precisely his incentive for not holding back: he *was* prepared to increase the level of risk for leverage in other areas of East-West conflict, namely Berlin.[22]

Khrushchev's deployment of nuclear weapons to Cuba was a U.S.

intelligence failure, but it was also a striking Soviet intelligence success. Operation ANADYR, named after an Arctic river, was a massive logistical undertaking, conducted under impressive secrecy and deception. As part of the deceit, in keeping with the operation's code name, soldiers were equipped with Arctic gear. To avoid aerial reconnaissance, they were hidden belowdecks in sweltering merchant ships crossing the Atlantic. On one occasion, a Soviet soldier suffering from appendicitis while at sea was not permitted to disembark and seek medical attention for fear of compromising the military operation.

Soviet vessels operated under a complete communications blackout: orders were given verbally, and captains only discovered their destination by opening sealed envelopes at staging posts on the journey. There was nothing for NSA and GCHQ eavesdroppers to intercept. As the NSA official history acknowledged, Soviet "security was almost perfect."[23]

In his self-aggrandizing account of the crisis, *Thirteen Days*, edited and published posthumously, Robert Kennedy, who had served as attorney general under his brother, claimed: "No official with the government had ever suggested to President Kennedy that the Russian buildup in Cuba would include missiles." That is false. In fact, John McCone, who replaced Dulles as DCI after the Bay of Pigs debacle, did exactly that. Despite the best efforts of Soviet intelligence to conceal its missiles, McCone began reviewing intelligence about Cuba and correctly grasped what was going on. A Republican and a friend of Dulles, McCone was a former businessman and chairman of the Atomic Energy Commission. According to Ray Cline, appointed by McCone as the CIA's head of analysis, the director "absorbed more from complex briefings than any senior official I have ever worked with." Kennedy's presidential appointment book in 1962 shows that McCone was a close adviser, frequently visiting the White House (79 times that year), though not as often as Dean Rusk (137 times) or national security adviser McGeorge "Mac" Bundy (246 times). The DCI was a significant adviser, though McCone and President Kennedy were not close friends.[24]

McCone's intelligence on Cuba derived from agents reporting on the island and the CIA's interrogation of refugees in Florida. The increased number of Soviet "agricultural technicians" on the island, wearing matching civilian clothes, sunburned, and with similar haircuts, stood out as suspicious.

McCone's strategic assessment of Cuba, we can now see, was also shaped by signals intelligence. Since the beginning of 1962, the NSA had been monitoring, with increasing alarm, the unprecedented Soviet surge of matériel in Cuba. The NSA was targeting Cuba as part of President Kennedy's covert action directive in 1961 to remove Castro from power, Operation MONGOOSE, which we shall discuss in the next chapter. While the NSA did not have access to any high-level encrypted Soviet communications, it did—along with GCHQ and Canadian SIGINT, CBNRC—intercept the communications of Soviet military and merchant vessels crossing the Atlantic. Intercepted manifests revealed that ship captains were falsifying their destinations and cargo weights. An NSA report from May 1962, for example, noted that during that year's first quarter, sugar and nickel-concentrate imports increased on Soviet ships by 50 percent from the same period the previous year. Gross tonnage of vessels from the Soviet Union to Cuba increased from 151,577 in the second quarter of 1961 to 340,151 in the second quarter of 1962. This led NSA analysts to surmise, correctly, that the ships, which were actually traveling to Cuba, were laden with military equipment. But what kind? Routine interception of Soviet bloc traffic also revealed that Cuban pilots were training in Eastern Europe on Czech fighter planes.

Then, in June 1962, the NSA identified the existence of MiG-21 fighters in Cuba. It also had another major source of intelligence: bulk access to the entire Cuban national telephone system. This was a result of a decision by the U.S. telecommunications giant RCA, perhaps with the NSA's encouragement, to build a system using vulnerable microwave transmitters rather than invulnerable landlines. In July 1962 a U.S. "technical research ship," USS *Oxford*, in fact a floating SIGINT collection platform with 116

SIGINT officers aboard, was dispatched to Cuban waters to collect military and civilian microwave telephone communications.[25]

Since the previous year, July 1961, the NSA team dedicated to Cuba had been run by Juanita Moody. In the NSA's male and military-dominated environment, Moody, a thirty-eight-year-old civilian, stood out. Without a degree—she attended Western Carolina Teachers College, but never graduated—or advanced technical background, she owed her rise to skill and hard work. Medium height, with curly brown hair and a round face, Moody had joined U.S. SIGINT (ASA) at Arlington Hall during World War II to work on German codes, where her superiors quickly spotted her skills as a cryptanalyst. In the 1950s, she became a senior officer in the NSA, leading groups on various aspects of the "Soviet problem," chief of European satellites, Russian manual systems, and Russian and East European high-grade manual systems. In 1961, Moody was transferred to be chief of a group called B1, whose responsibility was SIGINT collection on Cuba. Despite Moody's formidable skill, and her correct assessments of Soviet military buildup in Cuba, NSA failed to detect the disappearance, in internal Soviet communications traffic, of parts of the Soviet arsenal: the Soviet Fifty-First Rocket Division, and five medium- and intermediate-range missile regiments, vanished, only to appear in Cuba in October.[26]

On August 10, McCone dictated a memorandum for the president "expressing the belief that installations for the launching of offensive missiles were being constructed on the island." He continued to send the president his assessments, warning of Soviet missiles in Cuba, from his honeymoon in the South of France, where his new bride was confronted with the reality of marriage to a distracted DCI. In the so-called honeymoon cables from Cap Ferrat, McCone pressed for aerial reconnaissance using U-2 spy planes over Cuba.

Kennedy had first been briefed about U.S. aerial reconnaissance by President Eisenhower. His initial briefings included sessions with two highly talented U.S. intelligence officers, Art Lundahl and Richard Bissell. They described the remarkable progress that had been made with imagery intelligence in the mid-1950s. Lundahl's relationship with Kennedy became as close as it had been with Eisenhower. Instead of displaying large photographic briefing boards on easels, as he had done for Eisenhower, Lundahl, usually smoking a pipe, spread them out on the coffee table in the Oval Office for Kennedy. The president would leave his desk, sit in the rocking chair specially designed to ease his back pain, and study them through a magnifying glass.

Kennedy's newly energized President's Foreign Intelligence Advisory Board (PFIAB) increasingly turned its attention to imagery intelligence, or IMINT. Its most influential members were the two scientists we met earlier, William Baker, of Bell Labs, and Polaroid's Edwin Land, who had been instrumental in the development of the U-2 program. At a meeting of the PFIAB in August of 1960, before Kennedy became president, Baker and Land presented some of the earliest ultra-high-resolution satellite photographs, taken by America's first photo-reconnaissance space satellite, the *Discoverer*. "We were awed and amazed," recalled Clark Clifford, Truman's former counsel, who also advised Kennedy, "as we gazed for the first time upon photographs taken of the tennis court from one hundred miles above the ground, with resolution so clear that one could clearly see a tennis ball lying on the court!"[27]

The problem for U.S. IMINT analysts, Baker and Land explained to PFIAB and later to Kennedy, was that the volume of product risked overwhelming the interpreters. Lundahl explained to Kennedy that a U-2 camera photographing an area of about 125 nautical miles wide and 3,000 miles long would produce roughly ten thousand feet of film. "Imagine," he told the president, "a group of photo interpreters on their hands and knees scanning a roll of film that extended from the White House to the Capitol and back." Kennedy regularly asked Lundahl to repeat the analogy at briefings of his advisers so they could understand the depth of the challenge.

Due to the risks to U-2 planes from surface-to-air missiles, and "another U-2 incident" like that of Gary Powers, there were no U-2 overflights of Cuba for five weeks, from late August to early October 1962. On August 29, a U-2 had identified a Soviet SA-2 SAM missile site in Cuba. McCone, in the South of France, correctly reasoned that its purpose was to protect something: with no airfields to guard, he inferred that the site must contain medium-range ballistic missiles (MRBMs) capable of striking the United States. At CIA director McCone's urging, U-2 flights finally resumed in October.[28]

CIA agents on the ground, reporting from Cuba, described sightings of convoys carrying "long canvas covered objects" approaching the San Cristóbal area. On the basis of intelligence received, on September 4 the president announced in a White House statement that a missile defense system had been installed in Cuba. "The gravest issues would arise," Kennedy said, "if offensive missiles were introduced there." Soviet ambassador Anatoly Dobrynin gave the president and his brother, Robert, Khrushchev's personal pledge that there would be "no ground-to-ground missiles or offensive missiles placed in Cuba." But Khrushchev was lying. On September 15, NSA electronic intelligence, sweeping for emissions from radar, detected SA-2 signals going operational. At a news conference, Kennedy warned that if Cuba became an offensive military base, the United States would do "whatever must be done" to protect its security.

CIA and the NSA continued to report Soviet merchant vessels sailing for Cuba. After protracted delays due to cloud cover, on October 14, a U-2 flight finally succeeded in photographing suspected sites in Cuba. It confirmed the existence of a Soviet SS-4 MRBM missile site at San Cristóbal. The SS-4 had a range of 1,200 miles and was thus capable of striking major U.S. cities along the East Coast. The U-2's film was processed and analyzed by photographic interpreters at the CIA overnight. The next day, Monday, October 15, Ray Cline briefed Mac Bundy. On October 16, Bundy informed the president, while Cline briefed Robert Kennedy. This began the world's most dangerous thirteen days, which threatened to end civilization. Upon hearing news of the missiles in Cuba, and realizing that Dobrynin had lied to them, Robert Kennedy said: "Shit."

The president met with his advisers in the Cabinet Room of the White House on the morning of October 16. As sometimes happened, four-year-old

Caroline Kennedy was hiding beneath the table. A brief, lighthearted conversation between the president and his daughter eased the tension at the start of one of the most anxious meetings in White House history. As Caroline skipped out of the room, those present were reminded that the fate of future generations, as well as their own, depended on the decisions they would make in the intervening days. On a scheduled meeting two days later, Soviet foreign minister Andrei Gromyko again lied to the president about the Soviet deployment of missiles in Cuba.[29]

NUCLEAR BRINKMANSHIP

What the U.S. agencies failed to detect in Cuba was the Soviet Union's deployment of a hundred or so tactical nuclear weapons. How Kennedy would have reacted if that had been discovered is impossible to know. But better intelligence may have made the crisis even more dangerous. Castro, for one, was willing to die in a nuclear holocaust, as he told Khrushchev during the crisis. Throughout it, the available intelligence informed the president and his advisers serving on the ExComm. It first met on October 16 and remained in session for the next twelve days, until the East-West standoff was resolved. Its members lived on coffee and sandwiches, slept in their offices, did not tell their families where they were, and carpooled to avoid suspicious numbers of vehicles arriving at and leaving the White House. While the input of U.S. intelligence was important, it was the president's ability to keep his cool under intense pressure that was, according to Dean Rusk, secretary of state, Kennedy's "greatest contribution in the crisis." The president was under intense physical and mental pressure, while trying to maintain an outward air of calm.[30]

CIA accounts of the Cuban Missile Crisis naturally emphasize the intelligence provided by Penkovsky, its star asset. But the intelligence given to Kennedy during the crisis was derived from a combination of human and technical collection. At least some of the weight that the CIA later publicly ascribed to Penkovsky was probably a deliberate ploy on the part of the U.S. intelligence community to disguise the secret role of U.S. SIGINT during the crisis. On Kennedy's instructions, NSA reporting (code-named FUNNEL) about Soviet ballistic missiles in Cuba was so secret and compartmentalized that, until recently, it had been airbrushed from public records. SIGINT remains missing from even some of the most recently published accounts of the crisis. In November, Admiral Robert Dennison, who had been tasked with blockading Cuba during the crisis, wrote to the NSA and expressed his gratitude for the "unique and vital intelligence" of SIGINT, which was "one of the most important single factors in supporting our operations." The NSA's director, Gordon Blake, forwarded the admiral's note to NSA staff, telling them that the secret "nature of our business prevents public recognition," but they should consider this "well done."[31]

On the evening of Friday, October 19, an analysis of the photographs taken by U-2 planes from the air indicated that eight of the missile launch sites in Cuba were operational. Kennedy was campaigning in Chicago at the time for Democratic candidates running in the midterm elections. He made an excuse, saying he was suffering from a cold, and returned to the White House. He asked Jackie Kennedy, his wife, who was at their horsey Virginia country retreat with the children, to do likewise in case there was a sudden emergency. "If we were only thinking about ourselves, it would be easy," he told an aide and friend, Dave Powers, about the situation: "But I keep thinking about the children whose lives would be wiped out."

The next day, he chaired an expanded National Security Council meeting in the Yellow Oval Room, rather than the Cabinet Room, to avoid press attention. The First Lady had recently redecorated the Yellow Oval Room; filled with priceless antiques provided by private donors, it was an unlikely setting for a meeting that could potentially lead to nuclear war. Ray Cline began the meeting with an overview of the current state of missile sites. He concluded: "In summary, we believe the evidence indicates the probability that eight MRBM missiles can be fired from Cuba today." Art Lundahl next displayed the latest U-2 photographs on his usual briefing boards. "During the past week," he announced, "we were able to achieve coverage of 95 per-cent of the island and we are convinced that because of the terrain in the remaining 5 percent, no additional threat will be found there." When he finished, the president crossed the room to Lundahl and shook his hand: "I want to extend to your organization my gratitude for a job very well done."

The president asked David Ormsby-Gore, Britain's ambassador in Wash-ington, to come to the White House on Sunday afternoon, October 21. They had known each other since Kennedy's youth, in England, when his plutocrat father was the U.S. ambassador there. According to a Foreign Office file declassified in 2017, in a private meeting at the White House, Kennedy told Ormsby-Gore that he was the first person outside the U.S. government to know what was going on. The president laid out the intelligence that had been gathered on Soviet missiles in Cuba, and, seeking his friend's counsel, set out the two alternatives that his advisers had given him: strike Cuba, to take out the missiles, or blockade Soviet ships making their way there. Wrapping his head around the magnitude of the crisis, the British ambassador said that, in his view, quarantine was the best option. Relieved, Kennedy said that was likewise his decision. The president confided that he could not help admiring Khrushchev's strategy for Cuba: if the U.S. responded violently, it would give him the excuse to move against West Berlin.[32]

Kennedy then shared the U-2 photographs with Harold Macmillan. A CIA officer, Chester Cooper, previously the liaison officer in Britain during the 1956 Suez crisis, delivered the photographs to London on Air Force One. He was met at the airfield by the U.S. ambassador in London, David Bruce, himself an OSS veteran. Cooper reminded the ambassador that he had been instructed to travel with an armed escort. According to Cooper, "Bruce pulled up his jacket and pointed to the pistol that he was carrying. He was the armed escort."

The next day, Monday, October 22, Bruce and Cooper briefed Macmil-lan at 10 Downing Street and showed him the U-2 images. Cooper later recalled, "He studied them for a while and then said, more to himself than to us, pointing to the missile sites, 'now the Americans will realize what we here in England have lived through for the past many years.'" Macmillan's response to the U.S. president that day, in a telegram now tucked away among his papers at Oxford, echoed the same sentiment. Pledging to do anything to help, he cautioned that news of Soviet missiles in Cuba would not be so shocking to European audiences, who had lived in the shadow of nuclear war for years and had "got accustomed to it." In subsequent daily phone calls and cables during the crisis, Macmillan took on an avuncular role, addressing Kennedy as "My Dear Friend."[33]

On the evening of October 22, Kennedy delivered the terrifying news to Americans. In a brief television broadcast, he raised the specter of thermonuclear war on American soil. He denounced the "secret, swift and extraordinary" Soviet buildup in Cuba and announced a massive U.S. naval blockade of Cuba—he used the term "quarantine," because blockades were illegal under international law—composed of nearly two hundred naval vessels. Doing so risked Khrushchev responding in kind, for example, blockading Berlin, but it was the least bad option for the White House. Kennedy repeated his charge of "deliberate deception" by the Soviet government and described the world as being at the edge of a nuclear abyss. Although he did not reveal the existence of the U-2 images, only referring in the speech to "closest surveillance" and "unmistakable evidence," the photographs were soon disclosed to the media.[34]

The NSA—working with GCHQ—provided the White House with precise intelligence on the movements of Soviet vessels as they approached the blockade. The USS *Oxford*, an "NSA ship," according to Robert Kennedy, was patrolling the waters around Cuba, vacuuming up SIGINT and ELINT. NSA also produced information, unavailable from other sources, about the operation of Soviet forces in Cuba, their command and control, and some insight into the reactions of Soviet leadership to the crisis. Kennedy weighed the advice of the hard-liners, hawks who were pushing for a U.S. military strike against Cuba, against the doves who were resisting intervention. Robert Kennedy's now-opened papers reveal a scrawled tally of the hawks and doves on the ExComm. U.S. intelligence gave the president time to find a diplomatic solution to the crisis, even as his and Khrushchev's fingers hovered over the nuclear triggers.[35]

President Kennedy declassified real-time intelligence to win a major propaganda victory against the Soviets. On the afternoon of Thursday, October 25, at the UN Security Council during a debate on the crisis, the Soviet representative, Valerian Zorin, claimed U.S. photographs in the press were "falsified information of the United States Intelligence Agency." Kennedy, watching the debate on television, instructed the U.S. ambassador at the UN, Adlai Stevenson, to "stick him" with the evidence. Stevenson began by asking: "Do you, Ambassador Zorin, deny that the USSR has placed and is placing medium- and intermediate-range missiles and sites in Cuba? Yes or no? Don't wait for the translation. Yes or no?"

When Zorin prevaricated, Stevenson ordered some U-2 photographs to be displayed on easels in the UN Council's chamber. When confronted with this evidence, Zorin replied weakly, "Mr. Stevenson, we shall not look at your photographs." As Kennedy watched Stevenson present U.S. intelligence publicly exposing the Soviet deception, he said: "I never knew Adlai had it in him."[36]

Juanita Moody's team at the NSA was working a grueling twenty-four-hour cycle. The NSA's director, Gordon Blake, who had taken command just three months before, came to her office and asked what help she needed. Moody replied that she needed some additional staff. Next she heard the NSA director calling, from a nearby desk phone, her subordinates at home: "This is Gordon Blake calling for Mrs. Moody. Could you come into work now?"

In *Thirteen Days*, Robert Kennedy expressly referred to the importance of SIGINT guiding the ExComm: "During the course of this meeting [on Tuesday, October 23], we learned that an extraordinary number of coded messages had been sent to all the Russian ships on their way to Cuba. What they said we did not know then, nor do we know now, but it was clear that the ships as of that moment were still straight on course." In the early hours of Wednesday, October 24, U.S. naval intelligence intercepted more urgent transmissions from Moscow. Although the NSA was unable to decrypt them, the emergency ciphers appeared to contain instructions. Later that day, SIGINT direction-finding equipment indicated that Soviet vessels heading for Cuba had stopped dead in the water, while others were turning around. At that point, the director of naval intelligence, one of the few with clearance for FUNNEL, demanded verification of this crucial report before it went to the White House.

In the middle of that night, October 24, CIA head John McCone was woken up by aides who told him that naval intelligence was sitting on crucial unconfirmed intelligence. It was not until noon on Thursday, twenty-four hours after the initial SIGINT report, that U.S. naval intelligence finally told Robert McNamara that twenty-two merchant ships had either halted or turned back. The defense secretary was outraged when he discovered that the navy had sat on this information. As the NSA's official history acknowledges, it was inexplicable that this intelligence was delayed when it was critical to the president. Consequently, as the historian Max Hastings has recently noted, ExComm was making decisions based on intelligence that was not live.

At the 10:00 a.m. National Security Council meeting Thursday morning, DCI McCone delivered the NSA's crucial preliminary SIGINT report indicating that Soviet vessels were stopped or retreating. Kennedy asked for the information to be confirmed through naval reconnaissance and surface vessels. Secretary of State Rusk, upon hearing the report, famously whispered to Bundy: "We're eyeball to eyeball, and I think the other fellow just blinked." In reality, as the NSA's intercepts indicated and Soviet archives now confirm, Khrushchev had by then already decided to back down.[37]

DANGEROUS LIAISONS

During the crisis, the U.S. intelligence community thus provided information that guided the president's decision-making. This lay in sharp contrast to the systemic failures of Soviet intelligence. Khrushchev, who was only semiliterate—he could read but not write—effectively performed his own intelligence assessments during the crisis. The KGB chairman, Vladimir Semichastny, had been appointed in 1961 to ensure the KGB's loyalty to Khrushchev rather than to tell truth to power. During the thirteen days of the missile crisis, Semichastny did not have a single meeting with Khrushchev. Nor was he invited to attend meetings of the Presidium, as the expanded Politburo was known at the time. There is no evidence in available Soviet intelligence archives that the KGB ever delivered to Khrushchev an assessment of what Kennedy's reaction would likely be to the Soviet Union's placement of missiles in Cuba. The same seems to have been true for the GRU. The sycophantic Soviet system did not allow for unorthodox intelligence assessments.

Unlike their wartime predecessors during the Stalin period, the KGB and the GRU failed to collect valuable human intelligence during the crisis. Stalin's services had penetrated deep inside Roosevelt's wartime administration; now, two decades later, neither the KGB nor the GRU had any agents inside Kennedy's administration capable of betraying the National Security Council's secrets. The KGB *rezident* in Washington, Alexander Feklisov, the man who had served as Julius Rosenberg's handler, relied on sources among Washington's press corps and foreign embassies. His reports to the Center before and during the nuclear standoff contained little more than gossip. At the height of the crisis, the KGB's head of foreign intelligence wrote dismissively on Feklisov's telegrams: "This report does not contain any secret information."[38]

KGB and GRU SIGINT seem to have been more successful breaking American codes, as suggested by the Soviet medals awarded to officers in the KGB's SIGINT division, the Eighth Chief Directorate. Closed Soviet intelligence archives make it impossible to draw firm conclusions, but it is reasonable to assume that, as his own intelligence assessor, Khrushchev would have relied only on SIGINT that confirmed his thinking about arming Cuba with Soviet missiles. According to his speechwriter years later, Khrushchev was always irrational when it came to Cuba. Worse, not only did the KGB and the GRU fail to collect and deliver accurate intelligence for Khrushchev during the crisis, they actually made things more dangerous.

Robert Kennedy claimed in *Thirteen Days* that it was his back-channel diplomatic initiatives with Moscow that helped the world avoid nuclear catastrophe. The reality was quite different. The source of Robert Kennedy's dealings with the Kremlin before and during the crisis was a GRU officer stationed in Washington, Georgi Bolshakov, who worked undercover as a TASS reporter. Jovial, hard-drinking, blue-eyed, with a barrel chest, Bolshakov was introduced to the U.S. attorney general through an American journalist in May 1961. Between then and November 1962, the two men had a bewildering total of fifty meetings, for which no official U.S. records apparently exist. These took place at Robert Kennedy's office and in expensive hotels, like the Carlyle in New York, where the two men swapped manila envelopes. According to Robert Kennedy: "Unfortunately—stupidly—I didn't write many of the things down. I just delivered the messages verbally to my brother and he'd act on them. And I think sometimes he told the State Department and sometimes perhaps he didn't."[39]

Bolshakov successfully persuaded Robert Kennedy that, between them, they could bypass cumbersome diplomatic channels between East and West and influence Cold War statecraft. The attorney general convinced himself that "an authentic friendship grew" between them. He ignored warnings from the FBI and the CIA that Bolshakov was a Soviet intelligence officer, professionally trained in deception. Meanwhile, Khrushchev's Kremlin viewed Bolshakov as a messenger—for disinformation. Bolshakov's superiors in Moscow viewed his friendship with Robert Kennedy as suspicious. Before the 1961 Vienna summit, Bolshakov fed the attorney general what the historian Michael Beschloss has described as "bald disinformation" about Khrushchev's negotiation points. The fact that Kennedy's meetings with Bolshakov were secret left the attorney general unable to check the intelligence officer's reliability—exactly what the CIA would be able to assist with.

The head of CIA operations, Richard Helms, did not know about

Kennedy's meetings with Bolshakov until 1964. Rusk, Mac Bundy, and the U.S. ambassador in Moscow knew about them and were all alarmed by them. But they did not know the half of it. Before the crisis, Bolshakov assured Robert Kennedy that no Soviet missiles would be placed in Cuba. When U-2s detected SS-4s on October 14 and Kennedy confronted Bolshakov about them, he changed his tune to suggest that the missiles were purely defensive. That, too, proved to be false. Although he realized that he had been duped, the U.S. attorney general myopically continued to turn to Bolshakov as a back channel to the Kremlin.[40]

Robert Kennedy later claimed that he helped to resolve the crisis by conveying a back-channel message to the Kremlin. The deal that resolved the crisis was that, in exchange for Moscow removing its missiles from Cuba, Washington would secretly remove its Jupiter missiles from Turkey. Robert Kennedy's claim about his role is misleading. Although the missile swap was the basis of the agreement eventually reached between the two superpowers, they reached this agreement through a dangerously circuitous route—and not, it seems, by design. The attorney general first conveyed the idea of a missile swap to Bolshakov, through two journalist intermediaries, on Tuesday, October 23—even though by then the GRU officer was known to have previously deceived the White House about Soviet missiles in Cuba.

The historian Philip Zelikow, who has scrutinized tape recordings made in the White House during the crisis, has noted something astonishing: it does not appear that the president authorized his brother's offer for a Cuba-Turkey missile swap on October 23. The attorney general's offer nevertheless reached the Kremlin, both through Bolshakov himself and through a column published two days later by the American journalist Walter Lippmann. The column described the proposed deal, using information from an unknown source, perhaps Bolshakov himself. The offer from "RFK and his circle" influenced Khrushchev's decision to introduce the idea of a missile swap publicly on the morning of Saturday, October 27. By that stage, however, the crisis was nearing a resolution.[41]

The White House was presented with a dilemma: two separate letters arrived from Khrushchev, a "reasonable" one, in which the Kremlin promised to withdraw arms if Washington foreswore an invasion of Cuba, and a more extravagant one, which now included the Turkey missile-swap proposal. Which one should Kennedy respond to? Introducing this new dynamic, about Turkey, into negotiations already moving toward a resolution made the situation more dangerous. It increased the chances of misunderstanding.[42]

The president asked his brother to deliver a warning to the Kremlin through the Soviet ambassador in Washington, Dobrynin, which he did the evening of Saturday, October 27. Kennedy warned that he was prepared to launch a U.S. military attack on Cuba in the next twelve to twenty-four hours—involving, it seems, a D-Day-like invasion of the island with 125,000 American combat troops—if Moscow did not agree to withdraw its missiles. Soviet records reveal, however, that Khrushchev had already decided to back down before he received Dobrynin's message. That day, "Black Saturday," a U.S. U-2 plane was shot down over Cuba, apparently by mistake, and the American pilot was killed. Receiving this news, Khrushchev "shit his pants," according to Vasili Kuznetsov, the Soviet deputy foreign minister. At that point, the crisis could have ended, with Khrushchev conceding defeat—though doubtless described as a victory, in Soviet Orwellian doublespeak. But at that moment, Khrushchev, acting on Bolshakov's message, and the suggestion contained in Lippmann's article, proposed a Turkey missile swap to the White House.

Knowing that removing U.S. missiles from Turkey would be a violation of America's NATO obligations, according to Bundy, the Kennedy brothers responded that the Turkey missile swap could only be done in secret. On Saturday, October 27, when Kennedy sent a telegram to Khrushchev laying out the standards of the agreement, he added that once world tensions eased, he would be open to "a more general arrangement regarding 'other armaments.'" It was President Kennedy's warning of an imminent invasion of Cuba, sent to Dobrynin, not Robert Kennedy's confusing back-channel intervention, which finally ended the crisis. (According to Bolshakov, after Robert Kennedy met Dobrynin on October 27, he then also met with Bolshakov in his car. This would have set off an entirely separate line of GRU reporting, further increasing chances of confusion between Washington and Moscow.)

To resolve the crisis, the Kennedy brothers were prepared secretly to trade away U.S. NATO obligations in Turkey (which they had been considering even before the crisis). U.S. Jupiter missiles were secretly removed from Turkey and Italy in April 1963, though this was publicly denied. There is no evidence in British records or Macmillan's personal papers that Kennedy told the prime minister about his secret Turkey missile swap with Khrushchev. As Bundy later wrote, "We misled our colleagues, our countrymen, our successors, and our allies."[43]

Matters, however, were even worse. There was actually *another* Soviet intelligence back channel in Washington, this time involving Alexander Feklisov, the KGB Washington *rezident*, who went under the alias Alexander Fomin. On October 26, Feklisov inserted himself into the nuclear eyeball-to-eyeball negotiations between the two superpowers. He requested an urgent meeting with a well-connected ABC News correspondent, John Scali. Over cocktails, steak, and potatoes at Washington's Occidental Restaurant, Feklisov proposed a deal whereby Moscow would withdraw its missiles from Cuba in return for an end to the U.S. blockade and its guarantee of Cuban integrity. According to Feklisov's memoirs, he also issued a warning to Scali: if U.S. forces invaded Cuba, the Soviets would attack West Berlin within twenty-four hours. Feklisov, however, admitted that his message about West Berlin was "something I had no intention of saying," and conceded: "I had clearly gone beyond my mission."

To this day, available Soviet intelligence archives do not reveal whether Feklisov was acting on instructions from the KGB's Moscow headquarters or operating on his own during the crisis. This much we can say with confidence, however: the Cuban Missile Crisis reveals the dangers of clandestine diplomatic freelancing, using journalists as messengers over cocktails, and setting up meetings for which there are no records, instead of leaving it to intelligence professionals or seasoned diplomats to open channels of communication between two nuclear-armed adversaries.[44]

STEPPING BACK FROM THE ABYSS

Far from being a case study in diplomacy, the Cuban Missile Crisis is really a history of how close the world came to being blown up. In retrospect, the Cuban Missile Crisis was even more dangerous than most at the time realized. On Black Saturday, an American warship began dropping depth charges to force a Soviet submarine, armed with nuclear warheads, to the surface. Cut off from outside communication, Soviet submarine officers believed the explosions above them meant war had already broken out. They debated whether they should use their nuclear torpedo against the U.S. ship. Apparently three officers on the submarine took a vote—one voted for, two against.[45]

Both superpowers recognized that the risks of nuclear warfare were too great to be repeated. And each claimed victory after the crisis: Kennedy said that Khrushchev had removed Soviet missiles from Cuba, while Khrushchev proclaimed that, for the first time, the Soviet Union and the United States spoke to each other as equals. In June 1963, Kennedy made a conciliatory speech in which he called for a "fresh start" in Soviet-American relations, articulating what became a new American grand strategic doctrine of "peaceful competition." Khrushchev said it was the "greatest speech" by any American president since Roosevelt. The two established a "hotline" for communications during crises and signed a major arms limitation agreement, the Partial Test Ban Treaty, in 1963, which barred nuclear tests in the atmosphere, outer space, and underwater. Both governments would later initiate Strategic Arms Limitation Talks (SALT), starting negotiations in Helsinki in 1969 that became the SALT I treaty in 1972. It imposed numeric limits on submarine-launched ballistic missiles, while the Anti-Ballistic Missile Systems Treaty, also signed in 1972, restricted missile defenses.[46]

PART FOUR

THE CLASH OF EMPIRES

INTRODUCTION

One of the Damascenes who went with me to Najd has arrived
in Basrah and has telegraphed to me asking if he may come
to me. We could very profitably use him I've no doubt but the
Intell. Dept.– the misplaced name!– won't let him come lest he
should prove to be a spy. As if spies were not shouldering one
another in Baghdad!

–Gertrude Bell

IN 1945, THE UNITED STATES AND BRITAIN HAD DIFFERENT
strategies for the postwar world. Their differences centered on Europe's
empires. As Churchill roared, he did not become prime minister "to preside
over the liquidation of the British Empire." By contrast, the U.S. government, with its long anti-colonial heritage, saw future George Washingtons
in anti-colonial leaders. In Indochina, British and U.S. intelligence agencies
ended the war supporting opposite sides—the former helping to reimpose
French rule, the latter supporting anti-colonial forces.[1]

In Moscow, Stalin, like Lenin before him, considered European empires
as the highest form of capitalism. But neither leader had done much about
them, despite the Comintern's professed goal of supporting anti-colonial
movements. That dramatically changed under Nikita Khrushchev. As
the East-West conflict reached deadlock in Europe, Khrushchev looked to

the so-called Third World as a new theater for fighting the Cold War. In the Middle East, he rested his hopes on Egypt's Gamal Nasser, the leader of Arab nationalism. The KGB, through an officer, Vadim Kirpichenko, brokered relations with Nasser.

Nasser was a target of failed British covert action, as the world saw in 1956, when the British secretly colluded with the French and the Israelis—while excluding the United States—to try to remove him, creating the Suez Crisis. Eisenhower knew more about British, French, and Israeli military action against Egypt from U.S. intelligence, U-2 IMINT and SIGINT, than he let on at the time—and subsequently claimed. British-U.S. relations were soon repaired. MI6 and the CIA planned coups in other Middle Eastern countries together, like Syria. The Suez Crisis began Britain's subsequent withdrawal from empire "east of Suez," which over the next two decades saw the British evacuating from far-flung holdings. In places like Aden, the British evacuated under gunfire and heavy shelling.[2]

The Suez Crisis also invigorated Khrushchev's strategic interest in the Third World, where he and the KGB came to believe the Cold War could be fought and won. According to the KGB officer Nikolai Leonov, Khrushchev believed the destiny of the world lay in the Third World, whose name derived from the rebellious underdogs of the French Revolution. In the summer of 1960, Khrushchev bear-hugged new African delegates at the UN in New York. There the world came to know the Soviet premier's loquacity firsthand. Under his successor, Leonid Brezhnev, Soviet interest in what today is called the Global South further increased. This was a result of a crisis of Soviet communism in Europe, revealed when the Red Army had to intervene in Prague in 1968 to shore up the Soviet bloc.[3]

In April 1961, the same month of the CIA's Bay of Pigs fiasco, the KGB head Alexander Shelepin, forty-three, darkly handsome, devised a grand strategy to use national liberation movements as the spearheads of a Soviet "forward" policy in the Third World. The Soviet strategy, approved by the

Politburo, hoped to suck the U.S. into far-flung struggles and discredit it on the world stage. This would allow the Soviet government to campaign for a peace treaty over East and West Germany on favorable terms—that is, leading to the unification of Germany within the Soviet orbit.

The Cold War thus became a North-South conflict as well as an East-West one. It was really a global war, a clash between the debris of Europe's empires and fought by two empires in all but name, the United States and the Soviet Union. As we shall see in the next three chapters in this part, the West and East superpowers used intelligence services to undertake subversion and covert actions, or active measures, as part of their respective grand strategies to influence governments in the Third World.[4]

For Washington, the Cold War was a struggle for the "Free World." That meant an epic fight in developing nations for democracy over communist red neocolonialism. In U.S. foreign policy, it is impossible to disentangle where sincerity and legitimate fears of Soviet communism in countries in the Global South finished and commercial business opportunities began. Eisenhower's cabinet consisted of eight millionaires, supposedly men who could not be bought, but they saw little distinction between earning money and public service. By 1960, the U.S. constituted 40 percent of the world's economy. The postwar occupants of the Oval Office knew they had to continue fueling the U.S. economic boom. Exploiting Third World markets was an obvious way to do so.

Back in 1953, the CIA and MI6 had instigated a coup in Iran (Operations AJAX and BOOT, respectively) that overthrew its prime minister, Mohammad Mosaddegh, and installed a Western-friendly leader. Mosaddegh—whom Churchill insisted on calling "Mussy Duck"—was many things, including a flamboyant, pajama-wearing secular aristocrat, but he was no communist. The communist party in Iran, Tudeh, was not as powerful as some suggested in Washington and London. As State Department records released in 2017 now show, the success of the CIA and MI6 coup was more touch-and-go than either spy agency later claimed—and valorized. It owed much to luck.* While the British and U.S. governments could point to legitimate fears about Stalin's ambitions for Iran, control of oil reserves was what loomed large. In 1951 Mosaddegh, then a member of parliament, had pushed through a vote to nationalize his country's valuable oil supplies, including the assets of the Anglo-Iranian Oil Company, namely its massive refinery at Abadan on the Persian Gulf. The loss of AIOC blew a hole in the British Exchequer's cash flow. The shah of Iran, newly ascendant after the coup, granted the U.S. and British governments access to Iran's oil reserves, with the Anglo-Iranian Oil Company (later renamed British Petroleum). The new oil arrangements for Iran were brokered by John Foster Dulles's Wall Street law firm, Sullivan & Cromwell. It is no coincidence that one of the CIA's architects of the 1953 coup, the impossibly named Kermit Roosevelt Jr., grandson of President Theodore Roosevelt, later worked as an adviser to the new Iran-UK-U.S. oil consortium.[5]

There was a similarly slippery penny-loafered slope between U.S. intelligence and business interests the following year in Latin America. Ever since the Monroe Doctrine of 1823, the U.S. government had proclaimed hemispheric hegemony, decades before it had the navy to enforce it. In March 1954, amid McCarthyism, John Foster Dulles extended the Monroe Doctrine to include U.S. intervention against foreign ideologies (read: communism) in the Latin American republics. Three months later, the CIA launched Operation PBSUCCESS, a covert action that overthrew Guatemala's democratically elected leader, Jacobo Árbenz. Try as they might later to rewrite history—a document recovery program in Guatemala was revealingly code-named PBHISTORY—the CIA could not find evidence of Soviet support for Árbenz, who hardly posed any credible threat to the United States. That did not stop Eisenhower's national security team from speaking of "commies" in Guatemala, as contemporary handwritten national

---

* For more about the CIA and MI6 coup in Iran, see this book's website: www.spieshistory .com.

security notes in his library reveal. A more decisive force behind the coup was the role of the United Fruit Company and its powerful Washington lobbyists. Eisenhower's secretary, Ann Whitman, was married to United Fruit's chief Washington lobbyist. In a move that would be repeated time and again in Latin America, Árbenz's regime was replaced by a military dictatorship. "Tell me what to do and I will do it," said Guatemala's new leader, Carlos Armas, Washington's man, when Vice President Richard Nixon visited.[6]

The coup in Iran had nearly failed and Guatemala was only a success if measured against a nonexistent Soviet enemy. But both coups created a myth in Washington of the efficacy of covert action. The CIA told anyone willing to listen that it could do the impossible, that covert action was a panacea for failed U.S. diplomacy. A more sober and honest assessment would have been that a U.S. covert action could only succeed if accompanied by broader U.S. foreign policy. Essentially it could only provide a nudge to processes that were already underway, as the head of CIA analysis, Ray Cline, later noted. Such subtleties were lost on decision makers in Washington in need of quick political victories.

Both sides used their intelligence services to try to influence countries in the nonaligned movement (NAM), which grew after an Asian-African conference in Bandung, Indonesia, in 1955. The two superpowers believed the nonaligned countries would be attracted irresistibly to the other side, like metal filings to a magnet. Contrary to its name, the NAM was very much aligned—especially when Fidel Castro later became its leader. NAM countries tended to vote with the Soviet bloc at the UN. But the intelligence war in the Third World was more complex than the East-West clashes between the superpowers. Regional actors, whether national independence leaders or their intelligence services, frequently worked to attract the backing of one or the other superpower to better pursue their own policy aims. Exactly who was using whom is a vital and subtle question, which historians are only just starting to explore. Within the Third World, different actors frequently pursued policies independent of their sponsor. Soviet intelligence, as revealed by KGB records, was alarmed by the revolutionary activism promoted by Fidel Castro.

Another theme within Soviet foreign policy was resistance against the encroachment of Maoist communism in the Third World. In the end, the proxy wars engaged in by the superpowers in Third World countries did more to poison relations between East and West during the Cold War than anything else. Their covert actions also did immense damage to the governments and societies targeted.[7]

CHAPTER ELEVEN

RED HEAT

"The other day I was offered money."

"Yes?"

"To get information."

"What sort of information?"

"Secret information."

Dr. Hasselbacher sighed. He said, "You are a lucky man, Mr. Wormold. That information is always easy to give."

"Easy?"

"If it is secret enough, you alone know it. All you need is a little imagination, Mr. Wormold."

–Graham Greene, *Our Man in Havana*

WE HAVE ALREADY ANALYZED THE CUBAN MISSILE CRISIS OF October 1962, and noted in passing the Bay of Pigs debacle the previous year, in April 1961. It is useful, however, for covert action to be addressed together, thematically. Hence why the Bay of Pigs comes here. Our historical camera needs briefly to move backward before we continue forward.

In January 1959, Fidel Castro marched into Cuba's capital, Havana, and seized control from Fulgencio Batista, the country's corrupt pro-Western leader. Six foot three, bearded, wearing olive-green fatigues, Castro was a captivating presence. He could talk extemporaneously for hours, as the world discovered when, in the fall of 1960, he delivered the longest speech in the history of the UN.[1]

Despite Castro's later efforts to rewrite his biography, the Cuban Communist Party initially looked askance at his apparently moderate politics. His transformation—from a background of privilege to living the life of a revolutionary and becoming the most committed and reliable Soviet ally of the Cold War—owed much to Soviet foreign minister Anastas Mikoyan's visit to Cuba in February 1960. Mikoyan, from the Bolshevik old guard, was a former comrade of Lenin's. At Castro's hunting lodge on a lagoon, with frogs croaking and mosquitoes buzzing, the two men fished, drank rum and strong coffee, slept on concrete floors, and wore green army tunics to keep warm. The experience took Mikoyan back to his early revolutionary days in Russia. He left fully committed to Cuba. Castro, for his part, realized that he needed the backing of the Soviet Union to bring discipline to his young revolutionary government. In December 1960, to the surprise of his brother Raúl and Che Guevara, their fellow revolutionary desperado, Fidel proclaimed himself a Marxist-Leninist. As a newly minted Marxist, Castro, the "Maximum Leader," announced that there was no further need for elections, as the will of the people had manifested. The revolution had arrived. He presented his cabinet with agrarian reforms. He canceled Christmas.[2]

Castro would have close relations with the KGB throughout the Cold War. This was largely the work of two men, the KGB *rezident* in Havana, Alexander Alexeev, later Soviet ambassador to Cuba, and Nikolai Leonov, wunderkind in the KGB's First Chief Directorate. Photographs of Leonov show a striking man with swept-back blond hair, like Edward Fox's assassin in the film *The Day of the Jackal*. A keen fisher, Leonov reeled in the biggest possible catches for Moscow in Latin America. He initially sparked a friendship with Raúl Castro in 1953 as they traveled by boat to Mexico; Raúl was returning from a socialist youth festival in Prague, and Leonov, a twenty-five-year old translator, was en route to learn Spanish. Later, as a

KGB recruit, Leonov accompanied Mikoyan on his trip to Cuba, where he acted as the Soviet statesman's translator. He would later be Fidel Castro's translator when the Cuban leader was fêted on visits to the Soviet Union. Leonov's relationship with Fidel helped to propel him in his own career; he would rise to become deputy head of KGB foreign intelligence, responsible for agent operations in North and South America.[3]

While Fidel thus had a close friend and ally at the Center, he was arguably even closer to Alexeev, who arrived in Cuba in October 1959. The two men often cooked together in the Soviet embassy and "enjoyed the company of women." The Soviet code name for Cuba was AVANPOST ("bridgehead"). Cuba under Castro was Khrushchev's foothold into the Americas.

Did Cuba pose a genuine threat to U.S. national security at the time? William Fulbright, chairman of the Senate Foreign Relations Committee, later said that the Castro regime was a "thorn in the flesh, but it is not a dagger in the heart." Truer words have rarely been spoken. A rational policy toward Castro's Cuba would have been based on the U.S. strategy of containment. Rationality, however, was lacking in the Eisenhower and Kennedy administrations when it came to Cuba. Kennedy's secretary of defense, Robert McNamara, a former president of the Ford Motor Company, liked to say, "You can't substitute emotion for reason." But that is exactly what happened with Cuba. McNamara later recalled that the Kennedy White House was "hysterical" when it came to Castro, the target of a sustained offensive of U.S. covert action to remove him from power. Eisenhower set out his thinking in a secret letter to Harold Macmillan in August 1960: the U.S. would use every means short of outright intervention to remove Castro. The CIA drew up plots to assassinate him at both Eisenhower's and Kennedy's direction. In Washington, both sides of the political divide outdid themselves to be tough on Castro. Richard Nixon came under sustained pressure on the subject from the anti-communist Arizona senator Barry Goldwater. Meanwhile, John F. Kennedy had made much of the fact in his election campaign that the Iron Curtain was now within ninety miles of the United States.[4]

In April 1961, just three months into his presidency, Kennedy authorized the CIA's plans for a paramilitary invasion of Cuba, with the aim of achieving a popular uprising and installing a U.S.-friendly government. The Bay of Pigs invasion, Operation ZAPATA, failed miserably. Eisenhower had pushed the CIA for drastic action. When Kennedy arrived in the White House, he inherited the plans and an intelligence disaster in the making. He wondered, after the invasion, how he could have been so stupid. "If someone comes in to tell me this or that about the minimum wage bill," he said, "I have no hesitation in overruling them. But you always assume that the military and intelligence people have some secret skill not available to ordinary mortals."[5]

Those who planned the invasion were in fact ordinary mortals, with no secret skills when it came to executing regime change. But with his display boards and pointer in hand, Richard Bissell, CIA director of operations, gave convincing presentations. One of the more perplexing facts about the invasion is that the CIA's Directorate of Operations deliberately excluded the Directorate of Intelligence from the plan. As we have seen, a criticism leveled at Soviet intelligence before the Cuban Missile Crisis was that the KGB and the GRU did not provide Khrushchev with an assessment of the likely U.S. reaction to Moscow placing nuclear missiles in Cuba. A similar criticism can be leveled against the CIA regarding the Bay of Pigs.

How did this arise? In December 1959, President Eisenhower had begun pressing CIA director Dulles to take drastic action against Castro, according to a note from national security adviser Gordon Gray. In March 1960, Eisenhower approved a four-point program of covert action against the Cuban regime. It involved creating a unified Cuban opposition to Castro based outside of the island, propped up by a powerful propaganda offensive, a covert intelligence action organization within Cuba, and the development of a paramilitary force. In the spring and summer of 1960, Bissell devised a series of assassination plots. Unlike the KGB, at the time the CIA had no professional assassins. He thus decided to pull in the American Mafia. Mob bosses had their own reasons for wanting to remove Castro. They had lost revenue when he shut down gambling in Havana.

The CIA's "Family Jewels" report, kept secret for three decades, reveals that the courtly and well-mannered Bissell put out a contract with the Mafia to kill Castro. Through the CIA's chief of security, Sheffield Edwards, Bissell contacted a former Al Capone triggerman, the Italian-born John "Handsome Johnny" Roselli (whose real name was Filippo Sacco). Edwards also contacted the Chicago boss Sam Giancana, one of the FBI's ten most wanted criminals, and Florida boss Santo Trafficante Jr. Bissell's Hollywood-inspired vision of a gangland killing, in which Castro would be mowed down in a hail of bullets, put off the Mafia bosses. Instead, Giancana, who turned down payment on grounds of "patriotic duty," suggested an untraceable poison, not dissimilar to the KGB's preferred method of killing. On Bissell's instructions, the CIA's medical service prepared a botulinum toxin that "did the job" when tested on monkeys. Bissell's task force devised other schemes to kill Castro as well, including inserting a deadly toxin in his cigars.[6]

The CIA's plans against Castro, pushed forward by Eisenhower, were based more on wishful thinking than cold analytical assessment. By November of 1960, Bissell knew that most of the guerrillas who had landed in Cuba to "stiffen local resistance" had been picked up by Castro's regime. It had become clear there was "no true organized underground in Cuba." As Bissell said, "If there was to be any chance of success, we would have to place main reliance on the landing force, and only minor reliance on any resistance force." In November 1960, President-elect Kennedy received his first briefing on the Cuban operation. He viewed it at this stage as a contingency plan, one to which he was not yet committed.

The problem was, the plan had a momentum of its own. Kennedy believed that he retained the "right to stop this thing up to 24 hours before the landing," but the further along the plan steamrolled, the harder it became to call off. Bissell continued to sell snake oil to the president about a "growing" opposition to Castro. The decision to proceed with the operation, however, was Kennedy's alone.

At a key NSC meeting in March 1961, Bissell recommended sending an amphibious and airborne assault force to the Cuban coastal town of

Trinidad. The landing would demoralize Castro's militia, he claimed, and lead to widespread rebellion. To the dismay of CIA planners, Secretary of State Rusk convinced Kennedy to change the landing location, which the president felt was "too spectacular." They settled on a beach on the Bay of Pigs on the southern coast, a site surrounded by crocodile-infested swamps. DCI Dulles unhelpfully reminded the president that if he backed out of the operation, the 1,500-strong CIA Brigade, which had assembled and trained in Guatemala, would likely disperse and tell the world that Kennedy was weak on Castro. The Joint Chiefs, who should have known better, went along with the CIA's inept plan. Kennedy was never able to devote sufficient time to studying the operation. In one of the most crowded legislative programs in American history, he and his advisers never gave it sustained attention for more than forty-five minutes at a time.[7]

In March 1961, while in Palm Beach, Florida, for Easter weekend, Kennedy, between playing golf, going to church, swimming, and watching films at his father's house, made a firm decision to proceed. Key to the operation, it seems, was that Kennedy believed the CIA's Mafia assassins would already have killed Castro before the invasion force landed. According to Rusk, "very little" of what Dulles and Bissell had told the president about plans to assassinate Castro was put on paper, in keeping with the principle of plausible deniability.

According to Kennedy's friend George Smathers, a Florida senator, Kennedy told him while they were walking the White House grounds that he had "been given to believe" by the CIA that Castro would no longer be alive by the time the armed forces landed at the Bay of Pigs. As it transpired, the assassins never got close to killing the Cuban leader. A bartender was bribed to put a capsule of botulinum into Castro's milkshake, but he stored the capsules in a freezer and could not dislodge them in time. The farcical attempts on Castro's life—yes, including exploding cigars, as well as a walking cane designed to inject a poison gas—led Fidel to dub the CIA the "Central Agency of Yankee Cretins."[8]

In early April 1961, the *New York Times* published a leaked account of the CIA's plan for Cuba. As Eisenhower later admitted, it was pretty close to the original. Kennedy was clinging to the illusion that a guerrilla action in Cuba could achieve its objective in secret. In reality, the only way that Castro could have been removed was by an overt invasion force, sending in U.S. marines against his sixty-thousand-man army, tanks, and artillery. Kennedy really only had two viable options: to sanction an overt invasion or call the whole thing off. He lacked the profile of moral courage to do either. Instead, he settled on the worst of the alternatives, a secret operation that was not secret, and which lacked the overt military power to make it effective.

It resembled a sad parody of the massive Allied D-Day invasion. Operation ZAPATA began on April 15, got off to a rocky start, and went downhill from there over the next two days. CIA officer E. Howard Hunt, later involved in the Watergate burglary that helped to bring down President Nixon, gave the go order. Initial U.S. airstrikes against Cuban airfields, using poorly disguised U.S. planes, failed to knock out Castro's air force. Kennedy, who was spending the weekend in Virginia to avoid arousing suspicions, did not sanction further airstrikes. To do so, he felt, would reveal America's hand in the operation. That left the CIA invasion force fatally exposed, cut down by Castro's forces, as they stood knee-deep in seawater at the landing zone.

The invasion flotilla crashed into coral reefs, ran into a couple of Cuban patrols, and then came under heavy fire. It stood no chance. On the evening of April 17, dressed in white tie and tails, Kennedy received guests at the annual White House reception for members of Congress. After the band played "Mr. Wonderful," Kennedy went to the Cabinet Room for an emergency meeting about the operation. Radio communications aired pleas to send reinforcements. The following evening, the brigade commander radioed, "I have nothing left to fight with . . . I'm heading for the swamp." He cursed and shot his radio. Approximately 100 members of the brigade were killed, while 1,189 were captured by Castro's forces. They were taken to a sports stadium in Havana, where for four days Castro interrogated and harangued them on television. News outlets across the world broadcast images of U.S. prisoners being forced to applaud the man they had come to overthrow. In the CIA's war room, officers vomited into their wastepaper baskets. Castro could now legitimately describe himself as defending against American imperialism. Meanwhile, Western pilgrims to Castro's Cuba would show similar myopia about its brutality as those a generation earlier with the Soviet Union.[9]

ZENITH TECHNICAL ENTERPRISES

Kennedy's finest moment during the greatest debacle of his presidency was his decision to take public responsibility for the Bay of Pigs. To his surprise, he saw his popularity among Americans skyrocket after doing so. In these circumstances, it never occurred to anyone in Congress to conduct an inquiry into the failure in Cuba. It was a missed opportunity, which could have provided policymakers and Americans with insights into reasonable expectations for a covert action. In the wake of the Bay of Pigs, Kennedy fired Dulles and Richard Bissell. He told Bissell: "If this were the British government, I would resign, and you, being a senior civil servant, would remain. But it isn't. In our government, you and Allen have to go, and I have to remain." Kennedy replaced Dulles with the white-haired John McCone. Richard Helms, known as the "eminence grease" to his detractors, took over from Bissell as the head of operations (and in 1966 he became DCI himself).

U.S. aggression against Cuba did not push Castro into the arms of the Soviet Union, but it did strengthen their embrace. It also strengthened Moscow's claim that it was defending Cuba by placing "defensive" nuclear missiles there a year later. We might assume that choosing Helms (ex-OSS and with a traditional view of intelligence gathering) as director of operations was an effort to move the agency away from "kinetic" paramilitary activities, toward more patient and careful espionage. That, however, was not the intention of Kennedy's White House. Instead of pulling back from covert action against Cuba after the Bay of Pigs, Kennedy's national security advisers increased it. Kennedy was quick to resort to covert action as part of his statecraft. Over his eight years as president, Eisenhower had authorized 170 CIA covert operations. Kennedy authorized 163 in less than three years. Far from teaching the Kennedy brothers the dangers, and folly, of attempting to instigate regime change in Cuba, the Bay of Pigs fiasco seemed only to motivate them to pursue Castro with a vengeance. The Kennedy brothers were not used to being losers. Two weeks after the Bay of Pigs, it was agreed in an NSC meeting that "the U.S. policy toward Cuba should aim at the downfall of Castro." The administration attempted to handcuff the island's economy by banning Cuban imports, but not before Kennedy's counselors, the Wise Men, had stocked up their own private supplies of Cuban cigars.[10]

Robert Kennedy's papers, and others declassified by the JFK Assassination Records Review Board, reveal that there would have been a crisis in Cuba in 1962 even if Khrushchev had not placed nuclear missiles on the island. Seven months after the Bay of Pigs, President Kennedy put his brother—America's chief federal law enforcement officer—in charge of covert action to remove Castro from power in Cuba (Operation MONGOOSE). The group in charge of doing so was the National Security Council's Special Group (Augmented), so called because it was expanded to include Robert Kennedy and the Treasury secretary, Douglas Dillon. The centerpiece of America's anti-Castro operations was the largest CIA station in the world, code-named JM/WAVE, located on the campus of the University of Miami. Disguised as Zenith Technical Enterprises, it housed three hundred CIA officers, who recruited thousands of Cuban exiles as agents. Its annual budget of over $50 million was four times the total that the CIA spent on spying in the rest of Latin America.[11]

The head of MONGOOSE was a counterinsurgency specialist, Edward Lansdale, who had formidable paramilitary experience in the Philippines and Indochina. His nickname was "Colonel Landslide," a nod to his ability to rig elections. Others in the group included the CIA's pistol-toting William K. Harvey, whom we met earlier digging the Berlin spy tunnel. Lansdale produced a highly restricted plan for MONGOOSE, which included the use of chemicals and biological weapons to sabotage Cuba's harvest. These were not fringe antics, however, but Kennedy's chief foreign policy initiative in early 1962. This was the ugly reality of Kennedy's presidency, which, because of its tragically truncated end, posterity tends to forget.

The president is rightly remembered for his inspiring rhetoric, his courage, and the idealism of his New Frontier domestic agenda. But there was a dark side to the tawdry musical that gave Kennedy's White House its name, Camelot. Speechwriter Richard Goodwin became convinced there "was an inner hardness, often volatile anger beneath the outwardly amiable, thoughtful, carefully controlled demeanor of John Kennedy." One of Kennedy's alleged mistresses, Hollywood star Marilyn Monroe, died of an apparent suicide. Judith Campbell, another of the president's mistresses, was also the mistress of Chicago mobster Sam Giancana, the Mafia chief tasked with killing Castro. She later claimed to carry sealed envelopes between the two men to orchestrate his assassination. The truth of her claim is uncertain. What is clear is that the Kennedy brothers were cavalier about Cuba. Robert Kennedy's handwritten notes on a November 1961 meeting recorded: "My idea is to stir things up on [the] island with espionage, sabotage, general disorder, run & operated by Cubans themselves with every group but Batistaites & Communists. Do not know if we will be successful in overthrowing Castro but we have nothing to lose in my estimate."[12]

In fact, the Kennedy administration would have everything to lose in pursuing a covert action agenda against Castro. This attitude in the Kennedy White House did not change even during the East-West nuclear standoff in the autumn of 1962. On October 16, when ExComm had its first meeting, Robert Kennedy headed two meetings of the Special Group (Augmented) to discuss removing Castro; in fact, breathing fire, he berated its members about the lack of progress with Operation MONGOOSE. Those meetings continued throughout the crisis. On Black Saturday, Robert Kennedy chaired a meeting about MONGOOSE, a memo of which records him asking: "Is the end objective the removal of the Castro/Communist regime or to bring it to its knees?" The memo states that sabotage teams were being sent by submarine. To do what is not clear.

Even allowing for the coffee-fueled exhaustion and adrenaline during the Cuban Missile Crisis, the fact that those who attended the MONGOOSE meeting did not have a clear picture of their aims defies belief. Ray Cline, the CIA's director of analysis, was never informed of MONGOOSE or asked to evaluate it. Fortunately for all, Robert Kennedy's plans for MONGOOSE did not materialize. They would have made reaching a reconciliation during the missile crisis between the U.S. and the Soviet Union immeasurably more difficult. A central part of the resolution of the crisis was a pledge by the U.S. government for Cuba's territorial integrity. In early 1963, in the wake of the crisis, MONGOOSE was suspended. That did not stop the Kennedy brothers from continuing to pursue a covert action campaign of harassment against Castro, however. According to James Reston, Robert Kennedy "monkeyed around with amateur plots to assassinate Castro" until the last day of his brother's life.[13]

On November 22, 1963, the day President Kennedy was assassinated in Dallas, the CIA—doubtless on presidential authority—was embarking on another assassination attempt against Castro. Nearly five thousand miles away, the CIA's Desmond Fitzgerald was meeting in Paris with one of Castro's heavy-drinking former comrades-in-arms, Rolando Cubela Secades (code-named AM/LASH). Fitzgerald gave him a ballpoint pen within which was a hypodermic needle filled with poison. When he asked for "something more sophisticated," Fitzgerald offered Cubela "everything he needed (telescopic sight, silencer, all the money he wanted)" to assassinate Castro. Cubela was later arrested, imprisoned, then quietly released in Cuba. All mention of his dealings with the CIA was suppressed at Castro's command. As the historian Michael Burleigh has noted, it is difficult to resist the conclusion that Cubela was really planted by Castro's Soviet-trained intelligence service, the DGI.[14]

BREAKING COMMUNISTS' TEETH

In 1953, British Guiana, on South America's tropical North Atlantic coast, democratically elected Cheddi Jagan, the first Marxist leader of a British territory. Jagan became the target of a sustained British "special political action," and later CIA covert action, to prevent him from leading the colony to independence.

Jagan, slim and handsome, was the son of Indian immigrants to the colony and the leader of the People's Progressive Party (PPP). He had done well for himself, attending university first in the colony's capital, Georgetown, and then in the United States. He trained as a dentist at Northwestern University, outside Chicago, where he met his wife, Janet, an avowed Marxist. The couple's Marxism placed them on the FBI's radar. In 1947, the bureau began sharing intelligence on the Jagans with MI5, given that Cheddi was a British colonial subject. That year, back in British Guiana, Cheddi Jagan contacted the Soviet embassy in Washington, and, MI5 noted, he also contacted the British Communist Party in London. MI5's rolling surveillance of the Communist Party revealed, however, that Jagan was in no sense a communist. Its investigations, eventually contained in thirty-nine volumes of files, showed no indication that Jagan was a committed fellow traveler. According to MI5, he "wields great influence over a large number of people who have never been, and in all probability never will be, communists or have the slightest sympathy with communist aims and ideals." But subtle distinctions between Marxism and Soviet-controlled communism were lost in the Cold War's atmosphere, especially when Churchill once again became prime minister in 1951. As Churchill and Eisenhower were authorizing the CIA and MI6's plans for a coup in Iran, the British leader considered asking for American help to oust Jagan from power. In May 1953, Churchill wrote to his colonial secretary, Oliver Lyttelton: "We ought surely to get American support in doing all that we can to break the Communist teeth in British Guiana," adding caustically: "Perhaps they would even send Senator McCarthy down there."

The colony was too important for British commerce to be left to chance. It had the most valuable bauxite deposits in the world, essential for munitions. In September 1953, Churchill approved Operation WINDSOR, which saw the landing of British troops the following month. Britain's governor in the colony declared an emergency and suspended the constitution. Jagan was removed after just 133 days in office. Churchill's government justified its action on the nonsensical grounds that Jagan and his ministers intended "to turn British Guiana into a totalitarian state subordinate to Moscow."[15]

Despite Britain's best efforts to keep Jagan from power by suspending the colony's constitution, then redrafting it, and then redrawing electoral boundaries to force people off the electoral rolls, he continued to win elections. Six years later, Castro's seizure of power in Cuba transformed Washington's view of Jagan and the "communist" threat he posed. Jagan visited Cuba in 1960, as he would also the Soviet Union and China. In 1961, he again won a national election. Soon after, in October, he traveled to Washington, where he met President Kennedy in the Oval Office. Photos show them earnestly talking, as Kennedy sat in his cushioned rocking chair. Jagan described himself as a socialist in the British tradition. After their meeting, Kennedy said that although Jagan might be a Marxist, the United States "doesn't object, because that choice was made in an honest election, which he won."

Kennedy lied. He did object. By the time of their meeting, he was in fact already tasking the CIA to plan his guest's removal from power. Kennedy's administration viewed Jagan as a serious menace within America's "backyard." As Kennedy put it to Prime Minister Macmillan in early 1962: "We must be entirely frank in saying that we simply cannot afford to see another Castro-type regime established in this Hemisphere. It follows that we should set as our objective an independent British Guiana under some other leader." According to his brother, the president thought Jagan was "probably a communist." There was in fact no contemporary intelligence available to support that view. No evidence has emerged from Soviet archives that its intelligence services regarded Jagan as a reliable communist or a Soviet agent. Eastern bloc services did, it seems, naturally try to influence him, but without success.[16]

As well as commercial relations in the colony, Washington also maintained two naval bases in British Guiana, obtained under the wartime "destroyers for bases" agreement reached between Churchill and Roosevelt. In June 1961, the Kennedy administration urged the British to agree "to influence the outcome of the elections" in British Guiana. The precise means suggested are still classified, but they seem to have involved bribery of local politicians to instigate a vote of no confidence in Jagan. The British agreed to redistricting inside the colony, with the aim of reducing votes for Jagan. In early 1962, Jagan introduced austerity measures to help Guiana's dire economy. A tax increase fell mainly on the colony's African and mixed-ethnicity populations, which soon led to riots in Georgetown. In February 1962, on crisp embossed State Department stationery, Secretary of State Rusk wrote to his British counterpart, Alec Douglas-Home, calling for "remedial steps" to counter Jagan's "Marxist-Leninist" policy there: "I must tell you now that I have reached the conclusion that it is not possible for U.S. to put up with an independent British Guiana under Jagan."

Reading Rusk's letter, Macmillan felt exasperated that Washington was now undertaking the same policy, delaying colonial emancipation, for which it had previously lambasted Britain at the UN. Macmillan told Douglas-Home that the U.S. secretary of state's letter was "pure Machiavellianism," exposing a "degree of cynicism" that he found surprising given that Rusk was "not an Irishman, nor politician, nor millionaire." Replying to Rusk sharply, Douglas-Home described America's historic role as "the first crusader and the prime mover in urging colonial emancipation" and said it was not possible to stop Guiana from gaining its freedom without subverting democracy:

> You say that it is not possible for you to put up with an independent British Guiana under Jagan "and that Jagan should not accede to

power again." How would you suggest that this can be done in a democracy? And even if a device could be found, it would almost certainly be transparent.

Instead of preventing his rule, Douglas-Home said it would be better to steer Jagan in a Western direction. In the White House, Kennedy adviser Arthur Schlesinger Jr. poured cold water on the notion that Jagan was a communist. Back in September 1961, on the eve of Jagan's visit to the Oval Office, the State Department had labeled him a Soviet "sleeper agent." Schlesinger had argued against this: "Sleeper is a technical term meaning a disciplined agent who pretends to be one thing and then, at a given moment, tears off his mask and reveals himself as something entirely different." He continued: "I have not heard this seriously suggested about Jagan, and I hope that David [Bruce, U.S. ambassador in London] does not, on the basis of this cable, convey to the British the idea that our government seriously entertains this idea."[17]

In February 1962, Schlesinger met with Britain's Conservative Party luminary and former colonial secretary Iain Macleod, a dour bridge player who brought that gamesmanship to diplomacy. He told Kennedy's adviser that he disagreed with U.S. assessments that Jagan was a communist. "Jagan is not a communist; he is a Marxist and there is a distinction," said Macleod. He explained that it would be impossible to "dislodge a democratically elected party." Echoing Macleod, Schlesinger argued about Jagan with hawks like Rusk. The man was not a communist, Schlesinger said; instead, he was simply a naive "London School of Economics Marxist filled with charm."[18]

Schlesinger was in a distinct minority in Kennedy's White House, which saw Jagan—whose Georgetown headquarters was the "Red House"—as a menace. The U.S. intelligence community (Office of National Estimates) produced a Special National Intelligence Estimate on British Guiana. It stated that the "PPP leadership" had a clear record of "Communist-line policies" and that Jagan was a communist—based on what intelligence remains unclear to this day. The executive branch's covert action committee, the 5412

Special Group, began to consider ways to drive Jagan from power using international labor unions. In the summer of 1962, McGeorge Bundy was skeptical as to whether a U.S. covert action could work, doubtless thinking of the Bay of Pigs debacle: "I think it is unproven that CIA knows how to manipulate an election in British Guiana without a backfire."[19]

For assistance, Kennedy turned to David Ormsby-Gore. There was evidently a quid pro quo deal negotiated between Washington and London, not revealed in publicly available documentation. Despite Macmillan's previous "wind of change" speech in 1960 about colonial independence in Africa, which stressed the importance of the direction of newly independent states, East or West, and the prime minister's acceleration of British withdrawal from empire in Africa, Kennedy got Macmillan to delay independence in British Guiana. That left a window open for U.S. covert action. In 1962, Kennedy authorized a program, which would cost approximately $2 million over the next six years, to drive Jagan from power before the colony became independent. As the historian Richard Drayton has noted, Guiana was thereafter the only British colony in which the CIA, not British intelligence, took the lead.[20]

In October 1962, during the Cuban Missile Crisis, Britain's colonial secretary, Duncan Sandys, agreed that the CIA should be allowed to approach Jagan's political rival in the colony, the London School of Economics–educated lawyer Forbes Burnham. His party, the People's National Congress, duly received American funding. At least some funds were channeled through Congress under the pretext of conducting topographical surveys in the colony. This scheme was pushed forward by Democrat senator Thomas J. Dodd, who saw Jagan as another Castro. (Dodd, from Connecticut, was later censured by Congress for improper use of campaign funds.) In April 1963, the Guyana Trades Union Congress, with American financial support, instigated a crippling general strike that was to last for eleven weeks—longer than a general strike anywhere in the world before. As many as two hundred people died in riots in Georgetown. In July 1963, Macmillan once again noted the ironies of Kennedy's policies: "We shall not give B. Guiana 'independence' only to create Cuba on the mainland. It is, however, rather fun making the Americans repeat over and over again their passionate plea to us to stick to 'Colonialism' and 'Imperialism' at any cost."[21]

By 1963, MI5 had reversed its previous non-alarmist assessments of Jagan and was now warning Whitehall that he posed a threat to the security of British Guiana. That year, Britain's JIC noted the deteriorating situation in the colony amid Jagan's "enthusiastic Marxism" and his open admiration toward Castro. It is unclear, however, whether the observed deteriorating situation in British Guiana was a result of CIA covert action. Separating cause and effect presents perennial problems when assessing covert action. Jagan's embrace of Castro may have been a response to the effects of U.S. covert action.

In June that year, Macmillan hosted Kennedy for a weekend at his ivy-clad home in West Sussex, Birch Grove. Photographers snapped pictures of the president and his wife. Kennedy went to church on Sunday morning. Behind this peaceful setting, the two statesmen agreed to steal an election. Kennedy got Macmillan to agree to impose unilaterally proportional representation (rather than direct ballots) in Guiana's forthcoming election, in December 1964, which was believed to favor Jagan's rival, Burnham. They also agreed the colony could become independent after the election. The ethics of U.S. and British electoral meddling was summarized by a U.S. economic-development official in Guiana, indoctrinated into how U.S. development aid was being used there: "Can we maintain that we respect freedom of ballot, and accept the choice of people in a democratic election, even if not one we would make; and then coerce a people into choosing a government according to our wishes?"[22]

The British agreed to continue with the covert action plan even after Kennedy was assassinated and Lyndon Johnson took power. The plan worked. In the election that year, the U.S. administration achieved what President Kennedy had previously called "a good result": Burnham formed a coalition government and became the colony's premier and national leader-in-waiting, before independence. In May 1966, British Guiana was renamed Guyana and gained independence, with Burnham as its first prime minister.

As Washington's man, Burnham was welcomed by President Johnson to the Oval Office. When he got sick in 1968, LBJ sent him flowers. The U.S. government, however, had created a monster. Its protégé had learned well from the British and Americans, using similar tactics, forcing people off electoral rolls and rigging elections, in order to hold power. Burnham would rule Guyana corruptly and incompetently for twenty years, wrecking its economy and encouraging hostility between its Afro-Caribbean and Indian communities. Within a decade, Burnham was, in a bitter irony, gravitating toward the Soviet Union, thereby undermining Washington's primary strategic objective. In the 1970s he announced that Guyana was "on the road to socialism." He nationalized the sugar plantations and formed friendly ties with the Soviet bloc. It was not until after the end of the Cold War that the U.S. government permitted Jagan, and then his wife, to lead their country. Decades later, Schlesinger admitted, "We misunderstood the whole struggle down there."[23]

HUNTING GROUND: CHILE

Chile became a theater for Cold War intrigue between the superpowers. With its four thousand miles of Pacific coastline and rich deposits of copper and iodine, it drew the attention of both the United States and the Soviet Union, each seeking to subvert the government and counter the other's influence. On September 11, 1973, Salvador Allende, the country's democratically elected leader, was overthrown. Conventional wisdom holds that the CIA was responsible for the coup that led to Allende's death in the presidential palace that day. The CIA was indeed responsible, at the behest of the White House, for carrying out a sustained covert action program against Allende. But in fact, as we shall see, it did not plot with the Chilean army in 1973 to overthrow Allende.

Although most studies fail to mention it, the CIA was not operating in a vacuum in Chile. As the research of the historian Kristian Gustafsson has shown, the KGB was also active, instigating parallel covert actions to support Allende. While both sides did what they could to influence Allende's government, ultimately his downfall was a Chilean affair. It was Allende's mishandling of the Chilean economy, more than a foreign hidden hand, that led the army to plot against him.[24]

Well educated and well dressed, Allende held a medical degree from the University of Chile. With his thick black glasses, full head of hair, well-cut suits, and love of female companions, Allende was not a figure cast in the gritty revolutionary style of Castro. But the two men embraced each other, setting off alarm bells in Washington. U.S. policymakers feared that Allende's suave speaking ability could be a winning formula at the ballot box—which it proved to be. While Khrushchev, and later Brezhnev, never publicly backed Allende as they did Castro, Washington feared what was going on covertly. Chile was a valuable market for U.S. businesses and a central part of Kennedy's $20 billion Alliance for Progress in Latin America. Kennedy appears to have authorized the CIA to run a covert action against Allende in 1962. Two years later, in 1964, President Lyndon Johnson directed the CIA to instigate a second covert action program against Allende, trying to split those on the left and galvanize support for moderates in the country, particularly the Christian Democrats, led by Eduardo Frei, Washington's man in Santiago. The agency's action involved cash, propaganda, and other stock-in-trade clandestine tools like smear campaigns. It led to a "happy result"—according to one official on the National Security Council. Frei was elected. Britain's MI6 also played a hidden hand in Chile, as British records opened in 2021 reveal. Allende was kept at bay, for the time being at least, and Frei became president. By the end of the decade, however, despite U.S. and British efforts, Allende was emerging as a front-runner, now at the helm of a coalition of socialists, communists, radicals, and renegade Christian Democrats known as Popular Unity.[25]

As revealed by Russian archives, as well as KGB secrets smuggled to the West, the Soviet government and its principal ally in Latin America, Cuba, supported Allende. The KGB established a *rezidentura* in Chile in 1964. The

KGB had first contacted Allende back in 1953, through an officer named Svyatoslav Kuznetsov (LEONID). Allende was never a Soviet agent, only a confidential contact, which in KGB lexicon meant someone who provided information but would not, like an agent, perform requested intelligence activities. According to Nikolai Leonov, the KGB's leading expert on Latin America, Chile was a hunting ground for Soviet intelligence. The objective was not so much to export a communist revolution there, but to use Allende to resist "Yankee" influence in Latin America. The Soviet government funneled $400,000 (approximately $2.6 million today) to Allende through the local Communist Party and provided Allende with a personal subsidy of $50,000 (about $330,000 today). They also paid off at least one left-wing rival senator to keep him from running against Allende. The CIA was thus not chasing Soviet phantoms in Chile. The agency threw similar funds (approximately $475,000) to oppose Allende. The stage was set for a KGB-CIA showdown.[26]

In his memoirs, Richard Nixon was unapologetic about secretly supporting anti-communists in foreign countries—that is, meddling in the domestic affairs of other states. "As long as the Communists supply external funds to support political parties, factions, or individuals in other countries," the president wrote, "I believe that the United States can and should do the same and do it secretly so it can be effective." When Allende won the election in Chile in September 1970, Nixon was furious at the CIA. A postmortem report demanded by Henry Kissinger set out, in black and white, what went wrong. The CIA's assumption was that it could steal elections: any failure to do so was the result of covert efforts that were insufficiently strenuous. It apparently never occurred to anyone on Kissinger's national security team to question whether, and in what circumstances, covert action could be successful.

In a top secret report titled "Why Did the U.S. Government Not Take More Vigorous Political Action Measures to Prevent the Election of the Marxist Candidate, Salvador Allende, as President of Chile?," Kissinger's team concluded that there had been no systematic analysis of the threat posed by Allende because, at the time, Allende's political rival, Jorge Alessandri, seemed to be ahead going into the election. This was a sleight of hand. In fact, six months before the election, Kissinger himself had decided only to sanction a limited covert action in Chile, having analyzed the situation. Instead of supporting another candidate, Kissinger authorized a discrediting and smear ("spoiling") operation against Allende's Popular Unity party, ultimately costing $300,000. The U.S. ambassador to Chile at the time, Edward Korry, pushed for more aggressive "political action" before and after the election, to buy votes and influence people—something that he subsequently denied. For Kissinger, however, the risk was not worth the reward: if the U.S. action was exposed, it would strengthen Allende. The prospects of his rival, Alessandri, seemed good.[27]

With the popular vote split between three candidates, Allende won a tight election victory with a margin of 1.5 percent. Soviet active measures may have helped his coalition, if only by blunting CIA activities and splitting Allende's conservative opponents. The documentary evidence available does not allow us to draw firm conclusions. In Washington, however, Nixon called in the CIA director, Richard Helms, and berated him. Nixon had made a career out of criticizing the Democrats for losing Cuba to communism, and now he had lost Chile. According to notes that Helms took at the meeting, there was $10 million available for covert action in Chile. The CIA's mission was to "make the economy scream."[28]

Thus began the so-called Track I and Track II U.S. covert actions in Chile. Track I involved trying to find a way for the Chilean Congress not to vote in Allende as president, despite his victory at the ballot box. There was a way to do so. The fact that he had not collected more than 50 percent of the votes cast meant that a joint session of Chile's Congress would have to vote to ratify the election. Convention (but not law) said that he would be voted through, but it opened a door for the Nixon administration to buy votes to prevent Allende from actually taking office. The plan envisioned by Nixon, Kissinger, Helms, and the CIA's head of covert operations, Thomas

Karamessines, was to convince the Chilean Congress to vote Jorge Alessandri into power. Track II was a military coup to overthrow Allende. As
with much in Nixon's White House, it was a secret within a secret. It was
not known to the White House's Forty Committee, which was supposed
to oversee U.S. covert actions, nor was it known to the State Department
or to Edward Korry.

In the end, both tracks failed. Eduardo Frei, the Christian Democrat
leader, refused to violate the constitution when approached—presumably
by a CIA officer—about voting in Allende's rival. Nixon later claimed that
Track II, fomenting a coup, was shut down in October 1970, when a group
of retired Chilean military officers tried to launch their own coup. Chile's
military commander, René Schneider, was killed in a botched kidnapping. As
a result, people rallied around Allende, who was sworn in twelve days later.

In public, Nixon welcomed Allende's election and stated he would
respect it. In fact, he continued to sanction CIA covert actions. Track II
never really ended. MI6 played second fiddle, creating and dispersing propaganda, as records kept secret for fifty years now reveal. The CIA used
private U.S. companies like the multinational telephone company ITT to
funnel $8 million to anti-Allende forces. As it would do across the Third
World, the CIA planted stories in Chile's press espousing the importance
of democratic freedoms—while suborning a free press to do so. Moscow
viewed Allende's election as a strategic victory for socialism. Soviet intelligence siphoned funds to communist parties in other countries in Latin
America in the hope that they would follow Chile. Approximately half of
the 351 Soviet officials assigned to Latin American countries were known
or suspected Soviet intelligence officers. Soviet archives reveal that in total
the KGB funneled $1 million toward Allende while he was in government.[29]

Contrary to what is often popularly believed, the CIA did not orchestrate the coup that overthrew Allende in September 1973. The agency had
failed to penetrate the Chilean military, which carried out the coup led by
General Augusto Pinochet, and only learned about plans for the coup two
days before it took place. According to Jack Devine, a CIA officer stationed

in Santiago at the time, however, the CIA did create the climate in which the hard-line coup took place. The White House and CIA may not have lit the match, but they provided the fuel. But if we are to look for overall blame for the events in Chile in September 1973, we really need look no further than Allende himself. It was his own mishandling of the national economy—in 1973 inflation was between 350 percent and 650 percent—that galvanized opposition against him. For its part, the Soviet government and its intelligence services never supported Allende to the degree it did Castro. Soviet policy in Chile was also to resist Chinese influence. The KGB used Cuban intelligence, the DGI, to train hard-line militant groups in Chile, one of which was called MIR, but its fighters were decidedly nonconformist to the Soviet line. After Nixon's famous visit to Moscow in May 1972, and Brezhnev's return visit to the United States the following year, the Soviet government pulled back from backing Allende publicly.

On September 11, 1973, Allende sat on a couch in La Moneda Palace, placed an automatic weapon—a gift given to him by Castro—to his head, and blew his brains out. His shattered iconic eyeglasses showed the force of the shot. Allende's suicide—not an assassination, as often described—was a resounding defeat for the Soviet Union. The new Chilean leader, Pinochet, was initially greeted with optimism by the Nixon administration. Devine recalls the aftermath of Allende's fall: "In the heady days immediately following, we took pride in having helped thwart the development of Cuban-style socialism in Chile and having prevented the country's drift into the Soviet orbit. We expected that Pinochet's junta would hold on to power only long enough to stabilize the economy and would soon thereafter call for elections and step aside."[30]

Far from ceding power, as Washington hoped, Pinochet would rule Chile as a military dictatorship for about seventeen years, until the end of the Cold War, conducting a "dirty war" with gross violations of human rights. He was responsible for murdering at least 2,200 people and imprisoning about 40,000 others, many of whom were tortured, or thrown from helicopters. Countless more "disappeared," in a repression known as the

Caravan of Death. The U.S. government knew about Pinochet's human rights violations, and in some cases, it seems, helped to cover them up. As Jeane Kirkpatrick, later the U.S. ambassador to the UN, put it, there are degrees of evil; sometimes Washington had to back bad people to defeat worse ones. It was a line of thought not dissimilar to that expressed by President Roosevelt about the U.S.-backed tyrant in Nicaragua, Anastasio Somoza: "Somoza may be a son of a bitch, but he's our son of a bitch."

Nixon's obsessions with countering communism, which motivated his authorizations of U.S. covert actions against foreign democratic elections, eventually spilled over into his domestic politics. The Watergate scandal that started in 1972, and led to his resignation in 1974, was effectively a White House covert action. The scandal involved the kind of dirty tricks—bugging, burglary, wiretapping—that were commonplace U.S. practices overseas. But Nixon used them inside the United States against his Democratic presidential opponents—and then tried to cover them up. The means employed by Nixon, declared the subsequent articles of impeachment against him, included "endeavoring to misuse the Central Intelligence Agency." Both Nixon and Kissinger were convinced that the left-leaning Georgetown liberals in the CIA, the "clowns in Langley," were undermining them. Nixon believed the CIA had cost him the election in 1960, leaking intelligence to his opponent, John F. Kennedy. In the first five months of his presidency in 1969, according to Nixon's memoirs, at least twenty-one major stories based on leaks from the NSC appeared in the press. (How many were leaked by Kissinger himself is unclear.) When presented with leaks (other than his own) coming from within the White House, Kissinger's bullfrog baritone turned to screams.

In the summer of 1971, the *New York Times* published the Pentagon Papers, an official classified history of America's secret war in Vietnam before 1968. They were leaked by a former Pentagon aide, Daniel Ellsberg. When the story broke, Kissinger went into a spectacular White House rage. It was his "premier performance," recalled Nixon's chief of staff H. R. "Bob" Haldeman. Another aide, Charles Colson, recalled Kissinger pounding a

Chippendale table as he denounced "forces at work bent on destroying this government." The Nixon White House responded by instigating a covert action to smear and discredit Ellsberg. They instructed the FBI, and other helpers, to wiretap NSC staffers to find who was leaking secrets. In July 1971, Nixon created a top secret group in the White House known as the "plumbers," made up of former CIA and FBI operatives, to plug leaks. Their targets were soon Nixon's political opponents.[31]

Thus began Nixon's walk on the dark side, as his operatives burgled Democratic headquarters in the Watergate building in June 1972 to try to find political dirt on his rivals. The burglary, when exposed, eventually cost Nixon his presidency. He became the only president ever to resign from office (in the face of a congressional impeachment). As one history of U.S. intelligence has described, the most powerful government to fall because of a presidentially sanctioned covert action was thus not a foreign one, but Nixon's own. For its part, the Soviet government was bemused that something so trivial as spying on political opponents could have such profound consequences. As the Soviet ambassador in Washington, Anatoly Dobrynin, later mused, "His [Nixon's] use of the CIA, the FBI, and the considerable powers of his own office to remain in the White House was considered in the Soviet Union at the time a fairly natural thing for the chief of state to do. Who cared if it was a breach of the Constitution?" In Beijing, Mao wondered what "all the fuss" was about.[32] *

In Washington, fears of Soviet subversion in Latin America festered and metastasized. In the 1980s, under President Ronald Reagan, they would lead to another amateur White House covert action scheme: the Iran-Contra scandal, a harebrained plot by the White House against

---

* In Britain, Prime Minister Harold Wilson harbored similar fears to Nixon about a "deep state." Like Nixon, Wilson was highly intelligent and was convinced that there was a plot being waged by his country's intelligence services to unseat him. There was not. Unlike Nixon, Wilson resigned from office before his conspiracy theories (and mental deterioration) got the better of him: Christopher Andrew, *The Defence of the Realm*, chap. 10.

the Marxist Sandinista regime in Nicaragua. Despite what Reagan and his DCI, William Casey—the last ex-OSS officer to head the CIA—believed, the Sandinistas were not really a KGB or Cuban force. Reagan's team tried to find ways around congressional restrictions imposed on U.S. agencies, known as the Boland Amendment, to fund the inept contras fighting the Sandinistas. The plot they dreamed up involved illegally selling arms to Iran, a state sponsor of terrorism. The hard truth was that, like Castro in Cuba, the only way the Sandinistas could have been overthrown was by overt U.S. military action, which Reagan, like Eisenhower and Kennedy with Cuba, would not sanction. When exposed, the result was the worst scandal of Reagan's presidency. It was another sobering illustration of the dangers of private executive branch covert actions taking place beyond congressional oversight.[33]

CHAPTER TWELVE

SUNNY PLACES, SHADY PEOPLE

> They had been corrupted by money, and he had been corrupted
> by sentiment. Sentiment was the more dangerous, because you
> couldn't name its price. A man open to bribes was to be relied
> upon below a certain figure, but sentiment might uncoil in the
> heart at a name, a photograph, even a smell remembered.
> –Graham Greene, *The Heart of the Matter*

AS THE COLD WAR IN EUROPE REACHED A STALEMATE IN THE 1950s, both Eastern and Western superpowers looked to Africa as a new frontier. Lenin and Stalin had spoken of exporting communism to Africa but had done little. That changed with Khrushchev. According to Soviet foreign intelligence officers, when Khrushchev looked to sub-Saharan Africa as part of his grand strategy for the Third World, he saw a blank sheet of paper. In 1960, the KGB's foreign intelligence directorate, under the KGB's relatively youthful and energetic chairman, Alexander Shelepin, opened an Africa division. That summer, as Congo slipped into chaos, Khrushchev made himself the Soviet representative to the United Nations in New York, banging on the table in hours of speeches as he welcomed new countries in Africa to the UN.[1]

In the West, MI6 and the CIA were equally slow to turn their attention to Africa. Once the starter pistol had been fired, however, both sides began to influence leaders in Africa, which effectively meant meddling in the domestic affairs of colonies seeking independence, not always as successfully as they hoped. In essence, the two superpowers and their allies used newly independent states in Africa as proxy battlefields in the Cold War. Once again, their intelligence services were at the front lines, leaving a trail of destruction in their wake.[2]

RED SHADOW IN AFRICA

In 1957, the Gold Coast in West Africa was reborn as the Republic of Ghana. It was the first sub-Saharan Black African state to gain independence from European colonization. The Dutch, British, Danish, and Swedish had settled there beginning in the fifteenth century in search of gold. It came under Britain's colonial rule in the nineteenth century. The colony stretched from the Gulf of Guinea north toward the Sahara. As a wartime MI6 officer, Graham Greene was posted to Sierra Leone, to the west of the Gold Coast. His description in *The Heart of the Matter* of an anonymous British colony in West Africa fit the Gold Coast to a tee. It was the "original Tower of Babel," whose inhabitants were "West Indians, Africans, real Indians, Syrians, Englishman, Scotsmen in the Office of Works, Irish priests, French priests, Alsatian priests."

Britain's last governor in the Gold Coast, Charles Arden-Clarke, was tall and tanned, a clergyman's son, an ex-army officer, and a dog lover. The man who opposed him, fighting for the Gold Coast's independence, was an anti-colonial nationalist leader, Kwame Nkrumah. The son of a goldsmith from the neighboring French colony, the Ivory Coast, Nkrumah traveled to the United States, where he studied at a predominantly black college, Lincoln University in Pennsylvania, paying his tuition and board by working as a dishwasher, bellhop, soap maker, and fish peddler. Sometimes he slept on subway trains shuttling between Harlem and Brooklyn. In 1945, at the age of thirty-six, Nkrumah left for Britain to lead a crusade for Gold Coast independence. The strategic question for London and Washington was whether he was doing so with Moscow's help.[3]

As the historian Mark Matera has shown, the imperial metropolis, London, was central for groups that opposed colonialism, many of whose members were black students who came to study and work there. They debated, ate, socialized, drank together, and plotted anti-colonial political campaigns. The groups included left-wing African and West Indian students and intellectuals, like George Padmore, a self-described Marxist-Leninist who lived a comfortable lifestyle in Hampstead, and his fellow Trinidadian, the author C. L. R. James. Some, like Nkrumah, and Jomo Kenyatta of Kenya, attended the Pan-African Congress held in Manchester in October 1945, where crowds rallied behind impassioned speakers calling for national liberation and African political unity. Undercover Special Branch officers roamed the crowd, keeping notes on speakers.[4]

Following the congress, Nkrumah established the West African National Secretariat (WANS) in Gray's Inn, London, near the Dickensian cobble-stoned Inns of Court. It was, he later recalled, the "rendezvous of all African and West Indian students and their friends." He used the WANS office "to discuss our plans, to voice our opinions and air out our grievances." Through telephone taps and mail interception, MI5 was privy to many of these plans, opinions, and grievances. It ran surveillance on WANS not because of its anti-colonialism, which after all was a legitimate political expression, but because of its connections with the British Communist Party.

MI5's telephone taps revealed that Nkrumah, and other members of WANS, were indeed in contact with the CPGB. In his memoirs, Nkrumah recalled that he had difficulty leaving Britain in 1947, when he returned to the Gold Coast; the police questioned him at length. He believed that the police had "quite a file" of information about his political activities and attendance at communist meetings in London. Indeed, MI5's dossier on him ran to multiple volumes.[5]

Nkrumah drew inspiration for the Gold Coast's independence from Mahatma Gandhi's theories of passive resistance and Jawaharlal Nehru's influential tract *The Discovery of India*. Nkrumah resisted using violence to oppose colonial rule; his policy of "positive action" instead involved acts of nonconfrontation, like organizing strikes. He formed his own party, the Convention People's Party, or CPP, whose slogans were "Freedom" and "Self-Government Now." In February 1948, soon after he returned to the Gold Coast, riots broke out in the capital, Accra, killing 29 people and injuring 237 others. In defiance of British rule, protesters marched toward the governor's residence at Christiansborg Castle. Coinciding with a communist insurgency in Britain's colony of Malaya, in the Far East, it seemed to some in London that a red mist of communism was falling across the empire. Britain's governor in the Gold Coast declared a national emergency and arrested Nkrumah. He continued to direct the CPP from inside his Accra jail cell, smuggling out directives written on toilet paper.

For those in Accra and London who worried about the spread of communism in Africa, there was much to fear. When Nkrumah was arrested, he was found carrying an unsigned membership card to the British Communist Party. He was, it seemed, a secret member. Some CPP leaders called each other "comrades." Stalinism seemed to be gaining steam as regimes in Eastern Europe fell before the Soviet dictator and East and West squared off in Berlin. As Richard Rathbone, the leading historian of British West Africa, has noted, many in Whitehall believed that if the Gold Coast were granted independence, it would become a Soviet satellite.

It is here, however, that we find something surprising within MI5's declassified dossier on Nkrumah, the same thumbed file that Britain's spy chiefs used to assess his political sympathies years ago. Far from confirming their fears that Nkrumah was a closet communist, MI5 provided the colonial office in London and the governor in Accra with a non-alarmist analysis of Nkrumah's political beliefs. Its telephone checks and intercepted mail gave MI5 a unique eye into Nkrumah's "communism." Four months after the riots in the Gold Coast, in June 1948, MI5 concluded that his main motivations were nationalism and his own career advancement. He was a Marxist, but not a communist. His interest in communism, according to MI5, was likely prompted by his desire to enlist aid from the Soviet Union to further his political career and advance his cause in West Africa. There was not a single well-organized communist party in any of the British territories in Africa, MI5's Roger Hollis told the Joint Intelligence Committee. Communism in Africa was "not killed, but scotched," as he put it to the JIC.[6]

Britain's intelligence reports about Nkrumah shaped London's strategy toward the Gold Coast. MI5's assessments doubtless calmed the fears that Arden-Clarke had about Nkrumah, though we do not know if they actually changed his mind. Arden-Clarke arrived in the Gold Coast after the 1948 riots, having witnessed violence firsthand in Britain's counterinsurgency against communists in Malaya. He was determined to do everything possible to prevent similar violence breaking out in the Gold Coast. He wanted to channel, not check, the country's advancement to self-government. "You cannot slow down a flood," he said, "the best you can hope to do is keep the torrent in its proper channel." In 1951, Nkrumah won a general election in the Gold Coast. He did so again three years later.

As the Cold War intensified, questions about Nkrumah's "Marxism" periodically reemerged. In October 1950, seven months after Klaus Fuchs was found guilty in London of passing nuclear secrets to Moscow, London's *Daily Telegraph* ran a story titled "Red Shadow over the Gold Coast," claiming that Nkrumah's CPP was being orchestrated from Moscow, which wanted to turn the country into a Soviet outpost. Nkrumah's letters, intercepted by MI5, revealed a more reassuring story. By 1951, the colonial office came to view Nkrumah as a moderate. This was due in large part to British intelligence.

In February 1951, Arden-Clarke released Nkrumah from jail. A year later, Nkrumah became prime minister. Arden-Clarke believed there was no alternative to Nkrumah and his CPP: "We only have one dog in our kennel," he wrote to the colonial office. On New Year's Eve 1951, the governor stayed up until 2:00 a.m. talking on the phone with the head of MI5's overseas section, Sir John Shaw, an old colonial hand. It was doubtless a relief for Arden-Clarke to learn from Shaw that Nkrumah had fallen out of favor with the British Communist Party in London. In fact, they described him as a "busted flush."[7]

Independence for the Gold Coast, amid the intensifying Cold War, happened quicker than anyone in London or Accra thought possible. Historians have noted that Britain's peaceful transfer of power there owed largely to Arden-Clarke's ability to get on with Nkrumah. The two men hit it off as best they could given their different backgrounds and opposing interests. There was, however, another side to Arden-Clarke's bonhomie. In 1952, Nkrumah asked whether his mail was being intercepted. The governor gave his personal assurance that it was not. In fact, as we can now see from MI5's dossier, the Accra Special Branch did continue to intercept Nkrumah's mail, operating it "unofficially . . . against the written orders of the Governor, who receives the product in a form which he is not obliged to recognize as the fruits of disobedience of his own orders." Arden-Clarke, like other colonial governors, had no interest in playing a fair game of cricket when the stakes were so high. (There is some evidence that in nearby Nigeria, Britain's governor general, James Robertson, rigged an election on the eve of independence so the most conservative northern province, traditionally closely aligned with Britain, would hold the balance of power.)[8]

In the Gold Coast, relations between Arden-Clarke and Nkrumah were so close that, as the African colony approached independence, the governor was described as Nkrumah's "chief propaganda officer." Arden-Clarke helped him fend off political rivals. Six months before independence, MI5's liaison officer in Accra, John Thomson, revealed his true position as a British intelligence officer to Nkrumah. Ghana's leader-in-waiting accepted Thomson's offer to remain in place after independence. The work of British intelligence officers for the governments of colonies that gained independence—initially MI5 officers, then MI6—was a secret chapter of British decolonization and its geopolitical context, the Cold War. Thomson was present in Accra in March 1957 as the British flag was lowered and Ghana was born. President Eisenhower sent Vice President Richard Nixon and Martin Luther King Jr. to the ceremony.

Before Britain's transfer of power, Thomson also convinced Nkrumah's future cabinet to allow the British to continue to manufacture their cipher pads. The British were thus able to read Ghana's communications like open books. Ghana also used Crypto machines—which, as we know, were rigged by the U.S. government—for enciphering its communications. It is likely that Soviet code breakers also read Ghana's traffic. Between 1960 and 1967, the number of countries whose communications the KGB's SIGINT department, the Eighth Directorate, could read grew from fifty to seventy-two, as colonial states in Africa and elsewhere gained independence. Both sides of the Cold War watched as Nkrumah's rule lurched from promise to tyranny.[9]

After independence, Nkrumah became intoxicated by power. In private, he compared himself to Christ; in public, he referred to himself only as a living deity. Neon-lit statues of him appeared around the country. He became increasingly corrupt, a trait that MI5 and MI6 had noted earlier when they learned that he had been involved in diamond smuggling. In a story that would be replicated in other African countries during the Cold War, Nkrumah tried to play the two superpowers, East and West, off against each other. Both the U.S. government and the Soviet Union provided his new government with funds. The Soviets pushed to show they were more reliable for Africans than Mao's China.[10]

Moscow established an embassy in Accra, with KGB and GRU *rezidents*, and soon Nkrumah accepted a multitude of Eastern bloc security "technical advisers." Based on their advice, his security service was run along Eastern bloc lines, using informants and blackmail. But his Soviet advisers had no experience in building anything other than heavy-smokestack industries; as the historian James Scott showed, Soviet central planners had a history of grafting industries onto unsuitable environments.

In Sierra Leone, Soviet officials provided toilets for homes with no plumbing, snowplows in the hot African climate that were left famously to rust (apparently intended for brush cutting), a printing press that operated at 5 percent capacity, a radio station built over an iron-ore vein that interfered with its signals, and a tomato cannery built in an area without water or tomatoes. With Soviet help, Nkrumah wrecked the Ghanaian economy. He was not a Soviet stooge, however. During the Cuban Missile Crisis, he refused to allow Soviet aircraft to land in Ghana. (Nkrumah admired President Kennedy.) After the execution by firing squad of Congo's leader, Patrice Lumumba, in 1961, and Kennedy's own assassination in November 1963, Nkrumah became convinced that dark forces were out to kill him. The KGB accentuated his fears by supplying him with forged documents suggesting that the CIA wanted him removed.[11]

The KGB may have deceived Nkrumah with their forged documents, but they were not wrong about CIA covert action against him. As his rule in Ghana became increasingly authoritarian, the agency funded his political opponents, mirroring the support Soviet intelligence provided him. While British officials declined to support a coup to overthrow him, Britain's clandestine propaganda unit, the Information Research Department (IRD), did publish pamphlets smearing him. Its hand in them was so secret that, ironically, Britain's High Commission in Accra reported them to London, unaware of their provenance. Drawing on British tradecraft from World War II, like the Political Warfare Executive discussed earlier, the IRD created entirely bogus political groups in Africa to disseminate anti-Soviet propaganda.[12]

Nkrumah was deposed in a coup led by the Ghanaian army in February 1966. The U.S. government was not directly involved—emphasis on the word "direct." The reality was revealed by one member of the National

Security Council, Robert Komer, when he wrote to McGeorge Bundy the previous year. He noted that America played an indirect role: "We and other Western countries (including France) have been helping to set up the situation by ignoring Nkrumah's pleas for economic aid." After the coup, Komer wrote to President Lyndon Johnson describing it as a "fortuitous windfall" for the West. The new regime in Ghana cut ties with the Soviet Union, expelled Eastern bloc technicians, and banned Aeroflot flights from Moscow. The country remained within the Commonwealth and sided with the West for the rest of the Cold War. That did not stop Soviet intelligence and its Eastern bloc counterparts like the Czech StB, however, from trying to restore Nkrumah to power.[13]

There was a similar story four thousand miles away, in East Africa, in Kenya and Tanganyika (later Tanzania). British intelligence held thick files on their respective anti-colonial leaders, Jomo Kenyatta and Julius Nyerere. As with Nkrumah in Ghana, hawks in London and Washington viewed Kenyatta and Nyerere as communist stooges, especially after the Mau Mau revolt in Kenya in 1952. The British fought a violent counterinsurgency there. Despite the accurate information it had on file, British intelligence was unable to change the prevailing views about Kenyatta himself. The colonial office, and the local government in Nairobi, labeled him a communist, even calling him the devil, and imprisoned him after a sham trial. Kenyatta was released in 1961, whereupon the British government rehabilitated him; he now became "Old Jomo."

It has been claimed that, in the months preceding Britain's peaceful transfer of power in Kenya in December 1963, MI5 bugged independence negotiations that took place in London, in the ornate setting of Lancaster House, in St. James's. That claim was first made by Peter Wright in his book *Spycatcher*. Previously classified papers tucked away in the Ministry of Works, and uncovered for this book, suggest that Wright was correct. MI5 apparently bugged diplomatic negotiations of other countries as well. After independence, Kenya, and Kenyatta, remained firmly on the Western side.[14]

MURDER IN CONGO

Congo was a vast, sweltering country of savannah, jungle, and rain forest straddling the equator and stretching from West Africa to the continent's interior. Its capital, Léopoldville, was a modern Belgian city, with wide boulevards, cafes, and tall residential buildings transplanted into the heart of Africa. In 1960, it became a new front line in the East-West Cold War. In July of that year, its first democratically elected leader, Patrice Lumumba, appealed to the Soviet Union for help in keeping the country, rapidly disintegrating into chaos, from falling apart. In doing so, he played a dangerous game. By appealing to Khrushchev for aid, he pulled Congo into the world's superpower conflict at a time when Cold War tensions were at their height. Lumumba held office as prime minister for less than three months. He was killed in January 1961, at the age of thirty-five.[15]

In the late nineteenth century, King Léopold II of Belgium ruled Congo as his own fiefdom, although he never set foot in it. His dominion over Congo was the most brutal of any European nation in Africa, as Joseph Conrad depicted in his novella *Heart of Darkness*. In the twenty-three years of Léopold's rule, an estimated ten million Congolese died from disease or starvation or at the hands of death squads. When workers performing backbreaking work failed to meet rubber quotas, Belgian officials would hack off a daughter's hand or foot. Entire villages were massacred; killing was treated as sport. The native heads on spikes that Conrad wrote about outside the house of the mad colonist, Kurtz, were not far from reality. The king sold the country to the Belgium government in 1908. At independence five decades later, there were about 112,000 Europeans in Congo, out of a population of approximately 14 million, who ruled over a highly segregated and stratified society. Europeans held all the important posts. By the late 1950s, there were only about twenty black African university graduates. This sharply contrasted with the more integrated French Congo, on the other side of the vast, winding Congo River, whose broadening waters, as Conrad described, flowed through a "mob of wooden islands," causing European travelers to get lost like in a desert.[16]

Patrice Lumumba was a handsome, bespectacled young man, slight, with short hair, a goatee, and a mustache. He was invariably dressed in a jacket, tie, and pressed white-collar shirt. Belgian colonial officials insisted that "evolved" men like Lumumba, working for the administration, dressed to look "European." After a missionary-school education, he attended the government's nine-month post office training school, passing with distinction. Although he would be arrested for embezzlement from the post office, that would do little to harm his future political career—in the eyes of his countrymen, it was not a crime to steal from a kleptocratic regime to send one's children to a European school, as he proclaimed before a crowd. A fine orator, he could whip up the enthusiasm of listeners, and soon he had a political following. Like many African nationalist leaders, Lumumba dabbled in Marxism. At its core, however, his political creed was not communism but national liberation and Pan-Africanism. In January 1959, riots broke out in Léopoldville. Panicking, the Belgians announced consultations with the Congolese to create a constitution. Lumumba's anti-colonial scars were deepened when Belgian authorities detained him and beat him up in the riots.

Lumumba led a delegation to Brussels for constitutional consultations. The Belgian government first hoped that independence would take place over the course of thirty years. But observing France's protracted and calamitous withdrawal from Algeria, they decided on a quick exit. They would be out by June 1960. Independence became a rushed and ruinous affair.

In May 1960, Lumumba was elected prime minister of Congo. At the independence ceremony at the end of June, attended by the king of Belgium, Lumumba attacked Belgium's segregated rule: "We have known sarcasm and insults, endured blows morning, noon and night, because we are niggers," he proclaimed. "Who can forget the volleys of gunfire in which so many of our brothers perished, the cells where the authorities threw those who would not submit to a rule where justice meant oppression and exploitation?" Looking at the king, he said: "We are your monkeys no more." It took two hours to convince the king to attend the scheduled official lunch. He flew home immediately after.

Less than a fortnight after independence, however, Congo started to fall apart. A country made up of two hundred tribes and boasting four hundred dialects had little to hold it together. In July, the mineral-laden southern province of Katanga declared its own independence. Though it only had 12 percent of the country's population, it held 60 percent of its enormous mineral reserves. Stripped of Katanga's riches, Lumumba knew, Congo could not survive. The Belgian government sent in paratroopers to support Katanga (and protect its economic interests). Lumumba decided to crush Katanga's leader, Moïse Tshombe. Needing help, he appealed to the UN. Its secretary-general, Dag Hammarskjöld, dispatched the first of what would be the UN's peacekeeping forces there: twenty thousand troops under strict instructions of neutrality. That month, Lumumba traveled to the United States to seek support.

The trip did not go well. Eisenhower was away from Washington, playing golf, but Lumumba met with U.S. diplomat George Ball. His appeals for aid fell flat. He rambled irrationally, according to U.S. officials. At the National Security Council, Allen Dulles said—without evidence—that Lumumba was in Soviet pay, while Undersecretary of State Douglas Dillon, a wealthy banker known as "Mr. Congo," claimed that he was working for Soviet purposes. State Department officials thought him a lunatic ("psychotic") and a drug addict. Richard Bissell called Lumumba a "mad dog." The stench of racism was surely lurking behind such slurs.[17]

The same month, July 1960, following his meetings in New York, Lumumba formally appealed to the Soviet Union for military aid. "We will take aid from the devil or anyone else," said Lumumba, "as long as they get the Belgian troops out." The Soviet Union's first ambassador to Congo, Mikhail Yakovlev, and three KGB officers soon arrived in Léopoldville. From mid-August, Soviet aircraft based in Ghana, loaded with Eastern bloc "technicians," flew into Congo. The Soviets also delivered ten Ilyushin transport aircraft to Lumumba. To decision makers in London, Washington, and Brussels, it looked like the enormous country at the strategic center of Africa might become a communist satellite. If the Soviets controlled Lumumba, they could use Congo as a power base to spread Soviet influence to its nine bordering countries. Congo's size—roughly equal to all of Western Europe—its strategic position in Africa, and its natural resources meant that neither side, East or West, could afford to ignore it. Along with rubber, cotton, copper, and diamonds, Congo was rich in uranium and cobalt (used in missiles and weapons systems). Sixty percent of the world's cobalt supply came from a single Belgian company in Katanga.

No evidence has emerged from intelligence archives to suggest that Lumumba was in fact a Soviet agent. London's policymakers, however, were as convinced as Washington's that Lumumba was working for Moscow. Harold Macmillan described him as a "Communist stooge as well as a witch doctor." The prime minister was under pressure from London business leaders throughout the summer crisis to recognize the independence of the mineral-laden breakaway province of Katanga. Britain's ambassador in Congo, Ian Scott, compared Lumumba to Hitler, though he also saw the hidden hand of Egypt's leader, Nasser, at work. Britain's cabinet feared that Congo could become a catalyst for war between the superpowers.

The stage was set for a covert action to remove Lumumba in Congo. Beginning in 1960, the CIA started its largest covert action to date—exceeded only by Afghanistan, two decades later. Its purpose was to minimize communist influence and create pro-Western leadership. It involved "subsidies" (bribes) to local politicians. The CIA had only established an African division the previous year, led by the wonderfully named former OSS officer Bronson Tweedy. He reported to the agency's director of operations, Richard Bissell, who in turn reported to the DCI, Allen Dulles. Tweedy dispatched the CIA's thirty-eight-year-old Brussels chief of station, Lawrence Devlin, to Congo, where he worked under diplomatic cover as agricultural attaché at the U.S. embassy. He arrived there as Katanga declared independence, and the country teetered on the edge of disintegration. Devlin, a Harvard graduate, knew as little about Africa as his boss, Tweedy, but he was good at his job: recruiting and running agents. Wearing dark suits, white shirts, and shades, he looked the part of a CIA man, rarely seen without a cigarette in his hands.

It is difficult to imagine a greater contrast between the CIA's Devlin and MI6's head of station in Congo, Daphne Park, who looked, and acted, like Miss Marple from Agatha Christie's novels. She seemed more like someone we might find in a village tea shop in England's home counties than on the Cold War's intelligence front line in Africa. Her appearance was a brilliant piece of disarming deception. Who would suspect this unremarkable chancery official in Britain's embassy in Léopoldville of being a spy? Park's otherwise nondescript appearance masked the fact that she was a skillful operator. Like Jane Archer in MI5, and Juanita Moody in NSA, Daphne Park got ahead in MI6 by determination and talent. Being outside British territory, Congo fell under MI6's jurisdiction. Arriving in Léopoldville in 1959, Park chose not to live with the other European diplomats in the segregated area of the city patrolled by Dobermans, but instead in a modest house on the road to the airport, among the Congolese. It would be impossible to meet anyone useful, she reasoned, if she lived in a fenced-off compound.[18]

Despite appearances, Daphne Park was, in many ways, at home in Africa and among its people. She had grown up in East Africa, where her father hunted for gold. They lived in a mud hut without electricity in a village where the nearest white family was a ten-mile walk away. Moving to England for education, she graduated from Oxford and was recruited into Britain's wartime sabotage agency, the SOE, and then MI6. After a Russian-language training course at Cambridge, Park was transferred to Moscow, under diplomatic cover as second secretary at the embassy. She was there during the tumultuous year of 1956, which saw the disastrous Suez campaign, the British lion's last roar, and the Soviet Union crushing the uprising in Hungary. She insisted that intelligence work was built not on betrayal, as John le Carré describes in his novels, but on trust. Bonds of loyalty were, and are, essential between intelligence officers and agents.

Devlin and Park were tasked with recruiting agents close to Lumumba and his opponents, to understand their intentions. Often working in parallel, they knew and respected each other and became lifelong friends. As always, collaboration between MI6 and CIA in the field only took place when sanctioned by headquarters. Their missions were increasingly to destabilize Lumumba's regime. The money they distributed to his rivals was effective; anti-Lumumba chants began to crop up at his political rallies. On one occasion, Park helped one of Lumumba's political opponents escape the security forces, hiding the man in the back of her Citroën. She reported back to MI6 headquarters that Lumumba was indeed looking for closer alignment to the Soviet Union after independence. Devlin came to a similar conclusion. On August 18, 1960, after just six weeks in the country, Devlin cabled to Langley a fateful message:

EMBASSY AND STATION BELIEVE CONGO EXPERIENCING CLASSIC COMMUNIST EFFORT TAKEOVER GOVERNMENT. MANY FORCES AT WORK HERE: SOVIETS, COMMUNIST PARTY, ETC . . . WHETHER OR NOT LUMUMBA ACTUALLY COMMIE OR JUST PLAYING COMMIE GAME TO ASSIST HIS SOLIDIFYING POWER—ANTI-WEST FORCES.[19]

Devlin's reference to a communist takeover, when Cuba had fallen to Castro the previous year, lit a fire under Eisenhower's national security team. His cable convinced the president that action needed to be taken to remove Lumumba. The day the cable arrived, the president chaired a macabre national security committee meeting about doing "whatever is necessary to get rid of" Lumumba. According to subsequent secret testimony, during the meeting Eisenhower turned to Dulles and said flatly that Lumumba should be eliminated. After a moment of silence, the meeting continued. According to the later recollection of Richard Bissell, Gordon Gray came to the NSC meeting and said his "associate"—the president—"is very eager indeed that Lumumba be got rid of." Others at the meeting, including Douglas Dillon, could not remember Eisenhower issuing such an order. Contemporary notes show that the president said Congo's problem revolved around one man—with the obvious implication that the problem would disappear if he were removed. Bissell had "no doubt" that Eisenhower wanted him killed, but that did not necessarily mean having the CIA pull the trigger. Eisenhower would have realized, Bissell said, that "if you go out to kidnap a guy in the middle of Africa and he's your enemy, the chances of him getting killed are very good indeed." Though he did not care who pulled the trigger, Eisenhower wanted Lumumba dead.[20]

The president's message to eliminate Lumumba was relayed eight days later by Dulles in a cable to Devlin:

> IN HIGH QUARTERS HERE IT IS THE CLEAR-CUT CONCLUSON
> THAT IF LLL [LUMUMBA] CONTINUES TO HOLD HIGH OFFICE, THE
> INEVITABLE RESULT WILL AT BEST BE CHAOS AND WORST PAVE THE
> WAY TO COMMUNIST TAKEOVER OF THE CONGO . . . CONSEQUENTLY
> WE CONCLUDED THAT HIS REMOVAL MUST BE AN URGENT AND
> PRIME OBJECTIVE AND THAT UNDER EXISTING CONDITIONS THIS
> SHOULD BE A HIGH PRIORITY OF OUR COVERT ACTION.[21]

The CIA code-named its assassination of Lumumba Project WIZARD. But as we saw with Castro, the CIA and MI6 were amateurs when it came to assassinations. They did not have trained killers on staff. In September, Devlin received a cable from Bissell stating that a senior CIA officer, identifying himself as "Joe from Paris," would arrive in Léopoldville at the end of the month. Devlin was to carry out his directions. Joe from Paris was the CIA chemist Sidney Gottlieb. He was the agency's in-house expert on toxins, known as "Dr. Death" around Langley, where he led the agency's dryly named Health Alteration Committee, responsible for "biologically immobilizing" targets. A fat man with a clubfoot, a stutter, and a Bronx accent, Gottlieb looked like a cross between the James Bond villain Blofeld and Dr. Strangelove. With a doctorate in biochemistry from the California Institute of Technology, Gottlieb was the mastermind of the CIA's mind-control program (MKULTRA), which used electroshock and drugs like LSD on subjects, experiments that led to at least one death.

Gottlieb arrived in Congo fresh from devising ways to remove Fidel Castro in Cuba.[22]

Devlin met Gottlieb at a café in Léopoldville. They got into his car and turned the radio up, as Gottlieb explained that he had brought poisons to assassinate Lumumba. "Isn't this unusual?" asked Devlin, who had never been asked to kill anyone. "Who authorized this operation?"

Gottlieb replied, "President Eisenhower. Dick Bissell said that Eisenhower wanted Lumumba removed."

The chemist handed Devlin a kit bag, which, he explained, contained lethal poisons from the U.S. military biological-research facility at Fort Detrick in Maryland.

"It's your responsibility to carry out the operation, you alone," Gottlieb said. "The details are up to you, but it's got to be clean—nothing that can be traced back to the U.S. government."

One of the poisons, a neurotoxin from a cobra, was contained in a packet of toothpaste; it was designed to make it look like Lumumba had died from polio, which was rampant in Congo at the time. Gottlieb gave Devlin accessories like hypodermic needles, rubber gloves, and gauze masks, because the poison was dangerous to handle.

"Jesus H. Christ," Devlin exclaimed when he received his order. He cabled back to Washington: "Don't you know the Belgians are going to kill him?" According to Devlin's later own account, he was aghast and refused to commit murder. He locked the lethal toxins in his office safe, and, once they had degraded, threw them in the Congo River. "Poor Lumumba," recalled Devlin. "He was no Communist. He was just a poor jerk who thought 'I can use these people,'" Devlin later said in an interview.

The Church Committee, which uncovered and investigated the assassination plot, noted that Devlin's cables to Langley at the time were more enthusiastic about eliminating the Congo leader than he subsequently maintained. After the Church Committee's revelations of CIA assassinations and other abuses, Congress was given oversight for U.S. covert action.[23]

Instead of killing Lumumba, Devlin thought of ways to deliver him to his enemies to do the job. The ace up his sleeve was that, even before arriving in Congo, he had cultivated Lumumba's twenty-nine-year-old friend Joseph Mobutu, a former journalist whom Lumumba made his chief military assistant. Thus began a long, tragic relationship between Mobutu and the U.S. government. He was "the only man in the Congo able to act with firmness," Dulles told the president at an NSC meeting. Mobutu met Devlin in September and worked out a plan. Mobutu said that Lumumba had failed to keep the Soviets out of Congo: "We didn't fight for independence to have another country recolonize us." Mobutu said that he would be prepared to overthrow Lumumba if the U.S. government recognized his government. Lumumba would thereafter be "neutralized."

Mobutu launched his coup that month. Within a few weeks, the CIA had delivered $250,000 in cash to him. Meanwhile, as Devlin dragged his feet over his orders to kill Lumumba, Langley grew frustrated and in November dispatched others to energize the operation. They sent two Europeans, one an "'essentially stateless' soldier of fortune . . . and former bank robber," and the other a man who had an unspecified criminal background. The mercenary was given plastic surgery, and a toupee, to carry out the job.[24]

At the end of September, Britain's foreign secretary, Alec Douglas-Home, spoke with President Eisenhower, who said that he wished that Lumumba "would fall into a river of crocodiles." Douglas-Home replied that "regretfully, we have lost many of the techniques of old-fashioned diplomacy." A week later, Macmillan met Eisenhower in New York. Douglas-Home, who was also at the meeting, led the charge, stressing that "now is the time to get rid of Lumumba." Britain's ambassador in Congo, Ian Scott, sent a telegram to London: "It seems to me that the best interests of the Congo (and the rest of us) would be served by the departure of Lumumba from the scene either to jail (sufficient evidence exists to convict him of treason and of complicity in attempted murder of Colonel Mobutu) or abroad."

One response to that telegram came from the hand of a Foreign Office official, Howard Smith, who would later become MI5's director general. He doubted that Scott's proposed remedies would solve the problem because, whether Lumumba was in jail or abroad, he would still have a following. Instead, Smith suggested, Lumumba should be killed. Another official, an old SOE hand, scribbled: "There is much to be said for eliminating Lumumba."[25]

Years later, Daphne Park, retired from MI6 after four decades of service and serving in the House of Lords, reportedly claimed that she had helped to coordinate Lumumba's murder. The documentary evidence for her apparent claim is patchy. Instead, the evidence suggests that neither MI6 nor the CIA pulled the trigger that killed Lumumba, but that they did help to put him in harm's way at the hands of his local enemies.[26]

At the end of November 1960, during a thunderstorm, Lumumba tried to escape. He hid himself in the back of a car, attempting a hundred-mile journey back to his power base in Stanleyville, Congo's second-largest city. He never made it. He was intercepted by Mobutu's men and brought back to Léopoldville, where UN peacekeepers failed to stop him from being beaten with rifle butts. With John F. Kennedy a vocal supporter of African nationalism in his campaign, due to be sworn in as president in Washington, Lumumba's opponents wanted to get rid of him immediately in case Kennedy tried to intervene. At Belgium's urging, Lumumba was flown in a DC-4 to Elizabethville in Katanga. He was tied to his seat, with tape over his eyes and mouth; his goatee was shaved off and he was forced to eat it. He was so savagely assaulted by the drunk African guards during the flight that the Belgian radio operator vomited, and the terrified crew locked themselves in the cabin. At Elizabethville Lumumba was further tortured, with splinters rammed under his fingernails. Three days before Kennedy took office in Washington, Lumumba's captors drove him out onto a dirt track in Katanga, where they shot him and two other accomplices with submachine guns under vehicle headlights. Although evidence is imperfect, it appears his killers sawed up his body and dissolved it in vats of sulfuric acid, so that there would be no grave to attract his followers. Other accounts suggest that his body was buried, then disinterred, his bones and teeth pulverized, and blown to the winds.[27]

Lumumba became a martyr of African national liberation. The Soviet government renamed the Peoples' Friendship University in Moscow in his honor. Its first rector, and several of its staff, were KGB officers who used the university to recruit African, Asian, and Latin American students. Khrushchev spoke with the U.S. ambassador in Moscow, who sent an eyes only cable to Washington: "With respect to Congo K said what had happened there and particularly murder of Lumumba had helped communism. Lumumba was not Communist and he doubted if he would become one."

Mobutu gained power in Congo after a five-year-long power struggle. With U.S. support, he ruled the country, renamed Zaire, for three decades. He was a brutal and corrupt dictator. Clad in leopard skin, describing himself as "the all-powerful warrior, who goes from conquest to conquest leaving fire in his wake," he slaughtered opponents and bled the country's resources dry for his personal gain. He amassed a personal fortune thought to be the size of Zaire's national debt, most of which ended up in Swiss bank accounts, used on his shopping trips to Paris. He remained, however, Washington's man for the rest of the Cold War, America's tyrant, who received something like a billion dollars from the United States over the next three decades. True to his word, he kicked out Soviet officials, personally staging a mock execution of the KGB *rezident*, Boris Voronin, after he had him beaten and expelled.[28]

Capitals of countries in Africa seemingly worlds away from the Cold War, like Harare in southern Rhodesia (Zimbabwe), became hunting grounds for Eastern and Western intelligence agencies. They correctly assumed it was easier to recruit agents there than in each other's closely surveilled capitals. As the Portuguese empire in Africa broke up, Marxist regimes came to power in Angola and Mozambique. Both sides of the Cold War used their intelligence services and allies to wage proxy wars there. Mobutu's Zaire was a valuable staging post for the CIA's covert war against the Soviets and their tireless allies, the Cubans, in Angola, until CIA operations were exposed in 1974. Congress cut off the CIA's operations in the region, just as Brezhnev and Castro were making their moves, much to Kissinger's fury.

To the northeast, in the Horn of Africa, following the overthrow of the emperor of Ethiopia, Haile Selassie, Soviet intelligence backed ruthless Marxist leaders like Mengistu Haile Mariam. In the 1970s, both sides of the Cold War, East and West, shipped vast amounts of arms to African countries. The value of weapons imports to sub-Saharan Africa jumped from an annual average of about $150 million in the late 1960s to almost $2.5 billion in 1977, chiefly because of massive Soviet arms shipments to Ethiopia. This was a huge drain on the Kremlin's finances, when the Soviet economy was already faltering. These arms shipments did not strengthen, but weakened, and in some cases eventually destroyed, the nation-states that received them. The recipients of Cold War arms in the 1970s and 1980s became the failed states in Africa after the Cold War.[29]

CHAPTER THIRTEEN

DOMINOES

The intelligence gathered from roving spies shall be collected
together in the establishments of spies based in one place
and shall be transmitted by code.... Double agents are those
clandestine operatives who, while employed by a king, spy
for another king.... Miraculous results can be achieved by
practicing the methods of subversion.

—*The Arthashastra*

THE "LOSS" OF CHINA TO COMMUNISM IN 1949 DEFINED SUB-
sequent U.S. Cold War strategy. Suddenly, it seemed, there was the prospect
of three-quarters of the world's landmass turning red, from behind the Iron
Curtain in Europe, to China, and spreading from there to Southeast Asia.
Fears about communism in this vast swath of territory made up the essence
of the "domino theory," a metaphor espoused by Eisenhower in 1954. The
Soviet government unleashed a barrage of active measures to influence
nonaligned nations in these regions. Their governments, however, were
often fiercely nationalist, many only having recently gained independence
from European colonial powers. The domino theory, which failed to appreciate that communism was not monolithic, was thus a flawed concept. In

this chapter we will see how the U.S.—and to a lesser extent the British government—tried using covert action to prop up "dominoes" in Asia and the Middle East, and the nature of the Soviet active measures there.[1]

In 1949, Mao Zedong and the Chinese Communist Party (CCP) seized power after a two-decade-long war against the Chinese Nationalists (the Kuomintang). The Nationalist leader, Chiang Kai-Shek, and his forces fled to Taiwan. The red ink on British imperial maps now appeared to be matched by a different hue, a communist red, stretching from Europe to the Pacific and the South China Sea. When Mao emerged victorious, some in the United States blamed the Truman administration, mostly in the person of Secretary of State George Marshall, for "losing" China to communism. In reality, there was nothing that the U.S. government could have done through diplomacy or covert action to prevent Mao's victory. After all, Mao had the support of Stalin. The president was not willing to risk World War III over China.

Leading up to Mao's victory, the British had a valuable source of intelligence about Mao's secrets. His radio operator happened to be an eccentric British man, Michael Lindsay, later Lord Lindsay, whom MI6 appears to have recruited. Lindsay's espionage seems to have been responsible for allowing British code breakers at GCHQ to read Mao's communications. The British shared the decrypts with the U.S. government. By March 1947, however, those decrypts had dried up. Thereafter, British and U.S. intelligence were without eyes or ears when it came to Mao and the People's Republic of China (PRC). The British territory of Hong Kong became essential for collecting intelligence on the PRC and would remain so for the rest of the Cold War. It offered a small ray of light in the otherwise dark landscape of mainland China.[2]

Fifty-five years old at the time he gained power in China, Mao was a military strategist, a poet, a Leninist revolutionary, and a founding member of the Chinese Communist Party. His picture, made famous by Andy Warhol, would adorn the walls of countless credulous student dorms in the West in the coming decades, like similar pictures of Che Guevara and Fidel Castro. In the real world, Mao was a ruthless dictator, responsible for the single greatest human catastrophe of the twentieth century: his Great Leap Forward initiative to transform rural China into an industrial powerhouse. It effectively became a great leap backward. Approximately forty-five million people died from the resulting famine; it is estimated that in total seventy million Chinese died under Mao's regime through purges and famine. Mao was a devoted Stalinist but surpassed even his hero's monstrous crimes against humanity. Countless victims were sent to the *laogai*, a Mandarin abbreviation for "reform through labor." This calamitous experiment in "socialism," which led to the deaths of tens of millions of Chinese, was enforced by Mao's Moscow-trained security chief, Kang Sheng. A talented calligrapher who helped Mao publish his poetry, Sheng was "China's Beria." Like the homicidal Soviet intelligence chief, Sheng took sadistic pleasure in torturing his victims.[3]

Mao's continued devotion to Stalinism even after the Soviet leader's death in 1953 became a major cause of his regime's ideological split with the Soviet Union. Mao was shocked when Stalin's successor, Nikita Khrushchev, denounced the former Soviet dictator in his "Secret Speech" to the Politburo in 1956. (The Polish party leader had a fatal heart attack when he read the speech.) Viewing Khrushchev's denunciation of Stalin as heresy, Mao set about doing his utmost to humiliate the Soviet leader. During Khrushchev's visit to Beijing in 1958, Mao insisted on going for a swim, knowing that Khrushchev had never learned how. Tensions between the two communist powers finally came to a head in 1961. The so-called Sino-Soviet split proved to be the most important strategic rupture of the Cold War.[4]

Washington policymakers were slow to appreciate the growing fissure between the world's two communist titans. After McCarthyism, there was little place in Washington for nuance between communist regimes or the interplay between nationalism and communism. Washington's prevailing strategic thinking was of a monolithic communist bloc. This was the essence of the domino theory in Indochina: that one country falling to communism would lead to a succession of others doing so.

The CIA's Directorate of Intelligence (analysis) provided more accurate and sophisticated assessments, cutting across the grain of most Washington thinking. In 1956, it established the Sino-Soviet Studies Group, which produced a series of assessments known as the Esau studies. They took their name from the story in Genesis of Esau, Isaac and Rebecca's son, who lost his birthright to his older brother, Jacob. The implication was clear: fraternal enmity. By 1960, the CIA's unorthodox thinking about Soviet and Chinese fraternal antagonism was fed into a National Intelligence Estimate, produced by the chief assessment body, ONE. It was given to the most senior decision makers in Washington.

There were, however, still powerful skeptics of the CIA's assessment, who believed there was no rupture between China and the Soviet Union. The CIA's head of counterintelligence, James Angleton, ever the conspiracist, was convinced that the Sino-Soviet split was actually an elaborate deception. Other skeptics included none other than CIA director John McCone and President Kennedy himself. Washington's prevailing mood remained fixated on a homogeneous communist movement. By at least 1962, it was obvious that relations between Moscow and Beijing were fractured. It would take the U.S. government nine more years to exploit their split. That delay was due, to a large degree, to the Vietnam War. As Nixon put it in a conversation picked up by White House tape recorders: "You can't put your arms around the Russians at a time when they're kicking the hell out of us in Vietnam."[5]

Nixon's opening to China in 1971–72 was a turning point in the Cold War. By exploiting ideological differences between Moscow and Beijing, Nixon and Kissinger were able to thaw East-West relations. The two statesmen were arguably the most knowledgeable and experienced political team to run U.S. foreign and security policy since World War II. The German-born Kissinger was an academic heavyweight from Harvard. Nixon was a skillful politician and lawyer; if anything, he was too clever for his own good, willing to bend the rules for his own purposes. Since his days as a congressman on the House Un-American Activities Committee, taking up the case against Alger Hiss and others, he was obsessed with Soviet conspiracy.[6]

U.S. espionage played a significant role in Nixon's diplomatic opening with China. The spy in question in this case was a GRU officer, Dmitri Polyakov. His motivation for spying for the United States was personal despair. The GRU sent him to New York in 1951, where he worked under diplomatic cover at the Soviet mission at the UN. While there, one of his young sons became gravely ill with a heart condition. An initial operation failed. Polyakov needed money for a second, more expensive procedure. The Soviet government refused to foot the bill, and his son died. Polyakov never forgave his Moscow superiors. Their miserliness effectively drove him into the hands of U.S. intelligence.

Polyakov approached the FBI through a U.S. official at the UN, in the summer and autumn of 1961. His anger at the Soviet leadership was exacerbated by the Berlin Wall's construction that summer. Polyakov, like Oleg Penkovsky, the West's other spy in the GRU in our story, believed that Khrushchev was a reckless warmonger. It did not take long for the FBI to enroll Polyakov, calling him TOP HAT. Later, during his postings for the Soviet government in Cambodia and India, and in Moscow itself, he was transferred to the CIA and run under a new code name, BOURBON.* Polyakov became the U.S. government's longest-serving agent inside Soviet intelligence. For two decades, he provided what a later DCI called the "jewel in the crown" of U.S. intelligence. In total, he disclosed some 1,500 GRU and KGB officers, as well as upward of 150 agents and 19 operatives working under deep cover (as illegals). Some of the most important intelligence he produced, however, occurred when he returned to Moscow in 1969. The CIA ran him there, under the noses of the KGB. Fortuitously for his American case officers, and the U.S. government, he became head of the GRU section on China. The U.S. intelligence community thus had a spy at the heart of Soviet intelligence dealing with China at precisely the moment when relations between Moscow and Beijing plummeted.[7]

Moscow remained a hostile "denied area" for foreign espionage. The KGB

---

* BOURBON is the same code name given to an earlier UK-U.S. SIGINT operation: see p. 162.

would routinely send twenty surveillance operatives to shadow a single CIA officer. Sometimes the CIA resorted to hiding messages for agents in fake dog turds in the city's parks, sprayed with synthetic scents to ward off people. For Polyakov, the agency pulled out all the stops. Langley's technicians devised a way for Polyakov to communicate directly with the CIA station, housed inside the U.S. embassy in Moscow, without direct contact or elaborate dead-drop sites. They gave Polyakov a special handheld transmitter that sent encrypted communications in 2.6-second-burst transmissions. Known as "Discus," it was effectively the world's first text messaging system, invented by the CIA in the 1970s. Polyakov sent the messages while taking public transportation down Tchaikovsky Street, past the U.S. embassy.

Thanks to Polyakov's intelligence, Nixon and Kissinger could calibrate their moves for a U.S. rapprochement with China according to Moscow's reading of the situation. Specific details about how Polyakov's intelligence was fed into the briefings given to Kissinger are still classified. Documents in the Kissinger papers and the Nixon presidential library are riddled with redactions. According to those who worked his case, however, Polyakov's intelligence contributed to a key National Intelligence Estimate in August 1969. That estimate, now declassified, notes it was based on a "body of recent evidence." For security reasons, the CIA analysts who drafted the NIE almost certainly did not know Polyakov's identity—only that the CIA had a valuable and reliable source, BOURBON. The NIE set out for its readers that Sino-Soviet relations had deteriorated to such levels, as witnessed by recent border clashes on the Ussuri River, in March, that war between the two powers seemed, for the first time, possible in the near future. The Soviets were intent on attracting new allies to contain the Chinese, the NIE noted, while the Chinese faced "stiff competition" trying to expand their influence in Asia.[8]

The time was ripe for the U.S. to act. With some fancy footwork, the United States could place itself closer to the Soviet Union and China than they were to each other. Papers held in Nixon's presidential library reveal that, when Kissinger made his secret trip to China in July 1971, flying there from Pakistan, he liaised closely with Thomas Karamessines, the CIA's director of operations. The same was true before Nixon's own groundbreaking diplomatic trip to China in February 1972. Although the relevant files are still classified, it is likely that CIA briefings given by Karamessines to Kissinger included intelligence from BOURBON. During Nixon's trip to China, which opened diplomatic relations between the two East and West powers, Kissinger used U.S. intelligence to win over his hosts. He provided Marshal Ye Jianying, one of Mao's military commanders and a founder of the People's Liberation Army, with an intelligence briefing about Soviet forces on the Chinese border that was so highly classified, Kissinger claimed, that many senior U.S. intelligence officials had not received it. There are few better ways to befriend someone than to let them in on a secret. Sharing secrets builds trust—at least with those trustworthy.[9]

Later in the Cold War, U.S. and Chinese intelligence would collaborate *against* the Soviet Union. One such operation, CHESTNUT, involved joint monitoring of Soviet forces in Afghanistan from surveillance sites on Chinese soil. After Nixon's trip, China also became a principal target for Soviet espionage and active measures. The KGB briefly considered making China a main adversary, like the United States, but eventually settled for making it a "major adversary."

Polyakov continued to spy for the CIA until 1980, when he was recalled to Moscow. KGB counterintelligence, the Second Chief Directorate, came to suspect there was a mole inside the GRU, and Polyakov's fate was sealed by a traitor within the CIA, Aldrich "Rick" Ames. Polyakov was executed in Moscow. As with Penkovsky before him, Polyakov's story was one of bravery and betrayal—for which he paid the ultimate price.[10]

VIETNAM

The greatest domino supposedly threatening to fall was, of course, Vietnam. Presidents Kennedy and Johnson were convinced that America's engagement against North Vietnam—the country was divided in 1954 along the 17th parallel following the French defeat there—was essential within the context of the Cold War. One of modern history's great counterfactuals is whether, if he had lived longer, Kennedy would have escalated U.S. involvement in Vietnam as Johnson did. U.S. forces in Vietnam eventually reached half a million troops. There is little to indicate that Kennedy, before his death, was changing his convictions about Vietnam as a Cold War battlefield. He lapped up *The Stages of Economic Growth*, by the former OSS officer and MIT economic historian Walt Rostow, which argued that "traditional" societies were susceptible to communism as they were transitioning to modernity. Kennedy moderately increased U.S. personnel in Vietnam and instigated a village pacification program. He authorized the use of defoliants to deny the enemy forest cover and herbicides to kill off their food crops. Whether all this meant he would have surged U.S. forces there, like Johnson, is impossible to know.[11]

Whatever might have happened, Lyndon Johnson viewed Vietnam as an existential Cold War struggle. His administration continued many of Kennedy's policies, and some of Kennedy's advisers, like McGeorge Bundy, stayed on. But Johnson was his own man. Raised from humble beginnings in rural central Texas, he was a far cry from the polished, urbane Kennedy; his advisers viewed Johnson as something of an interloper in the White House. LBJ overcame his own perceived shortcomings by working harder than anyone, effectively cramming two working days into one. Kennedy ran university seminar-style discussions, a "floating crap game," as Dean Rusk called them. LBJ, who had been Senate majority leader before becoming vice president, was more focused. He used his six-foot-three, 230-pound frame to tower over people and bully them to get his way. He preferred to read intelligence reports than to be talked at by a briefer. He called members of his cabinet "sons of bitches" when they were not straight with him. He burped and farted in public. LBJ was determined not to lose Vietnam to communism in the way Truman had "lost" China in 1949. As a Texan, he was not going to be the man who lost the Asian Alamo.[12]

America's strategy for Asia under Kennedy and Johnson centered around the domino theory. In reality, the Vietnamese had been defending themselves against outsiders for two millennia. They were not going to be directed by Beijing, or Moscow, any more than they had been directed by Paris. Soviet records reveal that the Kremlin was nervous about the Vietnam War from start to finish. Although the Soviet Union supplied the North Vietnamese with most of their armaments, above all, it did not want to risk getting into a direct conflict with the United States.

Nuances about nationalism and communism were lost on Washington. America's prestige and honor, Johnson felt, was on the line. National security files, in rows of boxes at LBJ's library, reveal that U.S. intelligence provided Johnson with reams of operational and analytical assessments about Vietnam. The NSA collection was particularly valuable. As well as military intercepts, and order-of-battle intelligence, it provided the White House with diplomatic communications about the South, North—and also the French. CIA analytical assessments of Vietnam were generally more sober—that is, pessimistic—about the war than U.S. military intelligence. The CIA never said that the United States could not win the war in Vietnam, but its analysts did conclude that it would be a much more difficult task than acknowledged. Agency experts on Vietnam, like George Carver Jr. and Ray Cline, stressed that America was embarking on restructuring and reshaping a society in Southeast Asia. That was not something capable of happening quickly. It would require a long-term commitment.[13]

Johnson, however, was not interested in creating another Great Society in Vietnam like the one he was attempting to implement at home. His cabinet, particularly Robert McNamara, secretary of defense, myopically viewed the war through statistics about body counts and other metrics like munitions. They do not reveal the willingness of a population to fight against the odds—as Ukraine is showing today. The CIA was pessimistic that the president's bombing campaign against North Vietnam would reduce the will or ability of the North Vietnamese to fight. When North Vietnam launched its massive 1968 Tet Offensive, this pessimism proved to be warranted. America ultimately failed in Vietnam because the Vietnamese were willing to put up with more pain, over a longer period of time, than the U.S. government was willing to inflict—or the American people were willing to endure.[14]

The Vietnam War was a tragedy for every actor. It is estimated that approximately 2 million civilians on both sides were killed, along with 1.1 million North Vietnamese and Vietcong fighters and approximately 200–250,000 South Vietnamese. Some 58,000 U.S. personnel sent to Vietnam never returned. The war was also a tragedy for the CIA, which was involved in Operation PHOENIX, a counterinsurgency program to root out the Vietcong; it became a torture and assassination program.

President Johnson, elected in 1964 with an unprecedented majority, found that his domestic policies, his civil rights legislation and his Great Society reforms, were overshadowed by Vietnam. The war was a major reason why he decided not to run for reelection in 1968. Meanwhile the Soviet government, particularly its intelligence services, was only too happy to exploit the Vietnam War to discredit the United States on the world stage. Vietnam and American imperialism became running themes of KGB active measures to smear the United States before Third World audiences.[15]

DÉTENTE

From Kissinger's basement office in the West Wing, he and President Nixon instituted détente, the use of diplomacy to lessen tensions and improve relationships between East and West. Over the next decade, the U.S. government signed more treaties with the Soviet government than it had since diplomatic relations between the two countries began in 1933. The cornerstone was the SALT I treaty, signed by Nixon in May 1972 in the ornate setting of the Grand Kremlin Palace in Moscow. Nixon became the first U.S. president to visit the Soviet Union—and China. U.S.-Soviet arms limitation and reduction agreements during the period of détente were made possible by the East and West spying on each other. It was a Texas standoff, to use

President Johnson's former inevitable Texan depiction. "National Technical Means," expressly referred to in U.S.-Soviet arms treaties, was a euphemism for intelligence collection from SIGINT and IMINT by both sides. Without intelligence "NTMs," neither side could verify the other's compliance.[16]

Oil shocks in the Middle East in the early 1970s caused ripple effects in the Third World and between the superpowers. Amid an economic downturn, the Nixon, Ford, and Carter administrations all encouraged U.S.-Soviet trade relations, through which the Soviets could access U.S. agricultural goods, computer technology, and commercial credit facilities needed to purchase them. East-West trade skyrocketed under détente, rising sixfold from 1970 to 1979. For the Republican right, détente became a dirty word of acquiescence, like *appeasement* a generation earlier. In his radio broadcasts, the former California governor Ronald Reagan called détente the kind of deal that a farmer has with a turkey before Thanksgiving. There was more to it than Reagan's homely simile suggests, however. Amid a U.S. economic downturn, with spiking inflation in the 1970s, Kissinger and Nixon used détente to play for time. They pulled the Soviets into costly Third World adventures they could not afford, while innovating at home in ways that, as Kissinger's biographer Niall Ferguson has noted, would "leave the Soviets in the dust." Apple, Charles Schwab, Microsoft, Oracle, Visa—all started under détente.

Kissinger and Nixon's grand strategy was to use commerce to force the Soviet Union to reform as it was exposed to outside economic pressure. Under Nixon, and then Gerald Ford, who retained Kissinger as national security adviser and secretary of state, the U.S. government used the issue of human rights as a weapon against Moscow. Ford drove détente forward like the football player he was. He and Kissinger skillfully got Leonid Brezhnev, the Soviet Union's befuddled premier, to incorporate a declaration of human rights at an East-West summit held at Helsinki in 1975. Brezhnev dozed through it and thought he was agreeing to criticism of the West. It turned out, five years later, that the West and Soviet citizens themselves could criticize the Soviet government about human rights: in Poland. (The

KGB also seized on the subject of human rights, using it to discredit the U.S. government, particularly over African Americans.)

In Moscow, "peaceful coexistence," détente's core principle, meant something different than it did to Western audiences. It had a specific Marxist-Leninist meaning. A British Foreign Office paper on détente, declassified in 2021, set this out for senior Whitehall officials in 1973. Under the Marxist dialectic, "peace" meant peace for the proletariat. That was to be achieved through revolutionary struggle—namely, the success of the communist revolution. Meanwhile, "coexistence" meant parity, but only temporarily, until "peace" could be achieved. Lenin, after all, had said that it would be necessary to zigzag in the journey to build "socialism." Far from being something benign or positive, as the term sounded to Western ears, in Soviet lexicology peaceful coexistence in fact meant the long-term success of the communist revolution. Brezhnev believed that coexistence represented an opportunity for the Soviet Union to regroup and improve its beleaguered economy through the purchase of grain, foreign credits, and technology. Peaceful coexistence thus made no practical difference to the Soviet regime's long-term Marxist strategy of class warfare.[17]

Kissinger appreciated the Soviet perspective. But in his assessments for Nixon, he underplayed the significance of ideology for leaders in the Kremlin. More important, in his view, was the Soviet Union's realist interests as a great power. Overlooking ideology was an easy mistake to make with Brezhnev, who appeared to enjoy life to the fullest. But it was a mistake nonetheless. In fact, Brezhnev and his long-serving intelligence chief, Yuri Andropov, viewed détente as an opportunity to increase Soviet espionage on the United States. Under the cover of détente, they stole as much scientific and technical intelligence as possible. It is no coincidence that Andropov appointed the experienced KGB illegal, Yuri Drozdov, as *rezident* in Washington in 1975. Drozdov's experience made him ideal for Andropov's purpose: to take the offensive without worrying about the niceties of East-West relations. When he arrived in New York, there were about fifteen hundred Soviet citizens attached to its mission there. The FBI struggled to keep up with them.[18]

Détente offered opportunities for Soviet espionage similar to the wartime Grand Alliance, when East-West relations had ostensibly thawed. The opening of commercial relations offered low-hanging fruit for the KGB's Science and Technology Directorate, Line X, in the First Chief Directorate. It was child's play for Line X. A goodwill agricultural delegation sent to the United States, for example, was composed of about a hundred Soviet officials. An estimated one-third of them were known or suspected intelligence officers. During a tour around a Boeing factory, a Soviet official had Sellotape on his shoes in the hope of picking up loose metal filings. In 1972, the KGB hacked the phones of grain dealers and surreptitiously bought 25 percent of the U.S. grain harvest, causing a spike in domestic prices. As one U.S. official later noted: "Those of us observing these arabesques began to question the USSR's total commitment to the spirit of détente." Within the KGB, commercial interactions with the West also offered endless possibilities for corruption. It was something that the KGB's successors in Russia learned well.

Kissinger and Nixon knew that the Soviets would try to exploit commercial openings. But they could not have guessed the scale of the intelligence attack on U.S. science and technology, revealed by the opening of secret Soviet archives. At the time, the sale of Western technologies to the Soviet bloc was controlled through the Coordinating Committee (CoCom) of NATO, which embargoed certain products on the grounds of national security. In at least one instance, involving the sale of computers behind the Iron Curtain, Kissinger had to balance the benefits of improving East-West relations with restricting sensitive technologies like computers with greater processing power. He was also being pressured by U.S. and British computer manufacturers to allow them access to new markets behind the Iron Curtain. A resulting March 1974 National Security Decision Memorandum, "U.S. Policy on the Export of Computers to Communist Countries" (number 247), moderately relaxed the power of computers sold, while restricting and preventing more powerful hardware.[19]

Whatever suspicions Kissinger harbored about Soviet intentions were confirmed in March 1978, when Arkady Shevchenko became the highest-ranking Soviet official ever to defect to the West. He was a senior Soviet diplomat, and, since 1973, had been undersecretary-general for political affairs at the UN in New York. He knew how the KGB worked at the UN and received its intelligence. Three years before his defection, U.S. authorities had recruited and run him as a penetration agent. The KGB *rezident* in New York, Yuri Drozdov, suspected that U.S. intelligence had a mole in the Soviet ranks, who he suspected—correctly—was Shevchenko. With Drozdov closing in on him and finding himself recalled to Moscow, Shevchenko defected. Several years later, he published a memoir in which he claimed that Brezhnev was running a gangster economy dominated by the KGB, and that the UN was a collection platform for Soviet intelligence. His motivation for defecting was, he revealed to his U.S. handlers, that the Soviet government was cheating when it came to détente. A bigger Western breakthrough into Soviet efforts to steal science and technology would occur when Vladimir Vetrov, a KGB officer who worked at the heart of its efforts in Line X, revealed secrets to the West—more on which in our story later.[20]

According to a later U.S. estimate, approximately one-third of all Soviet delegates on official visits to commercial and industrial plants in the United States, including Fortune 500 companies, were actually undercover Soviet intelligence officers. In one instance, the Department of Commerce discovered a dummy corporation set up by the Soviets to obtain an embargoed computer. Officials intercepted the computer that had been purchased and substituted it with sandbags and a note saying, "Fuck You." Under Ronald Reagan, the U.S. government would take matters to a new level, sabotaging supply chains known to be targeted by Soviet spies.[21]

INDIA

It was not Vietnam but India that the Soviet Union viewed as the most important battlefield of the Cold War. Stretching from the freezing

Himalayas in the north to the steaming tropics of the South, India had been for two hundred years the jewel in the crown of Britain's empire. Intelligence was essential to the British Raj and the "great game" between the British and Russians on the North-West Frontier, as memorably described by Rudyard Kipling, Britain's great bard of empire. India had a history of intelligence that stretched back for millennia, as described by the *Arthashastra*, a tract that is as significant in India today as Machiavelli's *The Prince* is in Europe and America, or Sun Tzu's *The Art of War*—and happily lacking the tiresome clichés attached to the latter in the West. The Cold War brought a new chapter to the long-term East-West "great game" in India.

In August 1947, India gained independence from Britain. "Long years ago we made a tryst with destiny," proclaimed the country's first prime minister, Jawaharlal Nehru, "and now the time comes and we shall redeem our pledge. . . . At the stroke of the midnight hour, when the world sleeps, India will awake to life and freedom." The English-educated lawyer was right. As the world slept, the largest democracy on earth, about 340 million people, and the second-most populous country, was born. Britain's expedited withdrawal from India led to the country's partition and involved scenes of horror. Up to two million people were slaughtered and about fifteen million more displaced.

Just as we saw in Africa, Britain's intelligence services maintained close relations with the new nation's intelligence service, the IB. Before India's independence, spy chiefs in London reached an agreement with Nehru's government-in-waiting that MI5 would maintain a liaison officer in Delhi after the transfer of power. The IB's liaison with British intelligence was so close that, according to its head in the 1950s, B. N. Mullik, when it came to Soviet and communist influence in India, he had closer relations with the British than he did with his own government. Mullik shielded aspects of his work from Nehru, who was deeply suspicious of intelligence and security agencies, particularly the British, after years of incarceration by them. The IB also brokered good relations with the CIA. The principal architect of containment, George Kennan, grasped India's strategic significance for the

Cold War. At his urging, the CIA rolled out the red carpet when the IB's first director, T. G. Sanjeevi Pillai, visited Washington in 1947.

Nehru was never a communist, but some of his close advisers were. He was one of the founders of the nonaligned movement, which unambiguously drifted toward the Soviet Bloc. Nehru also aligned India with the Soviet Union. In 1956, Nehru was quick to denounce Britain's attack on Suez as an act of colonialism. He remained silent, however, when Soviet troops crushed the anti-Soviet uprising in Hungary, killing approximately 2,500 Hungarians, that same year.[22]

British intelligence and Mullik, India's spy chief, feared the Soviet-friendly beliefs of Nehru's advisers. A case in point was Krishna Menon, the Congress Party's left-wing firebrand and one of Nehru's closest confidants. With a hawklike face, and a large forehead, Menon became India's first representative (high commissioner) in London after independence. He went on to become India's ambassador in Moscow. As India's representative at the UN, he also effectively served as foreign minister.

Harold Macmillan described Menon as "smooth and false," a claim that rings true. Menon was an odd duck. Although he loathed the British, by the time of Indian independence, he had been thoroughly Anglicized, having lived in Britain for twenty-two years. Having forgotten much of his native Hindi, he spoke English. He preferred British food to spicy Indian cuisine, and wore tweed jackets and flannel trousers, not traditional Indian dress. MI5 had assembled a thick file on Menon because of his associations with the British Communist Party and known Soviet fellow travelers. Its periodic interception of his telephone calls and correspondence revealed Menon to be corrupt and a drug addict. His personal and business accounts were so entangled that, as one MI5 report noted, an audit was unlikely ever to unravel them.

With his appointment as India's high commissioner in London, MI5 and the IB became increasingly concerned about his pro-Soviet views. Mullik decided to liaise directly with MI5 rather than go through the High Commission. He feared that sensitive information passing Menon's desk there might find its way to the Kremlin. As later Indian ambassador in Moscow,

Menon would speak warmly of "technical assistance" and "goodwill" flowing between the two countries. Soviet intelligence did indeed try to cultivate him. On at least one subsequent occasion during his later political career, the KGB paid for his election expenses. As Nehru's minister of defense, Menon purchased Soviet MiG aircraft rather than Western fighters. Soviet hopes for Menon's political career were dashed, however, when war broke out between China and India in 1962. As minister of defense, he was blamed. To Moscow's frustration, his political career never fully recovered.[23]

Another of Nehru's advisers who set off klaxons in London and the IB was Arathil Nambiar. He was willing to cut deals with anyone who would help advance Indian independence. During the war, Nambiar was part of the Free India Movement, founded by the national hero Subhas Chandra Bose. In fact, Nambiar was Bose's personal representative in Nazi Germany. His Berlin-based Free India Center directed the India Legion, which fought with the Axis powers *against* the Allies; in 1944 it was absorbed into the Waffen SS. Nambiar and Bose's hatred of the British had led both men to side with the Nazis against the Allies. Nambiar's wartime collaboration led to his imprisonment by the British in Germany after the war, but he escaped to Switzerland. After independence, his old friend Nehru gave him an Indian passport. He would become Indian ambassador to Scandinavia and later to West Germany. In 1954, MI5 received information from the FBI, based on a Soviet defector, that Nambiar was a Soviet agent, stretching back to the 1920s. Nambiar visited Moscow back in 1929 and admitted to being recruited as a journalist by TASS. Nambiar thus had apparently made a deal with the devil in Moscow as well as in Berlin. Russian archives, uncovered for this book, suggest that the FBI's suspicions about Nambiar were correct. He was associated with the GRU agent Agnes Smedley, who later worked with the famous GRU illegal Richard Sorge. One of Nehru's senior diplomats, Nambiar thus appears to have been a Soviet spy.[24]

These were just two cases among many of Soviet espionage and influence in India. The KGB had countless sacred cows in the subcontinent. Spying there became even more important for Moscow after the Sino-Soviet split. Moscow needed an ally. According to one former KGB officer, Oleg Kalugin, the youngest general in KGB history, India was "a model of KGB infiltration of a Third World government." As Kalugin continued: "We had scores of sources throughout the Indian government—in intelligence, counterintelligence, the defense and foreign ministries, and the police . . . The entire country was seemingly for sale."[25]

The story of KGB infiltration of India is revealed by a tranche of Soviet secrets smuggled to the West, the Mitrokhin Archive. It shows that the focus of the KGB's efforts in India was Nehru's daughter, Indira Gandhi. She had been impressed in her youth by a visit to the Soviet Union, which the Kremlin carefully stage-managed, and believed the industrialization she saw there was a model for India to follow. She was the only non-communist prime minister to attend the fiftieth anniversary of the October Revolution in Moscow in 1967. As Moscow's relations with Beijing deteriorated, India, in the person of Indira Gandhi, came to the rescue. In March 1971, she won a landslide victory for her Congress Party, overturning the hopes of a conservative group.

Five months later, in August 1971, Gandhi secretly signed a Treaty of Peace, Friendship and Cooperation with the Soviet Union. It became a founding charter for India's alignment with Moscow. It served as a counterweight to America's opening with China, Chinese and Western influence in India, and the U.S. government's strategic "tilt" to Pakistan under President Nixon and Secretary of State Henry Kissinger, who supported Pakistan in its war with India in 1971. Pakistan was a reliable U.S. ally during the Cold War, while India was seen as suspiciously pink (at best). White House tape recordings caught Nixon and Kissinger hissing that Gandhi was "a bitch," and calling Indians "those bastards" who were starting a war with Pakistan. A year later, with Nixon's game-changing opening of U.S. diplomatic relations with China, Moscow's relationship with New Delhi took on even greater importance.[26]

According to a recently declassified 1972 British assessment of Soviet aims in India, Soviet military equipment was estimated to have made up

60 percent of the Indian Air Force's frontline strength and 55 percent of its frontline armored divisions. Indira Gandhi herself acknowledged that Soviet aid counted for 30 percent of India's steel output and 55 percent of its oil imports; Moscow was thus throwing resources at India. Brezhnev, whose health was deteriorating, largely left Soviet clandestine foreign policy to KGB chairman Yuri Andropov and the party's collegium of gray cardinals who oversaw it. India's critical importance to the Soviet Union is revealed by the fact that it housed the greatest number of KGB officers anywhere in the world outside of the Eastern bloc. At the end of the 1970s, there were at least five hundred Soviet officials based in New Delhi, Calcutta, Madras, and Bombay; in addition there were Soviet economic and technical advisers, and visiting Soviet-bloc "tourists."[27]

Moscow funded the Indian Communist Party, but its cash spread much wider. Corruption in India's ruling circles was a gift for the Center. Kalugin recalled: "Using bribes, confidential ties, and liberal financing of election campaigns, the KGB had played an important role in keeping India among the Soviet Union's friends and partners on the international scene." On one occasion in 1971, a KGB officer named Leonid Shebarshin delivered in the dead of night a secret payment of two million rupees (approximately $1.1 million today) from the Soviet Politburo to India's Congress Party. U.S. intelligence later estimated that approximately 40 percent of Indira Gandhi's government received Soviet political contributions.

The KGB also used front groups and India's free democratic press to spread forgeries and carry out other active measures. In 1969, Andropov wrote to the Central Committee in Moscow: "The KGB residency in India has the opportunity to organize a protest demonstration of up to 20,000 Muslims in front of the U.S. embassy in India. The cost of the demonstration would be 5,000 rupees and would be covered in the 1969–1971 budget allocated by the Central Committee for special tasks in India." Brezhnev replied: "Agreed."

By 1973, the KGB claimed to have ten newspapers in India on its payroll and planted 3,789 articles there that year alone. In addition, there were Soviet-funded publishing houses, magazines, books, pamphlets, and friendship societies. By the end of the decade, Western intelligence estimated that Moscow was placing 160,000 items overtly and covertly in the Indian press per year. Indian publications like *Blitz* and the *Patriot*, the latter with a circulation of 27,000, were run as fronts for Soviet intelligence, churning out propaganda and disinformation. Articles claimed that the U.S. government would balkanize India and was planning to use biological weapons in the country in the event of war with the Soviet Union. At a time when the U.S. military was using napalm and Agent Orange in Vietnam, such stories found receptive audiences. The U.S. government had only closed its (very real) biological weapons program in 1972.[28]

Of course, the CIA and British intelligence were not sitting on their hands. London and Washington poured aid into India and their intelligence agencies actively countered Soviet operations and propaganda. The CIA mouthpiece, the Congress for Cultural Freedom, usually associated with Europe, was active in India. Outfits like the Asia Foundation and the Friends of India Committee received CIA covert funding. Other charitable groups, like the Ariel Foundation, existed in a murky world between intelligence and development programs in the Third World. By 1958, MI6 had a policy of special political action to expose and discredit Soviet front groups in India and the developing world. It is difficult, if not impossible, to measure the direct impact of such activities. Ironically, because of KGB material smuggled to the West, we know more about its secrets in India than we do about corresponding Western activities. (Almost all MI6 and CIA secrets about Cold War India remain hidden in archives in London and Langley.) Nevertheless, it is inconceivable that the two agencies were not channeling rupees toward Gandhi's government in the same way the Soviets were. A cottage industry of memoirs by former CIA "agents" grew in India; some were written with the KGB's help, however, which makes unpacking fact from fiction in them a fool's errand.[29]

As always with Western covert actions, and corresponding Soviet active measures, it is next to impossible to measure success. Agencies on both sides had interest in exaggerating their successes, which they measured by the volume of information produced rather than its impact. We also do not know whether politicians in India who received bribes from the KGB, or Western services, altered their behavior, for example by voting as they were instructed. That is not a subject that decision makers discuss in memoirs. If those who took bribes did any soul-searching, they would probably have told themselves that they were the ones using the KGB, or the CIA, not the other way around. The reality of that nexus between agency and target, briber and bribed, propagandist and audience, who was using whom, will likely never be known when it comes to India—or elsewhere in the Third World. The documentary record is incomplete for this most secret area of statecraft.

Some light was nevertheless cast onto CIA activities in India when President Kennedy appointed the Harvard economist John Kenneth Galbraith as ambassador to the country in 1961. Given a briefing on agency activities in India in March that year, Galbraith was incensed. He later launched a public broadside on the CIA: "During my term in New Delhi, I learned that almost no information of any kind was uncovered by our intelligence operatives that wouldn't have come to us in the ordinary course of events." He later recalled that the CIA was proposing to siphon millions of dollars to non-communist candidates in elections in India. What Galbraith did not mention in his public criticism of the agency, nor in his memoirs, was the colossal similar efforts undertaken by the KGB in India.[30]

One area where the Soviets were clearly successful in India was cultivating Indira Gandhi's conspiracy theories about the CIA. According to her biographer, Gandhi's fears about Langley's hidden hand grew to an obsession. The KGB fueled them with forgeries. But the U.S. government did much of the work for the Moscow Center. Gandhi's fears were fanned by headline-grabbing revelations of CIA abuses in 1975 (dubbed the "Year of Intelligence") following the Senate Select Church Committee into intelligence abuses. The agency was subjected to greater outside scrutiny and criticism that year than any intelligence service in the world.

Grandstanding for his own presidential aspirations, Idaho Democratic senator Frank Church, who headed the committee, famously described the CIA as "a rogue elephant on the rampage" (though in private he admitted that the elephant was really acting at the direction of U.S. presidents).[31]

The revelations that his committee produced included some of the CIA's assassination attempts and coups in the Third World, which we have already encountered, against Castro in Cuba and Allende in Chile. The committee's work created a dangerous illusion that the CIA was alone in resorting to the dark arts of coups and assassinations. Of course, the Soviet government paid no similar scrutiny to its own intelligence services. Reading about the CIA's covert activities, Indira Gandhi became convinced that the agency was out to get her, possibly because she knew the levels of Soviet penetration in her government. Ultimately, however, it was not the CIA but her own bodyguards who did her in. Gandhi's assassination in October of 1984 is a reminder that the greatest danger can come from those close at hand rather than from the hidden hand of a foreign government.

AFGHANISTAN

Soviet adventures in the Third World began in the Middle East and ended there. Afghanistan, the "graveyard of empires," was to become exactly that for the Soviet Union, as it had been for the British before and would later become for the Americans. Afghanistan was an avowedly nonaligned country after the collapse of the British Raj in 1947, but Moscow feared that it would tilt toward the United States, like neighboring Pakistan. In 1979, Moscow's fears centered on Afghanistan's Hafizullah Amin. Educated at Columbia University, he appeared to Moscow to be an "agent of imperialism"—and probably a CIA asset, reasoned KGB chairman Yuri Andropov. Did Amin have contact with the CIA? We do not know. If the CIA were doing its job, it would be surprising if he did not.

In April 1978, a group of communists led by two KGB agents, Babrak

Karmal and Nur Muhammad Taraki, took power in a coup in the Afghan capital of Kabul. In September the following year, Amin countered by seizing power for himself. Moscow feared he would follow in Mao's path, or "do a Sadat," referring to Anwar Sadat, the Egyptian leader who pivoted to the West. Leaders in the Kremlin responded by deciding to remove Amin from power and install their loyalist, Babrak Karmal, backed by an invasion force. The Soviet decision to invade Afghanistan seems to have been taken by a troika of hard-liners: KGB chairman Andropov; Dmitri Ustinov, the minister of defense; and Andrei Gromyko, foreign minister. They did so against the advice of the generals in the Red Army, and apparently some in the KGB, who feared being sucked into a Vietnam of their own. Brezhnev, suffering from cerebral palsy, was in no state to make such decisions.[32]

The Soviet invasion of Afghanistan was to enforce the Brezhnev doctrine—to impose, with an iron fist, conformity to Soviet rule within the Eastern bloc and the Soviet sphere of influence. Creating a client state in Afghanistan would allow Moscow a route to the Indian Ocean. The Kremlin leaders deluded themselves that they could impose Soviet rule in Afghanistan, a fiercely nationalist and staunchly Islamic culture, with just a small invasion force. The invasion started in December 1979. KGB and GRU special forces (*spetsnaz*) stormed the presidential palace and after bitter fighting managed to kill Amin, although not before approximately one hundred members of the six-hundred-strong KGB special forces unit, Alpha Group, were killed.

Following the prearranged plan, Moscow's man, Karmal, then invited the Soviet Red Army to provide "fraternal assistance" to his regime. For the next nine years, Moscow waged a bloody war in Afghanistan: some fifteen thousand Soviets lost their lives there, which pales in comparison to the approximately one million civilians killed, as well as ninety thousand mujahedeen fighters and eighteen thousand Afghan troops. The Soviet government hid the scale of its casualties from Soviet citizens; fallen soldiers were buried in secret funerals. Later, President Mikhail Gorbachev would tritely describe Afghanistan as "a mistake." In truth, it accelerated the decline and fall of the entire Soviet empire.[33]

Via live-feed satellite imagery, President Jimmy Carter's national security team watched with more than a little satisfaction as the Soviets were dragged into a costly protracted counterinsurgency. The CIA embarked on what became its biggest ever covert action: a proxy war to support Afghan forces, including the mujahedeen, fighting the Soviets. Operation CYCLONE cost $2 billion, and would later famously under Reagan include providing Stinger surface-to-air missiles to the Afghans. The CIA's chief of station in Pakistan later recalled that his brief, when sent there, was unlike any he had received before: to kill Soviets. Langley also launched a disinformation campaign, circulating stories in the Afghan press that the Soviets considered the war a fight against Islam. British intelligence played a hidden helping hand, as documents opened in 2021 reveal, publishing details about Soviet atrocities. The CIA, supported by MI6, sought to smear the Soviet regime to Third World audiences in the same way the KGB had previously discredited the United States during Vietnam.[34]

Two months before the Soviet invasion, Victor Sheymov, a senior officer in the KGB's SIGINT department, Directorate Eight, secretly contacted the CIA. He offered to provide information in return for guarantees of his and his family's escape from Moscow. The CIA code-named Sheymov CKUTOPIA. He had a prized position in the KGB, being responsible for cipher links between KGB legal *rezidentury* overseas and the headquarters of its foreign (First Chief) directorate at Yasenevo, its Y-shaped Finnish-designed headquarters half a mile beyond Moscow's outer ring road.

After striking a deal with Sheymov, an exfiltration team at Langley went to work. His escape was overseen by a CIA officer named David Rolph. Taking advantage of the fact that KGB counterintelligence was focused on the expected influx of foreigners to Moscow for the summer Olympic Games, the CIA orchestrated Sheymov's escape in a breathtaking operation in which he was dressed as an airline pilot. His wife and daughter were hidden in a container that the U.S. embassy placed on board a plane. Once safely in the U.S., Sheymov provided the CIA and NSA with expert inside knowledge about Soviet communications and cryptology. A year later, in 1980, the U.S. intelligence community was able to tap cable traffic in and out of Yasenevo itself. This was probably the origin of some of the intelligence that landed on President Carter's desk about Afghanistan. The U.S. breakthrough into the nerve center of KGB foreign intelligence would continue for another five years, until it was sabotaged by another twist in the East-West intelligence war: a KGB agent deep inside the CIA, Aldrich Ames. That is the next part of our story.[35]

PART FIVE

THE CLASH OF REIGNING SUPERPOWERS

CHAPTER FOURTEEN

THE MAIN ADVERSARY

> We know that no one ever seizes power with the intention of
> relinquishing it. Power is not a means; it is an end. One does
> not establish a dictatorship in order to safeguard a revolution;
> one makes the revolution in order to establish the dictatorship.
> –George Orwell, *1984*

ON A DAMP WINTER'S DAY IN DECEMBER 1984, ORWELL'S INFA-
mous year, Margaret Thatcher entered the great hall of Chequers, the
British prime minister's country retreat, and greeted the world's assembled media. Her guest that day was a visiting member of the Politburo
and rising star in Moscow, Mikhail Gorbachev. Their four-hour meeting
at the sixteenth-century manor house in Buckinghamshire, northwest of
London, had been tough but productive. In a BBC interview afterward,
Thatcher said: "I like Mr. Gorbachev. We can do business together."
She acknowledged that Gorbachev believed in his political system of
government as firmly as she believed in hers, and they would not change
each other's views. But they had mutual interests: to do everything they
could to make sure that war never broke out again. East-West disarmament talks were going to be key in this endeavor, she said. But for

them to succeed, it was essential that both sides have confidence and trust in each other.[1]

Thatcher was not being completely honest, however, about how she came by her trust in the future Soviet leader. Before she met with Gorbachev, her foreign secretary, Geoffrey Howe, had been secretly briefed about Gorbachev's strategy by a British spy inside the KGB: Oleg Gordievsky. Gordievsky's importance for the West during the later Cold War was equivalent to earlier espionage of the Cambridge Spies for the Soviets. Gordievsky had been working for MI6 for a decade by the time Thatcher and Gorbachev met. He had risen up the KGB's ranks during that time to become its head of political intelligence (Line-PR) in the London *rezidentura*. This produced a remarkable situation, perhaps unique in the history of espionage: when Gorbachev arrived in London, he received a routine briefing on British politics by Gordievsky. Gordievsky then secretly informed MI6 about his briefing with the future Soviet leader. When Thatcher and Gorbachev sat down together at Chequers, Gordievsky had thus given briefings to them both. Armed with the knowledge of Gorbachev's KGB briefing, Thatcher confidently told the world that he was someone with whom she could do business.[2]

Thatcher's breakthrough with Gorbachev, facilitated by British espionage, represented a major shift in East-West relations. Over the previous five years, that relationship had plummeted to depths not seen since the early days of the Cold War. The Soviet Union's continuing fiasco in Afghanistan, combined with the elections of Margaret Thatcher in Britain in 1979 and Ronald Reagan in the United States the following year, brought détente to a crashing end. When Reagan entered the Oval Office, he was the first U.S. president to see past the Cold War, believing that he could end it by putting intense pressure on the Soviet Union. With charisma honed by years spent in front of the camera, Reagan knew how to deliver a powerful and effective message to Americans. He had become convinced of the threat posed by communism while working in Hollywood in the 1930s. Originally a Democrat, Reagan was so certain of the communist dangers in Hollywood that he acted as an FBI informant.[3]

By the time he was elected governor of California, he had become a Republican, serving two terms from 1967 to 1975. In 1975, President Gerald Ford appointed him to the Rockefeller Commission on CIA activities, where Reagan took a sympathetic view of the abuses that were being uncovered, concluding that the agency needed more dynamism, not less. In campaigning for the presidency in 1980, he promised to unleash the CIA and take a hard stance toward the Soviet Union, drawing on a good guys, bad guys metaphor. Reagan electrified U.S. foreign policy, like MTV's neon lights, which debuted in 1981.[4]

After winning the presidency, Reagan was true to his campaign pledges. In his first speech as president, he savagely attacked Soviet policy. He claimed that Moscow reserved "the right to commit any crime, to lie, to cheat" to achieve its goal: "the promotion of world revolution and a one-world Socialist or Communist state." By the end of 1981, he had placed trade sanctions on the Soviet Union after it imposed martial law in Poland. The Soviets were acting like international brigands, Reagan claimed.

The man he chose to unleash the CIA on the Soviet Union was his sixty-eight-year-old campaign manager, William Casey, former OSS officer, Wall Street lawyer, and chairman of the Securities and Exchange Commission. Like the president, Casey viewed Soviet communism as a source of evil in international relations. Reagan made the DCI, for the first time, a cabinet member—a move that Reagan later expressed regret. Like the president, Casey believed that the U.S. government needed an overt diplomatic assault on the Soviet Union, accompanied by covert action from the CIA. The agency would become the primary vehicle for turning back Soviet expansion and attacking its intelligence network. CIA insiders surmised that, with Casey at the helm, the CIA would see a resurrection of Wild Bill Donovan. Like his OSS predecessor, whom Casey admired, the new DCI saw his duty as bringing the fight to the enemy. Riding his critique of détente into the Oval Office, Reagan authorized National Security Decision Directive (NSDD) 32, finalized in 1982, which called on the United States "to contain and reverse the expansion of Soviet control and military presence through the world." Reagan further refined his global strategy against the Soviet Union in NSDD75 in January 1983. In Moscow, the KGB was aghast at Reagan's offensive policies. In March 1983, Reagan famously called the Soviet Union an "evil empire." Between 1981 and 1988, the U.S. intelligence budget more than doubled. Its covert action element went up more than threefold.[5]

For U.S. intelligence in the Reagan years, the Soviet Union and the Eastern bloc were the primary strategic enemy. As we observed earlier, the Soviet government likewise saw the United States as its Main Adversary, with Britain a close second. Moscow saw Thatcher's and Reagan's elections as twin shocks to Soviet security. The KGB used its time-honored tradition of spies and active measures to undermine them both. The KGB *rezidentura* in London, as Gordievsky revealed to MI6, organized active measures to discredit the "Iron Lady" (a nickname coined as an insult by a Soviet army newspaper, but one that Thatcher relished), placing negative articles with sympathetic left-wing British journalists.

Moscow viewed Thatcher as bad for the Soviet Union, but Reagan was considered the greater menace, given his country's vast military and economic resources. Reagan caused Brezhnev and his intelligence chief, Andropov, more anxiety than any U.S. president during the Cold War. His hard-line anti-Soviet rhetoric incensed and terrified Andropov. The spy chief had instructed the KGB to instigate active measures to discredit Reagan during his first bid for the Republican presidential nomination in 1976 (which he lost to Gerald Ford, who then lost the election to Democrat Jimmy Carter). The KGB's three *rezidentury* in the U.S. tried and failed to find compromising material on Reagan to leak to the press. The KGB chairman did less to meddle in the 1980 election between Carter and Reagan, largely because Brezhnev was fed up with Carter.

But once Reagan took office, Andropov instructed the KGB U.S. *rezidentury* to do anything they could to undermine the president and prevent him from running for a second term. He instructed them to recruit agents in either party, Democrat or Republican, to run against Reagan. Anyone else would be better, from Andropov's point of view. *Rezidentury* around the world were instructed to disseminate the slogan "Reagan means war." As the 1984 election approached, the KGB instigated a rally of protesters outside the Democratic National Convention in San Francisco, who marched under that slogan. The FBI and CIA discovered, from agents recruited inside KGB *rezidentury* in North America, that the Soviet government *intended* to undermine Reagan in the upcoming election. But as CIA analysts admitted to Casey, whether or not the Soviets had the *capacity* to do so was a subject they had not seriously explored. As it turned out, Reagan won the 1984 election in a landslide, winning forty-nine of the fifty states against the Democratic nominee, Walter Mondale. It revealed the limitations of Soviet active measures to interfere with, and swing, a U.S. presidential election, at least before the advent of the digital age and social media.[6]

HUMANS VERSUS MACHINES

By the late 1970s, the NSA and GCHQ were making inroads against Soviet enciphered traffic using state-of-the-art computers. While the Soviets excelled at theoretical computing, as we have seen, the Americans and British dominated its application. A Soviet research institute later known as Kvant built a powerful computer for the Soviet Union. Called the Bulat ("sword"), it paled in comparison to the supercomputers that the U.S. government developed. "We did not even dare dream, like the Americans, of putting each interception through computer analysis," recalled one Eighth Directorate officer, which did much of the analytical work. By contrast, U.S. and British intelligence communities had the use of a supercomputer, the Cray-1A. The $8.8 million machine weighed 5.5 tons. It vastly outgunned the Soviet M-10, the most powerful Soviet computer, designed for early warning of a missile attack. The maximum number of processor cycles for the M-10 was 5.3; the Cray, at 27.6, was five times as powerful. U.S. companies like IBM produced models even more effective at intercepting encrypted traffic, giving the West a significant technological advantage in SIGINT collection. But even as U.S. and British code breakers pulled ahead in the technology race, the ground fell from under their feet. Soviet espionage nullified and sabotaged their achievements. The KGB managed to recruit an agent at GCHQ.[7]

Geoffrey Prime was a social outcast and a pedophile. He was also a Soviet spy. He first offered his services to the Soviets in 1968, while stationed with the RAF in West Berlin, throwing a message out of a Berlin train window to a Soviet border guard, with an offer to work for them. The Soviets, unsurprisingly, embraced him. The KGB's security division, the Third Directorate, was his handler—it was they, not the First Chief Directorate, who received Prime's note as it sailed out of that train window.

They urged him to apply to GCHQ. He did so and was accepted into the service. For a decade, Prime (code-named ROWLANDS) provided Moscow with high-grade secrets from inside GCHQ. The quality of the intelligence he produced became increasingly valuable when he was transferred to GCHQ's J Division, which was responsible for eavesdropping on the Soviet Union. Prime's job gave him (and thus Moscow) access to ultrasensitive American SIGINT satellites and joint NSA-GCHQ submarine-tracking technologies. Prime later claimed he was motivated by ideology, the promise of communism. But at heart he was a mercenary, accepting cash for the British and American secrets he stole. Buckling under the stress of living a double life, and receiving little emotional support from the KGB, Prime resigned from GCHQ in 1977 and worked as a taxi driver. He considered defecting to the Soviet Union. Short of money, he renewed his contact with the KGB in 1980, traveling to meet a handler in Vienna that May. There he provided five hundred secret documents, contained in fifteen reels of film, which he had compiled three years earlier while still working at GCHQ.

Prime's intelligence was a treasure trove for the Kremlin. It revealed Washington's and London's ongoing attacks on Soviet communications through their supercomputers. In an instant, the West's hard-won advantage in computing was lost. As with the atomic bomb, the Kremlin had evened up the odds against the Main Adversary through human intelligence. Prime was ultimately identified and apprehended as a Soviet agent by sheer luck. He was arrested in 1982 for sexually assaulting underage girls. Upon searching his belongings, the police found, in addition to 2,287 index cards he compiled of potential victims, a satchel full of spy paraphernalia—onetime cipher pads, miniature cameras, microdot equipment, radios, and invisible ink. Without his arrest for pedophilia, it is unlikely that he would have been detected. He was charged with breaking the Official Secrets Act, and, after his trial and conviction, sentenced to thirty-eight years' imprisonment.[8]

U.S. SIGINT was betrayed by yet another Soviet agent, John Walker, a navy communications officer responsible for monitoring at the submarine-fleet message center (NAVCAMS) in Norfolk, Virginia. Walker, like Prime, volunteered his services to the Soviet Union. Facing bankruptcy from a failed business venture, he walked into the Soviet embassy on Sixteenth Street in Washington, DC, in 1967 and offered to become a Soviet agent. "I'm a naval officer. I'd like to make some money and I'll give you some genuine stuff in return," Walker told a surprised Soviet official. Despite his relatively low rank, he had access to some of the most prized secrets in the U.S. government: keys to NSA ciphers. Over the next seventeen years, in return for the high-value SIGINT that he stole, the KGB provided him, and other agents he recruited, a total of $1 million. Walker made his espionage venture a family affair, eventually recruiting his son and brother, and then a close friend, as well as trying (unsuccessfully) to recruit his daughter. The Walker brothers enabled the Soviets to read U.S. naval codes for close to eighteen years.

Walker's espionage allowed Soviet SIGINT to decrypt approximately one million U.S. communications, according to Oleg Kalugin. "His information was so good that our side had access to battle plans of the U.S. Atlantic fleet," the former KGB officer later recalled. Thanks to Walker, the Soviets had advance knowledge of U.S. naval exercises and secret maneuvers, including the timetable of B-52 bombing runs in Vietnam. The full scale of Walker's espionage was never exploited. His most important secrets would have only been used if war broke out between East and West. The information would have given the Soviet Union devastating knowledge of U.S. naval operations if the Cold War had turned hot. Walker was identified to the FBI in 1984 by his ex-wife, who had suffered years of abuse at his hands. He was arrested, convicted, and received a life sentence, dying in prison in 2014.

DISILLUSIONMENT

As we have seen, the most effective spies are often those who work with ideological conviction. A deeply held philosophical belief in a type of government, be it communist or democratic, can inspire a spy's selfless devotion. The Cambridge Five were driven by ideological conviction, as was Oleg Penkovsky. By the 1970s, however, the myth of the Soviet Union as a worker's paradise, which had inspired and fueled foreign agents a generation earlier, had disintegrated. The corruption and decrepitude of Brezhnev's regime were so apparent that only the most hard-line true believers could deceive themselves to its reality and work for it. Instead, Soviet intelligence later in the Cold War had to rely on money to lure recruits. The KGB strove to perpetuate its past glories with its Cambridge and Ivy League spies. But the likes of a pedophile like Geoffrey Prime, or a gun for hire like John Walker, were far cries from ideologically motivated agents—despite the Kremlin's efforts to paint them differently.

The shift from ideological to mercenary spies is documented in a study of known American spies in the postwar years. Of the seventy-four Americans who are known to have spied for the Soviet Union during the later Cold War, money was the sole or primary motivation for most. As Oleg Kalugin recalled:

> In my thirty-two-year tenure with the KGB, the great spies who
> came to us because they believed in Communism, such as Kim
> Philby, dwindled steadily and finally disappeared altogether. At the
> same time, the number of KGB officers who grew disaffected with

Soviet Communism and defected to the West rose sharply. The KGB was hit by a devastating double-whammy in which the number of good spies was shrinking while the number of defectors was soaring.[9]

If we look behind the money that passes hands, there are usually other underlying reasons why someone turns to espionage—a sick child, unmanageable medical bills, an expensive divorce. Rather than resorting to spying to buy luxuries or enjoy a better lifestyle, often money is used to address a life-damaging event. And while many of those who spied for the West against the Soviet Union in the later Cold War were ideologically committed agents, disgusted by their government, it is also true that both sides, East and West, used career failings to recruit: a feeling of disgruntlement, envy, being overlooked in their agencies by less intelligent superiors. Human frailties offer endless opportunities for treachery. Both sides preyed upon such character traits among those who had access to state secrets.[10]

SUPPLY CHAIN SABOTAGE

In July 1981, President Reagan met the new French president, François Mitterrand, in Ottawa. In a private, hushed meeting, the French leader revealed to Reagan that French intelligence was running a well-placed agent inside the KGB's science and technology department, Directorate T, within the First Chief Directorate. Code-named FAREWELL, the agent's true identity was Vladimir Vetrov. He was a senior officer in KGB's Line X, which was responsible for stealing Western science and technology secrets for Directorate T. A handsome man in his early fifties with thick black hair, Vetrov had become a Francophile during a posting in Paris, where he worked undercover as a Soviet commercial businessman. He loved the Parisian lifestyle, keeping a case of champagne in his car trunk "just in case." The contrast between the freedoms he enjoyed in Paris and the scale of Soviet theft of Western intellectual property that he saw occasioned a crisis of faith. Back in Moscow, in 1980 he sent a message with a visiting French businessman offering his services to French intelligence. As FAREWELL, Vetrov was run by the French security service (DST), with the help of MI6.

Mitterrand's spy chief gave intelligence obtained by FAREWELL over the previous year and a half to Reagan's DCI, Bill Casey, and to Vice President George H. W. Bush, who was himself a former DCI. The resulting haul of Soviet secrets, known as the FAREWELL dossier, confirmed the CIA's "worst nightmare," in the words of one officer: "our science was supporting their National Defense." Vetrov's dossier contained four thousand documents of KGB technology espionage directed against Western countries. The Soviet Military-Industrial Commission (VPK), he revealed, had tasked Directorate T and Line X with a broad espionage attack on Western governments across various sectors and fields.

The hunting grounds for Line X officers were routine trade fairs. But their espionage also reached into space: the joint U.S.-Soviet space venture that led to the dramatic Apollo-Soyuz docking in 1975, which symbolized détente to the world and is considered to have brought the space race to an end, had been used as a Soviet spying effort on the U.S. space program. One of the cosmonauts was a suspected KGB officer who stole everything he could get his hands on. Vetrov identified two hundred KGB Line X officers operating from ten *rezidentury* in Western countries, as well as one hundred additional agents who were being cultivated. Vetrov's intelligence has since been confirmed by KGB archives exfiltrated from Russia.

Espionage, rather than innovation, was the engine of the Soviet defense sector. Soviet space technology, for example, relied heavily on what was stolen from NASA. We know that in 1986 a KGB recruit breached sensitive U.S. databases, at the Lawrence Berkeley National Laboratory, in what may be the first known case of "online" hacking. In 1979, more than half the projects underway in Soviet defense and industrial sectors were based on technology obtained from the West. In 1980, the VPK ordered 3,617 "acquisition tasks," to obtain specific information from the West, of which 1,085 were completed within a year.

The United States was a more productive Soviet target, in terms of scientific and technical secrets stolen, than the rest of the world combined. According to Pentagon estimates—which appear to have been correct—70 percent of Warsaw Pact weapons systems depended on Western technologies. U.S. science and technology thus effectively drove both sides of the Cold War. The East German (Stasi) foreign intelligence chief, Markus Wolf, later claimed that one East German computer technology firm, Robotron, depended so much on stolen Western commercial secrets that it was effectively an unofficial IBM subsidiary. The Stasi's head, Erich Mielke, used a Robotron computer, which can be seen on his desk, in the Stasi museum in Berlin, to this day.[11]

Looking back, it appears that the FAREWELL dossier contributed to Reagan's major national security doctrine, NSDD 75, which further spelled out U.S. strategy to contain and roll back communism. Vetrov's intelligence also helped to prevent the loss of existing and future technology to the Soviet Union. Armed with it, the CIA went to work. In January 1982, Bill Casey authorized a plan put forward by a CIA economist, Gus Weiss, to sabotage the technologies that KGB's Line X was known to be targeting and stealing.[12]

"It was a brilliant plan," Richard V. Allen, Reagan's first national security adviser, said: "We started in motion feeding the Soviets bad technology, bad computer technology, bad oil drilling technology. We fed them a whole lot, let them steal stuff that they were happy to get." The CIA sabotaged supply chains that they knew the Soviets were targeting, from radar and mechanical tools to semiconductors. Quietly working with U.S. companies, the CIA delivered compromised computer chips to the Soviet military. Soviet chemical plants and equipment were disrupted by carefully constructed defective plans, as were their state-of-the-art turbines. The Soviet space shuttle used a rejected NASA design, setting the project back. Unsurprisingly, when the Soviet space shuttle Buran was unveiled, it looked like a clone of the U.S. space shuttle.

According to Weiss, the greatest Trojan horse created by the CIA was a software time bomb for a natural-gas pipeline that the Kremlin wanted to build from Siberia to Eastern Europe. Governments in Europe were concerned that such a pipeline would allow Moscow to hold foreign states hostage over fuel supplies—a strategy continued by Putin against the West today. Soviet engineers needed computers to control the pressure valves of the pipeline and sought software for doing so on the open Western market. The U.S. government rejected their request, but subtly pointed engineers to a certain Canadian company that might be able to provide what Moscow wanted. The Soviets took the bait and sent a Line X officer to steal the software. It worked well for a few months. But in June 1982, it malfunctioned. The pipeline blew apart in a three-kiloton blast. Repairs cost the Kremlin tens of millions of rubles that it could ill afford.

The quality of science and technology secrets Vetrov provided made him a major Western agent in the Cold War. Like many other spies, Vetrov was a flawed individual. His career as a French spy came to a disastrous end in 1982 in circumstances that still remain murky. His French handlers knew that he had a violent temper, but misjudged its magnitude. He got into an argument with his girlfriend in a parked car on a Moscow street. When a passing policeman approached, Vetrov, fearing that he had been identified as a spy, stabbed both the policeman and his girlfriend, killing the former. In prison, he boasted that he was involved in "something big." This soon brought him to the attention of the KGB. Harshly interrogated, he confessed and was convicted of treason. In 1985, shortly before his execution, he said that his only regret was not being able to inflict more damage on the Soviet government. It is possible, but cannot be proved from available records, that he was betrayed by a Soviet agent in MI6 or the CIA who had access to his intelligence.[13]

END OF DAYS: NUCLEAR WAR

Brezhnev and KGB chairman Andropov were aghast at Reagan's public hard-line stance against the Soviet Union. The president supported the deployment of 108 Pershing II and 484 Gryphon missiles in Europe, capable of striking targets in the Soviet Union. Reagan's tough speeches about the Soviet Union fed Brezhnev and Andropov's fears. In May 1981, they called together senior KGB officers for a major conference. Brezhnev, by then visibly ailing, denounced Reagan as a serious threat to world peace. Andropov went even further. He claimed, to the startled audience, that America was preparing to launch a nuclear first strike and obliterate the Soviet Union. Since the early Cold War, the U.S. military had plans (like BROILER) envisioning nuclear war. Such plans were not based on the U.S. striking first, initiating an attack, but envisioned nuclear war arising from miscalculation or Soviet offensive. The Soviet military had corresponding plans.[14]

Soviet leaders nevertheless had been haunted by a fear of a U.S. first strike since the early 1960s. In 1961, the GRU erroneously claimed that the Soviet detonation of a 50-megaton hydrogen bomb had deterred the United States from launching a preemptive nuclear attack. Fear of a first strike was one reason Khrushchev took the gamble of placing nuclear warheads in Cuba in 1962. By the end of the 1970s, Brezhnev and Andropov knew that although the Soviet arsenal was catching up, the United States was still ahead in the East-West nuclear arms race. The KGB carried out an analysis of the geopolitical situation in early 1981, using a newly developed computer program. It concluded that militarily, scientifically, and economically, world forces were moving in favor of the West. As Moscow was pulled into its own unwinnable war in Afghanistan, the Soviet Union appeared to be losing the Cold War.

Andropov announced that, by a decision of the Politburo, the two branches of Soviet intelligence, the KGB and GRU, would collaborate for the first time in a global intelligence program, code-named RYAN, an acronym in Russian for a "nuclear missile attack." It was the biggest peacetime Soviet intelligence operation ever mounted. With Brezhnev at his side, Andropov proclaimed that because the United States and NATO were actively preparing for nuclear war, the task for Soviet intelligence was to detect and provide an early warning about such attack plans. Though he did not state it expressly, the implication was that early detection of a

U.S. nuclear attack would allow Moscow to deter or dissuade Reagan from taking the fatal step to launch.

"The slogan," remembered Oleg Kalugin, was "do not miss the moment when the West is about to launch war." Had the Soviets had better intelligence on the Main Adversary, it would have discovered that the U.S. government had no plans for a nuclear first strike. In the 1960s and 1970s, the KGB and GRU had not managed to recruit agents with access to Washington's innermost secrets, as they had in the early years of the Cold War. But even if they had, it is doubtful whether Andropov would have trusted intelligence that undermined or conflicted with his own strategic thinking about the United States' plans for a preemptive attack.[15]

Secret Soviet documents stolen by Gordievsky, and later published, reveal the logic, and paranoia, feeding RYAN. It was an effort to detect deviations from routine activities in NATO countries. It could, its architects believed, indicate preparations for a preemptive strike. Instead, it became a monument to fear and loathing, and a vicious circle of intelligence collection and assessment. RYAN was not designed to discover whether America's plans for a nuclear attack existed, but to collect evidence to support the theory that they did. Instead of using genuine intelligence to inform their decision-making, Brezhnev and Andropov used RYAN to confirm their worst fears. In early 1982, Andropov instructed all KGB *rezidentury* overseas to make RYAN a top priority. They were instructed to keep close surveillance on "key nuclear decision makers" in Western countries. In London, the KGB *rezidentura* was ordered to watch for activities indicating preparations for a nuclear attack: suspicious things like lights staying on late at night at the Ministry of Defense, or a rise in the "price" of blood at blood banks—preparing for mass casualties and stockpiling, ran the theory. The Soviets evidently believed that in the capitalist West, blood was bought by "banks," not donated. In Washington, telltale signs that Soviet personnel were instructed to look for included a sudden increase in cars being parked at the Pentagon. The Main Adversary would not be able to hide its preparations for attack, you see.[16]

Some Soviet foreign intelligence officers stationed in the West, acclimatized to the realities of life there, scoffed at the Center's instructions. East German foreign intelligence chief Markus Wolf later recalled that he resented the waste of time caused by KGB demands for his assistance in discovering nonexistent plans for a U.S. first strike. But Wolf knew better than to complain. Orders were orders in the Eastern bloc.

In November 1982, eighteen months after delivering his alarming speech to the KGB, Brezhnev died. Andropov, who was suffering from what would prove to be fatal liver failure, succeeded him as Soviet leader. The "Butcher of Budapest" was the first KGB chief to become general secretary of the Soviet Communist Party. A devoted Marxist, Andropov, usually bedecked in a snow-white shirt and dark suit, understood English and German, was a jazz aficionado, and was extremely well read. Secretary of State George Shultz said that Andropov reminded him of Professor Moriarty, the evil genius in the Sherlock Holmes stories, "all brain in a disregarded body . . . a formidable adversary." With Moriarty at the helm in Moscow, Operation RYAN went into overdrive.[17]

Tensions ratcheted higher in 1982 in response to Moscow's deployment of powerful SS-20 missiles in the Eastern bloc to replace their aging SS-4s and SS-5s—a move that gave them a military advantage in Europe. NATO countered by deploying intermediate-range nuclear missiles (Pershing IIs and Gryphons) in Europe in order to, in their eyes, rebalance the scales. Soviet leaders saw the placement of these "Euromissiles" as a serious threat, if not a prelude to war. Like an exhausted boxer, the Kremlin feared that Washington would end the Cold War with a knockout punch, like one delivered by Rocky Balboa in *Rocky*, which hit the screens two years earlier. The new American-made NATO missiles could strike targets in the Soviet Union, including Moscow itself, in as little as six minutes. The only way to stop their deployment, announced Reagan, was for the Soviet Union to remove all its SS-20s from European Russia. In March 1983, Reagan unveiled a massive new strategy, the Strategic Defense Initiative (SDI), dubbed "Star Wars" by the president's opponents. It was a plan to construct a defensive shield above the United States using satellites and lasers to shoot down incoming Soviet missiles. Reagan was terrified of nuclear war. He saw SDI as a way to make a nuclear strike against his country impossible.

In Moscow, the Center interpreted Reagan's announcement of SDI as part of the government's preparation for atomic war. If successfully deployed, Reagan's missile defense would make the United States invulnerable to nuclear attack, able to launch against the Soviet Union without fear of retaliation. Andropov's new KGB chairman, Viktor Chebrikov, and his head of KGB foreign intelligence, Vladimir Kryuchkov, made it clear to *rezidentury* overseas that RYAN was a matter of Soviet survival. Their instructions to *rezidents* were addressed to them by name, which was rare. Andropov's strategy was twofold: first, to prevent the deployment of the Pershing II missiles at the end of November 1983. He placed his hopes on anti-nuclear "peace" movements throughout Europe, which the KGB supported. When such protests failed to stop the deployment of Pershings, his second strategy, RYAN, became his best defense. Andropov, terminally ill, ordered the KGB sabotage unit to prepare for terrorist attacks on British, American, and NATO targets in Europe in retaliation to any U.S. nuclear strike. It planned to send letter bombs to Margaret Thatcher's office and to prominent U.S. and NATO representatives. In August 1983, RYAN reached a new level in Europe, as KGB and GRU officers scoured for NATO teams thought to be armed with nuclear, biological, and chemical weapons, secretly infiltrating Soviet territory.[18]

In this toxic brew of paranoia, on September 1, 1983, a Soviet fighter plane shot down a Korean passenger jet, KAL 007, traveling from New York to Seoul via Anchorage. The plane had blundered badly off course over Soviet airspace. All 269 people on board were killed. The news shocked Reagan and Shultz. To them, it was as if the evil empire had shown its true stripes. From listening posts in Japan, working night shifts, the NSA had managed to intercept radar and communications from the Soviet fighter pilot announcing that he had fired and had destroyed the target. It was a striking success for U.S. SIGINT collection. The day after the plane was shot down, the secretary of state, with Reagan's blessing, went public with the incriminating SIGINT. Visibly angry and waving an intelligence report, Shultz told a press conference that the Soviet fighter could not have failed to realize it was a civilian aircraft. The Soviets had killed hundreds of civilian passengers in cold blood. The SIGINT showed that Soviet radar had tracked the plane for two hours.

It was the first time a U.S. secretary of state had publicly referred to SIGINT. Reagan's White House followed, over Labor Day weekend, with a media blitz. The president followed Shultz with his own televised address on Labor Day itself. Unhappy with the initial draft of his speech, which he read beside the White House pool, Reagan went to his study, still wearing his damp swimming trunks, laid a towel over the chair at his desk, and rewrote it. That night, he declared the attack an "act of barbarism, born of a society which wantonly disregards individual rights and the value of human life and seeks constantly to expand and dominate other nations." The next day, the U.S. ambassador at the UN, Jeane Kirkpatrick, "acerbic even in calm waters" according to the NSA's secret history, delivered an audiovisual presentation using selected intelligence of the plane being shot down before the General Assembly. It was like Adlai Stevenson's use of intelligence to secure a propaganda victory against the Soviets during the Cuban Missile Crisis. (In retaliation, the KGB attempted to smear Kirkpatrick's reputation using forged documents.) The Reagan administration, however, undermined its powerful case against the Soviet Union by overstating it. Much of what Shultz initially claimed turned out to be wrong. As the Reagan White House was releasing intelligence in real time, NSA analysts were still trying to produce accurate translations. In fact, the NSA translations showed that the Soviets believed they were tracking a U.S. reconnaissance aircraft. The CIA corrected the picture for Reagan in the Daily Brief. As Robert Gates later phrased it, the Reagan administration's rhetoric outran facts known to it. KAL 007 is a salutary tale for governments declassifying and spinning intelligence.[19]

In Moscow, the reaction to the downing of the Korean passenger jet took a predictable form: initial denial followed by a torrent of misinformation, with the Kremlin offering some facts while falsifying others, to make it seem that the U.S. government was to blame. Soviet state press outlets reported that KAL 007 was an American spy plane, operated by the CIA, whose secret mission was espionage on Soviet territory. Its call sign, 007, was surely evidence of its espionage. Dmitri Ustinov, a marshal of the Soviet Union, and Viktor Chebrikov, the KGB chairman, repeated this claim in a secret memorandum to Andropov. Nine days after KAL 007 was shot down, Nikolai Ogarkov, chief of the Soviet general staff, held a press conference in which he asserted that the Korean passenger jet had deliberately strayed into Soviet territory. On September 19, the KGB deputy chairman, Kryuchkov, told the head of the East German Stasi that the Soviet pilots and ground control genuinely thought that KAL 007 was a spy plane. Kryuchkov even outrageously suggested that, even though it turned out to be a civilian aircraft, it had been deliberately sent into Soviet airspace—to be shot down, thus provoking world fury. KGB active measures would continue to expose the truth, he said. In reality, there was no such conspiracy. The shootdown of KAL 007 was a tragic mistake.[20]

In its aftermath, Andropov disappeared from public view, never to reemerge. From his sickbed, on a dialysis machine, he issued a withering denunciation of U.S. policy, couched in apocalyptic language: "outrageous military psychosis" had taken over the United States, he said. "The Reagan administration, in its imperial ambitions, go so far that one even begins to doubt whether Washington has any brakes at all preventing it from crossing the point at which a sober-minded person must stop." Tensions mounted further the following month when Lech Wałęsa, the leader of the Solidarity trade union movement in Poland, which the Kremlin viewed as a central part of Reagan's plan to destabilize the Soviet bloc, was awarded the Nobel Peace Prize. The CIA did indeed support the Polish opposition movement, helping to keep Solidarity alive after the Soviets drove it underground.

In November 1983, NATO forces in Europe launched a training exercise, AUTUMN FORGE. Stretching from Norway to Turkey, it involved one hundred thousand NATO troops, sixteen thousand flown in from the

United States. AUTUMN FORGE's final part, ABLE ARCHER, culminated in a practice exercise of NATO nuclear launch procedures. Such events were routine for both sides, East and West, during the Cold War, and each scrutinized the other. The CIA was running a valuable agent inside Warsaw Pact forces, a Polish colonel named Ryszard Kukliński; the Soviet bloc had its own spy at NATO headquarters, Rainer Rupp, who was run by East German intelligence. NATO launched ABLE ARCHER at a moment when the Soviet government most feared a U.S. nuclear strike. To make matters worse, the exercise was conducted November 2–11, which included a holiday weekend, Veterans Day, something NATO had not done before. NATO left no doubt that it was only an exercise, but the Center saw it differently. On November 5, it told the London *rezidentura* that there was a possible timetable for a nuclear strike. As ABLE ARCHER unfolded, it sent an urgent telegram, either on November 8 or 9, which claimed—erroneously—that U.S. and NATO forces had been placed on alert. In fact, they were on heightened security following the massacre of 307 American and French troops in a truck bombing in Beirut. One of the possible explanations for the alert, the Center advised, was that NATO had begun the countdown for a nuclear first strike "under the cover of ABLE ARCHER."

The Soviet Union put fighter-bombers with nuclear weapons on twenty-four-hour alert in East Germany. According to U.S. intelligence documents, only declassified in 2021, the Soviet alert included "preparations for the immediate use of nuclear weapons." MiG-23s, equipped with missiles capable of shooting down Gryphon intermediate-range missiles, were also placed on alert. Soviet submarines carrying nuclear ballistic missiles dived below the Arctic ice to avoid detection, and crews stood at battle stations. On the day ABLE ARCHER began, the Soviet chief of the general staff, Nikolai Ogarkov, moved to his wartime command bunker deep under Moscow, where he secretly ordered a "heightened alert" for some of his nuclear forces. Victor Yesin, a commander of Soviet missiles trained on Western Europe, later revealed that his men had also been placed on heightened alert. His missiles were moved to their camouflaged wartime firing positions.[21]

THE ART OF BETRAYAL

The source of Britain's intelligence on RYAN, and the warning about the alarm that ABLE ARCHER caused in Moscow, was Britain's spy inside the KGB: Oleg Gordievsky. He was born into the KGB: his father and brother were officers. When it came time for him to decide on a career, there was only one choice. In 1968, he was stationed in the KGB *rezidentura* in Copenhagen. The sleek, friendly, and prosperous Danish capital enticed him, as did the freedoms he enjoyed there. There was no need to carry papers, people could watch and read whatever they wanted, and choose their job. The city obliterated the crude Soviet propaganda myth about life being superior behind the Iron Curtain. But it was the Soviet Union's crushing of the Prague Spring in 1968 that crystallized Gordievsky's disillusion. Drawing on extensive background research, the Danish Security and Intelligence Service and its close liaison partner, Britain's MI6, identified Gordievsky as a potential recruit. Robert Browning, MI6's ebullient head of station in Copenhagen, initially contacted Gordievsky at what appeared to be a chance encounter at a badminton game in 1974. In fact, it was meticulously choreographed—and successful.

Gordievsky—SUNBEAM, later code-named NOCTON, HETMAN, and OVATION—became a unique source for MI6, and the Western allies it shared his intelligence with, for twelve years. He was MI6's answer to Kim Philby, someone just as ideologically committed—in this case, to a free, democratic world—and equally skillful at hiding his true allegiances to friends and colleagues.[22]

In 1982, the Center posted Gordievsky to the London *rezidentura*. With MI6's help, Gordievsky's KGB career in the city took off. His MI6 handlers, who included John Scarlett, later MI6 chief, provided him with "chicken feed," genuine but not damaging information, which helped to advance his Soviet career. For its part, MI6 obtained a flow of secrets from Gordievsky about KGB agents and operations in Britain.[23]

It was Gordievsky who delivered Moscow's flash telegrams about ABLE ARCHER into MI6's hands. According to Britain's foreign secretary, Geoffrey Howe, "Gordievsky left us in no doubt of the extraordinary but genuine Russian fear of a real-life nuclear strike." To this day, historians disagree about whether or not the Kremlin really was on a nuclear trigger during ABLE ARCHER. Was the world on the brink of nuclear Armageddon like the contemporary made-for-TV film *The Day After*, which showed the town of Lawrence, Kansas, wiped out in a nuclear war with the Soviets? Was there a credible belief within the Politburo and the Soviet military that the United States was planning a nuclear first strike against the Soviet Union during a NATO training exercise? And did Moscow place Soviet forces on high alert as a result? Or was this merely Gordievsky's impression, or what the GRU thought (as opposed to what the KGB thought)? Or were the Soviets attempting to signal to the West how dangerous it was to deploy intermediate nuclear missiles aimed at the Soviet Union?

It is possible that the Soviet government, knowing that NATO was scrutinizing its forces, took them to the brink of a nuclear launch to signal its alarm about the Euromissiles. While some historians have tried to draw definite conclusions, in fact, the paper trail of Andropov's thinking about ABLE ARCHER remains hidden, if it exists at all, in closed archives in Moscow. The Soviet documents may be forever lost to history, having stemmed from the mind of a terminally ill leader clouded by the effects of dialysis and kidney failure. (At the Kuntsevo clinic in Moscow, Andropov rested in a dentist's chair, with a button on the armrest allowing him to shift positions to try to ease his pain.)

It is impossible to draw firm conclusions about ABLE ARCHER due to incomplete records. Recently opened U.S. records, however, show that Soviet forces were indeed on unusually heightened alert during the exercise. It was not just Gordievsky's intelligence that revealed Moscow's deep concerns during ABLE ARCHER. Although most scholars who have scrutinized this moment have failed to notice it, in fact NSA and GCHQ collection, indicated with the code name UMBRA on reports, was used in U.S. and

British assessments. They revealed that Soviet forces undertook unusual actions. One NSA report, which only came to light in 2021, showed Reagan's national security advisers that nuclear-capable SU-17 fighter-bombers in East Germany were equipped with electronic jamming pods for protection. More alarming, the NSA reported that the squadron leaders asked to do without those electronics because of "an unexpected weight and balance problem." The NSA concluded: "This message meant that at least this particular squadron was loading a munitions configuration that they had never actually loaded before, i.e., a warload." GCHQ's official history also notes that it conducted an analysis of traffic concerning ABLE ARCHER. It reflected fear and alarm among Soviet decision makers.[24]

British and U.S. intelligence would not have been so stupid just to use Gordievky's intelligence about ABLE ARCHER. A later all-source investigation by the President's Foreign Intelligence Advisory Board (PFIAB), in 1990, drawing on Gordievsky's material and SIGINT, drew the following terrifying conclusion: "In 1983 we may have inadvertently placed our relations with the Soviet Union on a hair trigger," with the risk that the Soviets "might have launched a preemptive strike against the U.S. in response to a perceived but non-existent threat." As Robert Gates, then deputy director of intelligence (analysis) at the CIA, later put it: "My first reaction to the reporting was not only that we might have had a major intelligence failure, but further that the most terrifying thing about Able Archer was that we may have been at the brink of nuclear war and not even known it." The KGB continued Operation RYAN, searching for a U.S. nuclear first strike, until at least 1987. Its leaders evidently really believed the U.S. had such plans.[25]

Gordievsky's intelligence led to a significant shift in British intelligence assessments about the Soviet Union. In September 1983, the JIC, undoubtedly acting on material provided by Gordievsky, commissioned a major paper to understand Soviet fears—that is, an exercise of strategic empathy. The report told its senior Whitehall readers that, whether founded or not, the Kremlin's fears were genuine: "Soviet foreign policy is driven by a mixture of nationalism, great power ambition, a sense of historical mission, and a desire to compete on equal terms with the West, together with an underlying sense of insecurity."[26]

Meanwhile, in Washington, the intelligence that Reagan received from his national security advisers, about the Kremlin's heightened alarm over ABLE ARCHER, seems to have had a profound effect on him. The kopek finally dropped. Although Reagan's memoirs do not expressly refer to ABLE ARCHER, he identifies November 1983 as the moment when he finally grasped "something surprising about the Russians: Many people at the top of the Soviet hierarchy were genuinely afraid of America and Americans. Perhaps this shouldn't have surprised me, but it did."

Seven days after ABLE ARCHER, Reagan wrote in his diary: "I feel the Soviets are . . . so paranoid about being attacked that without in any way being soft on them we ought to tell them no one here has any intention of doing anything like that." Reagan abandoned his rhetoric of the evil empire virtually overnight, realizing it was counterproductive because it stoked Moscow's worst fears. Instead, he softened the wording of his foreign policy speeches about the Soviet Union. Following discussions with George Shultz, he approved the creation of a small team within the national security planning group whose goal was "opening new channels to the Kremlin" and calming Soviet fears about an American first strike.[27]

Reagan was beginning a far greater détente with the Soviet Union than any of his predecessors in the Oval Office had ever dreamed of—but one through which, he believed, reversing Trotsky's aphorism, Soviet communism could be tossed into the dustbin of history. In January 1984, in a televised address, he gave his most conciliatory speech on East-West relations since he had entered politics. Big Brother was nowhere to be found. The president expressed astonishment that his views on the Soviet system should have "come as a surprise to Soviet leaders who've never shied from expressing their views of our system." He insisted, however, that "this doesn't mean that we can't deal with each other." It was in the interests of both countries to "avoid war and reduce the level of arms." There was no alternative, he told Americans, looking at the camera, to finding areas of "constructive cooperation": "We must and will engage with the Soviets in a dialogue as serious and constructive as possible. . . . We have a long way to go, but we're determined to try and try again. You may have to start in small ways, but start we must."

Some historians, like William Inboden, have questioned whether intelligence about ABLE ARCHER really led to a reversal of Reagan's strategy toward the Soviet Union. But from the perspective of the Soviet ambassador in Washington, Anatoli Dobrynin, Reagan's speech in January 1984 was a watershed. Dobrynin observed that, by Reagan's standards, it was a "remarkably conciliatory television address."[28]

In February 1984, MI6 started to share its intelligence with the CIA about the Soviet war-games scare, disguising the identity of its source in the KGB. Even among close intelligence allies like MI6 and the CIA, the identities of its most important sources are closely guarded. The fewer people who know an agent's identity, the less risk there is to his or her security (or the less "threat surface" there is, in the current vernacular of Western agencies). Sharing intelligence means assuming the security risk of those with whom it is shared. MI6's hesitance to disclose Gordievsky's identity proved to be a wise decision. In the spirit of its transatlantic rivalry, however, the CIA set up its own task force to identify the British secret source. It was a move that would have chilling consequences.

Gordievsky's intelligence was unique. In the assessment of Robert Gates:

> Our sources in the Soviet Union tended to be those who provided
> us with information about their military and research R&D. What
> Gordievski was giving us was information about the thinking of the
> leadership—and that kind of information was for us as scarce as hen's
> teeth.[29]

In the aftermath of ABLE ARCHER, Gordievsky's KGB career in the London *rezidentura* soared. It did so with MI6's assistance. In 1984, Gordievsky's superior, KGB *rezident* Arkady Guk, was publicly revealed to be involved in the case of a disaffected MI5 officer, Michael Bettaney, who had offered to spy for the Soviet Union. The information came to light in court, causing news headlines. MI6 had an ingenious plan to help advance Gordievsky's career. The British government declared Guk persona non grata. He and others were expelled from London. Removal of his superior opened a path for Gordievsky's promotion.

Gordievsky's secrets made a "powerful impression" on foreign secretary Geoffrey Howe: "The Soviet leadership really did believe the bulk of their own propaganda," Howe recalled. "They did have a genuine fear that 'the West' was plotting their overthrow—and might, just might, go to any lengths to achieve it." His intelligence was sent directly to Margaret Thatcher, who knew Gordievsky as Mr. Collins. In the words of Thatcher's biographer: "Gordievsky's dispatches . . . conveyed to her, as no other information had done, how the Soviet leadership reacted to Western phenomena and, indeed, to her."

Gordievsky opened a curtain for Thatcher and her foreign policy advisers into the Kremlin's thinking. "Probably no British prime minister has ever followed the case of a British agent with as much personal attention as Mrs. Thatcher devoted to Gordievsky," notes her biographer. When Andropov died in February 1984, after a mere fourteen months in power, Thatcher used suggestions provided by Gordievsky to make the best possible impression at his funeral in Moscow. With a hot-water bottle under her coat in the freezing Moscow winter, she struck a reasonable tone in her meeting with Andropov's successor, Konstantin Chernenko. At seventy-two, Chernenko was the oldest Soviet leader to take office, and his tenure would be shorter even than Andropov's. He was terminally ill himself and would die of emphysema thirteen months later.

Three walking-dead Soviet leaders over a two-and-a-half-year period symbolized the sclerosis of the Soviet system, and the decrepitude of the Politburo. But a young Politburo member, Gorbachev, caught Thatcher's attention. Gorbachev was energetic. He was to be the first party leader born after Lenin's death, and the first since Lenin with a university education. And so it was that at the end of the year, Thatcher, with Gordievsky's secret help, invited Gorbachev to London as part of a "parliamentary" debate. That is how they had their "doing business" meeting at Chequers. After their meeting, Gorbachev dramatically stated: "The Soviet Union is prepared . . . to advance towards the complete prohibition and eventual elimination of nuclear weapons." It was a breakthrough.[30]

At Chequers, Thatcher also urged Gorbachev to view Reagan differently. Although Moscow might think Reagan was "a monster," he was not, she assured Gorbachev: "He is a reasonable man who wants to reach an understanding with the Soviet Union. You must talk with him, but don't think you can ever drive a wedge between us, because we are absolutely one." Meanwhile, Thatcher urged Reagan to reach out to Gorbachev. Three months later, in March 1985, Gorbachev became the new Soviet leader. Reagan met this momentous change in Moscow with a conviction that not only did East-West tensions have to be reduced, but the Cold War must be brought to an end.

In May 1985, two months after Gorbachev rose to power, Gordievsky was appointed KGB *resident* in London. It was the culmination of a decade of work by both Gordievsky and MI6. But even as he became KGB station chief in London, Gordievsky's career came off the rails. That same month, the Center recalled him to Moscow. The cable summoning him home suggested that the trip was a formality involving his promotion. But he and his MI6 handlers suspected something was wrong.

When he got to Moscow, Gordievsky, an old hand at the espionage game, realized that he was under surveillance. The KGB evidently suspected he was a British spy. He was pressured into spending a weekend at a dacha belonging to his KGB superior. There he was harshly interrogated and given a truth serum to get him to confess. His inquisitors included the head of security (Department K) in the KGB's First Chief Directorate, Sergei Golubev, a "quiet, dour man" whose specialty was poisons and assassinations, and Viktor Budanov, whom Gordievsky later described as the "grimmest and most dangerous person" in the KGB. Despite the drugs, Gordievsky kept his tongue. He was released but placed under close surveillance. Knowing his life was on the line, he instigated an escape plan that he and his MI6 handlers had devised years before when he was first recruited in Copenhagen.[31]

The operation, code-named PIMLICO, was the brainchild of an MI6 officer, Valerie Pettit, whose taste for homely wool sweaters, among other things, set her apart from the public image of James Bond's MI6. Thatcher personally authorized Gordievsky's exfiltration from Moscow; she was prepared to take the political fallout for the safe passage of Mr. Collins. To initiate PIMLICO, Gordievsky was to give a preassigned signal by standing on a particular Moscow street at a specific time, carrying a plastic bag from the British supermarket Safeway. An MI6 officer would then acknowledge Gordievsky's signal by eating a chocolate bar while carrying a green Harrods bag. It was a tense mission, involving missed signals, but eventually Gordievsky made contact with MI6. They had given Gordievsky an escape plan, hidden in a book of Shakespeare's sonnets. Gordievsky followed it. He caught the train from Moscow to Leningrad (as St. Petersburg was known then), where he met the MI6 head of station in Moscow, Raymond Asquith—the Earl of Oxford and the great-grandson of a former British prime minister. Asquith drove a British diplomatic car with Gordievsky hidden in a secret compartment in the trunk, and together they made for the Finnish border.

After changing diplomatic cars, Asquith approached the Finnish border. He was accompanied by his wife and their newborn daughter, to give border guards the impression of a routine family holiday. Their secret passenger, terrified and drenched in sweat, was wrapped in a thermal blanket to avoid detection by heat sensors. As they lined up at the border crossing, Soviet guards and dogs approached the car. Asquith's wife, thinking quickly, resorted to an improvisation unique in the history of espionage: she threw one of her daughter's used diapers out of the window. The dogs turned away at the smell. As the car moved forward and cleared the border, Asquith put Sibelius's *Finlandia* on the car's stereo system as a signal to let Gordievsky know they had reached freedom. As Gordievsky later recalled, that moment transformed his life. It was like the scene in *The Wizard of Oz* when Dorothy opens the door of her fallen farmhouse and steps into Munchkinland, and the movie shifts from black-and-white to Technicolor.

Britain's ambassador in Moscow, Bryan Cartledge, was left in an agonizing position after Gordievsky's exfiltration. He had to deny that his embassy was a "nest of spies," while trying to prevent the spy case from jeopardizing improving Anglo-Soviet relations. Both countries thereafter undertook tit-for-tat expulsions. The British expelled twenty-five Soviet officials from Britain, identified by Gordievsky as non-declared intelligence officers, while the Soviets responded in kind. Cartledge was aghast, losing all his Russian speakers at the embassy and one-third of his staff: "Never engage in a pissing match with a skunk," he wrote to the Foreign Office in September 1985, "he possesses important natural advantages."

Once safely in Britain, Gordievsky met MI6's chief, Christopher Curwen, and Margaret Thatcher herself. The prime minister wrote to him, thanking him for his "personal courage and stand for freedom and democracy." That same month, MI6 revealed to the CIA that Gordievsky was its source, his sensitive reports about Soviet paranoia and policy having been received by Langley for the last one and a half years. Bill Casey flew to London to meet with Gordievsky, who supplied insights into how Reagan might best approach Gorbachev at an upcoming summit in Geneva. Gordievsky stressed that Reagan should not agree to arms cuts, unless Gorbachev agreed to accept the Strategic Defense Initiative, or until it was clear that Gorbachev was genuinely changing the leadership of the Soviet Union and its foreign policy.

Four days later, at a meeting of the National Security Council, Casey warned the president and Shultz of the line that Gorbachev would take. In July 1987, Reagan received Gordievsky in the Oval Office—a first for a former KGB officer—and thanked him for his work. The burning question in London and Washington intelligence circles, however, was how the KGB had identified Gordievsky, whose star had seemed to shine so bright.[32]

CIRCLE OF TREASON

Aldrich Ames was an alcoholic. Born in River Falls, Wisconsin, he flunked out of the University of Chicago, but later scraped together a degree from

George Washington University. His father, a former CIA officer, suggested that he apply to Langley. Ames did so, joining the officers' training program. Mustachioed and slightly built, Ames, who went by the name "Rick," loved the notion of being a dashing secret agent. Reality soon disabused him of his romantic dreams. He joined the CIA at its lowest ebb, following the Church Committee's disclosure of the agency's abuses. He settled into a gray bureaucratic lifestyle, and undertook Russian-language training. During a posting to New York, Ames handled the West's star Soviet defector, Arkady Shevchenko, whom we met earlier.

Ames never got the recognition he craved from his work with Shevchenko. His drinking undermined his career. On one occasion, after boozing at the Oyster Bar in Grand Central Terminal, he left a briefcase containing photographs of Soviet agents on a train. Despite such blemishes, his career progressed in the CIA's Soviet division. By 1985, he was part of a small team at Langley trying to identify Britain's spy in the KGB. At that point, Ames was going through an expensive divorce from his first wife. He had fallen in love with a Colombian woman, Maria del Rosario, whom he had met during a posting in Mexico, and whom he married. Her tastes were as expensive as his. By the spring of 1985, Ames was in debt to the tune of $42,000, on a CIA salary of $60,000. He was living a life that he could not afford.

In April of 1985, the month before Gordievsky was recalled to Moscow, Ames decided to solve his life's problems: he contacted the local KGB *rezident* in Washington, Victor Cherkashin, and volunteered to provide the names of Western agents for cash. He did it under the CIA's nose. His agency position offered him legitimate reasons for meeting with Soviet arms control officials, using an alias. Ames chose a Soviet diplomat in Washington who was "clean" (not involved with intelligence), and whom he used as a go-between. Two months after his initial approach, Ames met the *rezident*, Cherkashin, at a restaurant in Alexandria, by the Potomac, called Chadwick's. During a low-key happy-hour meeting, Ames inflicted more damage at that point to U.S. intelligence than any other individual act of espionage. In a notepad, he wrote down the name of every CIA agent within the Soviet Union known to him. According to Cherkashin, "that piece of paper contained more information about CIA espionage than had ever before been presented in a single communication." It was the mother lode of CIA secrets.[33]

Because Ames was a walk-in, Cherkashin had to get approval from the Center to recruit him. (Ames showed off his knowledge of Russian history by suggesting his own code name—KOLOKOL, or "Bell," the name of a journal edited by Russia's nineteenth-century exiled socialist Alexander Herzen.) Ames became the most destructive spy in American history. While a later account by Cherkashin inevitably included retrospective aggrandizement of his own career, he was correct in claiming that Ames tipped the balance in the East-West intelligence war in the last stages of the Cold War. He operated as a traitor inside the CIA from 1985 until he was suspected of being a Soviet and then Russian—that is, post-Soviet—agent in 1993. Ames was well placed in the CIA's counterintelligence effort against the Soviet Union, though he never rose to the apex like Philby had in MI6 a generation before. Cherkashin later suggested that Ames became disillusioned by the Church Committee findings and the CIA's treatment of its own assets. Ames was in fact motivated by greed. As he said at his trial nine years after his first contact, he did it for money. For his initial delivery of the CIA agent names inside the Soviet Union, he received $50,000—a paltry sum for selling out one's country.[34]

Ames would become the best-paid spy in American history. He evidently realized he could keep asking for more. He supplied information at dead-drop sites throughout Washington. By the time he was arrested in 1994, the KGB and its successor, the SVR, had paid him $2.5 million—with a further $2.1 million earmarked for him in a Moscow bank account. Ames admitted to having compromised "virtually all Soviet agents of the CIA and other American and foreign services known to me," and to having provided a "huge quantity of information on United States foreign, defense and security policies." He is known to have betrayed at least twenty-four Western agents targeting the Soviet Union, ten of whom were executed. They included the CIA's key asset in the GRU, Dmitri Polyakov, whose fate we learned earlier.

For the best part of a decade, to the amazement of his KGB handlers, Ames was able to take highly classified files out of CIA offices without arousing suspicion. Flush with Soviet cash, he enjoyed a lavish lifestyle. He lived in an upscale neighborhood in Arlington, Virginia, drove a Jaguar, had his teeth whitened, got a Rolex, and wore monogrammed shirts. His wife amassed $100,000 worth of jewelry, which Ames passed off as gifts from Rosario's family in Colombia. It is unclear why his lifestyle, given his modest CIA salary, did not set off alarm bells within Langley's security. With the help of his KGB handlers, Ames managed to get through CIA polygraph tests. He maintained his security clearance. When one polygraph interrogator asked if he had ever met a Soviet official, Ames admitted calmly that he had, at Chadwick's. But Ames did not reveal the secrets he had given him. By revealing half-truths, he hid the greater truth.[35]

Ames claimed to have betrayed Gordievsky. He figured out who MI6's agent was in the spring of 1985, a month before he volunteered to start working as a Soviet agent. To this day, however, there remains a mystery at the center of Ames's espionage. After he was detected, Ames insisted that he did not provide Gordievsky's name to the KGB until June 1985, when he gave the "big dump" of agent names at Chadwick's. Gordievsky, however, had been recalled to Moscow a month earlier. In the Kremlin's narrative, this is explained by careful KGB counterespionage work.

A more sinister interpretation is equally possible: that Gordievsky was identified by another agent. Members of the CIA damage-assessment team, interviewed for this book, remain convinced that an unidentified Russian agent existed either in the CIA or MI6, whose identity has never been exposed. Apart from Ames, none of the other *known* Soviet agents inside the U.S. intelligence community operating at the time had access to Gordievsky's name. Thus, based on the timeline of events, the established narrative about Ames betraying Gordievsky does not, on its own terms, make sense. According to Ames's KGB case officer, Victor Cherkashin, it is "undeniable" that Soviet intelligence had another source along with Ames, and the other Soviet spies later exposed. Cherkashin claims to have been tipped off about Gordievsky in April 1985 by a British journalist in Washington "who occasionally provided us with information," which is an odd claim to say the least. It leaves open the possibility that such a tip, if it did take place, was at the direction of someone in Moscow, in the KGB or GRU, who had access to another mole's information about Gordievsky.

The fact that Gordievsky was interrogated by Budanov, who had served in Britain and who later looked after Kim Philby, suggests a possible British connection with such an agent. When confronted about this possibility in interviews for this book, a former senior MI6 officer said, on the condition of anonymity, that the possibility of an unidentified Soviet agent in MI6 has hung like a sword over the service. As we have seen, the best way to catch a spy is with a spy, by recruiting an agent in a foreign intelligence service, rather than through technical collection (though this does happen). The identification and execution of the French agent Vladimir Vetrov, whose intelligence MI6 and the CIA had access to, may also be explained by the work of this unidentified Soviet mole. If that agent did exist, he or she may have been operating at the time of ABLE ARCHER two years before. That, if true, would offer a startling new interpretation of the NATO war games: the Kremlin may have been pushing its forces to the edge of nuclear alert, watching the West's reaction from within.[36]

CHAPTER FIFTEEN

COLLAPSE

They received with surprise, with indignation, and perhaps
with envy, the extraordinary intelligence that the Pretorians
had disposed of the empire by public auction; and they sternly
refused to ratify the ignominious bargain.
–Edward Gibbon, *The Decline and Fall of the Roman Empire*

IN ONE-PARTY AUTHORITARIAN STATES, PERSONALITIES AT the top are decisive. If Stalin had not succeeded Lenin, the Soviet Union would have been a different country. If Khrushchev had not come to power after a court intrigue, there may not have been a period of de-Stalinization. If a hard-liner had come to power in 1985 instead of Mikhail Gorbachev, the Soviet Union and the Cold War may have lasted for another decade or more.

Gorbachev tried to save the Soviet Union from itself. He tried to impose discipline on the Soviet nation to overcome the economic stagnation created under his predecessors. When his attempts failed, he launched reforms under the banner of perestroika ("rebuilding"). When bureaucrats in the vast Soviet government apparatus obstructed his orders, he used glasnost, or open discussion, to counter them, and democratization to reform the country's bureaucracy. By 1987, however, it was clear that his liberalizing economic reforms were failing. The Warsaw Pact nations accumulated vast debt, held by Western creditors. "We are integrally tied to the capitalist economy," Soviet adviser Anatoli Chernyaev wrote. Amid a plunge in oil prices, the Soviet Union's economy was worse off than before Gorbachev.[1]

In foreign policy, Gorbachev's grand strategy and "new thinking" were more successful—they directly contributed to the Cold War's end. His immediate goals were to end the arms race with the United States and the war in Afghanistan, both of which he believed were draining the Soviet economy. He received a secret briefing revealing that the Soviet defense industry was consuming one-third of the Soviet economy and absorbed 75 percent of its most talented citizens. Gorbachev faced a vast military-industrial complex in the Soviet Union whose purpose was focused on conflict with the United States. While Eisenhower had warned Americans in his farewell address about the military-industrial complex in America, the Soviet Union *was* a military-industrial complex.

It took courage to argue with the Politburo that Reagan's Star Wars program was likely more fantasy than fact, and that therefore the Soviet defense industry did not need to plow resources into matching it. Gorbachev thought cooperation would benefit all. He proclaimed a new doctrine of sufficiency—holding only a minimal number of nuclear weapons for protection. Gorbachev hammered out reductions in arms starting at the summit he held with Reagan in Geneva in November 1985, at the elegant lakeside Villa Fleur d'Eau. Reagan, dapper and trim, upstaged Gorbachev, who emerged from his tanklike limo in standard Politburo "uniform"—hat, scarf, and heavy overcoat, looking like an old man. In fact, he was twenty years younger than the president.

There was no clearer indication of Gorbachev's attempts to reform the Soviet government than the demands he placed on Soviet intelligence. Eight months after he became Soviet leader, he had a meeting with the KGB chairman, Viktor Chebrikov, in which Gorbachev castigated the KGB for providing sanitized, politically correct reporting. The KGB report of the meeting was titled "On the Impermissibility of Distortions of the Factual State of Affairs in Messages and Informational Reports Sent to the Central Committee of the CPSU and Other Ruling Bodies." Existing records do not reveal what prompted Gorbachev to demand intelligence reform. It may have been his accumulated exasperation with Soviet intelligence "pleasing the ear" of policymakers, as the head of KGB analysis put it, or "loyal information," as one of Gorbachev's allies, Alexander Yakovlev, recalled. Whatever the reason, his instructions were clear: "all chekists" (the KGB) should ensure that objective reporting, the whole truth, was delivered to the Central Committee. Gorbachev's instruction added this was a "Leninist requirement"—a nice touch.

To appease their superiors in the Center, and their new political master in the Kremlin, some Soviet officers at least paid lip service to Gorbachev's reforms. The KGB tried to present itself in a new light, going on a PR offensive to style itself as a modernized professional intelligence service, capable of enacting and following Gorbachev's changes. It even created a television program that was available for sale to Western broadcasters, called *KGB Today*, and published a picture of a striking young lady called "Miss KGB," all to portray the secret police in a better light. Whether these reforms were genuine, or hollow gestures for Gorbachev, is impossible to know. The KGB's in-house journal suggests it was taking reform seriously, though we should always be careful of people who mark their own homework. There was soon a backlash among the old guard, including its head of the First Chief Directorate, Vladimir Kryuchkov, who became KGB chairman in 1988. He outwardly professed reform for the KGB, but in fact was a reactionary hard-liner. The demands that Gorbachev placed on Soviet intelligence produced an irony presumably not lost on the Soviet leader: the KGB agreed sycophantically on the need to avoid sycophantic reporting. There was another reason why Gorbachev's attempts to reform the Soviet intelligence apparatus were unsuccessful. He needed the KGB; he knew it and they knew it. The KGB was the devil he knew.[2]

Under Gorbachev, the KGB continued to be a state within a state. The Soviet leader knew firsthand about its history of terror and repression; his father had been tortured by the NKVD. Along with the Red Army, the KGB was nevertheless one of the two iron pillars of the Soviet state. The weight of seven decades of history meant it would be difficult, if not impossible, to change the KGB. As events transpired, Gorbachev was right to be afraid of trying to change it.

Although Gorbachev disliked and probably feared the KGB, its foreign intelligence was important for him as he embarked on his colossal diplomatic maneuverings with President Reagan, and later Bush, to carry out his major foreign policy strategy: to wind down the East-West arms race. Until his death in August 2022, Gorbachev remained tight-lipped about the intelligence he received during the Soviet Union's closing stages. One of the KGB's top secret annual reports to Gorbachev, for 1987, was disclosed after the Soviet Union collapsed. It describes "packets of briefing materials" provided to him during the major summits he held with Reagan: in Geneva in November 1985 and Reykjavik in October 1986. Although it was not obvious at the time—especially after they glumly parted ways at Reykjavik, where Gorbachev and Reagan had failed to reach a breakthrough nuclear arms control agreement—the summits were milestones in bringing the Cold War to an end. We do not know what the packets of briefing materials contained. They may have been drawn from KGB human intelligence, though its other available annual reports suggest the importance of SIGINT.[3]

After the defection of Gordievsky, no Western intelligence service again had an agent inside capable of revealing Gorbachev's secret intentions. Washington, compared to Moscow, was a walk in the park for Soviet spies—often literally. The Center, meanwhile, had not one, but two, high-level agents deep inside the U.S. intelligence community. Aldrich Ames might have appeared to be "one in a million" to his KGB case officer in Washington. But within months of his recruitment, Cherkashin had another valuable source on his hands: Robert Hanssen. He was the most senior FBI agent ever to spy for a foreign power. He came from two generations of crooked cops in Chicago, according to one FBI officer who later interrogated Hanssen. Both his father and grandfather had been on the take. The apple did not fall far from the tree. But unlike them, Hanssen was entrusted with high-level

U.S. state secrets; he operated at a whole different level. He would spy for Moscow, on and off, for two decades.[4]

Hanssen trained as a dentist at Northwestern University, got an MBA, worked as an accountant, and then, in 1976, joined the FBI. Pudgy and unremarkable—"what do you expect, I've got six kids," he would tell colleagues—he found himself assigned to the FBI's Soviet counterintelligence program in New York. He later claimed that he was motivated to spy for the Soviet Union after reading Kim Philby's (misleading) autobiography, *My Silent War*. But unlike Philby, Hanssen detested Marxism-Leninism. In fact, he spied for money—lots of it. Part of his work for the FBI division in New York was to create a computer database of undercover Soviet intelligence officers. Having done so, in November 1979 he walked into the New York office of the Soviet trade organization AMTORG, the long-standing Soviet intelligence front outfit for the GRU. Hanssen offered to provide intelligence in return for cash. In his first communication, addressed to Cherkashin, he promised to deliver "certain of the most sensitive and highly compartmented projects of the U.S. Intelligence Community." Calling himself only *B*, later *Ramon Garcia*, not his true name, Hanssen was true to his word.* Among the secrets that he betrayed was information about Dmitri Polyakov, who had been spying for the United States since 1961. The KGB identified Polyakov from Ames, which Hanssen then confirmed. Polyakov was recalled to Moscow, where it seems he was used to pass disinformation to the CIA, then arrested and executed.[5]

In 1981, Hanssen stopped spying for Soviet intelligence when he was confronted by his wife, who noticed his erratic behavior and suspected he was having an affair. A good Catholic, she told him to donate his ill-gotten proceeds to Mother Teresa's Missionaries of Charity. (It is unclear whether he did so.) Four years later, however, in October 1985, Hanssen was back sinning again. This time he began spying not for the GRU but for the

---

* CIA insiders say that Hanssen chose the name *Garcia* because its end three letters, "cia," would throw the Soviets and anyone else off.

KGB. At that point in his FBI career, Hanssen had become a supervisor in the bureau's New York counterintelligence office. He was a mole among the mole hunters. Although he did not know it, he was working in parallel with Ames in the CIA. Hanssen was careful never to meet with his Soviet handlers face-to-face. Instead, he communicated with them through anonymous letters, signal sites, and dead drops. It was, and still is, unusual for an agent never to meet his or her handler. In fact, when the KGB accepted and ran Hanssen, they did not even know his true identity—only that *Ramon Garcia* was providing top U.S. secrets. They did not, apparently, even know if he was in the FBI or CIA. The KGB took a major risk with Hanssen, a "write-in," similar to the CIA's own, Goleniewski.[6]

Hanssen's espionage was devilishly brilliant, as even his FBI colleagues later admitted. He knew both sides of the East-West intelligence war inside out; CIA and FBI tradecraft when it came to Soviet intelligence, and the latter's methods against them. Hanssen artfully played both sides against each other. While he did not trust the KGB and refused their equipment, the KGB came to trust him, especially when the value of the secrets he was betraying became clear. He set the agenda for when and where he would provide information drops; over time, he offered up about twenty-seven letters and twenty-two packages, and provided six thousand pages of classified reports and twenty-seven computer disks, which contained high-grade U.S. secrets. According to a later review by the U.S. Justice Department's inspector general, Hanssen compromised the identities of dozens of human sources to Soviet intelligence, at least three of whom were executed. On one occasion, he communicated with the KGB by placing an advertisement in a newspaper about a car repair, with a phone number to call. He gave the KGB the names of three FBI agents operating in the KGB's North American *rezidentury*. Two of them, Sergei Motorin and Valeri Martynov, were recalled to Moscow, arrested, and executed, no doubt after being brutally tortured. A third FBI agent he betrayed, Boris Yuzhin, was imprisoned in Moscow, but survived and later emigrated to the United States. In return, Hanssen got $50,000 in cash.[7]

By August 1987, Hanssen had become supervisory special agent in the intelligence division's Soviet Analytical Unit at the FBI's Washington headquarters. He was responsible for strategic and operational analysis, policy and budget formulation, and counterintelligence training. In July 1991, he became program manager in the unit responsible for countering efforts by the Soviets (and particularly the KGB's Line X) to acquire U.S. scientific and technical intelligence. In short, Hanssen was right at the heart of American attempts to thwart Soviet intelligence. Cherkashin, and the others in the Washington *rezidentura* and at the Center who knew of his existence, referred to him simply as "The Source," though he was also assigned the code name KARAT. According to Cherkashin, Hanssen was like a funnel: he "saw everything that came in" on the FBI's Soviet program. Even allowing for Cherkashin's crowing recollections, Hanssen was in many ways a perfect spy: senior enough to have access to highly restricted U.S. secrets, and still junior enough to actually read them. He lacked sufficient charisma to rise to the top of the FBI, but that suited the KGB just fine. He was an invaluable bureau support agent, always hovering in the background. It was just where Soviet intelligence wanted him to be.[8]

Hanssen gave the KGB a compendium of double-agent operations, a description of secret U.S. spy satellite technology (and code words) used to intercept and decrypt Soviet satellite transmissions, and U.S. plans for continuity of government in the event of war. He also revealed the FBI's and NSA's most expensive and technologically advanced eavesdropping operations. The most breathtaking was code-named MONOPOLY, costing nearly $1 billion: it was an FBI-NSA tunnel constructed under the new Soviet embassy being built on a high hill in Washington, DC, Mount Alto. U.S. agencies assumed, with good reason, that the Soviets would use the new embassy's elevation for radio interception. Mirroring Soviet bugs in the U.S. embassy in Moscow, the FBI and NSA were using U.S. contractors to cram the tunnel with advanced eavesdropping equipment. Following in the footsteps of the Cambridge spy Anthony Blunt, who looked himself up in MI5's registry, as we saw, Hanssen would later search for his own name in the FBI's state-of-the-art searchable database, the Automated Case Support System, to see what information or suspicions the bureau had on file about him. There was nothing incriminating.[9]

Like Ames, Hanssen was a mercenary. He received diamonds, a Rolex watch, and more than $600,000 in cash over the course of his spying career. His Moscow contacts assured him that he had at least another $800,000 waiting for him in a Soviet escrow account. As with other spies, money was a means to solve a deeper wrong in his life. Hanssen was never the high-flying FBI special agent that he wanted to be. So he became an escapist, fashioning an inner life for himself that his day-to-day life lacked, besting his FBI colleagues in terms of money and adventure, even as they, in his mind, looked down on him as second-rate. He saw himself as a consummate outsider at the FBI. Unlike many at the bureau, he did not carry a firearm. He did not hit the gym, building towel-whipping camaraderie with colleagues. He lived a kind of Jekyll and Hyde existence, nondescript and dour at work but daring as a spy. Vain, and a sexual exhibitionist, Hanssen set up a closed-circuit video hookup so a friend could watch him having sex with his wife (without her permission). He used some of the money he obtained from the KGB to carry on a relationship with a Washington stripper; he bought her jewelry and a Mercedes, and bankrolled her life with an American Express card he gave her. She left him.

It is inconceivable that Viktor Chebrikov and his head of foreign intelligence, Vladimir Kryuchkov, did not inform Gorbachev about their high-level agents inside U.S. intelligence. Kryuchkov, a former protégé of Andropov, was a hard-line communist. Despite their different worldviews, Gorbachev had confidence in Kryuchkov—a confidence that he would later bitterly regret. One measure of the importance that Gorbachev attached to KGB foreign intelligence was that Kryuchkov accompanied Gorbachev on his historic visit to Washington in December 1987, where he and Reagan signed the Intermediate-Range Nuclear Forces treaty (INF). It was the first arms control agreement to reduce East-West nuclear arsenals between the superpowers. It was also the first time a KGB foreign intelligence head had accompanied a Soviet leader on a visit to the West. During the trip, Kryuchkov had a hushed dinner with CIA deputy director Robert Gates at an upscale Washington French restaurant, Maison Blanche, appropriately near the White House. As Gates later wrote:

> Looking back, it is embarrassing to realize that, at this first high-level CIA-KGB meeting, Kryuchkov smugly knew that he had a spy— Aldrich Ames—at the heart of CIA, that he knew quite well what we were saying to the President and others about the Soviet Union, and that he was aware of many of our human and technical collection efforts in the USSR.[10]

As Gorbachev negotiated with Reagan and his successor in the Oval Office, George H. W. Bush, there were echoes of Stalin's tactics at Yalta: espionage kept Gorbachev more aware of the inner workings of the U.S. government than it was of him. He had enough confidence in Kryuchkov that he appointed him KGB chairman in 1988—the first foreign intelligence (FCD) leader ever to become head of the KGB. Kryuchkov again accompanied Gorbachev to Washington in 1989. That September he was made a member of the Politburo. But just under two years later, Kryuchkov would lead a coup against Gorbachev.[11]

SOVIET ACTIVE MEASURES

KGB active measures, like their Western counterparts, covert action, involved a spectrum of political warfare. They ranged from propaganda at one end, to influence and bribery operations somewhere in the middle, to kinetic activities, including kidnappings and assassinations at the other end. They were the alpha and omega of the KGB's work, the clandestine corollary to Soviet diplomacy, no less important, but unavowed. One active measure, in the middle of that spectrum of dirty tricks, was disinformation (*dezinformatsiya*): perpetrating false or misleading information where the hand of its author is hidden. Usually that would require the involvement of an intelligence service. A 1972 top secret Soviet dictionary defined "disinformation" produced by the KGB as "especially prepared data, used for the creation, in the mind of the enemy, of incorrect or imaginary pictures of reality, on the basis of which the enemy would make decisions beneficial" to the Soviet Union. "*Deza*" included documentary fraud, literary hoaxes, and broadcasting false information, as well as acts of sabotage for psychological effect. Soviet active measures involved the equivalent of putting a boulder on a road and then publicly taking credit for its removal.[12]

The purpose of Soviet *dezinformatsiya* against the United States was to discredit its government, delegitimize its institutions, disorient or polarize its society, and cast doubt on the true account of events. It aimed to undermine the U.S. government's effective functioning as a democracy, as well as discrediting Western alliances like NATO. In the Kremlin's strategic conception, the Cold War was a zero-sum game; if the United States and its allies were weakened, the Soviet Union was strengthened. To disseminate disinformation, the KGB used a constellation of Soviet front groups in Western countries, many purportedly "peace" organizations, like the World Peace Council (WPC). They were forgery factories. U.S. intelligence identified about a dozen in May 1988, the largest of which was the WPC. When exposed as a fraud, the World Peace Council admitted that it obtained 90 percent of its income from the Soviet Union. In conceiving and disseminating disinformation, the KGB's methodology was not to create a false story out of nothing, but instead to amplify existing grievances in Western societies. Exploiting U.S. race relations, for example, was stock-in-trade for the KGB during the Cold War. The wounds that Soviet intelligence exploited in the United States were American-made, not foreign.[13]

The KGB foreign intelligence department responsible for conducting active measures was Service A ("A" for active measures). When Yuri Andropov became Soviet leader, Service A was staffed with approximately eighty officers at the FCD's headquarters, in Yasenevo, the "house in the birch woods" (equipped with medical and sports facilities, cinemas, and conference rooms). But the officers in Service A were only part of the KGB's overall resources devoted to active measures. In April 1982, as one of his last acts as KGB chairman before becoming Soviet leader, Andropov decreed that it was the duty of all Soviet foreign intelligence officers, whatever their "line," or department, to participate in active measures like disinformation.

The FCD as a whole, which had approximately fifteen thousand officers in the 1980s, thus became a delivery platform for active measures. Service A was given access to FCD files, agents, and operations. As a result, we can confidently say that about fifteen thousand KGB officials were working on disinformation in the 1980s. But it did not stop there. Added to this number was the Soviet Communist Party's International Department, the Central Committee's Propaganda Department, and Soviet state media outlets like TASS, which all helped to undertake active measures. The KGB considered their purpose as defensive, protecting the Soviet government from Western—principally U.S.—information warfare to split up the Soviet Union. In 1980, U.S. intelligence conservatively estimated that the Soviet Union had an annual budget of approximately $3 billion for active measures. By contrast, the body established under Reagan in the U.S. to counter Soviet disinformation, the Active Measures Working Group (AMWG), had approximately twenty officials drawn from other U.S. government departments. The CIA's overall budget in 1980 was around $2.2 billion (approximately $80 billion in today's values), while its entire covert action budget was in the tens of millions. It was like fighting a swarm of bees with a flyswatter, according to one U.S. official.[14]

The Reagan administration knew it was in the crosshairs of Soviet active measures. The obvious question was whether those measures posed a genuine national security threat. In 1985, the first year into Reagan's second term, the head of CIA analysis, Robert Gates, was called to the Senate Committee on Foreign Relations to testify openly about exactly that. His conclusion: generally, Soviet active measures did not pose a strategic threat to the United States, but were instead more of a tactical nuisance. He added, however, an important caveat, with ominous repercussions. Gates stated that "in a close election or legislative battle, they could spell the difference." The person asking Gates most of the questions about active measures was the junior senator from Delaware, Joe Biden.[15]

PANDEMIC DISINFORMATION

The most reckless and dangerous disinformation operation perpetrated by the KGB and its satellite service in East Germany, the Stasi, involved a novel disease first detected in the United States in 1981, which then spread into a pandemic: the AIDS virus. The outbreak offered the KGB an unprecedented opportunity to amplify a long-standing trope of its disinformation: a conspiracy theory that the U.S. government was secretly running an illegal bioweapons program. Service A laid the groundwork for the operation, code-named DENVER but also known as INFEKTION, in July 1983, when it manufactured a front-page article in the Indian periodical the *Patriot* titled: "AIDS May Invade India: Mystery Disease Caused by U.S. Experiments." The story was a letter from an anonymous source, described as a "well-known American scientist and anthropologist," stating that AIDS was a bioweapon created by the Pentagon. "Now that these menacing experiments seem to have gone out of control," the letter went on, "plans are being hatched to hastily transfer them from the U.S. to other countries, primarily developing nations where governments are pliable to Washington's pressures and persuasion." In reality, Service A wrote the letter and planted it in the newspaper. The *Patriot*, as we have seen, was itself a Soviet front.[16]

Eighteen months later, as the AIDS pandemic grew, the mainstream Soviet press picked up the *Patriot*'s story, reporting it as fact. Within the Center, the recycling and repackaging of disinformation was known as an "echo effect." As a U.S. official and expert on Soviet disinformation later stated, it was like a pinball game: "a fake story ran in country A and then was picked up as a legitimate story in country B and C." Service A organized pseudoscientific support for the story by recruiting a retired Russian-born East German biophysicist, Jacob Segal, described as a French researcher. He produced a fifty-two-page booklet claiming that the U.S. military created AIDS by experimenting on prisoners at a top secret U.S. military facility at Fort Detrick, artificially synthesizing two natural viruses, VISNA and HTLV-1:

> It is very easy using genetic technologies to unite two parts of completely independent viruses . . . but who would be interested in doing this? The military, of course. . . . How it occurred precisely at this moment and how the virus managed to get out of the secret, hush-hush laboratory is quite easy to understand. Everyone knows that prisoners are used for military experiments in the U.S. They are promised their freedom if they come out of the experiment alive.[17]

The KGB's conspiracy theory fed on existing distrust, particularly in African American communities, about public health officials. In the "Tuskegee Study of Untreated Syphilis in the Negro Male," conducted in 1932 and exposed by the Associated Press in 1972, the Public Health Service had experimented on six hundred men, recruited on the promise of free medical care, to find a cure for syphilis. The KGB's AIDS-virus disinformation exploited these fears, highlighting the prevalence of AIDS—"made in the USA"—in Africa. In mid-1986, the "Segal Report" took off, becoming what we can legitimately call fake news in Third World countries, particularly those in Africa, where similar "proof" appeared in letters to newspapers— actually Service A products, disseminated by other Soviet front groups. The conspiracy theory was more successful than Service A officers could have dreamed. In October 1986, the conservative-leaning British *Sunday Express* tabloid made the KGB narrative its front-page story. After that, it was picked up by an international newswire. By 1987, the story received coverage in major media outlets in eighty countries and in thirty languages.[18]

The U.S. intelligence community was eventually able to expose the KGB's AIDS-pandemic disinformation. As interviews for this book reveal, the U.S. intelligence community detected the Soviet conspiracy story through the CIA's Foreign Broadcast Information Service, responsible for monitoring Soviet media outlets. Its work is a testament to the value of open-source intelligence collection. It identified the wave of stories about AIDS being spread by the KGB. The U.S. government countered the conspiracy theory through the interdepartmental Active Measures Working Group. In the spring of 1987, the group published a report about AIDS disinformation and publicly attributed it to the Kremlin. According to Lawrence Eagleburger, a key supporter of the AMWG, the best way of countering active measures was through public exposure: "They are infections that thrive only in darkness, and sunlight is the best antiseptic."[19]

In October 1987, George Shultz had what he later described as a "sour and aggressive" meeting with Mikhail Gorbachev. The Soviet leader produced the AMWG report about AIDS and angrily said that it went against the spirit of glasnost. The secretary of state replied that when the Soviet Union stopped spreading lies, Washington would stop exposing them. Two months later, during a summit meeting in Washington, the Soviet leader pulled aside another AMWG official, Charles Wick, and told him: "No more lying. No more disinformation; I don't want politicians and bureaucrats creating all of these tensions anymore, disinformation and all that. It's going to be a new day."[20]

The Reagan administration accompanied its face-to-face confrontations about Soviet disinformation with a threat of sanctions, informing the Kremlin that U.S.-Soviet AIDS research collaboration, which Soviet scientists needed for their country's own AIDS epidemic, would be closed down unless the disinformation stopped. The Soviet stories disappeared practically overnight. It was like a faucet turning off, said one U.S. official involved with the AMWG, Herbert Romerstein. Soon after, facing public outcry from scientists across the world, the Kremlin officially disowned the AIDS story.[21]

Although the U.S. government ultimately exposed Soviet AIDS disinformation, the damage to public health was already done. Soviet lies during a public health crisis had a corrosive effect on public understanding about the causal links between HIV and AIDS. If AIDS was man-made, then it was not related to HIV, ran the argument. Despite efforts by U.S. medical experts to debunk the Soviet AIDS conspiracy theory, it continued to infect public thinking long after Moscow disowned it. In 2005, polling showed that 50 percent of African Americans still believed that AIDS was a man-made virus. That claim featured in a 2005 Kanye West hit song, perhaps unsurprising given "Ye"'s more recent airing of conspiracy theories. HIV-AIDS denialism had damaging consequences in African countries as well. In South Africa, President Thabo Mbeki denied a causal link between HIV and AIDS. By the time he left office in 2008, almost 330,000 preventable HIV deaths had occurred in his country. HIV-AIDS denialism may have also contributed to Russia's own AIDS epidemic. After the Soviet Union's collapse, Yevgeny Primakov, the first head of Russia's new foreign intelligence service, the SVR, admitted that the AIDS story had been a Service A fabrication. It was also, we now know, supported by the East German Stasi.[22]

NUCLEAR DISINFORMATION

On April 26, 1986, reactor number four at the Soviet nuclear power plant of Chernobyl, near the town of Pripyat, in Ukraine, suffered a catastrophic meltdown. Twenty-eight members of the power plant's staff died of acute radiation sickness soon afterward, though the actual total number of fatalities remains difficult to establish. A poisonous cloud blew from Ukraine toward Europe. Along with the radiation also came a cloud of Soviet disinformation. The 2019 HBO series *Chernobyl* showed in chilling detail how Soviet authorities covered up the leak. But that was not half of it, as we can now see from previously secret Ukrainian records.[23]

Immediately after the Chernobyl disaster, the Kremlin used its intelligence services, and state-run media outlets, to manufacture alternative facts to protect the regime's reputation and cast doubt on the disaster's cause and fatalities. Chernobyl threatened to strike at the heart of the Soviet government's legitimacy. According to a secret report on the accident by Britain's ambassador in Moscow, Bryan Cartledge, unsealed in 2018, as late as May 6, ten days after the Chernobyl disaster, the Soviet government was still not forthcoming about fundamental facts like "what actually happened at the plant," radiation levels in the area, or whether the fire at the reactor was in fact extinguished.

Soviet efforts to conceal knew no bounds. In one instance, KGB officials broke into a hotel room where French journalists were staying, stole radiated soil samples they had taken from the radioactive disaster zone, and swapped them for noncontaminated samples. In another, the KGB targeted *Newsweek*'s Moscow correspondent, Steven Strasser, who travelled to Kiev in June 1986. According to Ukrainian records, the KGB sent eight officers and nineteen members of the local volunteer brigade to look "into [Strasser's] actions" and prevent his "collection of slanderous information." In an interview for this book, when presented with these intelligence reports on him, Strasser said that information in the KGB dossier correctly identified his sources, but the KGB's efforts were not as clandestine or sophisticated as the files suggest: a phalanx of "KGB goons" surrounded him as he tried to interview people on Kyiv's streets. The KGB's active measures against Strasser were coordinated by a female agent, code-named ROTA (meaning "squadron"), probably his official minder from the Soviet Intourist (foreign tourists) agency. It was an open secret that Intourist housed intelligence officers and agents. The KGB was unsuccessful in manipulating Strasser's reporting, though it did prevent him from talking with useful people. It shows the lengths that a one-party state will go to in order to protect its reputation from Western investigative journalists.[24]

In another instance, to confuse U.S. press reporting about Chernobyl, the KGB planted a fabricated document to smear a U.S. official, Herbert Romerstein, who was trying to expose Soviet disinformation. The Soviets were thus producing disinformation about disinformation, a world where up was down. The KGB's efforts backfired; Romerstein was able to expose its forgery, and held a press conference revealing *Soviet* attempts to concoct lies after Chernobyl. Soviet intelligence nevertheless continued. It accompanied these specific active measures with broader alternative narratives to the disaster. Through a constellation of Soviet-supported "peace" groups in Western countries, the KGB promulgated the message that Chernobyl could happen anywhere. In the Kremlin's narrative, Chernobyl was the inevitable result of nuclear power anyplace. Soviet state media pointed to the partial meltdown of the Three Mile Island nuclear reactor in Pennsylvania in March 1979. Chernobyl, in Moscow's narrative, was not the result of Soviet negligence. Soviet intelligence propagated their message through agents and "useful idiots"—as the KGB called witting and unwitting people acting as mouthpieces—in Western countries in groups like the Campaign for Nuclear Disarmament. Moscow's alternative narrative for Chernobyl had some success. With the KGB's help, Chernobyl became a byword in Western countries for problems in the nuclear power industry generally, rather than its real cause: Soviet mismanagement.[25]

Distraction and deceit could only go so far, however. Chernobyl gutted the Soviet regime's reputation on the world stage. Gorbachev later described it as the single greatest cause of the Soviet collapse five years later. When the British diplomat Rodric Braithwaite visited Moscow in 1987, a year after the meltdown, people on the streets openly talked about the fact that the Soviet experiment had failed. Chernobyl convinced Gorbachev that something had to be done to break the deadlock about nuclear arms reductions with the United States.[26]

SOVIET DECLINE AND FALL

Two ostensibly simple questions that scholars still grapple with are: When did the Cold War end—at least this chapter of it? And who was responsible? Three decades after the succession of events in Eastern Europe that swept away the Soviet bloc in 1989, and led to the disintegration of the Soviet

Union two years later, historians are still divided on the answers to those two questions. That should not be surprising, given that fifteen hundred years later we still debate the decline and fall of the Roman Empire. Some see the revolutions of 1989 in Eastern Europe and the subsequent Soviet collapse as products of the relentless pressure applied by Ronald Reagan. In the face of it, the Soviet regime buckled. America won the Cold War. Others see the Soviet Union collapsing under its own weight, like a knight dying in his own armor, to use John le Carré's metaphor.

The Soviet Union was bankrupt and indebted to the West. Its satellite countries in Eastern Europe, effectively an empire in all but name, were draining Moscow's finances to the tune of between $5 billion and $10 billion a year. Then there was its "forward" policy—vast financial and military-aid subsidies to countries in Africa, Asia, and Latin America. Like other empires, it suffered dearly from overreach. But this does not mean that the Soviet Union's unwinding and downfall between 1989 and 1991 were inevitable. History is rarely, if ever, monocausal. Major world events are cumulative, even when a spark apparently ignites them.[27]

Reagan did place insufferable pressure on the Soviet Union, symbolized by his SDI strategy. But if we have to choose which actor in the final stages of the East-West superpower showdown did most to end the Cold War, it would have to be Gorbachev. His reforms de-escalated the East-West arms race. In February 1987, in the face of Reagan's intransigence in reducing or delaying SDI, Gorbachev bravely agreed to a treaty on intermediate-range nuclear forces without having it tied to other disarmament issues. In doing so, he blew apart decades of Cold War thinking—that gains for one side were losses for the other. When Reagan visited Moscow at the end of May 1988 and was asked if he still believed that the Soviet Union was an evil empire, the president replied that that remark was from a different era.

The Cold War effectively ended with Gorbachev's dramatic speech to the UN in December 1988. He announced that over the next two years, Soviet forces would be reduced by five hundred thousand, six of its armored divisions would be disbanded, and Moscow would no longer use force in Eastern

Europe or elsewhere. The Brezhnev doctrine, which had shored up the Eastern bloc by force, was dead. In the spring of 1989, former national security adviser Zbigniew Brzezinski heralded the dawn of the "post-Communist era." In April 1989, during a state visit to Cuba, Gorbachev declared—to the disgust of his host, Castro—that Moscow was renouncing its traditional policy of exporting socialism in favor of nonintervention.[28]

Gorbachev's early memories were of Stalin's Great Terror. Khrushchev's denunciation of Stalin in 1956, at the Twentieth Party Congress, had a profound effect on him. Like others, he hoped it would lead to "socialism with a human face." He found no such humanity, however, when he visited the Czech Republic soon after the 1968 Prague Spring. He rose up the party ranks in Stavropol, in southwest Russia, and later became a member of the Central Committee, and then the Politburo. Gorbachev's window to the outside world further opened as he read intelligence reports and books banned for most Soviet citizens. He was permitted to travel to Europe. The specter of nuclear war with the West terrified him—just as it did Reagan. Gorbachev came to believe that only by cooperating with the outside world could the Soviet Union stamp out the isolationism that had blighted it.[29]

Fundamentally, though, Gorbachev remained a believer in the Soviet Union. He wanted to reform and reinvent it, adapt its structures and incorporate liberalizing reforms from the West—not wreck and replace it. His task was unprecedented, peacefully reforming an authoritarian state in deep crisis, while negotiating with a superpower rival that held many of the cards. His reforms failed, we can now see, but he made possible what was previously unimaginable and made it ultimately seem inevitable: allowing countries in Eastern Europe to become independent and non-communist.

But the monumental reforms he instigated to eliminate the Stalinist legacy and create a prosperous Soviet state, a socialist democracy, led to the Soviet Union's unwinding and collapse. With hindsight we can see Gorbachev as a Shakespearean tragic hero, trying to change his regime but stuck in circumstances beyond his control. The author of massive Soviet reforms, he was also the architect of the Soviet Union's demise. The changes in the Soviet Union that Gorbachev instigated snowballed into a revolution driven from below, rather than one controlled from above. In trying to repair communism, he punched a hole in it. And, as with a dam holding back a vast body of water, pressure on the hole began to widen and then tore the entire structure apart.

The causes of the Soviet collapse were both external pressure and problems intrinsic to the Soviet government—the decline of communist ideology, economic failure, and running out of steam. In the postwar years, communists were seen by many as the brave resistance front against fascism in Europe, and people believed that Soviet communism was the wave of the political future. But that ideological faith had all but died out by the time Gorbachev came to power. The exposure of Stalin's genocide, the Soviet Union's brutal repression in Hungary in 1956, in Czechoslovakia in 1968, and in Poland in 1981, produced a fatal crisis of faith for all but the truest believers.

Travelers to the Soviet Union did not have to look far to find poverty and corruption. Living standards in the Soviet Union were equal to those of the poorest country in Western Europe, and in Soviet Russia itself, the situation was even worse. It was a country where things like oranges or bananas were exotic rarities. Stalin had created a command economy that emphasized heavy manufacturing and smokestack industries, making it inflexible. Inefficiency was the norm. The giant steel plant at Magnitogorsk employed sixty thousand workers and produced sixteen million tons of steel annually. A steel plant at Gary, Indiana, produced eight million tons while only employing seven thousand workers. As George Shultz told Gorbachev in 1987, they were living in the information age, and if the Soviet Union wanted to prosper, it had to be a part of it. That year, the United States counted some thirty million personal computers, for the most part the latest and most powerful models, while in the Soviet Union there were only fifty thousand, and most were of poor quality. The Soviet Union was the only developed country where health care was deteriorating and mortality increasing. Outside Moscow, the poverty of Russia was painfully apparent: villages had no running water, sidewalks were still constructed of wood. The Soviet Union may have been a nuclear superpower, but by other standards it was a Potemkin one.[30]

Contrary to conventional wisdom, the CIA did see the Soviet collapse coming. As early as 1985, CIA analysts were telling the president that the Soviet system could not survive. Gorbachev's attempts to reform an unreformable system, combined with accelerating economic decline, threatened the demise of the Soviet Union itself. According to Robert Gates, in the summer of 1989 the CIA created a tightly held contingency group planning for the Soviet Union's collapse—nearly two and a half years before it transpired. Neither U.S. nor British intelligence, however, predicted the chain of events that would lead to the unravelling of the Eastern bloc and the Soviet Union itself. Nobody knew that the events unleashed in 1989, with people in the streets and at the polling stations, would lead so quickly to the Soviet Union ceasing to exist. The heads of U.S. and British intelligence were watching events play out on CNN like everyone else. The history of the rise and fall of great powers, after all, did not suggest that such things happened so quickly. In January 1989, a NATO winter exercise (Wintex) envisioned scenarios that included economic crisis in the Soviet Union, a Stalinist coup against Gorbachev, mobilization across the Eastern bloc, and limited nuclear war in Germany. Those participating were so alarmed that the war game, scheduled for eight days, ended after just six. The nightmare was all too realistic. Germany, West and East, was the site of the highest concentration of nuclear arms anywhere in the world.[31]

We should not be too surprised that events in Berlin caught Western intelligence agencies off guard. As the historian Mary Sarotte has shown, the opening of the Berlin Wall in November 1989 was largely accidental, driven by ordinary Germans, not grand design. The East German government was on the verge of bankruptcy, in need of further loans from West Germany. To secure them, the government was willing to allow more East Germans to emigrate. In the first nine months of the year, two hundred thousand East Germans did so. But it was not clear at the time what the overnight easing of restrictions from East to West would mean. Forty thousand East Berliners burst through the wall on November 15. In hindsight, we can see that the East German border guards at Bornholmer Strasse, who opened the gates of the wall, set off a chain reaction. Eastern Europeans liberated themselves. But for contemporaries at the time, the opening of the Berlin Wall did not seem to indicate that Germany would be reunified, let alone that the Soviet Union would collapse. One CIA officer interviewed for this book, Paul Kolbe, was in training for an assignment to East Germany when the wall fell. At the time, it did not seem like the wall's opening would significantly change the CIA's mission for the Soviet Union itself. Only with hindsight is it clear that the German reunification in October 1990 started a succession of events that would sweep away the entire Soviet bloc. Europe was on the move. Gorbachev was powerless to stop Germany's reunification. With shelves empty of goods in major Soviet cities, he needed financial loans from Helmut Kohl's West German government.[32]

With German reunification, NATO's borders moved east across the Cold War's decades-old front line. As Germany moved from a confederation to unification, the CIA's mission was now to knock on the doors of former Stasi officers to get their information about Soviet intelligence and the former East German regime. The information they obtained was chilling. They discovered that the Stasi, and its foreign intelligence wing, the HVA, had been devastatingly efficient. Before the fall of the wall, the CIA had discovered, presumably from a source—those interviewed for this book would not be drawn—that none of its agents previously run against East German targets were genuine spies: every single one had been controlled by the Stasi. East Germany was a colossal U.S intelligence failure. What the CIA did not know until its officers pounded on doors in East Germany was the Stasi-HVA's reach into NATO. The alliance was thoroughly penetrated.

U.S. and British intelligence raced to keep up with fast-moving events.[33] They provided decision makers with running assessments about future possibilities as history unfolded before them: the opening of the Berlin Wall in 1989; the execution of the Romanian dictator, Nicolae Ceaușescu, who was shot (after a trial lasting less than two minutes) in a hail of bullets along with his wife, Elena, against a wall on Christmas Day 1989 as he sang the Communist "Internationale"; jubilant crowds four days later celebrating the former dissident playwright Václav Havel, previously imprisoned by the Czech StB, becoming president of the Czechoslovakian parliament; the reunification of Germany in 1990; and the failed coup against Gorbachev in August 1991.

Fortunately, the United States had a chief executive during these epic geopolitical events who was an experienced intelligence professional—the only former DCI ever to become president—George H. W. Bush. When Bush reached the Oval Office, he knew more about U.S. intelligence than any previous incoming president: how it worked, what was reasonable to expect, and what questions to ask. Bush usually met CIA briefing staff, frequently headed by DCI William Webster, at 8:00 a.m. each day. His foreign policy objective was to continue pressuring the Soviet Union without pushing so hard that he weakened Gorbachev's position and exposed him to hard-liners. As one of Bush's advisers described, the president was afraid to light a match in a gas-filled room. Bush aimed to facilitate a soft landing for the Soviet Union, on terms that were favorable to the West. As Bush later wrote, he did not want events to turn violent. Thatcher cautioned Bush that the Warsaw Pact should remain intact, as a fig leaf for Gorbachev, amid the humiliation of Soviet collapse. Intelligence was more important than ever. Without accurate reports, Bush had no way of knowing whether Gorbachev's arms reduction promises were genuine or what Gorbachev was likely to do in the face of nationalist protests in the Eastern bloc.

Gorbachev used intelligence similarly. His new head of foreign intelligence at the KGB was Leonid Shebarshin, the old India hand. Shebarshin later claimed that his principal initial task was to "ensure the West did not cheat on arms control." Both sides acknowledged each other's need for SIGINT and IMINT verification of arms reduction—trust, but verify: "*doveryai, no proveryai*," as Reagan liked to say. In East Berlin, the CIA placed radiation sensors in boxes next to railways to monitor the movement of Soviet nuclear weapons back home to Russia from East Germany, in compliance with treaty obligations.

CIA assessments of the epic events leading to the Soviet Union's demise, which reached the desks of Bush's national security team and James Baker, the secretary of state, included a cascade of alternative futures for Poland, Hungary, East Germany, Czechoslovakia, and the Baltic states. Most never happened. As Bush's national security adviser, Brent Scowcroft, said, "history, sadly, does not reveal its alternatives." Hindsight always blinds us with a light not apparent to those at the time: the past becomes tautology, what happened was bound to happen because it did. Decision makers at the time when the Soviet Union went into terminal decline, however, were living their history without the foreknowledge about events that now seems so obvious to us. A U.S. National Intelligence Estimate in April 1989, for example, concluded that the Soviet Union would remain the West's principal adversary for the foreseeable future. In fact, the hard-line coup against Gorbachev would come in just over two years.[34]

The KGB was better placed than other parts of the Soviet government to warn about the threat of nationalism to the Soviet system. But its analytic capabilities were sclerotic. Right up to the end, its purpose was to collect and send intelligence, not analyze or challenge views. When the Soviet Union eventually collapsed, the KGB had fewer than a dozen analysts in its ranks. The CIA had about two thousand.

The KGB's senior leadership saw Soviet economic ruin not as a failure of the Soviet system itself, but arising from a foreign hidden hand, a master plot perpetrated by the United States. The head of analysis, Nikolai Leonov, whom we met in Latin America, warned Gorbachev that the United States was a vulture swooping over the motherland, plotting to "incite our people to hate each other" and "pour oil on the flames of our internal discontent." When Gorbachev did not listen, Leonov took his "warnings" public, comparing Gorbachev's refusal to listen to Stalin's failure to heed intelligence about Nazi Germany half a century before. Similar conspiracies emerged from other members of the KGB old guard. The deputy chairman of the KGB, Viktor Grushko, attributed Soviet financial problems to a plot by Western banks. The prime conspiracy theorist, however, was the KGB chairman Kryuchkov, who blamed some of the appalling failures of Soviet grain storage on a (nonexistent) CIA plot to infect grain supplies. Reading a "classified" CIA report in public, he claimed the agency was recruiting agents in an elaborate plot to sabotage the Soviet government, the economy, and scientific research.[35]

Forty years of intelligence assessments about the Soviet Union had made CIA assessments of Gorbachev's reforms brittle and cynical. Evidence suggests that British JIC assessments were similarly jaundiced, though they have not yet been declassified. Fierce debates emerged in the CIA about whether Gorbachev's proposed arms reductions were in good faith, and his reforms genuine, or whether they were masking another agenda, like rearming; whether the elections in 1989 in the Soviet Union really would be free, as they largely turned out to be—the first in Russia since 1917, and the first in Eastern Europe since 1948—and whether or not Gorbachev's reforms really had changed basic elements of Soviet defense policy. Under Gorbachev, some billboards in Moscow proclaimed that the aim of perestroika was to *strengthen* military preparedness. A year after Gorbachev had become general secretary, the Politburo was still sending supplies to seventy thousand Sandinistas in Nicaragua.[36]

What was surprising then, and remains so today, is that Gorbachev did not send in the Red Army to suppress peaceful protests and shore up the Soviet bloc. Each of his seven Kremlin predecessors would have done so in the face of nationalist movements, and the Eastern bloc countries falling like dominoes. In January 1991, Gorbachev allowed the KGB and the Red Army to send in troops to Lithuania. They killed fourteen protesters in Vilnius. But this was an exception. Instead, Gorbachev sent his close adviser, Alexander Yakovlev, to the capitals of the disintegrating socialist commonwealth, to inform the governments that "our troops will not be used even though they are here. They will remain in their barracks and not go anywhere in any circumstances." Gorbachev chose not to crack down violently on pro-democracy protests, as the Chinese government had nineteen months earlier in Tiananmen Square.[37]

Gorbachev's popularity in Europe exceeded that of any twentieth-century

Western leader. Before his arrival in Washington in May 1990, Gorbachev had a 73 percent approval rating among polled Americans—higher than almost any U.S. president. He found himself more appreciated in Western capitals than in Moscow. In July 1991, he flew to London, where he was the first (and last) Soviet leader invited to a meeting of the leaders of G-7 (although he failed to gain a Marshall Plan type of aid package there for the Soviet Union, as he had hoped to do). He was cheered at Covent Garden Opera House, fêted at a Downing Street reception by Prime Minister John Major.[38]

Bush later stated that the "prime factor" in his foreign policy was signals intelligence. Most of the SIGINT provided to Bush, in his President's Daily Brief and other reports, remains classified. But we do know details. On August 17, 1991, Bush was informed about a communist hard-line coup against the Soviet leader whom Bush had banked so much on. Intelligence about the plot was derived from the NSA's monitoring of communications between the coup plotters in Moscow and military command posts around the country. They acted while Gorbachev was on holiday in Sochi, three weeks after he and Bush signed the START treaty, which cut strategic nuclear arsenals by roughly 30 percent and brought Cold War tensions visibly to an end. The previous month, with his steely gaze, Kryuchkov had begged Gorbachev to declare a state of emergency to stabilize the disintegrating political situation. Western governments were preparing to launch a coup against Gorbachev, his intelligence reports told the Soviet leader. At the Politburo, Kryuchkov denounced Gorbachev for losing the Eastern bloc countries, and now the Soviet Union itself. He was not taking seriously "intelligence" about a U.S. master plan to sabotage the administration and the economy, claimed the KGB chief. According to a later defector, as the Soviet Union was unwinding, Kryuchkov spirited billions of dollars from the Soviet Communist Party to unknown destinations overseas.

Gorbachev was attempting to preserve the Soviet Union on a voluntary basis, through a union treaty that was due to be signed on August 20. When Kryuchkov's pleas failed, he and other plotters took action on their own.

They met at OBJECT ABC, a KGB sanatorium, where they constituted themselves as an emergency committee, conjuring up connections to the original Cheka. Their stated aim was to "stabilize" the Soviet Union, effectively turning back the clock. Kryuchkov, along with defense and interior ministers Dmitri Yazov and Boris Pugo (formerly head of Latvian KGB), formed a powerful troika; they held the offices of previous kingmakers in Soviet history. The KGB had been instrumental in the ousting of Khrushchev in 1964. One of the military leaders involved in the 1991 coup was Sergei Surovikin, a hard-right Russian nationalist. Three decades later, from October 2022 to January 2023, Surovikin, known as the "Butcher of Syria" after Russia's savage war there, would be in charge of Putin's "special military operation" in Ukraine.

The attempted coup in August 1991 was effectively the last KGB active measure of the Cold War. This time, it was directed not against the Main Adversary but the Soviet Union's own secretary-general. Kryuchkov ordered Gorbachev to be placed under close surveillance, "for health reasons," and detained under house arrest in Crimea. The plotters were men "who have learned nothing and forgotten nothing," as one British official in Moscow noted. They drew up a list of 7,000 reformers to be detained. They ordered 300,000 arrest forms to be printed and requisitioned 250,000 pairs of handcuffs. Two floors of cells in the "shooting prison," Lefortovo, in eastern Moscow, were emptied to make room for important political prisoners. A secret bunker in the Lubyanka was created in case the coup escalated into violence.[39]

At the CIA, the head of the Office of Soviet Analysis, George Kolt, and the chairman of the National Intelligence Council, Fritz Ermarth, scoured the latest intelligence, especially from satellite and SIGINT, to understand the coup and its chances of succeeding. It became abundantly clear that the plotters were an ill-prepared, drunken, motley crew. When Bush was informed of the coup, he made a bold decision to pass the SIGINT, in disguised form, to Russia's recently elected president, Boris Yeltsin. Bush supported Gorbachev over his bearish and mercurial political rival, Yeltsin, the former Moscow party chief who had been sacked by Gorbachev for demanding too-radical reforms. In June 1990, Yeltsin had resigned from the Communist Party, dramatically walking out of the Twenty-Eighth Congress. A year later, he was elected president by the Russian people, becoming the first democratically appointed leader in Russian history. Unlike Gorbachev, who was elected by the Supreme Soviet, Yeltsin could style himself as a true Russian populist. Despite Bush's fondness for Gorbachev, he knew there was too much at stake not to warn Yeltsin about the coup. A U.S. intelligence official in Moscow was responsible for carrying the message to Yeltsin, and a communications expert was assigned to help make his calls with military leaders secure. Yeltsin helped to stop the coup, rallying a crowd of about fifty thousand people around the Russian parliament building in Moscow, standing on top of a tank, with Russia's white, blue, and red flag fluttering in the wind. What the coup plotters failed to realize was that in Moscow, unlike Beijing, it was too late to turn back the clock. "If the coup d'état had happened a year and a half or two years earlier," wrote Gorbachev afterward, "it might, presumably, have succeeded. But now society was completely changed." The coup crumbled farcically after four days. Pugo blew his brains out. Kryuchkov wrote a groveling letter to Gorbachev, asking for the putschists to be given lesser charges, and sentences like house arrest. Yeltsin became a hero after the coup.[40]

The KGB was no longer able to intimidate people. Large crowds, which a few years earlier would never have dared to assemble, gathered outside the headquarters of the Russian president to protect Yeltsin from attack. They later encircled the KGB's headquarters, the Lubyanka, cheering as a giant statue of Felix Dzerzhinsky, the Cheka's founder, was toppled from its plinth and trampled underfoot. A huge crane supplied by the Moscow City government carried the statue away, suspended by a noose, to a field near the New Tretyakov gallery, which quickly became a graveyard for statues of the fallen Soviet regime. Inside the Lubyanka, from the fifth floor, the head of KGB foreign intelligence looked out as "Iron Felix," the symbol of Soviet rule since 1926, was towed away. Leonid Shebarshin went home, realizing that the regime he had devoted his life to was falling around him. Protesters defaced the Lubyanka with graffiti: "Fuck this KGB"; a swastika was painted on its wall.

In Britain's embassy in Moscow, its ambassador, Rodric Braithwaite, cabled back to London: "The Soviet Union which had been stuck half way in the transition from totalitarianism to democracy may now be on the move again on the lines of the East European scenario of 1989." He was exactly correct.[41]

The August 1991 coup achieved the opposite of what the plotters wanted: far from stabilizing the Soviet regime, it accelerated both the collapse of the communist one-party state and the disintegration of the Soviet Union, which ceased to exist by the end of the year. In December, Yeltsin and the leaders of Ukraine and Belarus, Leonid Kravchuk and Stanislav Shushkevich respectively, secretly met in a forest hunting lodge in Western Belarus, choosing that remote spot to make an escape over the Polish border in case the KGB appeared, as they feared, to arrest them on Gorbachev's instructions. They agreed to create a Commonwealth of Independent States, which would effectively dismantle the Soviet Union. On December 1, 1991, Ukrainians, who had been central from the start of the bloody story of the pseudo-federal Soviet Union, as we have seen, voted 90 percent in a referendum to leave the Soviet Union. Within a week, the Soviet Union fell apart. On Christmas Day, power passed from Gorbachev, who was left without a job, to Yeltsin as president of Russia. At a ceremony to sign away the Soviet Union, Gorbachev's pen had no ink. He had to borrow one from a CNN reporter. The fifteen Soviet republics became independent countries. Watching the scenes on television in Cambridge, England, Oleg Gordievsky, MI6's former spy in the KGB, sat with his coauthor, the historian Christopher Andrew, as the hammer-and-sickle flag was lowered on the Kremlin for the last time and the Russian flag raised. For Gordievsky, it was a moment of celebration; it was what he had aimed the best part of his life toward, the dismantling of the Soviet Union and the end of the Cold War. In Langley, the CIA's Soviet–East European Division had a celebratory Christmas party. They passed out a party button with a red hammer and sickle and the words "The Party's Over."[42]

In Moscow, however, some feared the party was not over. In an erudite report back to London on New Year's Day 1992, "The Rubble of a

Dictatorship," only declassified thirty years after the events, Britain's ambassador Rodric Braithwaite wrote, "We must now gear ourselves for what may well be a decade of instability," with the rebirth of Russian nationalism, "frightening in its power." There will be trials of strength between Russia and Ukraine, he continued, with Moscow willing to fight to protect its people in breakaway republics. Ukraine's leader, Leonid Kravchuk, would not allow Russians to recreate their empire by a back door, reasoned Braithwaite. He concluded that Russians now fear the "Time of Troubles," prophesized by the Fool at the end of the nineteenth-century opera *Boris Godunov*: hunger, tears, and impenetrable darkness.[43]

Others in Russia felt similarly. Two years earlier, a KGB officer who went by the name Volodya was doing humdrum work as deputy *rezident* in Dresden, East Germany, near the Czech border. He collated files and watched for suspected Western spies. Dresden was a provincial sideshow for the KGB in East Germany. The real action was to the north, in Berlin-Karlshorst. In December 1989, Volodya watched nervously as crowds engulfed the gray Stasi headquarters in Dresden and then his KGB building across the street. He called the Center for reinforcements to defend his headquarters. There was, however, no reply. Moscow was silent. The shock of watching the Soviet Union disintegrate around him would scar that officer, better known as Vladimir Putin, profoundly. As Putin later put it, to his mind, the collapse of the Soviet Union was the greatest geopolitical catastrophe in the twentieth century. Everything was forever, until it was no more.

CHAPTER SIXTEEN

FALLOUT

"It's the oldest question of all, George. Who can spy on the spies?"
—John le Carré, *Tinker, Tailor, Soldier, Spy*

MOSCOW'S PARLIAMENT, THE SEAT OF RUSSIA'S FLEDGLING democracy, was being shelled by heavy T-72 tank artillery. Not far away, the U.S. embassy was caught in the crossfire between the Russian military and hard-liners attempting yet another coup, who had taken up positions in buildings nearby. Embassy staff barricaded themselves in, piling up furniture to protect themselves from the fighting outside. A group of marines stood at the front, prepared to fight any armed rebels who breached the embassy's perimeter. Moscow was experiencing the worst street fighting since the Bolshevik Revolution in 1917. Although numbers are difficult to determine, it seems some 147 people were killed, with about another 437 wounded.

In the early 1990s, Russia's government and society were in disarray. Scenes like this, in October 1993, revealed to the world the perilous state of Russia's democracy. After coming to power, Yeltsin had launched a series of economic reforms, but they backfired, plunging the country into economic and political crisis. Amid cries of "economic genocide," parliament tried to impeach Yeltsin. The effort failed. Following a referendum, Yeltsin attempted to enact constitutional reforms, but when those efforts failed as well, he announced that he intended to dissolve the parliament. At that point, hard-liners launched a coup against him. Yeltsin ordered a counter-coup; tanks rolled into Moscow and shelled the parliament.

The first night of the 1993 coup attempt, the CIA chief of station in Moscow, Rolf Mowatt-Larssen, accompanied by two other officers, took a car from the embassy's basement and plowed through acrid smoke, past bodies on the streets, to Spaso House, a circuitous three-mile drive away. There he and his CIA colleagues set up a secure satellite communication link with Washington. By dawn the next morning, the situation had further deteriorated. Elite Russian snipers were fighting building to building around Spaso House. Bullets rained down on the residency; rebels entered its grounds and broke windows. The Americans inside, including Ambassador Thomas Pickering, were cut off. It looked like Pickering and his staff might be taken hostage. The unflappable ambassador instructed Mowatt-Larssen to call his Russian liaisons and ask for help. Langley had a delicate, but live, liaison with Russia's new security service (the FSK, later known as the FSB). It was worth a try. The CIA man called FSK senior official (and later director) Sergei Stepashin, who sent a team of well-armed plainclothes FSB officers. They had strict instructions to protect the Americans, but nothing more. The FSB detail remained the Americans' silent partners throughout the thirteen-day crisis.[1]

Today, such liaisons between U.S. intelligence and its Russian counterparts after the Cold War are largely forgotten. But at the time, there were real efforts to shake off their Cold War past, or so it seemed. As usual, intelligence services were at the sharp end of broader geopolitics. Just five months after the CIA-FSB collaboration at the U.S. embassy, it was revealed that Russia's foreign intelligence service had penetrated the CIA's upper echelons. The exposure of Aldrich Ames in February 1994 dealt a blow to nascent U.S.-Russian intelligence relations.

Boris Yeltsin is mostly remembered in history for his physical and mental decline as Russia's leader. Frequently drunk, he was (literally) unable to stand up to the state security organs and the Russian Mafia. Under Yeltsin, Russia in the 1990s turned into the lawless "Wild East." At the end of the 1990s, Yeltsin chose an heir who would do well for him: the FSB's Vladimir Putin. True to his word, Putin granted Yeltsin amnesty. But before we conclude that Yeltsin's choice was a tragic mistake and that he was always the drunken clown he later became, it is worth remembering who the alternatives were at the time of his 1991 election.[2]

The Russian Communist Party came in second in Russia's 1991 election, offering Russians little more than a throwback to a nondemocratic past. Another contender, the person who came in third in the election, was Vladimir Zhirinovsky, of the Liberal Democratic Party of Russia. That party, influenced by KGB chairman Vladimir Kryuchkov, was neither liberal nor democratic. Zhirinovsky was, until his death in April 2022, a hard-line Russian nationalist and protofascist, often referred to as "the Russian Hitler." Zhirinovsky's despicable language about women, including Condoleezza Rice, Russia expert and later U.S. national security adviser, foreshadowed the "pussygrabber" language in later U.S. politics. From the beginning of Zhirinovsky's political career, he advocated for Russia's expansion into Eastern Europe, the Middle East, and beyond. Visitors to his Moscow office were treated to the sight of a large map of the world hanging on the wall, showing Russia's "empire" in red. It included not only the Baltic states but also Alaska. In Russia's Duma, Zhirinovsky later said that, if elected leader, he would instigate a police state with summary executions. At the end of the 1990s, he called for Russia's use of napalm and tactical nuclear weapons over the Balkans, threats which he repeated about Ukraine in 2022.[3]

Given these alternatives, Boris Yeltsin does not look so bad. For much of 1992, Yeltsin's popularity in Washington rivaled earlier "Gorbymania." Speaking to a Joint Session of Congress in Washington in June, he was welcomed by chants of "Boris, Boris, Boris" and given thirteen standing ovations as he vowed that "the idol of Communism . . . has collapsed, never to rise again." American lawmakers could now trust Russia, he claimed: "There will be no more lies, ever." It all sounded good.

THE WEST'S PEACE DIVIDEND

The collapse of the Soviet Union anointed the United States as the world's only superpower. The end of the Cold War, consigning communism to history's trash heap, also heralded what some in the West called the end of history. Liberal democracy had prevailed. America was now the world's hegemon, in what would become known as a unipolar world. The "peace dividend," a phrase popularized by President Bush and prime minister Thatcher, would enable all governments to cut back their defense spending after the Cold War. Bush requested his DCI, Robert Gates, to conduct an overall national security review to meet the peace dividend. In March 1992, Gates presented him with its results, for a "top to bottom transformation of the mission, role, and priorities of the intelligence community." Washington took a carving knife to U.S. intelligence agencies, gutting U.S. intelligence resources not dissimilar to demobilizations of Western secret services after the world wars.

To carry through the peace dividend, by the mid-1990s, the CIA's budget was cut by 17 percent. The greatest cuts were to those departments focusing on the now-dead Soviet bloc. John McLaughlin (later acting DCI) cut staff in the office of Slavic and Eurasian Analysis by 42 percent. The proportion of the intelligence community budget allocated to the former Soviet republics declined from about half in the fiscal year 1990 to a third in 1993. In fact, according to Michael Morell (another acting DCI), in the decade between 1991 and September 11, 2001, the CIA's staff was reduced by 50 percent. This involved more than just reallocations. Cuts were absolute. Between 1992 and 1995, NSA lost one-third of its labor force.[4]

Much like after 1945, the U.S. government was once again on the defensive against the Kremlin's espionage. Russia's continued running of two agents inside the U.S. intelligence community, Aldrich Ames and Robert Hanssen, was evidence enough that the U.S. government did not (yet) have a well-placed agent in Moscow. "We were on the backfoot, penetrated by them [Russian intelligence]," Rolf Mowatt-Larssen told me. The saving grace for U.S. intelligence in the 1990s was that, as the Russian economy collapsed, former Soviet intelligence officers were willing to offer secrets for cash. A busy marketplace for Kremlin secrets opened in the 1990s for Western governments. Insiders say that, in the decade after 1991, the CIA recruited more Russian spies than during the Cold War—though it is not possible to confirm this with documentary evidence.[5]

It is likely that, had Bush not lost the election in November 1992, which almost all pundits a year before believed he would win, the budget cuts in the U.S. intelligence community would have been better handled. When he spoke at Langley in November 1991, Bush told his audience that "intelligence remains our basic national instrument for anticipating danger, military, political and economic. Intelligence is and always will be our first line of defense, enabling us to ward off emerging threats whenever possible before any damage is done." His successor in the White House, Bill Clinton, had little interest in his intelligence chiefs. He was not close to his first DCI, James Woolsey, and rarely met him. In Clinton's thousand-page memoirs, Woolsey appears just once. When, in September 1994, a Cessna crashed onto the White House grounds, Washington wits joked that the pilot was Woolsey, trying to get a meeting with Clinton. Tony Lake, then being considered to succeed Woolsey, repeated the joke in the White House. The CIA was founded in the Cold War and designed to fight it. With the conflict's end, Langley seemed to have lost its role.

The end of the Cold War brought a degree of openness to both sides of the Atlantic that was unimaginable a few years before. Washington avowed the existence of its satellite agency, the National Reconnaissance Office (or NRO), which it hitherto had refused to admit existed. This was nothing compared to the seismic change underway in Britain, however. In the aftermath of the Cold War, the British government brought its intelligence services in from the cold, finally avowing their existence and ending the frequently farcical situations that occurred during the previous eight decades in which their existence was an open secret. Ministers and members of Parliament frequently had to perform linguistic acrobatics to avoid discussing them publicly. It was a state secret and a violation of the Official Secrets Act to reveal matters as trivial as whether MI5 had a canteen.

The government placed MI5 on an express statutory footing, under legislation, in 1989, which it followed five years later, in 1994, for MI6 and GCHQ. The new openness in Whitehall was seen most clearly in 1992, when, for the first time, MI5's new director general was publicly named. Even more surprising—shock and awe—was the fact that the new DG was a woman, Stella Rimington, whom we met in chapter seven. MI5 in fact had a long (but nonpublic) history of talented female officers, dating back to Jane Archer, Philby's nemesis. Rimington was inevitably decried in sexist terms in the tabloids as the spy who came in from doing the shopping. MI5 obtained an equally talented next female head, Eliza Manningham-Buller. The role of senior female officers in MI5 contrasted with contemporary Russian services. Gender remains one of the most striking differences in the intelligence war between East and West today. Gina Haspell as DCI; Avril Haines as the director of National Intelligence; Stephanie O'Sullivan, Susan Gordon, and Stacey Dixon as principal deputy directors of National Intelligence; or National Intelligence Council senior official, Fiona Hill, have no equivalent in Moscow or Beijing. The intelligence services of Russia and China do not reflect the countries of which they are a part. They are doubtless less effective because of it.

In 1992, John Major's government brought MI6 in from the shadows, publicly naming the chief of MI6 for the first time, Colin McColl. Major said it was time to sweep away "some of the cobwebs of secrecy which needlessly veil too much of government business." While British intelligence was entering a new era of openness, the peace dividend also led to a cutback of its resources, though less acute than in the United States, where the budgets were colossal (at the end of the Cold War, the U.S. was spending sixteen times as much on SIGINT as the British). MI5's staff was reduced from approximately 2,300 in 1989 to 2,000 in 1994. By the mid-1990s, the budget of Britain's intelligence services was declining by 3 percent per annum.[6]

LOOSE NUKES

Massive threats to world security, however, continued to exist, despite the peace dividend. The disintegration of the Soviet system actually made the proliferation of weapons of mass destruction in its former arsenal—nuclear, chemical, and biological—more likely, not less. Bush called this a "life-and-death" mission for the U.S. intelligence community. During the August 1991 attempted coup in Russia, the hard-line plotters had taken the Soviet nuclear codes, contained in a small attaché case, the "*chemodanchik*," away from Gorbachev. Immediately after the coup, Britain's prime minister, John Major, flew to meet President Bush at his family compound in Kennebunkport, Maine. Major then flew to Moscow, where he met with Gorbachev. The Soviet leader said that he would not reveal the nature of Soviet nuclear command and control to Major. But he assured Major that the *chemodanchik* was now safe. According to a British report of the meeting, unsealed in 2021, Major then revealed to Gorbachev: "Both British and U.S. intelligence knew that not a single dangerous step had been taken." Britain and America's National Technical Means evidently allowed them to scrutinize the Soviet nuclear arsenal. Gorbachev's last phone call with President Bush, on Christmas Day 1991, was to reassure him that he had safely passed control of the Soviet nuclear codes to Boris Yeltsin. A photo reveals Yeltsin, and his ashen-faced advisers, somberly receiving a briefing about the doomsday nuclear suitcase now under their control.[7]

The most surprising thing about the Cold War was that it did not end with nuclear apocalypse. The demise of the Soviet empire ended peacefully (except for civil war in Yugoslavia). Western intelligence services were essential to that. As the Soviet Union was dismantled, the greatest threat to global security was what would happen with its nuclear arsenal. In the U.S., two senators, Sam Nunn and Richard Lugar, spearheaded efforts to prevent nuclear proliferation. Their plausible nightmare was of Soviet nuclear weapons falling into the wrong hands—rogue regimes, terrorists, or criminals. That this did not happen was largely due to the efforts of U.S. intelligence. "Without the U.S. intelligence community," Ash Carter, former U.S. secretary of defense, who worked on counter-proliferation then, told me, "counter-proliferation would have been impossible." As usual with security intelligence, success was measured by what did not happen—a dog that revealingly does not bark.

James Baker informed President Bush that a disintegrating empire with "30,000 nuclear weapons presents an incredible danger to the American people—and they know it and will hold us accountable if we don't respond." The Soviet Union's dismemberment led to the creation, along with the Russian Federation, of three new nuclear powers: Ukraine, Kazakhstan, and Belarus. The Soviet nuclear arsenal in Ukraine, trained on Western Europe and the United States, meant that it had nearly two thousand strategic nuclear warheads. This was more than Britain, France, and China combined. U.S. and British intelligence were instrumental in countering their proliferation. As they had during the Cold War, their intelligence communities were able to identify the precise locations of former Soviet nuclear weapons scattered across those countries. They did so through a combination of Five Eyes SIGINT, satellite imagery (IMINT), electronic intelligence (ELINT), and old-fashioned espionage by MI6 and the CIA. In 1992, the CIA's Directorate of Intelligence established a Nonproliferation Center. Thanks to successful intelligence, President Clinton, at a meeting in Moscow in January 1994, reached an agreement with Yeltsin and Ukraine's president, Leonid Kravchuk, for the destruction of all warheads in Ukraine—at America's expense.

Western intelligence officers posed as arms dealers on the black market to buy nuclear weapons in former Soviet republics. This was euphemistically termed, in Washington and Whitehall vernacular, as "entering into the illicit purchasing chain" for nuclear weapons. Details about how, where, and when most such undercover operations took place are still classified, as well they should be due to their sensitivity, but one has been officially revealed: a project code-named SAPPHIRE. In the summer of 1993, a U.S.

official—presumably posing as an arms purchaser—discovered enriched weapons-grade uranium for sale from a factory in Kazakhstan, which manufactured fuel for nuclear reactors. The CIA reported that Iranian agents were on the trail of the 600 kilograms of uranium, capable of making more than twenty nuclear weapons, which was stored in a warehouse in Ust-Kamenogorsk, protected by little more than barbed wire. The resulting operation, SAPPHIRE, involved the clandestine transportation of a thousand containers from Ust-Kamenogorsk to the Oak Ridge laboratory, in Tennessee. With the permission of the Kazakh president, Nursultan Nazarbayev, a team of U.S. Department of Energy officials loaded the potential weapons-grade uranium onto American C-5 transport planes bound for Dover Air Force Base in Delaware, refueling several times en route. From there they were loaded into large, unmarked trucks and transported to Oak Ridge, where the uranium was deposited for safekeeping. In November 1994, U.S. Secretary of Defense William Perry revealed the operation: "We have put this bomb-grade nuclear material forever out of reach of potential marketeers, terrorists or a new nuclear regime."[8]

The program was an astounding success. Monitored by U.S. intelligence, and largely paid for with American dollars ($400 million), the former Soviet atomic weapons in Belarus, Kazakhstan, and Ukraine were either destroyed or relocated to Russian soil. Meanwhile, U.S. and British intelligence scrutinized Russia's own nuclear arsenal.[9]

SOVIET LAB LEAKS, BIOWEAPONS

As Western governments brokered relations with Moscow for a post-Soviet future, British and U.S. intelligence discovered a terrifying secret of the last two decades of Soviet rule: the Soviet government had operated a vast, illegal, biological weapons program. Worse, it was still operational. The Soviet program, the largest and most technically advanced in the world, was not just tactical but strategic, capable of altering the outcome of an entire conflict. It was designed to produce microbial, bacterial, and viral agents, transmissible person to person, like smallpox and plague, which could be delivered in intercontinental ballistic missiles to Western countries. They could hit British and American homelands, disabling and killing civilian populations, reducing their ability to fight, and rendering them helpless to a military takeover. The Soviet program was in direct violation of the 1972 Biological Weapons Convention banning their production and use, to which the Soviet government was a signatory.[10]

The first indication that the Soviet Union had biological weapons occurred in April 1979, when an anthrax outbreak took place in the city of Ekaterinburg (or Sverdlovsk, as it was known at the time), a thousand miles west of Moscow. It was the city where the Bolsheviks had shot, bayoneted, and incinerated with acid Tsar Nicholas II and his family. At least sixty-six people are known to have been killed when a plume of anthrax spores was accidentally released and drifted 50 kilometers, leaving a trail of human and animal deaths. It was later known as the "biological Chernobyl," the worst documented biolab leak in history.[11]

The Soviet government at the time insisted that it had been caused naturally, by contaminated meat, and refused outside, independent inspections. The KGB instigated active measures to confuse Western scientists, even establishing a bogus biochemical facility to deceive Western agencies investigating. With little positive evidence to the contrary, Western observers accepted the Soviet story. British and U.S. intelligence agencies were skeptical but were unable to confirm what happened at the site. In reality, as we now know, the Soviets covered up the lab leak. The top Communist Party official in Sverdlovsk at the time was Boris Yeltsin.

A decade later, as the Eastern bloc was crumbling, British intelligence received evidence that the Soviet government had a "huge, sophisticated, expensive, extensive and highly secret bioweapons program throughout the Soviet Union," which had been functioning uninterrupted since the 1970s. The intelligence came from one of the program's scientific directors, Vladimir Pasechnik, who defected to MI6 in October 1989. Pasechnik was a talented scientist who worked for the Soviet ministry of defense, which offered him an unlimited budget to set up a biotechnology laboratory. Only later did it dawn on him that his laboratory was part of a network producing deadly pathogens. Pasechnik wanted to defect, but was not allowed to travel abroad. Finally, in the summer of 1989, he was permitted to attend an academic conference in Paris in the autumn and purchase equipment for his laboratory. While there, he walked into the British embassy and defected. MI6's head of station exfiltrated him to Britain on a false passport. Under close protection and with a new identity, he revealed the horrors of his work to intelligence officers and scientists at Britain's top secret weapons institute, Porton Down.[12]

The illegal Soviet program was housed in a commercial organization, Biopreparat, which had about fifty facilities spread across the Soviet Union, from Leningrad to Siberia. Biopreparat was dual-use: one aspect of its work was legitimate, developing vaccines, new methods of crop protection, and pharmaceuticals. But as Pasechnik revealed, Biopreparat's other, true purpose was its secret military side: to create an offensive-weapons program. It had been secretly created under Brezhnev in 1973, the year after the Soviet government agreed to ban bioweapons. The Soviet government created the program believing that the U.S. government would never really close down its own sophisticated, successful bioweapons program. In fact, this is exactly what President Richard Nixon did. Biopreparat was thus a chilling illustration of Soviet deception at the heart of détente. Scientists at Biopreparat were indoctrinated to believe that their research was essential to defending the Soviet Union against a secret (nonexistent) U.S. bioweapons program. Bioweapons were attractive to Soviet leaders because they were cheaper than nuclear bombs. They allowed the possibility of attacking even a large country with relatively few weapons, delivering a live pathogen on a missile—a feat of engineering. After exploding and infecting victims, the disease would then spread exponentially throughout the population, effectively weaponizing a country's own people.

Western intelligence agencies had failed for two decades to detect the

Soviet bioweapons program. It was a monument to Soviet secrecy and deception, revealing how successfully a closed state can house and hide its secrets. Biopreparat was a system the likes of which the world had never seen. A military program under civilian cover, it employed tens of thousands of people, was self-contained, and had been built up over the years with inter-related, but independent, facilities. Many were buried deep in the Soviet countryside. Most facilities were not on their own producing bioweapons, but instead innocuous-looking constituent parts. When combined into the sum of their parts, however, the facilities produced such weapons. The biological weapons produced were designed for battlefield use. They included about a dozen highly lethal diseases: anthrax, Ebola, Marburg virus, bubonic plague, glanders, Q fever, and smallpox. Pasechnik revealed that Soviet scientists were working on a synthesized "super-plague," more virulent than previous viral strains, genetically engineered to better resist antibiotics and release biochemicals into a victim's immune system so they would more quickly become sick and die. The labs were also working on a chimera virus, created by genetically splicing smallpox with other viruses like Ebola, creating Ebola-pox. It was bioengineering at the edge of known science.

Most of Pasechnik's revelations thankfully remain secret, but we know he disclosed that his institute had carried out research on modifying cruise missiles to spread germs. Flying low to avoid early-warning detection, they were intended to spray clouds of pathogens over enemies. His lab had produced an aerosolized plague microbe that could survive outside the laboratory. By 1987, Biopreparat had the capacity to make 200 kilograms of super-plague a week—enough to kill five hundred thousand people. Pasechnik's revelations were later confirmed when his supervisor, the first deputy director of Biopreparat, Ken Alibek, emigrated to the United States and exposed even more details. When Alibek visited the United States in 1991, he was shocked to find that, contrary to what he had been led to believe, the U.S. did not have a bioweapons program.[13]

Biopreparat worked in conjunction with the GRU and the KGB. The KGB's Twelfth Directorate was responsible for conducting biowar and collecting intelligence about foreign programs. According to one of its veterans, it was preparing for "Day-X": when illegals would deploy bioweapons to sabotage NATO forces in Europe.[14]

In the spring of 1990, the British and U.S. ambassadors in Moscow confronted Gorbachev's foreign policy adviser, Anatoli Chernyaev, about the weapons labs. U.S. Secretary of State Baker did so with Soviet foreign minister Eduard Shevardnadze. When Gorbachev came to Washington in May, Bush broached the subject with him in a private discussion at Camp David. Gorbachev reportedly claimed that he believed the U.S. government was running a similar program. We do not know what KGB and GRU intelligence Gorbachev was receiving. Thatcher raised the issue with Gorbachev when she visited Moscow in June 1990. According to one account, she threatened to put Pasechnik on television if Gorbachev did not cooperate. The Soviet leader agreed to mutual inspections. It remains unclear whether Gorbachev was deceived by the Soviet military about Biopreparat or was himself deceiving Western governments. For his part, Britain's ambassador in Moscow, Braithwaite, who knew Gorbachev fairly well, later rejected the idea that there was any "false dealing" on the part of the last Soviet leader about bioweapons.

A Soviet team visited the U.S. government's abandoned facility at Pine Bluff, Arkansas, where officials explained how they had closed it down. In Russia, however, British and American teams encountered obfuscation and deception. Biopreparat scientists believed their Western visitors were trying to steal their secrets. Some were oblivious about the 1972 convention. Finding the truth at the Biopreparat facilities was "like grabbing a bar of soap in the shower," according to one British inspector. Because Biopreparat was ostensibly a commercial organization, and was conducting some legitimate work, scientists in Russia claimed they could not disclose their work because it was a commercial secret.[15]

The visits were carefully choreographed to show Biopreparat's benign capabilities. To the trained eye, however, it was clear that the facilities housed offensive bioweapons. One enormous facility at Obolensk had an explosive dissemination test chamber. At one end of the blast chamber was a long tube, with spaces in the wall where animal heads could be placed to expose them to an aerosolized explosion. At the other end of the chamber was a large steel door, like a submarine hatch, with double-thick armor; it was heavily dented, indicating blasts. Another facility, at Koltsovo, a Biopreparat group known as Vector, specializing in virology and viral agents, was found to have produced and tested smallpox as a bioweapon.

A breakthrough seemed to occur in early 1992, when President Yeltsin publicly admitted that the Soviet military had caused the 1979 Sverdlovsk incident and promised there would be "no more lies—ever" about "biological weapons experiments." It soon became clear, however, that hawks in Moscow kept the program secretly running. Unlike nuclear weapons, bioweapons offered Russia an asymmetrical advantage against Western governments. According to a secret report, opened in 2022, in July 1993 Britain's prime minister, Major, confronted Yeltsin about Russia's biological weapons program at a meeting in Tokyo. Major said that he had been pleasantly surprised by Yeltsin's candor admitting, at a previous meeting, that Russia had operated an illegal biological weapons program. Now Western inspections were stalling. Turning to his aides, Yeltsin replied this was just a "technical glitch." The extent to which Yeltsin was lying to Major, or ignorant about Russia's biological weapons program, is not revealed from the existing documentary record.[16]

By 1994, Russia's biowarfare program was known in the West to be operational again. British ministers and the U.S. Congress were kept informed of the program in classified briefings. U.S. intelligence revealed that the Soviet Union also had an illegal chemical weapons program, code-named FOLLIANT. It is not inconceivable to think the two programs contributed to the U.S. and British governments' decisions not to grant financial assistance to Russia in the 1990s without political reform. Russia's biological and chemical weapons programs would later produce next-generation "newcomer" (*Novichok*) pathogens, which Russia would use on Western soil two decades later. The failure of Western intelligence to discover Biopreparat would also leave a poisoned legacy when it came to assessing weapons programs of other countries, like that of Iraq in the 1990s and in 2003.[17]

RUSSIA'S NEW NOBILITY

As the Soviet Union receded into history, what was exposed in Russia did not make an attractive sight. When Soviet psychiatric facilities were opened to outside inspectors after 1991, they were found to contain perfectly healthy political prisoners. Then there were the intelligence services. Even before the Soviet Union fell, democratic politicians in Russia and policymakers in Washington recognized the need to draw a line under Russia's repressive security apparatus of the past, if the country were to have a democratic future. In October 1991, Yeltsin dissolved the KGB, the most powerful and fearsome security organization ever created. Western politicians visiting Moscow, like Senator John Kerry of Massachusetts, toured the Lubyanka, where he saw thousands of files on shelves. How many of the people contained in those files had been sent to their deaths in Siberian work camps? he wondered.[18]

For anyone visiting Moscow in the early days of Yeltsin's government, it was painfully apparent how weak and destitute the country was. Moreover, Russia was humiliated, having lost the Cold War and its status as one of the world's two superpowers. By any reasonable standard, it was not close to being a great power. In the 1990s, it was in the odd position of having a national anthem, but with no agreed words to it. It was just one sign among many of Russia's national identity crisis. Amid hyperinflation and rampant corruption, people starved to death; former Russian soldiers in Red Army coats begged for food and money in Moscow's streets, outside newly opened Western fast-food outlets like Pizza Hut and McDonald's. Into this grim, dystopian world, Russia's security and intelligence agencies (*organy*) offered a steel capability to enforce Russian interests. Intelligence and security officers—*siloviki*—became Russia's new nobility.[19]

In former Soviet bloc countries in the 1990s, there was a reckoning with the secret police that made those regimes possible. That did not happen in Russia itself. Many of the half-million former KGB officials bitterly resented the 1991 collapse of the system for which they, and their predecessors, had served as the sword and shield. They lost their jobs. Many ordinary

Russians felt similar, preferring the old order, when at least Russia was formidable. Western intelligence services exerted huge efforts through liaison relationships to help shape the new security and intelligence agencies of the Eastern bloc countries, through legislation, regulations, and constitutions, to avoid the scourge of secret police reappearing in other guises. In Russia itself, this did not happen. The speed with which the Soviet Union collapsed, and the chaos that ensued, made it impossible to plan Russia's post-Soviet intelligence establishment. It was done on the fly. The dangers of the Wild East made it all the more important, Yeltsin's officials urged Western policymakers, to allow the Kremlin to have residual intelligence and security capabilities. They were necessary, Yeltsin's Kremlin claimed, if only to prevent the proliferation of weapons of mass destruction.

Following the August 1991 coup, the last KGB chairman, Vadim Bakatin, advocated significant reforms to quash the KGB's power in Russia, dividing its many functions into different entities, as well as depoliticizing its work (so that it was not driven by ideology), and making it as transparent as possible. Bakatin, handsome and energetic, revealed his forward-looking reforms in a meeting with Robert Strauss, the U.S. ambassador in Russia, in December 1991. He gave the ambassador a dossier, including blueprints, for how the Soviets had installed bugs throughout the U.S. embassy in Moscow back in 1969, when the new embassy was being built. The building was dubbed the "giant microphone." Bakatin's disclosures made him despised as a traitor in Putin's Russia.[20]

Yeltsin implemented Bakatin's reforms in August 1991, and four months later, in December, the State Council of the Soviet Union abolished the KGB. Conspiracy theorists believed that Russia lost the Cold War as much by the actions of reformists like Bakatin as from the popular uprisings that toppled communist governments. At its demise, the KGB boasted a staff of 480,000 officials (officers and other ranks), but as we have seen, that excluded even more agents and co-optees working for it. When the KGB was abolished, half of its officers lost their jobs; the others were transferred to new security agencies.

Yeltsin, for the first time, placed Russian foreign intelligence on a legal basis—ironically, before Britain's MI6. New light is thrown on the contortions of this period by a secret British assessment in 1991, only opened in 2021, thirty years after events. In it, MI6's razor-sharp head of station in Moscow, John Scarlett, previously one of Gordievsky's handlers, noted that a year after the August coup, for the first time, political, judicial, and some operational constraints were being imposed on Russia's intelligence services. Scarlett hastened to add, however, that their independence would hinge on whether Russia's leaders interfered with them, like Andropov or Kryuchkov did, and whether they made themselves indispensable to the Kremlin. Sadly, Scarlett was correct on both fronts. They became political monsters. With hindsight, it is a tragedy for the Russian people and Western security that the KGB was not truly abolished. Unlike the Axis powers in 1945, Russia was not an occupied country where the U.S. government could impose its will and dictate how the Kremlin should use its security and intelligence agencies. Yeltsin's strategy, supported by the U.S., was to disperse the KGB into different agencies in the hope that it could not be put back together. In retrospect, as now seems so obvious, it did exactly that, reconstituting itself like the liquid metal of the T-1000 in *Terminator 2*, which captivated moviegoers in 1991.[21]

The eighteenth-century philosopher and statesman Edmund Burke famously noted that political revolutions tend to consume the regimes they overturn, producing continuities with them. This happened with the French Revolution in the eighteenth century, and with the Bolsheviks in Russia in 1917, as we saw, and also the revolution that swept away the Soviet Union. During the Cold War, the KGB had combined responsibilities for both foreign intelligence (the First Chief Directorate) and domestic security (the Second Chief Directorate). In December 1991, Yeltsin authorized the First Chief Directorate's functions to pass to a new foreign intelligence service, later called the SVR. (The SVR was not burdened with any baggage from the August 1991 coup attempt because its head, Shebarshin, had refused to join the plotters, spending the first day of the coup playing tennis.) Meanwhile, the Second Chief Directorate's responsibilities passed to a new domestic security service, the FSB, as it became known, after different acronyms.

The Lubyanka, under the watchful gaze of Yuri Andropov from his portrait on the wall, became the FSB's headquarters. The SVR and FSB inherited the KGB's infrastructure, archives, agents, skill set, ideology, and operational approach. FSB officers used the same KGB training textbooks, with the ideological sections about communism now simply ripped out. Meanwhile, the GRU continued to operate seamlessly, housed in "the Aquarium," the same headquarters, on the outskirts of Moscow. In one of the few breaks with the past, however, Russia finally obtained a dedicated SIGINT service, known as FAPSI. The work of Soviet SIGINT, in the KGB's Sixteenth Directorate and the GRU's Eighth Directorate, was passed on to it. The United States continued to be FAPSI's focus, as the Main Adversary, but the collapse of the Warsaw Pact led to the loss of 150 SIGINT stations.[22]

The mastermind behind the FSB and its 75,000-person workforce, its ideological founding father and professor, was a former senior KGB SCD officer, Rem Krassilnikov. He was a KGB true believer. His father was an NKVD officer, and he had chosen Rem's name in honor of a Soviet folk song—it is an acronym for the Russian phrase meaning "world revolution"—so that, as he correctly predicted, it would show his loyalty during Stalin's terror. Like his father, Rem continued to be a loyal servant of the Soviet regime. Rem's wife's name, Ninel, was Lenin spelled backward. With a thick mane of white hair and a soft, lined face, Rem Krassilnikov seemed like a kindly Russian grandfather. But his appearance was deceiving. In Langley, he gained almost mythic status. He was as close to an omniscient fictional spymaster in a novel as we can find. Over forty years, he rolled up countless Western intelligence operations against the Soviet Union. In the mid-1980s, Krassilnikov led both the British and American desks in KGB security (the SCD), where he hunted down and eliminated agents identified by the CIA's Aldrich Ames and the FBI's Robert Hanssen.[23]

Under Krassilnikov's direction, Russia's FSB adopted the tradecraft, and sins, of its Soviet predecessor. A case illustrating the seamless transition from the KGB to the FSB involved one of Krassilnikov's protégés, Alexander "Sasha" Zhomov. Back in May 1987, Zhomov met the CIA's chief of station in Moscow, Jack Downing, aboard the overnight Red Arrow (Krasnaya Strela) express train from Moscow to Leningrad, smoking cigarettes in the train's caboose. As they looked out at the Russian countryside, exhaling smoke, Zhomov handed Downing a note, offering to provide information from inside the KGB's security division revealing how it managed to unravel CIA operations in the Soviet Union. He offered to spy for the CIA in return for passage to America. To whet his appetite, he provided Downing with a grainy surveillance photograph of Downing himself.

In fact, Zhomov was the KGB case officer tasked with monitoring Downing. The hunter had offered to work for the hunted. He appeared to be a genuine defector, and the CIA Soviet Division assigned him the code name PROLOGUE. The agency's Moscow station, and its Soviet Division in Langley—known as the "Russia House" in honor of le Carré's same-named novel—tied themselves in knots trying to figure out if Zhomov was legitimate or a controlled agent. In the intelligence business, this is known as a "dangle," someone sent to lure foreign recruiters out into the open. When Zhomov backed out of a proposed CIA exfiltration plan, offering excuses, it became clear that he was a KGB dangle sent to draw out CIA officers and expose their recruitment techniques. But in the case of Zhomov the KGB broke a cardinal rule: it dangled an officer in the service, not an agent. Officers had access to all sorts of secrets, one of the reasons they were not supposed to be dangles—in the event they actually defected. Downing decided to play out PROLOGUE, passing and receiving information to and from Zhomov on the Red Arrow and in prearranged Moscow sites.[24]

Zhomov, with piercing gray eyes, thick hair, and caterpillar eyebrows, saw his primary mission as destroying U.S. spies by any means necessary. He symbolized the continuity from the Soviet KGB to Russian intelligence. His real mission, set forth by Krassilnikov and his deputy, Valentin Klimenko, who later became an FSB chief, had been to confuse the CIA in order to protect its agent, Aldrich Ames. After the Soviet collapse, Zhomov became the head of the FSB section targeting the U.S. and its agencies, where he attempted to track down the agent who betrayed Ames. At the time of writing this book,

Sasha Zhomov is still a senior Russian intelligence officer, heading the FSB's counterintelligence operations. In the CIA, he has a phantomlike reputation.

What about Russian foreign intelligence? From the outset, Russia's foreign service, the SVR, regarded itself as the proud successor of the KGB's FCD. KGB *rezidentury* in overseas embassies, and even its deep-cover illegals, simply changed the name of the service they worked for from one three-letter acronym to another.

Yeltsin appointed a foreign affairs expert, Yevgeny Primakov, to be the SVR's first director. A graduate of the Moscow Institute for Oriental Studies, Primakov was an expert on the Arab world, a former head of the Institute of World Economy and International Relations, one of Gorbachev's close foreign policy advisers, and a member of his presidential council. Unlike the KGB's FCD, which sent intelligence to the Center, then for dissemination to Soviet leaders, Primakov reported directly to Yeltsin. His briefings were doubtless enhanced by his talent for amateur dramatics.

According to Soviet archives smuggled to the West, while previously working as a journalist in the Middle East, Primakov had been a KGB co-optee (code-named MAKSIM). We do not know how Primakov was co-opted to work for the KGB, just that he did. He knew its methods. Unsurprisingly, therefore, while claiming that the SVR was charting a new course, Primakov adopted the KGB's playbook. He told Rodric Braithwaite in May 1992 that the SVR had 50 percent less staff than the KGB's FCD, which was estimated to have between twelve thousand and fifteen thousand. This decrease for the SVR was largely thanks to the exodus of former KGB officials to the private sector. But after aggressive recruitment drives, by the end of the decade the SVR's staff was back up to the KGB's Cold War numbers, even as the Russian economy tanked—or perhaps because of it. At the same time, the SVR embarked on a major PR offensive to change the public perception of Soviet intelligence officers as uneducated, violent thugs. In fact, according to their press releases, SVR officers, like their KGB foreign intelligence predecessors, were Westernized, cultured, and educated, professionals not unlike the fictional James Bond, and almost a chivalric order. Former Soviet spy chiefs published memoirs depicting themselves as knights carrying out daring operations, fulfilling a calling to enable Russia to advance its historical mission as a great power.[25]

Senior British intelligence officers traveled to Moscow to meet their now-friendly Russian counterparts. One was Stella Rimington, who had spent much of her previous twenty-year career investigating Soviet espionage, including the web of the Cambridge spy ring. Now, in December 1991, as the Soviet Union was unwinding, she flew to Moscow and was hosted by the KGB's reformist chief, Bakatin. The Cold War was over. In September 1992, DCI Robert Gates similarly visited Moscow and St. Petersburg, where Russia's new intelligence tsars, Primakov and FSB director Sergei Stepashin, likewise hosted him for dinner. Old Cold Warriors, CIA and KGB officers, drank, toasted, and played billiards together. In October 1993, Bill Clinton's DCI, James Woolsey, also visited Russia. It was not a success. Insiders remember Woolsey as largely uninterested in the trip. They say he showed little respect to his Russian hosts, who muttered an old Russian proverb that even a small tablespoon of vinegar spoils a pot of honey.[26]

As the U.S. intelligence community turned its gaze away from the former Soviet Union, the SVR fought hard for its own and Russia's future. It redoubled its efforts against the U.S. At the same time the SVR was talking about peace dividends with the Americans, it was running Aldrich Ames inside the CIA. Old KGB hands like Vadim Kirpichenko, whom we met earlier in the Middle East, were embraced and advised the SVR. Kirpichenko's sidekicks became known as the "Middle East" mafia within the SVR. In 1994, the State Duma, with Yeltsin's support, granted amnesty to the leader of the failed August 1991 coup, Kryuchkov. Once released from jail, he denounced the former Soviet leader as a traitor for instigating reforms, allowing the reunification of Germany, and losing Eastern Europe.

The greatest threat to Russian security, Primakov argued, was NATO expansion beyond its Cold War frontier. Primakov's fears were based on long-standing suspicions of NATO, and Russia's encirclement by Western powers. German unification, and its entry into NATO, brought the Alliance's frontier eastward into Russia's traditional sphere of influence, as Moscow saw it. In March 1993, the SVR, under Primakov, published a study that NATO's expansion eastward posed a threat to Russian national security. This occurred even as Yeltsin's foreign minister, Andrei Kozyrev, was propagating a more conciliatory tone with the West. Primakov later claimed to have information that U.S.-backed initiatives, like the Partnership for Peace, more on which later, were vehicles for admitting new members to NATO, but "not Russia." At the same time, the SVR continued to distribute propaganda to Russian audiences about American "vulture capitalism" and the CIA's expanding "attack" on Russia.

Western powers were striving to undermine Russia, just as they had after 1917, the SVR claimed. While there was no plot at work by the CIA or Wall Street to bring down Russia, there did exist a callous indifference among some to the country's plight. A small army of Western businessmen, consultants, and Wall Street lawyers arrived in Russia in the early 1990s to strike lucrative deals for the country's rich resources, seeking a huge payday. There were shysters on both sides. None of the Western lawyers or consultants, who privatized (effectively asset-stripped) Russia's industries, had better ideas than anyone else about how to dismantle a communist command economy covering eleven time zones and convert it into free-market capitalism. In 1992, G-7 countries agreed to loan commitments of $24 billion to Russia, with the U.S. providing $4.8 billion. Unquantifiable amounts ended up in the hands of the Russian Mafia, as the 2019 documentary film *Red Penguins* reveals.[27]

Privatizing Soviet state industries turned into a nightmare for Russia. Yeltsin hired a team of market-orientated economists, led by Igor Gaidar and Anatoli Chubais, who put in place what became known as "shock therapy," the rapid and unprecedented opening of Russia to liberal market reforms, to accelerate change and lessen the duration of economic contraction. But they were confronted by a Duma dominated by communists, with deputies in the middle who could be swayed (bribed) either way. Russia's experiment with democratic reforms ended in flames when Yeltsin's forces stormed the parliament in October 1993. In many ways, democracy in the motherland never recovered. Yeltsin's military intervention in Chechnya the following year was supposed to be a pacifying police action to prevent a domino effect among separatists within the Russian territories. It turned into a terrible war, in which Russian forces levelled Grozny, raped women, dropped cluster bombs, and killed civilian refugees carrying white flags.[28]

The main method for privatizing the Soviet Union's vast former state resources involved giving ordinary people vouchers, which they could swap for shares in newly privatized companies. This method of "hyper capitalism" opened the floodgates for corruption, as shown by Adam Curtis's remarkable 2022 documentary, compiled from raw contemporary BBC footage from Russia. Enterprising individuals—especially in Russia's gangland, St. Petersburg—traded people's vouchers for bottles of vodka, cigarettes, and bread. They were soon able to aggregate vouchers into share holdings of colossal value in oil refineries, mines, and steelworks. The former Soviet ministry of gas, for example, was privatized as Gazprom in 1993. It issued shares through the voucher system and was valued at about $250 million. Its real value was closer to the tune of $40 billion, with reserves of gas worth hundreds of billions. When shareholders of companies refused to relinquish their shares in a company in exchange for food and other commodities, no problem: they were threatened or murdered. Oligarchs would asset-strip companies, spiriting the proceeds overseas into foreign investments. Football clubs in the West, newspapers, or super-yachts were all playthings for Russia's new tsars.

Corruption in Russia in the 1990s was pervasive. Organized crime flourished: in arms dealing, narcotics and people trafficking, and the rise of "protection services" for the new private sector. Far from preventing corruption and crime, the FSB facilitated and drove it. The gamekeepers became poachers. FSB officers in its economic security division—an oxymoron—would meet with Mafia contacts on the pretext of being introduced to informants, but then end up working with them. According to one FSB defector, interviewed for this book, corruption in the service was so pervasive that, if you were not on the take, you were suspicious. Corruption was a way of creating loyalty in the FSB. In 1996, the chief of the FSB's economic counterintelligence directorate, Vladimir Tsekhanov, was said to be removed from his position because he dared to do his job properly. Meanwhile, Vladimir Putin, having lost the KGB job that helped him support his family, became an official in the St. Petersburg government. This placed him between the Russian government and booming organized crime in that city.[29]

One of the least appreciated chapters in post-Soviet East-West relations is the way Russia continued to run its former Cold War spies. The SVR picked up where the KGB left off: with Aldrich Ames, in the CIA, and Robert Hanssen, in the FBI. On the day when KGB chairman Kryuchkov initiated his coup in Moscow against Gorbachev, in 1991, Hanssen left a dead drop of classified material under the CIA's nose, a few miles from its headquarters in Virginia. A CIA liaison officer in Moscow at this time remembers how frequently Primakov would come to visit him. Only in hindsight would the CIA officer realize that, because of Ames, Primakov knew what the officer's cables back to Langley said about their meetings.

In February 1994, the CIA and the FBI finally caught up with Aldrich Ames. Eight years earlier, the agency had established a team of mole hunters to investigate its espionage failures against the Soviet Union, witnessed in the "Year of the Spy," 1985. The group, which included Paul Redmond, Sandy Grimes, and Jeanne Vertefeuille, were convinced there was an unidentified Soviet mole inside the agency. By 1992, they began to suspect Ames was that mole. His ostentatious lifestyle suggested that he was getting money from another source beyond his relatively modest government salary. His explanation—that Rosario's Colombian family was wealthy and had given them money—seemed far-fetched. In reality, Rosario at a minimum knew about her husband's espionage. There is some evidence to suggest that Ames's polygraph results were inconclusive, but the CIA allowed him to remain employed anyway. "There was a lot of denial about Ames," recalls a CIA counterintelligence officer interviewed for this book, who knew Ames: "The CIA had not been penetrated like this before, and we refused to think it was possible." Although the secret of how the CIA detected Ames has been tightly held, we now know that the CIA pitched former KGB officers who might know the mole's identity, in an operation known as PENNYWISE. They got lucky with KGB-SVR officer Aleksander Zaporozhsky, who was able to provide the CIA with enough information to identify Ames as the mole. The CIA and FBI reportedly gave Zaporozhsky $2 million and resettled him in America.[30]

Ames's exposure as a Russian spy, similar to Philby's at MI6 three decades before, caused years of wreckage and conspiracies in agencies on both sides of the Atlantic. The CIA and FBI launched damage-assessment investigations into Ames; oversight committees on Capitol Hill were out for blood. There were calls for the CIA to be closed down, especially with the end of the Cold War. The agency became the butt of jokes by late-night comedians. A subsequent investigation by the agency's inspector general harshly criticized the CIA's Office of Soviet Analysis (SOVA, meaning "owl" in Russian) for incorporating Soviet disinformation into its assessments—information obtained from dangles like Zhomov—and for failing to make clear that their reports may have been tainted. That said, the CIA did not deliberately peddle false information about the Soviet Union, as was claimed by some at the time, and since. It was a failure, not a conspiracy.

Russia's heightened espionage against its Main Adversary, even as America's defenses were lowered amid the peace dividend, mirrored the way Soviet intelligence exploited its supposed ally during World War II. In June 1994, just four months after Ames's arrest, the SVR recruited Harold J. Nicholson. Motivated by money, not ideology—for Russia in the 1990s had no ideology—Nicholson became the most senior CIA officer ever convicted of spying for a foreign power. Soon after his recruitment, he was made branch chief of the Counterterrorism Center at CIA headquarters. The fact that Ames had been able to get away with spying on the U.S. government for nine years probably encouraged Nicholson to turn to espionage to make money. Suspicion fell on him when he failed a polygraph test. He was arrested at Washington's Dulles Airport in November 1996, carrying classified information that he planned to hand over to the SVR in Zurich. Seven months later, he was sentenced to nearly twenty-four years in prison. It would take the CIA and the FBI another six years to catch the FBI's Robert Hanssen.[31]

The machinations of the FSB and the SVR, rising from the ashes of the old KGB, bled over into Russian politics at the highest level. The fusion of secret service and politics in Russia was unlike anything in the West. George H. W. Bush is the single example of a DCI becoming a U.S. president. No head of a British service has ever occupied Downing Street. In 1996, SVR director Yevgeny Primakov became Yeltsin's foreign minister. In 1998, he rose to become prime minister. He wanted to be Russia's president, a prospect that made Yeltsin look to safer hands. FSB director Sergei Stepashin was made prime minister the following year. And it was to the FSB that Yeltsin looked for his successor, Vladimir Putin, who had not only demonstrated his loyalty to Yeltsin but had offered him political protection.

Three weeks before Putin became FSB director, a vocal critic of Yeltsin's, Lev Rokhlin, was found shot in bed at his dacha. When assassination was not required, kompromat—the collection of compromising material to discredit or manipulate someone in political office—would suffice. For instance, when the general prosecutor Yuri Skuratov investigated Yeltsin's family for corrupt links to a Swiss construction firm, it did not take long for grainy footage of Skuratov scampering on a bed with two women to emerge on state TV, leading to his resignation. Putin critic Alexander Litvinenko maintained that similar compromising material existed of Putin himself. As the FSB's new director, Putin kept a statute of "Iron Felix," the Cheka's founder, on his desk.[32]

Some in Britain saw the warning signs. Lord Nicholas Bethell, a tireless human rights campaigner, warned Tony Blair in September 1997: "We need the help of the Russian police, and even the FSB, the KGB's successor. But we do not want the good name of Britain to be used to justify the terrible things that still happen in Russia." As revealed in Blair's newly opened cabinet papers, released in 2022, Bethell forwarded the prime minister an April 1997 Amnesty International report about torture in Russia's prison colonies. Blair replied that reforms in Russia had to be "incremental" and "realistic." At a later meeting in Moscow, Blair and Yeltsin issued a joint declaration to cooperate on organized crime. It was the equivalent of a robber guarding a bank. Blair told Yeltsin that building economic relations with Russia was at the top of his agenda. In late 1997, BP and Shell signed lucrative contracts for oil exploration in Russia.[33]

As Russia's economy tanked, the Clinton administration told Yeltsin that it was "no longer 1993," and that the United States would not automatically bail Russia out unless it improved its foreign policy—by ceasing coordination with Iran, for instance. Russia had to be "part of the team, not the opposition," said the U.S. administration. As Russia slid into chaos, its foreign intelligence became correspondingly more aggressive. SVR director Vyacheslav Trubnikov, another old KGB hand, was quoted in 1997 saying: "Confrontation between intelligence organs never ended but with the end of the Cold War, contrary to expectations, actually intensified." Old players like Leonid Shebarshin joined the chorus, warning that the world was less safe after the Soviet Union's demise and that the U.S. was using "democracy" as a form of imperialism. A year later, a global financial meltdown hit Russia hard; the government defaulted on its debts, and Russia's pension funds collapsed. The following year, when Putin came to power, the SVR was discovered to have planted a listening device in a conference room at the U.S. State Department, hidden behind a radiator, where it eavesdropped on sensitive conversations. To this day, it is unclear how it got there.[34]

In October 2000, the CIA and the FBI reeled in a major catch. Sergei Tretyakov, known as Comrade J, was a former KGB officer, now SVR deputy *rezident* working under diplomatic cover at Russia's mission to the UN in New York. During CIA and FBI debriefings, the stocky Russian produced close to five thousand secret Russian cables, not dissimilar to the haul by the Soviet defector Igor Gouzenko five decades earlier. Tretyakov revealed that active measures were as important for the SVR as they had been for the KGB. The SVR *rezidentura* sent officers to the New York Public Library, where they logged on to the internet from its public computers, and used email to bombard U.S. media outlets with pro-Russia news stories. They posted messages on chat boards designed to present Russia in the best possible light. Russia was already realizing that the internet, then in its infancy, could be used for spreading disinformation.[35]

PART SIX

THE CLASH OF
A NEW GLOBAL ORDER

CHAPTER SEVENTEEN

PUTIN'S WAR ON THE WEST

The streets of Petersburg possess a most indubitable quality:
they turn passers-by into shadows; shadows, however, the streets
of Petersburg turn into people.
We saw that in the instance of the mysterious stranger.
–Andrei Bely, *Petersburg*

VLADIMIR PUTIN, THE FORMER INTELLIGENCE OFFICER WHO rules Russia as president, is a small man, at five foot seven. But his ambition is unlimited. Whatever his title, he has ruled Russia since 1999, the longest reign of a Kremlin leader since Stalin. His early KGB career has shaped his worldview and his subsequent rule. He has used his security and intelligence agencies to turn Russia into a great power again, correcting what he sees as the catastrophe that befell Russia when the Soviet regime collapsed in 1991. He is trying to force a new European security arrangement. Like Stalin after 1945, Putin's strategy has been dominated by fear of Western encirclement and subversion. His policy has been to "contain" perceived Western subversion, which in practice means undertaking military and hybrid warfare against those he sees as preventing Russia's greatness: NATO, the EU, and the United States. Putin's election meddling in the United States in 2016, and beyond, was part of his larger escalation to reclaim Russia's past and to seek revenge against his enemies—impose his rule on Russia's "near abroad," countries in the previous Soviet "sphere of influence," the former Soviet bloc, silence his critics, and smite capitalist democracies in the West.

Putin's increasing tyranny, however, is not a straightforward continuum of the Soviet past. In terms of intelligence, he has updated Soviet spycraft for the new digital world, weaponizing social media to spread disinformation. Unlike past Soviet leaders, who had the Politburo, he treats Russia as his personal fiefdom, which he rules with a small number of sycophantic oligarchs and *siloviki*. Under Putin, Russia has become a Mafia state, as he married its intelligence services with organized crime. His obsession with recreating the Soviet past, seen in his occupation of Georgian territories in 2008 and his annexation of Crimea in 2014, reached its apotheosis with his bloody military invasion of Ukraine in February 2022.

◆

"We're in the middle of a cyber war," claimed the U.S. deputy secretary of defense, John Hamre. This was in 1999, not 2019. For about three years, Russian hackers had breached some of the most sensitive computer networks in the U.S. federal government, NASA, the Pentagon, the Department of Energy, and a dozen U.S. universities and other research centers. It was a colossal security failure. Pentagon officials described the high-tech espionage as a "state-sponsored Russian intelligence effort to get U.S. technology." It was, they said, "sophisticated, patient and persistent."

The hackers were only identified by accident, as part of a U.S. simulation game against its own systems. After a detailed forensic investigation, NSA experts discovered that the hackers had stolen passwords, logged in, and covered their tracks by erasing the logs. They gained access denied to all but the most senior administrators. They created back doors so they could enter and leave largely without trace, stealing information at will. Some federal employees saw files disappearing in real time before their eyes. NSA and

Pentagon officials played cat and mouse with the hackers in the systems. They were eventually identified as Russian—for one thing, their keystrokes spelled in Cyrillic, and they worked from 8:00 a.m. to 5:00 p.m. Moscow time. They were traced to sites linked to Russia's Academy of Sciences, the old stamping ground of former SVR director Yevgeny Primakov.[1]

Russia's unprecedented cyber hack into U.S. federal computer systems, detected in 1999, and code-named MOONLIGHT MAZE, was a wake-up call to the new intelligence war being waged by the Kremlin. Or at least it should have been. Russia was conducting espionage by new means, across networks, and Pentagon officials feared they might move from espionage, observing data, to sabotage—changing it. The volume of information stolen was so great that, if printed out and stacked up, it would reach as high as the towering obelisk of the Washington Monument.

Most of the details about MOONLIGHT MAZE remain classified. In their efforts to identify the hackers, it appears that the NSA followed the example set a decade earlier by the Berkeley-trained astronomer and author Cliff Stoll. A long-haired free spirit, Stoll looked after computer networks in his lab. He noticed that someone was logging on to use the computer without paying. Stoll set up a honeypot of appealing material in the system, which pulled in the hackers. He traced the login to a group in East Germany who sold their access to the KGB. When Stoll gave a presentation of his sleuthing to the NSA, he was given a standing ovation.[2]

MOONLIGHT MAZE officially came to an end when it was exposed by the U.S. government. Insiders say, however, that it lives on under another name. At the time of writing this book, more than two decades later, it is apparently still an active U.S. investigation, as data analysts unpack the scope of secrets stolen from U.S. networks. It is equally difficult to establish what the U.S. government's corresponding internet capabilities at that time were, as details are opaque. In 1997, the NSA was authorized to collect intelligence over the internet, in what was termed "computer network exploitation." It was also authorized to conduct "computer network attacks," a polite term for sabotage: disrupting and degrading external computer networks. With that, U.S. espionage and sabotage formally moved from the physical world to the cyber realm. Rumors have swirled since the late 1990s that the NSA has installed back doors on Microsoft operating systems and software.

Russia's hack into the U.S. government in 1999 revealed significant differences between the uses of the internet in Russia and the United States. From the moment the first web page went live, created by Tim Berners-Lee at the Swiss research facility CERN in 1991, Russians and Americans viewed it in starkly different ways. In an atmosphere of U.S. global digital dominance, Silicon Valley conceived of the internet as a positive advance toward life, liberty, and the pursuit of happiness. The web supported free speech and offered its architects and corporate users the chance to earn vast sums of money. The road to utopia went through Silicon Valley. In Russia, the opposite was true. The internet was used to create a dystopia. Russia's security and intelligence services—the FSB, SVR, GU, and FAPSI—viewed it as a means for domestic surveillance, repression, censorship, bribery, blackmail, foreign espionage, and the trafficking of narcotics, people, and sex. Russia's "red web" offered new opportunities for transnational organized crime and foreign intelligence, which fused under Vladimir Putin.[3]

PUTIN'S MAFIA STATE

Russia's intelligence services in the 1990s, reconstituted from the KGB, became the vehicle for the Kremlin to reassert itself on the international stage—to make Russia great again. By the end of the decade, Russia was not a great power, but instead becoming a Mafia regime, where intelligence, state security, and organized crime coalesced. Putin personifies the ranks of the *siloviki*: men with former connections to security and intelligence services and Russia's military. He was the ideal spokesman for that caste of men. It is estimated that the number of Kremlin officials with backgrounds in security rose from 2.5 percent in 2003 to 42 percent in 2007, and to an incredible 77 percent in 2019, if agents, as well as officers, are included.

Within Putin's presidential administration, the "overwhelming" number of technocrats, who help run Russia's economy, have backgrounds in the security and intelligence services, according to a CIA officer who served in Moscow until 2021, whom I interviewed for this book.[4]

Putin symbolizes all that is resentful, paranoid, and revanchist about Russia. After a career spent studying Russia in the CIA, Robert Gates has observed in his memoir: "I believe Putin is a man of Russia's past, haunted by lost empire, lost glory, and lost power." Putin was raised a true believer in the Soviet Union. His grandfather cooked for Lenin and Stalin; his father, a minor policeman, fought in an NKVD unit in wartime Leningrad, where both of his parents suffered terribly. He lost his brother there. In his youth, he was attracted to espionage novels and films, imagining himself a secret agent. He volunteered for the KGB at the age of fourteen, while still in school, but did not make the cut and was told to come back when he was older. He trundled off to college, studying law at Leningrad State University. His studies gave him the skills to use the law as a weapon, to rig elections and criminal prosecutions, falsify evidence, abuse the human rights of Russian citizens and foreigners, and conduct massive state-backed corruption. He joined the KGB upon graduating, in 1975, at the age of about twenty-three. He trained at the elite FCD training school, the Andropov ("Red Banner") Institute, where recruits were indoctrinated into KGB spycraft, espionage, and active measures.[5]

Putin's background in Soviet intelligence shaped his rule in Russia. So too did his leadership of the FSB, "putting his foot in the same river twice," as was later said about him. But equally important was Putin's time in the 1990s in St. Petersburg and Moscow. Having left the KGB and witnessed the Soviet Union collapse around him, he found work with one of his former law professors, Anatoli Sobchak, Leningrad's mayor. Sobchak put his former student in charge of the city's economic relations, which brought him in touch with the security agencies and St. Petersburg's Mafia. Putin galvanized both by opening municipality-owned casinos. The contracts for the holding companies owning the casinos were drawn up by a lawyer,

Dmitri Medvedev. He was later rewarded for his loyalty to Putin by becoming president of Russia in 2008, and, in 2012, prime minister, though he was always in the shadow of the country's true leader. Under Putin's guidance, helped by Medvedev, the municipal casinos were loss-reporting undertakings whose profits disappeared. They were crooked operations. Some of Putin's companies were Mafia fronts. St. Petersburg rightly earned a reputation as Russia's most dangerous city. Next came Putin's shredding of the city's hundred-million-dollar reserves in cotton, scrap metal, and wood, supposedly to feed its inhabitants. If so, they never saw the food (or money); the huge commissions generated by the work vanished into shell companies, which declared bankruptcy after profits were siphoned away into hidden overseas bank accounts.[6]

"Russia is a rich country, especially in its raw materials and people," wrote Britain's ambassador in Moscow, Andrew Wood, in a cable to London in 1997. "That is one reason why it has in the past been able to make such a mess of its affairs." In 1996, when Sobchak lost reelection, Putin moved to Moscow, where Yeltsin gave him a mid-level job managing Russian presidential properties. It gave Putin inside knowledge of the Soviet Union's former real estate, Russian embassies overseas, and regional administrations. When Yeltsin appointed him FSB director in 1998, at the age of forty-five, Putin learned even more about Russian organized crime. A year later, on New Year's Eve, to the world's surprise, Yeltsin appointed Putin his successor. As the sun went down across the country's eleven time zones, Russia's intelligence agencies, and organized crime, were galvanized in Russian politics in a way the country had never seen before. Nobody had predicted Putin's meteoric rise to power. In the early 1990s, to make ends meet, Putin had worked part time as a taxi driver. The SVR's Primakov later recalled that, as head of Russian foreign intelligence, he had never heard of Putin. In 1997 his name did not feature among those given to Tony Blair by the prime minister's advisers as a potential Yeltsin successor. Now, as president of Russia, Putin offered Russian oligarchs a straight deal—stay out of politics, and in return they would accumulate unimaginable wealth. Most took the deal. The *siloviki* viewed Putin as malleable and trusted that he would go soft on Yeltsin once he was out of power. They were right.[7]

According to one U.S. official who worked as a translator at the U.S. consulate in St. Petersburg between 1993 and 1995 and interacted with Putin, even back then his hostility toward the United States was "palpable." At a Fourth of July celebration at the consulate, Putin told the American that he would prefer to be anywhere else than there. On another occasion, Putin revealed to the same official that he had gone to the trouble of ghost-writing a press article criticizing a visit by Republican stalwart Bob Dole to Russia. That U.S. official, whom I interviewed for this book and asked to remain anonymous, later became the CIA's chief of station in Moscow. "There's a direct continuum between Putin's animosity towards the U.S. then and what we've seen play out in recent years," said the CIA officer in an exclusive interview. He added that pundits who claim that Putin has gone crazy during Covid isolation overlook the almost "maniacal hatred" that he has harbored against the U.S. since the early 1990s.[8]

Since 1999, Russia under Putin has returned to authoritarian rule, which has now bled into a Stalinist-style dictatorship. In leading Russia, Putin has relied on people loyal to him from his KGB days, the social and political circles he moved in while in St. Petersburg, his Smolny gang and "Ozero circle," those who owned dachas on the lake outside the city; as well as those loyal to him in Moscow, later in the 1990s, and at the FSB. These men include Viktor Zolotov, former KGB border trooper, who became Putin's bodyguard, and now a member of Putin's security council; Nikolai Patrushev, former FSB director, who called FSB officers Russia's "new nobility"; Alexander Bortnikov, former head of the FSB's powerful economic division, who then became FSB director himself; Sergei Ivanov, previous head of the security council and minister of defense; Sergei Lebedev, an old KGB officer, and a colleague of Putin's in East Germany, who became SVR director; Sergei Shoigu, former chief of police, head of eighty thousand interior troops, and minister of defense in 2022; Viktor Zubkov, chairman of

Gazprom, before 2022 one of the largest public gas companies in the world and the largest company in Russia; Sergei Chemezov, chief executive of the tech conglomerate Rostec; and Igor Sechin, head of the oil giant Rosneft and a former KGB officer in Mozambique. They became a rogues' gallery. At the time of writing this book, Putin and many of those *siloviki* men mentioned above have been sanctioned by the U.S. government because of the war in Ukraine.[9]

Putin and his inner circle emphasize their Chekist backgrounds and the commonality between Soviet and Russian services in personnel, operational know-how, agents, and archives. But there are also differences between Soviet intelligence and Putin's special services. The first concerns the nature of Putin's rule. In the Soviet era, the KGB was ruled by the (frequently decrepit) Politburo and kept in check by the party, which had informants in its ranks. By contrast, Putin's special services work for him: he directs them. Their purpose is to protect him and keep him in power; it's that simple. Beyond Putin and those he delegates, they operate with impunity. Special services in contemporary Russia are not subject to independent legal or parliamentary oversight, and, apart from a few brave reporters, like Yevgenia Albats, there is now no free press in Russia. Many Putin critics have wound up dead. The Kremlin has incrementally taken over Russian media outlets, starting with the independent TV broadcaster NTV. It had investigated bombings that were suspected to have been set off by the FSB, and the *Kursk* submarine disaster. In May 2001, the FSB and others searched NTV's offices and arrested its owner, who was forced to sell the company (improbably) to Gazprom.

Putin's Kremlin, where his intelligence chiefs hold center stage, operates more like a medieval court than the Politburo, as a 2012 case in the London High Court between two Russian oligarchs revealed. Like the medieval past, Putin's rule relies on patronage, feudal fiefdoms, and is riddled with intrigue and thieves. It also has its share of court idiots.

Another significant difference between Soviet intelligence services and those under Putin is ideology. Although FSB and SVR officers describe themselves as Chekists, Soviet communism is obviously dead in Putin's

Russia. Far from being Marxists, the *siloviki* embrace kleptocratic capitalism, where corrupt individuals, with Putin's blessing, enrich themselves through bribes, special favors, and plundering state resources. The FSB operates for the personal enrichment of Putin and his inner circle. Ever since his St. Petersburg days, Putin has understood the importance of cooperating with the Mafia. FSB officers provide the Russian Mafia with protection (*krysha*), for which they receive kickbacks. But this is not a story of a few bad apples. More than being a union of crooks and policemen, the FSB is an instrument for systemic state-run criminality. Through legislation passed in 2004, the FSB has had virtually unrestricted rights to intervene in Russian business and financial affairs. It has become effectively impossible to do business in Russia without FSB approval.

The FSB's Economic Security Division does the opposite of its professed role. It controls most sectors of the Russian economy and financial services, conducting and covering up financial crimes. An FSB defector interviewed for this book, who had worked in its finance division, explained that the FSB either has liaison officers with businesses in Russia (known as a "line") or officers actually embedded with them (known as an "object"). It works through Russian businessmen, so Western businesspeople do not know that the FSB is a silent partner. Ever since the 1990s, Russian real estate has been a ripe ground for targeting Western business leaders, explained the FSB officer, who must remain anonymous.[10]

It is thus fundamentally wrong to suppose the FSB is anything like Western services, like MI5 or the FBI. It permeates all aspects of Russia's corrupt economy. The charges leveled against the financier Bill Browder, who ran the investment firm Hermitage Capital in Russia beginning in the 1990s, offer a case in point. The FSB raided his offices in Moscow in 2007 and charged him with tax evasion. Browder's lawyer, Sergei Magnitsky, discovered that police, judges, and the criminal underworld were fraudulently claiming huge VAT refunds in Hermitage's name, using company seals taken during the raid. In total, they stole $230 million, money that was owed to Russian taxpayers. In 2008 Magnitsky was arrested and imprisoned. Russian officials demanded he make a deal to testify against Browder. He refused and died in prison eleven months later, apparently beaten and denied medical care.[11]

Money laundering has long been an FSB specialty, as it was for the Soviets from the outset. Old KGB hands in the FSB knew the techniques of shell corporations for Soviet industrial espionage. But now, in the 2000s, Russia was not a pariah, like the Soviet Union, but was being courted by well-dressed bankers on Wall Street or in the City of London. By one estimate, Danske Bank has laundered at least $230 billion, and Swedbank another $149 billion, from Russia and former Soviet countries. All this gives the FSB virtually unmatched financial and political power. In Putin's Russia we effectively find a state attached to a security service. Although Putin's official salary is approximately $140,000, rumors have his fortune ranging from $40 billion to $200 billion. According to aerial drone footage released by Putin's arch-critic Alexei Navalny, Putin has built a $1 billion seaside palace on the Black Sea, featuring a casino, ice rink, and vineyard. Putin's close friends and associates do almost as well. His "best friend," Sergei Roldugin, a cellist, and godfather to Putin's daughter Maria, plays a $12 million Stradivarius. He is worth an estimated $350 million but apparently controls much more in offshore accounts hidden in balmy destinations like Panama, the British Virgin Islands, and Cyprus.[12]

After the great financial crash of 2008, Britain became a favored haven for Putin's oligarchs. In "Londongrad," an army of lawyers, hedge fund and property managers, consultants, and art dealers have helped to wash dirty Russian money and turn it into respectable holdings, in properties in Mayfair and Chelsea ("Chelski"). In 2014, 60 percent of the business in London's commercial court was coming from Russian and Eastern European clients. The London laundromat made a killing for the City. With money flowing in, British leaders appeased Putin.[13]

Since coming to power in Russia, Putin has made much of his past as a KGB officer. But it is a carefully cultivated image, like his gunslinger gait, reminding everyone of his invisible sidearm. As one expert in the history of dictatorships has noted, the creed of Putin's *siloviki* is straight authoritarian:

nepotistic, nihilistic, cynical, ruthless, and eschewing the rule of law. It is entirely possible that the FSB organized the September 1999 bombings of apartment complexes in Moscow, and other cities, to justify Russia's war in Chechnya and boost Putin's patriotic profile. The buildings were demolished at night by an enormous cache of explosives in their basements, killing around three hundred people and injuring more. The bombings were blamed on Chechen militants; Putin's opinion polls soared in their wake. In October 2002, FSB special forces put an end to a theater siege in Moscow by using a synthetic opioid that acted as an incapacitating agent. Forty terrorists involved in the standoff died, but so did one hundred and thirty innocent hostages, who were denied the antidote either through secrecy or incompetence.[14]

FROZEN CONFLICTS

The terrorist attacks in the United States on September 11, 2001, transformed U.S. intelligence and national security. The war on terror was really a war against al-Qaeda in Afghanistan. But under the neoconservatives in George W. Bush's administration, the focus on counterterrorism became an expansive U.S. "war on terror." It involved an "axis of evil" that encompassed Iraq and Iran—despite the two countries being sworn enemies—and claims that Iraq was supporting al-Qaeda (which it was not) and had built "weapons of mass destruction" (which it also had not). No sensible standard was given for what "victory" would look like in the "war on terror"—the elimination of all terrorism?—to say nothing of the fact that it was impossible to wage war on a noun. America's war on terror was a messianic mission, impossible to win without addressing the underlying reasons why people commit terrorism.

Putin used the pretext of counterterrorism for his own actions against Chechens and Islamists in Russia. He shared intelligence with the U.S. during the war on terror, including during its engagements in Afghanistan, and the information "paid off in results" in some specific operations, as one former CIA chief of station in Moscow told me. In 2001, Bush met Putin and, in remarks he later regretted, said that he looked into the Russian leader's blue sharklike eyes and saw his soul. Two months after 9/11, the president welcomed Putin to his ranch in Crawford, Texas.[15]

But perhaps if Bush had looked more carefully into Putin's eyes, he would have recognized a more ruthless grand strategy: to make Russia a great power once again, and take revenge on the United States. To Putin, the collapse of the Soviet Union spelled the end of "historical Russia." The Soviet demise, he has said, remains a "tragedy" for most Russian citizens. With the Soviet Union's breakup, all the former Soviet republics gained something—independence—while Russia lost. After the Soviet Union's dissolution in 1991, the Kremlin found itself ruling half the territory that it had two years previously, and less than it had at any time since Catherine the Great in the eighteenth century. Russia's territorial dismemberment, and humiliation, seemed similar to after Brest-Litovsk in 1918. Twenty-five million ethnic Russians were marooned abroad, as the KGB had warned Moscow in the Soviet Union's final days. The Soviet collapse also unleashed Russian nationalism—which had largely been in abeyance during the polyglot Soviet Union—now personified by hard-liners like Zhirinovsky. The loss of the Soviet empire created phantom-limb syndrome for many of those within Russian political circles. Russia experienced all the dislocations that other world powers went through with their end of empires, but in two short years.[16]

◆

The deterioration of Russian-Western relations in the 1990s had not been inevitable. For a brief period, there was potential for Russia to be a partner with Western governments. The most viable of these opportunities was the now almost forgotten 1994 Partnership for Peace, which sought to bring Russia into close association with NATO. In the grandly titled "Charter for American-Russian Partnership and Friendship," Presidents Clinton and Yeltsin jointly committed themselves to defend and advance "common democratic values and human rights and fundamental freedoms." However, the partnership was soon effectively scuttled. For hard-liners in Moscow, it was little more than NATO by another name. Back in 1990, James Baker had made some kind of assurance during German unification to Gorbachev that NATO would not expand eastward "one inch." Baker overstepped his orders from the president, and the nature of his statement has been the subject of endless study ever since. The important point is that Yeltsin's foreign policy advisers, including the SVR, believed that the U.S. government had indeed made a promise not to expand eastward. Never mind that Gorbachev himself later publicly disagreed.[17]

Clinton was in principle opposed to the expansion of NATO. In the 1994 midterm elections, however, he lost control of the House and Congress to Republicans, who favored expanding NATO. To win a second term in the 1996 election, his stance on expanding NATO hardened. These decisions fell to Warren Christopher, secretary of state, and his successor in Foggy Bottom, Madeleine Albright. Two lobby groups influenced Clinton's thinking on the subject: leaders from newly liberated nations in central and Eastern Europe, who understandably did not trust the Russians and wanted a buffer zone, and U.S. defense industries, which stood to make a killing by selling hardware to new NATO members. Clinton tried to reassure Yeltsin by offering a Russian strategic alliance with NATO. The Partnership for Peace offered Moscow a seat at the table, along with twenty-one other nations—but no voice. Members of Congress saw it in geopolitical terms, Clinton would later explain to Tony Blair. The arrest of the CIA's Aldrich Ames as a Soviet-Russian spy in 1994 may have also contributed to Clinton's thinking. As Clinton noted in his memoirs, expanding NATO was "problematic."[18]

The opportunity to recast NATO, and former Warsaw Pact alliances, was not taken. At the end of 1993, Britain's foreign secretary, Douglas Hogg, told Russia's ambassador in London, Boris Pankin, an old Soviet hand, that NATO was central to Western security, so they would not "dilute" it.

However, according to records unsealed in 2022, Hogg hastened to add that NATO would be mindful of Russia's "sensitivities." Pankin replied that Russia wanted a comprehensive redrawing of European security, including NATO. Meanwhile, in Washington, after calculating the impact of Czech, Hungarian, and Polish American voters on winning a second term in 1996, President Bill Clinton announced the next year that, at the urging of the U.S., NATO would admit the Czech Republic, Hungary, and Poland. Tony Blair's now-opened cabinet papers reveal that he pressed Yeltsin to view NATO expansion as *inclusion* for Russia, not exclusion. It meant greater security in Europe, which was in Russia's interests, ran Blair's argument. Yeltsin replied that Russians had a "negative attitude" about NATO. He demanded that no nuclear weapons be stationed in the new NATO member territories, that Russia should have a veto in NATO decisions, and that Ukraine and the Baltic states be "off limits" for NATO expansion. Under pressure from Blair, Yeltsin dropped the latter two demands. In a secret circular to the foreign office in London, Britain's embassy in Moscow warned in no uncertain terms that NATO expansion was "painful" for Russia and seen as a "humiliating defeat." Although Yeltsin may formally accept its expansion, Russians did not. To placate Russia, it was admitted to the "big table" of G8 countries. The first wave, three countries, duly joined the alliance in 1999, the year Putin came to power, followed by nine more states over the next decade. Veteran Cold Warriors in the United States, including George Kennan, the architect of Soviet containment, publicly warned that expanding NATO was a mistake.[19]

Putin needed little convincing that NATO was, by definition, hostile to Moscow's interests. His point was proved to Russian voters when, at the end of the decade, in the name of humanitarian intervention, NATO fought two wars inside the former Yugoslavia. The latter had not attacked a NATO member (therefore had not triggered Article V) and was not part of NATO. Not long after offering Russia a strategic partnership, NATO thus rubbed dirt in Moscow's face by engaging in armed intervention in a region that Moscow considered a Russian sphere of influence. Scholars and

Western politicians can debate endlessly whether NATO actually poses a threat to Russia, to say nothing of soporific theoretical seminar discussions about balancing of power, but doing so misses the point. Trying to convince Russia's foreign ministry otherwise is fruitless. Putin and his inner circle *believe* NATO is a threat. They have been consistent in their view. The more they look, the less they like what they see. The U.S.-led invasion of Iraq in 2003 showed that Washington politicians and their allies in London were unashamedly engaged in the business of regime change. They are coming for us too, Putin could tell his fellow Russians.[20]

Today, Putin has been in power for more than two decades, during which time five U.S. presidents have come and gone from the Oval Office, and six British prime ministers entered Downing Street. For twenty-two years, Putin's rule has given him a consistency in leadership lacking in Western democracies. His primary mission has been to undo the "injustices" of the Soviet collapse and reach a grand bargain with the United States to right the wrongs of the past, as he sees them. To exert pressure, he has used a series of conflicts in Russia's near abroad, whose peoples wish they were further abroad. Putin can heat up, and cool down, these conflicts as suits his needs.

The term "great power politics," much in vogue in Washington as this book is being written, needs to be treated with caution when used in reference to Putin's Russia. His fierce desire certainly is to make Russia great again. But the rubric "great power politics" suggests a reversion, even nostalgia, to a balance of power between great powers found in nineteenth-century Europe. When it comes to Putin's Russia, however, that term does not do justice to the ugly reality: Putin and his clique are hooligans, domestically and on the international stage.

If we want a model for countering Putin, we should look not just to past "balances of power," but to the history of bringing down Mafia leaders. The career of Al Capone is a useful precedent to apply with Putin: follow the money—and use that as a weapon. Like many dictators, Putin is thin-skinned, in his case about his colossal wealth. Putin was pained by the Panama Papers and Alexei Navalny's revelations. The former KGB officer uses the full levers of his authoritarian security state to push through his agenda to destabilize neighbors by kidnap, murder, and election rigging, to project Russian power in the Middle East and farther afield. Putin seeks revenge on the United States for undermining Russia's position as a world power.

Putin views himself as containing the U.S. from subverting and meddling in Russian affairs—all of which requires robust security. For a naturally inclined conspiracist, it would be difficult for Putin not to believe the U.S. was out to get him. From his KGB days, he is aware of the hidden hand of the U.S. government in toppling foreign regimes and supporting centrist and democratic groups in Europe. He sees the CIA's hand in fomenting "color revolutions" inside Georgia in 2003 and Ukraine in 2004, traditional spheres of Russian influence, which he had to defend against. Putin blamed the defeat of his loyalist in Ukraine, Viktor Yanukovych, on U.S. meddling.

In February 2007, at the Munich Security Conference, Putin laid out his worldview in a blistering thirty-minute speech: he rejected the post-Soviet world order and accused the United States of being a hegemon, which was imposing its will on others, like Iraq. This unipolar world, Putin proclaimed in his clipped Russian, "in which there is one master, one sovereign," was not true democracy for other nations, because it did not reflect and respect their will. The United States was making the world more dangerous, not less. Putin called for a rebalancing of the international security landscape.

It is difficult to conclude anything other than, after Munich, Western governments were following Neville Chamberlain's footsteps of appeasement. The Western response was just enough to inflame Putin's fear of subversion, but insufficient to cause him to think twice about further territorial annexations. The next year, in 2008, Putin invaded Georgia. It produced a lackluster overt response from Western powers. President Bush's national security team had to decide whether to send U.S. troops and risk a war with Russia. They decided against military intervention, but based on national security records about Georgia at Bush's presidential library, the U.S. government was evidently doing something covert there, judging from the redactions. Was that sufficient? Evidently not. Meanwhile, Putin's indictment of U.S. regime change was heightened in 2011 after the beginning of the Arab Spring, which saw the U.S.-backed removal and killing of Libya's leader, Muammar Gaddafi. Putin was reportedly "disgusted" when he was killed, and watched the video clips, broadcast to the world, of Gaddafi's bloodied last moments countless times. The situation was hardly improved when Senator John McCain said that Putin should be nervous.[21]

The Maidan revolution, which erupted in Ukraine in February 2014, led to the ousting of Putin's loyalist in power, Yanukovych. Putin responded in 2014 by seizing Crimea and parts of the Donbas, in a military intervention using non-uniformed special forces, who seized control in just nineteen days. A leaked audiotape appeared online in 2014, doubtless intercepted by Russian intelligence, in which U.S. assistant secretary of state Victoria Nuland was heard talking about working with Ukrainian opposition leaders. That cemented, in Russian eyes, the notion of U.S. meddling in Ukraine. Since then, Putin initiated "repatriation" of Russians from "historic" Russian areas like the Donbas in Ukraine.[22]

THE WEST TAKES ITS EYES OFF THE BALL

The month after George W. Bush's inauguration in January 2001, the CIA and FBI caught Robert Hanssen, the Soviet-Russian mole inside the FBI who betrayed so many American secrets. It did so, it seems, by recruiting a down-on-his-luck former KGB officer. When Hanssen was arrested, in February 2001, he asked FBI special agents: "What took you so long?" Hanssen was sentenced to life in prison without the possibility of parole. U.S. counterespionage officers were convinced there was still an unaccounted-for Russian agent in Washington. FBI investigators alighted on a wholly innocent and professional CIA officer, Brian Kelley, as the Russian spy. It was another illustration of the damage that a spy discovered in an intelligence agency can cause, undermining the careers of trustworthy officers and agents who become collateral damage. In reality, Hanssen had learned about the

FBI's investigation of Kelley. Hanssen thought he had discovered a fellow spy and warned Moscow, which then planted clues pointing to Kelley.[23]

Briefed about the damage that Hanssen had done over a quarter of a century, President Bush decided, in Texan slang, to "go big" on Russia. He expelled fifty Russian diplomats, six of whom had been directly involved in running Hanssen. Seven months later, on 9/11, America was attacked by al-Qaeda terrorists, in an act that would transform both U.S. intelligence and national and global security. With the U.S.-led invasion of Iraq, America's war on al-Qaeda turned into a global war on terror. And as we saw earlier, U.S. and British intelligence communities cooperated with Russia's intelligence services in combating terrorism. After Putin visited London in December 2001, Prime Minister Tony Blair described U.K.-Russian relations as "unprecedentedly close" and announced efforts to enhance intelligence liaisons. These liaisons did produce some tangible results, according to insiders in the U.S. National Counterterrorism Center and Britain's Joint Terrorism Analysis Centre.[24]

After 9/11, as well as subsequent attacks in Europe and Britain, and the threat of terrorist groups obtaining chemical, biological, or even nuclear weapons, there were legitimate and understandable reasons why governments devoted enormous resources to counterterrorism. Four coordinated terrorist suicide attacks in July of 2005 in London resulted in the deaths of fifty-two people, while injuring almost eight hundred more. That year, 92 percent of MI5's work was focused on counterterrorism. MI6 and GCHQ threw similar resources at counterterrorism. It is important to consider the priority given to terrorism in a longer-term perspective. At the height of the Cold War, 70 percent of GCHQ's work, and about 75–80 percent of its budget, targeted the Soviet bloc. After 9/11, the pendulum swung sharp the other way. In 2006, GCHQ's work on all hostile foreign nations reached a low point of a mere 4 percent.[25]

Russia was not a true ally of the West in the war on terror, although it did have shared interests with Western governments. Before 9/11, George W. Bush had thought Putin was "one cold dude." The Russian leader's brilliance was to convince the Bush administration, and Blair's government, that he

was not pursuing two agendas at the same time. While he did assist Western governments with counterterrorism after 9/11, that did not deter him
from his long-term strategy: to restore Russia as a resurgent great power,
to dominate the former Soviet bloc countries Russia "lost" in 1991, and to
push back against foreign countries that were preventing the fulfillment of
Russia's historical mission, chief among them the United States. Twenty years
after 9/11, a British parliamentary investigation concluded that, although
there were understandable reasons why the British government devoted
overwhelming intelligence resources to counterterrorism, it did so at the
expense of the threat from Russia. British spy chiefs and policymakers at
Downing Street took their eyes off the ball, concluded the report.[26]

The clearest indication of Putin's ruthless agenda was revealed five years
after 9/11, when, using radioactive material as poison, a Russian hit squad
assassinated Alexander Litvinenko, a vocal Putin critic, on the streets of
London. Although leaders in the Kremlin had refrained from assassinations
during the Gorbachev and Yeltsin periods, with Litvinenko's death, Putin
was back in the business of targeted killings. Litvinenko's murder followed
in the KGB's earlier tradition of "wet affairs" (*mokrie dela*), whose Stalinist
motto was "no man, no problem" (*nyet cheloveka, nyet problemy*). Four
decades before, the Bulgarian critic Georgi Markov had been assassinated in
London under similar circumstances. While waiting for a bus on Waterloo
Bridge, Markov felt a sudden sting in his right thigh. Although he did not
realize it, it came from an umbrella, provided to Bulgarian intelligence by
the KGB, whose tip had been converted into a gun with a silencer, injecting
Markov with a lethal dose of ricin, a deadly poison. He died in agonizing
pain in a hospital four days later.[27]

Even the KGB, however, was never so reckless as to radiate the streets of a
Western capital. Litvinenko, a former KGB official, had worked in the FSB's
organized-crime division, where he caused a major public embarrassment for
Putin. In 1998, he led a group of FSB officers and agents from his division,
one masked, another wearing dark glasses, in a television appearance to accuse
the FSB—and by implication its director, Putin—of ordering the unsuccessful

assassination of one of Russia's oligarchs, Boris Berezovsky. Berezovsky, Yeltsin's former deputy national security adviser, had been a critic of Putin since 2000 and considered himself Russia's kingmaker. At the time of the Soviet breakup, he had made his fortune in cars, oil, and other ventures. He was one of the 110 oligarchs who owned 35 percent of Russia's wealth.[28]

Convinced—correctly—that FSB bosses were involved in organized crime, Litvinenko accused Putin of running an FSB crime syndicate. He was arrested and spent a year in prison. Litvinenko's allegations led to a spectacular falling-out between Berezovsky and Putin. Soon Litvinenko was on Berezovsky's payroll. Berezovsky relocated to London in 2000, and Litvinenko, with the oligarch's help, found his way there that same year. He was granted political asylum and became a naturalized British subject. He coauthored a book, *Blowing Up Russia*, in which he accused the FSB of bombing, in 1999, the two Moscow apartment buildings mentioned earlier, as a false-flag operation, blaming Chechens.

In London, Litvinenko ("Sasha") worked as Berezovsky's security consultant, as well as reportedly advising MI6 on Russian organized crime, for which he was paid £2,000 per month. In October 2006, he publicly accused Putin of being responsible for the assassination of the Russian investigative journalist Anna Politkovskaya, who was killed in the elevator of her Moscow apartment building. At that point, Putin had had enough of the London thorn in his side. A former KGB bodyguard turned successful businessman, Andrei Lugovoi, and a sidekick of his, Dmitri Kovtun, traveled to London to meet with Litvinenko. On a crisp autumn afternoon, the three men sat at the Pine Bar in the Millennium Hotel, in Grosvenor Square in Mayfair, a stone's throw from the U.S. embassy. They had cocktails and cigars. As they left, Lugovoi and Kovtun ordered a pot of tea for Litvinenko, which they laced with radioactive polonium.

That night, at his home in north London, Litvinenko became violently ill. Two days later, he was admitted to University College Hospital, vomiting and in great pain. Over the coming days, his hair fell out and vital organs failed. As he lay on his deathbed, spitting blood, he solved the riddle of his own murder. He denounced Putin with these words: "As I lie here I can hear the beating of the wings of the angel of death at my back. . . . You may succeed in silencing one man but the howl of protest from around the world will reverberate, Mr. Putin, in your ears for the rest of your life. May God forgive you for what you have done, not only to me but to beloved Russia and its people."[29]

Because of the polonium he ingested, Litvinenko's body was so radioactive that it had to be sealed in a specially prepared coffin. Berezovsky's team saw to it that images of Litvinenko, and his deathbed denunciation of Putin, were beamed around the world. Two hundred and fifty people from the hotel had to be tested for radiation poisoning. The two Russian assassins left a trail of radiation across London's underground stations and trains and on the planes in which they flew home. A discarded hotel towel was so contaminated that it had to be sent to Britain's Atomic Weapons Research Establishment.

A later British inquest concluded that Litvinenko's assassination was probably—more likely than not—authorized by FSB director Patrushev and approved by Putin himself. Kovtun suffered radiation poisoning but survived. British police unsuccessfully demanded Lugovoi's extradition for murder. Lugovoi moved into Russian politics; he holds a seat in the Duma as a member of Zhirinovsky's Liberal Democratic Party, giving him immunity from extradition.[30]

There is another bleak coda to the affair. Berezovsky, Litvinenko's patron, lost an epic legal battle, mentioned earlier, over ownership of the Russian oil producer Sibneft at London's High Court against fellow oligarch Roman Abramovich, former owner of Chelsea Football Club. Thereafter, in 2013, Berezovsky was found hanged in the bathroom of his Berkshire mansion. The inquest recorded an open verdict, meaning that his death was suspicious, but could not establish homicide. Investigative reporting suggests that Russia's intelligence services have been linked to fourteen deaths in Britain.[31]

In 2016, Montenegro, formerly a part of Yugoslavia, held a referendum on becoming NATO's twenty-ninth member. To prevent this from happening, the GRU planned a coup: to assassinate the country's prime minister, Milo Đukanović, and install an anti-NATO leader. The GRU coup failed, and Montenegro joined NATO in 2017. Two GRU operatives were arrested and prosecuted. The GRU was humiliated again the following year when it tried to assassinate a former MI6 spy in its ranks, Sergei Skripal, in Salisbury, England. Using Novichok, as we have seen, it did so with homicidal indifference to public safety. The two GRU officers involved, looking more like nightclub bouncers than intelligence officers, were identified by British authorities. They then appeared on Russian media, implausibly claiming to have been on a sightseeing tour of the English countryside and enchanted by Salisbury cathederal.[32]

DEEP-COVER ILLEGALS—AGAIN

One way that the SVR recreated KGB spycraft lay with its recruitment, and running, of deep-cover illegals in foreign countries. In June 2010, ten such Russian sleeper agents were exposed in the United States. Their mission, for more than a decade, had been to pose as American citizens and infiltrate what the Center called the country's "ruling circles." The operation had all the hallmarks of Cold War espionage: the use of invisible ink, clandestine meetings in parks, buried bags of money, and an attractive redheaded female operative named Anna Chapman. In one case, the agents deceived their own children about their true identity.

Code-named Operation GHOST STORIES by U.S. intelligence, the investigation was one of the longest and most elaborate counterespionage efforts in American history. After it was exposed, it became the basis for the hit series *The Americans*. Much of the media attention about the spy ring describes its unraveling as an FBI success story—which it was. But it was also a CIA success. Sometime around 1999, when Putin came to power, the FBI recruited an officer who had spent his career working in one of the SVR's and the KGB's most sensitive units, Directorate S, responsible for running illegals. Alexander Poteyev offered his services while working undercover at the Russian mission to the UN in New York, where he oversaw Department S operations in North America. The FBI routinely pitched Russian officials in New York. Eventually it worked with Poteyev, who seems to have preferred life in the United States. Sometime after being recruited by the FBI, he returned to Moscow, where he was promoted to deputy head of Department S, which gave him (and thus his American handlers) access to SVR illegal operations globally. Poteyev had a ten-year career as a U.S. agent in place. According to some of those involved, interviewed for this book and who ask to remain nameless, CIA handlers met him in various locations around the world—hotels, airport lounges. They often wore disguises. For Poteyev's services, the CIA paid him handsomely—an amount rumored to be $5 million—and promised to resettle him in the U.S. and give him a new life.[33]

In June 2010, U.S. intelligence officials evidently calculated that the time had come to exfiltrate Poteyev to the United States. He escaped through Belarus and Ukraine. His exfiltration, after more than a decade of espionage work, led the CIA and the FBI to pull the trigger and arrest the undercover agents he had identified. The oldest of the illegals, whose alias, or legend, was Juan Lazaro, had begun working as an illegal for the KGB thirty-four years before. When the arrests took place, he had actually retired from the SVR. Another of the illegals, Donald Heathfield, posing as a Canadian businessman, had graduated from Harvard's Kennedy School of Government in 2000 and was living in Cambridge, Massachusetts. Once exposed, Harvard revoked Heathfield's degree—on grounds that it had been obtained on false pretenses.[34]

The most glamorous agent in the GHOST STORIES network was Anna Chapman (née Kushchenko). She was born in Volgograd, where her father was a KGB agent (and perhaps officer). After obtaining a degree from a university in Moscow, she moved to London, where she picked up a husband, whom she met at a rave in London's Docklands. Her marriage gave her a British passport. They divorced four years later, and Chapman moved to New York, where she worked in real estate, although her real job was for the SVR. She was far from the femme fatale Jane Bond that Russian state media subsequently tried to portray her to be. She communicated with the Center while dining out in bustling New York restaurants, in a Starbucks, and at a Barnes & Noble bookstore, using a laptop with a wireless connection. She and her SVR handlers, who usually sat nearby, were incompetent. On one occasion, she complained to her contact that her computer was not working properly; he offered to take it in for repair, to which she agreed. Unfortunately for her, and the SVR, her contact that day was actually an undercover FBI special agent. When he returned the computer, the FBI and CIA were able to intercept her instructions from the Center and the material she passed to her handlers.

The network of Russian illegals in the United States was a failure on two counts: none of the agents gained access to classified information, and they were caught and publicly paraded in a way that embarrassed Russian spy chiefs. Ostensibly there was not much that people living in suburbia, or working in real estate in New York, could do to impact U.S. national security; none had managed to penetrate the American corridors of power. But it had the makings of another Portland spy ring. As the FBI was quick to point out, the illegals could act as talent spotters for those who did have access, not unlike Kim Philby decades before. Over time they may have been able to make contacts in academia, political think tanks, financial services, and the federal government. And their children could have potentially carried on their work and applied for positions in the U.S. government, military, and intelligence community.

The arrest of the Russian illegals had to be carefully choreographed. A year before, in 2009, the Obama administration had attempted a "reset" with Russia. The spy ring threatened worsening relations. As Poteyev was escaping Russia and the FBI decided to roll up the spy ring, Russia's new president, Dmitri Medvedev, Putin's old ally from his St. Petersburg days, was visiting Washington. He met Barack Obama, who spoke warmly of his hope for modernization and innovation for Russia. The two went to a burger joint in Arlington, where photographers caught them having cheeseburgers and sharing fries. But before meeting the Russian president, Obama had been briefed on Operation GHOST STORIES, as had his National Security Council. The president agreed to a phased approach to the unwinding of the network. He could not risk a major Russian spy ring being uncovered while the Russian president was in town, just a year after Obama's secretary of state, Hillary Clinton, famously embarked on a reset of U.S.-Russian relations with Russia's foreign minister, Sergei Lavrov. The arrests went down as Medvedev's flight left North American airspace. On July 4, Independence Day, CIA director Leon Panetta called the SVR director, Mikhail Fradkov, an old KGB hand, to tell him that his agents in the United States had been apprehended.[35]

For the FBI and CIA, the intention was never to bring Russian agents in the GHOST STORIES network to trial. Doing so would, after all, require them to disclose their Russian spy, Poteyev. Instead, they wanted to use the arrests of the Russian agents as leverage. Panetta informed the SVR that he wanted an exchange. Again, it had all the hallmarks of the Cold War. The spy swap took place in July 2010 on a sweltering airport tarmac in Vienna, ten going from Russia to the West and four from the U.S. to Russia. It was not quite Checkpoint Charlie, or the Glienicke Bridge in Berlin, but the ramifications were similar. "We were back at the levels of the Cold War," Paul Kolbe, chief of the CIA's Central Eurasia Division, told me. "For Russia, the idea that the Cold War was over was fantasy," said Kolbe, who was integrally involved with GHOST STORIES. One of those spies exchanged from East to West was an MI6 agent in the GRU, Sergei Skripal. His story, too, was like another page taken from a Cold War book. After Skripal's attempted assassination in 2018, the British government responded by expelling twenty-three Russian diplomats, who, Prime Minister Theresa May said—doubtless on MI5's advice—were intelligence officers. It was the largest such expulsion since the Cold War.

GHOST STORIES was a public relations disaster for the SVR, for Russia, and for Putin. The SVR had expended significant resources on running the illegals, which some Western intelligence observers could not fathom, given that so much information was available online without requiring elaborate espionage schemes. But for Putin, illegals were the epitome of Russian foreign intelligence, an important department worthy of support. "I know what kind of people these are," recalled Putin. "These are special people, people of special qualities, of special conviction, with a special character. To give up their life, their nearest and dearest and leave the country for many years, and to dedicate one's life to the Fatherland, not everyone is capable of doing that." Putin would later claim that he worked in the illegals section, Department S, of the KGB. There is no reliable evidence to support this claim. On the contrary, CIA insiders have told me that evidence exists that Putin wanted to be a KGB illegal—but he failed the language training. One does not need to be a psychologist to see how Putin's failure to become an illegal would have led to a chip on his shoulder and a belief that they have impossibly high standards.

Putin blamed the failure of the SVR sleeper network on "traitors." And he is reported to have said, chillingly: "Traitors will kick the bucket, trust me. These people betrayed their friends, their brothers in arms. Whatever they got in exchange for it, those thirty pieces of silver they were given, they will choke on them."[36]

After disappearing, Poteyev became public enemy number one for the Kremlin. A spokesman told the newspaper *Kommersant*: "We know who he is and where he is," and added: "A Mercader has already been sent after him," a reference to the Soviet operative Ramón Mercader, who killed Stalin's nemesis Leon Trotsky in Mexico in 1940 with an ice pick. True to his arrangement with the CIA, it seems, Poteyev was resettled in the United States and assumed life under an alias. In 2016 Russian media reported that he had died, but an investigative journalist revealed that he was still alive two years later, living in Florida. Despite the Kremlin's claims, a Mercader has not (yet) got to him.

In February 2022, the Department of Justice disclosed a case of a Mexican national, Hector Fuentes, who had pled guilty to acting as a Russian agent in Florida. Fuentes, who had spent significant time in Russia, was instructed by someone he believed was a Russian government official to travel to Miami, where he conducted surveillance on a "U.S. person," including taking a close-up photo of that person's license plate and parking location. The tradecraft in the case was, according to the DoJ, "consistent with the tactics of the Russian intelligence services for spotting, assessing, recruiting, and handling intelligence assets and sources." The target of his reconnaissance, the "U.S. person," is described by the DoJ as someone "who had previously provided information about the Russian government to the United States Government."[37]

Was this the beginning of a modern-day Mercarder sent to kill America's spy, Poteyev—an assassination on U.S. soil?

For Putin, the only thing worse than failure is being ridiculed. That is exactly what happened when the SVR's sloppy—and sexist, as it transpired—spy ring was exposed to the world in 2010. It emerged that the SVR code name given to Anna Chapman by her male handlers was her body size measurements. The SVR's operational failure and public humiliation may have contributed to Putin taking even more brazen risks against the United States going forward.

CYBERIA

Russia is the largest country in the world by landmass. Yet despite its size and abundant natural resources, in 2022, before Putin's war in Ukraine, Russia had an economy roughly the size of Italy's. (Between 2014 and 2022, Putin largely managed to sanction-proof Russia's economy.) Although Russia is a country of remarkable achievements in the arts and sciences, except for oil and natural gas it produces little that the world wants. As he reached his third decade at Russia's helm, Putin failed to diversify the economy. In 2015, Senator John McCain accurately described Russia as "a gas station masquerading as a country." It is precisely because Russia is so weak economically that Putin fostered a more aggressive foreign policy. As long as he himself is secure, what has he got to lose?

Putin's strategy regarding Western powers was a return to the zero-sum game: any time Western nations were doing badly, by default, Russia was winning. He has sought to split Western alliances, like NATO and the European Union, discredit Western governments and liberal democracies, sow chaos and confusion, and undermine the rules-based international order. He has sponsored separatist movements from Catalonia to far-right neo-Nazi movements in Bulgaria; he uses disinformation and money to influence audiences in Africa (shades of the Cold War), as well as dispatching paramilitary outfits like the Wagner Group there; he aids any country or organization that will help him advance his goals against the West, in accordance with the old Cold War playbook, updated and modernized for the digital era. Today, Russia's intelligence services use the internet to conduct espionage and to carry out acts of subversion and sabotage. Simply put, the internet has acted as a force multiplier for hostile states like Russia to conduct operations from afar. Putin's predecessors in the Lubyanka could only have dreamed of such a resource.[38]

Russian hackers were just getting started with Operation MOONLIGHT MAZE. As the internet exploded over the next decade, so did a hacker's potential to attack individuals, groups, and governments. In 2007, Estonia suffered a devastating Russian cyberattack on its critical infrastructure. It was an act of digital sabotage. Russian hackers affiliated with the country's intelligence services also used the cyber realm for other old Soviet strategies: subversion. One tool to subvert or influence targets, as we have seen, is disinformation: an effort to foment deliberately false, distorting, or distracting information or narratives, while hiding true authorship. The growth of social media has provided unprecedented opportunities to spread disinformation. Facebook was created in 2004, Twitter in 2006, Instagram four years later, Snapchat in 2011. They offer cheaper, quicker, easier, and arguably more effective ways to spread disinformation than ever before. There have always been lunatic fringes in societies, throughout history, willing to believe conspiracy theories. Social media platforms provide them with ways to amplify their voices and reach audiences not previously obtainable, giving them megaphones to disseminate bizarre and often violent theories.

Russia's intelligence services—the FSB, the SVR, and the GU—can now create false Twitter and Facebook accounts in an instant rather than going through the laborious process of creating physical front groups and launching publications, as their predecessors did. The new capabilities afforded by the internet has been combined with a seemingly endless appetite to accept disinformation. Western audiences have become avid consumers of such theories, accepting spurious stories, without evidence, as truth. A corrosive impact of disinformation on democratic societies is its assault on truth and facts themselves. As the journalist Peter Pomerantsev has shown, Russia has a long history of contorting the truth to fit the policy of the day. In Western countries, debates over what constitutes truth used to be safely confined to university seminars or navel-gazing op-ed pages. In the era of social media, facts themselves have become subjective, with audiences willing to believe falsifiable nonsense provided it accords with, or confirms, preexisting beliefs.

Following their Soviet predecessors, Russian intelligence hackers have targeted highly partisan wedge issues in Western societies to polarize citizens, poison public discourse, and short-circuit the democratic process. They amplify existing divisions rather than attempting to create new ones: Brexit in Britain; gun rights, abortion, anti-immigration, and Black Lives Matter in the United States. More recently, online trolls have targeted anti-vaccination movements during the Covid-19 pandemic. Online trolls and bots use a technique called "astroturfing" on social media, in which they present a viewpoint claiming to belong to a genuine group but cover up their true identity.

A case in point was the "Lisa affair," in January 2016, a story about a thirteen-year-old Russian-German girl who was reportedly raped by Arab migrants, which caused a scandal in the German press. In fact, it was a fake story. Lisa was not abducted or raped by "Arab migrants." The story was nevertheless amplified by Russian online trolls and state media, to exacerbate anti-immigration feelings, discredit the German government, and inflame Russian nationalism. The more that Putin could portray Western countries as places where young girls are raped, and whose societies are divided and consumed with hatred, the easier it was for him to rally his domestic audiences against liberal democracy. Meanwhile, Putin's Russia, at least until his invasion of Ukraine in February 2022, has successfully styled itself as an attractive alternative for Western alt-right extremists, offering a socially "conservative," white, anti-gay, and anti-immigration European model.[39]

Putin's presidential "election" in 2012 transformed his agenda with regard to the United States and irrevocably changed his diplomatic relationship with Secretary of State Hillary Clinton. The previous legislative (Duma) elections in December 2011 took place amid widespread electoral fraud—ballot stuffing, in the former Soviet tradition—which, for the first time, was filmed by Russians on their smartphones and spread online. Protests erupted in Moscow. Putin, ever the conspiracy theorist, viewed the protests not as the result of legitimate grievances, but as the work of a foreign hidden hand. When Clinton publicly criticized the 2011 legislative election and discussed promoting democracy, Putin viewed it as overreach—interference in Russia's domestic affairs. He would never forgive her.

Putin's humiliation from failed operations like GHOST STORIES, and Clinton's public criticism of Russia's election, seems to have increased his risk appetite. By 2014, Russian hackers were identified conducting malicious cyber activities. The Fancy Bear hacking group (also known as APT28) attempted to influence the Scottish independence referendum in 2014, seeking to promote independence groups online and thus break up the United Kingdom. In April 2015, APT28 hacked the French television network TV5Monde, almost destroying the company. The group then tried to disrupt the 2015 British general election, threatening Whitehall government servers and British media.

According to an independent investigation into British bulk intelligence collection, conducted after Edward Snowden's leaks, GCHQ used bulk interception to identify and thwart those Russian hacks in 2015. Moscow also sought to influence the 2016 Brexit referendum, promoting "Leave" messaging.

Putin's strategy in supporting Brexit was to break EU cohesion. The impact of Russian disinformation on the Brexit referendum remains unclear to this day. It has apparently never been investigated by any British government department. When a subsequent parliamentary investigation into Russian malign activities asked Britain's intelligence services for an analysis of hacking during the referendum, MI5's reply was a grand total of six lines of text. Extremely cautious about being seen as interfering in the democratic process, the service did not want to go anywhere near an election. Russian meddling in Brexit was, the parliamentary investigation concluded, too hot to handle.

Elected governments on both sides of the Atlantic have little interest in knowing whether Russian skeletons are lurking in the cupboards of elections they won. It constitutes a major shortcoming of British national security: interference in elections goes to the heart of a country's democratic process, its sovereignty. It is inconceivable that intelligence services should not have a role in identifying, attributing, assessing, and stopping foreign malign influence in British elections. If not them, then who?

Beginning in 2015, Britain's eavesdroppers at GCHQ also detected Russian hacking groups targeting the forthcoming U.S. presidential election. Then, in 2016, routine intercepts of known or suspected Russian intelligence operatives revealed suspicious contacts with the campaign team of the Republican candidate, Donald J. Trump.[40]

PUTIN AND TRUMP

According to a subsequent investigation by special counsel and former FBI director Robert Mueller, Russia's intelligence services conducted a "sweeping and systematic" attack on the 2016 U.S. presidential election. They did so, according to his report, U.S. intelligence assessments, and congressional investigations, to help Donald Trump win the election and denigrate his Democratic opponent, Hillary Clinton. Given the long history of the Kremlin's interference in U.S. presidential elections, which we have encountered earlier, it was unsurprising that Russia's intelligence services would attempt to do so again. What was surprising was their skill. The catalyst for Putin authorizing the 2016 election meddling seems to have been to exact revenge on Clinton for her comments about the 2011 Duma elections. Russia's election meddling involved tradecraft straight from the KGB's past: recruiting assets on Trump's campaign team, smearing a candidate hostile to the Kremlin (Clinton), and spreading disinformation.

Sometime in early 2016, Putin ordered an active-measures influence operation to undermine "the Clinton campaign, tarnish an expected Clinton presidential administration . . . and undermine the U.S. democratic process," according to a U.S. intelligence assessment, confirmed by a bipartisan Senate Intelligence Committee investigation. The intelligence assessment was made with "high confidence"—the gold standard for the U.S. intelligence community. It was apparently based on SIGINT and a well-placed CIA source with access to high-level Kremlin decision-making. The agent, whose identity has not been disclosed, was apparently exfiltrated by Langley from Russia in early 2017. Some suggest that U.S. agencies feared that Trump, by then in the Oval Office, might leak the name of the source to the Kremlin.[41]

In June 2016, before his election, the Trump campaign received a request from a Russian Kremlin-connected lawyer offering "dirt" on Clinton. A meeting took place at Trump Tower in New York, arranged by the Russian oligarch Aras Agalarov and his son, business partners with Trump in a lucrative 2013 beauty pageant in Moscow. They had, according to the Senate's bipartisan intelligence committee report, "significant ties to Russian organized crime" and to those in the Russian government attempting to influence the 2016 election. Members of the Trump campaign at the meeting, including Donald Trump Jr., welcomed the Russian assistance: "If it's what you say I love it," he emailed an opportunistic British publicist helping to broker the meeting. That was a different reaction from when previous U.S. presidential campaigns received offers of support from the Kremlin. (When Democratic candidate Hubert Humphrey was approached during his election campaign in 1968, he politely declined on the grounds that it was inappropriate, probably illegal.)[42]

The month after the Trump Tower meeting, at a press conference at his Doral resort in Florida, candidate Trump stated: "Russia, if you're listening, I hope you are able to find the 30,000 emails that are missing," referring to emails that Clinton reportedly deleted from a personal server while serving as secretary of state, one of Trump's major campaign rallying calls. After Trump's speech, Russian hackers got to work. WikiLeaks acted as a delivery platform for Russian intelligence. In October, on the eve of the election, it released a tranche of hacked Democratic emails with the aim of discrediting Clinton's campaign.[43]

Trump's campaign chair from June to August of 2016 was Paul Manafort, who, before 2014, had worked for pro-Russian Ukrainian president Viktor Yanukovych. Manafort had also worked for the Russian oligarch metals baron, Oleg Deripaska, and was indebted to him. While managing Trump's campaign, which he did for free, apparently as payment-in-kind of Deripaska, Manafort remained in contact with former business associate Konstantin Kilimnik. He was in fact a Russian intelligence officer, according to the Senate intelligence report. Manafort shared sensitive internal campaign polling data with Kilimnik, which would have been useful for the Russians in their disinformation campaign. In August 2018, in charges arising from Robert Mueller's Russia probe, Manafort was found guilty of conspiracy, tax and bank fraud, and obstruction of justice. The Senate Intelligence Committee's unambiguous conclusion was that "Manafort's presence on the Campaign and proximity to Trump created opportunities for Russian intelligence services to exert influence over, and acquire confidential information on, the Trump Campaign."[44]

American voters were subjected to a firehose of Russian disinformation, which reached millions of people on Facebook alone. Its delivery vehicle was the Internet Research Agency, a "troll farm" based in a nondescript building in St. Petersburg. It was funded through other entities by the businessman and Putin's "chef" Yevgeny Prigozhin, whose trolls effectively sliced and diced American public opinion before the election. The IRA industrialized the art of trolling, pumping out conspiracy theories and half-truths, hijacking social media and blog posts. Its workers operated in eleven-hour shifts, with set quotas. They started to spread disinformation about the

U.S. election and its process as early as 2014, posing as U.S. activists and encouraging American voters to attend protest rallies.

The single greatest thrust of IRA targeting was domestic race relations. This was again grafted from the Soviet playbook, as we have seen. The IRA set up bogus online groups supposedly linked to legitimate antiracism groups in America, like Black Lives Matter, to suppress black votes and denigrate Clinton. Masquerading online as Americans, the Russians managed to stage rallies in key states to support Trump, calling for Clinton to be jailed. It was an updated version of the rallies the KGB orchestrated against Reagan in 1984. Did Russian intelligence swing the 2016 election for Trump? No one knows. Trump won the electoral college by about 78,000 votes, in five key swing states, all of which were targets of Russian disinformation. Beyond that, although some have tried, we cannot draw any more certain conclusions.[45]

It is easy to say that President Obama should have done more to "stop" Russian electoral interference in 2016. In truth, Obama was placed in an impossible position: declassifying real-time intelligence about Russian election meddling would have been politically cataclysmic, inevitably leading to criticism of being an unprecedented intrusion—meddling—by a president in the election of his successor. "We did everything we could to communicate confidentially to Putin to knock it off," Secretary of State John Kerry told me. In September 2016, President Obama told Putin to "cut it out" with election meddling.[46]

Special counsel Robert Mueller conducted a multiyear probe into possible connections between the Trump campaign and Russia. He did not find sufficient evidence of a criminal conspiracy (the term "collusion" is meaningless in U.S. law), but his investigation resulted in the indictment of thirty-four individuals and three companies, including six Trump associates and campaign officials and twenty-six Russian nationals. Five of the six indicted Trump advisers pled guilty, including Trump's first national security adviser, Michael Flynn, his campaign chairman, Manafort, who later pled guilty to a count of conspiracy, and Roger Stone, a former Washington lobbyist, Nixon aide, and Trump ally. Upon leaving office, Trump subsequently pardoned many of these people, including Flynn, Manafort, and Stone, on the grounds that the Russia investigation was a "hoax." Under U.S. law, however, a presidential pardon constitutes an admission of guilt.

While Mueller's investigation concluded that there was insufficient evidence to bring criminal charges of conspiracy between Trump and his campaign, the bipartisan Senate intelligence report shows that there was coordination, cooperation, and convergence between the Trump campaign and the Kremlin. As the then director of National Intelligence, James Clapper, told me: "I saw a lot of bad things in my fifty years in intelligence, but nothing got me so viscerally as what the Russians did to us in 2016."

When the "Steele dossier" was published in January 2017, compiled by a former MI6 officer, Christopher Steele, with long-standing expertise on Russia, but now working in private business, it caused a media explosion. As you may recall, coming just ten days before Trump took office, the dossier suggested that the Kremlin held salacious, compromising material (*kompromat*) over Trump. Contrary to subsequent claims, in fact the Steele dossier was not part of the key US Intelligence Community Assessment (ICA), declassified on January 6, 2017, which concluded that Russia sought to interfere in the 2016 presidential election to assist Trump and undermine Clinton. The classified version of the ICA report had about 420 footnotes, and not one drew on the Steele dossier. As Clapper explained to me: the only place where the Steele dossier featured was in another, even more highly classified, version of the ICA report. It was discussed in one annex, of eight, which explained why the U.S. intelligence community was not relying on the dossier for its assessment—they only had "limited corroboration" for the dossier's claims. (This annex was later, ironically, declassified by Trump's own DNI, John Ratcliffe.) There are few, if any, parallels in history for the position that Obama's intelligence officials, like Clapper, were placed in regarding Trump and Russian electoral interference: briefing a president-elect on a national security threat at which he is the center.[47]

Despite the political storm at the center of the Steele dossier, its central question—namely the links between Trump and Russia—remains alive. This constitutes a counterintelligence subject, distinct from the parameters of Mueller's investigation, which focused on whether there was conspiracy between Trump and the Kremlin. A conspiracy requires criminal standards of evidence, beyond reasonable doubt, while counterintelligence operates at a lower evidential level. To this day, to the best of my knowledge, it is unclear what happened to the FBI's counterintelligence probe into Trump. It was known to exist. It was not, however, subsumed into Mueller's investigation. The situation is made more suspicious with news in January 2023 that a senior FBI officer in New York on the Trump-Russia probe, Charles McGonigal, allegedly took money from Putin's favorite oligarch, Deripaska, once he left office. Again, Trump's campaign chief, Manafort, was indebted to Deripaska. Through Manafort, Trump was thus one person (Deripaska) removed from the FBI's New York Russia probe and from Putin. Presumably the FBI is investigating whether McGonigal was a Russian agent while in the FBI's New York office, following in Robert Hanssen's footsteps.

Does Putin hold compromising material over Trump? It is possible that Trump is indebted to Russian oligarchs arising from the 2008 financial crisis, when U.S. and European banks refused to extend credit to him. Trump's reputation, after all, has frequently not lived up to that of the successful businessman he presented himself as on *The Apprentice*. His businesses have reportedly declared bankruptcy at least six times. His companies are also known to have done significant business with Russians dating back to at least 2006. The Trump Organization was actively exploring building a Trump Tower in Moscow during the 2016 campaign, even as Trump was claiming, "I have nothing to do with Russia."[48]

As president, Trump consistently expressed admiration for Putin and took positions that advanced Putin's foreign policy agenda. He disparaged NATO, and the European Union, denigrated U.S. allies like Germany, and supported Brexit. In May 2017, Trump invited foreign minister Sergei Lavrov and the Russian ambassador in Washington, Sergei Kislyak, an old

Soviet hand, to the Oval Office. He told the two that he had just fired FBI director, James Comey, "a nut job," saying that he hoped that would take the heat off. In fact, it triggered special counsel Mueller's investigation.

In his meeting with Lavrov and Kislyak, Trump disclosed sensitive intelligence about counterterrorism, reportedly gleaned from the Israelis. The Israeli government was, it seems, distraught, fearing that Russia would pass the disclosed intelligence to Putin's ally in the Middle East, Iran. Meanwhile, Trump disregarded assessments from the U.S. intelligence community about Russian election meddling, most brazenly at a joint press conference with Putin in July 2018 in Helsinki. After a private meeting with Putin, Trump publicly took his side about Russian election meddling, denying it, which flew in the face of the U.S. intelligence community's conclusion.

Whatever the reasons for his embrace of Putin, the relationship between U.S. intelligence agencies and the presidency reached all-time lows under Trump. The president called their work "something that Nazi Germany would have done" and accused U.S. intelligence, the deep state, of spying on him. In fact, U.S. intelligence agencies were spying on Russians with whom members of the Trump campaign were liaising. As the 2020 election approached, Trump amplified Russian disinformation, claiming that it was Ukrainians, not the Russians, who were meddling. U.S. society under Trump became so hyper-partisan that some U.S. intelligence officials failed their duty to remain nonpolitical. In the FBI's investigation into the Trump campaign's links with Russia, CROSSFIRE HURRICANE, one FBI officer falsified evidence to obtain a surveillance (FISA) application on a U.S. person on Trump's campaign. A later investigation by a U.S. intelligence community's ombudsman concluded that intelligence became politicized during Trump's presidency: his senior political appointees suppressed intelligence about Russian meddling while emphasizing that about China, and some lower-level analysts committed sins of omission or commission while delivering intelligence up the chain of command about malign activities.[49]

ALL THE TSAR'S MEN

On the centenary of the founding of Soviet foreign intelligence, in 2020, the SVR conducted a hack to the future: it carried out a massive data breach into the U.S. federal government's software supply system. As we noted in chapter one, the SVR targeted a software company, SolarWinds, to hijack a routine software update to insert malware on millions of downloaded systems. At the time of writing this, it is thought that computer systems of some one hundred companies (including Microsoft, Cisco, and Intel) have been compromised, as have those of the Pentagon and a dozen U.S. government agencies, including the Treasury, Justice, and Energy Departments. SolarWinds was a fitting culmination of the one-hundred-year intelligence war between Russia and Western powers. What started with Comintern spies on the ground in Europe's capitals moved to the skies, to space, and deep under the sea; the conflict is now being waged in the cyber world, persistent and largely unseen by the public.

The SVR was doubtless pleased to get good publicity for SolarWinds, especially against its rival services, the FSB and the GRU. At the same time, the Kremlin has tried to deflect attention from its incompetent intelligence operations in preceding years, particularly by the GRU (such as its failed assassination of Sergei Skripal in 2018 and the poisoning of opposition leader Alexei Navalny by placing a toxin in his underpants, but who survived by being medically evacuated to Germany, where he was successfully treated, only to be arrested when he returned to Russia in 2021). Part of the Kremlin's effort to distract from intelligence embarrassments has been to revert to imagined glories from the Soviet past. The SVR continues to place flowers on Philby's grave in Moscow; in 2017, it unveiled a new portrait of Philby in a Russian state art gallery in Moscow. The city's mayor has renamed a square for Philby, located, appropriately, near SVR headquarters. The death of the KGB's former spy in MI6, George Blake, at the age of ninety-eight, in December 2020, was met with predictable sanitized and misleading adulation by the SVR press bureau about his life and espionage.

The SVR's director, Sergey Naryshkin, is a former dud KGB officer, who has known Putin since working at the regional KGB headquarters in Leningrad, the "Big House" on the Neva. Naryshkin was kicked out of Brussels in the late 1980s, after his cover was blown as a KGB officer. Following the Soviet Union's demise, Naryshkin found work with Putin in the St. Petersburg government. According to one CIA chief of station in Moscow, interviewed for this book, who knew Putin and Naryshkin there since 1993 and 1995, Naryshkin was "knee deep" in money laundering. Naryshkin later authored an apparently plagiarized graduate degree dissertation from a Russian university. Along with serving as SVR director, Naryshkin also doubles as the head of Russia's historical society. Unsurprisingly, the latter produces little more than Russian hagiography. SVR's stage-managed public image and history avoid an ugly reality: in the last century, Soviet intelligence services were instruments of suppression and terror, which helped to imprison Soviet citizens, and in doing so protracted the Cold War.[50]

Putin's carefully sanctioned application of history reveals his descent from authoritarian rule to dictatorship. In Kremlin-authorized books, Stalin noticeably came back. The SVR's centenary included publications that rehabilitated Stalin. An SVR booklet from 2021 contained quotes from Stalin on its cover, something that would have been unthinkable in the recent past. In 2021, Putin closed Memorial Human Rights Centre, which for three decades had exposed Stalin's crimes. In Putin's narrative, Stalin, the former Soviet dictator, was not so bad after all.[51]

Like Stalin himself, Putin is responsible for a colossal intelligence failure. His decision to invade Ukraine in February 2022 ranks alongside Stalin's miscalculation before Hitler's invasion as an epic strategic failure. Putin's war in Ukraine has produced more cohesion among NATO than anything else in its history. Even previously neutral Sweden and Finland are now joining the alliance. Unless or until Russian—or Western—records are one day released, we cannot know what intelligence Putin was receiving before his decision to invade. We can, however, make some educated guesses. It seems likely that, as with Stalin before him, the nature of Putin's sycophantic court guaranteed that he received intelligence that confirmed, not challenged, his thinking. He relies on an echo chamber of *siloviki* advisers. It may be that Putin's public humiliation of the tongue-tied Sergey Naryshkin, in the choreographed and scripted National Security Council meeting preceding the invasion, owed to the SVR director having challenged his boss's thinking about Ukraine.

Whatever was going on with the intelligence reaching Putin, that arriving before President Joe Biden was some of the most effective in modern history. The U.S. intelligence community's forewarning of Putin's war plans for Ukraine constitutes an intelligence success—words we do not often hear. We do not know how U.S. intelligence stole Putin's secret war plans, nor should we at this stage; they will be revealed one day in Biden's presidential library. (I will be the first in line, when they are.) It is safe to assume, however, that they derived from a combination of human, technical, and open-source intelligence collection. Whatever its source, this much is clear: U.S. intelligence delivered accurate, timely, and relevant assessments to the commander in chief, who listened to it. Biden's White House then boldly declassified that intelligence in real time, preempting Putin's use of false flags as a pretext for his invasion. Doing so limited the Russian dictator's room for maneuver. More failures followed. Since the invasion, more than four hundred Russian intelligence officers have been expelled from embassies in Europe and North America and Russian illegals rolled up in the Netherlands, Norway, Sweden, and Poland.

A LOOK BACK

Looking at the grand sweep of the hundred-year intelligence war between East and West described in this book, we can draw three conclusions. The first relates to Putin. If the dictator were removed from power, by a putsch or assassination, would that improve Russia's relations with the West? To put the question bluntly: Does the West have a Putin problem or a Russia problem? As noted in chapter one, in my view, unfortunately the answer is the latter. Putin's nationalist message—that the West has undermined Russia's destiny as a great power—is not unique to him. It is shared by hard-liners like Nikolai Patrushev, head of Putin's Security Council. If Putin were to disappear and someone like Patrushev were to take over, Russia would have slim prospects for a democratic future. The West needs to brace itself for a long struggle with Russia.

My second conclusion concerns what lawyers call a "but for" test: What would have happened but for—that is, without—the subject under consideration? In this case, what would the Cold War have been like without the input of each side's intelligence services? This requires counterfactual thinking. In the case of the Soviet Union, it is impossible. Soviet security and intelligence services were so ingrained in the regime's existence that it is impossible to imagine the world's first one-party state without them. What we can say for certain is that, without the KGB's iron fist, populations in Eastern Europe and Russia would have been able to reject Soviet rule earlier than they did, as they tried to in 1956 in Hungary, 1968 in Czechoslovakia, and 1981 in Poland.

Due to the nature of Soviet rule, which generally eschewed telling truth to power and imposed crippling conformist intelligence assessments, Soviet leaders failed to receive objective assessments from their intelligence services at key moments during the Cold War. Until the end, Soviet leaders were effectively victims of KGB disinformation, which the system created, as the U.S. ambassador in the Soviet Union, Jack Matlock Jr., noted. While U.S. intelligence sometimes became politicized, in the Soviet Union those traits were institutionalized. In that respect, Soviet intelligence had a marginal impact on decision-making during the Cold War: Soviet leaders like Stalin, or Khrushchev, who excluded the KGB during the Cuban Missile Crisis, were going to do what they did anyway. They were their own intelligence analysts. Intelligence services made the Soviet regime possible, but were also instruments of its ultimate downfall.[52]

It is easier to imagine what would have happened in the West without intelligence services. After all, the U.S. government did not have a peace-time foreign intelligence agency until as late as 1947. The disaster of Pearl Harbor illustrates what can happen when a country lacks a dedicated foreign intelligence service. When President Jimmy Carter entered the Oval Office in 1977, he was worried about CIA abuses, which had been exposed by the Church Committee over the previous two years. In Carter's campaign, he promised Americans to correct three things, "Watergate, Vietnam, and the CIA." The agency, he claimed, tended to snuff out human rights. But even as skeptical as Carter was, after receiving briefings while campaigning for president, he publicly admitted that he was opposed to dissolving the CIA, as some were pushing for, or to ceasing its covert actions: "We need them, I regret to say; I wish we didn't, but we do."[53]

Of course, U.S. and British governments experienced intelligence fail-ures, and abused intelligence, politicizing it at times to suit their ends. But these distortions were not systemic, as they were in the Soviet Union. Without the daily stream of intelligence provided for the president and senior decision makers in the President's Daily Brief, they would have been less informed, and less prepared to handle key decisions during the Cold War. During the Cuban Missile Crisis, President Kennedy was provided with valuable assessments, based on all-source collection, human intelli-gence (from Oleg Penkovsky), and technical intelligence (from U-2 and SIGINT). That intelligence gave Kennedy room for diplomatic maneuvers.

Without Oleg Gordievsky's espionage for MI6, the British and U.S. governments would not have been given a window into the genuine fear felt by those in the Kremlin about Western powers—and the U.S. in par-ticular. Although U.S. intelligence failed to predict the events that swept away communism in Eastern Europe and then the Soviet Union itself, as the events unfolded the CIA provided President George H. W. Bush with timely, relevant, and accurate intelligence that assisted him and his national security team as they navigated those seismic upheavals.

Both sides of the Cold War, West and East, used their intelligence services to instigate covert actions in Third World countries. Without their clandestine services, neither side would have been able to conduct non-avowed foreign policy in pursuit of their national interests. The KGB believed that the Cold War could be won in the Third World. CIA and MI6's strategy was to use covert actions, developed during World War II, against Soviet influence in those countries, both real and imagined, though both the British and the Americans also used the specter of communism to leverage commercial interests in those countries.

The most successful covert action during the Cold War was that conducted by the CIA to support anti-Soviet insurgents in Afghanistan. The Red Army's defeat there was symbolized in February 1989 by the image of the last Soviet commander in Afghanistan, Boris Gromov, walking alone over the Friendship Bridge, between Afghanistan and Uzbekistan, behind the last armored Soviet vehicles, with Soviet flags flapping in the cold wind, as they left the country. Afghanistan, Moscow's Vietnam, contributed to the Soviet Union's overall downfall. Most covert actions, however, were not as successful as those of the CIA in Afghanistan. They did little more than antagonize relations between East and West and damage the societies and economies of Third World countries targeted.

Intelligence during the Cold War was asymmetric. Throughout the seven decades of the Soviet period, it was far easier for Soviet intelligence services to spy on Western democracies than the other way around. The Soviet Union and its Eastern bloc satellites were police states, patrolled by heavily armed borders and with pervasive security services. Western services were out in the cold in Moscow. Even posting a letter to an agent there, containing a message hidden in microdots or secret ink, was an elaborate business for a foreign intelligence service. The Soviet government riddled foreign embassies behind the Iron Curtain with listening devices, as we have seen. The relative freedoms in the West provided Soviet services with built-in advantages over their Western adversaries.[54]

At three moments when the West considered relations to have thawed, during World War II, during détente, and after the demise of the Soviet Union, the Kremlin continued—and in fact increased—its spying on the West. But perhaps the greatest deception conducted by Soviet spy chiefs occurred at the end of the Soviet Union's existence: the KGB convinced Russians, and the outside world, that the service had ceased to exist. In the 1990s, while U.S., British, and other Western intelligence services wound down their old Cold War bureaucracies focused on the former Soviet bloc, the KGB reconstituted itself as Russia's new intelligence services. They continued to use the same officers, methodologies, and even agents embedded in Western governments. More than that, they were now driven by a sense of revenge against the West and the former Gorbachev regime for allowing the collapse of the Soviet Union. It was from this bitter, revanchist stew in Russia that Putin emerged.

My third conclusion relates to the successes of Soviet and Russian intelligence. They achieved some of the greatest successes in the history of espionage. The Cambridge Five rank among the best spies ever. They and other Soviet agents in the West equipped Stalin with some of the West's innermost secrets as the Cold War set in. Stalin's spies stole the plans for the world's first atomic weapon. Scratch the surface, however, and we find something other than the carefully sanitized versions of these spies disseminated by the Kremlin today. In reality, some of the most important Soviet spies in the West achieved what they did despite, not because of, the Soviet intelligence services. The KGB was not ten feet tall. Some of the best intelligence came from ideologically committed communists, who threw secrets at Soviet intelligence.[55]

At key moments, Soviet intelligence officers badly let down the Cambridge Spies, failing to appear at meetings and placing so much pressure on them that at least one, Donald Maclean, had a nervous breakdown. (Philby, Burgess, and Blunt eased the pressures of living double lives by drinking themselves into oblivion.) Furthermore, British intelligence came astonishingly close to catching some of the key spies in the Cold War. On the day Guy Burgess and Donald Maclean defected behind the Iron Curtain, an undercover MI5 officer was standing next to them in a pub, trying to hear what they were whispering. With a bit of luck, British and U.S. counterespionage could have made history go differently. (Scholars generally do not like discussing, or analyzing, the role of luck in history. But why not? Luck happens when preparation meets opportunity.)

An unsentimental analysis of Russian intelligence reveals a succession of failures and humiliations: from deep-cover illegals in the United States rolled up by the FBI and the CIA in 2010 to inept GRU assassination attempts in Europe and Britain. Russia's electoral interference in 2016 was detected by U.S. intelligence. Even with Donald Trump, and whatever the nature of his relationship is with Putin, Russia's services appear to have bitten off more than they could chew. According to reporting, Putin said that Trump was mentally imbalanced—though after two years' isolation during Covid, Putin appears equally imbalanced. Putin's disastrous decision to invade Ukraine fits into a much longer history of Soviet intelligence failures, from Operation BARBAROSSA onward. Russia's initial operations there were being overseen by the FSB's notoriously corrupt Fifth Department (also known as the Fifth Service), responsible for active measures in former Soviet states. Its head, Sergei Beseda, was sacked and has been placed under house arrest, where he would be advised to keep away from windows, for risk of defenestration. Russia's once famed doctrine of hybrid warfare—really as old as warfare itself—is in tatters, nowhere to be seen in Ukraine.

Even Russia's much-celebrated cyber capabilities have apparently underperformed against NATO countries since the war in Ukraine. Why has Putin not launched cyberattacks on Western countries that are effectively in a proxy war with Russia in Ukraine? Perhaps Western services have thwarted massive attacks. More likely, I think, Putin failed to give his services time to prepare for offensive cyber capabilities. Cyber is not a perfect weapon. It is a new medium, and tool, for the use of much older tradecraft: espionage, subversion, and sabotage.

CHAPTER EIGHTEEN

NEW COLD WAR

When a state has weathered many great perils and subsequently
attains to supremacy and uncontested sovereignty, it is evident that
under the influence of long established prosperity, life becomes
more extravagant and the citizens more fierce in their rivalry
regarding office and other objects than they ought to be . . . they
think they have a grievance against certain people who have shown
themselves grasping . . . they are puffed up by the flattery of others
who aspire to office. . . . When this happens, the state will change
its name to the finest sounding of all, freedom and democracy, but
will change its nature to the worst thing of all, mob rule.
—Polybius, *Histories*, VI

THE PERSON AT THE CENTER OF THE OPERATION WAS A CHI-
nese national, Fang Fang. Over the course of four years, from 2011 to 2015,
she patiently cultivated a wide circle of local and national politicians in
San Francisco's Bay Area, home to the world's leading software companies. She built relationships, intimate and otherwise. One of the politicians
whom Fang met with on several occasions, and helped to fundraise for in
2014, was Representative Eric Swalwell. He would later make a run for the

Democratic nomination in the 2020 U.S. presidential election. According to the FBI, Fang was a Chinese agent, working with the Ministry of State Security (MSS). The FBI identified Fang during her meetings with her MSS contact and in 2015 began a probe into her activities, putting her under surveillance. She abruptly returned to China that year. Swalwell cooperated with the FBI about his contacts with her.[1]

Seven years later, in 2022, MI5 made an unprecedented public intervention in British political life. After a "significant, long-running" investigation, it warned that a British-Chinese lawyer named Christine Ching Kui Lee was an agent for the Chinese government and had infiltrated Parliament with the aim of interfering in British politics. Lee funded British MPs, which is not illegal under English law. In one case, she gave donations of over £450,000 in five years to the Labour MP Barry Gardiner.[2]

Two incidents of alleged Chinese influence in Western politics. Big deal, you might think. All states conduct influence campaigns to pursue their national interests. Spies spy. International law is generally permissive of espionage, unless expressly prohibited by treaty or custom. But there are differences between how, and for what ends, states use their clandestine services. Not all intelligence services play by the same rules. The Chinese government plays by very different rules compared to Western services. The methodologies used by Chinese intelligence against Western countries are not always sophisticated; the Chinese "spy balloon" that floated across America in February 2023 had a distinct nineteenth-century feel, though it was equipped with high-tech collection capabilities. But what Chinese services sometimes lack in sophistication, they always make up for with brazenness and sheer brute force of numbers.

◆

When it comes to writing a book, there is a general rule that authors should not introduce a new subject at the end. Rules, however, exist to be broken. The reason I am doing so here, as we approach this book's closing credits, is because the West's future balances on a knife-edge. We are currently in the opening stages of a new chapter in the epic intelligence war between East and West: this time, between the United States and the People's Republic of China. The outcome of the story is unknown, events still in progress. Hence it must come at the end.

My colleague, the historian Niall Ferguson, has been a prominent voice warning that the clash between global titans this century—the U.S. and China—constitutes a new Cold War. Ferguson's argument inevitably led to a cascade of op-ed pieces about whether the Cold War is a useful paradigm for understanding present U.S.-China relations. From the perspective of intelligence and national security, such discussions are quaint, like discussing the nature of smoke in a burning house. As far as intelligence is concerned, Niall Ferguson is correct. We are already engaged in a new Cold War—and Western public policy conversations about Chinese espionage have hardly begun. The real question is whether the U.S.-China struggle remains cold or turns into a hot war—for example, over Taiwan, the one "legacy" issue that China's authoritarian leader Xi Jinping has left to fix.[3]

Like Soviet intelligence during the last century, Chinese agencies are waging a persistent, integrated, and asymmetric onslaught on Western countries. This can be seen in three areas—espionage, subversion, and sabotage—which were through lines in the last century's intelligence war between East and West, as we have seen. They are again today. Like the last century's Cold War, the Chinese-West intelligence struggle today is asymmetric because it is disproportionally more difficult for Western governments to collect intelligence on China than the other way around. China exploits the relative freedoms in the West to steal as many commercial, industrial, and military secrets as possible. China's intelligence services, operating in an authoritarian one-party state, are not bound by the rule of law (as recognized in the West), independent political oversight, or public accountability.

Xi's China presents colossal challenges for foreign services. It is a digital authoritarian police state, a closed society with ubiquitous technical surveillance. Xi's zero-Covid policy, which saw entire cities shut down and quarantined long after such actions ceased in Western countries, presented a nightmare for foreign services trying to recruit sources. The clash between Chinese and Western intelligence is also asymmetric because the Chinese government, like the Soviets beforehand, integrates intelligence and commerce in ways without parallel in countries like Britain or the United States. In China, as in the Soviet Union, spying and buying are fused. China employs a "whole of society" approach to espionage, using both its intelligence services, as well as purportedly private Chinese companies, Chinese nationals, and diaspora communities. China's strategy is to overwhelm Western counterintelligence, if not through sophisticated espionage tradecraft, then by volume. Though not perfect, the best analogy for understanding China's intelligence onslaught on the West is the Soviet Union. The history of the last century's East-West intelligence war informs the new one underway today.[4]

———

China has featured tangentially in our story so far, like a large tanker ship on the horizon, edging ever closer to shore. But now, it is towering over us. In 2022, the heads of the FBI, CIA, MI5, and even GCHQ and MI6 (traditionally two of the world's most secretive agencies) all went public to say that China presents the single greatest challenge to Western democracies in the twenty-first century. The challenge stems from China's size—the country contains one-fifth of humanity on the planet—and its wealth. China has the world's second-largest economy. Some analysts suggest that China's GDP, measured at market exchange rates, will displace that of the U.S. early in the next decade.

The United States has been the target of a pervasive, sustained, multi-faceted, and accelerating intelligence onslaught from China during the first two decades of the twenty-first century. By 2020, the FBI was investigating more than 2,500 China-related cases, opening a new case every ten hours, in all fifty U.S. states, and in each of its fifty-six field offices. That makes Soviet intelligence look childlike.[5]

Since coming to power in March 2013, Xi has not hidden his grand design for China's national rejuvenation: to make it the greatest power in the world. He is a true believer, born into communism and molding himself in the image of Mao, the Great Helmsman. He used a platform of "anti-corruption" to strengthen his regional, then central, and now supreme hold on power. Now in an unprecedented third term in office, after the Twentieth Party Congress in October 2022, Xi's goal is for China to displace the United States as the world's greatest power both in Asia and the world.

The year 2049, the centenary of communist rule in China, seems an obvious deadline for Xi. In order to become the number one power, China must catch up with the West and overturn the U.S.-led rules-based international order. Xi's strategy is to protect his own rule and "unite" China—which means absorbing Hong Kong and Taiwan, by force if necessary. In his public strategic plan, "Made in China 2025," Xi identified ten key technology areas that he wants China to excel in, including robotics, green energy production and vehicles, aerospace, and biopharma. Xi has said that in those areas of core technology, where it would be otherwise impossible for China to catch up with the West, the country must "research asymmetrical steps to catch up and overtake" Western powers. Xi has thus made no secret of having given his authorization to steal technological secrets.[6]

In the decade after 2010, the FBI witnessed a 1,300 percent increase in China-related economic espionage cases. Some of that may be explained by increased FBI collection, discovering more espionage going on anyway, but that cannot explain it all. China's cyber-hacking operations, targeting every sector of Western society, are greater than *every other major nation combined*, according to the FBI. In July 2022, MI5's director general, Ken McCallum, gave an unprecedented joint public briefing with FBI director Chris Wray at MI5's London headquarters, Thames House. Wray put it bluntly to the audience of assembled business leaders: "The Chinese government is set on stealing your technology, whatever it is that makes your industry tick, and using it to undercut your business and dominate your market."[7]

In October 2022, President Biden effectively declared economic war on China by imposing restrictions on high-end chips. Biden's strategy is to sabotage China's race for dominating artificial intelligence (AI). As the commentator Edward Luce pointed out, when the history of this period comes to be written, it will likely see this as the moment when the U.S.-China rivalry came out of the closet.[8]

How did we get here? Before 9/11, the U.S. intelligence community was sounding the alarm about the national security threat posed by Chinese espionage. At the turn of the century, China's intelligence services were conducting sustained efforts to steal American S&T, like nuclear secrets, as national security papers held at President Bill Clinton's library reveal. Then 9/11 happened. Thereafter, Western intelligence agencies overwhelmingly focused their resources on kinetic counterterrorist operations—while downgrading collection on resurgent states like China and Russia. According to a report published in 2020 by Britain's parliamentary intelligence oversight committee, in 2006–7 some 92 percent of all of MI5's work effort was devoted to counterterrorism, with the remainder thinly spread across all other areas, including hostile state activities.

According to MI6's deputy chief Nigel Inkster, who retired in 2006: "In my three-decade career with Britain's Secret Intelligence Service, China was never seen as a major threat." In the United States, the downgrading of hostile states like China after 9/11, at the expense of counterterrorism, was less acute than in Britain, but there was a "downward glide," according to one NSA official interviewed for this book on the condition of anonymity.

The U.S. intelligence community had more resources than the British, more capacity, so shifts are less acute. But even the U.S. intelligence community did not give China the attention it deserved after 9/11. According to Sue Gordon, a career CIA officer and later one of the most senior American intelligence officials, the U.S. intelligence community failed to respond to what was going on in China after 9/11. That period ushered in the digital revolution, which, Gordon noted, permanently changed the nature of intelligence and national security. The Chinese government grasped the opportunities provided by the digital revolution and operationalized them. The U.S. did not. It was still overwhelmingly focused on terrorism and was trying to address new threats with leftover resources. According to Michael Hayden, DCI from 2006 to 2009 (and previously director of NSA): "Every day [at CIA] I woke up thinking I had to do something about China, but there was never enough time." The priority given to counterterrorism within U.S. intelligence continued until as late as 2017. Former DCI James Clapper told me that when he retired that year, counterterrorism was still the greatest recipient of funds within the U.S. intelligence community.[9]

In 2005, the principal civilian Chinese intelligence services, the Ministry of State Security (MSS), declared war on the U.S. intelligence community. From that point, according to CIA insiders interviewed, all the MSS's best personnel and resources were marshaled at the U.S, with the long-term strategic aim of supplanting America in Southeast Asia. As the U.S. was distracted if not consumed by the War on Terror, the MSS's gains were largely undetected or appreciated by U.S. spy chiefs. China's strategy followed a saying, *GeAnGuanHuo* (隔岸观火), "watch the fires burn from the safety of the opposite river bank which allows you to avoid entering the battle until your enemy is exhausted."

Soon the CIA was experiencing failures in China. They stemmed from the CIA station in the U.S. embassy in Beijing. Those failures were exposed between 2010 and 2012, when Chinese intelligence broke up a CIA spy network, reportedly leading to the detection, imprisonment, or death of around thirty agents. Insiders describe this case as the tip of an iceberg of still-classified U.S. intelligence failures in China in recent years. Their causes remain unclear. They may have arisen from Chinese technical collection of CIA covert communications (COCOM). More chillingly for Langley, according to some insiders, they may have come from a Chinese mole inside U.S. intelligence. The spy in question may have been a former CIA case officer in China, Jerry Lee, now convicted of espionage. If Xi makes a move on Taiwan, we shall find out whether the U.S. intelligence community has penetrated his regime in the same way it did Putin's. I think it is unlikely—but hope I am wrong.[10]

China's economic rise this century has been meteoric. At the turn of the century, its GDP was around $1.2 trillion. It is now $17.7 trillion. When I traveled there twenty years ago, it was clear that a jaw-dropping industrial transformation was underway. Taking a boat down the Yangtze River, as I backpacked around China, it was obvious from the smog-belching heavy industry on either side of the banks that China meant business.

Between 2011 and 2013, China used more cement than the United States consumed in the entire twentieth century. The country's high-speed trains leave Amtrak, with its rattling carriages, even on the "express" Acela, in the dust. The widespread belief in the West, at least at the time of the 2008 Beijing Olympics—that China's economic development and integration with the world economy would lead to greater political freedom and make it into a responsible stakeholder in global affairs—has proven to be mistaken.

Chinese espionage against Western countries has accelerated since Xi took power. Of the 160 reported cases of Chinese spies in the United States from 2000 to 2020, over half are since Xi took the helm. Those are, of course, just the cases detected by U.S. authorities. China's industrial explosion this century was propelled by foreign intelligence collection. This has taken the form of traditional human espionage combined with cyber exploitations. These offensive efforts have allowed the Chinese government to reverse-engineer manufacturing and save time and resources on research and development. According to U.S. intelligence (ODNI) estimates, Beijing's spying has saved China $320 billion in R&D costs. China's massive Belt and Road Initiative, a political and economic program to advance their interests in other regions of the world through large investments in infrastructure, has been accompanied by a barrage of espionage, subversion, sabotage, and disinformation. All are designed to further China's grand strategy to make itself into a superpower rivaling America.

Xi's "China Dream," his "Made in China 2025" platform, and the "Thousand Talents" program are amped-up Soviet-like economic plans. They are designed to make China independent of Western technology, invert the existing world order, make the West dependent on Chinese technology, and establish China in its rightful place as the middle kingdom, all while containing the United States and its "imperialism."

As usual with counterespionage, we only know about spies who are caught. Take the case of a Chinese national, Xu Yanjun, who in November 2021 was successfully prosecuted in the U.S. for stealing technology in Europe and the United States. Beginning in at least 2013, Xu presented himself as a businessman interested in joint ventures with U.S. and European companies specializing in aviation. His patient recruitment strategy eventually worked with GE Aviation, which developed an advanced composite aircraft engine. In March 2017, he recruited an agent in the company, a GE engineer, who gave him sensitive IT data. Xu threw money, and a trip to China, at his recruit. Xu was of course not a businessman but a Chinese intelligence officer (again, part of the Ministry of State Security). In 2018, Xu started to task his recruit for GE technical secrets. By this time, however, the GE employee had alerted the FBI. Xu was arrested in April 2018 in Belgium, where he traveled to meet his agent. If it had been successful, Xu's espionage would have allowed the MSS to steal valuable GE Aviation secrets, and the Chinese government to leapfrog over a decade of hard work and billions of dollars spent in research and development. The case shows the fusion of human and cyber intelligence—"hyber."

There are countless other cases of Chinese "businessmen" seeking joint ventures with Western companies, using the prospect of cooperation to obtain intellectual property—maybe an underlying source code—but then withdrawing from an agreement once it is obtained. Western companies are left like empty shells, having given up their IP. They often have to declare bankruptcy, with resulting job losses, in the face of Chinese firms selling products based on their own IP on the market. To add insult to injury, sometimes Chinese companies sell Western IP back to the communities from which they stole it.

The former head of counterintelligence at the CIA, Mark Kelton, has put the current Chinese espionage storm in perspective: a scale such that the United States government has not seen since Soviet intelligence in the 1930s. Kelton's remarks deserve widespread attention. Among the government and private sector secrets that have been appropriated by China in the twenty-first century are U.S. missile and military aircraft designs (F-35 and F-22), Silicon Valley software and hardware secrets, pharmaceutical patents, and research from U.S. universities and other institutions. A cursory glance at the J-20, a Chinese fifth-generation fighter, reveals its similarity to the F-22. That is not surprising, given that a Chinese national was prosecuted for stealing its plans from Lockheed Martin. (This follows in the tradition of the Tupolev Tu-4, a Soviet bomber, which was a clone of the famous glass-fronted Boeing B-29 Superfortress.) It remains to be seen whether Western governments have secretly learned the lessons of the Cold War from the FAREWELL case described earlier: to sabotage U.S. supply chain secrets being targeted and stolen by a hostile state. There are rumors that the NSA sabotaged software made by Cisco Systems that ended up in China.[11]

To carry out their intelligence offensive, China's spy chiefs are deploying some of the apparatus and methods of their Soviet predecessors. Legal intelligence officers are stationed in Western countries under diplomatic cover. Deep-cover illegals, without diplomatic cover, pose as students at U.S. universities, businesspeople, or tourists. They recruit agents in the West with access to political and economic secrets.

China's spy chiefs keep diaspora communities in Western countries under surveillance, appeal to their "patriotic" duty, and, when that fails, use family members who remain in China to bribe and blackmail their relatives into collecting intelligence and influencing targets. China's intelligence services also use a constellation of front groups in Western countries, such as the five hundred or so Confucius Institutes across the world, to engage in illicit activities. As the scholar Alex Joske has shown, although they are not ostensibly under the control of the Chinese Communist Party, they are in fact directed by the CCP's United Front Work Department (UFWD) in Beijing. The UFWD, described by Mao as one of the party's "Magic Weapons," is the equivalent of the Comintern. The country's influence campaigns have reached U.S. and British universities, think tanks, media organizations, and politicians, all with the aim of recruiting future leaders and promoting platforms favorable to China.[12]

There are good reasons for China's use of tradecraft similar to that of the Soviets. China's intelligence services—the Ministry of State Security, the Ministry of Public Security, and PLA military intelligence—have their origins in the Soviet period. The CCP famously scrutinizes Soviet history, especially the Soviet Union's collapse. In 2006 it produced an eight-volume DVD set, *Consider Danger in Times of Peace: Historical Lessons from the Fall of the CPSU (Communist Party of the Soviet Union)*. The CCP would undoubtedly look askance at the suggestion that it needed to learn about intelligence from the Soviets or Russia. China has its own ancient history of espionage, deception, and subversion on which to draw. We do not know the extent to which China's spy chiefs have educated themselves through their friends in Moscow, past and present, and/or are themselves innovating. So far as we know publicly, the West does not yet have the Chinese equivalent of Western spies in the KGB, such as Oleg Gordievsky or Vasili Mitrokhin, who can reveal Beijing's innermost intelligence secrets. It seems fanciful to suppose, however, that there are not such defections. Perhaps that person is Ling Wancheng, who defected to the U.S. in 2016. The brother of a disgraced senior CCP official, Ling reportedly shared Chinese nuclear secrets with the U.S. In 2021, rumors swirled that one of China's top intelligence officials, Dong Jingwei, defected to the United States, but the story has since gone (suspiciously) silent.[13]

Chinese intelligence is also naturally seeking to penetrate Western agencies themselves. The MSS has recruited agents to infiltrate the CIA the way the KGB recruited the Cambridge Spies eight decades ago. Glenn Duffie Shriver was an American in his twenties, who studied and worked in China. He was recruited by the MSS for money and tasked with entering the U.S. Foreign Service or the CIA. He was only detected—and subsequently charged and imprisoned—in 2010, following his dramatic failure of a CIA polygraph test. We do not know whether there are undetected Shrivers inside U.S. intelligence. The case of Jerry Lee, mentioned above, a CIA officer who became a Chinese agent after he left the agency, shows Chinese intelligence has certainly got close. If or when Chinese intelligence archives are one day opened, or a defector's secrets published, it would alas be unsurprising to discover that a Chinese Kim Philby or Rick Ames is already working inside U.S. or British intelligence, disclosing Western secrets. For all we know, China's provocative actions in the South China Sea may be calibrated on intelligence from deep inside Washington, just as Stalin's provocations were in postwar Europe. In 2019 alone, three *former* U.S. intelligence officials (from the CIA and the Defense Intelligence Agency) were prosecuted for revealing secrets to the Chinese. Chinese intelligence is also known to have recruited *former* French intelligence officers. Has Chinese intelligence gone further and recruited *current* officers?[14]

Chinese intelligence has a database of potential kompromat for recruiting American spies of which the KGB could only have dreamed. Beginning in November 2013, it seems, Chinese hackers breached the databases of the U.S. Office of Personnel Management (OPM). They contain the most sensitive information about holders of U.S. security clearances—personal information that those who go through background checks want to keep secret, sometimes even from their own families: personal finances, substance abuse, extramarital affairs, psychiatric care, sexual behavior, even notes to polygraph tests.

It is estimated that the OPM data stolen by Chinese hackers pertains to millions of Americans. It includes twenty-two million security clearance files and five million fingerprints. All this data is now in Beijing. Former FBI director James Comey has stated that his own security clearance form has likely been stolen, providing Chinese hackers with the addresses of every place he has lived since he was eight, and a list of everywhere he has traveled to outside of the United States. Chinese hackers followed the OPM breach by conducting, in 2017, one of the largest data breaches in history: the theft of confidential data on approximately 150 million Americans from the consumer credit reporting agency Equifax. If you are an American, it is now more likely than not that China has stolen your personal data. In 2021, the Chinese government conducted a massive hack of Microsoft Exchange email server software. It compromised the networks of thirty thousand American companies. According to the FBI in 2022, China has stolen more personal and corporate data from Americans than hackers from every other country combined.[15]

The marketplace for foreign intelligence recruitment is now LinkedIn. In some instances, former U.S. government employees and contractors make it all too easy for Chinese operatives. Some proudly display on LinkedIn that they have security clearances, effectively putting a For Sale sign on their profiles. They are comparatively easy targets for Chinese false-flag operations, wherein officers pose as innocuous "risk consultants" offering lucrative contracts. With relatively small government salaries, piling mortgage debts, and eye-watering college tuition bills, for some it will not be hard to sell out the American dream for Chinese cash. Divided loyalties, not ideology, are the key motivation for Americans known to have become spies since the end of the Cold War.

Fair enough for China, we might say. They are doing what anyone else would—perhaps just better. But that is to discount a fundamental asymmetry. The U.S. government does not collect economic and industrial intelligence to give its companies a competitive advantage. By contrast, the Chinese government has integrated "national security"—a slippery term—and commerce. Through legislation passed since 2014, all Chinese citizens and companies are required, when requested, to collaborate in collecting intelligence. In effect, this has produced a whole-of-society espionage effort. The Chinese technology giant Huawei, the largest manufacturer by revenue of telecom equipment in the world, constitutes a latent platform for bulk Chinese intelligence collection.

In China, because of a series of national security laws passed since 2015, there is no such thing as a truly independent business. The country's intelligence services are hidden partners in commercial enterprises with the outside world. The story of Crypto AG, discussed in chapter nine, reveals how *Western* governments colluded with a private encryption company to collect bulk data. It is fanciful to think that China is not undertaking similar activities. Huawei's hardware, integrated into homes and offices worldwide, in appliances that are part of the Internet of Things, provides China with unprecedented opportunities for bulk collection through billions of interconnected and interdependent global data points. TikTok constitutes an advanced Chinese government collection tool, masquerading as a social media platform. It provides Beijing with a tsunami of global information, behind the endless dance videos posted on it. It also allows China the opportunity to shape and suppress online narratives, should it wish to do so. It does not take much to imagine what Chinese data scientists can do with this information, using machine learning and data mapping techniques like social network analysis.[16]

As with the Soviets, a major priority for Chinese intelligence is domestic control and repression: intrusive surveillance of citizens, the suppression of pro-democracy dissent, indoctrination, and the incarceration of enemies, even those who pose little credible security threat. China's internment of about one million ethnic Muslim Uighurs in Xinjiang, and its forced labor programs, recall the Gulag.

The CCP goes to comparable lengths to silence opposition and airbrush away its human rights abuses, creating what the author Louisa Lim calls the "People's Republic of Amnesia," committed to destroying all popular memory of the 1989 democracy movement in China. Just as the KGB jammed British and American radio transmissions into the Soviet Union, today Chinese intelligence operates the great firewall, censoring internet traffic, with online sensors preventing all internet search terms of Tiananmen Square and any online reference to the massacre of June 4, 1989, by blocking all combinations of searches of the numbers 6, 4, and 1989. They also blocked the Chinese word for "jasmine," the synonym for Tunisia's color revolution in 2011, incredible for a nation of jasmine tea lovers. China sells its digital playbook, including facial recognition software used for ubiquitous surveillance, to authoritarian regimes across the world—offering a tried-and-tested blueprint for social control, ready for dictators to use. Made-in-China surveillance technology is being found around the globe.

China's doctrine of "winning without fighting" (like Russia's active measures) is designed to influence foreign affairs to its advantage. The two countries do, however, have different aims: Russia uses covert action to divide Western alliances, and create chaos in Western democracies, while China seeks to project a positive image of itself as an alternative to its Western competitor, pulling foreign countries away from the U.S. and into its orbit. As with so much else, though, when it comes to spying and covert actions, the CCP has taken matters to an entirely new level compared to the past. The MSS is staffed with approximately eight hundred thousand officials, dwarfing the KGB even at its height.

The Chinese government has regurgitated for Covid the same conspiracy theory cooked up by the KGB about AIDS. Whether by design or coincidence, Beijing has pushed disinformation that Covid-19 was a bioweapon developed by the U.S. military. The Chinese government has even claimed that Covid-19 originated at Fort Detrick, the same U.S. military research facility where the KGB claimed AIDS was engineered. What's old is new again.

But today there is no need for Chinese services to plant disinformation in obscure publications, as the KGB did. Social media now provides a quick, easy, and cheap torrent of disinformation about the coronavirus. As with AIDS, China's Covid disinformation exploits existing divisions in the U.S. and other Western societies. Western anti-vaxxers did the heavy lifting for Chinese trolls. Meanwhile, if we are to look for a laboratory that may have manufactured the novel coronavirus, we should look to Wuhan, not Maryland. The Soviet Union, after all, produced disinformation about *American* bioweapons when *it* was secretly conducting the world's largest illegal secret biological weapons program, Biopreparat.

At the same time, due to the nature of the Chinese one-party regime, Xi's foreign affairs may be undermined by the same crippling sycophancy that beleaguered the Soviets. Xi's regime does not incentivize intelligence officers to think independently and challenge political orthodoxy, but instead places a premium on filtering out anything the Chinese leader does not want to hear. If history is any guide, when Chinese archives are one day hopefully opened, we are likely to find a similar chasm between the Chinese government's ability to collect intelligence and its ability to accurately assess it—just as we saw in the Kremlin. Former MI6 deputy chief Nigel Inkster, a China expert, put his finger on the issue when he noted: "Rather as with the KGB, the difficulty has been in telling truth to power." After the Twentieth

Party Congress in 2022, Xi's politburo is stacked with loyalists. This raises the alarming prospect that Xi is making consequential decisions, such as about Taiwan, based on yes-men—his politburo is all male—and warped intelligence. Doing so increases the chances of a Chinese miscalculation.[17]

Chinese industrial espionage, stealing Western research and development, was *the* story before the coronavirus pandemic. Since then, China's Belt and Road projects have stalled. Beijing has pivoted from traditional infrastructure investment abroad to new health, digital, and green silk roads initiatives, which emphasize the benefits of trade with China. But something else is now also underway. China has identified thirty-five strategic technologies that it depends on from imports, so-called chokepoint technologies, vulnerable to supply chain disruption. China is innovating those technologies for itself, insulating itself from Western disruptions. We shall see whether Xi's strategy is successful. The latest information available as this book goes to print, from leading U.S. cybersecurity companies like Crowd-Strike, is that Chinese hackers are moving from theft of Western R&D to insertion of malware. This can be used to sabotage infected systems.[18]

I write this chapter while looking out at the skyline of Hong Kong, China's "special Administrative Region." Previously one of the most enterprising societies in the world, Hong Kong now offers a chilling indication of what Beijing has in store for territories it considers its own—like Taiwan, the democratic island off China's coast. Hong Kong's latest new national security law, rammed through its compliant, handpicked parliament during the Covid pandemic in June 2020, effectively ended political opposition here, allowing Chinese authorities sweeping jurisdiction to surveil, detain, and arrest "subversives"—invariably pro-democracy activists. The British consider it a breach of the 1984 Sino-British Joint Declaration, which provided for Hong Kong to remain autonomous—"one country, two systems"—for fifty years after the 1997 handover. A watershed moment occurred in March 2022, when British judges withdrew from Hong Kong's top court, the Court of Final Appeal, where they had sat since the handover (as they had under British rule). Hong Kong's new national security law made their presence "no longer tenable," because the administration had "departed from values of political freedom, and freedom of expression," according to the head of Britain's Supreme Court in London. Meanwhile, Singapore, with its rule of law, vibrant culture, and efficient government, seems set to take on Hong Kong's mantle as Asia's most dynamic city-state.[19]

In February 2022, on the eve of Russia's invasion of Ukraine, Putin held a meeting with President Xi in which they declared themselves to be in a partnership with "no limits." Russia and China's partnership is an express effort to overturn the U.S.-led liberal democratic order. According to Xi and Putin, the U.S. uses democracy and human rights as a pretext to impose its will on other nations. The U.S. "attempts at hegemony," wrote Xi and Putin, "pose serious threats to global and regional peace and stability and undermine the stability of the world order." The West is decadent, and in decline. As Russian foreign minister Sergei Lavrov put it in a tweet: "We are at the beginning of a new era, a movement towards real #multilateralism, not the one which West tries to impose based on the 'exceptional role' of the Western civilization in the modern world. The world is much richer than just Western civilization." Putin has been howling similar words since his 2007 Munich speech.[20]

Putin and Xi mean what they say: that liberal democracy is not up to the task of responding to a world in crisis. Xi reportedly told Joe Biden that only autocracies can provide the rapid responses needed to address the challenges of the modern world, from pandemics to disinformation. The United States, with its pesky freedoms, performed badly when it came to the Covid pandemic. (Earlier Chinese propaganda, criticizing America's handling of the pandemic, has since become a distant memory given the brave, open criticism in the fall of 2022 by Chinese citizens of their own government's disastrous zero-Covid policy.) The painfully apparent dysfunction of the United States political system nevertheless offers endless, easy propaganda victories for the CCP, whose membership is larger than

Britain's population: Donald Trump's torrent of lies and conspiracy theories, in and out of office, the polarization of U.S. society, which culminated with a white supremacist insurrection on the Capitol in January 2021.

The Cold War is not a perfect analogy for the world's contemporary superpower clash. Cold War 2.0 is not simply a repeat of Cold War 1.0. China's economic and technological integration with the rest of the world, and other countries' dependence on Chinese manufacturing, makes geopolitical relations with China significantly more complex—and more dangerous. Unlike contemporary China, the Soviet Union never made much that the rest of the world wanted. The country was a pariah. The U.S. economy was a goliath. That is not the same now. China is the top trading partner for more than half of all countries, and is Europe's biggest source of imports. At the end of 2021, China held roughly $1 trillion of U.S. debt. Little wonder that Secretary of State Antony Blinken performs linguistic acrobatics to avoid calling U.S.-China relations a "Cold War." (He knows how trade can be used as weapons between East-West superpowers, having written a book about the Soviet-Siberian natural gas pipeline in the 1980s.) The Biden administration's 2022 national security strategy likewise emphasizes that the U.S. does not seek a new Cold War. That, of course, overlooks one of this book's central conclusions: Western powers can be in a Cold War irrespective of whether they seek one and before they recognize it.[21]

There are other differences too. The Cold War was characterized by universalist, incompatible ideologies. Unlike the Soviet Union, the Chinese politburo today does not espouse a universalist philosophy. Like Russia, China's bid for global power is based on ethnonationalism. Someone who looks like me can never become Chinese, though I could have become a Soviet fellow traveler and even a citizen (Russian racism, however, was never far from the surface in the Soviet days). China's intelligence offensive today is also more expansive than anything the Soviets could muster. The latter's intelligence offensive during the Cold War was traditionally focused on specific targets. China's strategy is much broader, a whole-of-state approach, using a "human wave," or a "mosaic," or "a thousand grains of sand" to vacuum up foreign intelligence and overwhelm American counterintelligence.[22]

That said, the Cold War is still a useful paradigm. It is the only precedent we have for a sustained intelligence superpower clash. Both sides today, East and West, have nuclear weapons. (China wishes to increase its warheads from about 350 to 1,000 in 2030, compared to America's reported 5,500.) Unlike with the Soviets, there are no effective nuclear arms limitation agreements between the U.S. and China. As in the Cold War, relations between both sides today rest on the principle of mutually assured destruction. "A nuclear war cannot be won and must never be fought," as Reagan liked to say. While there is not a clash now between communism and capitalism, this century's struggle does have an ideological component to it: between authoritarianism and liberal democracy. This is not just rhetoric, or talking points for pundits on CNN. Both sides, East and West, espouse the benefits of their different, divergent forms of government. They are each seeking to contain the other, in yet another struggle for the future order of the world.

The full scale of the Chinese onslaught on the West is only now being appreciated. In 2020, the House Intelligence Committee reported that, without a significant realignment of resources, the U.S. intelligence community would not be prepared to meet the challenge posed by China this century. The U.S. government has only recently awakened to the nature of this onslaught, and the damage done, and is struggling to catch up. If I were to situate where we in the West are today compared to the last century's Cold War, based on public information and trends, I would place us at approximately the year 1947: Western intelligence services are alert to the nature of the national security threat, are turning their sights to it, but they are chasing a horse that has already bolted the stables.[23]

Matters are improving. In October 2021 the CIA, under the leadership of the veteran diplomat William "Bill" Burns, established a China Mission Center. According to Burns in 2022, the CIA plans to double the number of Mandarin speakers in the coming years, though that does not tell us much, without knowing how many Mandarin speakers were in the agency before. MI5 tells us that its Chinese investigations have grown sevenfold since 2018—but again, from what number is unclear. Intelligence collection, especially espionage, alas cannot be turned around quickly.[24]

What about the future? How this century's clash of superpowers turns out is, of course, impossible to know. As Joseph Nye, former chairman of the National Intelligence Council, has reminded us, there are only future scenarios, not certainties. But I will leave you with observations about where we seem to be heading, based on where we have been. History, as Churchill noted, is a guide for the present and what may lie ahead. Applied history is most usefully understood as history that informs the present—a phrase I have borrowed from Paul Kennedy.[25]

As I suggested in this book's opening chapter, history does not repeat itself, but it does rhyme. In the geopolitical standoff between the United States and China, we can already see what those rhymes will be: emerging technologies that will define our lives in the twenty-first century, artificial intelligence, quantum computing, and biological engineering. They are this century's equivalent to atomic secrets in the last. While last century's superpower contest involved an arms race for nuclear superiority and computing, this century's contest will involve a race for the control of data. The West does not appear to be winning the sprint for AI. According to the Pentagon's former software chief, who resigned in November 2021, the U.S. government has already effectively lost the battle to China over AI.

China's massive data collection strategy, across the globe, is "collect and store now, decrypt later." This is where the East-West race for quantum computing poses such dangers. By using subatomic particles, quantum computing will render obsolete our existing public key encryption systems, which hitherto have been the backbone of internet cryptology. Whoever masters quantum will be able to decrypt the data they have stolen and stored that uses public key encryption. China is currently trailing Western companies like IBM in the race for quantum computing—but it is catching up. The threat that quantum computing poses to existing cryptology, however, is not as dire as even recently thought. As of the fall in 2022, private Western companies are offering on the open market encryption services invulnerable to quantum computing. The task for Western companies, and governments alike, is to migrate existing and future data into such protected systems starting *now*.

While there is thus a "fix" to quantum, another looming threat, as one Western SIGINT expert has told me, lies with the vulnerability of the five or six big private companies that provide security certificates for the internet. The internet relies on them. The companies are vulnerable to human penetration or sophisticated cyberattack. One company, RSA, already has been exploited. Penetrating them would allow an actor to read encrypted communications, using their certificates.[26]

Another rhyme with the Cold War is likely to be the influence of non-aligned countries, which will again doubtless use the East-West clash for their own ends. India has chosen to align itself, yet again, with Moscow. Will Xi and Putin's alignment with "no limits" develop into a Bloc, a kind of Warsaw Pact 2.0, to rival NATO? Will there be a split between China and Russia, like the Sino-Soviet rupture? Will Western intelligence agencies be able to help policymakers exploit such a split? Perhaps the war in Ukraine will become like the Korean War, a hot conflict in a broader Cold War. And so on. It is unknown. Whatever the future has in store for us, however, it is not difficult to see Hong Kong or Taiwan becoming last century's Berlin, contested cities, similarly buttressed by battalions of spies.

The application of history does have limits when it comes to informing the present. Just as it is frequently a mistake to claim something is "unprecedented," it is equally mistaken to think there is nothing new under this century's rising red sun. We really do live in a brave new world. We are on the brink of the fourth industrial revolution, witnessing blurring boundaries between physical, digital, and biological realms. This will fundamentally change how we live, work, and interact with each other, in a way that will be as disruptive to our societies as the first industrial revolution previously was.

Today's interconnected digital world is changing not only how we live, but also the nature of intelligence and national security. All intelligence agencies are having to rethink tradecraft. Maintaining espionage cover in an age of global digital information is more difficult than it was even in the recent past. The time of an analog intelligence operation is over. Social media, and the digital dust we emit as we use our phones—and are caught on CCTV, door- or dashcams—offer ubiquitous technical surveillance, forcing agencies to rethink how they conduct traditional business.

In the past, Soviet intelligence planned for sabotage operations for the outbreak of hostilities between East and West, World War III, by conducting physical reconnaissance of critical infrastructure in Western countries and secretly planting arms caches there for use during war. Today, there is no need for such physical operations (though they do continue). Chinese hackers in the PLA's cyber unit, known as 61398—as well as corresponding Russian, Iranian, and North Korean units—can vault into the heart of Western governments and critical infrastructure, planting malware on computer operating systems for activation like delayed-action booby traps. Today approximately 85 percent of U.S. critical infrastructure lies in the private sector, which dramatically increases the attack surface for a hostile state like China.[27]

Our new globalized information environment has inverted the nature of intelligence. During the Cold War, it is estimated that U.S. intelligence derived 80 percent of all its collection on the Soviet Union from secret sources, namely technical collection and espionage, and 20 percent from open sources. Now those proportions are believed to be reversed. Governments no longer hold a monopoly on intelligence. The future of intelligence lies with the private sector, not with governments. Open-source (or commercially available) data is already transforming the landscape of intelligence, leading to an existential crisis among Western agencies. Outfits like Bellingcat and C4ADS are revealing secrets about Russia and China, respectively, that traditionally would have taken an intelligence service huge resources and time. (Even then, success would not have been guaranteed.) Another open-source intelligence start-up, Strider Technologies, has shown that the Chinese government is exploiting scientific research collaborations at Los Alamos to advance its defense industries in dual-use technologies like hypersonics. The echoes with the first Cold War—Los Alamos, home of the Soviet atom spies—are blindingly obvious. As in the last Cold War, the U.S. government is effectively funding an adversary's defense industry. U.S. government research grants for Chinese scientists at Los Alamos have advanced Chinese S&T and undermined American competition. Public information about parking tickets, and patents, shines a light on what is going on behind the digital and bamboo Iron Curtains. To stay relevant and continue to provide a margin for decision makers, traditional secret services like MI6 are having to come out of the shadows, embrace, and integrate with new technologies that can turn complex data into insights. This reiterates that this century's East-West intelligence war will be about data and who can best exploit it, through machine learning and AI.[28]

The history of the last century's epic intelligence war offers seven lessons for the superpower struggle now unfolding between the United States and China.

First, the best defense is good intelligence. Given the unprecedented Chinese assault on U.S. secrets, good intelligence—timely, accurate, and relevant information—will be key for Western policymakers to act decisively about Chinese intentions and capabilities.

Second, intelligence this century will increasingly be dominated by open-source information. There will continue to be a niche for traditional espionage. A well-placed spy like Oleg Gordievsky can give insights into a foreign leader's mindset, and thinking, that would remain mysterious with even the best open-source intelligence. The West must seek such sources. An ironclad rule from the last century is that spies catch other spies; the same will be true this century, requiring Western intelligence services to penetrate China's intelligence agencies to protect our own secrets. But outside this niche area for traditional espionage, this century's intelligence war will be about open-source data and the scientists who can exploit it. The age of a secret service is over.

Third, Western strategy regarding China must be based on strategic empathy. It would be a mistake to put forth a grand strategic doctrine like NSC 68, which set out the U.S. government's strategy to contain the Soviet Union but failed to address how that doctrine would appear to those in Moscow. NATO made a similar strategic miscalculation after the Soviet

Union's collapse when it failed to understand Russia's deep sense of humiliation and its intense desire to protect its "national interests."

Fourth, Western policymakers must use covert actions cautiously: they have limited practical effect, can result in unforeseen consequences ("blowback"), and tend to embitter relations between superpowers. Whether it is regime change, degrading alliances, or discrediting targets, covert actions are only effective when they supplement diplomacy and statecraft. Seductive as they are as a quick fix for failed diplomacy, covert actions cannot replace overt foreign policy. Outside of the Soviet-Afghan war, and perhaps U.S. support for the anti-Soviet Solidarity movement in Poland (QRHELPFUL), it is difficult to think of a single U.S. covert action that provided a long-term strategic success.

Fifth, information warfare in this century's cyber age will continue to involve the insidious spread of disinformation, which can cause us to question the existence even of facts and truth. "Truth decay" cannot be solved by Western clandestine services alone—that is the true lesson of U.S. efforts to counter Soviet disinformation. Intelligence agencies of democracies can do their best to counter online disinformation. But their efforts will never be sufficient; like chopping off a hydra's head, more spring up on social media. The answer to the challenge of algorithmically driven disinformation lies with patient, long-term education about online information—digital literacy. What is required is a broad-based public-private effort, a new Marshall Plan of the Mind.

Sixth, the intelligence war between East and West will persist whatever happens overtly with relations between China and the U.S., whether they improve or deteriorate. Russia, past and present, has used its intelligence services offensively against Western countries when their defenses were down, as a result of improved relations, or when they were distracted elsewhere. There is no reason to believe that China would not do the same. Western governments must be alert to this and expect it.

Seventh, and finally, the U.S. government must be as transparent as possible about the known nature and scope of Chinese espionage and other illicit activities. Chinese clandestine efforts must be disclosed, challenged, and debated.

One of the major conclusions from last century's intelligence war between East and West is that two apparently incompatible things can be true at the same time. Just as with Soviet espionage, Chinese espionage can be real—*and* Western democracies can create McCarthyite witch scares. Chinese intelligence actively recruits from Chinese diaspora populations, but few Chinese Americans become spies. In fact, they are frequently victims of Xi's regime. Operation FOXHUNT involves Chinese intelligence officers targeting, capturing, and repatriating Chinese citizens overseas who are considered to be political threats, often by using threats to family still residing on the mainland. Over eight years, about nine thousand people worldwide were hauled to China as part of FOXHUNT, some of them U.S. nationals. While the Chinese government undertakes every kind of covert activity, the FBI also makes mistakes. The FBI wrongly accused a professor at Temple University, Xiaoxing Xi, a naturalized American citizen and world-renowned expert on superconductor technologies, of being a Chinese agent. The same happened to Gang Chen, an MIT professor. He was cleared in January 2022 after a lengthy DoJ investigation, but is stepping away from federally funded research because of anxiety about being racially profiled.[29]

There is a real prospect of a new Red Scare, targeting U.S. citizens who happen to be of Asian descent, chilling free speech and academic freedom, with innocent citizens of Western countries wrongly accused of being Chinese spies. We do not know whether Charles Lieber, former chair of Harvard's Department of Chemistry and Chemical Biology, was a Chinese agent. He has been convicted of taking Chinese money, which he hid from Harvard and the National Institutes of Health. That does not necessarily make him a spy—he may simply have made bad decisions. It is time for an urgent public policy conversation about the nature of Chinese illicit activities in the West, and the balance that Western democracies are prepared to strike between national security and civil liberties. Sunlight remains the best disinfectant.

The American Century, if we understand that to mean the age of America's global leadership, so termed by the American media magnate Henry Luce, is now over. When the history of this period comes to be written, we may well conclude it came to an end in 2016. Under a president willing to ride rough-shod over norms and laws, the United States experienced the seductive pull of authoritarianism. Strong leaders, the cliché says, can "get things done." One of America's foremost experts on Russia, Fiona Hill, has concluded that the United States risks becoming like Russia. Given the levels of nativist populism, violence, partisan divide, political corruption, and a recent coup attempt in the U.S., it is hard to disagree with her. (Trump, inevitably, dismissed Hill, who is English-born, as a "deep state stiff with a nice accent.") In 2017, the Economist Intelligence Unit downgraded the United States to be a flawed democracy. It has remained such in reports since. In fact, American democracy has arguably gotten worse, rather than better, in the years since. America has many similarities to the corruption and mob rule that the ancient historian Polybius wrote about (in the quote at the beginning of the chapter) when explaining the rise of the Roman republic (read: China) to replace the Greek city-states (America) as the dominant Mediterranean power.[30]

The ultimate damage that Trump inflicted on American democracy lies with the Big Lie: his claim, without evidence, that he did not lose the 2020 election—that it was "stolen" from him. The refusal of Trump to concede that he lost, fearing he would be branded a loser, was insidious enough. But then, on January 6, 2021, he helped to instigate a coup attempt at the Capitol with the intention of overturning the election result. He was apparently indifferent about his vice president being killed for his "betrayal"—for not being loyal enough to the president to ignore U.S. law and join in Trump's plan.

This is the stuff of tin-pot dictatorships. In fact, it has a direct precedent, as we saw earlier in Chile, when the U.S. government tried to rig the election of Allende. Swap the name Biden for Allende, and the parallels with Trump's effort to suborn electors to overturn the 2020 election hit you in the face. Both tried to pressure electors not to ratify a democratic election. What the U.S. government did overseas in the past is now being done at home. Speaking in October 2022, former CIA director Michael Hayden, who spent a career analyzing dangerous foreign regimes, said that he believes the U.S. has a fifty-fifty chance of surviving.[31]

Turning on the news in America today with children in the room is a risky business. Our screens show gun violence, with children being shot to death in schools, a churn of revelations about systemic racism, and polarization over our freedom to make intensely private choices about our bodies, our partners, and our lives. If you traveled overseas as an American during Trump's presidency, it became quickly apparent that his administration made our country into a laughingstock on the world stage. Trump's America appeared like a crumbling edifice, like his former Taj Mahal in Atlantic City. Since Putin's war in Ukraine, the Republican Party has tried to rewrite its recent past, but we should not forget that in the 2020 U.S. election, Trump used Russian disinformation, claiming that Ukraine, not Russia, was responsible for meddling in the 2016 election. He then tried to withhold crucial weapons for Ukraine and attempted to blackmail the Ukrainian president, Volodymyr Zelensky, earning Trump the first of his two unprecedented impeachments by the House of Representatives.

When Barack Obama was elected president in 2008, I thought—naively—as an American who has lived overseas most of my life, that the issue of racism in the United States had finally been consigned to history. Instead, Obama's presidency threw fuel on a simmering fire of racism in U.S. society. Trump's presidency appealed openly to the country's nativist fears, and to white nationalists, who were eager for a champion. He encouraged fringe ideas and conspiracy theories, like QAnon, which holds that Democrats are a cabal of satanic pedophiles and cannibals out to sabotage Trump, to become respectable and mainstream. (Its leader, Q, holds a Q-level security clearance, used for nuclear secrets, and therefore knows what is "really" going on, you see.) Hostile foreign governments like Russia saw the paranoid strain in U.S. politics and exploited it.

A Trump second term, it is reasonable to assume, would see a conspiracy-driven administration seeking revenge for his "unfair" loss in 2020. Five Eyes partners are bracing themselves; under a second Trump presidency, they may no longer be able to count on the U.S. government as a reliable ally, given Trump's previous embrace of Putin, threat to pull out of NATO, and attacks on the U.S. deep state.

The U.S. domestic situation is dire. That said, China's continued economic rise is not guaranteed. Xi may be physically imposing, at nearly six feet, but China is not ten feet tall. Beijing has had to impose emigration restrictions to stop a brain drain from China. As Elon Musk, the billionaire who wants to colonize Mars, put it in his usual blunt way to his millions of Twitter followers: "The acid test for any two competing socioeconomic systems is which side needs to build a wall to keep people from escaping? That's the bad one!" Covid may become the Chinese Communist Party's Chernobyl, contributing to its decline and unwinding, possibly even its collapse. The protests that erupted in China in November 2022 against Xi's zero-Covid policy suggest opposition to his rule. We don't know how far protests in China will go. Xi's "China Dream" may already be over, and could become a nightmare through a war with Taiwan, for example. Worryingly for the rest of the world, a China in decline may become an even more dangerous player. As Russia shows, a superpower that never achieves the global dominance it believes it deserves is a dangerous one, capable of unleashing an aggressive clandestine foreign policy. Decline increases risk-taking.[32]

For all the West's problems, most people, I believe, would still rather live in the United States, Britain, or, if you are lucky enough, Europe, with their democratic freedoms, than under China's digital authoritarianism. I am free to criticize the U.S. government in ways that would land me in jail in China or Russia. As Winston Churchill said, democracy remains "the worst form of government—except for all the others that have been tried." Democracy and freedom are also worth fighting for, as Ukrainians are bravely showing. Russia's war in Ukraine will hopefully lead to a renaissance of democracy over authoritarianism. With luck, that will be the history of our future, the next chapter of the epic intelligence war between East and West.

ACKNOWLEDGMENTS

IN THE COURSE OF WRITING THIS BOOK, I HAVE INCURRED debts to countless people. First and foremost, I would like to thank Christopher Andrew, at Cambridge University, my doctoral supervisor, mentor, friend, and collaborator, who read the entire manuscript and provided invaluable comments. Harvard's Kennedy School of Government, where this book grew from start to finish, is a remarkable intellectual home. I have benefited richly from its unique combination of scholars and practitioners. My colleagues in the Applied History Project at the Kennedy School, Graham Allison, Niall Ferguson, and Fred Logevall, have kindly supported my research and been polite enough not to mention the war. I was able to test some of the ideas for this book at one of our Applied History Working Group sessions in the fall of 2022, where colleagues, now including Steven Kotkin, provided constructive criticism.

My heartfelt thanks go to other colleagues, at the Kennedy School's Intelligence Project: Paul Kolbe, Rolf Mowatt-Larssen, Kevin Ryan, Maria Robson-Morrow, and Michael Miner. Under Paul, Rolf, and Kevin's leadership, and with Graham's backing, we have made the Intelligence Project the leading center for the public policy study of intelligence in North America. The Intelligence Project is made possible by the generous and unfailing support of Thomas Kaplan. This book would not be possible without it: thank you, Tom. I've been lucky enough to receive help from outstanding research assistants at the Intelligence Project along the way: Sean Power,

Maya Cotton, Charlie Arnowitz, Caroline Kristof, and Nidal Morrison. I'd like to thank the following, who also gave me valuable comments on various drafts: Nicholas Dujmovic, David Sherman, Rory Cormac, Shaun Walker, Eyck Freyman, Jacob Forward, Adam Shelley, and Kevin Quinlan. My thanks go to members of the British and U.S. intelligence communities, whom I interviewed, and must remain anonymous. You know who you are. Like everyone else, I was grounded during the Covid pandemic, unable to travel to archives. My thanks go to the archival staff at U.S. presidential libraries and the UK National Archives. Ivan Grek, and his network of researchers at The Bridge, have been priceless.

My literary agents, Bill Hamilton and Michael Carlisle, helped turn the idea for this book into a reality. It's been a privilege to work with my editors, Robert Messenger at Simon & Schuster, Richard Beswick at Little, Brown, and my wonderful external editor, Roger Scholl. The senior production editor at Simon & Schuster, Yvette Grant, has done the impossible. I'd like to thank Bill Frucht, Pronoy Sarkar, Clive Priddle, Sam Nicholson, and Celina Spiegel, whom I enjoyed meeting during the book's auction process. Beck & Stone have done sterling work with communications and in designing the book's website. In the editorial process, Adrian Ho and Janet Byrne caught an embarrassing number of factual errors in the manuscript. As always, any errors that do appear in the text are solely mine. My heart goes to my family in England, father, mother, and dynamo sister, Lia, who even went to the National Archives for me to find records; and to all the DiPesas in Scituate, Massachusetts. Mary McCafferty has done more than any sister-in-law should, helping me with the bibliography.

My utmost thanks to my wife, Catherine, for putting up with me as I became monomaniacal writing this book, which has been living with us. I owe you more than I can express, Catherine. The book is dedicated to my son, Hayden, who came along at just the right moment and has lived his whole life with this project, putting up with a distracted father. He helps me put everything in perspective and gives me hope for the future.

—Cambridge, Massachusetts

GLOSSARY

AFSA	ARMED FORCES SECURITY AGENCY	U.S. SIGINT BODY
ASA	ARMY SECURITY AGENCY	U.S. ARMY SIGINT BODY
ASD	AUSTRALIAN SIGNALS DIRECTORATE	AUSTRALIAN SIGINT SERVICE
ASIO	AUSTRALIAN SECURITY INTELLIGENCE ORGANIZATION	AUSTRALIAN SECURITY SERVICE
BND		WEST GERMAN FOREIGN INTELLIGENCE SERVICE
BRUSA	BRITISH-UNITED STATES COMMUNICATION INTELLIGENCE AGREEMENT	ANGLO-AMERICAN SIGINT SHARING AGREEMENT, WORLD WAR II AND COLD WAR
BSC	BRITISH SECURITY COORDINATION	WWII BRITISH INTELLIGENCE BODY ESTABLISHED IN THE U.S.

CIA	CENTRAL INTELLIGENCE AGENCY	U.S. FOREIGN INTELLIGENCE AGENCY
CHEKA	ALL-RUSSIAN EXTRAORDINARY COMMISSION FOR COMBATING COUNTERREVOLUTION AND SABOTAGE	KGB PREDECESSOR, SOVIET STATE SECURITY AND INTELLIGENCE SERVICE FROM 1917 TO 1922
CIG	CENTRAL INTELLIGENCE GROUP	IMMEDIATE PREDECESSOR TO THE CIA
COI	COORDINATOR OF INFORMATION	WORLD WAR II INTELLIGENCE ADVISER TO U.S. PRESIDENT, PREDECESSOR TO DCI
COMINTERN	COMMUNIST INTERNATIONAL	STALIN-ERA UNDERGROUND COMMUNIST GROUP, CONTROLLED BY MOSCOW
CPGB	COMMUNIST PARTY OF GREAT BRITAIN	
CPUSA	COMMUNIST PARTY OF THE UNITED STATES OF AMERICA	
DCI	DIRECTOR OF CENTRAL INTELLIGENCE	HEAD OF THE CIA, COORDINATOR OF U.S. INTELLIGENCE ACTIVITIES, AND PRINCIPAL INTELLIGENCE ADVISER TO THE U.S. PRESIDENT FROM 1946 TO 2005
DNI	DIRECTOR OF NATIONAL INTELLIGENCE	POST-9/11 SENIOR U.S. GOVERNMENT OFFICIAL WHO SERVES AS THE EXECUTIVE HEAD OF THE U.S. INTELLIGENCE COMMUNITY AND COORDINATES U.S. INTELLIGENCE ACTIVITIES; PRINCIPAL INTELLIGENCE ADVISER TO U.S. PRESIDENT
DST		FRENCH SECURITY SERVICE

ELINT	ELECTRONIC INTELLIGENCE	INFORMATION GATHERED THROUGH THE INTERCEPTION OR MONITORING OF ELECTRONIC SIGNALS OTHER THAN THOSE USED FOR COMMUNICATION
FAPSI		RUSSIAN SIGINT SERVICE FROM 1991 TO 2003
FBI	FEDERAL BUREAU OF INVESTIGATION	U.S. LAW ENFORCEMENT AND INTELLIGENCE AGENCY
FCD	FIRST CHIEF DIRECTORATE	KGB FOREIGN INTELLIGENCE BRANCH
FSB		RUSSIAN SECURITY SERVICE FROM 1995 TO THE PRESENT; SUCCESSOR TO THE KGB
GC&CS	GOVERNMENT CODE AND CIPHER SCHOOL	PREVIOUS NAME FOR GCHQ
GCHQ	GOVERNMENT COMMUNICATIONS HEADQUARTERS	BRITISH SIGINT SERVICE
GRU		SOVIET MILITARY INTELLIGENCE
GU		POST-SOVIET (RUSSIAN) MILITARY INTELLIGENCE SERVICE
HVA		EAST GERMAN STASI FOREIGN INTELLIGENCE WING
HUMINT	HUMAN INTELLIGENCE	INFORMATION COLLECTED OR DERIVED FROM HUMAN SOURCES

ICBM	INTERCONTINENTAL BALLISTIC MISSILE	BALLISTIC MISSILE WITH A RANGE GREATER THAN ABOUT 5,500 KM, MAINLY DESIGNED FOR NUCLEAR WEAPONS DELIVERY
IMINT	IMAGERY INTELLIGENCE	INTELLIGENCE DERIVED FROM THE EXPLOITATION/ANALYSIS OF VISUAL IMAGERY
INO		EARLY SOVIET (CHEKA) FOREIGN INTELLIGENCE DEPARTMENT
JIC	JOINT INTELLIGENCE COMMITTEE	"HIGH TABLE" OF BRITISH INTELLIGENCE COMMUNITY
KGB		SOVIET SECURITY AND INTELLIGENCE SERVICE, COMBINING SECRET POLICE AND FOREIGN INTELLIGENCE
LCS	LONDON CONTROLLING SECTION	WORLD WAR II BRITISH INTELLIGENCE BODY FOCUSED ON STRATEGIC DECEPTION AGAINST THE AXIS POWERS
MGB		KGB PREDECESSOR; SOVIET SECURITY APPARATUS FROM 1946 TO 1953
MI5	THE SECURITY SERVICE	BRITISH SECURITY INTELLIGENCE SERVICE RESPONSIBLE FOR COUNTERESPIONAGE, COUNTER-SUBVERSION, AND COUNTER-SABOTAGE IN BRITISH TERRITORY
MI6 (SIS)	SECRET INTELLIGENCE SERVICE	BRITISH FOREIGN INTELLIGENCE SERVICE
MPS	MINISTRY OF PUBLIC SECURITY	CHINESE DOMESTIC INTELLIGENCE BODY

MRBM	MEDIUM-RANGE BALLISTIC MISSILE	BALLISTIC MISSILE WITH A RANGE BETWEEN ABOUT 1,000 AND 3,000 KM
MSS	MINISTRY OF STATE SECURITY	CHINESE SECURITY INTELLIGENCE SERVICE
NASA	NATIONAL AERONAUTICS AND SPACE ADMINISTRATION	U.S. GOVERNMENT AGENCY RESPONSIBLE FOR THE CIVIL SPACE PROGRAM AND AERONAUTICS AND SPACE RESEARCH
NATO	NORTH ATLANTIC TREATY ORGANIZATION	INTERGOVERNMENTAL WESTERN MILITARY ALLIANCE
NIE	NATIONAL INTELLIGENCE ESTIMATE	AUTHORITATIVE U.S. INTELLIGENCE ASSESSMENT
NKVD		KGB PREDECESSOR, SOVIET STATE SECURITY AND INTELLIGENCE SERVICE FROM 1934 TO 1943
NPIC	NATIONAL PHOTOGRAPHIC INTERPRETATION CENTER	CIA-LED IMINT ANALYSIS BODY, PREDECESSOR TO U.S. NATIONAL GEOSPATIAL-INTELLIGENCE AGENCY
NRO	NATIONAL RECONNAISSANCE OFFICE	U.S. IMINT AGENCY
NSA	NATIONAL SECURITY AGENCY	U.S. SIGINT AGENCY
NSC	NATIONAL SECURITY COUNCIL	PRINCIPAL FORUM USED BY THE PRESIDENT OF THE UNITED STATES FOR CONSIDERATION OF MATTERS OF NATIONAL SECURITY, MILITARY, AND FOREIGN POLICY

ODNI	OFFICE OF THE DIRECTOR OF NATIONAL INTELLIGENCE (U.S.)	U.S. SENIOR-LEVEL CABINET AGENCY THAT OVERSEES THE U.S. INTELLIGENCE COMMUNITY AND PROVIDES SUPPORT TO THE DNI
OGPU		KGB PREDECESSOR, SOVIET STATE SECURITY AND INTELLIGENCE SERVICE FROM 1923 TO 1934
OPC	OFFICE OF POLICY COORDINATION	CIA DEPARTMENT RESPONSIBLE FOR COVERT ACTION FROM 1948 TO 1952
OP-20-G	OFFICE OF CHIEF OF NAVAL OPERATIONS, 20TH DIVISION OF THE OFFICE OF NAVAL COMMUNICATIONS, G SECTION/ COMMUNICATIONS SECURITY	WORLD WAR II–ERA U.S. NAVY SIGINT UNIT
OSO	OFFICE OF SPECIAL OPERATIONS	DEPARTMENT OF CIG (AND LATER CIA) RESPONSIBLE FOR FOREIGN INTELLIGENCE COLLECTION
OSS	OFFICE OF STRATEGIC SERVICES	WORLD WAR II–ERA U.S. FOREIGN INTELLIGENCE SERVICE
PDB	PRESIDENT'S DAILY BRIEF	TOP SECRET ASSESSMENT DELIVERED TO U.S. PRESIDENT PRODUCED BY THE DCI AND POST-9/11 DNI
PLA	PEOPLE'S LIBERATION ARMY	CHINESE ARMED FORCES
PWE	POLITICAL WARFARE EXECUTIVE	BRITISH WORLD WAR II CLANDESTINE SERVICE CREATED TO DISSEMINATE AVOWED AND NON-AVOWED PROPAGANDA
RCMP	ROYAL CANADIAN MOUNTED POLICE	CANADIAN LAW ENFORCEMENT AND INTELLIGENCE AGENCY

SALT	STRATEGIC ARMS LIMITATION TALKS	SERIES OF BILATERAL CONFERENCES AND TREATIES SIGNED BETWEEN THE U.S. AND THE USSR INTENDED TO REDUCE THE NUMBER OF LONG-RANGE BALLISTIC MISSILES EACH COUNTRY COULD POSSESS AND PRODUCE
SDI	STRATEGIC DEFENSE INITIATIVE	PROPOSED MISSILE DEFENSE PROGRAM TO PROTECT THE U.S. FROM BALLISTIC STRATEGIC NUCLEAR WEAPONS
SIGINT	SIGNALS INTELLIGENCE	INTELLIGENCE DERIVED FROM INTERCEPTION AND ANALYSIS OF SIGNALS
SLBM	SUBMARINE-LAUNCHED BALLISTIC MISSILE	BALLISTIC MISSILE CAPABLE OF BEING LAUNCHED FROM SUBMARINES, WHICH CAN ALSO CARRY A NUCLEAR WARHEAD
SOE	SPECIAL OPERATIONS EXECUTIVE	BRITISH WORLD WAR II SERVICE RESPONSIBLE FOR COVERT ACTION, RECONNAISSANCE, AND SABOTAGE
SPG	SPECIAL PROCEDURES GROUP	UNIT WITHIN THE CIA'S OSO RESPONSIBLE FOR CLANDESTINE PSYCHOLOGICAL WARFARE; PREDECESSOR TO OPC
STB		CZECH SECURITY AND INTELLIGENCE SERVICE
SVR		RUSSIAN FOREIGN INTELLIGENCE SERVICE SINCE 1991; SUCCESSOR TO KGB'S FCD

METHODOLOGY AND SOURCES

The great Oxford historian, Keith Thomas, has said that historians do not like to talk about their methodology, in the same way that stage magicians do not speak of theirs: it ruins their tricks. I do not see any need for magic here, however. My methodology has been to synthesize contemporary records and newspapers, private papers, memoirs, and oral interviews. In the process of doing so, I have become something of a spy myself in the archives, trying to pull together the story from both sides, East and West, while always asking myself the questions: "So what? Why does this matter, and what difference did it make?" To my mind, history is a creative endeavor, not dissimilar to pointillist painting, with research and writing starting in minute detail, gradually expanding to a broader historical canvas. History is also inherently visual; trying to imagine how decisions looked to those at the time, who were of course living their lives imagining alternative futures now lost to posterity. The Anglo-American writer Christopher Isherwood once said, "I am a camera." While I would not go that far, I have tried to capture a visualization of events in the narrative, making it almost cinematographic, as we zoom in, pan out, and, in some cases, flash backward or forward. History is not a science. It is also more than a regurgitation of events, just "one fucking thing after another," as Alan Bennett so memorably put it in *The History Boys*.

My work has involved research trips far afield, from the boiling prairie land of Kansas, where President Dwight Eisenhower's library is located, to the National Archives in London (where I became such a regular visitor that an archivist thought I was on staff), to a garage in Toronto holding the private papers of a former Soviet defector, to cafes in Europe where I interviewed former Soviet intelligence officers, and to Singapore, where I had frank (and nonattributable) interviews with British and American officials about China. I have interviewed a former U.S. secretary of state, a head of U.S. intelligence, three former CIA heads of station in Moscow, one of whom only left the government after being expelled from Russia in 2021, a former chief of MI6, and fifty-three serving intelligence officers. As a former courtroom barrister, I know the limitations of interviews—memories are fallible, even when well-meaning, and depend on the questions being asked. I have therefore, so far as possible, based interviews on documentary evidence. The above pages are the story of what I discovered during my research, now with more gray hair, and perhaps slightly more of a stoop, than I had at the beginning.*

---

* Keith Thomas, "Working Methods," *London Review of Books* 32 (June 2010). For futures that never transpired, consider the U.S. intelligence briefings given to George H. W. Bush's national security team: SNIE 11-18-91 "The Republics of the Former USSR: The Outlook for the Next Year" September 1991, John Gordon Files Subject Files, National Security Council Files, Subject Files, SDI, July 1991, GHWL; on problems of memory as evidence, see Toby Landau, "Tainted Memories: Exposing the Fallacy of Witness Evidence in International Arbitration" (Kaplan lecture, Hong Kong Club, November 17, 2010).

NOTES

ARCHIVES
APRF: Archive of the President of the Russian Federation, Moscow, Russia
BL: British Library, London, UK
BOD: Bodleian Libraries, University of Oxford, UK
CHAC: Churchill Archives Centre, Cambridge University, UK
DDEL: Dwight D. Eisenhower Presidential Library, Abilene, KS, USA
GDA SBU: State Archives of Ukraine, Department of the Security Service, Kyiv, Ukraine
GHWBL: George H. W. Bush Presidential Library, College Station, TX, USA
GRFL: Gerald R. Ford Presidential Library, Ann Arbor, MI, USA
GWBL: George W. Bush Presidential Library, Dallas, Texas, USA
HIA: Hoover Institution Library and Archives, Stanford, CA, USA
HSTL: Harry S. Truman Presidential Library, Independence, MO, USA
JCL: Jimmy Carter Presidential Library, Atlanta, GA, USA
JFKL: John F. Kennedy Presidential Library, Boston, MA, USA
LBJL: Lyndon Baines Johnson Presidential Library, Austin, TX, USA
NARA: U.S. National Archives and Records Administration, Washington, DC, USA
RGANI: Russian State Archive of Contemporary History, Moscow, Russia
RGASPI: Russian State Archive of Socio-Political History, Moscow, Russia
RNL: Richard Nixon Presidential Library, Yorba Linda, CA, USA
RRL: Ronald Reagan Presidential Library, Simi Valley, CA, USA
TNA: The National Archives, London, UK
WCL: William J. Clinton Presidential Library, Little Rock, AR, USA
YAL: Yale University Library, New Haven, CT, USA

SPECIFIC COLLECTIONS
ACAD: Alexander Cadogan Papers, CHAC
DENN: Alexander Denniston Papers, CHAC
AMEJ: Julian Amery Papers, CHAC
MITN: Mitrokhin Archive, CHAC

ONLINE ARCHIVAL RESOURCES
U.S. intelligence agency archives
CIA CREST (portal for CIA historical records): https://www.cia.gov/readingroom/collection/crest
    -25-year-program-archive

FBI VAULT (portal for FBI historical records): https://vault.fbi.gov/

USG-NSA (portal for National Security Agency historical records): https://www.nsa.gov/Helpful-Links
/NSA-FOIA/Declassification-Transparency-Initiatives/

OTHER ARCHIVES

ADST: Association for Diplomatic Studies and Training Oral History Project, https://adst.org/oral-history/

FRUS: Foreign Relations of the United States, https://history.state.gov/historicaldocuments

GWU NSA: The George Washington University National Security Archive, https://nsarchive.gwu.edu/

DNSA: Digital National Security Archive, https://proquest.libguides.com/dnsa

SHAFR: Society for Historians of American Foreign Relations, https://shafr.org/

WCDA: Wilson Center Digital Archive, https://digitalarchive.wilsoncenter.org/

DBPO: Documents on British Policy Overseas, https://proquest.libguides.com/dbpo

U.S. Department of State Archive: https://2001-2009.state.gov/

Margaret Thatcher Archive: https://www.margaretthatcher.org/archive

A note for readers: To save space in this book, I have chosen not to give web page links to documents and most articles. Full notes, with all the web links and a bibliography, can be found on the book's website: www.spieshistory.com. In the following notes, I have, however, hopefully provided sufficient information for readers to find citations easily through a search engine. The CIA unhelpfully changed links on its previous CREST system for documents, which reinforced my reason for not providing links here, as they risk becoming outdated—though I have provided CIA document ID numbers so they can be easily found. For archival references, I have followed the following format: author, title, date, file number, archival citation, and archive. My British relatives and friends will, I also hope, forgive me for following America's unusual (and from an international perspective, annoying) date format: month, day, year. That format led to confusion among the Allies in World War II, but that is a story for elsewhere. Another note: for transliteration of Russian names, I have followed the simplified version used by BBC monitoring service, whose simplifications include "y" for "iy" in surnames (so, Trotsky) and "i" for "iy" in first names (so, Yuri). When a name is well-established in English, however, like Anatoly Dobrynin, I have used that.

CHAPTER 1: The Hundred-Year Intelligence War

1. Ukraine [name illegible], "Political and Economic Situation in the Ukraine," February 7, 1922, FO 688/12/6, TNA; [Envelope K-9] MITN 2/10, CHAC.

2. For sanitized versions of the Red Army in Ukraine, see, for example, Serov, *Zapiski iz chemodana*, pp. 41–42.

3. Author interview with FSB defector to the United States on condition of anonymity, April 12, 2022; Service, *Kremlin Winter*, pp. 229–43.

4. Author interview with Ladislav Bittman, July 24, 2018; for the KGB considering the CIA and MI6 as its primary opponents, see Krasilnikov, *KGB protiv MI-6: okhotniki za shpionami*; Bittman's comments about the significance of instructions from Moscow should not be taken to mean that Soviet intelligence services did not employ local nationals from its early days. They did, as the recent research of Alexandra Sukalo has shown: "The Soviet Political Police: Establishment, Training, and Operations in the Soviet Republics, 1918–1953" (PhD diss., Stanford University, 2021); for Anglo-American intelligence relations, see Smith, *The Real Special Relationship*; and Kerbaj, *The Secret History of the Five Eyes*.

5. MI5 discovered after World War II that the GRU had been collecting British military publications from as early as 1932. See B.2.b, "Collection of Economic Intelligence by the Soviet Union and Satellite Countries," September 6, 1948; s.24a "HQ Organization of the GRU," KV 5/81, TNA.

6. Typical commentary that one side recruited heroes, while the other recruited traitors, can be

found in Semichastny, *Spetssluzhby SSSR v taynoy voyne*, p. 154. For a more objective concession, see Lyubimov, *Zapiski, neputevogo rezidenta*, pp. 76–78; and Fabre, *Spying through a Glass Darkly*, pp. 113–41, for understanding treason and betrayal. For FBI statistics, see Christopher Wray, "The Threat Posed by the Chinese Government and the Chinese Communist Party to the Economic and National Security of the United States," remarks at the Hudson Institute, July 7, 2020; a valuable analysis of cyber as new medium for sabotage, espionage, and subversion can be found in Thomas Rid, "Cyber War Will Not Take Place," *Journal of Strategic Studies* 35 (2012): 5–32.

7. Albats, *The State Within a State*. For the revanchist anger of a former senior KGB officer in the mid-1990s, born from humiliation ("the death of Russian civilization, the extinction of one of the most important peoples"), see Leonov, *Likholet'ye*, p. 428; Semichastny, *Bespokoynoye serdtse*, pp. 7–9, 413–14. For comments on Russians rewriting their history, see Braithwaite, *Russia: Myths and Realities*, p. 249. For *siloviki*, see Jack, *Inside Putin's Russia*, pp. 316–17; Burleigh, *The Best of Times, the Worst of Times*, pp. 150–151.

8. "NATO Enlargement: Policy," DEFE 68/1493, TNA, sets out August 1996 UK Ministry of Defence role-play gaming scenarios for NATO expansion; they trigger Russian countermoves and counterattacks, which then led new NATO members to invoke collective security under Article V. "NATO Enlargement: Policy," draft, "NATO Enlargement: Who and When," June 1996. For Cook and Robertson's letter, see "NATO Enlargement," Robin Cook and Robert Armstrong, minute to prime minister, June 15, 1997, "Russia/UK Relations," PREM 49/149, TNA; Gates, *Duty*, p. 157. For debates on NATO enlargement, see Goldgeier, *Not Whether But When*; Marc Trachtenberg; "The United States and the NATO Non-Extension Assurances of 1990: New Light on an Old Problem?" *International Security* 45 (2021): 162–203.

9. Josh Rogin, "NSA Chief: Cybercrime Constitutes the 'Greatest Transfer of Wealth in History,'" *Foreign Policy*, July 9, 2012. A useful study for the role of covert action as an instrument of U.S. policy remains Godson, *Dirty Tricks or Trump Cards*; and Treverton, *Covert Action*.

10. For expert analysis of the Cold War, which has influenced my understanding, see Gaddis, *The Cold War*; Westad, *The Cold War*; Lüthi, *Cold Wars*; and Haslam, *Russia's Cold War*. For KGB and Middle Eastern terrorism, see MITN 1/6/5, CHAC. Among the cases that do not feature in this book are those of Vitali Yurchenko (see Brinkley, ed., *The Reagan Diaries*, p. 369 [November 15, 1985]); Edward Lee Howard; Ryszard Kukliński (see Weiser, *A Secret Life*); and Adolf Tolkachev (see Hoffman, *The Billion Dollar Spy*).

11. A useful new history of the Third World alternative to the Cold War can be found in Parrott and Lawrence, eds., *The Tricontinental Revolution*.

12. The classic account remains Andrew and Dilks, eds., *The Missing Dimension*.

13. Howard, *Safe House*, and Wise, *The Spy Who Got Away*; Desmond Ball, *Soviet Signals Intelligence (SIGINT)*, p. 2.

14. Zegart, *Spies, Lies, and Algorithms*, pp. 25–36; see also Raymond L. Garthoff, "Foreign Intelligence and the Historiography of the Cold War," *Journal of Cold War Studies* 6 (2004): 21–56. For KGB amplification and, in some cases, funding of New Left exposés of CIA abuses, see MITN 1/6/5, CHAC.

15. Bismarck's quote is from Kennedy, *The Rise and Fall of Great Powers*, p. 540.

16. For debates between historians as Soviet archives were opening, see John Lewis Gaddis, "Intelligence, Espionage, and Cold War Origins," *Diplomatic History* 13 (1989): 191–212. See D. Cameron Watt's response in "Intelligence and the Historian," *Diplomatic History* 14 (1990): 199–204.

17. Some KGB and SVR officers absurdly claimed that the Mitrokhin Archive was British disinformation and that no archivist could have known what Mitrokhin claimed: Kirpichenko, *Razvedka*, "Introduction." In fact, the value of the Mitrokhin Archive was tested by Western intelligence services, and its contents have been corroborated by other documents from opened Russian archives.

18. For Britain's intelligence services, and their functions, see "Report of Enquiry by Sir Norman Brook into the Secret Intelligence and Security Services," March 1951, CAB 301/17, TNA. For "the

friends," see Patrick Reilly memoirs (1981), "The Secret Service," p. 202, archive of Sir (D'Arcy) Patrick Reilly Ms. Eng. C. 6918, BOD.

19. Dallin, *Soviet Espionage*, pp. 14–15; Urban, *The Skripal Files*, pp. 1–4; Russia's foreign intelligence service (SVR) today evidently sees a direct continuum between itself and the Cheka: http://svr .gov.ru/history/history.htm.

20. Henry A. Kissinger memorandum to the president, "Defection in the UK by a Soviet KGB Official," September 24, 1971, National Security Files, Subject Files "Defectors and Refugees," box 318 RNL; Lyalin's recruitment of agents in his network, who knew him as "Alex," included at least one British civil servant and started at least in 1967. See Regina v Costo, "Statement of Constantinos Martinou," September 10, 1971, CRIM 1/5681/1, TNA; JIC(A)(72)13, "The Threat of Sabotage in the United Kingdom," March 20, 1972, CAB 186/11, TNA; MITN 1/6/4, CHAC; for the expulsion of Soviet officials from Britain in September 1971, Operation FOOT, see Bennett, *Six Moments of Crisis*, pp. 123–48; author interview with former Security Service (MI5) officer on condition of anonymity, April 4, 2016.

21. For SolarWinds, see David Sanger, Nicole Perlroth, and Eric Schmitt, "Scope of Russian Hacking Becomes Clear: Multiple U.S. Agencies Were Hit," *New York Times*, December 14, 2020.

PART I: THE CLASH BETWEEN DICTATORS AND DEMOCRACIES

CHAPTER 2: CHILL IN THE EAST

1. [Envelope K-9], MITN 2/10, CHAC; Service, *Lenin*, p. 434.

2. MITN 1/6/10, CHAC. Typical valorizations can be seen in Primakov, ed., *Ocherki ob Istorii Vneshnei Razvedki*, vol. 2, pp. 7–12.

3. [Envelope K-9] MITN 2/10, CHAC; Dziak, *Chekisty*; Primakov, ed., *Ocherki ob Istorii Vneshnei Razvedki*, 2, pp. 6–7. See Heller, *Cogs in the Wheel*, pp. 91–110, for the Cheka's institution of fear.

4. "Allied Military Intervention in Russia," FO 608/177 [no.3] TNA; Davis and Trani, *The First Cold War*; Foglesong, *America's Secret War against Bolshevism*. Churchill's anti-Bolshevism is well told in Kinvig, *Churchill's Crusade*. Also see Roberts, *Churchill*; Carley, *Silent Conflict*, chap. 1; Beevor, *Russia*, pp. 273–75; Jeffery, *MI6*, pp. 134–36; Stalin, *History of the Communist Party of the Soviet Union— Bolshevik (Short Course)*, chap. 8; *Sluzhba Vneshney Razvedki, Rossiyskoy Federatsii 100 let. D'kumenty i svidete'stva*; Leonov, *Razvedka*, p. 34. As the official history of Russian intelligence states: "In the 1920s, Western countries launched a fierce propaganda campaign against the USSR, grossly distorted its domestic policy, attributed its aggressive policy to foreign policy, and called for political and economic isolation of the Soviet Union in the international arena. All this inflicted noticeable damage on the international prestige of the USSR, prevented the development of its external relations, trade, and economic relations. The leading role in the organization and conduct of this campaign was played by Western intelligence agencies, who used their agents in the Soviet Union for this purpose, as well as white-emigre organizations": Primakov, ed., *Ocherki ob Istorii Vneshnei Razvedki*, vol. 2, p. 13.

5. Reilly's unclear origins, and bigamy, are laid out in his MI5 dossier, "Sidney Reilly," KV 2/827, TNA, which also shows the MI6 chief's support of him: see minute 3, February 20, 1919. Some of Reilly's intelligence reports from Russia can be found in "Russia," FO 371/3962, TNA, which also indicates MI6's lack of intelligence at the time in Russia; Lockhart to Gregory, May 2, 1919, "Russia," FO 371/4017, TNA; "Arthur Ransome," KV 2/1903 and 1904, TNA; "Notes on Sidney Reilly: Information Provided by George Hill," Robert Hamilton Bruce Lockhart Papers, box 11, folder, 1 HIA. For another of Cumming's agents in Russia, Paul Dukes, known as ST/25, see his embellished account in Dukes, *The Story of "ST 25,"* and his *Red Dusk and the Morrow*; Service, *Spies and Commissars*, pp. 146–65, 219–28, 239–41; Schneer, *The Lockhart Plot*, pp. 238–41; Young, ed., *The Diaries of Sir Robert Bruce Lockhart*, p. 41; Kennan, *Soviet-American Relations*, vol. 2: *The Decision to Intervene*, pp. 302–03; *Istoria Sovetskikh Organov Gosudarstvennoi Bezopasnosti*, chap. 2, pp. 84–85; Debo, *Revolution and*

Survival, p. 361. Robert Bruce Lockhart was the author of numerous books on politics, fishing, and Scotch whisky, though it was his memoirs that brought him celebrity. For his account of the plot, see his memoir, *Memoirs of a British Agent*. A central figure in U.S. clandestine activities in Russia, in parallel with Lockhart, was the wonderfully named Xenophon Kalamatiano. See Saul, *Friends of Foes?* p. 9. For Stalin's impression of British intelligence generally, and Lockhart in particular, see RGAPSI Stalin Fund F. 558 Op. 3 Case 25; and Roberts, *Stalin's Library*, pp. 118–19.

6. Debo, *Survival and Consolidation*, p. 401; Andrew and Mitrokhin, *The Mitrokhin Archive*, vol. 1, *The KGB in Europe and the West*, pp. 37–39.

7. Figes, *A People's Tragedy*, pp. 646–47; Beevor, *Russia*, pp. 304–05, 355, 488–90; Nicolas Werth, "The Red Terror," in Courtois et al., eds., *The Black Book of Communism*, pp. 71–80; Sebestyen, *Lenin*, pp. 386–88, 466–69; Volkogonov, *Lenin*, pp. 238–41.

8. MITN 1/6, CHAC; Suny, *Stalin*, pp. 3, 434.

9. The INO was established under Order No. 169, December 20, 1920, http://svr.gov.ru/history /stages/stage01.htm; Primakov, *Ocherki ob Istorii Vneshnei Razvedki*, vol. 2, p. 5; Kolpakadi, *Sovetskaya vneshnyaya razvedka*, pp. 8–9; Haslam, *Near and Distant Neighbors*, p. 23.

10. [Envelope K-9] MITN 2/10, CHAC; Primakov, *Ocherki ob Istorii Vneshnei Razvedki*, vol. 2, p. 3; Suvarov, *Inside Soviet Military Intelligence*, pp. 85–86.

11. British code breakers had notable prewar successes against Comintern radio traffic in the Far East: "Moscow and Shanghai Messages," HW 17/3, TNA.

12. "Soviet Illegal Espionage in US," August 1957, FBI Series, box 2, Records of the White House Office, Office of the Special Assistant for National Security Affairs, DDEL.

13. [Envelope 9] MITN 2/10, CHAC; Fitzpatrick, *The Russian Revolution*, p. 95. For Cheka disinformation, see *Istoria Sovetskikh Organov Gosudarstvennoi Bezopasnosti*, pp. 154, 175.

14. [Envelope K-9] MITN 2/10, CHAC, shows that Cheka officer Artur Artuzov was instrumental in TREST. This and MITN 1/6/4, CHAC, also show that an earlier Cheka operation, SINDIKAT ("Syndicate"), likewise targeted Boris Savinkov, former deputy minister of war in the provisional government overthrown by the Bolsheviks. The operation deceived Savinkov to return to Russia for talks with a bogus underground; when he did so, he was arrested by the Cheka, tortured, and executed after a show trial. Another operation, code-named CASE 39, targeted exiled Ukrainian leaders. For Savinkov, see Primakov, *Ocherki ob Istorii Vneshnei Razvedki*, vol. 2, pp. 7, 89–96, which predictably claims that he jumped out of a window while incarcerated. See Primakov, *Ocherki ob Istorii Vneshnei Razvedki*, vol. 2, pp. 94–95, also for TREST, which erroneously claims that Reilly was killed in an accidental clash with border guards in Finland. A standard history of TREST is in Gasparyan, *Operatsiya "Trest."* Also see *Istoria Sovetskikh Organov Gosudarstvennoi Bezopasnosti*, pp. 188, 211, 245.

15. Myths about Britain's secret service still found their place in Russia after the Cold War. See the Introduction to Krasilnikov, *KGB protiv MI-6*. For "the game," see MITN 1/6/5, CHAC.

16. "Historical Sketch of the Directorate of Military Intelligence during the Great War of 1914–1919," WO 32/10776, TNA.

17. Muggeridge, *Chronicles of Wasted Time*, p. 406; a description of MI6's headquarters found in Patrick Reilly memoirs (1981), p. 203, archive of Sir (D'Arcy) Patrick Reilly, Ms. Eng. C. 6918 BOD. See Jeffery, *MI6*, pp. 225, 231.

18. Stimson's quote can be found in Stimson and Bundy, *On Active Service in Peace and War*.

19. "Note for File," n.d., s.319a "Nicolas Klishko," KV 2/1415, TNA; "Russian Oil Products Ltd," KV 5/73, TNA. Another Soviet front commercial outfit in Britain was the Far Eastern Fur Trading Company: see KV 2/1655, TNA.

20. "GEORGE Reports and Decrypts for the Prime Minister, June to September 1920," HW 12/332, TNA. GC&CS started life in 1919 with just twenty-five officers: "The Government Code and Cypher School (GC&CS)," December 2, 1944, p. 3, DENN 1/4, CHAC. For Fetterlein, see ibid. (DENN), pp. 6, 8. For slightly different translations, see Ullman, *Anglo-Soviet Relations*, p. 117 n. 51.

21. The most forensic examination of the Zinoviev letter has been written by Gill Bennett: *The Zinoviev Letter*. Also see Roskill, *Hankey*, pp. 382–83; Morgan, *J. Ramsay MacDonald*, pp. 118–21; Marquand, *Ramsay MacDonald*, pp. 381–88; Haslam, *The Spectre of War*, pp. 64–69; *Sluzhba Vneshney Razvedki Rossiyskoy Federatsii 100 let*, pp. 30–31; Jacobsen, *When the Soviet Union Entered World Politics*, pp. 138–40.

22. MI5 and Scotland Yard note, "Russian Oil Products," March 5, 1930, KV 5/71, TNA; Guy Liddell, "Russian Oil Products Ltd," January 16, 1931, s.132a "Russian Oil Products," KV 5/72, TNA.

23. "Recovery of British Official Documents by Raids on ARCOS Ltd, May 1927," KV 3/15-16, TNA; "Federated Press of America," KV 1/1101, TNA; "History of a Section of the Russian Intelligence Service, Operating in This Country, under Management of William Norman Ewer," January 8, 1930, s.809a "Norman Ewer," KV 2/1016, TNA; Kocho-Williams, *Russian and Soviet Diplomacy*, p. 91.

24. Parliamentary Debates (Commons), cols. 1842–1854, May 24, 1927; *Documents Illustrating the Hostile Activities of the Soviet Government and Third International against Great Britain*, Cmd. 2847 (1927); Andrew, *The Defence of the Realm*, pp. 154–58.

25. L/P&J/12/359 India Office Records (IOR), BL; Bazhanov, *Bazhanov and the Damnation of Stalin*, pp. 104–13; Bohlen, *Witness to History*, p. 20; in 1927, MI6 also managed to obtain, presumably from an agent, the registry logbooks of the foreign department of the OGPU: KV 3/14, TNA.

26. MITN 1/6/1 and 1/6/5, CHAC; Agabekov, *OGPU*, pp. 195–97; Sibley, *Red Spies in America*, p. 61.

27. MITN 1/6/1, CHAC; Corson and Crowley, *The New KGB*, appendix I.

28. For the history of stealing and capturing code books, see, for example, "The Establishment of the Decoding Service and Room 40, 1917," DENN 1/2, pp. 3, 5, CHAC.

29. For Cheka recruitment strategies of foreign cipher clerks, see [envelope K-9]; for SPEKO and Boky, see *Near and Distant Neighbors*, p. 130.

30. Andrew and Mitrokhin, *The Mitrokhin Archive*, vol. 1, pp. 58–61.

31. [Envelope K-9] MITN 1/6/1, CHAC.

32. For Bazarov, see MITN 1/6/4, CHAC; Primakov, *Ocherki ob Istorii Vneshnei Razvedki*, vol. 3, p. 175.

33. "B" Minute July 1, 1933; H.L.A. Smith, July 15, 1933, s.5a, and s.7a; S.11 report, "Ernest OLDHAM," September 21, 1939, all in "Ernest Oldham," KV 2/808, TNA.

34. Applebaum, *Red Famine*, concludes that at least 5 million people died of hunger between 1931 and 1935 across the Soviet Union (p. xxix); Conquest, *The Harvest of Sorrow*, pp. 299–301; Snyder, *Bloodlands*, pp. 21–58; Nicolas Werth, "The Great Famine," in Courtois, ed., *The Black Book of Communism*, pp. 159–68; Dolot, *Execution by Hunger*. The subject of local ("substate") dictators, acting on behalf of Moscow, and their own ends, has been explored by Gorlizki and Khlevniuk, *Substate Dictatorship*.

35. Hastings, *Secret War*, p. 352; Toynbee was on MI5's radar as a communist before 1951, when his friendship with Donald Maclean made him the subject of surveillance, inquiries, and interrogation. See W. J. Skardon, "Guy Burgess. Donald Maclean," June 22, 1951, s.107 "Philip Toynbee," KV 2/4597, TNA; Tzouliadis, *The Forsaken*; Hollander, *Political Pilgrims*, pp. 141–67.

36. "D.3 Survey of Russian Espionage in the United Kingdom, 1935–1955," June 1956, p. 13, KV 3/417, TNA. For Deutsch, see MITN 1/6/1, CHAC; Primakov, *Ocherki ob Istorii Vneshnei Razvedki*, vol. 3, pp. 44–45 for Maly.

37. Primakov, *Ocherki ob Istorii Vneshnei Razvedki*, vol. 3, pp. 20–25; *Sluzhba Vneshney Razvedki, Rossiyskoy Federatsii 100 let*, p. 88.

38. "Information from THOMAS [Krivitsky]," January 25, 1940, s.1a "Arnold Deutsch," KV 2/4428, TNA. MI5's Jane Archer was able to show the Soviet GRU defector, Walter Krivitsky, a photograph of Deutsch: B.3 [Jane Sissmore/Archer], January 30, 1940, s.13a "Walter Krivitsky," KV 2/804, TNA. For later investigations into OTTO, see C. O. Shipp, February 8, 1968, s.134b "Jenifer Hart," KV 2/4639, TNA. A valuable history of the Cambridge Spies is in Davenport-Hines, *Enemies Within*, chap. 10; Ben Macintyre's *A Spy Among Friends* vividly tells the story of Philby.

39. B. Palliser, n.d., s.3a "Jenifer Hart," KV 2/4638, TNA; B. Palliser, K.3, April 28, 1969, s.139a "Jenifer Hart," KV 2/4639, TNA; and same file, 134b "Extract from Report on Interviews with Arthur Henry Ashford WYNN," by C. O. Shipp, October 3, 1967; and same file, C. O. Shipp, s.130a "Interview with Jennifer HART on 15 January 1968"; Hart, *Ask Me No More*, p. 71; Haynes, Klehr, and Vassiliev, "Spy Mystery Resolved," *Times*, May 13, 2009; *Sluzhba Vneshney Razvedki, Rossiyskoy Federatsii 100 let*, p. 88–89; Wright, *Spycatcher*, pp. 264–67; Damaskin, *Kitty Harris*, pp. 144, 146; Duff, *A Time for Spies*, p. 108.

40. Primakov, *Ocherki ob Istorii Vneshnei Razvedki*, vol. 3, pp. 27–38, for Deutsch and Philby, especially, p. 32; Haslam, *Near and Distant Neighbors*, pp. 73.

41. Only later was MI5 able to piece together Philby's association with communists in Vienna: B.2 "Edith Tudor-Hart," December 1, 1951, s.227b "Alexander Tudor-Hart," KV 2/1604, TNA; Milicent Bagot, "Edith Tudor-Hart," May 3, 1942, s.56a "Edith Tudor-Hart," KV 2/1013, TNA; Arthur Martin, October 3, 1951, s.143a "Edith Tudor-Hart," KV 2/1014, TNA; "Extract from an Interview of H. A. R. Philby by W. J. Skardon," December 28, 1951, s.117b "Maurice Dobb," KV 2/1759, TNA; intercepted letter from Maurice Dobb, Trinity College, Cambridge, to Alexander Tudor-Hart, December 2, 1930, s.5w "Edith Tudor-Hart," KV 2/1013, TNA; Home Office Warrant, October 2, 1951, s.146a "Edith Tudor-Hart," KV 2/1014, TNA; A. F. Burbridge, December 6, 1951, minute 228 "Alexander Tudor-Hart," KV 2/1603, TNA. For Anthony Blunt's recruitment on the basis of intellectual idealism, see Hollander, *Political Pilgrims*, p. 81.

42. Philipps, *A Spy Named Orphan*, pp. 45–46; Alexander Cadogan, "Report of Committee of Enquiry," November 1, 1951, p. 25, CAB 301/120, TNA; Kathleen Sissmore [Jane Archer] [MI5] to Valentine Vivian [MI6], March 16, 1938, s.8a "Paul Hardt," KV 2/1008, TNA. Anthony Blunt, the Soviet spy in MI5, recalled that he once looked himself up in its registry and found just two traces, one linking his name to the well-known communist in Cambridge, Maurice Dobb, and the other stating that he had visited the Soviet Union before the war. He was able to talk his way out of both: Carter, *Anthony Blunt*, p. 245.

43. For security considerations and homosexuality in Britain, when it was illegal, see "Action Taken on Cadogan Report," May 1952, Foreign and Commonwealth (hereafter FCO) 158/208, TNA. "Communist Activities in Universities, Cambridge," KV 3/442, TNA, contains minutes of meetings of the Cambridge University Labour Club, containing Maclean's and Burgess's names and also mentions of Philby. This information was not available to MI5 until after 1951.

44. Conquest, *Reflections on a Ravaged Century*, p. 152. The story of the Bolsheviks as millenarian sectarians, preparing for the apocalypse, who once in power were disappointed by a failed prophecy, is beautifully told by Slezkine, *The House of Government*.

CHAPTER 3: NEMESIS

1. Overy, *Blood and Ruins*, chap. 1; Mitter, *Forgotten Ally*, p. 212; Burleigh, *Moral Combat*, pp. 19–20; Damaskin, *Kitty Harris*, p. 47.

2. Curry, *The Security Service*, pp. 22–25, 148; "D. G. White's Lecture Notes regarding Counter-espionage Investigations and Organisation of RSS and GC&CS," January 9, 1943, s.1a "Mr. Dick White's Lecture for New Regional Security Liaison Officers [RSLOs]," KV 4/170, TNA; F. H. Hinsley et al., *British Intelligence in the Second World War*, vol. 1: *Its Influence on Strategy and Operations*, p. 57, and vol. 4: *Security and Counter-Intelligence*, pp. 11–12.

3. "The German Intelligence Service and the War," report by Hugh Trevor-Roper, 1945, p. 3, CAB 154/105, TNA; Collier, *Hidden Weapons*, p. 55.

4. For fears of Axis espionage in Britain and a Nazi invasion, see the following at TNA: JIC(40)73 "Invasion of the United Kingdom," May 17, 1940, CAB 81/97; JIC(40)101 "Summary of Likely Forms and Scales of Attack That Germany Could Bring to Bear on the British Isles in the Near Future," June 5, 1940, CAB 81/97; JIC(40)108 "Telephone Conversations in the United Kingdom

in Foreign Languages," June 7, 1940, CAB 81/97; and JIC(40)134 "Use of Smoke in an Invasion of Great Britain," June 21, 1940, CAB 81/97; Curry, *The Security Service*, pp. 145–46. For British plans to attack the Soviet Union, then effectively allies (through the Non-Aggression Pact of 1939) with the Axis powers, see Osborn, *Operation Pike: Britain versus the Soviet Union, 1939–1941*, and Kitchen, *British Policy towards the Soviet Union during the Second World War*, pp. 22–28, 274.

5. For breakdown of security and police in Malaya before the fall of Singapore, see "Japanese Espionage in Malaya," November 26, 1941, s.12a "Japanese Intelligence Activities in Malaya," KV 3/426, TNA; and a personal account found in ibid., KV 3/426, s.16a June 2, 1942; for the American Comintern agent Agnes Smedley, lover of the GRU prize agent in the Far East, Richard Sorge, see MI5 [name withheld] to Valentine Vivian (MI6), April 16, 1937, s.119a "Agnes Smedley," KV 2/2207, TNA; Price, *The Lives of Agnes Smedley*, chap. 9; Aldrich, *Intelligence and the War against Japan*, pp. 28–32.

6. Kotkin, *Stalin*, pp. 135–41; Steven Kotkin, "When Stalin Faced Hitler: Who Fooled Whom?" *Foreign Affairs* 96 (2017): 48–71. Even Pavel Fitin, the head of the INO, later politely observed the difficulties of passing Stalin intelligence before BARBAROSSA: Stalin's "unquestioned authority" would create an "unenviable position" if he received intelligence that he did not like. Primakov, *Ocherki ob Istorii Vneshnei Razvedki*, vol. 4, pp. 20–21; Kershaw, *Fateful Choices*, p. 258.

7. Statistics compiled from the Ukrainian archive of the SBU 0195–0196; 0197–0199; F. 16 O.1 D. 506, pp. 88–91; F. 16 O. 1 D. 0508, pp. 11–12, 212–21, 230–35, 236–41, 242–48, 259–64; F. 16 O. 1 D. 511, pp. 219–30, 231–33, 233–234; F. 16 O. 1 D. 516, pp. 5–11, 15–70, 82–93, 94–100, 157–61, 162–71, 183–86, 206–14, 215–24, 225–33, 234–37, 247–50, 257–59, 260–63, 264–66, 272, 285, 286–87, 308, 309–10, 311, 312–15, 316–18, 319–20, 321–22, 330–37, 345–47, 348–51, 361–62, 363–65, 366–67, 368–71, 372–74, 383–84, 387–90, 392; F. 16 O. 1 D. 517, pp. 259–80; F. 16 O. 1 D. 518, pp. 63–65; MITN 1/6/4, CHAC; Serov, *Zapiski iz chemodana*, pp. 78–80; on Trepper, see his *The Great Game*, pp. 74–76.

8. Primakov, *Ocherki ob Istorii Vneshnei Razvedki*, vol. 4, p. 21–22.

9. "Soviet German Relations," s.74 FO 371/29482, TNA. This is the record of the conversation·with Soviet ambassador Maisky, on June 13, 1941, in which Eden said that the intelligence about German troop concentrations was derived from "technical matters, which I was not qualified to handle." The chief proponent of the belief that Hitler would invade the Soviet Union was Churchill himself (as he not immodestly noted in his memoirs) after reading ULTRA. He disagreed with Britain's JIC, which concluded only in June 1941 that a German attack on Russia was likely. See COS 40 (350) "Likelihood of a German Attack on Russia," June 5, 1941, CAB 80/28, TNA, with a comment from Churchill that he was "unconvinced." But by June 9, the JIC was envisioning war between Germany and the Soviet Union: JIC(41)234 (Final) "The Possible Effect of a German-Soviet War," June 9, 1941, s.53 CAB 371/29483, TNA. For Churchill's disguise of ULTRA as "agents," see Churchill, *The Second World War*, vol. 3: *The Grand Alliance*, p. 317. The best and forensic analysis of Churchill's warning to Stalin remains Gorodetsky, *Grand Delusion*, pp. 160–61; now also Kotkin, *Stalin*, vol. 2, pp. 150–51. For Maisky's similar dismissal of warnings from Cripps on June 18, see Gorodetsky, *Stafford Cripps in Moscow*, pp. 111–13; Clarke, *The Cripps Version*, p. 214; Murphy, *What Stalin Knew*, pp. 148–49; Reynolds and Pechatnov, *The Kremlin Letters*, pp. 37, 41; and Gorodetsky, *The Maisky Diaries*, p. 361 (June 13, 1941), with editorial note.

10. "Comments by Alexander Orlov," August 26, 1955, s.64b "Alexander Orlov," KV 2/2879, TNA; [MI6] to M. Morton-Evans, November 9, 1949, s.19a "Ignace Reiss," KV 2/1898, TNA; Poretsky, *Our Own People*, pp. 236–37; Volodarsky, *Stalin's Agent*, pp. 345–51; Costello and Tsarev, *Deadly Illusions*, pp. 305–6. For a contemporary description of purges, see Davies, *Mission to Moscow*, p. 161.

11. Jansen and Petrov, *Stalin's Loyal Executioner*, chap. 4; Khlevniuk, *The History of the Gulag*, chap. 4; Khlevniuk, *Stalin*, p. 150; Nicolas Werth, "The Great Terror," in Courtois et al., eds., *The Black Book of Communism*, pp. 184–202; for Yezhov, see Burleigh, *Day of the Assassins*, p. 101–102. For

descriptions of the show trials, see Brands, *Inside the Cold War*, pp. 60–73, and Yakovlev, *A Century of Violence in Soviet Russia*. For the origins of the Terror as a conspiracy against Stalin, the "center of centers," see Jansen and Petrov, *Stalin's Loyal Executioner*, p. 75, and Lenoe, *The Kirov Murder and Soviet History*, chap. 11. For the number of prisoners in the Gulag, see Applebaum, *Gulag*, p. 579, and Rayfield, *Stalin and His Hangmen*, p. 329. The classic personal account of the Terror can be found in Ginzburg, *Into the Whirlwind*. See "Ivan Serov," KV 2/3830, TNA, for Serov's visit to Britain in 1956.

12. Primakov, *Ocherki ob Istorii Vneshnei Razvedki*, vol. 3, p. 18; Leonov, *Likholet'ye*, p. 40; Volkogonov, *Stalin*, p. 393.

13. Burleigh, *Moral Combat*, pp. 154–55; for British detection of Axis and Soviet intelligence collaboration, see "Liddell Diaries," August 16, 1940, KV 4/186, TNA; Roger Hollis, "Communism and the Position of the Communist Party," April 29, 1941, s.34b "Policy on Control of Communists—General," KV 4/265, TNA; Curry, *The Security Service*, p. 190; Hinsley, *British Intelligence in the Second World War*, vol. 4, *Security and Counter-Intelligence*, p. 38. For the secret annex of the Non-Aggression Pact, see Watson, *Molotov*, p. 170. For the Stalin quote, see Kershaw, *Fateful Choices*, p. 258. For Katyn, see Burleigh, *Moral Combat* (above); McMeekin, *Stalin's War*, pp. 146–52; Volkogonov, *Stalin*, p. 360; Birstein, *SMERSH*, p. 75; Roberts, *Stalin's Wars*, p. 170. For NKVD-German cooperation, see Johnson, *Faustian Bargain*, p. 113. Nazi-NKVD collaboration is inevitably airbrushed from Primakov, *Ocherki ob Istorii Vneshnei Razvedki*, vol. 3, p. 296ff.

14. For Kennedy's view of Britain as doomed, see "Memorandum of Conversation between President and Myself, 3pm August 1 1940," Joseph P. Kennedy Papers, Appointments and Diary, box 100, JFKL. For Donovan in London, see Waller, *Wild Bill Donovan*, pp. 59–60.

15. P. M. Loxley to H. Britten (H.M. Treasury), July 25, 1942, "USA: Liaison with Authorities in USA and London," FO 1093/238, TNA; Stephenson, *The Secret History of British Intelligence in the Americas*, pp. 55–65, 71–75; for Churchill's war strategy to bring the United States into the war, see Todman, *Britain's War, 1937–1941*, pp. 526–29, and Cull, *Selling War*, p. 145.

16. Andrew, *The Secret World*, pp. 610–12, 630–35; Toll, *Pacific Crucible*, p. 310; Hotta, *Japan 1941*, p. 278. Bletchley Park's decrypt from Tokyo, instructing the Japanese ambassador in London to destroy his cipher machine, on December 1, 1941, is in "C," [MI6 Chief] to Churchill, December 3, 1941, HW 1/290, TNA; Johnson, *American Cryptology* (available on USG-NSA), book 1, pp. 3–4.

17. Frederick D. Parker, "The Unsolved Messages of Pearl Harbor," *Cryptologia* 15 (1991), pp. 295–313.

18. Colville, *The Fringes of Power*, p. 294. Bletchley decrypts were also known as ISOS, BONIFACE, and Blue Jackets (BJs), after the color of their covers): "C," to H. M. G. Jebb, January 2, 1940, "Chief of the Secret Intelligence Service (SIS): reports and information; Blue Jackets (BJs)," FO 1093/309, TNA. GC&CS started life in 1919 with just twenty-five officers: "The Government Code and Cypher School (GC&CS), 1944," p. 5, DENN, CHAC.

19. William J. Friedman, "Report on E Operations of the GC&CS at Bletchley Park," August 12, 1943, p. 6, HW 14/85, TNA; E. T. Williams, "ULTRA (WWII Intelligence Information)," October 5, 1945, DDEL.

20. Roberts, *Churchill*, p. 687. Alan Brooke later visited Bletchley and noted, "I marvel at the work they are doing": Danchev and Todman, eds., *War Diaries*, entry for April 16, 1942, p. 250, and entry for April 1, 1942.

21. Kennedy, *Engineers of Victory*, pp. 62, 63, 69, 137, 243; Hinsley, *British Intelligence in the Second World War* (abridged), pp. 115–125. For U.S. industrial might for manufacturing bombes, see Alan Turing, "Visit to National Cash Register Corporation of Dayton, Ohio," December 1942, "Communications Liaison," HW 57/9, TNA; Patrick Reilly, "The Secret Service," archive of Sir (D'Arcy) Patrick Reilly, Ms. Eng. C. 6918, BOD.

22. Howarth, *Intelligence Chief Extraordinary*, pp. 114–16.

23. Andrew, *The Secret World*, p. 641, notes: From June 1941 to February 1943, 585 Allied ships were

lost in the Atlantic, but only thirteen U-boats were sunk. In February 1942, the German navy introduced a new code variant (SHARK) that defeated Bletchley's code breakers until the end of the year. But apart from this nine-month period, they were able to crack and read German naval communications, sometimes within hours of transmission. After that, Allied control of the sea route was never seriously threatened, and U-boat sinkings soared. From April 1943 to May 1945, just 178 Allied ships were lost, but 286 U-boats were sunk. SIGINT contributed to this reverse of fortunes for the Allies. German naval commander Admiral Dönitz ordered an investigation, which wrongly concluded that U-boat communications were still secure and that the Allies were probably gaining information from agents in French ports.

24. Harry Hinsley, "The Influence of ULTRA in the Second World War" (Annual Liddell Hart Centre for Military Archives lecture, February 18, 1992); Ferris, *Behind the Enigma*, pp. 223–24. For the Germans' "good source," Bernard Fuller, see "USA: Liaison with Authorities in USA and London," British embassy Stockholm to London, August 13, 1942, signed by Anthony Eden, FO 1093/238, TNA.

25. Dilks, ed., *The Diaries of Sir Alexander Cadogan*, p. 720 (February 22, 1945); Cadogan diary, September 6, 1941, ACAD 1/10, CHAC. For Churchill's disclosure of ULTRA, see "C," Reply to Prime Minister on Hitler's Order of the Day "Not to Be Passed to Stalin," HW 1/2385, TNA.

26. The preceding owes much to Hastings, *The Secret War*; Smith, *OSS*, pp. 200, 208; Petersen, ed., *From Hitler's Doorstep*, pp. 183–85.

27. Toll, *The Conquering Tide*, pp. 203–06; Smith, *The Emperor's Codes*, pp. 132–44.

28. H. T. Tizard memo for Prime Minister, October 19, 1940, PREM 3/475/1, TNA.

29. "Co-operation with the US Army Sigint Organisation Based at Arlington Hall, Washington," "Washington and E Traffic [1941]," HW 57/30, TNA; ibid. [HW 57/30]; J. H. Tiltman, "ENIGMA—Policy," May 5, 1942, HW 57/30, TNA. For vetting of Americans in Britain after December 1941, see Sir David Petrie (DG MI5) to Lord Swinton (Security Executive), December 19, 1941, s.5a "Control of Americans: Main Policy & Liaison with Security Authorities," KV 4/135, TNA; "Cross Reference: Liaison with FBI in Vetting Americans Coming to the UK," April 16, 1941, s.25b "Control of Americans," KV 4/136, TNA; "Brigadier John Tiltman: A Giant among Cryptanalysts" (Fort George G. Meade, MD: NSA Center for Cryptologic History, 2007), USG-NSA; David Sherman, "The First Americans: The 1941 US Codebreaking Mission to Bletchley Park" (Fort George Meade, MD: NSA Center for Cryptologic History, 2016), USG-NSA; "Early Papers Governing the US-UK Agreements," William Friedman to Corderman, February 6, 1943, s.65b, USG-NSA; "Agreement between British Government Code and Cypher School and US War Department in Regard to Certain 'Special Intelligence,'" June 1943, USG-NSA. For the integration of Bletchley and U.S. SIGINT, see chief MI6 [Menzies] to Peter Loxley, August 31, 1944, s.44 "B.J.'s," FO 1093/329, TNA; Eisenhower, *Crusade in Europe*, p. 68.

30. William J. Donovan, "Accomplishment of OSS," memo for the president, July 1945, William J. Donovan Papers, microfilm reel 188, CHAC; Herrington, *Special Operations in Norway*, pp. 100–02.

31. For MI6 bribes, "Bribes to German Supply Vessels," CAB 301/33, TNA; and "SIS: Finance," FO 1093/185, which uses the term *subsidies*; Cruickshank, *The Fourth Arm*, pp. 80, 108; Garnett, *The Secret History of PWE*, pp. 195, 308; Office of Strategic Services, *Morale Operations Field Manual*; Smith, *The Shadow Warriors*, pp. 205–06; Cave Brown, ed., *The Secret War Report of the OSS*, chap. 19; "PSB, Short History of (by Dr. Lilly)"; White House Office of the National Security Council Staff Papers, December 21, 1951, OCB Secretariat Series, box 6, DDEL.

32. Hastings, *Secret War*, pp. 260–82; Kochanski, *Resistance*; Cipher telegrams: SOE Director ["CD"] "Tito," November 21, 1943, "SOE/OSS Policy and Liaison—the Middle East," HS 8/7, TNA; Balkans and Middle East Director SOE to SO [Cairo], June 18, 1943, "SOE/OSS Policy and

Liaison," HS 8/5, TNA; "America—SOE/OSS Policy and Liaison: London Agreement," July 1943, HS 8/9, TNA; "America—SOE/OSS Policy and Liaison: SOE Donovan Treaty," HS 8/10, TNA; "O.S.S. Mission to Moscow," [July 1944], s.14 "SOE/FO/NKVD/OSS Liaison" HS 4/350, TNA. For SOE's daring wartime operations, see "SOE Albanian Diary," AMEJ 1/1/31, Julian Amery Papers, CHAC; Maclean, *Eastern Approaches*, pp. 439–40.

33. "America—SOE/OSS Policy and Liaison," HS 8/9, TNA. For hostility between OSS and SOE, see Leo Amery to Anthony Eden, October 16, 1944, "Far East; India/General," HS 1/211, TNA. Aldrich, *Intelligence and the War against Japan*; Cruickshank, *SOE in the Far East*, p. 242; Thorne, *Allies of a Kind*.

34. Burleigh, *Moral Combat*, pp. 306–7.

35. O'Sullivan, *Espionage and Counterintelligence in Occupied Persia*, pp. 170–94; Gary Kern, "How 'Uncle Joe' Bugged FDR," *Studies in Intelligence* 47 (2003) [available on CIA CREST].

36. Hastings, *The Secret War*, p. 281.

37. Burleigh, *Moral Combat*, p. 241; Snyder, *Bloodlands*, pp. 187–224.

38. For the ROTE KAPELLE, see "The Case of the Rote Kapelle," October 17, 1949, "The Rote Kapelle," KV 3/349, TNA. For Trepper, see his same-named dossier KV 2/2074, TNA; MI5 had only two traces of Leopold Trepper before the war in its files: "Leopold Trepper," ss.1a, 2a, KV 2/2074, TNA. Primakov, *Ocherki ob Istorii Vneshnei Razvedki*, vol. 4, pp. 130–42.

39. Hastings, *The Secret War*, pp. 54–55, 193, 244; Stephan, *Stalin's Secret War*, chap. 6; Primakov, *Ocherki ob Istorii Vneshnei Razvedki*, vol. 4, pp. 109–20; MITN 1/6/4, CHAC. On NKVD tactics in the borderlands, see Statiev, *The Soviet Counterinsurgency in the Western Borderlands*, chap. 9.

40. Burleigh, *Moral Combat*, p. 349.

41. Roberts, *Churchill*, p. 678; Breitman, *Official Secrets*, p. 57ff; Burleigh, *Moral Combat*, p. 444; Wheatley, *British Intelligence and Hitler's Empire in the Soviet Union*, p. 179.

42. For Bletchley decrypts revealing Nazi atrocities and deportations of Jewish populations, including children, see "German Language Message Extracts, Reflecting German Police Atrocities Both in Russia and Concentration Camps," HW 16/44, 16/45, 16/46, 16/47, TNA; "Jewish Children in South of France Being Deported to Eastern Europe," 1943, HW 12/295/26, TNA.

43. Serov, *Zapiski iz chemodana*, pp. 182–85, 190–92; Rayfield, *Stalin and His Hangmen*, p. 349; Andrew, *The Secret World*, p. 655.

44. Burleigh, *Moral Combat*, p. 251; Alexander and Kunze, eds., *Eastern Inferno*, pp. 112–13.

45. Howard, *British Intelligence in the Second World War*, vol. 5: *Strategic Deception*, pp. 26–27.

46. Sir David Petrie to Sir Anthony Eden, "Short Review by Sir David Petrie of the Activities of the Security Service 1939–1944, Prepared for the Foreign Secretary: A Report on the Work of the Service by the Director-General up to and including D-Day," June 26, 1944, p. 7, s.2a KV 4/87, TNA.

47. Masterman, *The Double-Cross System*, p. 3; "Comments by Sir Dick White on Wartime Record of the Security Service," [1955], CAB 301/131, TNA.

48. Howard, *British Intelligence in the Second World War*, vol. 5: *Strategic Deception*, pp. 21, 26–27. For Bletchley Park's praise of TREASURE's work, see Denys Page, Assistant Director, GC&CS, to J. C. Masterman (MI5), May 26, 1944, s.359a "Nathalie Sergueiew," KV 2/466, TNA; ibid. [KV 2/466] s.377a Mary Sherer (B1A), July 4, 1944; Sergueiew, *Secret Service Rendered*, pp. 207–10; Hesketh, *Fortitude*, pp. 340–50; Holt, *The Deceivers*, pp. 545–46.

49. "German Intelligence Reports Relating to Allied Troop Dispositions in the Run-Up to and Aftermath of Operation OVERLORD," marked with Churchill's initials and red underlining, HW 40/6, TNA; [MI6 Chief] to Churchill, May 31, 1944, HW 1/2866, TNA; "C" providing "special messages": No. 132013 Japanese Ambassador, Berlin to Minister for Foreign Affairs, Tokyo, May 28, 1944. On Ōshima, see Boyd, *Hitler's Japanese Confidant*. On FUSAG and BODYGUARD, see Overy, *Why the Allies Won*, pp. 150–52.

50. Eisenhower to Menzies, July 12, 1945, Principals File, box 77, Pre-Presidential Papers, DDEL;

E. T. Williams, "ULTRA WWII Intell Information," October 5, 1945 (8th Army report). Pre-Presidential Papers, box 20, DDEL.

CHAPTER 4: STALIN'S WARTIME ASSAULT

1. For a defense of Soviet espionage against its wartime Western Allies, "keeping abreast" of the Western powers, see Primakov, *Ocherki ob Istorii Vneshnei Razvedki*, vol. 4, pp. 275–86.

2. Kathleen Sissmore [Jane Archer], April 20, 1937, minute 78, "Ivor Montagu," KV 2/599, TNA; B.2.a, January 5, 1949, s.262a "MONTAGU Ivor," KV 2/601, TNA; Lota, *GRU i atomnaya bomba*, p. 123.

3. "Vassiliev Black Notebook," Alexander Vassiliev Papers, WCDA; Andrew and Mitrokhin, *The Mitrokhin Archive*, vol. 1, p. 167.

4. Cairncross, *The Enigma Spy*, pp. 85, 100–01; Primakov, *Ocherki ob Istorii Vneshnei Razvedk*, vol. 4, p. 183. For Dennis Proctor, see Peter Wright, "Note of Y by Mr. P. M. Wright with Mrs. Flora Soloman," December 6–7, 1966, s.111 "Flora Soloman," KV 2/4634, TNA. Blunt's NKVD handlers in London were Anatoli Gorsky and then Boris Kreshin.

5. GC&CS did collect some traffic on the Soviet Union through German communications: "Iscott," HW 17/53–66, TNA; for Liddell quote, see "Liddell Diaries," October 27, 1942, KV 4/190, TNA; Cadogan diary, August 13, 1943, ACAD, CHAC; Sir David Petrie to Anthony Eden, June 26, 1944, p. 4, s.2a KV 4/87, TNA; Hinsley, *British Intelligence in the Second World War* (abridged) p. 115.

6. For bugging, see "Report on the Operations of F Division in Connection with Subversive Activities," p. 3, KV 4/54, TNA; Curry, *The Security Service*, p. 364; "Liddell Diaries," October 27, 1942, KV 4/190, TNA. For Springhall, "Note on the Case of Douglas Frank Springhall," November 18, 1941, s.235x "Douglas Springhall," KV 2/1596, TNA; Court Proceedings against Douglas Frank Springhall, "Preliminary Observations by MI5," June 21, 1943, s.272b KV 2/1596, TNA; "Liddell Diaries," July 29, 1943, KV 4/192, TNA. One of Springhall's agents, Olive Sheehan, who worked in the Air Ministry, obtained classified information on a wartime radar system code-named WINDOW. For her prosecution in 1943, see E. B. Cussen, July 27, 1943, s.32b "Olive Sheehan," KV 2/4600, TNA. Springhall's case followed the prewar case of Percy Glading: "Percy Glading," s.1a, "Home Office Warrant Imposed on Percy Glading," July 22, 1925, KV 2/1020, TNA; "Secrets Case," *Times*, February 4, 1938; "Official Secrets Act," *Times*, March 15, 1938; Curry, *Security Service*, pp. 108, 361–62.

7. For Philby and Section IX, see Primakov, *Ocherki ob Istorii Vneshnei Razvedki*, vol. 4, pp. 174–75.

8. Andrew and Mitrokhin, *The Mitrokhin Archive*, vol. 1, pp. 157–58.

9. Primakov, *Ocherki ob Istorii Vneshnei Razvedki*, vol. 4, pp. 175–77.

10. Primakov, *Ocherki ob Istorii Vneshnei Razvedki*, vol. 3, pp. 439–47. Shebarshin, *Ruka Moskvy*. In fact, the British dossier on Rudolf Hess shows how perplexed MI5 and MI6 were about Hess's flight. Furthermore, it shows from an ULTRA decrypt that Ribbentrop told the Japanese ambassador, Ōshima, that Hess was deranged and made the flight on his own initiative: "Japanese Ambassador, Rome, to Foreign Ministry, Tokyo, May 14, 1941," s.11a "Rudolf Hess," KV 2/34, TNA; Dilks, ed., *The Diaries of Sir Alexander Cadogan*, p. 378.

11. Primakov, *Ocherki ob Istorii Vneshnei Razvedki*, vol. 5, p. 20; "Operation UNTHINKABLE," CAB 120/691, TNA.

12. For Duncan Lee, see "Vassiliev White Notebook #3," Alexander Vassiliev Papers, WCDA. For Larry Duggan, see "Vassiliev Yellow Notebook #2," Alexander Vassiliev Papers, WCDA. Haynes, Klehr, and Vassiliev, *Spies*, pp. 220–25.

13. MITN 1/6/1, CHAC.

14. For Akhmerov, see MITN 1/6/4, CHAC; Primakov, *Ocherki ob Istorii Vneshnei Razvedki*, vol. 4, pp. 216–26. For Browder and Bentley, see "Vassiliev White Notebook #2," Alexander Vassiliev Papers, WCDA.

15. For Dickstein, see "Vassiliev White Notebook #2," Alexander Vassiliev Papers, WCDA. For OGPU-NKVD in the Spanish Civil War, defense against fascism, see Primakov, *Ocherki ob Istorii Vneshnei Razvedki*, vol. 3, pp. 131–47; Hastings, *The Secret War*, p. 376.

16. Matthew Aid, "'Stella Polaris' and the Secret Code Battle in Postwar Europe," *Intelligence and National Security* 17 (2002): 17–86; Alvarez and Mark, *Spying through a Glass Darkly*, pp. 51–57.

17. Arnold Krammer, "Russian Counterfeit Dollars: A Case of Early Soviet Espionage," *Slavic Review* 30 (1971): 762–773; Leonard, *Secret Soldiers of the Revolution*, pp. 108–10, 112–17; Krivitsky, *I Was Stalin's Agent*, chap. 4; MITN 1/6/4, CHAC, which clearly identifies Duggan as "19." A fellow Soviet agent recruited by Hede Massing was Noel Field: Sharp, *Stalin's American Spy*, pp. 38–42.

18. White was also code-named RICHARD and LAWYER: USG-NSA Venona Release New York to Moscow (No. 590), April 29, 1944, for example; "Vassiliev Black Notebook," "Vassiliev White Notebook #1," "Vassiliev White Notebook #2," "Vassiliev White Notebook #3," Alexander Vassiliev Papers, WCDA; Steil, *The Battle of Bretton Woods*, pp. 291, 295–97.

19. SOE's mission in Moscow was opened in September 1941. It was part of the British mission there opened after BARBAROSSA, led by Noel Mason-MacFarlane, who experienced suffocating NKVD surveillance: Butler, *Mason-Mac*, pp. 136–37. SOE's mission in Moscow noted in 1944 that the NKVD had "done literally nothing for us": SOE Director ["CD"] letter to Orme Sargent (FO), August 22, 1944, s.85 "SOE Russia," HS4/350, TNA; "Security and OSS Leakages," December 1945, HS 8/12, TNA; for Donovan's visit to the Lubyanka, see s.10, cipher telegram Moscow to London, December 29, 1943, s.10 "OSS/SOE Liaison in Moscow," HS 4/332, TNA, in which Fitin's name was inaccurately transcribed as "Citine" or used by the NKVD deliberately to confuse. For impressions by SOE's mission in Moscow (led by George Hill since September 1941) about OSS liaison there, see ibid. [HS 4/332], "The O.S.S. Mission to Moscow," s.14, January 6, 1944; CAB 81/113 JIC(43)25 (Final) "British Military Mission in Moscow," February 2, 1943, CAB 81/113, TNA; JIC(44)81 (0) (Final) "No 30. Military Mission," March 8, 1943, CAB 81/121, TNA; MITN 1/6/3, CHAC; Smith, *OSS*, p. 253.

20. MITN 1/6/5, CHAC, for Belfrage and SOUND (Jacob Golos), his handler. After working for BSC, going through vetting for PWE, MI5 noted that Belfrage had communist views but erroneously concluded they were "mild and amounted to little more than interest in left wing affairs": W. Ogilvie, August 24, 1944, minute 7, "Cedric Belfrage," KV 2/4004, TNA. Belfrage claimed that the material he passed to Golos was part of an MI6 deception, which was never corroborated, Michael Serpell, minute 15, June 18, 1947. It is also notable that Kim Philby was involved in MI6's case on Belfrage: s.10, November 24, 1945.

21. For Hopkins, who was never a Soviet agent but who provided friendly warnings to the Soviets about U.S. counterintelligence, see MITN 1/6/5, CHAC.

22. Beria, *My Father*, pp. 103–105; Katz, *The Daughters of Yalta*, pp. 151–153; Montefiore, *Stalin*, pp. 497–98; Gill Bennett, "The Yalta Conference Opens: 4 February 1945," FCO Historians *What's the Context?* (blog), "What's the Context?" (blog), https://issuu.com/fcohistorians/docs/what_s_the_context_blog_collection/s/11682651.

23. Haynes, Klehr, and Vassiliev, *Spies*, pp. 1–31, which notes that the case against Alger Hiss is now "case closed"; Eduard Mark, "*In Re* Alger Hiss: A Final Verdict from the Archives of the KGB," *Journal of Cold War Studies* 11 (2009), 26–67; Plokhy, *Yalta*, pp. 353–57. For Hiss at Yalta, see Report of the Crimea Conference, "Operation ARGONAUT 1945: Meeting between President Roosevelt, M. Stalin and Mr Churchill (February 1945)," CAB 120/170, TNA. For Hiss as GRU agent, see USG-NSA Venona message 1822 Washington to Moscow, March 30, 1945; Romerstein and Breindel, *The Venona Secrets*, pp. 136–37; Bohlen, *Witness to History*, pp. 194–95; Hiss, *Recollections of a Life*, p. 98; Nitze, *From Hiroshima to Glasnost*, p. 20.

24. Hiss, *Recollections of a Life*, pp. 118–19. After Yalta, Churchill wrote to Stalin, expressing his sincere thanks for hosting the conference, in "agreeable and convenient surroundings": "You yourself said

that co-operation would be less easy when the unifying bond of fight against a common enemy had been removed. I am resolved, as I am sure the President and you are resolved that the friendship and cooperation shall not fade when victory has been won. I pray that you may long be spared to preside over destinies of your country, which has shown its full greatness under your leadership, and I send you my best wishes and heartfelt thanks": Prime Minister Churchill to Stalin, February 17, 1945, "ARGONAUT," CAB 120/170, TNA.

25. Reynolds, *Need to Know*, p. 217; Chambers, *Witness*, pp. 466–69; Berle, *Navigating the Rapids*, pp. 582–83; Tanenhaus, *Whittaker Chambers*, pp. 159–62; Evans and Romerstein, *Stalin's Secret Agents*, pp. 78–79. The GRU illegal resident in the United States was Boris Bykov, whom Whittaker Chambers knew as "Peters": "Boris Bykov," KV 2/2406, TNA. He was identified by GRU defector Walter Krivitsky in June 1939: Primakov, *Ocherki ob Istorii Vneshnei Razvedki*, vol. 3, pp. 176–78. See Roberts, *Churchill*, p. 654, for Churchill's comments that he was willing to enter an alliance with anyone, even the devil, to defeat Nazism. The inference of who was the devil was clear; see Burleigh, *Moral Combat*, p. 77.

26. Baker, *Rezident*, p. 195.

27. Weiner, *Enemies*, p. 182; MITN 1/6/5, CHAC; J. A. Cimperman [FBI], U.S. embassy London, to Freda Small, MI5, January 27, 1947, s.5a "Steve Nelson," KV 2/3827, TNA; Nelson, *American Radical*, p. 294, for his denial of Soviet espionage.

28. Craig and Radchenko, *The Atomic Bomb*, pp. 43–50; MITN 1/6/3, CHAC. See Stimson Diary, Henry Stimson Papers, December 31, 1944, YAL, for Stimson's suggestion of a real quid pro quo on atomic secrets with the Soviets.

29. Todman, *Britain's War 1942–1947*, pp. 376, 604–605.

30. "Engelbert Broda," s.148a Millicent Bagot to Major Dixon, RSLO Cambridge [no name], April 22, 1942, KV 2/2350, TNA; Haynes, Klehr, and Vassiliev, *Spies*, pp. 64–69.

31. MITN 1/6/3, CHAC; Primakov, *Ocherki ob Istorii Vneshnei Razvedki*, vol. 4, pp. 182–83; Gowing, *Britain and Atomic Energy*, pp. 107–8; Sudoplatov, *Special Tasks*, p. 173. See Farmelo, *Churchill's Bomb*, pp. 186–95, on Hankey—and thus Cairncross and the Kremlin—and the British atomic bomb project. There is some indication that the NKVD had another source, which does not appear to be Broda: Operational archive of the Foreign Intelligence Service of Russia (declassified on the SVR's website) 82 072/4/17, *"Spravka Pervogo upravleniya NKVD SSSR o soderzhanii doklada «Uranovogo komiteta», podgotovlennogo na osnovanii razvedyvate"nykh svedeniy, poluchennykh iz Londona, (ne raneye 3 oktyabrya—ne pozdneye 10 oktyabrya 1941)"* ["Information from the First Directorate of the NKVD of the USSR on the contents of the report of the 'Uranium Committee' prepared on the basis of intelligence information received from London (not earlier than October 3—not later than October 10, 1941)"].

32. Andrew and Mitrokhin, *Mitrokhin Archive*, vol. 1, pp. 150–52; Some intelligence on plutonium atomic research was brought to the New York *rezidentura* by a woman named Lucia (OLIVIA), the daughter of an antifascist Italian union leader, whose brother-in-law (MAR) worked on plutonium research at the DuPont company: MITN 1/6/3, CHAC; Primakov, *Ocherki ob Istorii Vneshnei Razvedki*, vol. 5, p. 495.

33. Copy of letter, registration office, Kiel, October 11, 1934, s.1a "Klaus Fuchs," KV 2/1245, TNA; ibid. [KV 2/1245] C-Division note. s.1b. June 2, 1942, "Emil Julius Klaus Fuchs"; ibid. [KV 2/1245] Hugh Shillito, minute 3, September 4, 1943; ibid. [KV 2/1245] Milicent Bagot to Chief Constabulary, Birmingham, s.6a, August 9, 1943; ibid. [KV 2/1245] Guy Liddell, minute 97, May 22, 1945; ibid. [KV 2/1245] Roger Hollis, minute 55, December 4, 1946; Max Born to Edinburgh tribunal, October 20, 1939, "Klaus Fuchs," KV 2/1259, TNA; Max Born to internment committee, May 29, 1940, "Klaus Fuchs," KV 2/1246, TNA; KV 2/1245, TNA; Gowing, *Independence and Deterrence: Britain and Atomic Energy, 1945–1952*, vol. 1, p. 140; Groves, *Now It Can Be Told*, p. 143. For Fuchs as REST and CHARLES, see "Vassiliev Black Notebook," "Vassiliev White Notebook #1," "Vassiliev Yellow Notebook #1," Alexander Vassiliev Papers, WCDA.

34. Hugh Shillito, minute 50, November 29, 1942, "Leon Beurton and Ursula Beurton," KV 6/41, TNA; Werner, *Sonya's Report*, pp. 251–52; Lota, *GRU i atomnaya bomba*, pp. 61–63. For the confusion that the Nazi attack on the Soviet Union in June 1941 caused the British Communist Party (and many of its members), see Banac, ed., *The Diary of Georgi Dimtrov*, p. 168 (entry for June 24, 1941).

35. "Vassiliev Yellow Notebook #1," Alexander Vassiliev Papers, WCDA; Sudoplatov, *Special Tasks*, p. 184.

36. Primakov, *Ocherki ob Istorii Vneshnei Razvedki*, vol. 5, pp. 275–83.

37. Haynes, Klehr, and Vassiliev, *Spies*; Andrew and Mitrokhin, *The Mitrokhin Archive*, vol. 1, p. 170. For Julius Rosenberg, see "Vassiliev Black Notebook," "Vassiliev White Notebook #1," "Vassiliev Yellow Notebook #1," Alexander Vassiliev Papers, WCDA.

38. Andrew and Mitrokhin, *The Mitrokhin Archive*, vol. 1, pp. 169, 194.

39. For George Koval, see his FBI file declassified on the FBI VAULT, which starts in 1956. Lota, *GRU i atomnaya bomba*, chap. 2, which does not identify Koval; Hagedorn, *Sleeper Agent*; H. A. R. Philby to R. H. Hollis, December 19, 1945, s.12a "Arthur Adam," KV 2/3787, TNA; U.S. House of Representatives, *Report on Soviet Espionage Activities in Connection with the Atom Bomb*, part III (1951); Michael Walsh, "Gorge Koval: Atomic Spy Unmasked," *Smithsonian Magazine*, May 2009.

40. Dobbs, *Six Months in 1945*, pp. 176–77. Maclean was transferred to Washington in April 1944: "Maclean: Burgess: Philby," p. 234, archive of Sir (D'Arcy) Patrick Reilly, Ms. Eng. C. 6920 BOD; D. D. Maclean, "Report on Members of Branch A of the Foreign Service," January 14, 1944, FCO 158/186, TNA; Archive; Primakov, *Ocherki ob Istorii Vneshnei Razvedk*, vol. 5, pp. 82–83. We do not know whether Donald Maclean had access to foreign office cables about the San Francisco conference, found, for example, in "UK Delegation to the San Francisco Conference on International Organisation: Briefs," FO 976/2, TNA. On Hiss at San Francisco, see Gladwyn, *The Memoirs of Lord Gladwyn*, p. 163; Halifax, *Fulness of Days*, p. 291. For later Soviet intelligence activities at the UN: "RIS Operating under UN Cover," FCO 168/5763, TNA.

41. "Minute from Mr. N. Butler to Mr. Bevin [F.O. 800/537]," October 12, 1945, DBPO, Series I, vol., II, doc no. 200, pp. 559–62; Resis, ed., *Molotov Remembers*, pp. 55–56; Primakov, *Ocherki ob Istorii Vneshnei Razvedki*, vol. 4, p. 12.

PART 2: THE CLASH OF CIVILIZATIONS

CHAPTER 5: FROM WORLD WAR TO COLD WAR

1. The British Parliament's secret vote, which funded its intelligence services, declined from £15 million in 1943 to £1.75 million in 1946: "Report of Enquiry by Sir Norman Brook into the Secret Intelligence and Security Services," March 1951, p. 4, CAB 301/17, TNA; "Future Organisation of Secret Intelligence Service (SIS): The Bland Report," October 8, 1944, CAB 301/45, TNA; Donaldson to Edward Bridges, December 8, 1948, "Security Service (MI5) Organisation Issues," CAB 301/30, TNA. For later figures of the KGB's size, see JIC(83)5 "The Soviet Global Perception," September 5, 1983, CAB 186/36, TNA.

2. For Kaltenbrunner, see "Nazi Bangs Stand," *Washington Post*, November 4, 1946; Trevor-Roper, *The Last Days of Hitler*.

3. For interrogations of Germans disclosing intelligence on Soviet intelligence, see, for example, R. V. Hemblys Scales, May 12, 1947, s.5a "HQ Organisation of the GRU," KV 5/81, TNA; "Field Interrogation of Horst Kopkow," Neumunster, June 7, 1945, s.10a "Horst Kopkow," KV 2/1500, TNA. For descriptions of rubbled Germany, see Victor Cavendish-Bentinck, "Weeded Papers," April 8, 1945, FO 1093/191, TNA.

4. "Miscellaneous Notes Taken from Grant's Safe, Telegram from Moscow to Ottawa," August 22, 1945, s.105a "Igor Gouzenko," KV 2/1427, TNA; *The Defection of Igor Gouzenko: Report of the Canadian Royal Commission* (Ottawa, 1946); for the report by Britain's scientific adviser, Sir

Henry Tizard, into "weapons of mass destruction," see Sir Henry Tizard, "Future Developments in Weapons of War," June 1945, CAB 80/94/116, TNA; Sibley, *Red Spies*, pp. 173–74; Andrew and Mitrokhin, *The Mitrokhin Archive*, vol. 1, pp. 180–81; Andrew, *The Defence of the Realm*, pp. 339–42; Gill Bennett, "The CORBY Case: The Defection of Igor Gouzenko, September 1945," in *From World War to Cold War: The Records of the FO Permanent Under-Secretary's Department, 1939–51* (2013); Kevin Riehle, "Soviet Intent at the Dawn of the Cold War: Igor Gouzenko's Revelations about GRU Intelligence Taskings," *Journal of Intelligence History* (2021): 1–18.

5. J. A. Meyer, "COMINT—Hard Facts in the Cold War," [A65655] (National Security Agency, 1958), USG-NSA; Guy Liddell, June 17, 1945, s.46a "Alan Nunn May," KV 2/2209, TNA; "Liddell Diaries," September 11, 1945, KV 4/466, TNA.

6. Orme Sargent to prime minister, March 2, 1946, "Corby Case," FO 1093/538, TNA; Liddell to Cadogan, September 24, 1945, and minutes, September 27, 1945, "Corby Case," FO 1093/539, TNA; DBPO, Series I, vol. II, no. 200, n.d., p. 125.

7. Marc Trachtenberg, "The United States and Eastern Europe in 1945: A Reassessment," *Journal of Cold War Studies* 10 (2008): 113. On the heritage of "peaceful coexistence," see Haslam, *Russia's Cold War*, p. 215; Jacobsen, *When the Soviet Union Entered World Politics*, pp. 17–26.

8. Blum, ed., *The Price of Vision*, p. 490; Butler to Cadogan, November 6, 1945, "Canadian Spy Case: Defection of Igor Gouzenko (Corby Case)," FO 1093/539, TNA; ibid. (Butler to Attlee, November 13, 1945); DBPO, Series I, vol. II, no. 200, p. 125; Hyde, *The Atom Bomb Spies*, p. 36.

9. SIS New York [Stephenson] to 48000 [Chief SIS], September 11, 1945, s.5a "Alan Nunn May," KV 2/2209, TNA. For their rendezvous, see "CXG Telegram 273, SIS Station New York to CSS, London," September 11, 1945, s.5a "Igor Gouzenko," KV 2/1420, TNA; telegram no. 244, "Grant" to the "Director," August 2, 1945, "Igor Gouzenko," KV 2/1427, TNA; Gouzenko, *The Iron Curtain*, pp. 238–247; Stevenson, *Intrepid's Last Case*, p. 106.

10. Chief of SIS [Menzies] to T. E. Bromley [foreign office], October 19, 1945, "The Case of Constantine Volokov," FCO 158/198, TNA, with note attached on Volkov by Philby; Philby, *My Silent War*, p. 118. Philby took over and sidelined British investigations into at least one other Soviet defector: Akhmedov, *In and Out of Stalin's GRU*, pp. 190–91; Borovik, *The Philby Files*, p. 239; West and Tsarev, *The Crown Jewels*, p. 238.

11. H. A. R. Philby [MI6] to R. H. Hollis [MI5], February 19, 1946, s.64a "Igor Gouzenko," KV 2/1421, TNA; ibid. [KV 2/1421] s.65a: Hollis to Philby, February 1946; "H. A. R. Philby to J. H. Marriott," May 13, 1947, s.1y "HQ Organisation of the GRU," KV 5/81, TNA; Stevenson, *Intrepid's Last Case*, p. 53.

12. With hindsight, it is clear that Krivitsky's information contained an amalgamation of different characteristics of the five Cambridge spies, who were educated at private schools (except Cairncross) and at Cambridge, one of whom (Maclean) was the son of someone knighted. Krivitsky described the agent as a young man "from one of our Universities," educated at "Eton and Oxford," an "aristocrat," with a source in the foreign office, "imperial council," and someone from a noble background (a vague reference to Maclean's father): Jane Archer to Valentine Vivian [MI6], January 30, 1940, s.17a "Walter Krivitsky," KV 2/804, TNA. In February 1941, Krivitsky was found dead in Washington, either by suicide or assassinated by the NKVD. To this day, his death has not been resolved: Kern, *A Death in Washington*, chaps. 6–8.

13. "Liddell Diaries," September 14, 1945, KV 4/466, TNA; "Statement by Atomic Scientists," September 7, 1941, and "FBI [Hoover] to Matthew Connelly, Sec. to Pres.," September 12, 1945, President's Secretary's Files ["PSF"], box 146, FBI File, 1945–1952 HSTL; Budiansky, *Code Warriors*, chap. 2; Johnson, *American Cryptology*, book 1: *Centralization, 1945–1960*, p. 161; Philby, *My Silent War*, p. 105.

14. After he was released from prison, Nunn May married Broda's Russian-born ex-wife, Hilde: "Statement of Alan Nunn May," February 20, 1946, s.289a "Alan Nunn May," KV 2/2213, TNA;

"Leakages in Canada," *Times*, March 5, 1946; "Soviet Spy Ring in Canada," *Times*, March 16, 1946; Burt, *Commander Burt of Scotland Yard*, pp. 29–45; Moorehead, *The Traitors*, pp. 40–42; Lota, *GRU i atomnaya bomba*, pp. 87–88, 265; R. T. Reed, October 14, 1953, minute 898, "Alan Nunn May," KV 2/2222, TNA; H. Phillimore, October 24, 1953, s.495b "Engelbert Broda," KV 2/2354, TNA; Butler to Cadogan and Butler to Attlee, n.d., "Canadian Spy Case: Defection of Igor Gouzenko (Corby Case)," FO 1093/539, TNA; Haynes, Klehr, and Vassiliev, *Spies*, pp. 64–69; Moorehead, *The Traitors*, pp. 18, 31; "Allan Nunn May," *Telegraph*, January 24, 2003; Broda, *Scientist Spies*, pp. xi, 120.

15. Andrew and Mitrokhin, *The Mitrokhin Archive*, vol. 1, pp. 139–140.

16. Information provided to the author by Igor Gouzenko's daughter; Gouzenko, *The Iron Curtain*, p. 12; Moorehead, *The Traitors*, p. 32.

17. Haslam, *Near and Distant Neighbors*, pp. 132–34; for Golos, see MITN 1/6/5, CHAC; "Role of the Communist Party, USA, in Soviet Intelligence" [CIA-RDP65-00756R000300080001-0], February 1953, pp. 35–37, CIA CREST; Bentley, *Out of Bondage*, p. 211; see pp. 99–100 and 153 for preceding narrative. "Elizabeth T. Bentley" [file 8 of 18] "New York Memo," October 18, 1944, FBI VAULT; Andrew and Mitrokhin, *The Mitrokhin Archive*, p. 110; Kessler, *Clever Girl*, pp. 62–63.

18. U.S. House Committee on Un-American Activities, *Hearings Regarding Communist Espionage in the United States Government*, 80th Cong., 2nd sess. (Washington, DC: Government Printing Office, 1948); Bentley, *Out of Bondage*, pp. 286–90; Lamphere, *The FBI-KGB War*, pp. 36–41.

19. Bradley, *A Very Principled Boy*, pp. xii–xiii; Olmsted, *Red Spy Queen*, chaps. 6, 7; "Role of the Communist Party, USA, in Soviet Intelligence" [CIA-RDP65-00756R000300080001-0] February 1953, p. 40, CIA CREST; Silvermaster (Julius Rosenberg) Summary [Part 4 of 7], "Underground Soviet Espionage Organization (NKVD) in Agencies of the United States Government," October 21, 1946, FBI VAULT; Nathan G. Silvermaster Summary [Part 1 of 7], "Underground Soviet Espionage Organization (NKVD) in Agencies of the United States Government," February 21, 1946, FBI VAULT; William Remington File 65-56402, n.d., FBI.

20. H. A. R. Philby to J. H. Marriott, November 2, 1945, "Igor Gouzenko," KV 2/1419, TNA; Telegram no. 765 from New York for MI5, Hollis, November 19, 1945, s.87b "Igor Gouzenko," KV 2/1425, TNA. Philby's hand is also probably seen here: CXG Telegram 963 SIS Station New York [Stephenson] to CSS [Menzies] London, January 5, 1946, s.18a "Ignacy Samuel Witczak," KV 2/1635, TNA. Bentley, *Out of Bondage*, pp. 297–301; Olmsted, *Red Spy Queen*, pp. 105–6; Weinstein and Vassiliev, *The Haunted Wood*, p. 104; Sibley, *Red Spies*, p. 127.

21. "Memorandum on the Hiss Case," November 1948, Congressional Period Correspondence, PPS 205, box 6, RNL. Hiss was prosecuted on perjury, not crimes relating to espionage. Feklisov, *The Man behind the Rosenbergs*, pp. 66–67; Albright and Kunstel, *Bombshell*, p. 180; Kessler, *Bureau*, pp. 78–79; "Spy Queen Names Aid to F.D.R.," *New York Daily News*, August 1, 1948; "Hiss Spy Paper Linked to Late Treasury Aid," *Chicago Daily Tribune*, November 29, 1949; U.S. House Committee on Un-American Activities, *Hearings Regarding Communist Espionage in the United States Government*, 80th Cong., 2nd sess., 1948, pp. 503–62, 563–86; Massing, *This Deception*, p. 332; Baker, *Rezident*, p. 475; "Woman Links Spies to U.S. War Offices and White House," *New York Times*, July 31, 1948; Rosenberg Cases, "Elizabeth T. Bentley," *Meet the Press* program, December 6, 1953, pp. 31–35, FBI VAULT.

22. Clifford, *Counsel to the President*, pp. 162–64, 166–71; Warner, ed., *The CIA under Harry Truman*: Truman Memo to Secretaries of State [Byrnes], War [Patterson], and Navy [Forrestal], January 22, 1946, Truman Papers OF, HSTL; [Souers] Progress Report on the Central Intelligence Group, June 7, 1946, Papers of Clark M. Clifford, HSTL; "Memo for File," July 17, 1946, Papers of George Elsey, HSTL. A good examination of the role of DCIs is given in Garthoff, *Directors of Central Intelligence as Leaders of the U.S. Intelligence Community*.

23. Andrew, *For the President's Eyes Only*, p. 165.

24. James Lay and Robert Johnson, "An Organizational History of the National Security Council," June 30, 1960, Papers of Sidney Souers, box 1—Admin of National Security, HSTL; "Gen. Hoyt S. Vandenberg," obituary, *New York Times*, April 3, 1954.

25. *FRUS, 1945–1950, Emergence of the Intelligence Establishment*, Memorandum from DCI [Vandenberg] to Secretary of State [Byrnes], September 12, 1946; Gordon, *Dirty Tricks*, pp. 34–35.

26. On the British rescinding of commitments to Greece and Turkey, see Bennett and Salmon, eds., DBPO, Series I, vol. XI, no. 28: Foreign Office to Sir A. Cadogan (UK Del New York), December 4, 1946, p. 73. On U.S. loans to Greece, see "United States Loan to Greece," FCO 162/1131, TNA; George C. Marshall, "Remarks by the Secretary of State at Harvard University," June 5, 1947, https://www.marshallfoundation.org/wp-content/uploads/2014/06/Marshall_Plan_Speech_Complete.pdf.

27. Don K. Price for Herbert Hoover, "Lessons to Be Learned from the British Cabinet Secretariat," "Note," March 17, 1948, National Security Council File, box 13, HSTL. In 1947, Vandenberg became vice chief of staff of the newly established U.S. Air Force, the second-youngest American to reach the rank of four-star general; only Ulysses S. Grant had been more rapidly promoted. "National Security Act of 1947," Pub. L. No. 80–253 (1947); U.S. Senate, Church Committee, *Final Report of the Select Committee to Study Governmental Operations with Respect to Intelligence Activities*, 94th Cong., 2nd sess., vol. 1, pp. 21–22.

28. The 1947 National Security Act purposefully did not expressly set out the CIA's jurisdiction of covert action but instead relied on a carefully chosen, but vague, formulation that it would "perform such other functions and duties related to intelligence affecting the national security as the National Security Council may from time to time direct." Clifford, *Counsel to the President*, p. 169; "Note on U.S. Covert Actions," *FRUS, 1964–1968, Dominican Republic, Cuba, Haiti, Guyana*; R. H. Hillenkotter [DCI] to Truman: Memo for President, June 30, 1948, Truman Papers, PSF Central Intelligence Files, HSTL; "NANA Article," December 11, 1965, SMOF Rose A. Conway Files, Truman Papers, HSTL.

29. W. B. Smith memo "Procedure for NSC 10/5 Matters," n.d., Truman Papers, PSF, HSTL; "Office of Policy Coordination," August 4, 1949, p. 170, Truman Papers, PSF, box 170, HSTL. For "War of Wills," see Gordon Gray to Truman, February 22, 1952, Truman Papers, Historical Files, HSTL; Gordon Gray interview, June 18, 1973, pp. 51–57, Oral History Project, HSTL; "Note on U.S. Covert Actions," in *FRUS Foreign Relations, 1964–1968*, vol. 32; *FRUS, 1945–1950, Emergence of the Intelligence Establishment*, NSC 10/2 National Security Council Directive on Office of Special Projects, June 18, 1948; Nicholas Dujmovic, " 'Drastic Actions Short of War': The Origins and Application of the CIA's Covert Paramilitary Function in the Early Cold War," *Journal of Military History* 76 (2012): pp. 775–808; Bianca Adair, "Rear Admiral Sidney Souers and the Emergence of CIA's Covert Action Authority," *Studies in Intelligence* 65 (2021).

30. Summary Report of the Paramilitary Study Group, May 22, 1961, Subject Series CIA Bay of Pigs Richard Bissell Papers, DDEL; NSAM box 4, "5412/2" [1955] National Security File, LBJL; "Report of Enquiry by Sir Norman Brook into the Secret Intelligence and Security Services," March 1951, p. 12, CAB 301/17, TNA; "Office of Policy Coordination," Truman Papers, PSF, box 170, HSTL; Cline, *Secrets, Spies, and Scholars*, p. 114; Prados, *Lost Crusader*, p. 44.

31. Weiner, *Legacy of Ashes*, p. 43.

32. "C" [MI6 Chief] to Sir William Strang, October 13, 1949, s.1 "Intelligence in the Soviet Union," FO 1093/474, TNA; ibid. [FO 1093/474] s.4 Sir David Kelley, October 31, 1949.

33. Stuart Menzies [Chief MI6], "Deception Organisation in Peace," May 6, 1946, "Deception Organisations," CAB 121/110, TNA; "Deception in Post-War Period," note, April 1, 1947, and "Re-organisation of the London Controlling Section," December 19, 1950, CAB 301/15, TNA; Huw Dylan, "Super-Weapons and Subversion: British Deterrence by Deception Operations in the Early Cold War," *Journal of Strategic Studies* 38 (2015).

34. "Report of Enquiry by Sir Norman Brook into the Secret Intelligence and Security Services," March 1951, p. 12, CAB 301/17, TNA; "Russia's Strategic Interests from the Point of View of Her Security," October 18, 1944, CAB 81/126, TNA; JIC(46)1(0) (Final), "Russia's Strategic Interests and Intentions," March 1946, CAB 81/132, TNA; Folly, *Churchill, Whitehall and the Soviet Union*, p. 142; Goodman, *The Official History of the Joint Intelligence Committee*, vol. 1, pp. 232, 239. John Curry, "Brief Notes on the Security Service and Its Work Prepared for Permanent Under Secretaries, Service Intelligence Departments etc.," minute 14a, October 1, 1946, KV 4/158, TNA.

35. Primakov, *Ocherki ob Istorii Vneshnei Razvedki*, vol. 5, chaps. 3, 4, pp. 34–46. For interpretation of Stalin acting defensively against the Truman doctrine, see Primakov, vol. 5, pp. 24–25.

36. Primakov, *Ocherki ob Istorii Vneshnei Razvedki*, vol. 5, appendix: "Note by the NKGB of November 6, 1945," pp. 507–34; "Communication of the Residency of One of the European Countries January 1948"; "N 11 Agent's Note of the Deputy Chairman of KI at the Council of Ministers of the USSR of April 1948," pp. 558–60; "N 12 Agent Note by a Resident of KI Dated April 1948," p. 561; "N 15 Message of the CI Residence of the North-Atlantic Security Pact Dated May 1948," pp. 566–68; "N 18 Message of the Residence of KI from May 1948," pp. 570–72; "N 22 Note from the Deputy Chairman of the KI at the Council of Ministers of the USSR, January 5, 1949," p. 592; "N 23 Note from the Deputy Chairman of the KI at the Council of Ministers of the USSR, February 19, 1949," pp. 592–93. Kathryn Weathersby, " 'Should We Fear This?': Stalin and the Danger of War with America," Cold War International History Project working paper no. 39 (July 2002); JIC(45)311(0), "Intelligence on Atomic Energy," November 6, 1945, CAB 81/131, TNA; "Comparison of UK and US Atomic Energy Acts, 1946," n.d., AB 16/202, TNA; "Proposed Co-Operation between US and UK on Development of Atomic Energy," n.d., FO 371/93198–93204, TNA.

37. Beevor, *Berlin*, p. 410; Naimark, *Stalin and the Fate of Europe*, pp. 159–65.

38. Eduard Mark, "The War Scare of 1946 and Its Consequences," *Diplomatic History* 21 (1997): 383–415.

39. For British counter-subversion, see "Brook Committee: Counter-Subversion in Commonwealth and Colonial Territories," DO 231/60, TNA; "Entry from Molotov's Diary on Reception of US Ambassador [Walter Bedell] Smith," May 4, 1948, USA folder, Moscow 11/558/387 RGAPSI; Chebrikov et al., *Istoriya Sovetskikh Organov Gosudarstvennoy Bezopasnosti*, pp. 294–95, 468–69.

40. Naimark, *Stalin and the Fate of Europe*, pp. 19–20; Moravec, *Master of Spies*, pp. 239–40.

41. Pucci, *Security Empire*, pp. 107–12, 116–17. Author interview with Ladislav Bittman, July 24, 2018; Andrew and Mitrokhin, *The Mitrokhin Archive*, pp. 355–58. The official history of Russian intelligence (predictably) styles NKVD actions as providing assistance to emerging "people's democracies" in Eastern Europe: Primakov, *Ocherki ob Istorii Vneshnei Razvedki*, vol. 5, p. 44.

42. Gaddis, *George F. Kennan*, pp. 294–95; "Europe–Italy: Measures Proposed to Defeat Communism in Italy" [0001380847], February 9, 1948, CIA CREST; *FRUS, 1948, Western Europe*, vol. 3, NSC 1/2, "Report by the National Security Council: The Position of the United States with Respect to Italy," February 10, 1948.

43. Corke, *US Covert Operations and Cold War Strategy*, pp. 47–50.

44. Cline, *Secrets, Spies, and Scholars*, pp. 98–101; Shimer, *Rigged*, pp. 23–43; "Daily Summary #61" [01068498], April 26, 1946, CIA CREST.

45. MITN 1/6/5, CHAC; Richard Drake, "The Soviet Dimension of Italian Communism," *Journal of Cold War Studies* 6 (2004): 115–119; Naimark, *Stalin and the Fate of Europe*, pp. 142–43; Mistry, *The United States, Italy and the Origins of Cold War*, pp. 149–52; "An Evaluation of Psychological Effect of U.S. Effort in Italy" (1953) [CIA-RDP80R01731R003300190049-7], pp. 5–6, CIA CREST; Colby, *Honorable Men*, pp. 108–11.

46. Powers, *The Man Who Kept the Secrets*, pp. 30–31; Rusk, *As I Saw It*, p. 563; Steil, *The Marshall Plan*, pp. 262, 315; Weiner, *Legacy of Ashes*, p. 32; Rositzke, *The CIA's Secret Operations*, pp. 156, 158–59; Gaddis, *George F. Kennan*, pp. 316–17; Costigliola, *Kennan*, p. 12; Kennan, *Measures Short of War*; U.S. Congress, *Church Committee Final Report*, vol. 1, p. 37; 94th Congress, Book IV, pp. 29, 31; "Summary of the Current Italian Political Situation" [CIA-RDP91T01172R000200280002-9], April 28, 1952, CIA CREST.

47. "Notes by Stalin and Other Materials on Soviet-American Relations," n.d., USA Folder, 11/558/387 RGAPSI.

48. Clifford, *Counsel to the President*, p. 224. For Wallace's earlier communications to Stalin, in October 1945, which justify his description as an agent of influence, see Zubok, *A Failed Empire*, p. 47.

49. "Notes by Stalin and Other Materials on Soviet-American Relations" cipher telegram by Gromyko with information about conversation with Wallace regarding the U.S. presidential election, April 4, 1948, USA folder, 11/558/387 RGAPSI; ibid. [11/558/387], USA Folder. "Notes by Stalin and Other Materials on Soviet-American Relations," cipher telegram from New York by Gromyko about points to be included in Wallace's open letter to Stalin, April 27, 1948, including publication in Pravda and responses; Gromyko, *Memoirs*, p. 48; Harry S. Truman, "St. Patrick's Day Address in New York City," March 17, 1948, HSTL; Schmidt, *Henry A. Wallace*, p. 75; Baime, *Dewey Defeats Truman*, pp. 121–22. On FBI inquiries into Wallace, see Sullivan, *The Bureau*, p. 37.

50. For later KGB efforts to smear U.S. candidates, like the anti-Soviet liberal Democrat Henry "Scoop" Jackson, in 1978, see MITN 1/6/5, CHAC.

CHAPTER 6: PUZZLE PALACES

1. "Report of Enquiry by Sir Norman Brook into the Secret Intelligence and Security Services," March 1951, p. 13, CAB 301/17, TNA; Ferris, *Behind the Enigma*, pp. 245, 542; CP (55) 89 "Templer Report," April 23, 1955, CAB 129/76 and DEFE 22/23, TNA.

2. For the above discussion of plaintext, see Carol B. Davis, "Candle in the Dark: COMINT and Soviet Industrial Secrets, 1946–1956," NSA Center for Cryptographic History, 2017. The evolution of the UKUSA agreement can be found in: GC&CS (Hut 3) to Washington (Eric Jones), August 31, 1945, "Co-Operation between GC&CS, Signals Liaison Unit (SLU), Washington and the Signal Security Agency (SSA)," HW 57/34, TNA; "Joint Meeting of the Army-Navy Communication Intelligence Board and Army-Navy Communication Intelligence Co-ordinating Committee," October 29, HW 80/1, TNA; "British-U.S. Communication Intelligence Agreement," March 5, 1946, USG-NSA; Hayden, *Playing to the Edge*, pp. 41–42, which describes that GCHQ acts as a backup for NSA in case of a catastrophic shutdown.

3. Douglas MacEachin, *The Final Months of the War with Japan*, CIA CREST; "Joint Meeting of the Army-Navy Communication Intelligence Board and Army-Navy Communication Intelligence Co-ordinating Committee, October 29, 1945," HW 80/1, TNA; "Technical Conference for the Implementation of the US-British Communication Intelligence Agreement, March 11–27, 1946," HW 80/6, TNA; "BRUSA Planning Conference, 2–19 March 1953," HW 80/10, TNA; "Amendment No. 4 to the Appendices to the UKUSA AGREEMENT (3rd ed.) Overview of UKUSA Agreement," HW 80/11, TNA; private information about Walter Mills, ed., *The Forrestal Diaries*; Ferris, *Behind the Enigma*, pp. 370–377.

4. Figures taken from: Ferris, *Behind the Enigma*, p. 277; Aldrich, *GCHQ*, p. 75; Budiansky, *Code Warriors*, pp. 38–42; Aid, *The Secret Sentry*, pp. 10–14; Johnson, *American Cryptology*, book 1, pp. 158–60; Benson and Warner, eds., *Venona*, Intro.

5. Johnson, *American Cryptology*, book 1, p. 10; for an insider's view, see NSA Oral History Juanita Moody, June 16, 1994 [4310433], p. 12, https://media.defense.gov/2021/Jul/15/2002763502 /-1/-1/0/NSA-OH-1994-32-MOODY.PDF; memorandum for Admiral King [from Chief of Staff Marshall] [Doc-ID 3983918], September 25, 1945, USG-NSA. DNSA: *National Security Agency*,

Organization and Operations, 1945–2009, memorandum for General Marshall [from Admiral King], October 2, 1945; memorandum for Admiral King [from Chief of Staff Marshall], October 10, 1945; and memorandum for General Eisenhower [from Admiral King], December 28, 1945. CIA CREST; "Memorandum for Admiral King [from Chief of Staff Eisenhower]," December 8, 1945. "Memorandum for Admiral Nimitz from General Eisenhower," January 2, 1946; "Memorandum for General Eisenhower [from Admiral Nimitz]" [CIA-RDP82S00527R000100100018-7], January 4, 1946; "Memorandum for Admiral Nimitz [from General Eisenhower]," January 16, 1946; memorandum for the files, March 29, 1949 (noting in March 1949 that the British already had a unified SIGINT system).

6. "Little experience" quote from Johnson, *American Cryptology*, book 1, p. 10.

7. Johnson, *American Cryptology*, book 1, pp. 158–60; Benson and Warner, eds., *Venona*, Intro.

8. Johnson, *American Cryptology*, book 1, p. 277–78; Killian Report, "Meeting the Threat of Surprise Attack," February 14, 1955, Records of White House Office, White House Staff Secretary, Subject Series, box 16, DDEL; NSC 5522—Technological Capabilities Panel, n.d., Records of White House Office of the Special Assistant for National Security Affairs, NSC Series, Policy Papers Subseries, box 16, DDEL; Weinstein and Vassiliev, *The Haunted Wood*, p. 291.

9. The following owes much to Christopher Andrew, "The VENONA Secret," in K. G. Robertson, ed., *War, Resistance and Intelligence*, pp. 203–25. Also see Blum, *In the Enemy's House*, p. 27; Douglas Martin, "Robert J. Lamphere, 83, Spy Chaser for the F.B.I., Dies," *New York Times*, February 11, 2002; "FBI Documents of Historic Interest re. VENONA That Are Referenced in Daniel P. Moynihan's Book *Secrecy*," n.d., [Part 1 of 1], FBI VAULT VENONA; "Jury to Hear Weisband's Plea September 11," *Washington Post*, August 23, 1950; Bart Barnes, "Meredith K. Gardner, 89; Cracked Codes to Unmask Key Soviet Spies," *Los Angeles Times*, August 21, 2002.

10. Michael Warner, "Did Truman know about Venona," *CIA Center for the Study of Intelligence Bulletin* (Summer 2000); Andrew, "The VENONA Secret."

11. Haynes, Klehr, and Vassiliev, *Spies*; for "red herring," see McCullough, *Truman*, p. 652; Truman, *Harry S. Truman*, p. 414.

12. Mitchell and Mitchell, *The Spy Who Seduced America*; Gage, *G-Man*, pp. 353–55. For VENONA, Soviet espionage, communism, and historians, see Haynes and Klehr, *In Denial*. It is notable that SIGINT was not mentioned in the congressional exposé of Soviet espionage in 1960: U.S. Senate Committee on the Judiciary, "Exposé of Soviet Espionage, May 1960," 86th Cong., 2nd sess., July 21, 1960; "Secrets, Lies, and Atomic Spies," *NOVA*, PBS, February 5, 2002; "Coplon Jury Told Judy 'Hated U.S.,'" *Baltimore Sun*, June 29, 1949.

13. Johnson, *American Cryptology*, book 1, p. 166; Haynes, Klehr, and Vassiliev, *Spies*, pp. xviii–xix, xxxvii; Lamphere, *The KGB-FBI War*, "Text of Statements Read in Moscow by Former U.S. Security Agency Workers," *New York Times*, September 7, 1960; "2 U.S. Defectors Turn Up in Russia," *Los Angeles Times*, September 4, 1960.

14. Robert Lamphere quoted in "Secrets, Lies, and Atomic Spies," *NOVA*, PBS, February 5, 2002.

15. For examination of McCarthy's list of "communists" and VENONA, see http://www.johnearl haynes.org/page62.html; preceding "Star Chamber" quote from "Robert J. Lamphere, 83, Spy Chaser for the F.B.I., Dies," *New York Times*, February 11, 2002; Tye, *Demagogue*, p. 261; Logevall, *JFK*, pp. 499–500.

16. Rusk, *As I Saw It*, p. 161; "No person" quote from Johnson, *American Cryptology*, book 1, p. 39; "Daily Summary—1950/04–1950/06" [06749478], 1950, p. 99, CIA CREST.

17. For British failure to predict the Korean War, see COS (48) 97th meeting, July 9, 1948, DEFE 4/14, TNA; "Basic Review of Foreign Policy and Strategy of the Soviet Union," October 9, 1950, CAB 158/9, TNA; Farrar-Hockley, *The British Part in the Korean War*, vol. 1: *A Distant Obligation*; Andrew, "The VENONA Secret"; "North Koreans Attack in Great Force," *Times*, July 29, 1950.

18. This is overlooked by Primakov, *Ocherki ob Istorii Vneshnei Razvedki*, vol. 5, pp. 389–90; JIC (47)76(0) (Final), "Possibility of War before the End of 1956," January 23, 1948, CAB 158/2, TNA; JIC(48)42(0) (Final), "Indications of Russian Preparedness for War," June 18, 1948, CAB 158/3, TNA; JIC(49)111 (Final), "Soviet Use of Atomic Bombs," March 14, 1950, CAB 158/8, TNA; "The Likelihood of War with the Soviet Union and the Date by Which the Soviet Leaders Might Be Prepared to Risk It," August 18, 1950, CAB 158/8, TNA. "Soviet Intentions and Capabilities and the Date When the Soviet Union Might Be Prepared to Engage in a General War," JIC(50)77 (Revise), December 21, 1950, JIC(50)100 (Final), CAB 158/11, TNA, which was an Anglo-American assessment. Truman resisted pressure from the U.S. military to use a nuclear weapon in Korea: Jones, *After Hiroshima*, pp. 66–69.

19. For the failure of U.S. intelligence before Korea, see Halberstam, *The Coldest Winter*, pp. 52–53; P. K. Rose, "Two Strategic Intelligence Mistakes in Korea, 1950," *Studies in Intelligence* (2001); Alexander Ovodenko, "(Mis)Interpreting Threats: A Case Study of the Korean War," *Security Studies* 16 (2007): 254–286; William McAfee, ADST oral interview with Charles Stuart Kennedy, September 9, 1997, pp. 29, 31.

20. Weiner, *Legacy of Ashes*, pp. 66–69.

21. Nicholas Dujmovic, "The Significance of Walter Bedell Smith as Director of Central Intelligence, 1950–53," CIA CREST.

22. Haslam, *Near and Distant Neighbors*, p. 173.

23. Haslam, *Near and Distant Neighbors*, p. 173; Primakov, *Ocherki ob Istorii Vneshnei Razvedki*, vol. 5, pp. 444–45; Gerovitch, *From Newspeak to Cyberspeak*, p. 133.

24. [Envelope K-9] MITN 1/7, CHAC; Andrew and Gordievsky, *KGB*, pp. 419–20; Torigian, *Prestige, Manipulation, and Coercion*, pp. 26–31; Montefiore, *Stalin*, pp. 647–648.

25. Walton, *Empire of Secrets*, p. 335; Aldrich, *GCHQ*, chapter 8; David Easter, "Soviet Bloc and Western Bugging of Opponents' Diplomatic Premises during the Early Cold War," *Intelligence and National Security* 31 (2016): 28–48.

26. For a critique of the creation of a Commonwealth "intelligence culture," see Gregory S. Kealey and Kerry A. Taylor, "After Gouzenko and 'The Case': Canada, Australia, and New Zealand at the Secret Commonwealth Conferences of 1948 and 1951," in Molinaro, ed., *The Bridge in the Parks*, pp. 22–44. Christopher Andrew, "The Growth of the Australian Intelligence Community and the Anglo-American Connection," *Intelligence and National Security* 4 (1989): 213–256; Ferris, *Behind the Enigma*, chapter 8; Maria Robson, "The Third Eye: Canada's Development of Autonomous Signals Intelligence to Contribute to Five Eyes Intelligence Sharing," *Intelligence and National Security* 35 (2020): 954–969.

27. For Kissinger and Chagos, see box 727, National Security File, Country File "United Kingdom," K. Wayne Smith, "Memorandum of Conversation with John Thomson," December 12, 1970, and box 727, National Security File, Country File "United Kingdom," "Memorandum for Major General Brent Scowcroft on US-UK Indian Ocean Talks," May 16, 1974, both at RNL. For the transition of power from Britain to the United States in the former's empire, see the classic essay by William Roger Louis and Ronald Robinson, "The Imperialism of Decolonization," *Journal of Imperial and Commonwealth History* 22 (1994): 462–511. More generally, see Schake, *Safe Passage*.

28. See, for example, these JIC reports at TNA: "Far East Defence," 1949, CO 537/5004; JIC(A)(69)23 (Final), "Chinese Foreign Policy," August 7, 1969, CAB 186/2; JIC(78)9, "The Threat to Hong Kong," August 29, 1978, CAB 186/26; Aldrich, *GCHQ*, pp. 151–155; Smith, *The Unknown CIA*, p. 86; William Roger Louis, "Hong Kong: The Critical Phase, 1945–1949," *American Historical Review* 102 (1997): 1052–1084. Desmond Ball, "Over and Out: Signals Intelligence (Sigint) in Hong Kong," *Intelligence and National Security* 11 (1996): 474–496; Cradock, *Know Your Enemy*, pp. 83–84.

CHAPTER 7: CLIMATE OF TREASON

1. Hiss's perjury conviction turned on his suit against Chambers for slander at the House Un-American Activities Committee. Chambers produced a microfilm of typed copies of secret State Department documents, hidden in a hollowed-out pumpkin at his Maryland farm—forever after called the "pumpkin papers." According to Chambers, the documents had been obtained from Hiss before the war, which his wife then typed, following instructions from their Soviet GRU handler, Bykov. For Burgess and Maclean, see Alexander Cadogan, "Report of Committee of Enquiry," November 1, 1951, "Report of Cadogan Committee of Enquiry and Consequences of the Burgess and Maclean Affair, 1951–1952," CAB 301/120, TNA.

2. *Sluzhba Vneshney Razvedki, Rossiyskoy Federatsii 100 let*, p. 98, and chaps. 7 [pp. 89–93], 13 [pp. 146–59]; Primakov, *Ocherki ob Istorii Vneshnei Razvedki*, vol. 3, pp. 20–60; Dolgopolov, *Kim Filbi*, p. 17.

3. OSI/SR-10/49/1 "Status of the U.S.S.R. Atomic Energy Project" [CIA-RDP80R01731R 000800100052-0], August 24, 1949, CIA CREST; "Liddell Diaries," September 24, 1949, KV 4/471, TNA. The declassified records of the PDB predecessors contain few mentions of Soviet atomic capabilities before its first detonation; one occurred in September 1949 (after the Soviet atomic test): "Daily Summary—1949/07–1949/09" [06749456], 1949, CIA CREST; "Text of President's Statement on 23 September 1949 RE: First Russian Atomic Explosion" [CIA-RDP80R01443R000100010002-9], September 23, 1949, CIA CREST; "Estimate of the Status of the U.S.S.R. Atomic Energy Project for the Joint Chiefs of Staff" [CIA-RDP80R01731R000800100051-1], October 1, 1949, CIA CREST; "USSR's Possession of Atomic Bomb and Its Influence upon Political Problems of Western Europe" [CIA-RDP83-00415R003800060010-2], November 17, 1949, CIA CREST; "Foreign Radio Reactions to the President's Statement about an Atomic Explosion in the USSR" [CIA-RDP78-04864A000100090050-6], September 29, 1949, CIA CREST; House of Commons Hansard, "Atomic Energy (Soviet Union)," September 27, 1949, vol. 468.

4. Holloway, *Stalin and the Bomb*, pp. 222–23; Haynes, Klehr, and Vassiliev, *Spies*, pp. 60–61; Close, *Trinity*, pp. 159–161; Moss, *Klaus Fuchs*.

5. See in the following volume of Fuchs's dossier, "Emil Julius Klaus Fuchs," KV 2/1245, TNA: minute 52, J. O. Archer, November 27, 1946; minute 57, Guy Liddell, December 20, 1946; minute 89, G. R. Mitchell, February 2, 1947; minute 97, Guy Liddell, May 22, 1947; "Vassiliev Yellow Notebook #1," Alexander Vassiliev Papers, WCDA; "Moscow: CHAR'Z's Information on the Atomic Bomb and Method of Separation of ENORMOZ; Moscow Requests Further Details," HW 15/28/100, TNA.

6. T. A. Robertson, minute 48, October 15, 1946, "Emil Julius Klaus Fuchs," KV 2/1245, TNA; Bew, *Clement Attlee*, pp. 420–21; Close, *Trinity*, p. 157.

7. [Air Chief Marshall] William Elliot, February 10, 1950, "The Klaus Fuchs Case," CAB 301/108, TNA.

8. For telephone and intercepts, see KV 2/1266-70, n.d., TNA. For surveillance and his driving, see KV 2/1246, TNA. The SVR today describes Fuchs as a pacifist: Primakov, *Ocherki ob Istorii Vneshnei Razvedki*, vol. 6, p. 182.

9. J. C. Robertson, Note, January 24, 1950, s.433a "Klaus Fuchs," KV 2/1250, TNA; W. J. Skardon, "Emil Julius Klaus FUCHS: Fourth, Fifth, Sixth, and Seventh Interviews," January 31, 1950, s.444b KV 2/1250, TNA; Klaus Fuchs, "Summary Brief on Dr. Emil Julius Klaus Fuchs," February 6, 1950, pp. 50–74, FBI VAULT; Yellow Notebook #1, Alexander Vassiliev Papers, WCDA: "Bras-Charles," n.d., KGB File 84490, vol. 1, p. 82; *Sluzhba Vneshney Razvedki, Rossiyskoy Federatsii 100 let*, p. 209; Close, *Trinity*, pp. 349, 400–03; House of Commons, Hansard, "Klaus Fuchs Debate," vol. 606, June 11, 1959; "Developments in London," n.d., pp. 34–35, Klaus Fuchs [Part 5 of 111], FBI VAULT.

10. "Guy Liddell Diary," January 25, 1950, KV 4/472, TNA; J. C. Robertson, s.433a KV 2/1250,

TNA; W. J. Skardon, "Emil Julius Klaus FUCHS: Fourth, Fifth, Sixth, and Seventh Interviews," January 31, 1950, s.444b KV 2/1250, TNA.

11. *Sluzhba Vneshney Razvedki, Rossiyskoy Federatsii 100 let*, p. 107; not discussed in ibid., pp. 147–48.

12. W. J. Skardon, "Note," August 15, 1947, KV 6/42, TNA; J. C. Robertson, "Leads for Further Investigation Provided by the Case of FUCHS," March 7, 1950, s.575a "Klaus Fuchs," KV 2/1253, TNA; W. J. Skardon, "Klaus Fuchs," December 1, 1950, s.759a "Klaus Fuchs," KV 2/1253, TNA; "Yellow Notebook #1," KGB File 84490, vol. 1, "Bras-Charles," 82–84, "Addendum to a letter to London dated 5.4.48," Alexander Vassiliev Papers, WCDA.

13. "Disappearance of Foreign Office Officials," Steel to Cabinet Office [Makins], June 21, 1951, PREM 8/1524, TNA. For criticism of British authorities in the United States, see F. Hoyer Millar [Washington] to Foreign Office, February 6, 1950, "Arrest and Conviction of Dr Fuchs on Charges of Spying for Russia; American Reactions," 371/82902, TNA; Memorandum from D. M. Ladd to Director [Hoover] on "Foocase," March 1, 1950, p. 29, "Klaus Fuchs" [Part 5 of 111], FBI VAULT; office memorandum from D. M. Ladd to Director [Hoover], April 28, 1950, p. 15, "Klaus Fuchs" [Part 38 of 111], FBI VAULT; office memorandum from D. M. Ladd to Director [Hoover], May 18, 1950, p. 11, "Klaus Fuchs" [Part 39 of 111], FBI VAULT; Clegg to Director [Hoover] Cable "Urgent: Foocase," May 20, 1950, "Klaus Fuchs" [Part 10 of 111], FBI VAULT; W. J. Skardon, "Interrogation of Dr FUCHS by the FBI," June 9, 1950, s.689ea "Klaus Fuchs," KV 2/1255, TNA; "Proposal to Permit the Strengthening of Intelligence Activities, Hillenkoeter to Hoover" [CIA-RDP80R01731R003500040001-3], March 17, 1950, CIA CREST.

14. Hopkins, *Oliver Franks and the Truman Administration*, pp. 145–46. For Britain's diplomatic recognition of the PRC, see "Mr Bevin to HM Representatives Overseas," vol. 8: *Britain and China* doc, no. 121, June 26, 1950, in DBPO, series I.

15. "Harry Gold," February 25, 1950, s.4a, A. S. Martin, KV 2/3797, TNA; Harry Gold, "Report by Brenton S. Gordon on Harry Gold, File No. 65-3319," [Part 20 of 108], June 1, 1950, p. 4, FBI VAULT; "Teletype to Bureau" [Part 1 of 108], November 28, 1949, p. 7, FBI VAULT; Harry Gold, "Statement of Harry Gold" [Part 4 of 108], May 22, 1950, pp. 15–24, FBI VAULT; "Harry Gold," "Vassiliev Yellow Notebook #1," Alexander Vassiliev Papers, WCDA; File "Zinger," Caliber no. 86192, v. 1: P. 121, NY— C 3.06.50," March 6, 1950, p. 49; "Memorandum from D. M. Ladd to The Director [Hoover]" [Part 4 of 14], June 26, 1950, p. 39, FBI VAULT; David and Ruth Greenglass; Close, *Trinity*, pp. 369–71; "Letter to Walter Bedell Smith from FBI" [CIA-RDP81R00560R000100090006-7], August 14, 1951, CIA CREST. C. D. Jackson, former OSS operative and Eisenhower's adviser on psychological warfare, pushed Attorney General Herbert Brownell to get "some really skillful Jewish psychiatrist" to gain the Rosenbergs' confidence, and confessions, in order to stay their executions, though he emphasized that they "deserve to fry a hundred times for what they have done." Some thought their executions would simply "seal their mouths forever" while turning them into martyrs for the communist cause. Ethel Rosenberg continued to adamantly assert their innocence, even writing a letter to President Eisenhower requesting pardons. Eisenhower was unpersuaded, remarking in a letter to Columbia professor Clyde Miller that the "action of these people has exposed to greater danger of death literally millions of our citizens. See "Memorandum for the File" "Julius Rosenberg" [Part 1 of 87], May 29, 1940, p. 17, FBI VAULT; "The Rosenberg Espionage Conspiracy," September 25, 1953, p. 4, "Ethel Rosenberg" [Part 2 of 10], FBI VAULT; "Refutation of Communist Charges in Connection with the Rosenberg Case" [0000014713], January 30, 1953, CIA CREST; Memorandum for the Attorney General Re: Report on Interview with Rosenbergs, June 5, 1953, Herbert Brownell Papers, box 75 B(3), DDEL; Typescript Copy of Letter, Ethel Rosenberg to President Eisenhower, June 16, 1953, DDE's Records as President, Official File, box 354, OF-101-R Amnesty-Pardons, Rosenberg, Julius and Ethel, DDEL; Memorandum Kirk to Smith "Re: Foreign Response to Rosenberg Case," January 16, 1953, NSC Staff Papers, PSB Central Files Series, box 26, PSB 383.4,

DDEL; Memorandum, Taquey to Johnson "Re: Influencing Foreign Response to Rosenberg Case," May 29, 1953, NSC Staff Papers, PSB Central Files Series, box 17, PSB 092(1), DDEL; "Letter, Response of Clyde Miller to President Eisenhower Urging Clemency for the Rosenbergs," June 8, 1953, Eisenhower Papers as President, Administration Series, box 32b, Rosenberg Case Statement, DDEL; "Letter, Herbert Brownell to President Eisenhower in the Matter of the Commutation of Sentence of Julius and Ethel Rosenberg, Attorney General," n.d., pp. 1–6, DDE's Records as President, Official File, box 354, OF-101-R Amnesty-Pardons, Rosenberg, Julius and Ethel, DDEL; memorandum from SA [Special Agent] Richard T. Kradsky to SAC [Special Agent in Charge], New York "Re: UNSUBS Recipients of Leica Camera and $7,000 from Ethel Rosenberg June, 1950," July 28, 1955, pp. 11–25, "Ethel Rosenberg" [Part 1 of 10], FBI VAULT; Henry Lee, "Spies Die in Chair," *New York Daily News*, June 20, 1953; letter from William H. McMillen, Associate Chief Investigation Division, to Director, FBI [Hoover], n.d., pp. 19–23, "Julius Rosenberg" [Part 1 of 87], FBI VAULT; letter from William H. McMillen, Associate Chief Investigation Division, to Director, FBI [Hoover], "Julius Rosenberg" [Part 1 of 87], FBI VAULT; "Announcement of Ethel Rosenberg's Arrest," "Julius Rosenberg" [Part 13 of 87], August 11, 1950, FBI VAULT.

16. MITN 1/6/4, CHAC; All from Alexander Vassiliev Papers, WDCA; "Yellow Notebook #1," KGB File 84490, vols. 2 and 3; "Bras-Charles," "Memorandum on K.F. from the GRU," "Possible Reasons for Failure," February 1950; report to S. R. Savchenko, "London 6.04.50"; V. Zorin [written by Raina] to comrade J. V. Stalin, February 5, 1950; A. Raina "Plan of Oper. Measures Connected with Ch-s's Case," February 5, 1950; "Addendum to the Plan of Oper. Measures with Regard to Ch-s's Case," February 21, 1950; V. Zorin "To Comrade J. V. Stalin," May 29, 1950, pp. 86–98; KGB File 86194, vol. 2, "Mad/Goose/Arno-Harry Gold," "Letter C-NY 23.02.50," p. 109; KGB File 84490, vol. 5, "Bras"–Klaus Fuchs, "To Comrade S. N. Kruglov," n.d., p. 56; Haynes, Klehr, and Vassiliev, *Spies*, p. 124; Albright and Kunstel, *Bombshell*, pp. 288–89.

17. G. A. Carey Foster to Sir Robert Mackenzie (British embassy London), "Leakages in Washington," April 7, 1951, KV 6/142, TNA; "Disappearance of Maclean and Burgess," n.d., PREM 8/1524, TNA; "Vassiliev Black Notebook," Alexander Vassiliev Papers, WCDA.

18. [Name redacted] MI6 to Carey Foster, Foreign Office, January 19, 1950, "Disappearance of Guy Burgess and Donald Maclean," CAB 21/3878, TNA; ibid. [CAB 21/3878], J. V. Strong [MI5] to Carey Foster, "Guy Burgess," January 20, 1950; D. Storrier, "CURZON," May 25, 1951, s.88a "Donald Maclean," KV 2/4140, TNA; "Liddell Diaries," May 29, 1951, KV 4/437, TNA; "Maclean Desk diary" [calendar], FCO 158/189; MITN 1/6/4, CHAC; Primakov, *Ocherki ob Istorii Vneshnei Razvedki*, vol. 5, pp. 84–85. Confirmation of Burgess and Maclean's arrival behind the Iron Curtain would come from the defection of a KGB officer, Vladimir Petrov, in *Australia: Petrov, Empire of Fear*, pp. 271–76.

19. For Philby as STANLEY, see MITN 1/6/4, CHAC; "Moscow; Comment on the Accuracy of 'STANLEY's Information,'" September 17, 1945, HW 15/16/15, TNA.

20. Philby's betrayal of his fellow Soviet agents is inevitably airbrushed from Primakov, *Ocherki ob Istorii Vneshnei Razvedki*, vol. 5, pp. 67–72; Dolgopolov, *Kim Filbi*, written with the SVR's assistance and declassified records relating to Philby; Andrew Higgins, "Even in Death, the Spy Kim Philby Serves the Kremlin's Purposes," *New York Times*, October 8, 2017; "Moscow Names Square after British Double-Agent Kim Philby," *Guardian*, November 8, 2018.

21. Andrew and Mitrokhin, *The Mitrokhin Archive*, vol. 1, pp. 205–06, 216–17; an FBI report to Hoover noted that as Burgess's roommate, "PHILBY should be able to furnish considerable information concerning BURGESS": Memorandum from SAC, WFO to Director, FBI [Hoover], June 15, 1951, p. 7, "Cambridge Five Spy Ring" [Part 2 of 42], FBI VAULT.

22. MI6 telegram, Washington, June 2, 1951, s.92b "Guy Burgess," KV 2/4102, TNA; ibid. [KV 2/4102] s.116f: MI6, Washington [Philby] to "C," June 4, 1951, forwarded to Director General MI5,

June 8, 1951; letter to Director, CIA [Smith] from Director, FBI [Hoover], June 16, 1951, p. 35, "Cambridge Five Spy Ring" [Part 3 of 42], FBI VAULT.

23. "Liddell Diaries," January 14, 1952, April 3, 1951, June 12, 1951, June 14, 1951, and December 12, 1951, KV 4/473, TNA; "Possible Return of Guy Burgess and Donald Maclean to the UK," minutes Patrick Dean, November 17, 1955, FCO 158/178, TNA; "Suede," November 30, 1951, "PEACH" [Philby], FCO 158/27, TNA; SIS [MI6] to Bedell Smith, January 14, 1952, and Milmo "Report of Enquiry," January 14, 1952, "PEACH," FCO 158/27, TNA; A. J. de la Mare, October 28, 1955, "Guy Burgess and Donald Maclean," FCO 158/175, TNA. For CIA (Walter Bedell Smith) concern over Philby, see Christopher Steel [British embassy Washington] to D. P. Reilly [FO], October 17, 1951, "Washington Leakages," FCO 158/21, TNA. Director Hoover, Note to Special Assistant to the President, Dillon Anderson "Brief on Donald Maclean, Guy Burgess, Harold Philby," November 8, 1955, Records of the White House, Office of the Special Assistant for National Security Affairs, FBI Series, box 7, DDEL.

24. Patrick Dean "Note," n.d., "Guy Burgess and Donald Maclean: Contacts with Other Foreign Office Officials, including Kim Philby (PEACH)," FCO 158/30, TNA; Andrew, *The Defence of the Realm*, pp. 428–429; Primakov, *Ocherki ob Istorii Vneshnei Razvedki*, vol. 4, p. 187.

25. "Statement of Morgan Goronwy REES," June 6, 1951, s.2a "Goronwy Rees," KV 2/4603, TNA; Primakov, *Ocherki ob Istorii Vneshnei Razvedki*, vol. 4, p. 194; "Extract from DDG's Note re. Visit of BLUNT & HARRIS," May 30, 1951, s.114b "Donald Maclean," KV 2/4140, TNA; "Liddell Diaries," May 30, 1951, and June 12, 1951, KV 4/473, TNA; Modin, *My 5 Cambridge Friends*, p. 222; Rees, *A Chapter of Accidents*, p. 207; Andrew and Mitrokhin, *The Mitrokhin Archive*, vol. 1, pp. 104–5, 111–12.

26. "PM's Statement," March 15, 1948, FCO 158/252, TNA. In 1940, MI6's counterespionage officer, Valentine Vivian, ironically rejected the idea that Kim Philby's father, St. John Philby, a noted Arabist, would be disloyal (he had been interned at the start of World War II), noting that Kim was at that point working in MI6 Section D, that he had met him, and that he seemed "able and charming": Valentine Vivian to Guy Liddell, September 24, 1940, s.57b "St John Philby," KV 2/1118, TNA; House of Commons, Hansard, "Foreign Service (Mr Guy Burgess)," vol. 489, June 18, 1951.

27. C Division Distribution, March 1949, s.42a "C Division: Organization and Duties," KV 4/166, TNA; Prime Minister's Personal Minute, December 21, 1947, s.25a "Policy on Investigation & Measures to Control Fascists in Government Contracting Firms," KV 4/203, TNA; Sir Percy Sillitoe to Sir Edward Bridges, July 9, 1948, s.49a KV 4/204, TNA; Cadogan Report, November 3, 1951, with Clement Attlee's initialed marginal note, "I agree," FCO 158/207, TNA; Alexander Cadogan, "Report of Committee of Enquiry," November 1, 1951, p. 25, CAB 301/120, TNA; "Security in the Foreign Service," July 1951, FCO 158/236, TNA. For stringent criticism of the old-boy network that allowed Philby into MI6 and how positive vetting would probably have caught him, see A. J. de la Mare to P. Dean, April 7, 1954, "PEACH," FCO 158/28, TNA; "Cabinet Committee on Subversive Activities" and "The Employment of Civil Servants Etc., Exposed to Communist Influence," May 29, 1947, GEN 183/1 CAB 130/30, TNA; Hennessy, *The Secret State*, p. 87; Hennessy and Brownfeld, "Britain's Cold War Security Purge: The Origins of Positive Vetting," *Historical Journal* 25 (1982): 965–74; House of Commons, Hansard, "Former Foreign Office Officials (Disappearance)," vol. 545, col. 1499, November 7, 1955.

28. Minutes "Security Enquires" about Positive Vetting Foreign Office Employees, n.d., FCO 158/237, TNA; Sillitoe, *Cloak without Dagger*, pp. v, xv; "Prime Minister Agreed to Receive a Deputation from the TUC Regarding Representation by Trade Union Officers at Proceedings before the Three Advisers on the Treatment of Communists and Fascists in the Civil Service," n.d., PREM 8/948, TNA; Williams, *Not in the Public Interest*, pp. 171–72.

29. SLO [MI5 liaison] Australia to H[ead] SIFE [Security Intelligence Far East], April 9, 1954, s.86a "Vladimir Petrov," KV 2/3439, TNA; Philby, *My Silent War*, chap. 13; "Statement to the Press,"

November 4, 1955, "Burgess, Maclean and Philby," FCO 158/178, TNA; "Reappearance of Burgess and Maclean," February 1956, FCO 158/125, TNA; Andrew and Mitrokhin, *The Mitrokhin Archive*, vol. 1, pp. 184–85.

30. As one MI5 report put it, Victor Rothschild, banker, scientist, and intelligence officer, was friendly with Philby and crops up "time and again in the course of our enquiries into the shadowy and tenuous web": A. M. MacDonald, minute 46, November 1965, "Victor Rothschild," KV 2/4531, TNA. For Rothschild and Soloman, see KV 2/4633, TNA; A. S. Martin (D.1), minute 60, "Flora Soloman," July 15, 1962; s.17b "Extract from T/C on PEACH," May 29, 1952; s.57a E. M. Furnival-Jones, "Flora SOLOMONS [sic]," July 5, 1962; s.66b "Transcript of Meeting between Lord Rothschild and Mrs. Soloman," July 19, 1962; s.71a "Note on Mr. Martin's Interview with Mrs. Flora SOLOMAN," July 8, 1962. For Elliot's interview of Philby, see s.38z "Extract from Notes Handed by PHILBY," January 11, 1963, "Arnold Deutsch," KV 2/4428, TNA; Peter Westlake to Sir Hugh Stephenson, February 15, 1963, "Philby" CAB 301/269, TNA; ibid. [CAB 301/269] "Case of H. A. R. Philby, Aide Memoire for the Prime Minister's Talk with Mr Harold Wilson," July 11, 1963, CAB 301/269, TNA; "The Case of Harold 'Kim,' Philby," Philip de Zulueta, February 15, 1963, PREM 11/4457, TNA. For Stella Rimington, see Stella Rimington (K.3/8), "Summary and Assessment of Flora SOLOMON," November 4, 1971, s.145a "Flora Solomon," KV2/4635, TNA; Philby, *My Silent War*, p. 200; "Philby 'Third Man,' Who Warned Maclean," *Times*, July 2, 1963; Macintyre, *A Spy Among Friends*, pp. 259–63; Primakov, *Ocherki ob Istorii Vneshnei Razvedki*, vol. 5, pp. 73–74; Serov, *Zapiski iz chemodana*, p. 420, suggests that "useful contact" between the Soviet services with Rothschild ended with the creation of Israel in 1948; Wright, *Spycatcher*, pp. 172–73.

31. For Michael Staight, see MITN 1/6/4, CHAC; "Vassiliev White Notebook #3," Alexander Vassiliev Papers, WCDA; Burke Trend, "John Cairncross," February 28, 1964, 301/270, TNA; J. E. D. Street minute, February 16, 1964, and B. A. B. Burrows, February 18, 1964, "John Cairncross," FCO 158/129, TNA; SAC, WFO to Director, FBI [Hoover] "Harold Adrian Russell Philby," June 14, 1966, pp. 41–42, in "Michael Whitney Straight" [Part 1 of 1], FBI VAULT, in which Straight asserted that he confronted Blunt about his espionage and Blunt confessed: Straight, *After Long Silence*, pp. 101–03. Straight also disclosed Leo Long's name, who confessed during an interview with MI5 in 1964: S. Webb (MoD) to David White (Cabinet Office), November 6, 1981, "L. H. Long," FCO 158/164, TNA. For the search for Soviet agent ELLI, described by Igor Gouzenko, who is believed to be Leo Long, see G. R. Mitchell, January 31, 1961, "Jenifer Hart," KV 2/4638, TNA; Andrew, *The Defence of the Realm*, p. 348.

32. Andrew and Gordievsky, *KGB*, pp. 665–666.

33. Lownie, *Stalin's Englishman*, pp. xii; Patrick Reilly, "Maclean: Burgess: Philby," p. 259, archive of Sir (D'Arcy) Patrick Reilly, Ms. Eng. C 6920 BOD; Purvis and Hulbert, *Guy Burgess: The Spy Who Knew Everyone*, chap. 10.

34. Cleveland C. Cram, "Of Moles and Molehunters," *Studies in Intelligence* (Summer 1994).

35. C. A. G. Simkins, B.2.a, October 17, 1951, "Tomas Harris," KV 2/4636, TNA; Primakov, *Ocherki ob Istorii Vneshnei Razvedki*, vol. 4, p. 171. Far from being a Soviet agent, Footman appears to have been an NKVD target to get Burgess recruited into British intelligence: Primakov, *Ocherki ob Istorii Vneshnei Razvedki*, vol. 3, p. 52.

36. "Stephen de Mowbray," obituary, *Telegraph*, October 7, 2017. The theory that Hollis was a Soviet agent rumbles on: Pincher, *Treachery*, pp. 611–21.

37. Macintyre, *Agent Sonya*, chap. 5; House of Commons, Hansard, "Security," vol. 1, March 26, 1981.

38. Private information from a former head of CIA counterintelligence; Turner, *Secrecy and Democracy*, p. 45; Holzman, *Kim and Jim*, pp. 208–09. The validity of Nosenko's defection and intelligence also rumbles on: Bagley, *Spy Wars*; Blum, *The Spy Who Knew Too Much*.

39. Interview with former senior CIA officer Paul Kolbe, November 15, 2021; "Nosenko Detection," February 1964, box 229, National Security File, Country File "Europe and USSR," LBJL;

Thomas Karamessines to McGeorge Bundy, February 11, 1964, "Family Jewels" [0001451843], April 3, 1973, CIA CREST; "The Monster Plot," https://www.archives.gov/files/research/jfk /releases/104-10534-10205.pdf; Morley, *The Ghost*; Richard J. Heuer, "Nosenko: Five Paths to Judgment," *Studies in Intelligence* 31 (Fall 1987): 71–101; Andrew and Mitrokhin, *Mitrokhin Archive*, vol. 1, pp. 404–5; Henry Kissinger memorandum to President-Elect Nixon, December 19, 1968, *FRUS, 1964–1968*, vol. XIV, *Soviet Union*; Kalugin, *Spymaster*, pp. 124–25. For the gradations of Soviet assets, from informants to paid agents, see Michael Weiss, "You Don't Have to Be Recruited to Work for Russian 'Intelligence,'" *New Lines Magazine*, February 4, 2021.

40. Andrew and Mitrokhin, *Mitrokhin Archive*, vol. 1, p. 270.

PART 3: THE CLASH OF ARMS

CHAPTER 8: BATTLEGROUNDS

1. Primakov, *Ocherki ob Istorii Vneshnei Razvedki*, vol. 5, pp. 120–27; Record Group [RG] 263 [Records of the Central Intelligence Agency], CIA Name Files, Second Release, boxes 22–23, and "Felfe, Heinz: Damage Assessment," National Archives, College Park, MD; RG 263, CIA Subject Files, Second Release, box 1, NARA. Otto John then bizarrely redefected back to West Germany in 1955, where he was tried: MI6 [name withheld] to G. R. Mitchell, July 22, 1954, s.99a "Otto John," KV 2/2465, TNA. The story can be found in "Defection to GDR from Berlin of Dr Otto John Head of the Federal German Security Office (BFV)," FO 371/109324, TNA; Kim Philby was involved in the British handling of Gehlen's case from the outset: H. A. R. Philby to J. H. Marriott, June 12, 1946, s.3a "Reinhard von Gehlen," KV 2/2862, TNA.

2. "Tokaev" (codename EXCISE), MI6 [name redacted], to M. G. L. Joy, September 14, 1948, "Defector from Berlin: Lieutenant Colonel Gregory Tokaev," FO 1093/549, TNA; "Tass Writer Calls Tokaev 'Traitor,'" *New York Times*, September 6, 1948. For financing of Soviet defectors in Britain, see "Working Party on Russian and Satellite Defectors," Harold Macmillan, September 22, 1950, CAB 301/136, TNA. For an inevitable effort to smear Toakev's reputation, see Serov, *Zapiski iz chemodana*, pp. 270–71. Generally for British policy, see Kevin Riehle, "Early Cold War Evolution of British and US Defector Policy and Practice," *Cold War History* 19 (2019): 343–361. On the role of ideological disillusionment as a motivation for defection, see Riehle, *Soviet Defectors*, pp. 264–67.

3. Orme Sargent to Secretary of State [Bevin], May 12, 1948, and W. G. Hayter to Percy Sillitoe [DG, MI5], July 5, 1948, "Tasoev," FO 1093/550, TNA; JIC(51)(76), minutes of JIC 76th meeting, July 19, 1951, CAB 159/10, TNA.

4. D. G. White to William Hayter [FO], September 17, 1948, "Defectors: General," FO 1093/551, TNA; "Peter Deryabin," FCO 168/5078, TNA.

5. Tromly, *Cold War Exiles and the CIA*, pp. 193–211, 214–15; Gaddis, *George F. Kennan*, pp. 316–17.

6. Menzies, "The capabilities of secret services in peace in support of an overall political plan," January 20, 1948, "Covert Propaganda," FO1093/375 TNA.

7. The preceding follows Cormac, *Disrupt and Deny*, part 2; Philby quote in *My Silent War*, p. 146.

8. Cormac, *Disrupt and Deny*, pp. 49–51; For Britain's coolness of the CIA's use of émigré groups: "We were afraid that most of the emigres had been too long out of touch with their countries and had little standing there and we considered that the only results of using them might be, if not entirely negative with consequent waste of effort and discredit to ourselves, then at the most only the arousing of premature and exaggerated hopes, with dangerous consequences, in the countries themselves": see Dennis Allen (British embassy Washington) to William Hayter (FO), April 18, 1949, "Cold War: UK Strategy in Eastern Europe," FO 1093/563, TNA, relaying a meeting with Frank Wisner at CIA. My analysis owes much to a major revision of British and U.S. operations in Albania, BGFIEND/ VALUABLE, by Stephen Long: "CIA-MI6 Psychological Warfare and the Subversion of Communist Albania in the Early Cold War," *Intelligence and National Security* 35 (2020): 787–807. The traditional

interpretation of Philby betraying MI6 and the CIA's Albania operations was given in Bethell, *The Great Betrayal*; glamorizations are found in Smiley, *Albanian Assignment*.

9. Cormac, *Disrupt and Deny*, pp. 60, 72, 272; [Name illegible] minute, July 8, 1950, and ensuing minutes, "Albania: Operation Valuable (July–December 1950)," FO 1093/636, TNA; for putting a frown on Stalin's face, see "Operation Kremlin Cracks," box 83, "Princeton Meeting May 1952," Eisenhower Papers as President, Ann Whitman File, Administrative Series, box 22, C. D. Jackson File 2, DDEL; Lulushi, *Operation Valuable Fiend*, pp. 85–86, 90–91.

10. For a softening of rollback, see NSC 174, "Policy towards Soviet Satellites in Eastern Europe," December 11, 1953, DDE, White House Office of Special Assistant for National Security Affairs, NSC Series, box 8, Policy Papers, DDEL.

11. Gaddis, *Strategies of Containment*, p. 96.

12. May, ed., *American Cold War Strategy*, p. vii; Bowie and Immerman, *Waging Peace*, pp. 28–30.

13. On 1953 protests, see "Policy towards Soviet Satellites in Eastern Europe"; Martha Mautner interview, November 1995, pp. 15–16, Oral History Project, ADST; "Full Division Is Patrolling Strikebound Soviet Zone," *Washington Post*, June 18, 1953.

14. Allen Dulles, memo, October 19, 1954, Eisenhower Papers as President, Ann Whitman File, Administrative Series, box 13, file containing report by James Doolittle, "Report on the Covert Activities of the Central Intelligence Agency," September 30, 1954, pp. 2–3, DDEL. A sanitized copy of the Doolittle Report is available in the Reading Room at DDEL. "Report to the National Security Council by the Executive Secretary (Lay)," NSC 162/2, October 30, 1953, doc. 1, in *National Security Affairs*, vol. 2, pt. 1, of *FRUS, 1952–1954*; Anderson, *The Quiet Americans*, p. 435; Hitchcock, *The Age of Eisenhower*, p. 108, for Solarium.

15. Eisenhower to Allen Dulles, December 11, 1957, Eisenhower Papers as President, Ann Whitman File, Administrative Series, box 22, C. D. Jackson File 2, DDEL; NSC 158, "United States Objectives and Actions to Exploit the Unrest in Satellite States," June 29, 1953, White House Office, OSA/NSA, DDEL; a reassessment of Radio Free Europe's messages of support in Hungary can be found in Johnson, *Radio Free Europe and Radio Liberty*.

16. Shebarshin, *Ruka Moskvy*, pp. 55–56. For earlier Soviet honeytrap operations, see [envelope K-9] MITN 2/10; MITN 1/6/1; MITN 1/6/4, all at CHAC.

17. Ashley, *CIA Spymaster*, p. 47; Haslam, *Near and Distant Neighbors*, pp. 184–85.

18. MITN 1/6/1, CHAC; Ashley, *CIA Spymaster*, pp. 132–33; Hood, *Mole*, pp. 297–98; Murphy, Kondrashev, and Bailey, *Battleground Berlin*, pp. 268–81; John L. Hart, "Pyotr Semonovich Popov: The tribulations of faith," *Intelligence and National Security* 12 (1997): 44–74.

19. Britain's JIC correctly forecast that Stalin would seek to overthrow Tito but would be unlikely to do so openly: JIC(49)73, "Possibility of Russian Armed Action against Yugoslavia," September 3, 1949, FCO 1093/561, TNA; Sudoplatov, *Special Tasks*, pp. 336–339.

20. Volodarsky, *The KGB's Poison Factory*, p. 33; Deriabin and Bagley, *The KGB*, pp. 361–62; Wilmers, *The Eitingons*, p. 413.

21. Haslam, *Near and Distant Neighbors*, p. 178; Burleigh, *Day of the Assassins*, pp. 222. On Bandera and wartime OUN collaboration with Nazi mass murder, see Statiev, *The Soviet Counterinsurgency in the Western Borderlands*, pp. 58–59; Taubman, *Khrushchev*, p. 193; Primakov, *Ocherki ob Istorii Vneshnei Razvedki*, vol. 4, p. 86; Serov, *Zapiski iz chemodana*, pp. 34, 56–57.

22. Memorandum for the Record "Assassination of Stefan Bandera," [519a6b2b993294098d511a08], April 22, 1976, CIA CREST; GDA SZR Ukraini "Kharakterystyka Na Ahenta-Boyovyka UMDB L'vivs'koyi Obl.'Oleh'; l. d. (Osobova Sprava) No. 27083," in *Sprava Operatyvnoi Rozrobki Ahenta KDB Stashyns πkoho B.M. ("Oleh" – "Taras")*, vol. 1, pp. 54–56; Anders, *Murder to Order*, pp. 53–54; Volodarsky, *The KGB's Poison Factory*, p. 187; Plokhy, *The Man with the Poison Gun*, pp. 59–65.

23. Burleigh, *Day of the Assassins*; Stashinsky was a KGB agent, not an officer. "Soviet Spy Trial at Karlsruhe," *Times*, October 9, 1962; "Germans Hold Russian; Ex-Soviet Agent Reported to Admit

to Bandera Killing," *New York Times*, November 18, 1961; "Poison Gas Pistol Shown to Court," *Times*, October 10, 1962.

24. Milton Magruder, "Ex-Assassin of Reds Heard Secretly Here," *Washington Post*, May 12, 1954; Volodarsky, *The KGB's Poison Factory*, p. 36.

25. MI6's debriefing of Khokhlov is revealed in PREM 11/772, TNA: Ivone Kirkpatrick, forwarding report from "C" (MI6 Chief) to Prime Minister, with Churchill's initials, "Nikolai Khoklov Sent to FRG by Soviet Government to Carry Out Assassination of Georgi Okolovich," May 8, 1954; "The Case of Nikolai Khokhlov," *US Congressional Record* 100:8, July 9, 1954, S10156; "Instruction in Murder and Assassination by the Former Soviet Ambassador to the United State," *Congressional Record* 100:11, August 11, 1954, S13992. Khokhlov, *In the Name of Conscience*, pp. 145, 163; de Silva, *Sub Rosa*, p. 80.

26. Haslam, *Near and Distant Neighors*, p. 178. On later KGB efforts against the OUN, including one KGB deception group calling itself "DOR 88," see Vasili Mitrokhin, "The Nationalism Case, Folder 57: The Chekist Anthology," WCDA.

27. The best account of the Portland spy ring has been written by Trevor Barnes, *Dead Doubles*. For Kroger's biography, and forged passports, see MITN 1/6/4, CHAC, and Snelling, *Rare Books and Rarer People*, pp. 206–9. For later piecing together of Kroger's movements, see Director General MI5 to Director of Security New Zealand SIS, July 3, 1970, s.2922a "Peter and Helen Kroger," KV 2/4575, TNA; Dolgopolov, *Abel Fisher*, pp. 184–201. For Rudolf Abel, see Drozdov, *Zapiski*, pp. 116–20.

28. MI5 assigned the code name LAVINIA to the CIA's agent, SNIPER: Goleniewski; "The Lonsdale Case: A Preliminary Report," March 1961, pp. 3–5, "Gordon Lonsdale," KV2/4466, TNA; D. H. Whyte (D.2), August 5, 1960, "Gordon Lonsdale," KV 2/4429, TNA.

29. D.2 minute, May 11, 1960, "Harry Houghton," KV 2/4380, TNA; B. A. Hill, L. A. [legal adviser], minute 98, August 2, 1960, "Harry Houghton," KV 2/4381, TNA; Andrew, *The Defence of the Realm*, pp. 485–88.

30. Surveillance reports of "Gordon Lonsdale" found in "Harry Houghton," KV2/4381, TNA.

31. MITN 1/6/4, CHAC.

32. See especially the note by W. J. Skardon, July 11, 1960, KV 2/4381, TNA; "Ethel Gee," KV 2/4377, TNA.

33. Signals received by TREK, December 9, 1960, "Gordon Lonsdale," KV 2/4437, TNA. C. J. L. Elwell, "Suggested Plan of Operation for the Arrest and Search of TREK, the KILLJOYS, REVERBERATE and TRELLIS," January 6, 1961, s.60c KV 2/4377, TNA.

34. "Little Suburban House Was Communication Centre for Spy Ring, Crown Alleges," *Times*, February 8, 1961.

35. "Nuclear Submarine's Details Shown," *Times*, February 10, 1961; Lonsdale, " 'Master Mind' Gets 25 Years," *Time*, March 23, 1961; Rositzke, *The CIA's Secret Operations*, p. 137.

36. C. J. L. Elwell, "Note," August 16, 1961, s.1094a "Gordon Lonsdale," KV 2/4452, TNA, and ensuing recorded conversation. One of the MI5 case officers on the Portland spy ring was Peter Wright. The now available British files on Portland constitute strong evidence that, contrary to claims made by Peter Wright in *Spycatcher*, Hollis was not a Soviet agent. If he had been, it seems inconceivable that Hollis, who oversaw MI5's handling of the Portland case, would not have warned the KGB that Lonsdale, its prize agent in Britain, was compromised. Soviet moles in British intelligence like Kim Philby typically managed to warn fellow Soviet agents when the net was closing on them.

37. MITN 1/6/4, CHAC; press cuttings re: KROGER's departure from Britain, October 24, 1969, "Peter and Helen Kroger," KV 2/4575, TNA. Primakov, *Ocherki ob Istorii Vneshnei Razvedki*, vol. 5, p. 190, claims Lonsdale died of a stroke after a long day of walking; see p. 203 for "the heroic" welcome for the Cohens in Moscow. "Mr. Greville Wynne Freed in Berlin Exchange," *Time*, April 23, 1964; "Gordon Lonsdale," obituary, *Times*, October 14, 1970.

38. [Envelope K-16] MITN, CHAC; John McCone, DCI, to LBJ, "CIA, Covert Action

Programs—Eastern Europe," August 8, 1964, Agency File, box 9, National Security File, LBJL; correspondence between Richard Helms, Walt Rostow, and Johnson, May 1968, National Security File, Country File "Europe and the USSR—Czechoslovakia," box 182, LBJL; Cabinet Papers, box 14, Cabinet Meeting, July 31, 1968, LBJL; minutes of Cabinet Meeting, August 22, 1968, NSAM 304 U.S. Relations with Eastern Europe, LBJL; JIC(68)54 (Final), "The Soviet Grip on Eastern Europe," December 2, 1968, CAB 158/71, TNA.

CHAPTER 9: RISE OF THE MACHINES

1. Dulles, *Craft of Intelligence*, p. 149; Taubman, *Secret Empire*, pp. 29–31; Killian Report, "Meeting the Threat of Surprise Attack," February 1955, White House Office of the Staff Secretary, Subject Series, Alphabetical Subseries, box 16, DDEL; U.S. Congressional Record, July 21, 1954, p. 1158.

2. Killian Report, December 20, 1954, Eisenhower Presidential Papers, Ann Whitman Files, box 13, DDEL; Killian, *Sputnik, Scientists, and Eisenhower*, pp. 79–81.

3. "Meeting the Threat of Surprise Attack," Eisenhower Presidential Papers, WHO Office of Staff Secretary Subject Series, box 16, DDEL; "Scientific Judgments on Foreign Communications Intelligence," Baker Report [January 23, 1958], Records of the White House Office of the Special Assistant for National Security Affairs (OSANSA), NSC Series, Subject Series, box 10 File, DDEL; DDE Diary Series, box 30, file folder "Staff Notes, February 1958," memorandum of a Presidential meeting, February 10, 1958, DDEL, regarding the Baker Panel report on special intelligence.

4. CIA Historical Paper, "The Berlin Tunnel Operation 1952–1956," 1964, pp. 4, 10, 15, 18, 25, CIA CREST, https://irp.fas.org/cia/product/tunnel-200702.pdf.

5. "Operation Regal: The Berlin Tunnel," United States Cryptologic History Special Series, No. 4 (1988) [Doc ID 3962741], p. 7, USG-NSA.

6. CIA Historical Paper, "The Berlin Tunnel Operation 1952–1956," 1964, p. 25, CIA CREST.

7. "Report of the Committee on Security Procedures in the Public Service (Radcliffe Committee), 1961," p. 2, CAB 301/258, TNA. I am grateful to Trevor Barnes for alerting me to this file's contents concerning Blake; Robert McFadden, "George Blake, British Spy Who Betrayed the West, Dies at 98," *New York Times*, December 26, 2020.

8. For Blake's biography, see Allen Dulles, DCI, to General Clifton, May 4, 1961, attaching memorandum, "George BLAKE," Papers of President Kennedy, President's Office Files, Countries [United Kingdom], box 127a, JFKL; "Report of the Committee on Security Procedures in the Public Service (Radcliffe Committee), 1961," p. 2, CAB 301/258, TNA; description of Blake taken from "The Very Strange Case of Britain's Super-Spy," *Washington Post*, May 21, 1961.

9. "Report of the Committee on Security Procedures in the Public Service (Radcliffe Committee), 1961," p. 5, CAB 301/258, TNA; meeting between Cram and Blake, private information.

10. "Tunnel of Love," *Washington Post*, May 1, 1956.

11. The best reassessments of the Berlin tunnel, and claims of "disinformation," can be found in Vogel, *Betrayal in Berlin*, pp. 452–54; Hermiston, *The Greatest Traitor*, pp. 194–96; Stafford, *Spies beneath Berlin*, pp. 188–90; Murphy, Kondrashev, and Bailey, *Battleground Berlin*, p. 236. See also Bagley, *Spymaster*, pp. 93–94. For persistent claims about disinformation, see Primakov, *Ocherki ob Istorii Vneshnei Razvedki*, vol. 5, p. 216; *Sluzhba Vneshney Razvedki, Rossiyskoy Federatsii 100 let*, pp. 262, 265, which also states that Blake was responsible for identifying more than two hundred British and U.S. agents who were rendered useless.

12. Blake, *No Other Choice*, p. 198; Quine's interview can be found here: https://soundcloud.com /quirpy/channel-4-tv-pilot-test-interview; Hermiston, *Greatest Traitor*, pp. 230–31; Papers of President Kennedy, President's Office Files, Countries [United Kingdom], box 127a, Allen Dulles, DCI, to General Clifton, May 4, 1961, attaching memorandum "George BLAKE"; Corera, *MI6*, p. 143, JFKL; Ashley, *CIA Spymaster*, p. 151; "John Quine: Counter-intelligence Supremo at MI6 Who Exposed the Double Agent George Blake," obituary, *Independent*, June 20, 2013.

13. For Martin and Mitchell, see "463rd Meeting of NSC October 13, 1960," Eisenhower Papers as President, Ann Whitman File, NSC Series, box 13, file folder, DDEL. The KGB inevitably used Martin and Mitchell's defection for active measures: MITN 1/6/5, CHAC.

14. Record of Conversation in the Prime Minister's room at the House of Commons on Thursday, October 27, 1966, p. 2; "George Blake's Escape from Prison (October 1966) and the Implications for National Security," CAB 301/264, TNA.

15. "Traitors," *Daily Mail*, August 4, 1975.

16. Andrew and Mitrokhin, *The Mitrokhin Archive*, vol. 1, p. 440; Kennan, *Memoirs 1950–1963*, pp. 154–57; State Department to Ambassador Kohler (Moscow) and Bohlen (Paris), National Security File—Intelligence File, "USSR—Hidden Microphones in Moscow Embassy," LBJL; Dobrynin, *In Confidence*, p. 357; Eisenhower Papers as President, White House Central File (Confidential), Subject Series, box 62, File "Russia," DDEL; Krasilnikov, *Prizraki s ulitsy Chaykovskogo*, pp. 77, 85; David Kahn, "Soviet Comint in the Cold War," *Cryptologia* 22 (1998). A pioneering article on bugging has been written by David Easter: "Soviet Bloc and Western Bugging of Opponents' Diplomatic Premises during the Early Cold War," *Intelligence and National Security* 31 (2016): 28–48.

17. Sharon A. Maneki, "Learning from the Enemy: The GUNMAN Project," NSA Center for Cryptologic History (2nd ed., 2018), https://media.defense.gov/2021/Jul/13/2002761779/-1/-1/0/LEARNINGFROMTHEENEMYGUNMAN.PDF; for electronic waves at the U.S. embassy in Moscow, and their health effects, see Kenneth deGraffenreid Papers, RAC, boxes 5, 6, RRL; Brent Scowcroft to Anatoly Dobrynin, December 17, 1975, and Brezhnev's reply, December 31, 1975, Kissinger-Scowcroft West Wing Office Files, "USSR—'D' File (Dobrynin)," GRFL.

18. Quoted in David Easter, "Soviet Bloc and Western Bugging," p. 47.

19. Wright, *Spycatcher*, pp. 84–86; Claude Boillot Papers Folder "Special Operations," boxes 1–2, various dates, DDEL; Mondale, *The Good Fight*, p. 146; David Easter, "Spying on Nasser: British Signals Intelligence in Middle East Crises and Conflicts," *Intelligence and National Security* 28 (2013): 824–844; Theoharis, ed., *From the Secret Files of J. Edgar Hoover*, pp. 127–30.

20. Johnson, *American Cryptology*, book 1, p. 204; Howard Champaigne, "Lightning" [Doc-ID 3991001] and R. L. Wiginton, "The LIGHTNING Program" [Doc-ID 3991005], both on USG-NSA; NSA staff figures given in Clark Clifford interview, May 28, 1971, tape 5, p. 25, Oral History Project, LBJL.

21. Burke, *It Wasn't All Magic*, chap. 10; "Before Super-Computers: NSA and Computer Development" [Doc-ID 3575750], USG-NSA; Johnson, *American Cryptology*, book 1, pp. 200, 204.

22. For Macmillan and counting the cost of empire, see Darwin, *Unfinished Empire*, pp. 363–66; Ferris, *Behind the Enigma*, pp. 298–304; Reilly Memoirs, "The Secret Service" [1981], p. 232, Archive of Sir (D'Arcy) Patrick Reilly, Ms. Eng. C. 6918 BOD. The difficulties of funding GCHQ from civilian funds (the secret vote in Parliament), as opposed to military, are set out in "GCHQ Working Party on the Interception Services" (Templer Report), 1961–1962, T296/279, TNA.

23. Aldrich, *GCHQ*, pp. 221–225.

24. John E. Griffith, "Foreign vs. U.S. Computers: An Appraisal" [Doc-ID 3991006], USG-NSA; Haslam, *Near and Distant Neighbors*, chap. 10.

25. Greg Miller, "The Intelligence Coup of the Century," *Washington Post*, February 11, 2020. The best studies of RUBICON are: Sarah Mainwaring, "Division D: Operation Rubicon and the CIA's Secret SIGINT Empire," *Intelligence and National Security* 35 (2020): 623–640; Richard Aldrich et al., "Operation Rubicon: Sixty Years of German-American Success in Signals Intelligence," *Intelligence and National Security* 35 (2020): 603–607.

26. Carter prioritized SIGINT and IMINT over HUMINT: Paseman, *A Spy's Journey*, p. 259. This was perhaps because of Carter's background in engineering.

27. Killian, *Sputnik, Scientists, and Eisenhower*, p. 84. For authorization of the U-2, see A. J. Goodpaster, "Memorandum of Conference with the President," November 24, 1954, Eisenhower Papers as

President, Ann Whitman File, Ann Whitman Diary Series, box 3, ACW Diary, November 1954, DDEL. For Bissell's character, see Rasenberger, *The Brilliant Disaster*, p. 57.

28. Gregory W. Pedlow and Donald E. Welzenbach, "The CIA and the U-2 Program 1954–1974," CIA History Staff (1998), pp. 154–57, CIA CREST; Killian, *Sputnik, Scientists, and Eisenhower*, p. 84; Eisenhower, *Waging Peace*, pp. 544–55; Church Committee, *Final Report*, book 4, p. 59.

29. Gregory W. Pedlow and Donald E. Welzenbach, "The CIA and the U-2 Program 1954–1974," CIA History Staff (1998), pp. 154–57, CIA CREST; A. J. Goodpaster, "Memorandum of Conference with the President," September 28, 1960, Eisenhower Papers as President, DDE Diary Series, box 53, Staff Notes, September 1960, DDEL.

30. Andrew, *For the President's Eyes Only*, pp. 223–34.

31. Allen Dulles, memorandum to Andrew Goodpaster listing all U-2 overflights of Soviet bloc from 1956–1960, August 18, 1960, Office of the Staff Secretary, Subject Series, Alphabetical Subseries, box 15, Intelligence Matters (17), DDEL.

32. MITN 1/6/5, CHAC; Ambrose, *Eisenhower*, pp. 506–8.

33. For Eisenhower's authorization of one more flight after May 1, see A. J. Goodpaster, "Memorandum for Record," April 25, 1960, Office of the Staff Secretary, Subject Series, Alphabetical Subseries, box 15, Intelligence Matters DDEL. For Eisenhower's cover story of the U-2 mission, a "scientific weather mission over Turkey," see Office of the Staff Secretary, Subject Series, Alphabetical Subseries, box 14, Intelligence Matters, DDEL; for Eisenhower agonizing about U-2 intelligence, see John S. D. Eisenhower, "Memorandum of Conference with the President," August 10, 1960, Office of the Staff Secretary, Subject Series, Alphabetical Subseries, box 15, Intelligence Matters, DDEL; for Soviet active measures following Gary Powers's capture, see MITN 1/6/1, CHAC; Khrushchev, ed., *Memoirs of Nikita Khrushchev*, p. 528; "Note from KGB Chairman to Central Committee of the Communist Party of the Soviet Union Regarding Plan to Discredit CIA Chief Dulles," June 7, 1960, WCDA.

34. Andrew, *For the President's Eyes Only*, pp. 228–35.

35. For U-2 and the CORONA project, see: A. J. Goodpaster, "Memorandum of Conference with the President," February 7, 1958, Office of the Staff Secretary, Subject Series, Alphabetical Subseries, box 14, Intelligence Matters, DDEL; Richard Bissell, "Project CORONA," March 11, 1959, Office of the Staff Secretary, Subject Series, Alphabetical Subseries, box 15, Intelligence Matters, DDEL; Taubman, *Secret Empire*, pp. 230–40. For OXCART, see Gregory W. Pedlow and Donald E. Welzenbach, "The CIA and the U-2 Program 1954–1974," CIA History Staff (1998), chap. 6, CIA CREST. For Soviet detection of U.S. *Discoverer* satellites in September 1959, seven months after the first launch, see "Report by Chairman for the Committee of State Security [Shelepin] on American *Discoverer* Satellites," September 26, 1959, WCDA.

36. For the U-2 ending the "bomber gap," see Gregory W. Pedlow and Donald E. Welzenbach, "The CIA and the U-2 Program 1954–1974," CIA History Staff (1998), pp. 111–12, and pp. 159–70 for U-2 and intelligence on the "missile gap"; on Kennedy's public speeches about the missile gap, see U.S. Congress, Senate, *Congressional Record*, August 14, 1958, p. 17574; "An Investment for Peace," Papers of John F. Kennedy, Pre-Presidential Papers, Senate Files Speeches and the Press Speech Files, 1953–1960, "Senate Floor, February 29, 1960," JFKL; Papers of John F. Kennedy, Pre-Presidential Papers, Presidential Campaign Files, 1960, box 1052, "Television Debates: ABC Transcript: Fourth Debate," JFKL.

37. Allen Dulles (DCIA), Memorandum for the President, August 3, 1960, Eisenhower Papers as President, Ann Whitman File, Administrative Series, box 13, File "Allen Dulles," DDEL; D. D. Eisenhower to John F. Kennedy, August 19, 1960, White House Central Files, Official File, Democratic Party, box 603, JFKL; Oral History Program, Earle Wheeler interview (1964), pp. 1–2, JFKL; McNamara, *In Retrospect*, pp. 20–21.

38. CIA memorandum, "Changes in National Intelligence Estimates on Soviet ICBM Forces," February 21, 1961, Papers of President Kennedy, National Security Files, Countries, box 298, File "The

Missile Gap," JFKL; Perry and Collina, *The Button*, p. 34. Nixon also believed that the CIA had briefed Kennedy on Eisenhower's plans for Cuba (the actual details of Kennedy's briefings on Cuba remain unclear) but continued to criticize the Republicans for being soft on Castro: Oral History Program, Allen Dulles interview, December 5–6, 1964, p. 9, JFKL. Nixon, *Six Crises*, pp. 354–55; for references to the missile gap after his briefings, see, for example, "Excerpts from Kennedy Talk to Legion," *New York Times*, October 18, 1960; "Transcript of the Third Kennedy-Nixon Television Debate on Issues of Campaign," *New York Times*, October 14, 1960.

CHAPTER 10: THE MISSILES OF OCTOBER

1. "Janet Chisholm," *Telegraph*, August 6, 2004.
2. A valuable, balanced summary of Penkovsky is in Garthoff, *Reflections on the Cuban Missile Crisis*, pp. 63–66; Horne, *Macmillan*, vol. II, pp. 369–70; Len Scott, "Espionage and the Cold War: Oleg Penkovsky and the Cuban Missile Crisis," *Intelligence and National Security* 14 (1999): pp. 23–47. Surprisingly, however, some otherwise excellent recently published histories of the Cuban Missile Crisis still omit the role of Oleg Penkovsky: Plokhy, *Nuclear Folly.*
3. Richard Helms [Deputy Director, Plans] to DCI, "Essential Facts of the Penkovskiy Case," May 31, 1963, Papers of President Kennedy, National Security Files, Departments and Agencies, box 271b, JFKL; Schecter and Deriabin, *The Spy Who Saved the World*; Maclean, *Take Nine Spies*, pp. 306–8.
4. Ashley, *CIA Spymaster*, pp. 154–64; "Meeting Number 2" [CIA-0000012393], April 21, 1961, CIA CREST.
5. Corera, *MI6*, p. 140.
6. "Meeting Number 1, Mount Royal Hotel" [CIA-0000012392], April 20, 1961, CIA CREST.
7. Corera, *MI6*, pp. 141, 151; interview with Joe Bulik, January 31, 1998, GWU NSA.
8. "Sir Dick Franks," obituary, *Telegraph*, October 20, 2008; Corera, *MI6*, pp. 141, 151. Detailed analysis of British and U.S. handling of Penkovsky has been done by David Gioe: "Handling HERO: Joint Anglo-American Tradecraft in the Case of Oleg Penkovsky," in Gioe, Scott, and Andrew, eds., *An International History of the Cuban Missile Crisis*, pp. 135–75. A vivid account of Penkovsky is Duns's *Codename: Hero*. The British code name for Penkovsky was YOGA, and his product was RUPEE. For Serov's visit to London, where the press dubbed him "Ivan the Terrible," see Serov, *Zapiski iz chemodana*, pp. 468–69. See also "Ivan Serov," ss.44a onward in his MI5 dossier, KV 2/3830, TNA; "Biography of Ivan Aleksandrovich Serov, Gordon Arneson (INR) to Allen Dulles (CIA)" [CIA-RDP80B01676R004200090028-9], September 30, 1958, CIA CREST.
9. For Khrushchev and a peace treaty over Berlin, see British Foreign and Commonwealth Office documents from the British Archives No. 3: Richard Smith, ed., *Britain and the Berlin Crisis, 1961*, document 1: "Memorandum by the Earl of Home for the Cabinet," July 26, 1961; Keith Hamilton, Patrick Salmon, and Stephen Twigge, eds., *The Invasion of Afghanistan and UK-Soviet Relations*, DBPO, Series III, 6, p. 84.
10. "Meeting Number 1, Mount Royal Hotel" [CIA-0000012392], April 20, 1961, CIA CREST; "Meeting Number 4, Leeds" [CIA-0000012394], April 23, 1961, CIA CREST; "Meeting Number 10" [CIA-0000012398], April 30, 1961, CREST; "Meeting Number 12, London" [CIA-0000012400], May 1, 1961, paragraphs 54–71, CIA CREST.
11. Oral History Program, Allen Dulles interview, December 5 and 6, 1964, pp. 15–16, JFKL. The evening before his assassination, Kennedy, like Lee Harvey Oswald, his assassin, was reportedly reading a James Bond novel.
12. Kennedy to McCone, and Richard Helms, acting for DCI, to Kennedy, "Essential Facts of the Penkovsky Case," May 31, 1963, Presidential Papers, National Security Files, Departments and Agencies, box 271, JFKL; Garthoff, *A Journey through the Cold War*, p. 113; Len Parkison, "Penkovsky's Legacy and Strategic Research," *Studies in Intelligence* 16 (Spring 1972): pp. 1–18; "Radio and Television Report to the American People on the Berlin Crisis," July 21, 1961, JFK speeches, JFKL;

"Joint Evaluation of Soviet Missile Threat in Cuba" [CIA-RDP78T05449A000200030001-8], October 18, 1962, CIA CREST; Schechter and Deriabin, *The Spy Who Saved the World*.

13. Gordievsky, *Next Stop Execution*, pp. 114–15.

14. Corera, *MI6*, pp. 160–162.

15. Emily Langer, "Hugh Montgomery, Spy with Exploits from Battlefield to Powder Room, Dies at 93," *Washington Post*, April 10, 2017; Christopher Andrew, "Remembering the Cuban Missile Crisis," in Gioe, Scott, and Andrew, *An International History of the Cuban Missile Crisis*, pp. 19–20; for Penkovsky dead drops, "under the lights and by the bridge," see William D. Morgan interview, June 23, 1995, p. 55, Oral History Project, ADST.

16. Crankshaw, ed., *Khrushchev Remembers*, pp. 493–95; Haslam, *Near and Distant Neighbors*, pp. 197–99; Semichastny, *Sovetskaya vneshnyaya razvedka*, p. 158; Serov, *Zapiski iz chemodana*; Richard Helms, "Essential Facts of the Penkovsky Case," May 31, 1963, Papers of President Kennedy, National Security Files, Departments and Agencies, box 271, JFKL.

17. *Sudebnyj protsess po ugolovnomu delu agenta angliyskoy i amerikanskoy razvedok grazhdanina SSSR Pe'kovskogo O. V. i shpiona-svyaznika poddannogo Velikobritanii Vinna G. M. 7-11 maya 1963 goda*; "Reflections on Handling Penkovsky" [CIA 000612251], CIA CREST; Schechter and Deriabin, *The Spy Who Saved the World*, pp. 372–73; Phillip Knightley, "Gervase Cowell," obituary, *Guardian*, May 15, 2000. Meanwhile, Wynne, after serving eighteen months in Lubyanka, was subsequently exchanged in a spy swap for the KGB officer known as Gordon Lonsdale, the illegal arrested in Britain in the Portland spy ring: "Central Intelligence Bulletin" [CIA-RDP79T00975A006900180001-6], March 21, 1963, CIA CREST. According to the GRU director at the time, Ivan Serov, before Penkovsky's arrest, the KGB had turned him into a Soviet agent against the West and used him to feed disinformation to Western intelligence. In Serov's memoirs, purportedly written secretly and later found at his family dacha and then published, Serov asserts that the KGB ran Penkovsky due to its endless rivalry with the GRU and to ensure Serov's downfall as GRU director. Even assuming his memoir's authenticity, Serov's claims seem implausible. First, before and during the Cuban Missile Crisis, the KGB was largely incompetent. Second, by claiming the existence of an elaborate conspiracy orchestrated by the KGB and directed against him, Serov seems to have been grasping for a convenient exculpatory narrative for Penkovsky, rather than the more plausible one: that under his leadership, the GRU suffered its worst security failure during the Cold War.

18. Oral History Program, Robert Amory Jr. interview no. 2, July 5, 1968, p. 37, JFKL; Helms, *A Look over My Shoulder*, pp. 216–22. A cautionary perspective on Penkovsky, however, was given by a key adviser to Kennedy—Llewellyn "Tommy" Thompson—who said, "I don't think it [Penkovsky's intelligence] had very much importance": Oral History Program, Llewellyn Thompson interview, February 27, 1966, p. 46, JFKL. This is contradicted by the documentary evidence set out in the next endnote (19).

19. For IRONBARK, see the following in McAuliffe, ed., *CIA Documents on the Cuban Missile Crisis*: Doc. 61 "Joint Evaluation of Soviet Missile Threat in Cuba," October 18, 1962, pp. 187–91; Doc. 65 "Joint Evaluation of Soviet Missile Threat in Cuba," October 19, 1962, pp. 203–8; Doc. 81 "Supplement 3 to Joint Evaluation of Soviet Missile Threat in Cuba," October 22, 1962, pp. 281–82; for CHIC[K]ADEE, see Doc. 52 "[McCone] Memorandum of Meeting Attended in Secretary Ball's Conference Room," October 17, 1962, p. 160; and "Introduction," Tuesday, October 16, 1962, Miller Center Presidential Recordings, digital edition.

20. Fursenko and Naftali, *Khrushchev's Cold War*, p. 435; Barrass, *The Great Cold War*, p. 138; similar "equalizing" comments found in Serov, *Zapiski iz chemodana*; Leonov, *Razvedka*. Some U.S. observers, like Richard Pipes, the Harvard historian and Reagan national security adviser, commented that "mutually assured destruction" meant different things in Washington and Moscow. If nuclear war broke out, the Soviet military thought they could still "win," presumably with survivors living in a nuclear holocaust, while Pipes contended that the U.S. military concluded

that both sides would lose. That view is misleading: the U.S. military also had similar plans for post-nuclear survival. See "How President Reagan Might Conduct His Policy towards the Soviet Union," October 1981, Richard Pipes Papers, box 3, RRL.

21. Johnson, *American Cryptology*, book 2, p. 317.

22. SNIE 85-3-62, "The Military Buildup in Cuba," September 19, 1962, *FRUS, 1961–63*, vol. X, *Cuba, January 1961–September 1962*.

23. Gribkov and Smith, *Operation Anadyr*; Plokhy, *Nuclear Folly*, p. 86, for the appendicitis story; Johnson, *American Cryptology*, book 2, p. 332; Britain's Joint Intelligence Committee appears to have discussed the Cuban Missile Crisis for the first time on Tuesday, October 23: COS (62) 66th meeting "Confidential Annex," October 23, 1962, DEFE 4/148/66, TNA. Kennedy, *Thirteen Days*, p. 23; Leonov, *Likholet'ye*, pp. 76–77; Taubman, *Khrushchev*, p. 549.

24. Cline, *Spies, Secrets, and Scholars*, pp. 188–189; Barrett and Holland, *Blind over Cuba*, pp. 12, 13, 124, 133. Statistics compiled about McCone's visits to the White House from JFK's appointment book: JFKL. Kennedy and McCone, however, were edgy, not friendly: Oral History Program, McGeorge Bundy interview, March 1964, pp. 17–18, JFKL. Notably, Kennedy's appointment book does not mention the MI6 head of station in Washington at the time, Maurice Oldfield, who some authors, like Richard Deacon, claimed had personal access to the president. It is possible he did in secret, but this cannot be substantiated. For McCone's appointment, see Kennedy handwritten note, September 26, 1961, Papers of President Kennedy, Regional Security, box 228, JFKL.

25. Aid, *Secret Sentry*, pp. 64–69; "Reference to Radar Tracking on Russian Radar in Cuba" [0/11370-62], April 18, 1962, USG-NSA; "Dry Cargo Shipments to and from Cuba in Soviet Ships (1 Jan–31 March 1962)," May 2, 1962, USG-NSA; "First Elint Evidence of Scan ODD Radar in Cuban Area," June 6, 1962, USG-NSA; "Further Unusual Soviet/Cuban Trade Relations Recently Noted," August 7, 1962, USG-NSA; "Spanish Speaking Pilots Training in Trencin Airfield, Czechoslovakia on 31 May 1961," June 17, 1962, USG-NSA; Johnson, *American Cryptology*, book 2, p. 323.

26. David Wolman, "The Once-Classified Tale of Juanita Moody," *Smithsonian Magazine*, March 2021; Johnson, *American Cryptology*, book 2, p. 322; NSA Oral History Juanita Moody, June 16, 1994, [ID 4310433], pp. 31–33, https://media.defense.gov/2021/Jul/15/2002763502/-1/-1/0/NSA-OH-1994-32-MOODY.PDF.

27. Andrew, *For the President's Eyes Only*, pp. 221–22.

28. Well told by Barrett and Holland, *Blind over Cuba*, and Absher, Desch, and Popadiuk, *Privileged and Confidential*, pp. 53–54. Lundahl would become the only American photographic analyst ever to be awarded both the U.S. National Security Medal and an honorary British knighthood.

29. Andrew, *For the President's Eyes Only*, p. 287; Schecter and Deriabin, *The Spy Who Saved the World*, p. 331; Robert Kennedy Papers, Attorney General's Confidential files, box 209, for Robert Kennedy receiving U-2 IMINT in June, July, and August 1962, JFKL; *FRUS, 1961-63*, vol. XI, *Cuban Missile Crisis and Aftermath* Doc 34: Minutes of the 505th Meeting of the National Security Council, October 20, 1962.

30. For Castro and willingness to die in a nuclear war, see Khrushchev Fund, F.52 O. 1 D.600, *Remarki Khrushcheva pered diktovkoy pi'ma F. Kastro k okonchaniyu kubinskogo krizisa (30 oktyabrya 1962)* ["Khrushchev's remarks before dictating the letter of F. Castro to the end of the Cuban crisis (October 30, 1962)"], RGANI; Getchell, *The Cuban Missile Crisis and the Cold War*, pp. 151–53; Ball, *The Past Has Another Pattern*, pp. 288; Perry, *My Journey at the Nuclear Brink*, p. 1; "Editorial Note," in *Cuba, January 1961–September 1962*, vol. 10 of *FRUS, 1961–1963*. On Dobrynin's ignorance of the missiles, see *In Confidence*, pp. 74–75. On Kennedy keeping his cool, also see Oral History Program, Lord Harlech (William David Ormsby-Gore) interview, March 2, 1965, p. 16, JFKL. The intensity of Kennedy's schedule is highlighted by Suri, *The Impossible Presidency*, pp. 196–205.

31. "Funnel: Project Involving the Forwarding of Special Cuban Traffic," September 12, 1962, USG-NSA; "NSA and the Cuban Missile Crisis," May 1998, p. 12, reproducing memo: Director, Gordon Blake, NSA director, to assistant director of production, John Davis, Memorandum "Appreciation," November 28, 1962, USG-NSA; Johnson, *American Cryptology*, book 2, p. 325.

32. Ormsby-Gore to Prime Minister (Top Secret enciphered), October 22, 1962, "Cuban Missile Crisis: Contacts between John F. Kennedy, President of the USA, and Harold Macmillan, UK Prime Minister," FO 598/29, TNA.

33. Oral History Program, Chester Cooper interview no. 2, May 16, 1966, p. 24, JFKL; "Situation in Cuba," British Washington embassy to Foreign Office, October 22, 1962, PREM 11/3689, TNA; Lord Harlech (William David Ormsby-Gore) interview, p. 15, JFKL; "Ms Macmillan Dep C.950," Macmillan to Kennedy, October 22, 1962, BOD; telegram 222308Z from the White House to Rusk, October 22, 1962, *FRUS, 1961–1963, American Republics, Cuba 1961–62, Cuban Missile Crisis and Aftermath*, vols. 10/12, *Microfiche Supplement*, Doc. 365; Lankford, *The Last American Aristocrat*, pp. 307–308, says that when Bruce met Acheson off his flight, Bruce produced a gun and bottle of whiskey; Sherman Kent, "The Cuban Missile Crisis of 1962: Presenting the Photographic Evidence Abroad," *Studies in Intelligence* 16 (1972): 19–42. Thorpe, *Alec Douglas-Home*, p. 240.

34. Robert Donovan, "Navy Prepared to Sink Ships—If Necessary: JFK Orders Cuba Blockade; If Castro Looses Rockets, U.S. Will Strike at Soviets; Soviet Convoy on Way, Will be Intercepted," *Boston Globe*, October 23, 1962.

35. National Security Files, box 315, Ex Comm meeting number 3, October 24, 1962, JFKL, for reports coming in that ships had stopped; NSA Oral History Juanita Moody, June 16, 1994, [4310433], pp. 38–39, https://media.defense.gov/2021/Jul/15/2002763502/-1/-1/0/NSA-OH-1994-32-MOODY.PDF.

36. "U.S. Makes Clear: Blockade Stays Till Reds Dismantle Cuba Missiles: U.S. Shows Photos to U.N., Russians Say They're Forged," *Boston Globe*, October 26, 1962.

37. Johnson, *American Cryptology*, book 2, p. 329; Hastings, *Abyss*, chapters 7, 9; Fursenko and Naftali, *Krushchev's Cold War*, pp. 484–86; Rusk, *As I Saw It*, p. 237, for his famous phrase; Serov, *Zapiski iz chemodana*, pp. 568–69, notes that he did not attend meetings of the presidium.

38. Philip Zelikow, "The Dangers of Backchannels," *American Interest* (June 7, 2017). For subsequent increases in KGB collection tacitly admitting previous failures, see MITN 1/6/3 and MITN 1/6/4, CHAC. For targeting of the White House under Khrushchev but failure to recruit agents there, see MITN 1/6/5, CHAC. "Aleksandr Feklisov: Spy Handler for the KGB," obituary, *Independent*, December 8, 2007. Serov claims to have run a source in the State Department (Serov, *Zapiski iz chemodana*), but that source did not have access to ExComm; Fursenko and Naftali, *One Hell of a Gamble*, p. 258; Fursenko and Naftali, "Soviet Intelligence in the Cuban Missile Crisis," *Intelligence and National Security* 13 (1998): p. 65.

39. Oral History Program, Robert Kennedy interview no. 1, February 29, 1964, pp. 67, 70, JFKL; Pierre Salinger, "Memo for the Record," October 4, 1961, Pierre Salinger Papers, box 173; Beschloss, *The Crisis Years*, p. 156; Naftali and Forsenko, *One Hell of a Gamble*.

40. Freedman, *Kennedy's Wars*, p. 53; Andrew, *For the President's Eyes Only*, pp. 278–79; Beschloss, *The Crisis Years*, pp. 255, 280; Salinger, *With Kennedy*, p. 198, for CIA's warnings about Bolshakov; on Robert Kennedy and disclosure of classified U.S. intelligence to Bolshakov, see Voorhees, *The Silent Guns of Two Octobers*, p. 59; Georgi Bolshakov, "The Hot Line," *New Times* nos. 4, 5, 6 (1989). Arthur Schlesinger recalled that Bolshakov "seemed to us all an honest fellow": Schlesinger, *A Thousand Days*, p. 820; Oral History Program, Robert Kennedy history interview no. 1, February 29, 1964, p. 71 and McGeorge Bundy oral interview RFK no.1, December 1, 1972, JFKL.

41. My narrative here follows Zelikow, "The Dangers of Backchannels."

42. For missile swap message, see Khrushchev message to Kennedy (14:00 Moscow time), October 27, 1962, Papers of President Kennedy, National Security Files, box 316, JFKL. For Khrushchev's claim of defensive missiles, see CIA US embassy, Moscow to Secretary of State, translating message from Khrushchev to Kennedy, October 23, 1962, *FRUS, 1961–63*, vol. 6, *Kennedy Khrushchev Exchanges*; James Reston, "Soviet Shift Poses a Mystery for U.S.: U.S. Is Perplexed by Soviet Moves," *New York Times*, October 28, 1962; Kennedy, *Thirteen Days*, pp. 81–83.

43. Zelikow, "The Dangers of Backchannels." For comment "shit his pants," see Barrass, *The Great Cold War*, p. 143. On Khrushchev backing down, see Dobbs, *One Minute to Midnight*, pp. 321–324; for Bolshakov and RFK meeting in his car, see Bolshakov "Hot Line" no. 6; on the idea of a Turkey missile swap, but apparently nothing more than an idea, as far as the British were concerned, see Oral History Program, interview with Lord Harlech (William David Ormsby-Gore), March 12, 1965, p. 49, JFKL; for Bundy quote, see Bundy, *Danger and Survival*, p. 434. For Kennedy's preceding consideration of removing missiles from Turkey, see RFK Papers, box 193, CIA Intelligence Coverage of Foreign Countries, Caribbean Survey Group (MONGOOSE), Central Intelligence Directive, Watch Committee of USIB, section 1, JFKL; Kennedy, *Thirteen Days*, p. 83, carefully glosses over Kennedy's secret undertaking to remove missiles from Turkey. Sorensen, who edited the account by Robert Kennedy posthumously, later said that he took out the Turkey missile swap. Sorensen in Ally, Blight, and Welch, *Back to the Brink*; Beschloss, *The Crisis Years*, p. 536.

44. Feklisov, *The Man Behind the Rosenbergs*, p. 378; Fursenko and Naftali, *Khrushchev's Cold War*, pp. 484–86; Semichastny, *Spetssluzhby SSSR v taynoy voyne*, p. 183. For Feklisov and Scali, see Fursenko and Naftali, *One Hell of a Gamble*, chap. 12.

45. Zubok, *A Failed Empire*, p. 148; Svetlana Savranskaya, "New Sources on the Role of Soviet Submarines in the Cuban Missile Crisis," *Journal of Strategic Studies* 28 (2005): pp. 233–59.

46. For Khrushchev's victory speech, see Khrushchev's speech to the Supreme Soviet, December 28, 1962, "Foreign Policy: Aftermath of the Cuban Missile Crisis," FO 371/171934, TNA. Mikoyan was dispatched to Cuba after the crisis to assuage Castro's criticism that Khrushchev conceded to Kennedy: *Telegramma A.I.Alekseyeva v MID SSSR o besede A.I.Mikoyana s F.Kastro, O.Dortikosom, R.Kastro, E.Gevara, E.Aragonesom i K.R.Rodrigesom*, November 4, 1962, GWU NSA. The SALT II Treaty was signed but never ratified: see Doc. 9, NFAC/ORPA Memorandum for Director, December 21, 1961, in Haines and Leggett, eds., *CIA's Analysis of the Soviet Union*, p. 67.

PART 4: THE CLASH OF EMPIRES INTRODUCTION

1. For the Churchill liquidation quote, see Clarke, *The Last Thousand Days of the British Empire*, p. xvii; Hamilton, *The Mantle of Command: FDR at War*, pp. 206, 209.

2. For Eisenhower's receipt of U-2 intelligence during the Suez crisis, see Gregory W. Pedlow and Donald E. Welzenbach, "The CIA and the U-2 Program 1954–1974," CIA History Staff (1998), pp. 112–19; Nikolai Leonov, "Soviet Intelligence in Latin America during the Cold War" (lecture, Centro de Estudios Públicos, September 22, 1998), https://jeffersonamericas.org/wp-content/uploads/2020/08/Leonov00.pdf; Kirpichenko, *Razvedka*, p. 46. For U.S. intelligence and the Suez crisis, see "The Suez Crisis: A Brief Comint History" [DOICD: 4165421], pp. 16–20, USG-NSA; "Britain East of Suez," June 18, 1965 [CIA-RDP79-00927A004900070004-0], CIA CREST; SNIE 30-4-56 "Probable Repercussions of British-French Action in the Suez Crisis," September 5, 1956 [CIA-RDP79R01012A007400030001-8], CIA CREST; Prados, "The Central Intelligence Agency and the Face of Decolonization under the Eisenhower Administration," in Statler and Johns, eds., *The Eisenhower Administration*, p. 37. For KGB and Egypt, through legal and illegal *rezidentury*, one of which was code-named EAGLE in the 1960s, see MITN 1/6/5, CHAC. For MI6 and CIA plans for a coup in Syria, including false flags, see Matthew Jones, "The 'Preferred Plan': The Anglo-American Working Group Report on Covert Action in Syria, 1957," *Intelligence and National Security* 19 (2004): 401–415.

3. On Lenin and Stalin's interest (but little more) in using Soviet intelligence in the British empire, see "Walter Krivitsky," s.20a, January 30, 1940, KV 2/804, TNA. On Khrushchev at the UN, see FO 371/153638, TNA, "15th Session of UN General Assembly" (1960), s.22912/153, and "Reflections on Mr. Khrushchev's Attendance at the Fifteenth General Assembly," November 12, 1960; Taubman, *Khrushchev*, p. 12; Leonov, *Likhole'ye*; Friedman, *Shadow Cold War*, p. 127. For the Cold War and the Third World, see Westad, *The Global Cold War*; Lüthi, *Cold Wars*; Friedman, *Ripe for Revolution*. For active measures, see MITN 1/6/5, CHAC.

4. Primakov, *Ocherki ob Istorii Vneshnei Razvedki*, vol. 5, p. 372.

5. New light has been cast on the CIA and MI6's coup in Iran with the declassification, in 2017, of a tranche of State Department records: *FRUS, 1952–1954, Iran 1952–1954*; Menand, *The Free World*; Osgood, *Total Cold War*, pp. 113–26; Robert McClure to C. D. Jackson, September 14, 1953, Jackson's Papers, box 73, File "Robert McClure," DDEL; Takeyh, *The Last Shah*, pp. 104–14; Burleigh, *Small Wars, Faraway Places*, pp. 269–74.

6. Records of White House Office of the Staff Secretary Cabinet Series, box 2, file folder C-16 (1), July 9, 1954, DDEL; Oral History Program, Richard Bissell Jr. interview, June 5, 1967, pp. 15–17, DDEL; Nicholas Cullather, "Operation PBSUCCESS: The United States and Guatemala 1952–1954," CIA CREST. The classic account of Guatemala remains Schlesinger and Kinzer, *Bitter Fruit*; Max Holland, "Operation PBHISTORY: The Aftermath of SUCCESS," *International Journal of Intelligence and Counterintelligence* 17 (2004): 300–32; LaFeber, *Inevitable Revolutions*, pp. 120–27. On a corporatist approach to John Foster Dulles's foreign policy from his time in private practice—and that of his brother, Allen—see Immerman, *John Foster Dulles*, p. 276; Burleigh, *Small Wars, Faraway Places*, p. 274.

7. Chamberlin, *The Cold War's Killing Fields*, pp. 556–57. The problems of the NAM, its lack of "glue" to stick its members together, have been examined by Lüthi, "The Non-Aligned: Apart from and Still within the Cold War," in Mišković, Fischer-Tiné, and Boškovska, eds., *The Non-Aligned Movement and the Cold War*, pp. 106–7; Willetts, *The Non-Aligned Movement*. On Sino-Soviet competition in the Third World, see Brazinsky, *Winning the Third World*, pp. 169–73; for Soviet defense against Maoist encroachment in Africa, see, for example, F.5 O.50 D. 603, pp. 65–75, RGANI: *Pi'mo v TSK KPSS ot zaveduyushchego 2-m afrikanskim otdelom MID SSSR M. Sytenko s napravleniyem pi'ma Posla SSSR v Gane G.M. Rodionova o rabote Poso'stva po razoblacheniyu podryvnoy rasko'nicheskoy deyate'osti rukovodstva Kitaya i spravka poso'stva «O formakh i metodakh raboty predstaviteley KNR v Gane»*, May 29, 1964.

CHAPTER 11: RED HEAT

1. Richard Nixon, "Conversation with Castro," Pre-Presidential Papers, Robert E. Cushman, files PPS 325, April 19, 1959, RNL; Oral History Program, Richard Bissell Jr. interview, June 5, 1967, p. 32, DDEL. This chapter's title owes inspiration to Alex von Tunzelmann's excellent eponymous study, *Red Heat*.

2. The best account of the KGB in Latin America is Andrew and Mitrokhin, *The Mitrokhin Archive*, vol. 2, *The World Was Going Our Way*, chaps. 3 and 4; Leonov, *Likhole'ye*, pp. 55–58; see also Sutherland, *From Moscow to Cuba and Beyond*, pp. 126–27; "Memorandum of Discussion at the 435th Meeting of the National Security Council, Washington," February 18, 1960, *FRUS, 1958–1960*, vol. 6, *Cuba*.

3. Andrew and Mitrokhin, *The Mitrokhin Archive*, vol. 2, *The World Was Going Our Way*, pp. 34–35; MITN 2/22 [envelope K-22], CHAC; Primakov, *Ocherki ob Istorii Vneshnei Razvedki*, vol. 5, pp. 233–34; Leonov, *Likhole'ye*, pp. 29–33.

4. Eisenhower to Macmillan, August 8, 1960, "Exchanges between President Eisenhower and Prime Minister Harold Macmillan on Cuba," CAB 301/158, TNA; "Letter from President Eisenhower to Prime Minister Macmillan," July 11, 1961, *FRUS, 1958–1960*, vol. 6, *Cuba*. Anti-communist

Arizona senator Barry Goldwater was a sustained target of Soviet active measures: MITN 1/6/5, CHAC; Burleigh, *Small Wars, Faraway Places*.

5. Andrew, *For the President's Eyes Only*, pp. 262–67.

6. Kornbluh, ed., *Bay of Pigs Declassified*, pp. 8–10; Roselli is also spelled "Rosselli." Sam Giancana is sometimes found with his first name Salvatore, and Santo sometimes spelled Santos. "CIA Policy Paper re Cuba," March 17, 1960, containing a paper "A Program of Covert Action against the Castro Regime," Eisenhower Office of Staff, Secretary International Series, box no. 4 file, DDEL. Eisenhower laid out his policy toward Cuba: to create conditions that would "bring home to the Cuban people the cost of Castro's policies." See Eisenhower to Macmillan, July 11, 1960, "Exchanges between President Eisenhower and Prime Minister Macmillan 1960," CAB 301/158, TNA; Kessler, *Inside the CIA*.

7. Oral History Program, Richard Bissell interview, February 25, 1967, p. 30, JFKL; Oral History Program, Dean Rusk interview, February 19, 1970, p. 19, JFKL; May and Neustadt, *Thinking in Time*, p. 1.

8. One of the prominent voices against a paramilitary invasion of Cuba was Arthur Schlesinger, who favored a surgical strike: Schlesinger, memorandum for president, April 5, 1961, Papers of Arthur Schlesinger, box WH31b, JFKL; Johnson, *The Third Option*, p. 100.

9. For CIA "self-delusion" about the Bay of Pigs, see Oral History Program, Richard Bissell Jr. interview, June 5, 1967, p. 24, JFKL; Tad Szulc, "Anti-Castro Units Trained to Fight at Florida Bases," *New York Times*, April 7, 1961; Hollander, *Political Pilgrims*, pp. 262–67; Andrew, *For the President's Eyes Only*, p. 262–67; Tunzelmann, *Red Heat*, pp. 252–53; Bowles, *Promises to Keep*, p. 392.

10. Burleigh, *Small Wars, Faraway Places*, p. 440; Andrew, *For the President's Eyes Only*, p. 266.

11. Burleigh, *Small Wars, Faraway Places*, p. 438; U.S. Senate, *Alleged Assassination Plots Involving Foreign Leaders*, 94th Cong., 1st sess., Nov. 20, 1975. p. 84.

12. Papers of Robert F. Kennedy, Attorney General Papers, box 215, JFKL: Excomm meeting RFK notes and memos, RFK Notes (10:00 a.m. Meeting), October 25, 1962; "Notes on Cuba Crisis," October 26, 1962; handwritten notes, July 11, 1961. For MONGOOSE plans after Bay of Pigs, see, for example, James Symington to Robert Kennedy, "Meeting in Lansdale's Office," Robert F. Kennedy Papers, Attorney General's Confidential Papers, box 211, July 10, 1962, JFKL. For Lansdale on counterinsurgency, see Boot, *The Road Not Taken*; Halberstam, *The Best and the Brightest*, pp. 124–29, and Beschloss, *The Crisis Years*, p. 375; for Camelot, see Burleigh, *Small Wars, Faraway Places*, p. 431; Hersh, *The Dark Side of Camelot*.

13. On RFK's meetings of MONGOOSE during the Cuban Missile Crisis, see Robert F. Kennedy Papers, Attorney General's Confidential File, JFKL: box 211, "Memorandum for the Record: Minutes of the Special Group (Augmented) on Operation MONGOOSE," October 26, 1962, and "Special Group (Augmented)," October 16, 1962; and box 208, John McCone to Robert Kennedy, October 30, 1962, "John McCone" folder; "Summary Record of NSC Ex Comm Meeting No. 6," October 26, 10:00 a.m., Presidential Papers, National Security File, box 316, JFKL; "16 October (Tuesday) (Acting DCI)" [CIA-RDP80B01676R001700180046-7], CIA CREST. For continuation of MONGOOSE, see Memorandum for Discussion of Covert Program against Cuba, April 7, 1964, National Security File, Country File "Latin America—Cuba," box 24, LBJL; Oral History Project, Ray Cline interview no. 2, October 3, 1985, p. 2, LBJL; George W. Ball, "JFK's Big Moment," *New York Review of Books*, February 13, 1992; GWU NSA Briefing Book 687, John Prados and Arturo Jimenez-Bacardi, eds., *Kennedy and Cuba: Operation MONGOOSE*, October 3, 2019.

14. Burleigh, *Day of the Assassins*, chap. 7, pp. 193–198; Schorr, *Staying Tuned*, p. 276.

15. Churchill to Lyttelton, May 2, 1953, "Suspension of Constitution in British Guiana and Declaration of a State of Emergency," PREM 11/827, TNA; House of Commons, Hansard, "British Guiana," vol. 518, col. 2186, October 22, 1953; for MI5's assessment that neither Jagan nor his party, the PPP, were controlled or directed by the outside communist influence, see Security Liaison Officer

(name withheld), Port of Spain, Trinidad (who at the time had jurisdiction over British Guiana for British security intelligence), January 18, 1951, s.45a "Cheddi and Janet Jagan," KV 2/3600, TNA; also Millicent Bagot [MI5] to C. G. Costley-White, Commonwealth Relations Office, November 16, 1953, "Cheddi and Janet Jagan," KV 2/3608, TNA; Drayton, "Anglo-American 'Liberal' Imperialism," in Louis, ed., *Yet More Adventures in Britannia*. For Kennedy and Jagan's meeting, see Schlesinger, *A Thousand Days*, pp. 776–77. For sympathetic treatment of Kennedy regarding Jagan, see Dallek, *An Unfinished Life*, pp. 440–41.

16. [Envelope K-9] MITN 2/10, CHAC; Jan Koura and Robert Waters, " 'They Are as Businesslike on That Side of the Iron Curtain as They Are on This': Czechoslovakia and British Guiana," in Muehlenbeck and Telepneva, eds., *Warsaw Pact Intervention in the Third World*, pp. 74–94.

17. Sources for the preceding two paragraphs are drawn from: U. Alexis Johnson memorandum for Arthur Schlesinger Jr., October 4, 1961, Papers of President Kennedy, National Security File Regional Security, box 228, JFKL; "Report of Anglo-American Working Party," September 1961, Ibid.; message to Prime Minister Macmillan from President, July 11, 1963, Papers of President Kennedy, National Security File, Countries [United Kingdom], box 174, JFKL; U. Alexis Johnson to Arthur Schlesinger, August 29, 1961, Arthur Schlesinger Papers, box White House 27, JFKL; Macmillan, minute on Rusk to Home, February 19, 1962, Dean Rusk to Lord Home, February 20, 1962, and Lord Home to Dean Rusk, February 28, 1962, PREM 11/3666, TNA; telegram from the Department of State to the Embassy in the United Kingdom, February 19, 1962, and "Letter from Foreign Secretary Home to Secretary of State Rusk," February 26, 1962, in *FRUS, 1961–1963*, vol. 12, *American Republics*; Catterall, ed., *The Macmillan Diaries*, vol. 2, pp. 500, 578.

18. Memorandum from the President's Special Assistant (Schlesinger) to the Ambassador to the United Kingdom (Bruce), February 27, 1962, Arthur Schlesinger Jr. Papers, White House Papers, box 27, JFKL; London (David Bruce) to Secretary of State, September 7, 1961, and memo, Schlesinger to U. Alexis Johnson, September 7, 1961, Arthur Schlesinger Jr. Papers, White House Papers, box 27, JFKL; Shepherd, *Iain Macleod*, p. 239, for Macleod's meeting with Kennedy about Jagan in the White House in 1961.

19. SNIE 87.2 62 "The Situation and Prospects in British Guiana," CIA CREST (also found in *FRUS, 1961–1963*, vol. 12, *American Republics*); McGeorge Bundy memorandum for president, July 13, 1962, National Security File, Staff Memoranda, Ralph Dungan, box 391, folder "British Guiana, 6/1/1962–8/15/1962," JFKL; Palmer, *Cheddi Jagan and the Politics of Power*, pp. 247–48.

20. Weiner, *Legacy of Ashes*, p. 192; McGeorge Bundy to Schlesinger, September 19, 1962, Arthur Schlesinger Jr. Papers, White House Papers box 27, JFKL; Oral History Program, William David Ormsby-Gore (Lord Harlech) interview, March 12, 1965, p. 46, JFKL; "Editorial Note," in *FRUS, 1964–1968*, vol. 32, *Dominican Republic; Cuba; Haiti; Guyana*; Rabe, *U.S Intervention in British Guiana*, pp. 75–103. For Macmillan's winds-of-change speech: Macmillan, Appendix One: "Address by Harold Macmillan to Members of Both Houses of the Parliament of the Union of South Africa, Cape Town, 3 February 1960," in *Pointing the Way*; Hyam and Louis, eds., *British Documents on the End of Empire Project: The Conservative Government and the End of Empire*, doc. [32] DO 35/10570, no. 3., address by Mr. Macmillan, February 3, 1960; for Macmillan and acceleration of decolonization in Africa, see Hennessy, *Having It So Good*, pp. 600–602.

21. Macmillan to Kennedy, May 30, 1963, Presidential Papers, National Security File, box 174a, folder 21, JFKL. McCone to Arthur Schlesinger attaching note, June 11, 1962, Arthur Schlesinger Jr. Papers, White House Papers box 27, JFKL; Drayton, "Anglo-American 'Liberal' Imperialism."

22. For the reversal of MI5's previous non-alarmist assessments, see "Note for File," March 17, 1961, attaching "An Assessment of the Progressive People's Party (PPP) and Its Leaders," s.1311a "Cheddi and Janet Jagan," KV 23638, TNA; "Security Liaison Officer's Reports: British Guiana," CO 1035/173, TNA; JIC915/63 "Economic Aid to British Guiana," December 30, 1963, and JIC(64)34 (Revised Draft), "The Outlook for British Guiana," August 14, 1964, both of which can be

found in "Threat to the Security of British Guiana," CO 1035/285, TNA; Harry Hoffman, Economic Development Mission to British G, to Ralph Dungan, White House, June 1, 1962, Arthur Schlesinger Jr. Papers, White House Papers box 27, JFKL.

23. "PM Home Visit," February 1964, and "Meetings with Walker," February 1964, National Security File, Country File "Europe and USSR—United Kingdom," LBJL. On Burnham rigging elections and LBJ's flowers, see Thomas Karamessines, DDP, to Walt Rostow, June 12, 1968, National Security File, Country File "Latin America—British Guiana," box 56, LBJL. Tim Wiener, "A Kennedy-C.I.A. Plot Returns to Haunt Clinton," *New York Times*, October 30, 1994.

24. Kristian Gustafson and Christopher Andrew, "The Other Hidden Hand: Soviet and Cuban Intelligence in Allende's Chile," *Intelligence and National Security* 33 (2018): 407–421; Gustafson, *Hostile Intent*; [Envelope K-22] MITN 2/22, CHAC; Leonov, *Likholet'ye*, pp. 65–66; Jack Devine, "What Really Happened in Chile," *Foreign Affairs*, July/August, 2014.

25. Gordon Chase memorandum for Bundy, August 25, 1964, National Security File, Country File "Latin America," box 21, s.6, LBJL; J. N. Henderson, September 13, 1962, and G. S. McWilliam, September 24, 1962, "SPA [Special Political Action] in Chile," FCO 168/674, TNA; [Envelope K-9] MITN 2/10, CHAC; Grow, *U.S. Presidents and Latin American Interventions*, p. 97; Rory Cormac, "The Currency of Covert Action: British Special Political Action in Latin America, 1961–64," *Journal of Strategic Studies* 45 (2020); "Chile 1964: CIA Covert Support in Frei Election Detailed; Operational and Policy Records Released for First Time," September 27, 2004, GWU NSA.

26. Gustafson and Andrew, "The Other Hidden Hand"; [Envelope K-9] MITN 2/10, CHAC; Nikolai Alekseev, "Podeba levykh sil na prezidentskikh v Chili," September 27, 1970, F.5 O.62 D.565, RGANI; and from the diary of Soviet ambassador to Chile, A. Anikin, January 11, 1966, F.5 O.50 D.764 67, RGANI; Church Committee, *Alleged Assassination Plots*, pp. 228–232. Harmer, *Allende's Chile and the Inter-American Cold War*, pp. 56–64; Haslam, *The Nixon Administration and the Death of Allende's Chile*, pp. 61–62.

27. Nixon, *The Memoirs*, p. 489; "Chile Wrap-Up and Post-Mortem," March 1971, esp. Viron P. Vacky, "Memorandum," March 25, 1970, and Viron P. Vaky, "Memo for Dr Kissinger," June 22, 1970, National Security Council Files, Henry A. Kissinger Office Files, Country Files—Latin America, RNL.

28. Church Committee Helms memo, September 15, 1970, in exhibit 2, *Covert Action: Hearings before the Select Committee to Study Governmental Operations* 94 Congress 1 Session, vol. 7, December 4 and 5, 1975, p. 96; Haslam, *The Nixon Administration and the Death of Allende's Chile*, p. 65, notes that between 1970 and 1973, the U.S. government spent at least $10 million on destabilizing the Allende government. "CIA, Notes on Meeting with the President of Chile, September 15, 1970," GWU NSA; [Envelope K-9] MITN 2/10, CHAC. For MI6 special political action, see "Recipient of IRD Material in Chile—La Prensa," FCO 168/6388, TNA.

29. [Envelope K-9] MITN 2/10, CHAC; Alexander Basov conversation with Salvador Allende, November 15, 1971, p. 89, F.5 O.63 D.736, RGANI; figures quoted about Soviet officials are taken from NIE 80/90-71 "The Soviet Role in Latin America," April 29, 1971, Senior Review Group Meetings, box H-059, file "SRG Meeting—Latin America," National Security Council Institutional (H) Files, RNL.

30. Gustafson and Andrew, "The Other Hidden Hand"; Jack Devine, "What Really Happened in Chile." "However unpleasant they act," Kissinger said about Pinochet, "the government is better for us than Allende." For figures for killings and deaths in Pinochet's Chile, see "Chile Recognizes 9,800 More Victims of Pinochet's Rule," BBC News, August 18, 2011; Kornbluh, *The Pinochet File*.

31. Ehrlichman, *Witness to Power*, pp. 300–302; Haldeman, *The Ends of Power*, pp. 110–13; Andrew, *For the President's Eyes Only*, pp. 377–79; Sullivan, *The Bureau*, pp. 235–37; Schorr, *Clearing the Air*.

32. The "most powerful" quote from Andrew, *For the President's Eyes Only*, p. 396; Dobrynin, *In Confidence*, pp. 265–66; Chang and Halliday, *Mao*, p. 583.

33. LaFeber, *Inevitable Revolutions*, pp. 296–99; Johnson, *The Third Option*, pp. 123–131; Treverton,

Covert Action, pp. 222–33; Baker and Glasser, *The Man Who Ran Washington*, pp. 269–70; Brands, *Latin America's Cold War*, p. 200, for CIA training of the Contras.

CHAPTER 12: SUNNY PLACES, SHADY PEOPLE

1. Shelepin was youthful compared to other KGB chiefs. Primakov, O*cherki ob Istorii Vneshnei Razvedki*, vol. 5, pp. 410–11; *Doklad sovetskoy delegatsii na 2-y konferentsii solidarnosti narodov Azii i Afriki*, F.5, O.50, D.273, April 28, 1960, pp. 19–30, RGANI. For KGB in Africa, see MITN 1/6/5, CHAC; Attwood, *The Reds and the Blacks*, pp. 17–18.

2. The slow approach of MI6 toward Africa was revealed in a tour of sub-Saharan Africa by a senior MI6 officer, setting out what contributions the service "might make" there in the future: Norman Brooke [cabinet secretary] to Prime Minister [Macmillan], December 16, 1959, forwarding the MI6 report "Notes on a Visit to Africa," PREM 11/2585, TNA.

3. Brendon, *The Decline and Fall of the British Empire*, p. 517.

4. Matera, *Black London*, pp. 220–37.

5. Nkrumah, *Ghana*, p. 63; "Tele-Check CPGB Headquarters," January 1, 1948 [s.33ab], and Sir Percy Sillitoe to R. W. H. Ballantine, Commissioner of Police, Gold Coast, January 28, 1948 [s.39a] "Kwame Nkrumah," KV 2/1847, TNA.

6. "Personality Note" June 1948, s.61b KV 2/1847, TNA; "Extract from SLO West Africa Report on Meeting with the New Governor of the Gold Coast," September 13, 1949, s.115a KV 2/1848, TNA. See also Rathbone, ed., *British Documents on the End of Empire Project: Ghana*, doc. [85], CO 537/5263, FO Research Department, "A Survey of Communism in Africa," June 1950; H. Loftus-Brown to Juxon Barton, Colonial Office, June 3, 1953, s.285a KV 2/185, TNA; "A Survey of Communism in Africa," August 1950, DO 231/124, TNA.

7. Sir John Shaw, January 1, 1952, minute 209, and SLO [MI5 liaison officer] West Africa to Director-General, s.245a, September 24, 1952, "Kwame Nkrumah," KV 2/1850, TNA.

8. H. Loftus-Brown, "Note for File," October 15, 1952, s.247a, and Sir John Shaw, December 1, 1952, minute 261, "Kwame Nkrumah," KV 2/1850, TNA. Hyam, *Britain's Declining Empire*, p. 149; "Rigging Nigeria," BBC Radio 4, July 30, 2007, *File on Four*, Mike Thompson, presenter.

9. For Nkrumah's lurch to the left after independence, see Rooney, *Kwame Nkrumah*, pp. 169ff; Mazov, *A Distant Front in the Cold War*, pp. 201–210; Muehlenbeck, *Czechoslovakia in Africa*, pp. 103–4.

10. Burleigh, *Small Wars, Faraway Places*, pp. 399–400; for the influence of China, rather than the Soviet Union, in sub-Saharan Africa, see Norman Brooke [cabinet secretary] to Prime Minister [Macmillan], December 16, 1959, forwarding MI6 report, "Notes on a Visit to Africa," PREM 11/2585/, TNA.

11. Rooney, *Kwame Nkrumah*, p. 226; Scott, *Seeing like a State*; Burleigh, *Small Wars, Faraway Places*.

12. J. B. Ure Minute, February 22, 1965, and correspondence between High Commission in Accra and Costley-White [Commonwealth Relations Office], "Ghana Leaflets," FCO 168/1858, TNA. On approaches to British officials, see "Ghana—1965–1969," PREM 13/2677, TNA; for CIA covert action against Nkrumah, author interview with former CIA Deputy Director of Operations, June 4, 2005.

13. J. K. Drinkall [IRD] "Ghana Leaflets," FCO 168/1858, TNA; RWK [Kromer] to McGeorge Bundy, May 27, 1965; National Security File, Country File "Latin America—Ghana," box 89, LBJL; Williams, *White Malice*, pp. 491–92. Also see comments by Sherman Kent, "Trends in Ghana," February 14, 1964, found in Robert F. Kennedy Attorney General Papers, box 208, JFKL.

14. For surveillance of Nyerere during independence negotiations in London in 1959, 1960, and 1961, see, for example, J. E. Day, minute 112, June 20, 1959, which shows that Nyerere liaised with someone later established to be a Czech (StB): British MP, John Stonehouse, "Julius Nyerere," KV 2/3889, TNA; s.22a and 22b, October 16, 1959, "Julius Nyerere," KV 2/3892, TNA. James Brennan, "The Secret Lives of Dennis Phombeah: Decolonization, the Cold War, and African

Political Intelligence," *International History Review* 43 (2021). For non-alarmist intelligence on Jomo Kenyatta, based on MI5's periodic surveillance of him in Britain, and its ongoing surveillance of the CPGB, see H. Loftus-Brown to Juxon Barton, colonial office, November 22, 1953, · s.357b "Jomo Kenyatta," KV 2/1788, TNA. For the Czech *rezident* in London, see MITN 1/6/4, CHAC; Wright, *Spycatcher*, p. 58, describes installation of bugs at Lancaster House in 1955. We can establish that Lancaster House was closed for installation of certain "technical installations" between two conferences, which was the same time when Wright claimed he installed bugs: see Webber (colonial office) to L. T. Vergin (conference and supply department), November 22, 1955, p. 160, "Lancaster House Conferences" WORK 12/444, TNA. Furthermore, F. D. Webber can be established as an MI5 officer; see, for example, E. N. Griffith-Jones to F. D. Webber, August 14, 1963, s.6 "Organisation of Intelligence Services in the Colonies—Kenya," CO 1035/187, TNA. For KGB in Kenya post-independence, see [Envelope K-17] MITN 2/17, CHAC. For MI6's role during later independence negotiations, see "Roger Horrell," obituary, *Times*, June 12, 2021. The colonial backgrounds of MI5 officers in the Cold War were illustrated by Patrick Walker, *Towards Independence in Africa*, a district officer in Uganda who later became MI5's director-general.

15. My narrative here owes much to, and follows, Burleigh, *Day of the Assassins*, pp. 133–143; and Charles G. Cogan and Ernest May, "The Congo, 1960–1963: Weighing Worst Choices," in May and Zelikow, eds., *Dealing with Dictators*, pp. 49–87; and Burleigh, *Small Wars, Faraway Places*.

16. This description of Congo follows Burleigh, *Day of the Assassins*, pp. 133–134; Lefever, *Uncertain Mandate*, p. 131; for Conrad's quote, see *Heart of Darkness*, p. 59.

17. Scott, *Tumbled House*, p. 36; Kalb, *The Congo Cables*, p. 53; Thomas, *The Very Best Men*, p. 221; L. D. Battle to Ralph Dugan, March 9, 1961, pp. 28–23, Papers of President Kennedy, National Security File, Countries [Congo], box 27a, JFKL; O'Brien, *To Katanga and Back*, p. 93.

18. For preceding discussion about CIA covert action, see David Robarge, "CIA's Covert Operations in the Congo, 1960–1968: Insights from Newly Declassified Documents," *Studies in Intelligence* 58 (2014); Mazov, *A Distant Front*, pp. 82–83; Burleigh, *Day of the Assassins*, p. 140; Hayes, *Queen of Spies*, pp. 164–68; Corera, *MI6*, p. 99.

19. Kalb, *The Congo Cables*, p. 53.

20. Oral History Program, Richard Bissell Jr. interview, November 9, 1979, pp. 19–23, DDEL; Bissell, *Reflections of a Cold Warrior*, pp. 143–44.

21. Kalb, *The Congo Cables*, pp. 64–65; Mahoney, *JFK: Ordeal in Africa*, p. 73; Eisenhower Papers as President, Ann Whitman File, NSC Series Memorandum of 456th Meeting of NSC, August 18, 1960, DDEL; Minutes of Special Group Meetings, Thomas A. Parrott Memorandum for the Record, September 8, 1960, U.S. National Security Council, Intelligence Files, box 1, DDEL; *Church Committee Interim Report*, pp. 60.

22. Kinzer, *Poisoner in Chief*, p. 175; Kinzer, *The Brothers*, pp. 248–50.

23. Devlin, *Chief of Station, Congo*, pp. 94–99. "Note on U.S. Covert Actions," in *FRUS, 1981–1988*, vol. 6, *Soviet Union, October 1986–January 1989*; Mondale, *The Good Fight*, p. 145; Smith, *Encyclopedia of the Central Intelligence Agency*, p. 76.

24. A similar plan—to get Lumumba's enemies to do the dirty work—was proposed by the British ambassador in the Congo: Ian Scott to Foreign Office, October 10, 1960, "Internal Political Situation" FO 371/146646, TNA; Macmillan, *The Macmillan Diaries*, vol. 2, December 3, 1960, p. 340; Urquhart, *A Life in Peace and War*, p. 157; Brian Urquhart, "Character Sketches: Mobotu and Tshombe—Two Congolese Rogues," *UN News*, n.d. (c. 2016?); Gerard and Kuklick, *Death in the Congo*, pp. 154–55; Stephen R. Weissman, "Opening the Secret Files on Lumumba's Murder," *Washington Post*, July 21, 2002; U.S. Senate, *Alleged Assassination Plots Involving Foreign Leaders*, 94th Cong., 1st sess., November 20, 1975, p. 45.

25. Smith and Ross minutes, September 28, 1960, "The Congo" FO 371/146650, TNA; "Editorial Note," *FRUS, 1958–1960*, vol. 14, *Africa*, September 21, 1960, p. 497.

26. David Lea, "Letters," *London Review of Books*, April 11, 2013; Hayes, *Queen of Spies*, pp. 164–168.

27. Burleigh, *Day of the Assassins*, p. 142; Wrong, *In the Footsteps of Mr. Kurtz*, pp. 80–81; Hochschild, *King Leopold's Ghost*, p. 301.

28. Kelly, *America's Tyrant*; Meredith, *The Fate of Africa*, p. 302–5; Primakov, *Ocherki ob Istorii Vneshnei Razvedki*, vol. 5, pp. 419–20, 429–40.

29. "*Po voprosu o kompensatsii postavkami iz SSSR Respublike Kuba vooruzheniya, kotoroye mozhet byt*," *Ostavleno Kubinskimi Voyskami v Narodnoy Respublike Angola*, F.89 O.10, D.20, January 31, 1989, pp. 2–3, RGANI; Westad, *The Global Cold War*, pp. 214–15; Isaacson, *Kissinger*, pp. 673–85 (p. 677 for CIA and Soviet influence in Angola); Gleijeses, *Conflicting Missions*, pp. 328–38, for Kissinger and CIA covert action in Angola. For KGB recruitment in third-party countries, see MITN 1/6/5, CHAC; Westad, *The Global Cold War*, pp. 214–15. For the KGB in the Horn of Africa, see Yordanov, *The Soviet Union and the Horn of Africa during the Cold War*, pp. 122–23; Stockwell, *In Search of Enemies*, pp. 19–23; Meredith, *The Fate of Africa*, pp. 148–49.

CHAPTER 13: DOMINOES

1. For Soviet active measures in nonaligned countries and statistics compiled by the KGB, which doubtless exaggerated its influence, see the Mitrokhin Archive (Andrew and Mitrokhin, *The Mitrokhin Archive*, vol. 2, *The World Was Going Our Way*) and MITN 1/6/4, CHAC. For "equality" of Western covert action and Soviet active measures in developing countries, see Primakov, *Ocherki ob Istorii Vneshnei Razvedki*, vol. 5, pp. 414–415.

2. MI6's reports ("CX") from a "delicate and reliable" source, possibly derived from Lindsay, can be found in WO 208/4403, "Chinese Communist Activity in Manchuria" (1946); Susan V. Lawrence, "Hsiao Li Lindsay," obituary, *Guardian*, June 1, 2010; Aldrich, *GCHQ*, p. 151.

3. Dikötter, *Mao's Great Famine*, pp. 324–34.

4. Previously Khrushchev had pledged to Mao his support in the event of a U.S. attack on China: *Zapiska Khrushcheva v Prezidium TSK o podgotovke pi'ma Mao Tszedunu*, F.52 O.1, D.350, p.3, RGANI.

5. Harold P. Ford, "Calling the Sino-Soviet Split," *Studies in Intelligence* 42 (1999); Brinkley and Nichter, eds., *The Nixon Tapes*, entry for May 1, 1972, also given in "Conversation among President Nixon, Secretary of State Rogers, and the President's Assistant for National Security Affairs (Kissinger)," May 1, 1972, document 180, in *FRUS*, vol. 14, *Soviet Union, October 1971–May 1972*; Oral History Project, Ray Cline interview, October 3, 1985, p. 12, LBJL; Pillsbury, *The Hundred-Year Marathon*, p. 24. On ideological differences, see Jian, *Mao's China and the Cold War*, pp. 8–9; Burleigh, *Small Wars, Faraway Places*, pp. 459–60.

6. For Kissinger's breakthrough with China, see Kissinger Memorandum for the President, "My Meeting with Chairman Mao," February 24, 1973, President's Personal File, box 6, file "China," RNL.

7. My telling of Polyakov's case follows Haslam, *Near and Distant Neighbors*, pp. 223–27; Grimes and Vertefeuille, *Circle of Treason*, pp. 27, 30–31; Krasilnikov, *Prizraki s ulitsy Chaykovskogo*, pp. 217–19; Shebarshin, *Ruka Moskvy*.

8. NIE 11/13-69 "The USSR and China" [0001095916], August 12, 1969, CIA CREST. It also appears that China had a spy in Washington: MacMillan, *Nixon in China*, p. 163.

9. On Karamessines and (redacted) intelligence provided to Kissinger, see "Exchanges Leading to HAK's First Trip to China," July 1971, National Security File, box 1031, RNL. On the intelligence shaping Kissinger and Nixon about Sino-Soviet clashes, which "might be an opening we want to explore," see State Department, "Memorandum for the President," October 8, 1969, National Security File, box 384, and President's Daily Briefs, National Security File, box 10, August 19, 1969, RNL; on Kissinger sharing intelligence, see Andrew and Mitrokhin, *The Mitrokhin Archive*, vol. 2, pp. 280–81.

10. For operation CHESTNUT, see Pillsbury, *The Hundred-Year Marathon*, pp. 74–75, and Dillon, *Spies in the Family*, pp. 262–63.

11. Burleigh, *Small Wars, Faraway Places*, p. 456; Logevall, *Embers of War*, pp. 665–66.

12. Halberstam, *The Best and the Brightest*, p. 458, for the contrast of Kennedy's and Johnson's leadership; Bowles, *Promises to Keep*, p. 518; Oral History Project, Clark Clifford interview, May 28, 1971, p. 6, LBJL; Andrew Latham, ed., *Nonproliferation Agreements, Arrangements and Responses: Proceedings of the 1996 Canadian Non-Proliferation Workshop*, p. 187.

13. Oral History Project, Ray Cline interview, October 3, 1985, pp. 21–32, LBJL; McNamara, *In Retrospect*, pp. 275, 292–94.

14. Adams, *War of Numbers*. For pessimism of U.S. bombing campaigns to reduce the will of the North Vietnamese, see "Memorandum: The Vietnamese Communists Will to Persist" [CIA-RDP79T00826A001100010052-6], August 26, 1966, CIA CREST; Oral History Project, Ray Cline interview no. 2, October 3, 1985, p. 21, LBJL; Nitze, *From Hiroshima to Glasnost*, p. 279; Ahern, *Vietnam Declassified*; Logevall, *Embers of War*, p. 364.

15. MITN 1/6/5, CHAC.

16. SNIE 11-13-68 "US Intelligence Capabilities to Monitor Certain Limitations on Soviet Strategic Weapons Programs," July 18, 1968, National Security File, box 11, LBJL. The sensitivity of NTMs is revealed in redactions in British JIC assessments; see, for example, JIC(84)5, "The Detection of Soviet Preparations for War against NATO," June 15, 1984, CAB 186/37, TNA. William P. Clark, "Material Supporting the President's Memorial Day Speech," May 29, 1982, Executive Secretariat, NSC Subject File "Arms Control" [1982], box 5; Niall Ferguson, "Dust Off That Dirty Word Détente and Deal with China," *Bloomberg*, June 5, 2022; Niall Ferguson, "Crisis, What Crisis? The 1970s and the Shock of the Global Order," in Ferguson, Maier, Manela, and Sargent, eds., *The Shock of the Global*, pp. 20–21; Sargent, *A Superpower Transformed*, pp. 131–61; Ford, *A Time to Heal*, pp. 325–28. For Soviet counteractions against U.S. "human rights" campaigns, see *Vypiska iz protokola, Ñň 50 zasedaniya Politbyuro TSK KPSS ot 24 marta 1977 O dal'neyshikh merakh diskreditatsii roli spetssluzhb SSHA v antisovetskoy kampanii o «Pravakh cheloveka»*, F.89, O.25, D.45, pp. 1–4, RGANI.

17. "Soviet Foreign Policy and Détente," October 1973, in same-named file FCO 168/6879, TNA. JIC(A)(69)18 (Final), "Soviet Policy on Disarmament and Arms Control," January 14, 1969, p. 2, CAB 186/2, TNA; Brezhnev and Kissinger, "Memo of Conversation," April 21, 1972, National Security Council Files, Henry A. Kissinger Office, Files, Country Files—Europe USSR, box 73, RNL.

18. For increased numbers of Soviet deep-cover "illegals" sent to the United States during détente, see MITN 1/6/4, CHAC. The flow of scientific and technical intelligence increased from 114 classified materials in 1961 from New York *rezidentura* to 24,000 in 1972: MITN 1/6/3, CHAC; Drozdov, *Zapiski*, pp. 39–40; Brezhnev and Kissinger, "Memo of Conversation," April 21, 1972, National Security Council Files, Henry A. Kissinger Office Files, Country Files—Europe USSR, box 73, RNL; Garthoff, *Détente and Confrontation*, pp. 117–19. On Kissinger's academic pedigree, see Ferguson, *Kissinger: The Idealist*, chapter 7. More broadly, see Mark Kramer, "Ideology and the Cold War," *Review of International Studies* 25 (1999): 539–576; Zubok, *A Failed Empire*, p. 337.

19. "Exports of High Technology End-Items and the Transfer of Technology to the Soviet Union," May 1973, National Security Council Institutional Files NSDMs, box H-244, NSDM 246, RNL; for above comments of U.S. officials, see Gus Weiss, "The Farewell Dossier: Duping the Soviets," CIA CREST.

20. Shevchenko, *Breaking with Moscow*, pp. 282–85. For KGB use of commercial relations during détente, see MITN 1/6/5, CHAC; National Security Council Institutional Files NSDMs, box H-244, NSDM 246, "Exports of High Technology End-Items," RNL; Moynihan, *A Dangerous Place*, pp. ix–x. Victor Rezun (Suvarov), a GRU officer, defected in Geneva in 1978 and disclosed to Britain's MI6 the nature of GRU industrial espionage tasking: Suvarov, *Inside Soviet Military Intelligence*, pp. 35–36.

21. MITN 1/6/3, CHAC.

22. For communism in India, see Frank Roberts (British High Commission New Delhi) to R. R. Sedwick (Commonwealth Relations Office), "Communist Party of India. Change in Policy," July 21, 1950, DO 231/1, TNA.

23. Director of Central Intelligence, "Comments on Memorandum from Ambassador Bowles," May 16, 1964, Papers of Robert Komer, box 26, LBJL; McGarr, *The Cold War in South Asia*, p. 161, for U.S. officials' earlier views of Menon. For Menon and fraternal assistance, see Gromyko, *Memoirs*, pp. 234–35.

24. Indian Security Unit to Colonel Vickery, December 1945, Statement by Nambiar, p. 5, "Arathil Nambiar," KV 2/3904, TNA; "Arathil NAMBIAR," s.27e "Copy of Letter from the American Embassy re. Ruth FISCHER Mentioning NAMBIAR," October 4, 1954, KV 2/3905, TNA. The file description suggests that in 1959, MI5 received intelligence from a defector source that Nambiar had been recruited as a Soviet military intelligence (GRU) agent in the 1920s, but that serial is now missing from his file. For Quit India and Bose, see Harper, *Underground Asia*, pp. 642–43; F.495 O.42 D3, pp. 43–54, 137, 160, 198–199; F.495 O.42 D13, p. 13, RGAPSI.

25. Kalugin, *Spymaster*, p. 141.

26. "Comments on Memorandum from Ambassador Bowles," May 16, 1964, Papers of Robert Komer, Director of Central Intelligence, LBJL. On Indira Gandhi's visit to the Soviet Union ("We had a tremendous time"): Gandhi, *My Truth*, pp. 67–68; MITN 1/6/5 CHAC; Brinkley and Nichter, *The Nixon Tapes, 1971–1972*, p. 312. For U.S. U-2 planes stationed in Pakistan, for example, see Kux, *The United States and Pakistan*, p. 91.

27. JIC(A)(72)33, "Soviet Aims and Influence in India," September 15, 1972, CAB 186/12, TNA; "Soviet Aims in India," July 1972, s.2 FCO 168/6604, TNA; B. E. Cleghorn to J. N. Allan, October 28, 1980, "Soviet Propaganda in India," FCO 168/5986, TNA; "The Soviets in India: Moscow's Major Penetration Program," December 1985 [CIA-RDP86T00586R000400490002-2], CIA CREST; U.S. Department of State, Foreign Affairs note, "Soviet Active Measures: The World Peace Council," April 1985, Kenneth deGraffenreid Papers, RRL; CIA memorandum for Henry Kissinger, "Soviet Military Assistance to India," Kissinger-Scowcroft West Wing Office Files, General Subject, box 13, file "India/Pakistan," December 1971, RNL.

28. MITN 1/4, CHAC; Volkogonov, *Autopsy for an Empire*, p. 281; Volkogonov, *The Rise and Fall of the Soviet Empire*, p. 281. One less sophisticated KGB forgery in India, in 1967, involved Britain's high commissioner, John Freeman, purporting to show that the United States was financing right-wing Indian politicians. In this case, however, the forgery was caught because it referred to him as "Sir" John Freeman, but he was not in fact knighted: Dennis Greenhill circular to Heads of Missions, September 15, 1970, "Soviet Disinformation," FCO 168/6087, TNA; Shebarshin, *Ruka Moskvy*, pp. 74–98. For the long history of Soviet forgeries, see Romerstein and Levchenko, *The KGB against the "Main Enemy,"* chap. 3.

29. The most reliable and detailed research on the CIA in India has been done by Paul McGarr. See, for example, his "Quiet Americans in India: The CIA and the Politics of Intelligence in Cold War South Asia," *Diplomatic History* 38 (2014): 1046–1082. See also Wilford, *The Mighty Wurlitzer*, pp. 84, 241; Lawrence, *The End of Ambition*, p. 174; note, November 1958, "Special Political Action against Communist Front Organisations," DO 231/116, TNA. For IRD work in India, see "India: Progress Report on IRD Work, Visits by Mr P Joy (IRD) to Bombay and Calcutta, Co-Operation with Counter-Propaganda Unit and Press Information Bureau," FO 1110/1698, TNA; C. F. R. Barclay to C. G. Costley-White, "India: Tour by Mr. E Joy (IRD) of South, proposal for Field Officer to Calcutta, book publishing, new 'Fact Sheets,'" FO 1110/1829, TNA. On discrepancies in the book by John Smith [alias?], *I Was a CIA Agent in India*, see "CIA in India," 1967, FCO 168/2649, TNA. For the "Ariel Foundation," see series in FCO 168/1050–1054, TNA; Kux, *India and the United States: Estranged Democracies*, p. 267; Bloch and Fitzgerald, *British Intelligence and Covert Action*, p. 151.

30. For "intrigues" left out of memoirs, see Moynihan, *A Dangerous Place*, p. x; Galbraith, *A Life in Our Times*, p. 395; Madan, *Fateful Triangle*, p. 258.

31. For correction of "rogue elephant," see Clarridge, *A Spy for All Seasons*, p. 159. For KGB (easy) exploitation of revelations by the Church Committee in the Third World (an operation the KGB code-named LEMON, approved by Kryuchkov in January 1977), see MITN 1/6/1 and 1/6/5, CHAC. On Gandhi's beliefs about the CIA plots, see U.S. Embassy New Delhi to Secretary of State, December 30, 1975, Presidential Country Files for the Middle East and South Asia, box 12, "India," GRFL; George Bush, DCI, to Brent Scowcroft, March 31, 1976, Kissinger-Scowcroft West Wing Office Files, Central Intelligence Agency—Communications, box 3, GRFL; Kux, *India and the United States: Estranged Democracies*, p. 339. The CIA was subjected to four separate investigations (plus lawsuits and subpoenas of individuals): its own investigation, led by William Colby; President Gerald Ford's investigation, conducted by his vice president, Nelson Rockefeller (June 1975); the House investigation (eventually known as the Pike Committee, in February 1975); and the Senate investigation (known as the Church Committee, in January 1976). See William Colby to President, December 24, 1974, National Security Adviser, Presidential Agency File, box 3; "Colby Report" file, GRFL; National Security Adviser, Presidential Agency File, box 5, Central Intelligence Agency File, "President's Commission on CIA"; Meyer, *Facing Reality*, pp. 217–19; Shackley, *Spymaster*, p. 76; John M. Crewdson, "Church Doubts Plot Links to Presidents," *New York Times*, July 19, 1975.

32. Vasili Mitrokhin, "The KGB in Afghanistan (updated 2009)," Cold War International History Project working paper 40, pp. 100–102; Braithwaite, *Afgantsy*, pp. 77–81; Solovyov and Klepikova, *Yuri Andropov*, pp. 268–69; Brown, *The Rise and Fall of Communism*, p. 354; Chamberlin, *The Cold War's Killing Fields*, pp. 432–34.

33. All this was predictably denied by Brezhnev at the time—FCO 168/5900 "Soviet Involvement in Afghanistan British High Commission Kuala Lumpur," May 22, 1980—and denied later: Gromyko, *Memoirs*, pp. 239–40. For Sadat and Kissinger, see Indyk, *Master of the Game*, pp. 264–67. For (apparent) KGB advice against Soviet intervention in Afghanistan, see Primakov, *Ocherki ob Istorii Vneshnei Razvedki*, vol. 6, pp. 49–50. For Afghanistan as a short-term mission, see Shebarshin, *Ruka Moskvy*, p. 154. For Soviet claims of fraternal assistance, see Richard Smith, Patrick Salmon, and Stephen Twigge, eds., *The Invasion of Afghanistan and UK-Soviet Relations*, DBPO, series III, vol. 8, doc. 7: "Record of a Meeting between Mrs Thatcher and the Soviet Ambassador (MR LUNKOV) at No. 10 Downing Street," January 3, 1980, pp. 35–39.

34. Satellite IMINT had the code name TALENT/KEYHOLE, which can be found in Brzezinski's communications to U.S. Secretary of State Cyrus Vance: "Soviet Allegations concerning US Role in Afghanistan," March 30, 1979, s.26 National Security Affairs, Brzezinski Material, Country File "Afghanistan," and s.27 Michael Oskenber to Brzezinski, "Afghanistan," JCL. For the code name, see White House Office of the Staff Secretary, Alphabetical Subseries, box 15, "Intelligence Matters," DDEL. For British covert propaganda in Afghanistan, see "Note for file: AFGHAN-ISTAN," March 28, 1980, s.45 "Soviet Involvement in Afghanistan Covert Propaganda by UK and US," FCO 168/5900, TNA; Bird, *The Outlier*, pp. 504–5.

35. Haslam, *Near and Distant Neighbors*, pp. 246–47. On Sheymov's exfiltration, see his memoir, which states it was through Czechoslovakia: *Tower of Secrets*, chap. 12; Krasilnikov, *Prizraki s ulitsy Chaykovskogo*, p. 80.

PART 5: THE CLASH OF REIGNING SUPERPOWERS

CHAPTER 14: THE MAIN ADVERSARY

1. The feeling of goodwill after Chequers was mutual: see Mikhail Gorbachev to Margaret Thatcher, October 12, 1985, "UK Soviet Relations" PREM 19/1647, TNA. For a positive description of Gorbachev ("eminently the right man for the job") by the long-serving and respected Foreign

Office interpreter K. A. (Tony) Bishop, see "Mikhail Gorbachev: A Personal Assessment of the Man during His Visit to the United Kingdom," December 15–20, 1984, PREM 19/1647, TNA; Thatcher Archive, "TV Interview for BBC ('I like Mr Gorbachev. We can do business together')," December 17, 1984, https://www.margaretthatcher.org/document/105592.

2. Moore, *Margaret Thatcher: At Her Zenith*, pp. 233–35; Howe, *Conflict of Loyalty*, p. 349.

3. Andrew, *For the President's Eyes Only*, pp. 457–458.

4. Prados, *William Colby and the CIA*, p. 301.

5. Brands, *The Twilight Struggle*, chapter 7; for CIA budget figures, private information, see Periscoe, *Casey*, pp. 100–102. For alarm caused in Moscow, see, for example, "KGB Report on New Elements in US Policy toward the European Socialist Countries," March 31, 1984, WCDA; Mastny and Byrne, eds., *A Cardboard Castle?*, p. 466. One British official in Washington noted that Reagan's anti-communist rhetoric, as displayed in his Westminster Hall speech in June 1982, had similar crudeness as Marxism: Derek Thomas, British embassy Washington, to Sir Julian Bullard, November 30, 1982, s.1 "Follow Up to President Reagan's Speech—Covert Aspects," FCO 168/6189, TNA. For Casey, see Fischer, *The Reagan Reversal*, pp. 88–90; Brenes, *For Might and Right*, pp. 207–9; Krasilnikov, *Prizraki s ulitsy Chaykovskogo*, chap. 6, pp. 168–189; "The President's News Conference," January 29, 1981, RRL; "Editorial Note," April 16, 1982, in *FRUS*, vol. 3, *Soviet Union, January 1981–January 1983*; Nicholas Dujmovic, "Ronald Reagan, Intelligence, William Casey, and CIA: A Reappraisal," available on CREST.

6. [Name redacted] Memorandum for DCI, "The Soviets and the 1984 US Elections" [CIA-RDP85T00153R000300020043-0], October 28, 1982, CIA CREST; [Name redacted] National Intelligence Officer for USSR, memorandum for DCI and Deputy DCI, through Chairman NIC, "Soviets Playing on US Election" [CIA-RDP86M00886R001000010026-5], August 1, 1984, CIA CREST; John Lenczowski to John Poindexter, "Statement on Soviet Intervention in the U.S. Electoral Process," August 16, 1984, RRL; Jack Matlock Papers, box 22, "USSR—Disinformation/ Deception," RRL. For KGB attempting to find kompromat on Reagan to smear him, see MITN 1/6/5, CHAC; Matlock, *Reagan and Gorbachev*, p. 88.

7. For description of Cray-1, see Johnson, *American Cryptology*, book 3, p. 153; Haslam, *Near and Distant Neighbors*, pp. 235, 244.

8. Cole, *Geoffrey Prime*, chap. 1; *R v. Geoffrey Arthur Prime*, 5 Cr. App. R. (S.) 127 (1983).

9. For preceding discussion of Walker, see Earley, *Family of Spies*; Romerstein and Levchenko, *The KGB Against the "Main Enemy,"* pp. 291–98; Kalugin, *Spymaster*; for the study mentioned, see PERSEREC study "Changes in Espionage by Americans, 1947–2007," Table 10, p. 32.

10. For personal observations of disillusionment within the Soviet Union under Brezhnev, see Kendall, *The Cold War*, p. 255.

11. For KGB archives, see Andrew and Mitrokhin, *The Mitrokhin Archive*, vol. 1, p. 283; Mitterand sent Thatcher a note about FAREWELL in April 1983, evidenced in Thatcher to Mitterand, September 12, 1985, "Soviet Union: UK/Soviet Relations," PREM 19/1647, TNA. The relevant underlying records, however, have not (yet) been declassified. Mitterand also expelled forty-seven Soviet officials from France identified as, or suspected of being, intelligence officers: Expulsion of Soviet Officials: Press and Political Reactions, April 6, 1983, s.42 "Franco-Soviet Relations," FCO 28/5314, TNA. For Line X, see MITN 1/6/4, CHAC; David Hoffman, "Reagan Approved Plan to Sabotage Soviets," *Washington Post*, February 27, 2004; the story of the KGB's hack is described in Stoll, *The Cuckoo's Egg*.

12. Gus W. Weiss, "The Farewell Dossier," CIA CREST; Reed, *At the Abyss*, pp. 266–70; MITN 1/6/3, CHAC.

13. Kostin and Reynaud, *Farewell*, pp. 282–83.

14. Andrew and Gordievsky, *KGB*, p. 598; Andropov Fund, *Proyekt vystupleniya Andropova na soveshchanii konsul'tativnogo soveta stran uchastnits Varshavskogo dogovora*, January 4, 1983, F.82, O.1, D.4,

pp. 1–19, RGANI; *Tekst vystupleniya Andropova na soveshchanii rukovoditeley stran Varshavskogo dogovora*, June 28, 1983, F.82, O.1, D.4, pp. 35–44, RGANI; emphasis on U.S. plans for nuclear war can still be found in official Russian publications, though similar Soviet plans are overlooked: Primakov, *Ocherki ob Istorii Vneshnei Razvedki*, vol. 6, "Introduction"; *Sluzhba Vneshney Razvedki, Rossiyskoy Federatsii 100 let*, p. 222.

15. Andrew and Gordievsky, *KGB*, pp. 588–89, 598–606; Shvets, *Washington Station*, pp. 73–75.

16. Committee for State Security (KGB), "Indicators to Recognise Adverserial Preparations for a Surprise Nuclear Missile Attack," November 26, 1984, WCDA; Garthoff, *Soviet Leaders and Intelligence*, pp. 62–63.

17. Volkogonov, *Autopsy for an Empire*, p. 333. For CIA assessments of Andropov, see the following in the papers of Jack Matlock, Series II, USSR Subject File, box 35, RRL: CIA Directorate of Intelligence, "The Soviet Political Succession: Institutions, People, and Policies," April 20, 1982; "Soviet Leadership in Transition," July 1982; John McMahon to Robert McFarlane, "Andropov's Leadership Style and Strategy," February 14, 1984; "Andropov," (1) John McMahon to Robert McFarlane, February 14, 1984; "Andropov's Leadership Style and Strategy," Jack Matlock Files, box 20, RRL; Ebon, *The Andropov File*, p. 69; Arbatov, *The System*, pp. 246–47; George Shultz to the president, "Andropov's Proposal to Destroy Missiles," August 29, 1983, Jack Matlock Files, series V, Head of State Correspondence, box 64, file August–November 1983, RRL. For analysis of Reagan's desire to abolish nuclear weapons, see Brinkley, ed., *The Reagan Diaries*, pp. 185–86 [October 10, 1983]; Melvyn P. Leffler, "Ronald Reagan and the Cold War: What Mattered Most," *Texas National Security Review* 1 (May 2018): 77–89.

18. Andrew and Gordievsky, *Instructions from the Centre*, chap. 4, pp. 85–90; the purpose of RYAN, to detect a surprise nuclear attack, was described by the then KGB deputy chairman, Kryuchkov, to the head of East Germany's foreign intelligence (HVA), Markus Wolf, Ministry of State Security (Stasi), "About the Talks with Comrade V. A. Kryuchkov," November 7, 1983, WCDA. For Wolf's continued collection on RYAN, following instructions from Kryuchkov, see "Deputy Minister Markus Wolf, Stasi Note on Meeting with KGB Experts on the RYAN Problem," August 14–18, 1984, WCDA.

19. Hersh, *The Target is Destroyed*; Reagan, *An American Life*, pp. 582–84; Shultz, *Turmoil and Triumph*, pp. 361–371; Gates, *From the Shadows*, p. 267; Garthoff, *The Great Transition*, pp. 119–20; Johnson, *American Cryptology*, book 5, pp. 332–334, edition with fewer redactions available at https://nsarchive.files.wordpress.com/2015/10/kal-007-nsa-history.pdf.

20. "Meeting between KGB Deputy Chairman Kryuchkov and East German Minister for State Security Mielke, including Discussion of the Shootdown of Korean Airlines (KAL) Flight 007," September 19, 1983, WCDA. For a valuable analysis of Soviet active measures and the KAL 007 shootdown, see Uri Ra'anan, "Soviet Active Measures in 1987: Innovative Techniques," in "Soviet Active Measures," FCO 28/7745, TNA. "Address to the Nation on the Soviet Attack on a Korean Civilian Airliner," September 5, 1983, RRL.

21. The above owes much to Barrass, *The Great Cold War*, pp. 298–301.

22. Macintyre, *The Spy and the Traitor*; the KGB (inevitably) pushed a myth that MI6 recruited Gordievsky through blackmail: Krasilnikov, *Prizraki s ulitsy Chaykovskogo*, chap. 7.

23. Garthoff, *The Great Transition*, p. 139; David Rose, "A Singular Spy," *Guardian*, May 8, 2004.

24. These new details about ABLE ARCHER were revealed with the publication, in February 2021, of a new volume of the *Foreign Relations of the United States* (*FRUS*), which included the "end of tour" memo written by retiring Defense Intelligence Agency (DIA) director, Leonard Peeroots, in January 1989. However, in October 2022, a federal judge ruled, agreeing with the CIA, that the Peeroots memorandum should not have been declassified because of the need to protect "intelligence activities" and "sources and methods." This is despite the fact that the *FRUS* volume underwent an extensive review process—with the CIA. As this book goes to print, the Peeroots memorandum has been withdrawn from *FRUS* online. To say that the resulting situation is

absurd is an understatement: countless people downloaded the relevant *FRUS* volume and press reporting on it was extensive. For discussion, see https://nsarchive.gwu.edu/news/able-archer-83 -foia/2022-10-04/public-document-federal-judge-and-cia-dont-want-you-see. In the meantime, see original reporting on the volume here: David E. Hoffman and Nate Jones, "Newly Released Documents Shed Light on 1983 Nuclear War Scare with Soviets," *Washington Post*, February 17, 2021. Useful, balanced overviews of ABLE ARCHER can be found in Colbourn, *Euromissiles*, pp. 88–90; Donaghy, *The Second Cold War*, pp. 208–12; Gordon Barrass, "Able Archer 83: What Were the Soviets Thinking?," *Survival* 58 (November 2016); Braithwaite, *Armageddon and Paranoia*, pp. 352–55. Among those who have tried to draw definitive conclusions about ABLE ARCHER—that it was or was not a genuine war scare—are Simon Miles, "The War Scare That Wasn't: Able Archer 83 and the Myths of the Second Cold War," *Journal of Cold War Studies* 22 (2020): 86–118; Simon Miles, "The Mythical War Scare of 1983," *War on the Rocks*, March 16, 2021; Miles, *Engaging the Evil Empire*, pp. 80–81. See Downing, *1983*, chap. 16. Also see Moore, *Margaret Thatcher at Her Zenith*, pp. 115–17; Garthoff, *Soviet Leaders and Intelligence*, pp. 66–68; Ferris, *Behind the Enigma*, p. 383. The first page of what appears to be a significant British JIC report on ABLE ARCHER has been declassified, but not the rest of the report: JIC(84)5, "The Detection of Soviet Preparations for War against NATO," June 15, 1984, CAB 186/37, TNA.

25. "The Soviet 'War Scare' ": Report by the President's Foreign Intelligence Advisory Board, February 15, 1990, p. xii, GWU NSA; Gates, *From the Shadows*, pp. 270–73. The designations on the PFIAB report, GAMMA and UMBRA, indicate that SIGINT contributed to it: Barrass, "Able Archer"; Brown, *The Human Factor*, p. 84. For continuation of RYAN, see Committee for State Security (KGB), "About Results of Intelligence Activities to Note Indicators for a Surprise Nuclear Missile Attack," January 1987, WCDA.

26. JIC(83)5, "The Soviet Global Perception," September 5, 1983, CAB 186/36, TNA.

27. Brinkley, ed., *The Reagan Diaries*, November 18, 1983, pp. 198–99; Reagan, *An American Life*, pp. 588–589.

28. "Address to the Nation and Other Countries on United States–Soviet Relations," January 16, 1984, RRL. Reagan, *An American Life*, pp. 585–86; Dobrynin, *In Confidence*, p. 545; Inboden *The Peacemaker*, pp. 181, 246.

29. Quoted in Barrass, "Able Archer 83."

30. Gordievsky's career and escape have been wonderfully told by Ben Macintyre, *The Spy and the Traitor*, esp. pp. 85–97 for PIMLICO; Howe, *Conflict of Loyalty*, pp. 349–50; Reagan's DCI, William Casey, and his leading Soviet analyst, Robert Gates, correctly predicted Gorbachev's eventual rise to power as early as April 1982: "If I had to bet money, I'd take Andropov on the nose and Gorbachev across the board": William J. Casey Memorandum for the President, "Soviet Political Succession: Institutions, People and Policies," April 22, 1982, Jack Matlock Files, box 20, "Andropov," RRL. On Brezhnev's decline (and medal mania), see Schattenberg, *Brezhnev*, pp. 333–36.

31. Andrew and Gordievsky, *KGB*, p. 16; Lyubimov, *Zapiski neputevogo rezidenta*; "Sir Christopher Curwen," obituary, *Telegraph*, December 23, 2013; Howe, *Conflict of Loyalty*, p. 436; Macintyre, *The Spy and the Traitor*, p. 299; "Valerie Pettit," obituary, *Times*, March 24, 2020.

32. For "Margaret's briefing to Ron," see Thatcher to Reagan, September 12, 1985, "Soviet Union: UK/ Soviet Relations," PREM 19/1647, TNA. For CIA/William Casey briefing, see ibid. [PREM 19/1647], MI6 [name withheld] to Charles Powell, September 26, 1985. For Thatcher's letter to Gordievsky, September 7, 1985, see Casey briefing, and for Cartledge's skunk comment (paraphrasing an earlier comment by Lord Brimelow in wartime Moscow), see ibid. [PREM 19/1647], flash telegram, September 16, 1985. The Soviet government sentenced Gordievsky to death in absentia. In an agonizing decision, Gordievsky decided that it would be safer for his wife and two small children to stay in Russia, while he tried to escape with MI6's help. After his successful exfiltration, the British government mounted a concerted effort to get them released, which finally succeeded in September 1991: "Oleg Gordievsky,"

FCO 28/10458–10460, TNA. The Gordievskys' marriage later failed, perhaps unsurprisingly given the pressure placed on it. For Gordievsky's meetings with Thatcher, see Moore, *Margaret Thatcher: At Her Zenith*, pp. 617–618; "Sir Christopher Curwen," *Times*, December 26, 2013.

33. Cherkashin, *Spy Handler*, p. 29; Soviet Foreign Policy at the UN, November 1984, "Russian Intelligence Service Operating under UN Cover," FCO 168/5763, TNA.

34. Weiner, Johnston, and Lewis, *Betrayal*, pp. 33–34. Primakov later gave an unconvincing explanation that Ames was also motivated by ideology for the Soviet Union: Primakov, *Russian Crossroads*, p. 107.

35. Cherkashin, *Spy Handler*, p. 29; Earley, *Confessions of a Spy*, p. 183; Grimes and Vertefeuille, *Circle of Treason*, pp. 126, 186; Wiehl, *A Spy in Plain Sight*, pp. 100–101.

36. Author interview with former CIA's damage assessment team, June 20, 2018, and with former MI6 officer, November 3, 2019. Grimes and Vertefeuille, *Circle of Treason*, pp. 169–70; Bearden and Risen, *The Main Enemy*, pp. 517, 516; "Aldrich Ames," FBI History, n.d., https://www.fbi.gov /history/famous-cases/aldrich-ames#:~:text=the%20KGB%20paid%20him%20%2450%2C000; Weiner, Johnston, and Lewis, *Betrayal*, pp. 91–92; Tim Weiner, "Why I Spied; Aldrich Ames," *New York Times*, July 31, 1994; David Wise, "Thirty Years Later, We Still Don't Know Who Betrayed These Spies," *Smithsonian Magazine*, November 2015; Cherkashin, *Spy Handler*, p. 179. The story of the "Fourth Man" has now been examined by Robert Baer in *The Fourth Man*, but see the cautionary review of his book by Joseph Augustyn, "The Forth Man and the Hunt for Proof," *The Cipher Brief*, June 7, 2022; Michael Sulik, Lucinda Webb, Mark Kelton in *The Cipher Brief*, February 5, 2023; Paul Redmond, "The Ghost of Angleton," *International Journal of Intelligence and Counterintelligence*, February 2023. Baer is concerned with showing that the "Fourth Man" (woman?) was in the CIA. But if s/he existed, s/he could have been in MI6.

CHAPTER 15: COLLAPSE

1. Anna Melyakova, trans., "The Diary of Anatoly S. Chernyaev, 1974," January 3, 1974, GWU NSA.

2. Remnick, *Lenin's Tomb*, pp. 342–43; Zubok, *Collapse*, p. 165; Shebarshin, *Ruka Moskvy*, p. 316; Braithwaite, *Across the Moscow River*, p. 83.

3. These reports to Gorbachev were first published by Raymond Garthoff, "The KGB Reports to Gorbachev," *Intelligence and National Security* 11 (1996): 224–244; F. 89, O.18, D.92, pp. 1–2, *Spravka o merakh organov KGB SSSR v svyazi s resheniyem Politbyuro TSK KPSS ot 29 noyabrya 1985 goda po zapiske General'nogo sekretarya TSK KPSS M.S. Gorbacheva o nedopustimosti iskazheniya fakticheskogo polozheniya del v soobshcheniyakh i informatsiyakh, postupayushchikh v TSK KPSS i drugiye rukovodyashchiye organy*, December 10, 1985, and F.89, O.51, D.16, pp. 99–107, *Doklad KGB SSSR ob itogakh operativno-sluzhebnoy deyatel'nosti za 1989*, February 14, 1990, RGANI. For intelligence given to Gorbachev, see Service, *The End of the Cold War*, pp. 266–67. For not being obvious at the time, see "Memorandum of Conversation," Jack Matlock Files, series III, "US-USSR Summits," November 19, 1985, RRL.

4. Weiner, *Enemies*, p. 346.

5. Bearden and Risen, *The Main Enemy*, pp. 122–29; U.S. Congress, Select Committee on Intelligence, 103rd Cong., 2nd sess., "An Assessment of the Aldrich H. Ames Espionage Case and Its Implications for U.S. Intelligence," November 1, 1994, pp. 1–3; James Risen, "Former F.B.I. Agent Gets Life in Prison for Years as a Spy," *New York Times*, May 11, 2002; "Excerpts from the F.B.I. Affidavit in the Case against Robert Hanssen," *New York Times*, February 22, 2001.

6. James Risen and David Johnston, "Wife Says Suspect Told a Priest 20 Years Ago of Aiding Soviets," *New York Times*, June 16, 2001.

7. Cherkashin, *Spyhandler*, pp. 235–37; Larry Ryckman, "Soviet FBI Spy Says He'd Do It Again," *Washington Post*, February 12, 1992; DOJ Office of the Inspector General, "A Review of the FBI's Performance in Deterring, Detecting, and Investigating the Espionage Activities of Robert Philip Hanssen," August 14, 2003, https://oig.justice.gov/sites/default/files/archive/special/0308/index.htm.

8. "Affidavit in Support of Criminal Complaint, Arrest Warrant and Search Warrants," *USA v. Robert Philip Hanssen*, https://irp.fas.org/ops/ci/hanssen_affidavit.html#:~:text=34.%20On%20July,and%20technical%20intelligence.

9. For KGB radio interception from Washington *rezidentura*, code-named POCHIN ("Start"), and PROBA (in New York), see MITN 1/6/1 and MITN 1/6/3, CHAC; Shultz, *Turmoil and Triumph*, p. 880; Wise, *Spy*, pp. 252–53.

10. Gates, *From the Shadows*, p. 426.

11. Archie Brown, "Vladimir Kryuchkov," obituary, *Guardian*, November 30, 2007.

12. MITN 1/6/5 CHAC; Bittman, *The Deception Game*, pp. 123–31; Bittman, *The KGB and Soviet Disinformation*, chap. 3; Shultz and Godson, *Dezinformatsia*; Wolf, *Man Without a Face*, chap. 12.

13. United States Information Agency, "Soviet Active Measures in the Era of Glasnost" (March 1988), pp. 57–60, Kenneth deGraffenreid Papers, RRL. For TASS and disinformation in India, see "Distribution in India of TASS Agency material," 1948, FO 1110/44, TNA; Dzhirkvelov, *Secret Servant*, pp. 303–304. For KGB exploitation of domestic U.S. race relations, see MITN 1/6/5, CHAC.

14. The figure of 15,000 is taken from U.S. Department of State, Soviet Influence Activities, *A Report on Active Measures and Propaganda*, p. 87, interview with Stanislav Levchenko; Service A numbers taken from Andrew and Gordievsky, *KGB*, p. 628; House Permanent Select Committee on Intelligence, Soviet Active Measures: Hearings, 97th Cong., 2nd sess., 1982, gives a lower figure, 200, in Service A headquarters in Moscow; Robert Gates in Senate Committee on Foreign Relations, Subcommittee on European Affairs, *Soviet Active Measures*, 99th Cong., 1st sess., 1985, gives a figure of 700 in total within Service A. Also see Levchenko, *On the Wrong Side*, pp. 236–37; "Soviet Disinformation," H. P. Kos to Mr. Fifoot, September 1, 1985, FCO 168/6087, TNA. Service A was led by a "dark" suspicious Armenian, Ivan Agyants: author interview with Ladislav Bittman, July 24, 2018; Primakov, *Ocherki ob Istorii Vneshnei Razvedki*, vol. 5, p. 13. Before 1970, Service A was known as Department D within the KGB.

15. "Soviet Active Measures," Hearings before the Subcommittee on European Affairs of the Committee on Foreign Relations, United States Senate, 99th Cong., 1st sess., 1985, pp. 18–22.

16. Douglas Selvage, "Operation 'Denver': The East German Ministry for State Security and the KGB's AIDS Disinformation Campaign, 1986–1989," *Journal of Cold War Studies* [part I] 21 (2019): 71–123 and [part II] 23 (2022): 4–80; Rid, *Active Measures*, pp. 298–311.

17. Copy of Segal Report in author's possession, given by a former CIA officer.

18. U.S. Department of State, "Soviet Influence Activities: A Report on Active Measures and Propaganda, 1987–1988," Publication 9720 (August 1989), pp. 2, 34–43; the papers of Kenneth DeGraffenreid, held at the Ronald Reagan Presidential Library, have significant holdings concerning the Active Measures Working Group, but almost all are still classified; for "sunlight" quote, see Lawrence Eagleburger, "Unacceptable Intervention: Soviet Active Measures," *NATO Review* 31, no. 1 (April 1983): 6–11. The AIDS fabrication is set out in Cull, *The Cold War and the United States Information Agency*, pp. 444–46; Thomas Boghardt, "Soviet Bloc Intelligence and Its AIDS Disinformation Campaign," *Studies in Intelligence* 53 (2009).

19. Kathleen Bailey, email message to author, June 30, 2020; author interview with CIA officer stationed in New Delhi at time of AIDS disinformation, February 12, 2019. Fletcher Schoen and Christopher J. Lamb, "Deception, Disinformation, and Strategic Communications: How One Interagency Group Made a Major Difference," *Strategic Perspectives* 11 (2012): 103, https://ndupress.ndu.edu/Portals/68/Documents/stratperspective/inss/Strategic-Perspectives-11.pdf; Shultz, *Turmoil and Triumph*, p. 997.

20. Schoen and Lamb, "Deception," p. 103.

21. Herbert Romerstein, "Disinformation as a KGB Weapon in the Cold War," *Journal of Intelligence*

History 1 (2001): 66; Charles Wick, "Soviet Active Measures in the Era of Glasnost: A Report to Congress," United States Information Agency (March 1988), p. 3.

22. David Robert Grimes, "Russian Fake News is not New," *Guardian*, June 14, 2017.

23. Higginbotham, *Midnight in Chernobyl*, p. 70; Plokhy, *Chernobyl*, pp. 46–49, 321–22, 347.

24. GDA SBU, F.11, D.1478, vol. 20, pp. 11–15; GDA SBU, F.11 D.992, vol. 29, p. 178; for Cartledge's report, see Cartledge to Foreign Office, May 6, 1986, "Chernobyl Disaster," PREM 19/3656 TNA. For KGB efforts to influence Strasser, see author interview with Steven Strasser, May 22, 2020; Steven Strasser, "Jitters in the Frontline," *Newsweek*, June 16, 1986; "In Chernobyl's Grim Shadow," *Newsweek*, June 29, 1986. For KGB and Intourist, see MITN 1/6/5 CHAC; Plokhy, *Chernobyl*, pp. 238–41.

25. "Soviet Active Measures," FCO 28/7745, TNA; Primakov, *Ocherki ob Istorii Vneshnei Razvedki*, vol. 6, pp. 70–71. For useful idiots and "hangers on," see MITN 1/6/5 CHAC.

26. Rodric Braithwaite, "Could Gorbachev Have Done Better?," in Vladislav Zubok et al., "A Cold War Endgame or an Opportunity Missed? Analysing the Soviet Collapse Thirty Years Later," *Cold War History* 21 (November 2021): 24. On the significance of Chernobyl for Gorbachev, see Mikhail Gorbachev, "Turning Point at Chernobyl," *Project Syndicate*, April 14, 2006; Gorbachev, *Memoirs*, pp. 189, 193; Palazchenko, *My Years with Gorbachev and Shevardnazde*, p. 49; Shevardnadze, *The Future Belongs to Freedom*, pp. 174–75.

27. Tudda, *Cold War Summits*, pp. 162–63. For Soviet aid to the Third World, see Jack Matlock Files, box 36, "USSR—Third World," RRL.

28. "Address by Mikhail Gorbachev at the UN General Assembly Session (Excerpts)," December 7, 1988, Cold War International History Project Archive, WCDA; Chernyaev, *My Six Years with Gorbachev*, pp. 293–94.

29. Gorbachev, *On My Country and the World*, p. 32; Malia, *The Soviet Tragedy.*

30. Ian Sutherland (British ambassador Moscow) to Geoffrey Howe (foreign secretary), March 12, 1985, "Soviet Union. UK/Soviet Relations," PREM 19/1647, TNA; Mallaby, *Living the Cold War*, p. 229; Spohr and Reynolds, *Transcending the Cold War*, pp. 160–71; Gorbachev, *What Is at Stake Now*, p. 106.

31. Gates, *Duty*, p. 31; Gates, *Exercise of Power*, p. 251; Bruce D. Berkowitz and Jeffery T. Richelson, "The CIA Vindicated: The Soviet Collapse Was Predicted," *National Interest*, September 1, 1995.

32. Sarotte, *The Collapse*; Sarotte, *1989*, pp. 40–43; Brent Scowcroft, "Memorandum for the President," November 29, 1991, Brent Scowcroft Papers, German Unification Files, GHWBL; Garton Ash, *The Magic Lantern*, pp. 61–77.

33. Author interview with former CIA officer Paul Kolbe, March 12, 2022; Eichner and Dobbert, *Headquarters Germany: Die USA-Geheimdienste in Deutschland*, p. 103.

34. See NIE 11-4-89, "Soviet Policy toward the West" (April 1989), reprinted in Fischer, ed., *At Cold War's End*, pp. 227–54; CIA Directorate of Intelligence, "The Gorbachev Succession," April 29, 1991, National Security Council, Nicholas Burns, Ed Hewett Files, Subject Files Russia Subject Files, File "Political Situation: Gorbachev," GHWBL. For alternative future scenarios, see, for example, SNIE 11-18-91 "The Republics of the former USSR: The Outlook for the Next Year," September 1991, National Security Council Files, John Gordon Files, Subject File SDI, July 1991, GHWBL; Brent Scowcroft Memorandum for the President, November 28, 1991, Brent Scowcroft Papers, German Unification Files, GHWBL. The CIA has produced a valuable collection: "The Collapse of Communism in Eastern Europe: A 30-Year Legacy," available on CREST. For the Scowcroft quote, see Kempe, *Berlin 1961*, p. x; Reagan, *An American Life*, pp. 633, 715. For Reagan, Gorbachev, and verification, see Shevardnadze, *The Future Belongs to Freedom*, pp. 89–91.

35. For analysis being a backwater within the KGB until the 1960s, see Leonov, *Likholet'ye*, p. 67. As head of KGB analysis thereafter, Leonov predictably tried in his memoir to show its work in the best possible light, though he concedes it was ultimately unsuccessful. A report by Kryuchkov,

highlighting for Gorbachev foreign intelligence agencies taking advantage of democratic reforms in the Soviet Union, is in F 89 [reel 1006] O 51 D. 15, February 17, 1989, HIA; Dobbs, *Down with Big Brother*, pp. 330–35; Andrew and Gordievsky, *Comrade Kryuchkov's Instructions*, pp. 219–20; Andrew and Gordievsky, *More Instructions from the Centre*, pp. 125–28; Korchilov, *Translating History*, pp. 74–75; figures on CIA and KGB private information; David Wise, "Closing Down the K.G.B.," *New York Times Magazine*, November 24, 1991.

36. Shultz, *Turmoil and Triumph*, pp. 864–65; Powell, *My American Journey*, pp. 375–76; for disagreements within the CIA about Gorbachev's arms reductions, see Saravanskaya and Blanton, *Gorbachev and Reagan*, pp. 456–57. For evidence that the JIC did not predict the August 1991 coup or know as much about it as the CIA and NSC in Washington, see: N. H. R. A. Broomfield to Secretary of State, August 19, 1991, s.28a "Overthrow of President Gorbachev (19/8/91)," FCO 28/10991, TNA; "Minute from Mr Adams (PS/PUS) to Mr Synott," June 12, 1989, p. 141, document 70, in Smith, ed., DBPO, Series III, vol. 12; minute from Sir P. Cradock to Mrs. Thatcher, June 19, 1990, in DBPO, Series III, vol. 7, doc. 211.

37. Spohr, *Post Wall, Post Square*, pp. 3–4; Mikhail Gorbachev, "Perestroika and New Thinking: A Retrospective," *Russia in Global Affairs*, August 9, 2021, https://eng.globalaffairs.ru/articles /perestroika-and-new-thinking-retro/.

38. Major, *The Autobiography*, pp. 231, 499; Grachev, *Gorbachev's Gamble*, pp. 207–10; Yeltsin, *The Struggle for Russia*, pp. 47, 49; p. 72 for a description of Kryuchkov. Beschloss and Talbott, *At the Highest Levels*, p. 421; Patrick E. Taylor, "U.S. Officials Weren't Convinced Coup Would Fail," *New York Times*, August 22, 1991; Service, *The End of the Cold War*, pp. 490–91.

39. For the British official's quote, see Charles Crawford, "Soviet Attempted Coup," August 19, 1991, s.16 "Overthrow of President Gorbachev (19/8/91)," FCO 28/10991, TNA.

40. Beschloss and Talbott, *At the Highest Levels*, pp. 424–25; Matlock, *Autopsy on an Empire*, pp. 593–95; Grachev, *Final Days*, pp. 90–91; Brown, *The Human Factor*, p. 253; Archie Brown, "Vladimir Kryuchkov," *Guardian*, November 30, 2007; Engel, *When the World Seemed New*, pp. 470–73. For CIA intelligence given to Bush about the coup, see Bruce Berkowitz, "U.S. Intelligence Estimates of the Soviet Collapse: Reality and Perception," in Central Intelligence Agency, *Ronald Reagan*, p. 25, available on CREST.

41. Brathwaite (Moscow) to FCO, August 23, 1991, s.72 "Overthrow of President Gorbachev (19/8/91)," FCO 28/10991, TNA; Shebarshin, *Ruka Moskvy*, introduction.

42. "Telecons with CIS Leaders: Telecon with Gorbachev 12/25/1991," National Security Council, Nicholas Burns, Ed Hewett Files Subject Files, GHWBL; Bearden and Risen, *The Main Enemy*.

43. Rodric Braithwaite, "The Rubble of the Dictatorship," January 1, 1992, s.60 "Control of Nuclear Weapons," FCO 179/911, TNA.

CHAPTER 16: FALLOUT

1. Rolf Mowatt-Larssen, "US and Russian Intelligence Cooperation during the Yeltsin Years," Harvard Belfer Center Paper, February 11, 2011.

2. Spohr, *Post Wall*, p. 121; Judah, *Fragile Empire*, p. 225; E. Wayne Merry interview, February 19, 2010, pp. 240ff, ADST. Generally low expectations for Yeltsin's leadership by 1997 are revealed in contemporary British Foreign Office and Ministry of Defense reports, which note when Yeltsin was in good form, "without signs of tiredness or drink": "NATO Enlargement," DEFE 68/1493, TNA. For organized crime in Russia, see "Crime in Russia," FCO 176/397, TNA; Seymour M. Hersh, "The Wild East," *Atlantic*, June 1994.

3. For Yeltsin looking better than alternatives, see G. D. Ferguson, "Policy towards Russia: Background Papers," February 9, 1993, s.7 "United Kingdom Policy towards Russia," FCO 176/303, TNA; Solovyov and Klepikova, *Zhirinovsky*, pp. 153–54; private information.

4. John McLaughlin, "The Changing Nature of CIA Analysis in the Post-Soviet World," speech given

at the Conference on CIA's Analysis of the Soviet Union, 1947–1991, March 9, 2001, CIA CREST; author interview with Rolf Mowatt-Larssen, June 2, 2017; other figures come from private information.

5. "Our First Line of Defense: Presidential Reflections on US Intelligence," p. 51, CIA CREST.

6. "The Secret's Out: Top British Spy Identified," *New York Times*, May 7, 1992; Andrew, *The Defence of the Realm*, appendix 2; the Spycatcher affair in 1986–1987, concerning the publication of Peter Wright's memoirs, had revealed the absurdities of secrecy surrounding MI5 and MI6. Margaret Thatcher's cabinet secretary, Robin Armstrong, was humiliated in an Australian court as he tried not to mention MI6's name by Wright's counsel, Malcolm Turnbull (later Australian prime minister); Moore, *Margaret Thatcher: Herself Alone*, pp. 230–61.

7. "PM's Visit to the Soviet Union: Meeting with President Gorbachev," September 1, 1991, s.18 "Control of Soviet Nuclear Weapons," FCO 179/505, TNA. Gorbachev revealed to Braithwaite that there were two *chemodanchiks*, one in his possession and the other held by the Soviet defense minister, Yevgeny Shaposhnikov: Braithwaite to FCO, "Secretary of State's Meeting with Yeltsin: 20 January: Security Issues," s.4 "UK Military Assistance to Russia," FCO 177/1041, TNA; Hoffman, *The Dead Hand*, chap. 12.

8. Perry, *My Journey at the Nuclear Brink*, pp. 100–101; Kassenova, *Atomic Steppe*, pp. 192–95; Michael E. Ruane and Knight-Ridder, "How U.S. Silently Quelled a Nuclear Threat," *Chicago Tribune*, November 24, 1994; "Transcript of Press Conference by Defense Secretary (William Perry), Secretary of State (Warren Christopher) and Energy Secretary (Hazel Leary) on Project Sapphire, November 23, 1994," November 23, 1994, GWU NSA.

9. For British payments to contain, degrade, and destroy Soviet nuclear material (£30 million over three years): "US-Russian Talks on Safety, Security and Dismantlement (SSD) of Soviet Nuclear Weapons," June 8, 1992, s.326 "Western Assistance to the Soviet Union," FCO 179/920, TNA.

10. A valuable summary of the Soviet illegal bioweapon program is in Zelikow and Rice, *To Build a Better World*, pp. 260–62.

11. Ralph Earle [U.S. Arms and Disarmament Agency] to Zbigniew Brzezinski, March 5, 1980, National Security Affairs Staff Material—Eastern Europe, USSR box 23, file "USSR: Sverdlovsk Incident," s.2a, JCL; P. S. Roland, "Biological Accident at Sverdlovsk," February 28, 1980, s.1 "Chemical and Biological Weapons in U.S.S.R.," FCO 28/4205, TNA; and ibid. [FCO 28/4205], s.52 P. S. Roland, "Sverdlovsk," November 25, 1980; MITN 1/6/1, CHAC; Alibek, *Biohazard*, p. 79; for earlier period, see Rimmington, *Stalin's Secret Weapon*; Service, *The Last of the Tsars*, pp. 254–57. For Western officials not convinced about the Soviets ending their biological weapons program, see Mark Palmer interview, October 30, 1997, p. 89, ADST.

12. Leitenberg and Zilinskas, *The Soviet Biological Weapons Program*, pp. 582–93; Hoffman, *The Dead Hand*, pp. 329–30; Adams, *The New Spies*, pp. 270–83; Moore, *Margaret Thatcher: Herself Alone*, pp. 481–82; Alibek, *Biohazard*, pp. 137–45, 149; Pearce Wright, "Vladimir Pasechnik," obituary, *Guardian*, November 28, 2001; Domardskij, *Biowarrior*.

13. Alibek, *Biohazard*, pp. x, chap. 19; Harris and Paxman, *A Higher Form of Killing*, p. 245; "Interview with Dr. Kanatjan Alibekov," *Frontline*, PBS, n.d., https://www.pbs.org/wgbh/pages/frontline/shows/plague/interviews/alibekov.html.

14. Kouzimov, *Biological Espionage*.

15. Roderic Braithwaite, "Soviet Biological Weapons," August 4, 1993, "Russia: Biological Weapons," FCO 176/372, TNA; Braithwaite, *Across the Moscow River*, pp. 141–43; "Interview with Dr. Christopher Davis," *Frontline*, PBS, https://www.pbs.org/wgbh/pages/frontline/shows/plague/interviews/davis.html; "Gorbachev (Dobrynin) Sensitive," n.d., Brent Scowcroft Papers, Special Separate USSR Notes File, GHWBL; Powell to Wall, April 15, 1990, "Prime Minister's Visit to Bermuda, April 1990: Meeting with George H. W. Bush, President of the USA," PREM 19/2913, TNA; Moore, *Margaret Thatcher: Herself Alone*, pp. 538–39, 545–46; Leonov, *Likholet'ye*, p. 189, for the "rape" of Soviet microbiology by outside inspectors.

16. Head, FCO Eastern Department, to British embassy, Moscow, July 13, 1993, "Russia: Biological Weapons," FCO 176/371, TNA; "BW Demarche—Yeltsin," April 1999, National Security Council, Michael Fry files, GHWBL; Russell Watson, "No More Lies—Ever," *Newsweek*, June 28, 1992; author interview with a British Ministry of Defence biological weapons expert on condition of anonymity, June 7, 2012.

17. R. Jeffery Smith, "U.S. Officials Allege That Russians Are Working on Biological Arms," *Washington Post*, April 8, 1994. For continued Russian obfuscation, see John Kerr (British embassy Washington) to FCO London, "Russia: Biological Weapons," September 15, 1997, "Russia: UK/Russia Relations: Internal Situation," PREM 49/59, TNA. Also see Raymond A. Zilinskas, "The Soviet Biological Weapons Program and Its Legacy in Today's Russia," Center for the Study of Weapons of Mass Destruction occasional paper no. 11 (July 2016): pp. 44–45. On the impact of decision makers in Washington, see Zelikow and Rice, *To Build a Better World*. It is known that Russia continued its chemical warfare program after 1993: see Mark Sedwell, UK national security adviser, to Jens Stoltenberg, NATO Secretary General, April 13, 2018, https://assets.publishing.service.gov.uk/government/uploads/system/uploads/attachment_data/file/699819/Letter_from_the_UK_National_Security_Adviser_to_the_NATO_Secretary_General_regarding_the_Salisbury_incident.pdf.

18. Kerry, *Every Day Is Extra*, pp. 195–96. Yeltsin had set out his views of reforming the KGB in *Against the Grain*, pp. 252–53; "Psychiatry in the Soviet Union," FCO 28/11155.

19. Gessen, *The Man Without a Face*, pp. 179–80.

20. Bakatin, *Doroga v proshedshem vremeni*, pp. 142–43; Krasilnikov, *Prizraki s ulitsy Chaykovskogo*, pp. 95–96; "Vadim Bakatin," obituary, *Times*, September 23, 2022; Garthoff, *The Great Transition*, p. 497; Clay Risen, "Vadim V. Bakatin, the Last Chairman of the K.G.B., Dies at 84," *New York Times*, August 20, 2022; on Bakatin's openness, see Baker, *The Politics of Diplomacy*, p. 534.

21. John Scarlett to FCO, August 26, 1992, s.13 "Russian Intelligence Services," FCO 176/128, TNA. A similar point, about the essential need for intelligence services staying out of politics, was made by Braithwaite to Crawford (Soviet Department), "Policy towards the Ex–Soviet Union: The Way Ahead," January 6, 1992, s.1 "UK Military Assistance to Russia," FCO 177/1041, TNA; Bakatin, *Doroga v proshedshem vremeni*, pp. 126–27; Gessen, *The Future Is History*, p. 104.

22. For the FCD and the August 1991 coup, see Shebarshin, *Ruka Moskvy*, "19.5.91," pp. 213–224; Suvarov, *Inside Soviet Military Intelligence*, p. 51; Plokhy, *The Last Empire*, p. 135.

23. For Krassilnikov and the Second Chief Directorate, see Krassilnikov, *Prizraki s ulitsy Chaykovskogo*, chap. 5, pp. 103–18; Cherkashin, *Spy Handler*, pp. 78–79; James Risen, "Rem Krassilnikov, Russian Bane of C.I.A., Dies at 76," *New York Times*, March 24, 2003.

24. Bearden and Risen, *The Main Enemy*, pp. 13–14, 396–405; Cherkashin, *Spy Handler*, pp. 260–361; Sam Roberts, "Jack Downing, C.I.A. Chief in Cold War Capitals, Dies at 80," *New York Times*, June 30, 2021; Benjamin Fischer, "Doubles Troubles: The CIA and Double Agents during the Cold War," *International Journal of Intelligence and Counterintelligence* 29 (2015): 51, 58; Russo and Dezenhall, *Best of Enemies*, pp. 160–69. For KGB tradecraft of identifying CIA officers, see MITN 1/6/1, CHAC. The case of the KGB officer and "defector" Vitali Yurchenko is still unresolved: he defected to the United States in Rome in 1985 but then redefected from the United States to the Soviet Union. It remains unclear whether he was a genuine defector who had a change of heart or was a dangle from the outset.

25. "Scarlett to Ms. P Major Eastern Department FCO," June 1992, s.9 "Russian Intelligence Services," FCO 176/128, TNA; Gordon Bennett, "The SVR: Russia's Intelligence Service," March 2000, https://irp.fas.org/world/russia/svr/c103-gb.htm; for Primakov and KGB ties, see Andrew and Mitrokhin, *The Mitrokhin Archive*, vol. 1; Talbott, *Russia Hand*, p. 18.

26. Robert Gates had also previously (in February 1990) traveled to Moscow to meet KGB chairman Kryuchkov: Memorandum of Conversation between Robert Gates and V. I. Kryuchkov,

February 9, 1990, Brent Scowcroft Papers, box 21, GHWBL; Gates, *From the Shadows*, p. 491. For Rimington, see Braithwaite, *Across the Moscow River*, p. 257; Rimington, *Open Secret*, pp. 232–239; Mowatt-Larssen, "US and Russian Intelligence Cooperation during the Yeltsin Years"; Mowatt-Larssen, *A State of Mind*, pp. 138–39.

27. Braithwaite, *Across the Moscow River*, p. 340; Clinton Presidential Records NSC Russia, Ukraine, and Eurasian Affairs, Nicholas Burns Transition, January 1993, WCL. For an account of Russian intelligence, which should be read with caution in my view, see Lunev, *Through the Eyes of the Enemy*; Primakov, "Perspektivy rasshireniya NATO i interesy Rosii," *Izvetisya*, November 26, 1993; Primakov, *Vstrechi na Perekrestakh*, p. 207. For U.S. aid, see Zubok, *Collapse*, pp. 235–36; FCO Economic Relations Department, April 3, 1992, "Statistics on Assistance to the Former Soviet Union," FCO 176/183, TNA, which shows that in 1991–1992, the UK government agreed to give $685 million. Zelikow and Rice, *To Build a Better World*, p. 399. For nonsensical claims that the CIA did not downgrade Russia but expanded its efforts after 1991, see Krasilnikov, *Prizraki s ulitsy Chaykovskogo*. See also James Goldgeier and Joshua Shifrinson, "The United States and NATO after the End of the Cold War: Explaining and Evaluating Enlargement and Its Alternatives," in Monteiro and Bartel, eds., *Before and After the Fall*, pp. 277–79.

28. "Revealed: Russia's Worst Crime in Chechnya," *Guardian*, March 5, 2000; "Russians Accused of Massacres," BBC News, February 23, 2000; Patrick Cockburn, "Russian Warplanes Kill Dozens of Villagers," *Independent*, October 11, 1999.

29. D. M. Jack, British consulate St. Petersburg, to George Ferguson, FCO London, March 8, 1993, s.1 "Russia—St. Petersburg," FCO 176/364, TNA; G. D. Ferguson, FCO Eastern Department, to W. Egerton, British embassy Moscow, August 5, 1993, "Crime in Russia," FCO 176/397, TNA; Adam Curtis, "Russia 1985–1999," BBC iPlayer; Pomerantsev, *Nothing Is True and Everything Is Possible*, p. 95. Putin's patron in St. Petersburg was its mayor, Anatoli Sobchak, who previously taught him law. Sobchak ingratiated contemporary British officials: S. L. Gass (FCO) to Stephen Wall, 10 Downing Street, September 19, 1991, s.73 "British-Soviet Relations," FCO 28/10996, TNA.

30. For Ames and polygraphs, see Bearden and Risen, *The Main Enemy*, pp. 456–57; Grimes and Ver-tefeuille, *Circle of Treason*, pp. 177–78; Weiner, Johnston, and Lewis, *Betrayal*, pp. 89–92, 162–63; U.S. Senate, Congress Select Committee on Intelligence, "Meeting the Espionage Challenge: A Review of United States Counterintelligence and Security Programs," 99th Congress, 2nd sess., October 3, 1986; for PENNYWISE, see Ellen Barry and Scott Shane, "Intrigue and Ambiguity in Cases of 4 Russians Sent to West in Spy Swap," *New York Times*, July 9, 2010; Russo and Dezenhall, *Best of Enemies*, pp. 279–80.

31. David Johnson, "Officials Outline 2-Year Betrayal within the C.I.A.," *New York Times*, November 19, 1994; Tim Weiner, "C.I.A. Traitor, Saying He Wanted Cash for Family, Gets 23 Years," *New York Times*, June 6, 1997; Denson, *The Spy's Son*, pp. 150–51.

32. Lucas, *The New Cold War*, pp. 25–46. For continuity of KGB and SVR, see Talbott, *Russia Hand*, p. 160; Julia Ioffe, "How State-Sponsored Blackmail Works in Russia," *Atlantic*, January 11, 2017.

33. Blair to Bethell, November 3, 1997, "Russia," PREM 49/160, TNA. Shebarshin, *Ruka Moskvy*.

34. Bennett, "The SVR"; David A. Vise, "State Department Bug Seen as Major Security Breach," *Washington Post*, December 9, 1999.

35. Earley, *Comrade J*, p. 194. For Bethell's correspondence with Blair, see Bethell to Blair, September 20, 1997, "Russia—Relations," PREM 49/159, TNA; Christopher Meyer (British embassy Washington) to FCO, "Russia: Economic Problems and the US Response," December 8, 1997, PREM 49/160, TNA. William Grimes, "Sergei Tretyakov, Spy Who Fled to U.S., Dies at 53," *New York Times*, July 9, 2010.

PART 6: THE CLASH OF A NEW GLOBAL ORDER

CHAPTER 17: PUTIN'S WAR ON THE WEST

1. Rid, *Rise of the Machines*, pp. 316–39; Buchanan, *The Hacker and the State*, p. 318; "We're in the Middle of a Cyberwar," *Newsweek*, September 9, 1999.

2. As set out in Stoll, *The Cuckoo's Egg*.

3. This story has been well told by Soldatov and Borogan in *The Red Web*; for Silicon Valley, see O'Mara, *The Code*.

4. Burleigh, *The Best of Times, the Worst of Times*, chap.5; author interview with former CIA chief of station in Moscow, on condition of anonymity, December 12, 2022.

5. Gates, *Duty*, p. 532. For the Red Banner Institute, see Leonov, *Likholet'ye*, p. 67; Reitschuster, *Putin's Demokratur*, pp. 38–41; Brzezinski and Scowcroft, *America and the World*, pp. 166–67.

6. Burleigh, *The Best of Times, the Worst of Times* p. 151; Belton, *Putin's People*, pp. 112–13.

7. Dominic Chilcott (Private Secretary, Foreign Secretary) to John Holmes (10 Downing St.), May 22, 1997, "Russia," PREM 49/159, TNA. For Andrew Wood's comment, see this same file, PREM 49/159, TNA, Andrew Wood to FCO, May 12, 1997; Primakov, *Russian Crossroads*, p. 3; Putin's name does not appear in David Remnick's excellent study, *Resurrection* (1997).

8. Author interview with CIA chief of station in Moscow, December 12, 2022.

9. Belton, *Putin's People*, pp. 181–87; Burleigh, *The Best of Times, the Worst of Times*, p. 150; Luke Harding, "Igor Sechin: Rosneft's Kremlin Hard Man Comes out of the Shadows," *Guardian*, October 18, 2012.

10. Author discussion with former FSB officer, April 3, 2022, and November 16, 2022.

11. Browder, *Red Notice*, pp. 276–77.

12. U.S. Congress, *Russian Money Laundering*, 105th Cong., 1st sess., September 1999; Kotkin, *Armageddon Averted*, p. 125; The Dossier Center, "Lubyanka Federation: How the FSB Determines the Politics and Economics of Russia," *Atlantic Council*, October 5, 2020.

13. Burleigh, *The Best of Times, the Worst of Times*, pp. 151–52; Ben Judah, "London's Laundry Business," *New York Times*, March 7, 2014; House of Commons, Foreign Affairs Committee, "Moscow's Gold: Russian Corruption in the UK," Eighth Report of Session, 2017–2019, May 21, 2018.

14. "The UK and Russia: What Is to Be Done?," RUSI *Commentary*, March 20, 2018; Satter, *The Less You Know, the Better You Sleep*.

15. Rumsfeld, *Known and Unknown*, pp. 306, 308–9; description of Putin from Cameron, *For the Record*, p. 455; "Crawford: Joint Statements etc," box 2, file CO139 "Russia," White House Office of Records Management Subject Files, GWBL.

16. A good account of the Russian end of empire can be found in Plokhy, *The Last Empire*; and Clover, *Black Wind, White Snow*. Gordon Brown noted that after Litvinenko's assassination, when he looked into Putin's eyes, "I did not see a good man": Brown, *My Life, Our Times*, p. 212. For Russia's loss of empire, see Yeltsin, *The Struggle for Russia*, p. 285. For loss of empire, see Dobrynin, *In Confidence*, p. 615; Lo, *Russia and the New World Disorder*, pp. 100–105; and, more generally, Mark Kramer, "The Soviet Legacy in Russian Foreign Policy," *Political Science Quarterly* 134 (2019–2020): 585–609.

For anyone doubting the dislocation caused by the loss of other empires, consider this memorable passage from Jan Morris's *Farewell the Trumpets* (pp. 508–10), about Britain's *homo imperialis*:

> But there, look, swinging briskly around the corner from the Abbey, courteously stepping into the gutter to overtake the pavement secretaries, oblivious it seems to the curses of taxi drivers—there is a figure you will not find in Copenhagen! He is not a young man now, in his 50s perhaps, and he is slightly stooped, as though a succession of fevers has warped his spine. But he is slim, stringy, rather rangy, and his face is so heavily tanned, not simply a sunburn but a deep, ingrained tincture

of brown, that physically he scarcely looks like an Englishman at all. But British he unquestionably is, the most British man in sight, his expression, his movement, his every gesture reflecting a Britishness that has almost vanished from England. Even his clothes are yesterday's. He wears a brown floppy trilby hat, looking as though it had been repeatedly soaked in rainstorms and dried in the sun, and slightly scuffed suede shoes. . . .

There he is. He looks out of touch, out of time. He meets nobody he knows, for he has few friends in London now; even at the Office it's all new faces, and he's never bothered with any of those damned clubs. He averts his eye from the passing crowd, for to be honest he doesn't much like the style of Londoners these days. . . .

He is a foreigner in his own capital. He is a true exotic among the cosmopolitans. Here's the last of the British Empire builders, home on leave and hating it.

17. For Partnership for Peace, see Gerhardt von Moltke, "Partnership for Peace: Framework Document," December 30, 1993, "NATO Partnership for Peace," DEFE 68/1443, TNA; Maxim Kórshunov, "Mikhail Gorbachev: I Am Against All Walls," *Russia Beyond*, October 16, 2014, https://www.rbth.com/international/2014/10/16/mikhail_gorbachev_i_am_against_all_walls_40673.html. The best account of Baker's statement, and ensuing confusion, can be found in Sarotte, *Not One Inch* (pp. 55–56 for Baker's statement); Primakov, *Russian Crossroads*, pp. 129–30; Primakov, *Vstrechi na Perekrestakh*, p. 207; Leonov, *Likholet'ye*, pp. 353–54; Michael R. Gordon, "The Anatomy of a Misunderstanding," *New York Times*, May 25, 1997; Weiner, *The Folly and the Glory*, pp. 170–71. For evidence of no pledge, see Mark Kramer, "The Myth of a No-NATO-Enlargement Pledge to Russia," *Washington Quarterly* 32 (2009): 39–61; Zelikow and Rice, *To Build a Better World*, pp. 230–31; Sarotte, *Not One Inch*, pp. 174–202, 208–10; Trachtenberg, "The United States and the NATO Non-Extension Assurances"; Goldgeier, *Not Whether But When*, p. 15; Sergey Radchenko, " 'Nothing but Humiliation for Russia': Moscow and NATO's Eastern Enlargement 1993–1995," in Radchenko, Sayle, and Ostermann, eds., *NATO in the Cold War and After*, pp. 7–50; Walt, *The Hell of Good Intentions*, p. 266.

18. Burleigh, *The Best of Times, the Worst of Times*, pp. 11–12, 151; Talbott, *The Russia Hand*, pp. 236–38. For two different views, see Jonathan Haslam, "Russia's Seat at the Table: A Place Denied or a Place Delayed?," *International Affairs* 74 (1998): 119–130, and William Odom, "Russia's Several Seats at the Table," *International Affairs* 74 (1998): 809–821. Philip Barton to Dominick Chilcott, "Russia," "Clinton Visit," May 29, 1997, PREM 49/149, TNA. In March 2002, Tony Blair told George W. Bush that Putin wanted "to be at the top table": Campbell, *The Blair Years: The Alastair Campbell Diaries*, p. 609; Hill, *No Place for Russia*, pp. 114–15; Clinton, *My Life*.

19. George Kennan, "A Fateful Error," *New York Times*, February 4, 1997; Costigliola, ed., *The Kennan Diaries*, p. 656. For Blair's efforts to persuade Yeltsin about NATO enlargement, Prime Minister's Meeting with Yeltsin, May, 27, 1997, see "Russia," PREM 49/159, TNA; Dominic Holmes to John Chilcott, "Telephone Call with President Yeltsin," May 13, 1997, "Russia," PREM 49/159, TNA; Wood (Moscow) to FCO, May 12, 1997, and s.2 "Russian Foreign Policy," May 12, 1997, "Russia: Relations," PREM 49/159, TNA; "Call on Mr. Hogg by Russian Ambassador, 7 December 1993," s.22 "Russia/Ukraine," FCO 176/337, TNA.

20. For KGB active measures to discredit NATO and the EEC/EU as militarist aggressors, see MITN 1/6/5, CHAC; Sayle, *Enduring Alliance*, pp. 243–44 for NATO's "out of area" operations after 9/11 (in Libya).

21. Burns, *The Back Channel*, pp. 222, 228–29, 238; NSC European Affairs (Georgia and Russia Conflict, 2008), GWBL; Bush, *Decision Points*, pp. 431, 435.

22. Burns, *The Back Channel*, p. 222; Rice, *No Higher Authority*, pp. 670–72; Walker, *The Long Hangover*, pp. 127–31, 138–42; Stent, *Putin's World*, pp. 189–204.

23. Jeff Stein, "Riddle Resolved: Who Dimed Out American Traitor and Super-Spy Robert Hanssen?," *Newsweek*, January 11, 2018; Kessler, *The FBI*, pp. 123–25; Wise, *Spy*, pp. 205–19; "Veteran FBI Agent Arrested and Charged with Espionage," February 21, 2001, https://archives.fbi.gov/archives/news/pressrel/press-releases/veteran-fbi-agent-arrested-and-charged-with-espionage.

24. Campbell, *The Burden of Power: Countdown to Iraq*, pp. 36–37; Meyer, *DC Confidential*, p. 178.

25. Ferris, *Behind the Enigma*, p. 312; UK Parliament Intelligence and Security Committee, "Russia," July 21, 2020, p. 21, available here: https://isc.independent.gov.uk/wp-content/uploads/2021/03/CCS207_CCS0221966010-001_Russia-Report-v02-Web_Accessible.pdf.

26. UK Parliament Intelligence and Security Committee, "Russia," July 21, 2020, p. 21.

27. The KGB's involvement with Markov's assassination was revealed in 1993 by Oleg Kalugin, the former KGB officer who oversaw the operation. According to documents released in 2022, the British Crown Prosecution Service decided not to prosecute Kalugin: "The Markov Affair," FCO 175/648, TNA. Also see Christopher Nehring, "Active and Sharp Measures: Cooperation between the Soviet KGB and Bulgarian State Security," *Journal of Cold War History* 23 (2021): 9–10.

28. Burleigh, *Day of the Assassins*, pp. 238–239, 243–247.

29. Sixsmith, *The Litvinenko File*, pp. 31–36, 52–54; Zygar, *All the Kremlin's Men*, p. 40.

30. Sir Robert Owen, *Report into the Death of Alexander Litvinenko* (January 2016), pp. 42–43, 246, https://assets.publishing.service.gov.uk/government/uploads/system/uploads/attachment_data/file/493860/The-Litvinenko-Inquiry-H-C-695-web.pdf; Service, *Kremlin Winter*, pp. 234–35; Gessen, *The Man Without a Face*, pp. 199–201, 221–24; Burleigh, *Day of the Assassins*.

31. Masha Lipman, "Boris Berezovsky: An Oligarch Dies," *New Yorker*, March 26, 2013; Joel Gunter, "Sergei Skripal and the 14 deaths under Scrutiny," BBC News, March 7, 2018.

32. Urban, *The Skripal Files*, pp. 1–4; Andrew Roth and Vikram Dodd, "Salisbury Novichok Suspects Say They Were Only Visiting Cathedral," *Guardian*, September 13, 2018; Shaun Walker, "Alleged Russian Spies Sentenced to Jail over Montenegro 'Coup Plot,' " *Guardian*, May 19, 2019.

33. The following owes much to Urban, *The Skripal Files*, pp. 174–85; Corera, *Russians Among Us*, pp. 76–78, 173–75, 233; also see Olson, *To Catch a Spy*, p. 25.

34. Nikolai Dolgopolov interview with Mikhail Vasenkov, *Rossiyskaya Gazeta*, March 29, 2020; Naveen N. Srivatsa, "Harvard Kennedy School Revokes Degree Awarded to Russian Spy," *Crimson*, July 16, 2010.

35. "Former CIA Senior Clandestine Services Officer Daniel Hoffman on Pursuing the 'Russian Ten,' " *Intelligence Matters* podcast, Michael Morell (presenter), August 26, 2020; Clinton, *Hard Choices*, pp. 230–45.

36. Alexandra Ma, "Traitors Will Kick the Bucket," *Business Insider*, March 7, 2018; previous discussion taken from author interview with former CIA chief of station in Moscow, December 12, 2022.

37. Alex Campbell, Jason Leopold, and Heidi Blake, "This Russian Double Is a Lot Less Dead Than He Seemed," *BuzzFeed News*, October 3, 2018; Department of Justice press release, "Individual Pleads Guilty to Acting within the United States on Behalf of Russian Government," February 16, 2022, https://www.justice.gov/opa/pr/individual-pleads-guilty-acting-within-united-states-behalf-russian-government.

38. For Russia in Africa, consider Michael Weiss and Pierre Vaux, *The Company You Keep: Yevgeny Prigozhin's Influence Operations in Africa* (Washington, DC: Free Russia Foundation, 2020); Andres Schipani, "Spying and Stability: Djibouti Thrives in 'Return to Cold War,' " *Financial Times*, May 11, 2021.

39. Stefan Meister, "The 'Lisa Case': Germany as a Target of Russian Disinformation," *NATO Review*, July 25, 2016.

40. UK Parliament Intelligence and Security Committee, "Russia," July 21, 2020, p. 12; David Anderson, QC [KC] Report of the Bulk Powers Review (August 2016), p. 164, for anonymized case study, but which can usefully be read in conjunction with: Tom Harper and Richard Kerbaj, "GCHQ Thwarted Russian Cyber-Attack on General Election," *Times*, September 25, 2016; Luke Harding, Stephanie Kirchgaessner, Nick Hopkins, "British Spies Were the First to Spot Trump

Team's Links with Russia," *Guardian*, April 13, 2017; author interview with senior GCHQ officer on condition of anonymity, May 3, 2018; David D. Kirkpatrick, "Signs of Russian Meddling in Brexit Referendum," *New York Times*, November 15, 2017.

41. Office of Director of National Intelligence, "Background to 'Assessing Russian Activities and Intentions in Recent US Elections': The Analytic Process and Cyber Incident Attribution," January 6, 2017; U.S. Senate, Select Committee on Intelligence, 116th Cong., 1st sess., *Report on Russian Active Measures Campaigns and Interference in the 2016 U.S. Election*, vol. 5, *Counterintelligence Threats and Vulnerabilities* (2020), p. vii.

42. *Report on Russian Active Measures Campaigns and Interference in the 2016 U.S. Election*, vol. 5, *Counterintelligence Threats and Vulnerabilities*, pp. 348, 943; Dobrynin, *In Confidence*, p. 196.

43. *Report on Russian Active Measures Campaigns and Interference in the 2016 U.S. Election*, vol. 5, *Counterintelligence Threats and Vulnerabilities*, pp. 232–52.

44. Ibid. endnote 43, immediately above, pp. vi–vii.

45. Kathleen Hall Jamieson, an expert in communication, has suggested that Russian disinformation was significant in tipping the 2016 election for Trump: Jamieson, *Cyberwar*; Perlroth, *This Is How They Tell Me the World Ends*, pp. 310–12.

46. Author interview with John Kerry, October 20, 2022.

47. Hill, *There Is Nothing for You Here*, pp. 184–85.

48. "Fact Check: Has Trump Declared Bankruptcy Four or Six Times?," *Washington Post*, September 26, 2016; for preceding quote from author interview with James Clapper, October 21, 2022; the U.S. intelligence officer who briefed Trump during the transition has been revealed to be Ted Gistaro; for the FBI counterintelligence probe, see Benjamin Wittes, "The Counterintelligence Gap: An Update," *Lawfare*, August 27, 2020; Snyder, *Road to Unfreedom*, p. 234; Christopher Steele can be identified from now-public records, declassified in 2021, working under British diplomatic cover in Moscow in 1991: Christopher Steele to George Edgar, April 4, 1991, s.31 "Soviet Economy General," FCO 28/11102, TNA.

49. Barry A. Zulauf, U.S. intelligence community's analytic ombudsman, ODNI, letter to U.S. Senate Select Committee on Intelligence, January 6, 2021, https://context-cdn.washingtonpost.com /notes/prod/default/documents/c3c41863-be9e-4246-9ed9-e43aedd013f9/note/4e677597-f403 -4c9b-b838-f5613d79b341.

50. Author interview with former CIA chief of station in Moscow, December 12, 2022; Leon Neyfakh, "The Craziest Black Market in Russia," *Slate*, May 22, 2016, https://www.slate.com/articles /news_and_politics/cover_story/2016/05/the_thriving_russian_black_market_in_dissertations _and_the_crusaders_fighting.html; Naryshkin has known Putin since working at the KGB regional headquarters in Leningrad, the "Big House" on the Neva.

51. For the rehabilitation of Stalin, see quotes from him in Kolpakidi, *Sovetskaya vneshnyaya razvedka, 1946–2020*.

52. Matlock, *Autopsy on an Empire*, pp. 152–53.

53. President Ford Committee Records, Carter quotes, quoting Carter in June 1976, GRFL; Carter, *A Full Life*, pp. 178–81.

54. A. S. Halford to G. W. Harrison, British embassy Moscow, February 2, 1949, s.1 "The Soviet Union: Intelligence Questionnaires," FO 1093/473, TNA.

55. This is disputed, of course, in commentaries such as Shebarshin, *Ruka Moskvy*, pp. 264–66.

CHAPTER 18: NEW COLD WAR

1. Bethany Allen-Ebrahimian and Zach Dorfman, "Exclusive: Suspected Chinese Spy Targeted California Politicians," *Axios*, December 8, 2020. The MSS's lack of tradecraft with Fang is not uncommon. In his study of 595 documented cases of Chinese espionage, Eftimiades (*Chinese Espionage*, p. 21), has shown that 218 used little or no tradecraft.

2. Gordon Corera and Jennifer Scott, "MI5 Warning over 'Chinese Agent' in Parliament," BBC News, January 13, 2022, https://www.bbc.com/news/uk-politics-59984380.

3. Gideon Rachman, "A new cold war: Trump, Xi and the escalating US-China confrontation," *Financial Times*, October 5, 2020; Niall Ferguson, "The New Cold War? It's with China, and Has Already Begun," *New York Times*, October 1, 2019; "The New Cold War: America, China, and the Echoes of History," *Foreign Affairs*, November/ December 2021.

4. Peter Martin, Jennifer Jacobs, and Nick Wadhams, "China Is Evading U.S. Spies—and the White House Is Worried," *Bloomberg*, November 10, 2021.

5. Christopher Wray, "The Threat Posed by the Chinese Government and the Chinese Communist Party to the Economic and National Security of the United States," remarks at the Hudson Institute, July 7, 2020, https://www.fbi.gov/news/speeches/the-threat-posed-by-the-chinese-government -and-the-chinese-communist-party-to-the-economic-and-national-security-of-the-united-states; Christopher Wray, "Countering Threats Posed by the Chinese Government inside the U.S.," remarks at Reagan Library, January 31, 2022, https://www.fbi.gov/news/speeches/countering -threats-posed-by-the-chinese-government-inside-the-us-wray-013122.

6. Eftimiades, *Chinese Espionage*, pp. 10–15, which demonstrates that Chinese S&T collection correlates to strategic planning documents: *Made in China 2025, Space Science and Technology in China, A Road Map to 2050, The National Key Technologies R&D Program,* and *The 13th Five Year Plan.* For Xi's grand strategy, see Doshi, *The Long Game.* Xi had become general secretary of the CCP and leader of the military in November 2012. My understanding of Xi has been greatly enhanced by the eight-part podcast *The Prince,* presented by Sue-Lin Wong for the *Economist* (September 2022); Chris Buckley and Paul Mozur, "What Keeps Xi Jinping Awake at Night," *New York Times*, May 11, 2018. For Xi's grand strategy, see Khan, *Haunted by Chaos*, p. 211; Cameron, *For the Record*, p. 620.

7. "Joint Address by MI5 and FBI Heads," July 6, 2022, https://www.mi5.gov.uk/news/speech-by -mi5-and-fbi; Mike Glenn, "FBI Director, U.K. Counterpart Say China Wants to Steal Business Tech," *Washington Times*, July 7, 2022; Wray, "Countering Threats Posed by the Chinese Government Inside the U.S."

8. Edward Luce, "Containing China Is Biden's Explicit Goal," *Financial Times*, October 19, 2022.

9. William Leary, "Technology Transfers to China," in box 2, "DOE National Laboratory Activity in the People's Republic of China," June 1994 National Security Council Access, Management, WCL; ibid. [WCL], Clinton Presidential Records, box 6, Counsel's Office Steven Reich Papers, "A Report on Security at the US Department of Energy," June 1999; deGraffenreid, ed., *The Cox Report*; on-record remarks by Sue Gordon and Michael Hayden at Cipher Brief Threat Challenge Conference 2022, October 10, 2022; author interview with James Clapper, October 21, 2022.

10. Zach Dorfman, "Botched CIA Communications System Helped Blow Cover of Chinese Agents," *Foreign Policy*, August 15, 2018; Zach Dorfman, "Beijing Ransacked Data as U.S. Sources Went Dark in China," *Foreign Policy*, December 22, 2020. For Chinese intelligence and takedown of CIA agents in 2010, also see Faligot, *Chinese Spies*, pp. 387–90; Gertz, *Deceiving the Sky*, p. 107; private information.

11. Mark Kelton, "The Coming Chinese Storm," *The Cipher Brief*, March 25, 2019; Department of Justice press release, "Chinese National Pleads Guilty to Conspiring to Hack into Contractors' System to Steal Sensitive Military Hardware," March 23, 2016, https://www.justice.gov/opa/pr /chinese-national-pleads-guilty-conspiring-hack-us-defense-contractors-systems-steal-sensitive. A leading Western expert on Chinese intelligence, Peter Mattis, has stated that the best word to describe China's approach to intelligence collection is *aggression*: Peter Mattis, "Prepared Statement," testimony before the U.S-China Economic and Security Review Commission, June 9, 2019, p. 34.

12. Joske, *Spies and Lies*; Peter Mattis, "The Analytic Challenge of Understanding Chinese Intelligence Services," *Studies in Intelligence* 56 (September 2012); Jamil Anderlini and Tom Mitchell, "Top China Defector Passes Secrets to US," *Financial Times*, February 4, 2016; John Feng, "China

Spymaster Dong Jingwei Makes First Public Appearance since Defection Rumors," *Newsweek*, June 24, 2021.

13. David Ian Chambers, "The Past and Present State of Chinese Intelligence Historiography," *Studies in Intelligence* 56 (September 2012).

14. For Glenn Duffie Shriver, Kevin Mallory (ex-CIA officer), and Jerry Chun Shing Lee (ex-CIA), see Mattis and Brazil, *Chinese Communist Espionage*, pp. 235, 237, 239. For Ron Rockwell Hansen (ex-DIA contractor), see Department of Justice (DOJ) press release "Former Intelligence Officer Convicted of Attempted Espionage Sentenced to 10 Years in Federal Prison," September 24, 2019, https://www.justice.gov/opa/pr/former-intelligence-officer-convicted-attempted-espionage-sen tenced-10-years-federal-prison. For Candace Marie Claiborne (ex-State Department), see DOJ press release "Former State Department Employee Sentenced for Conspiring with Chinese Agents," July 9, 2019, https://www.justice.gov/opa/pr/former-state-department-employee-sentenced-con spiring-chinese-agents. Also see the FBI video "Don't Be a Pawn: A Warning to Students Abroad," c. April 2014, https://www.fbi.gov/video-repository/newss-dont-be-a-pawn-a-warning-to-stu dents-abroad/view.

15. Christopher Wray, "Countering Threats Posed by the Chinese Government inside the U.S.," January 31, 2022, RRL; Christophe Cornevin and Jean Chichizola, "Les révélations du *Figaro* sur le programme d'espionnage chinois qui vise la France," *Le Figaro*, October 22, 2018.

16. For divided loyalties, see, for example, Katherine L. Herbig, "Changes in Espionage by Americans: 1947–2007," Department of Defense technical report 08-05, March 2008; for Chinese legislation, see, for example, mandatory provisions in Article 77 of the PRC's National Security Law (2015) and Articles 7 and 14 of the PRC's National Intelligence Law (2017) and the 2017 National Intelligence Law; Eftimiades, *Chinese Espionage*, p. 5; Demetri Sevastopulo, "US Intelligence Officials Warn Companies in Critical Sectors on China," *Financial Times*, October 22, 2021; Inkster, *China's Cyber Power*, pp. 45–48.

17. "China's Spies Are Not Always as Good as Advertised," *Economist*, June 1, 2022; the estimated size of the MSS, 800,000, was given to the author in an interview with an FBI officer on condition of anonymity, August 2, 2022; Nathalie Guibert and Brice Pedroletti, "Infektion 2.0, l'opération chinoise d'inspiration russe censée faire oublier l'origine du Covid-19," *Le Monde*, September 8, 2021.

18. Ben Murphy, *China's Self-Identified Strategic Technology Import Dependencies* (Washington, DC: Center for Security and Emerging Technology, May 2022).

19. For the Hong Kong judiciary under the Anglo-Chinese Joint Declaration and Basic Law, see Vogel, *Deng Xiaoping and the Transformation of China*, pp. 506–9. For the erosion of academic freedom at the University of Hong Kong, see Kirby, *Empires of Ideas*, pp. 369–75.

20. Lionel Barber, Henry Foy, and Alex Baker, "Vladimir Putin Says Liberalism Has 'Become Obso-lete,'" *Financial Times*, June 27, 2019; Sergei Karaganov, "We Are Witnessing the Birth of a New World Order Where West Will Have to Live within Its Means," *RT* [Russia Today], October 31, 2022. For background, see Rachman, *Easternization*, p. 205. For the Lavrov tweet (12:16 p.m., July 25, 2022): https://twitter.com/RussianEmbassy/status/1551602257464098817?s=20 &t=CpgpX_0nPMzPSoy95NqYpA; "Joint Statement of the Russian Federation and the People's Republic of China on the International Relations Entering a New Era and the Global Sustainable Development," February 4, 2022, http://en.kremlin.ru/supplement/5770#:~:text=serious%20 threats%20to%C2%A0global%20and%C2%A0regional%20peace%20and%C2%A0stability%20 and%C2%A0undermine%20the%C2%A0stability%20of%C2%A0the%C2%A0world%20order.

21. Blinken, *Ally Versus Ally*; U.S. National Security Strategy, October 2022, https://www.white house.gov/wp-content/uploads/2022/10/Biden-Harris-Administrations-National-Security-Strategy -10.2022.pdf.

22. House Permanent Select Committee on Intelligence, "The China Deep Dive: A Report on the

Intelligence Community's Capabilities and Competencies with Respect to the People's Republic of China," September 30, 2020, p. 8, Executive Summary, published on House Permanent Select Committee on Intelligence website, September 30, 2020.

23. "Fears over Mandarin Speakers in Whitehall," *Spectator*, November 23, 2021; "FBI and MI5 Leaders Give Unprecedented Joint Warning on Chinese Spying," *Guardian*, July 6, 2022.

24. William Burns, "The Role of Intelligence at a Transformational Period," speech given at Georgia Tech, April 14, 2022, https://www.cia.gov/static/21993f0aa96849f2dbdfafcc2d6598e6/Director-Burns-Speech-and-QA-Georgia-Tech.pdf.

25. The classic formulation of applied history can be found in Neustadt and May, eds., *Thinking in Time*; Joseph Nye, "Estimating the Future," in Godson, May, and Schmitt, eds., *U.S. Intelligence at the Crossroads*, pp. 86–96. For the difficulties of contemporary history, see Hennessy, *Distilling the Frenzy*.

26. For quantum computing, see Cyberspace Solarium Commission, "Final Report," March 2020, pp. 121–22; Daniel Politi, "U.S. Has Lost AI Race to China, According to Former Software Chief at Pentagon," *Slate*, October 11, 2021; Susan Gordon, John Richardson, and Mike Rogers, "The Quantum Computing Threat Is Real. Now We Need to Act," *CyberScoop*, October 20, 2022; Andy Greenberg, "The Full Story of the Stunning RSA Hack Can Finally Be Told," *Wired*, May 20, 2021.

27. U.S. National Counterintelligence and Security Center, "Protecting Critical and Emerging U.S. Technologies from Foreign Threats," October 2021, https://www.dni.gov/files/NCSC/documents/SafeguardingOurFuture/FINAL_NCSC_Emerging%20Technologies_Factsheet_10_22_2021.pdf.

28. See, for example, Christo Grozev, "The Remote Control Killers behind Russia's Cruise Missile Strikes on Ukraine," *Bellingcat*, October 24, 2022, https://www.bellingcat.com/news/uk-and-europe/2022/10/24/the-remote-control-killers-behind-russias-cruise-missile-strikes-on-ukraine/; Strider Technologies, Inc., "The Los Alamos Club," 2022, https://www.striderintel.com/wp-content/uploads/Strider-Los-Alamos-Report.pdf; Kissinger, Schmidt, and Huttenlocher, *The Age of AI*, pp. 207–27.

29. The issue of racial profiling and U.S. counterintelligence has been told by Hvistendahl, *The Scientist and the Spy*.

30. Hill, *There Is Nothing for You Here*, pp. 9–10; Fiona Hill, "The Kremlin's Strange Victory," *Foreign Affairs*, November/December 2021.

31. On-record remarks by Michael Hayden at Cipher Brief Threat Challenge 2022, October 19, 2022.

32. Pei, *China's Crony Capitalism*; some analysts see China declining after failing to escape the "middle-income trap." Others envisage it hitting a plateau because of demographic constraints, low-factor productivity, and Xi's policy of favoring state-owned firms over private companies. In addition, China faces serious problems of rising inequality and environmental degradation: see Joseph S. Nye Jr., "America's China Challenge," *Project Syndicate*, August 3, 2022, https://www.project-syndicate.org/commentary/america-successful-response-to-china-challenge-by-joseph-s-nye-2022-08.

INDEX

627

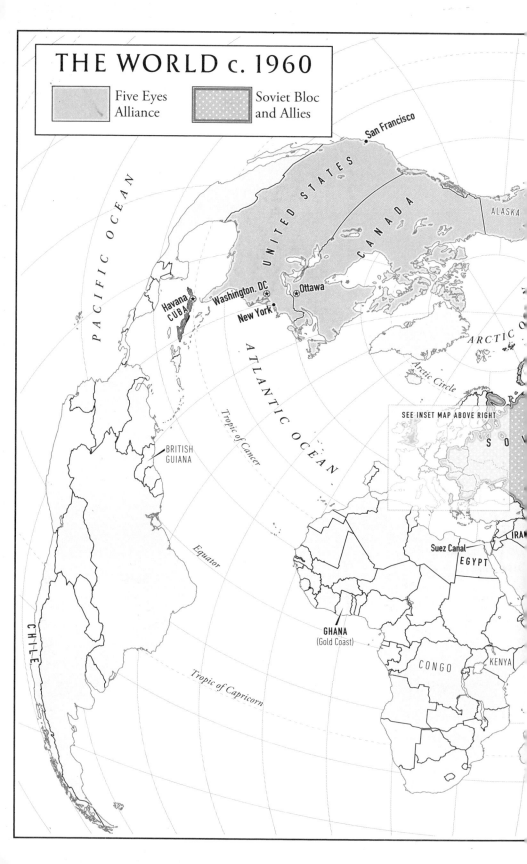

THE WORLD c. 1960

Five Eyes Alliance

Soviet Bloc and Allies

San Francisco

UNITED STATES

CANADA

ALASKA

PACIFIC OCEAN

Havana
CUBA

Washington, DC

Ottawa

New York

ARCTIC O

Arctic Circle

ATLANTIC OCEAN

Tropic of Cancer

SEE INSET MAP ABOVE RIGHT

S O V

BRITISH GUIANA

Equator

IRA

Suez Canal

EGYPT

GHANA
(Gold Coast)

CONGO

KENYA

CHILE

Tropic of Capricorn